R. F. DELDERFIELD

To Serve Them All My Days

SIMON AND SCHUSTER·NEW YORK

Dedicated to my friend and colleague
of the book world—
R O B I N
D E N N I S T O N

A Qualified Disclaimer

Almost every writer of fiction inserts the obligatory disclaimer in his work and some, I suspect, do it with tongue in cheek. The truth is, of course, no one ever *invented* anyone. Every character in fiction is an amalgam of factors drawn from the author's memory and imagination and this is particularly true of *To Serve Them All My Days*. No character here is a true portrait, or caricature, of any master or boy I ever encountered at my six schools and one commercial college, between 1917 and 1929, but aspects of people I met are embodied in all of them, and I have even used nicknames I recalled, as well as several scholastic backgrounds. To write fiction in any other way would be to divorce oneself from reality and what kind of book would emerge from that? In using, say, an average of six schoolmasters and six boys for every one between these pages, I intended, no slight or criticism, only to portray life at school as I saw it up to 1940, when I had entered my twenty-ninth year. I was glad to leave five of the six schools but there is one I still regard with the greatest affection. I leave it to the reader to sort the wheat from the chaff.

R.F.D.
February 1971

Contents

PART

ONE

Initiate

How soon hath Time, the subtle thief of youth,
  Stolen on his wing my three and twentieth year!
My hasting days fly on with full career,
  But my late spring no bud or blossom shew'th.
John Milton

Chapter One

The guard at Exeter warned him he would have to change at Dulverton to pick up the westbound train to Bamfylde Bridge Halt, the nearest railhead to the school, but did not add that the wait between trains was an hour. It was one of those trivial circumstances that played a part in the healing process of the years ahead, for the interval on that deserted platform, set down in a rural wilderness, and buttressed by heavily timbered hills where spring lay in ambush, gave Powlett-Jones an opportunity to focus his thoughts in a way he had been unable to do for months, since the moment he had emerged from the dugout and paused, rubbing sleep from his eyes, to glance left and right down the trench.

From that moment, down long vistas of tortured, fearful and horribly confused dreams, his thoughts, if they could be recognised as thoughts, had been random pieces of a child's jigsaw, no two dovetailing, no half-handful forming a coherent pattern. Yet now, for a reason he could not divine, they coalesced and he was aware, on this account alone, of a hint of reprieve.

*　　*　　*

The shell, a coal-box, must have pitched directly on the parados of the nearest traverse, filling the air with screaming metal and raising a huge, spouting column of liquid mud. He had no real awareness of being flung backwards down the slippery steps, only a blessed certainty that this was it. Finish. Kaput. The end of three years of half-life, beginning that grey, October dawn in 1914, when his draft had moved up through a maze of shallow ditches to a waterlogged sector held by the hard-pressed Warwickshires they were relieving.

Even then, after no more than two days in France, his sense of geography had been obliterated by desolation, by acres and acres of debris scattered by the sway of two battle-locked armies across the reeking mudflats of Picardy. There were no landmarks and not as many guidelines as later, when trench warfare became more sophisticated. The confusion, however, enlarged its grip on his mind as months and years went by, a sense of timelessness punctuated by moments of terror and unspeakable disgust, by long stretches of yammering boredom relieved by two brief respites, one in base hospital, recovering from a wound, the other when he was withdrawn for his commissioning course. Superiors, equals and underlings came and went. Thousands of khaki blurs, only a very few remaining long enough to make a lasting impression on him. Here and there he had made a friend, the kind of friend one read about in the classics, true, loyal, infinitely relished. But the mutter of the guns, the sour mists that seemed to hang over the battlefield in summer and winter, had swallowed them up as the wheels of war trundled him along, a chance survivor of a series of appalling shipwrecks.

Occasionally, just occasionally, he would be aware of conventional time. The coming of a new season. A birthday or anniversary, when his memory might be jogged by a letter from home, full of mining-village trivia. But then the fog would close in again and home and the past seemed separated from him by thousands of miles and millions of years, a brief, abstract glimpse of links with a civilisation as dead as Nineveh's.

And at the very end of it all that ultimate mortar shell, landing square on the parados and pitchforking him over the threshold of hell where, for the most part, he was unaware of his identity as a man or even a thing but floated free on a current of repetitive routines—shifts on a stretcher or in a jolting vehicle; daily dressings, carried out by faceless men and women; odd, unrelated sounds like bells and the beat of train wheels; the rumble of voices talking a language he never understood; the occasional, sustained yell that might have signified anger, pain or even animal high spirits.

The intervals of clarity and cohesion lengthened as time went on, but they were never long enough for him to get a firm grip on his senses. He learned, over the months, that he had been dug out alive, the only survivor of the blast, after being buried for several hours. Also that he had survived, God alone knew how, the long, jolting journey down the communication trenches to the dressing station, to advance base and finally to Le Havre and the hospital ferry. For a long time, however, he was unaware of being back in England, shunted from one hospital to another until he finally came to rest at Osborne, reckoned a convalescent among a thousand or more other shattered men as confused as himself.

Then, but very slowly, he became fully aware of himself again. Second Lieutenant David Powlett-Jones, 'A' Company, Third Battalion, South Wales Borderers; sometime Davy Powlett-Jones, son of Ewart and Glynnis, of No. 17 Aberglaslyn Terrace, Pontnewydd, Monmouthshire, a boy who had dreamed of scholarship and celebrity, of bringing a gleam of triumph into the eyes of a short, stocky miner who had worked all his life in a hole in the mountain and died there with two of his sons in the Pontnewydd-Powis explosion of August, 1913.

He was aware of his identity and, to some extent, of his past and present, but the future was something else. He could never attach his mind to it for more than a few seconds. The war surely would go on for ever and ever, until every human soul in the world was engulfed in it. He could never picture himself leading any different kind of life but that of trudging to and from the line, in and out of the mutter of small-arms fire and the sombre orchestra of the shells. Hospital life, as he lived it now, was no more than an interval.

Then Rugeley-Scott, the neurologist, infiltrated into his dream world. First as a white-smocked and insubstantial figure, no different from scores of predecessors who had paused, hummed and prodded during the last few months, but ultimately as a force where he could find not comfort exactly but at least relevance. For Rugeley-Scott had certain theories and persisted in putting them forward.

One was his theory of upland air and David's own Celtic roots responded to this, feeding a little vitality into the husk of his flesh and bone. For Rugeley-Scott said that a man could enjoy a sense of proportion in upland air that was denied the Lowlander, upland air being keen and stimulating and capable of clearing the fog in the brain and reanimating petrified thought-processes. It had a trick, he said, of making a man at one with his environment. Rugeley-Scott, of course, was a Highlander, whose boyhood had been spent in Sutherland and whose medical studies had taken him no further south than Perthshire. He believed passionately in upland air in the way a primitive savage believes in the witchdoctor's bones and amulets.

Rugeley-Scott's second theory grew out of the first, close involvement in a small, tightly knit community, where a personality was encouraged to flower as it could never flower in a city. It was concerned, also, with a specific purpose, enshrined in an ideal of some kind. In a creed, perhaps, or a crusade. In one or other of the arts that yielded an end product. Above all, in involvement with others but not too many others. A hundred or so, collectively breathing upland air.

David never afterwards recalled how these theories came to centre on the profession of schoolmaster, imparting to successive generations of the young such knowledge as a man accumulated through books, experience, contemplation. Yet somewhere along the line, in the first weeks of 1918, this concentration occurred, so that David Powlett-Jones, white hope of the Pontnewydd Elementary School, the miner's son who had won the first local scholarship to the Grammar School at thirteen, and had gone on to win another for university four years later, began to see himself, a little fancifully, as an usher on a rostrum, writing on a blackboard in front of an audience of boys.

It was no more than a silhouette at first but Rugeley-Scott, with Celtic obstinacy, persisted until a comprehensive picture emerged. And after that, a train of minor events was fired that involved letters and telephone calls, so that at length, on a still afternoon in early March, seven months after the coal-box had exploded below Pilckhem Wood, David Powlett-Jones found himself sitting on a paint-scarred seat on Dulverton Station, wondering who had dumped a rail junction in such an isolated spot. He wondered too how long he would have to order his thoughts before he boarded a train for a place he had never heard of be-

6

fore Rugeley-Scott gave him the envelope containing particulars for his interview with the Reverend Algernon Herries, Headmaster of Bamfylde School, Devon.

He thought then, with a mixture of bitterness and humility, "But what the hell am I doing here anyway? What headmaster in his senses would engage a wreck like me, who jumps a foot in the air every time a door bangs? That chap Herries, whoever he is, will take one look at me and show me the door, tut-tutting all the way to the motor, providing they have motors out here."

He then drew three deep breaths of upland air and despite the memory of the ward's wry jokes about it, found that it did have a noticeable effect upon his powers of concentration. At least it enabled him to evaluate the view of those hanging woods, part evergreen, part the skeletal branches of older, heavier timber, and remark on the astounding quietude of the little station. Quiet was something he had forgotten about, along with so many other things that belonged to his childhood and boyhood. Never once, not even on the blackest night in Flanders, had it been as quiet as this. Always there had been the scrape and shuffle of working parties, the plash of signallers slipping in flooded trenches, cursing at every traverse. And in the background, always, the guns had growled north or south of the sector, a thunderstorm roaming between Switzerland and the sea.

Here you could almost reach out and touch the quiet. It was a living thing that seemed to catch its breath up there in the hanging woods and then, at a wordless command, slip down the long hillside and gust over the rails to lose itself in the wood opposite. Its touch was gentle and healing, passing over his scar tissue like the fingers of a woman. He wanted to embrace it, press it into himself, swallow it, lose himself in it. And all the time the white clouds overhead kept pace with it, moving in massive formation across the blue band above the valley and the breeze smelled of resin and bracken and all manner of clean, washed, living things. No whiff of putrefaction here. And no hint of gas.

He surrendered to its benediction, and was sound asleep when the walrus-moustached stationmaster found him, studying him with the compassionate detachment of a sixty-year-old who had seen the passage of a thousand troop-trains. The long, slightly saturnine face was Celtic, one of the darker, taller, heavy-browed Celts who had little in common with West Countrymen this side of the Tamar. The limbs, relaxed now, seemed shrunken under the khaki gaberdine, the body pulled in by the worn Sam Browne belt. The face was that of a boy prematurely aged, with hollowed cheeks accentuated by deepset eyes and high cheekbones. The skin was tanned, but below the tan there was a hint of pallor. The railwayman muttered, "Osspittle. Somewhere up the line," and was tempted to let him sleep on but then, recollecting his duty, he shook him by the shoulder and said, "Tiz yer, lad. Vower minutes late. Your stop'll be fourth on, no more'n vifteen minutes."

The man's clumsy gentleness touched him. It was a long time since anyone had called him 'lad'. It was another short step on the road to resurrection.

2

The flint road wound upward through immense patches of wild rhododendron, then down again to culverts that carried a swirl of storm-water from the moor, along with a sludge of brown, decaying twigs and dead leaves. There had been no one to meet him at the halt and no sign of a conveyance of any kind but he did not mind walking. It set forward the time of the interview by half an hour, the time he calculated it would take him to walk the two miles to the crossroads marked on the map enclosed with the letter confirming his interview. The crossroads was marked as Barton Cross and when he reached it he saw that the barn or barton marked a junction of four roads that were really no more than half-surfaced cart-tracks. He thought, "Now who the devil would build a school right out here? Nothing lives here but rabbits," but then, as at the station, his awakening senses told him the wilderness was teeming with life, every kind of life, and that there was promise here, in a month or two, of an immensity of colour and movement under the touch of April.

Already the hedgerows were starred with campion and primrose, with dog violets showing among the thistles and higher up, where the rhododendrons tailed off on the edge of a little birch wood, the green spires of bluebell were pushing through a sea of rusty bracken.

He calculated the gradient at about one in six and the road kept twisting towards a brown-green summit that was the open moor. And then, coming at last to a level stretch, he saw the grey line of buildings on the southern edge of the plateau, and the twin ribbons of leafless beeches lining the two drives. He paused at a ruined five-bar gate that lacked a hinge and bulged outward. Beyond it was a playing field and on the rugby pitch a game was going on between two fifteens wearing identical red and black jerseys. The cries of the players came to him faintly on the freshening breeze and he had a sense of renewal, seeing the little figures over there not as part of the present but of a time a million years ago, when he had played in the Grammar School fifteen, and had worn a jersey rather like that, save that the stripes were red and yellow. The moment passed and he pushed on, passing up the east drive to the forecourt and pausing in front of the three-storey Gothic building that reared itself there, grey, rather gaunt and incongruous in that setting.

The façade itself was long and flattish but outbuildings straggled all the way up the slight rise to a quadrangle he could glimpse beyond an arched doorway. He remembered then that the place had been built at a period when no commercially minded architect would dream of using any but a Gothic design, a time when the missionaries of Arnold of Rugby swarmed south, carrying the Doctor's creed into every shire of the nation. You did not have to be told it was a school up there. It had, even at this distance, the smell of school, a compound of boiled greens, stale dust, steam-heat, spurned grass, sweat, socks and damp clothes. He moved along the forecourt until he came to an iron-studded door with a knocker fashioned in the shape of a dolphin. He raised the knocker, dropping it without resolution.

*　　*　　*

The Reverend Algernon Herries looked like an ageing, amiable clown. He had a cheerful, piping voice and a fruity bottle-nose, lined with a network of tiny veins and clothed, as though in crude jest, by a swathe of dark, curling hairs that reminded David of the legs of an insect. White hair rose from the forehead in a clownish peak, giving a false idea of his stature that was short and thickset but still suggestive of agility and precise movement. His face was an actor's face, that might have been seamed and burnished by years of make-up routine. The mobile eyebrows were clownish, too, tufted and pointed like the hair, but below them the eyes

9

were of piercing blueness, the one feature of the face that belonged in a world of earnestness and shrewdness, eyes, David told himself, that would miss little and were there to keep watch over tolerant excesses that could go with a face like that. The man might look eccentric but that did not mean he was anybody's fool. It therefore followed that he would not waste much time on an applicant lacking any kind of degree or experience, who had, moreover, the Twitch.

Yet the handshake was cordial, neither too firm nor too limp, and as he turned to lead the way down a stone corridor to his study he called, "Mr. Powlett-Jones, Ellie! Bring tea, m'dear!" and motioned his visitor into a room spilling over with books and dog-eared papers, indicating the one armchair beside the window, saying, "Sit you down. Ellie will be here with the tea in a jiffy. My apologies for your having to walk. We had a boneshaker until Christmas but then Stanbury, who drove it, took it into his head to do his bit and join the Army Service Corps. I do hope they don't trust him with one of those heavy Thorneycrofts you chaps use. He'll wreck it, for sure. He was always disputing passage with cromlechs and taking short cuts across patches of bog."

David began to warm towards him. It was impossible not to, for his geniality was so genuine. But there was rather more to it than that. He was the first civilian David had ever heard inject irony into that phrase 'do his bit'. For years now civilians had talked about 'doing their bit' as though they were on their way to church and wanted everybody to acknowledge their piety.

"I . . . er . . . enjoyed the walk, sir," he said, hesitantly. "The countryside . . . it's much wilder than the country around Osborne . . ." but then he stopped, biting his lip. He had been on the point of saying something bloody silly about the tortured Flanders landscape. Herries said, with unexpected gravity, "How long were you out, Mr. Powlett-Jones?"

"Three years."

"Three? Then you must have been under age when you enlisted."

"Only a week or two, sir. I went across with a Territorial draft in October. We were untrained but the regulars were badly hammered at First Ypres. I've been luckier than most."

"There's no possibility of your returning?"

"No, sir, I'm boarded." And then, with a touch of defiance, "I'd

10

be no use to anyone out there now." He noticed dismally, that his hands had begun to shake.

Herries got up suddenly and at first David assumed the movement was an excuse to prevent him noticing the Twitch. It was not. He crossed the room and pointed to a fading sepia photograph hanging above one of the bookshelves. It was a very conventional photograph, fifteen lumpish youngsters, ranged in three rows, one lad squatting and nursing a ball.

"There's no need to feel isolated from us, least of all from me. That was our 1913 First Fifteen. Twelve are dead and one of the survivors is legless. We've lost eighty-seven to date, seventy-two of them known to me personally. My boys." He was silent a moment. Then, "On July 8th, 1916, I recorded eight names in one week's casualty list. Does that help?"

It helped but it also embarrassed. Suddenly, inexplicably, David felt his throat constrict and whipped his right hand to his eye. For nearly a minute there was silence in the cluttered room. The bell saved him, saved them both perhaps. Its harsh, clanging note filled the room and then went jangling away to the north as the ringer, relishing his work, crossed the quad towards the longest of the red-brick outbuildings. Herries said, "That's Shawe. Nobody is allowed to touch that bell but Nipper Shawe. He was the smallest boy in the school when he came here, so I had to find something to invest him with dignity. It worked, as you see. He now has the strut of the professional town-crier."

A murmur reached them, swelling rapidly to a sustained clatter, as boys began to pass the window in twos and threes, boots scuffling, voices shrill and urgent. Herries pushed open the casement and hailed the nearest of them.

"Who won, Daffy?"

A breathless boy paused under the window. "Nicolson's, sir! Eleven-five."

"*Eleven*, you say? Great Scott! Outram's were leading five-nil at half-time, weren't they?"

"Yes, sir, but Monkey scored a try early in the second half and Dodger converted. Then Hutchinson scored two more tries far out in the last five minutes!"

"He did? Well, good for Hutch! That must have rattled Outram's. Thank you, Daffy."

The boy ran on, disappearing in a stream that was flowing

11

through the arch of the western face of the quad. Away in the distance Nipper Shawe was still swinging his handbell. Herries settled himself, reluctantly David thought, behind his littered desk.

The spate of nicknames, the obvious rapport between headmaster and boys puzzled him. In both his schools the headmaster had been a remote, austere figure. He had never heard either of them use a nickname, or address even a senior boy as a near-equal. His hands stopped shaking. He said, getting some kind of a grip on his nerves, "I've . . . er . . . no degree, sir. I was planning to go up to Cambridge in the autumn of 1914. I only agreed to this interview because the Osborne neurologist insisted. He has . . . er . . . some eccentric ideas on therapy."

"Really? Tell me."

"He said I could apply for a temporary post, and gain experience while the shortened ex-officers' courses are being arranged at Varsity. I wasn't even sure I wanted to teach. I'm certainly not equipped for the job."

The tufted eyebrows came up. "Any other career in mind?"

"No, sir."

"Then I'd say the neurologist knows what he's about."

Herries got up again. Behind a desk he seemed unable to express himself with characteristic directness. "Look," he said, suddenly, "why don't you give us a trial? As from now, and irrespective of whether that chap at Osborne is right or wrong? You'd be helping me no end. I'm stuck with a dozen tired men called out of retirement, and two C.3 trainees, rejected by the medicals twice over. Oh, they do what they can, but they come in for a lot of ragging. This overdose of jingoism we've had for so long, it's rubbed off on the boys. You'd have a distinct advantage over the rest of us there. Three years at the Front. Twice wounded. It's a flying start, man."

"I'm very far from fit, sir."

"You'll *get* fit up here. Everybody does." He expanded his barrel chest and David thought briefly of Rugeley-Scott, and his insistence on the benefits of upland air. "Besides, we'd make allowances. History is your main subject, isn't it?"

"Modern history was to have been, sir."

"Could you make a stab at English in Lower School? Ground work? Introductory stuff? As I say, we're in a rare pickle here.

Every school is, of course, but out here, miles from the nearest town, we're at the very end of the queue. Just how do you feel about hanging around Osborne until those shortened courses are set up, then going up for the minimum two years?"

"Frankly the prospect terrified me, sir. It's difficult to make the necessary effort when the only people you meet are crocks, as bad or worse than yourself. They tell me it'll be much the same at Cambridge. Every man on those courses will be ex-service."

"You're afraid of becoming institutionalised? Is that it?"

"More or less. I had thought about signing away pension claims, discharging myself and going it alone somewhere."

"Anywhere particular?"

"In the Welsh mountains. I had some good times up there when I was a boy but Rugeley-Scott insists . . ."

Herries flipped the cover of a buff file.

"It's only fair to tell you I had a lengthy letter from Mr. Rugeley-Scott. He was very explicit. Would you care to see his letter?"

"No, sir. I can guess what he said."

"The bit about an enclosed community?"

"I know the clinical symptoms of severe shell-shock. I should do, after seven months in hospital."

"Let's take it as read then. As to 'going into retreat', you could do that here if you cared to. Term ends in three weeks and you could stay around and nurse yourself for a month. It's very quiet during the holidays. I could show you the country on horseback. We still have a couple of old screws the requisitioners left behind. Or you could walk solitary if you preferred it."

For the first time since he had been fully aware of his situation David came to terms with his profound reluctance to go home to Pontnewydd. His mother, who had survived worse tragedies, would stay clear of him, but who else would in a close-knit mining community, where almost everyone knew him as 'Davyboy'? What was necessary, what was absolutely essential in the next few months, was privacy. Privacy, within a community of people cut off from the reality of what was still happening over there.

"Could you give me a moment to think it over, sir?"

"I can give you all evening. No need to pound down that road for the five-thirty. Be our guest and sleep in the President's Room —President of the Old Boys that is. We always keep a room for him, that's his privilege. I can lend you pyjamas and we'll root out a toothbrush, although I'm told they're in short supply like everything else except eggs and bacon. We're very privileged in that respect. We keep our own hens and pigs."

He opened the door and stepped out, calling to his wife Ellie for the tea. David went over to the window that opened on the quad. Behind what looked like the changing rooms the light was dying. Through a screen of leafless elms bordering the playing field he could see the orange glow of a heatless sun. Sunsets belonged to his earlier life. In the trenches the sun always set behind the British sectors. There was some kind of bath-house over there and every now and again a towel-draped boy darted across a flagged court and disappeared into a cloud of steam. It was as much a masculine world as Flanders but the difference showed in the speed of the boys' movements and their high spirits that reached him as half-heard sallies and short barks of laughter. Out there men still laughed but rarely in that way, rarely without bitterness. He thought, "It's what I need, I daresay, but how the devil do I know I could stand up to it? If any one of those kids tried it on, as boys always do with a new man, I might go berserk. Or I might crumple up and pipe my eye, as I nearly did when Herries mentioned that 1913 First Fifteen . . ."

He braced himself to take a closer look at the photograph. The boys were his contemporaries, their average age about seventeen when that picture was taken. It was even possible to fancy he could recognise one or two of them, so typical were they of all the youngsters who went west in the bloody shambles in 1916. That was the day Robin Barnes copped it two yards from the trench. And Nick Austin, too, although Nick had taken a night and a day to die, too far out to be brought in by the stretcher-bearers. A whole generation gone and here was the next, flexing their muscles for the show, looking forward to it, he wouldn't wonder. There was talk of a big Jerry offensive, with whole divisions released by the collapse of the Russian front. If things were desperate enough they might even come combing in places like this. Jerry already had. Two prisoners, brought in by trench raiders the night before he stopped the mortar blast, had been seventeen and looked much younger. He remembered them vividly, although he had never thought about them since, a pair of terrified starvelings in uniforms several sizes too big for them, their coal-scuttle helmets sitting on their shaven heads like extinguishers . . . Could anyone do anything about it at this stage? Suppose the war ended next year or the year after? Would there be anyone left to listen?

Herries and his wife came back together, the headmaster carrying a loaded tray. Mrs. Herries was four inches taller than her husband and thin as a beanpole. Her eyes were as kind and shrewd as his and he thought, as Herries introduced them, "He's holding on better than most and so is she . . . It must be a little like losing seventy-two sons . . ." and the reflection helped him to make up his mind. He said, "Could I wire for my things, sir? Enough to tide me over?" and Herries said, casually, "Better than that. We'll telephone the hospital as soon as you've had a meal and a look round. Crumpets? Why not? There are certain compensations in being marooned, my dear chap."

It was dusk in the quad when they went out. They had no electricity up here and a shuffling little man with buck teeth was lighting oil lamps suspended over the three arches and at intervals down the long, flagged corridor to the dining hall. David peeped in and made a rough calculation of numbers seated at tea. Four hundred, give or take a dozen. He followed Herries up two flights of slate steps to a landing giving access to two large dormitories, each sleeping about thirty boys. It seemed a very Spartan school. There were no floor coverings, apart from narrow strips of scuffed coconut matting, and no lockers beside the iron cots, each covered with a red blanket. Under each bed was a laundry basket and an enamel chamber-pot. It was very much like a barrack but some of the headmaster's brusque geniality had rubbed off on the fabric, enough to make it threadbare-friendly, like an old and shabby rectory. Herries, reading his thoughts, said, "We're not too well endowed and all the renovations we had in mind have been postponed for four years. The carpentry shop keeps us from disintegrating completely. Our numbers keep up, however, a third of them the sons of Old Boys. A few of their fathers were in Upper School when I came here."

"When was that, sir?"

"Summer term, 1904. I always say I came in on the radical tide. It was a year or so before a Liberal landslide. You would have been a child of eight."

"I remember for all that," David said, smiling. "You can't evade politics in the valleys. How did Bamfylde come to be built in a place as remote as this, sir?"

"Everyone asks that. It grew from a school for farmers' sons. About two dozen of them used to ride their ponies to a farm-house a mile or so nearer the village. Most of the day boys still ride. One of Arnold's disciples was rector here and talked the local people and county authorities into founding the place, in 1853. We're a direct grant school, and about a third of our income comes from the Ministry. They leave us pretty much alone, however, and I get my way in most things. Lord Hopgood—this is part of the Hopgood estate—and the Old Boys make all the real decisions. After I've primed them, that is. Some of the Governors are Old Boys, others are local government bigwigs, a few of them local tradesmen in the area. I'll give you some registers and a prospectus to lull you to sleep after dinner. Come on down now. We've just time to view the place from my thinking post before it's dark!" and he bounced down the stairs, into the passage, across the quad and through the arch leading to the changing rooms and bath-house, moving at a half-trot.

The red-brick block behind the school was shut and silent now. Herries, bustling ahead, pointed to a row of single-storey stone buildings. "Tuck-house, stables, junkroom, armoury—we have a very flourishing O.T.C.—and the fives court. Latrines opposite. Have to do something about them soon, war or no war. The only effective flushing we get is by moorland brook. Well enough this time of year, when it rains five days a week, but a problem in a dry spell. Take the left-hand path between those two elms. That's the cricket pavilion and swimming bath. We had the devil's own luck there. It was finished the week war broke out. Mind the roller —the chain-gang shouldn't have left it there. Along under the hedge towards the plantation. I've seen that grow. Local wise-acres said trees couldn't survive in the path of the north-easters but they did. We now have a windbreak I wouldn't care to be without. Here's the spot. My thinking post!" and he stopped, giving David time to catch his breath. Herries heard him wheezing and was instantly apologetic. "I say, old chap, I'm sorry . . . simply never occurred to me . . . I trot everywhere. Most of us do up here, except in summer term. Have to keep the blood circulating. But I should have remembered, you're still convalescent. Take a breather."

Herries's thinking post was the stump of an enormous beech, snapped off about twenty feet from the ground. He seemed to have a great affection for it and patted it as though it was a dog. "Getting on for three hundred years when it was struck by lightning, in 1912. Lucky job it happened in August, with no one about. Could have killed a dozen of us. Took the sawyers a month to cart it away but it's still very much alive for me. I used to climb it as a boy."

"You were a boy at Bamfylde?"

"Seventy-three to seventy-eight, but that was in Wesker's time. Wesker was a brute. I've seen him flog a whole class for spelling mistakes in dictation. Damned fool thing to do. Lucky I could spell." He paused for a moment, looking down on the scatter of orange lights some two hundred yards below. The outline of the main buildings was just visible, a blue-black blur, quickened by the last pulse of the winter sun. "I very rarely flog a boy and then only for two offences. Persistent lying, and persistent bullying."

David said, suddenly, "How do you see it, sir? Education, I mean, the real purpose of it? In all that time you must have formed some conclusions."

In the dusk he saw the man smile as he stroked his thinking post.

"How? Well, certainly not as a matter of hammering information into boys. That was the general idea when I was young, before Arnold's ideas had time to flower. He was an insufferable prig, of course, and most of his disciples were worse, but they were moving in the right direction. The important thing is to adapt their theme to the twentieth century, before the commercials move in and take over. I don't really regard myself as a schoolmaster, or not any longer. I've changed direction myself a good deal since I took charge here, particularly so in the last few years. I suppose I see myself as a kind of potter at the wheel but then, that's priggish too, wouldn't you say?"

"Not the way you mean it."

"Ah, but how *do* I mean it, precisely? It isn't easy to put these things on paper, or even convince yourself satisfactorily. Parents send their sons to a place like this for specific reasons. The main one is to get an education that will enable them to survive, I suppose. But once they settle in many other processes go to work. They learn a little tolerance, I hope, and how to see a joke against

17

themselves, and how to stand on their own feet. But, above all, the knack of co-operating. I'm not too insistent on scholarship. Scholars are dull dogs for the most part. When I was a boy here there were no organised games to speak of. We crammed and then mooched about, devising ways of avoiding punishment, and tormenting one another out of sheer boredom."

"Isn't that what everyone's engaged in now, sir?"

"Yes, it is. But there's a well-defined end product, thank God."

"What is it, sir?"

"A second chance. You're a history man, so let me ask *you* a question. Granted my thinking post is three hundred years old, what was happening when it was a foot high?"

"The Civil War was brewing."

"Precisely. And something very practical emerged from that. Parliamentary democracy for one thing. Two steps up, and one and a half down. That's my view of history. British history, at all events."

"But we've fallen down a long flight since 1914, haven't we?"

"We've taken a tumble certainly, but that's because we were too damned cocky in the first years of the new century. I daresay we'll learn from it. Dammit, we have to unless all those youngsters were the victims of an obscene practical joke, and I can't let myself believe that they were. As I say, I saw seventy-two of them grow up, and there weren't many fools among them. And no cowards, either, not in the true sense of the word."

The man's optimism was working on him like a drug. His staying power, the strength and simplicity of his faith, was something the men out there had lost long ago, as long ago as Neuve Chapelle and Loos. But a flicker of doubt remained. He said, "As to learning from it, I take it you mean internationally? Out there everyone below the rank of field officer has had a bellyful of patriotism."

"Ah, patriotism," Herries said, affably, and although the dusk now shrouded them completely, David divined a twinkle in the eyes. "Don't forget Edith Cavell, Powlett-Jones. 'Patriotism is not enough' . . . She could have amplified that, poor soul. Patriotism is a first step, I'd say. On the road to civic maturity that is. You had three years out there. I still believe in a Divine Purpose. You survived for a purpose, I imagine. To help head other survivors in the right direction, maybe."

18

Nipper Shawe was swinging his bell again. For prep probably, and its clamour terminated Herries's reverie. "Come, we'll look in on Big School and introduce you. It'll break the ice for man and beast. Then dinner. Ellie has shepherd's pie, with gooseberry fool to follow. We have fruit cages behind that copse and Ellie is a fanatical bottler."

They moved down the slight incline towards the scatter of lights and at the end of the path David barked his shin on the fender of the horse-roller. "Curse that chain-gang," Herries said, genially, "I'll have Masterson's press-gang move it in the morning. Masterson is down for Dartmouth in September. He's a natural leader of the press-gang."

Chapter Two

1

Never in the past or indeed in the years ahead was he so sharply aware of that heightened sense of time that accompanies the process of self-discovery; of new faces, new experiences, new dimensions of space, shape, texture, colour and relationship that lifted him out of limbo and set his feet squarely upon virgin ground.

There was that farcical incident the first day he took the Lower Fourth, that final refuge of extravagant humorists, who regarded any new tutor, especially an inexperienced one, as legitimate prey, a blind and bumbling bear, to be baited and tested for sharpness of tooth and claw. From the first he saw the various groupings of the boys in terms of sections in a muster of infantry, halfway through his front-line service, a time when the ranks of any sizeable unit included battle-tried veterans, work-shy barrack-room lawyers and any number of nervous eighteen-year-olds, fresh from school and recruit centre, all eager to show their mettle.

The scale began in the Second Form, composed entirely of first and second termers, ticking off the days as they adjusted to the pangs of homesickness. One looked for no trouble at all with these. All that was necessary was to slip into the role of jovial uncle, or brother separated by a wide age gap, and jolly them along, spicing the lesson with a few old chestnuts and injecting the spice of romance into pages of the text-books where all the tedious milestones of British history were marked in heavy, marginal print, a row of cromlechs tracing a road across a water- less desert.

In the Lower, Middle and Upper Third sights had to be ad- justed. Here were the thirteen- and fourteen-year-olds, who had played themselves in and were now in the process of separating into four streams, streams that he came to think of as the anxious- to-learners, the occasional-triers, the professional time-passers and the practical jokers, bent on making a reputation for them- selves.

It was in the Fourth Forms that trouble really began. The Fourth Forms were the school watershed, boys of fifteen and above, with two or three years of rough and tumble behind them and no immediate responsibilities ahead, a majority of skrim- shankers who reminded him of the crafty, time-serving men, whose experience earned them stripes one day that were taken away the next. And of the three Fourth Forms the Lower Fourth was the toughest, perhaps because the Cambridge examinations would be that much nearer after removes to the Middle and Upper Fourth were achieved, and pressures were applied by parents re- acting to end-of-term reports.

At all events, his first crisis came on his second morning at Bamfylde, when he introduced himself to some thirty blank-faced fifteen-year-olds in Big School, used as a formroom for the Lower Fourth during the day and as a communal prep room for the whole of the Middle School in the evenings.

It was a difficult room to overlook. The space between the rostrum and the first row of desks was unusually wide, so that he had a sense of being detached from the class in a way that did not happen elsewhere. The ceiling was high and arched and the three Gothic windows gave a clear view of the forecourt and east drive, an open invitation to idlers to concentrate on comings and goings out there rather than on the blackboard or the rostrum.

Boyer, a well-grown, rather saturnine boy with dark hair and high cheekbones, occupied a desk in the back row and even before the incident David marked him down as a jester. He had humorous, heavy-lidded eyes, grey, watchful and mocking. From the moment of making his first appearance, however, David was struck by the unusual passivity of the class. They sat very sedately, attentively awaiting his opening gambits, so that he was well launched on a survey of Elizabeth's foreign policy when there was a sudden stir at the back of the room. A glance, centring on Boyer, warned him he was in trouble, serious trouble if he let it get out of hand, for Boyer had turned very pale, blinking his humorous eyes rapidly as his limbs twitched and jerked, setting all the ink-pots in the communal desk leaping in their sockets. Before David could make even the briefest assessment of the situation the mouth began to twitch in sympathy so that one had the distinct impression that Boyer was in the grip of some form of palpitation or spasm that would bring him, in a matter of seconds, to a point of prostration. David stood up and made a single step towards the edge of the rostrum but at once a forest of hands shot up and reassuring advice was shouted at him from all directions.

"It's all right, sir!"

"Don't worry, sir!"

"Only one of Boyer's fits, sir . . . !"

"Shall I take him to Matron, sir?" And then, calmly stated above the chorus by Dobson, Boyer's right-hand neighbour, "It happens about once a week, sir! Fresh air always brings him round, sir. Shall I open the window and loosen his collar, sir?"

It was Dobson's unceremonious handling of the boy that alerted him for, as he bent over Boyer to loosen his tie, he overplayed his hand by tightening it. Boyer, choking on the knot, came to for a fleeting second, long enough to push his outstretched hand into Dobson's face with such force that Dobson reeled across the aisle until stopped by the water pipes. At the same time concern seemed to ebb from the boys crowding round and some of them began to titter, establishing beyond doubt that Boyer's performance was very much appreciated.

He took a chance then. He had nothing but instinct to tell him that Boyer's seizure was a well-rehearsed trick on the part of the Lower Fourth to relieve the tedium of an hour devoted to De Silva, Walsingham and the Dutch. He roared, at the top of his voice, *"Silence! Places!"* and the command at least had the effect of dispersing the crowd about Boyer's desk, giving him his first real chance to weigh the probabilities. Then Dobson rallied but again, a mere amateur alongside Boyer, he overplayed, saying, in an aggrieved voice, "I was only trying to *help, sir* . . . !" and that did it. Colour returned to Boyer's face and he sat upright, blinking and looking confused, a traveller who has awakened in a train to discover he has passed his station. And in a sense he had for David descending from the rostrum, and moving down the centre aisle, scented victory in the hush that fell in the class as he said, quietly but menacingly, "Stand *up*, Boyer! You too, Dobson!", and both boys raised themselves, looking, David thought, surprised and vaguely apprehensive. He said, in the same level tone, "*Quite* a performance! But it needs working on, Boyer! You're not bad but your partner is a terrible ham," and the astonished laugh, heavier and more sustained than the obligatory response to a master's quip, set the seal on his triumph. He paused then, savouring it and wondering if either Boyer or Dobson would have the nerve to carry the bluff a stage further. When they did not he said, mildly, "It's only fair to warn you I'm familiar with all forms of hysteria. In fact, I'm an expert, having spent the last seven months in shell-shock wards."

It was well below the belt. He was aware of that but he didn't care. It was a crossroads in his life, and victory was essential. In the uneasy silence that followed he weighed his words carefully, finally opting for a middle course, halfway between outrage and appeal, but choosing irony as the weapon best suited to the occasion.

"Well, now," he said, "Boyer being happily restored to full health, suppose I begin by being frank? This is my second day here but I'll add to that. It's also my second day in the teaching profession—teaching in school, that is, for I've been engaged, among other things, in teaching recruits how to deal with the Opposition. Think about that, because the Opposition, from here on, is *you*. Right, sit down, both of you, and let's have a show of hands. How many of you were in on Boyer's little relapse?"

Four hands were raised. Then eight and finally two more, near the front. Their readiness to admit complicity touched him. He said, easily, "Well, that's honest at all events. Boyer took the risks alone, so I don't really see why he should be expected to carry all the bacon home. Everyone concerned, including Boyer and his male nurse, can copy out the chapter we were doing and bring it to me at morning break tomorrow. You deserve far worse, of course, but they tell me every dog is allowed one bite."

The murmur told him all he wanted to know but Boyer still

had a surprise for him. He stood up again, red in the face but resolute. "My . . . er . . . apologies, sir . . . It was only . . . a . . . well . . . sir . . . a . . ."

"A tryout?"

"Well, yes, sir. None of us knew, sir. About the hospital, I mean."

"No reason why you should." He lowered himself on the edge of the desk for a moment. At any minute he knew that his hands would begin to shake and the prospect terrified him. He said, carefully, "You've no exams this term, have you?" and Youings, a studious-looking boy in the front row, said, "No, sir, not this term," and made it sound as if he regretted it.

"Has anyone here ever tried teaching you more up-to-date history? The basic causes of the present war, for instance?"

"A little, sir," from Youings, who continued, "Germany's commercial jealousy, and need for overseas markets, sir?" but then, to his surprise, Dobson's hand shot up and he said, in response to a nod, "Kaiser Bill's trying to rule the world, isn't he, sir?"

"According to the *Daily Mail* he is. Any other ideas?"

In their collective concentration he sensed a desperate eagerness to appease. Letherett, a red-headed boy, reminded the class of the assassination of the Austrian Archduke at Sarajevo. Gibson seemed to think it was all a bid on the part of Germany for naval supremacy. Hoxton was more subtle, stating categorically that Germany had gone to war in the belief that Britain would stand aside and let her occupy France. They were still having their say when the bell went and they seemed genuinely interested in his assessments of their answers. He said, by way of valediction, "We'll continue the inquest on Friday if my reading of the timetable is correct. Class dismissed," and he gathered up his books and left without a backward glance.

*   *   *

It was different again with the Classical Fifth but perhaps not so different from his point of view, for here again he deliberately pushed himself out on a limb.

The Classical Fifth were beyond the skylarking stage. Some of them, a sizeable minority he would say, were genuinely interested in the subject, and he was luckier here, for they were preparing for summer exam questions on the late nineteenth century, as far as the death of Queen Victoria. It was easy to introduce them to the same theme, and be sure of their attention. He took the same line, stating the basic causes of the war and inviting questions. Foster Major's question gave him his cue; Foster Major, six feet tall, and already sprouting golden hairs on his upper lip. He asked, eagerly, "How much longer will it take us to beat the Hun, sir?"

"We can't beat him now, Foster!"

The murmur that greeted this heresy dismayed him so he added, quickly, "Not in the real sense, not in the way we might have done if the Gallipoli show had been a success." He waited for that to sink in, then said, "Now we've no alternative but to crush him and don't fool yourselves into believing that that is a final answer. It'll buy us time but that's about all. Jerry is bled white, but then, so are we. I don't know what you fellows think of the Americans but I'll tell you what the chaps think of them over there. Our one chance of avoiding a stalemate."

They digested this. He could sense incredulity doing battle with other, less complicated reactions. Indignation, possibly, something that ran counter to everything they had been told over the years by men fighting the war from Fleet Street. Finally Gosse, a languid, smartly dressed boy, whose heavy horn-rimmed spectacles gave him a slightly aesthetic look, raised his hand. "Are you saying, sir, that we couldn't beat the Hun without the Yanks—without the Americans, sir?"

"I'm saying it would take us another two to three years, and that's only another way of saying there wouldn't be a victory. The object of war, as the men over there see it, is to preserve our way of life. That's what they've been told and that's what they believe, those of them that still believe in anything except each other. In three years there would be nothing worth preserving. One other thing, Gosse. Over there nobody uses the term 'Hun' any more. I stopped using it at a place called St. Quentin. Two Germans carried me in a blanket across four hundred yards of open ground under a box barrage. If they hadn't I wouldn't be here arguing the toss with you."

But Gosse, a diehard if ever there was one, stuck to his point. "I take it they were prisoners, sir?"

"Yes, they were. But shell-splinters aren't particular where they find a billet. They risked their lives to save mine."

"But in 1914 they burned Louvain, sir."

"Yes, they did. But I like to think they've learned since then. We've all learned something, or should have. If we haven't, getting on for a hundred chaps who occupied those desks of yours a few years ago died in a circus, not a war."

He hadn't meant to say as much as this but later he was glad. For two reasons, separated by a few hours. In the first place, when the bell sounded marking the end of morning classes, they crowded round him, asking all kinds of questions, a few baffled and even hostile, but every one of them prompted by a burning curiosity. Then, as dusk was setting in, and he was closeted in what Herries called Mount Olympus—the ground-floor lavatory in the head's house with its opaque window opening on to the covered part of the quad—he overheard Gosse and two other Fifth Formers discussing him. Dispassionately, as though they already accepted him as a queer fish. He made haste to get out then but before he could escape he heard one boy say, "All *right*, he's a Bolshie. But what he says makes sense to me, Starchy!"

He was getting to grips with the Bamfylde obsession for nicknames. There were two Gosse boys at the school. The elder, a beefy extrovert, was called 'Archibald', so it followed that he should be labelled 'Archy' and his elegant brother 'Starchy'. Starchy Gosse was a pedant but fair-minded, it seemed, for he said, mildly, "It depends on how long he's been out there," and the third boy asked, "Why Starchy?"

"They say it gets a man down in the end. That chap talks just like my Uncle Edward. He was invalided out two years ago, but my governor has stopped inviting him over. Seems to think he's . . . well, almost pro-Hun . . . pro-Jerry. I don't think he is. I mean, how the hell could he be, with one eye and one leg gone?"

David was sweating when he reached the stairs but in the privacy of his rooftop room, lent to him until he took up his quarters in Havelock's House at the start of the summer term, he found he was able to take a more encouraging view of the conversation. At least Gosse had begun to think outside his prejudices. And at least doubt had begun to cloud the Classical Fifth's conventional picture of the war, as drawn for them by Northcliffe and Bottomley. And also, as a bonus, Starchy had corrected himself when using the word 'Hun'. Did it matter a damn if they thought of him as a Bolshie?

* * *

26

The Sixth Forms had to be handled very differently. In a way he equated them with the very youngest boys in the school, for they were exceptionally vulnerable at seventeen-plus. If the war dragged on for a few months, some of them would be out there and they were all too aware of it. The Rupert Brooke approach—'Breast expanding to the ball'—spent itself long ago, and disillusionment was general among all but the fanatics and armchair strategists. Sometimes it seemed to him that the foul blight had already touched these youngsters, so that he saw them stripped of their high spirits, leading some forlorn attack on a German sector, defended by heavy machine-guns and belching mortar fire. They pressed him shyly for technical details, extensions of questions posed in the drill books of the Officers' Training Corps that paraded twice a week in the plantation and on the hillsides beyond. He humoured them, feeling his age here more than in any other part of the school. The gap between him and the eldest of them was no more than four years but it might have been fifty.

And then, towards the end of term, a week or two after Ludendorff's shattering breakthrough on Gough's Fifth Army front, with the appalling prospect of Paris falling, and the British being flung back on the Channel ports, there was another incident that left its mark on him yet encouraged him to see his presence here as something of real value.

Algy Herries told him at breakfast that young Briarley's father, a captain in the Rifle Brigade, had been killed on the Lys, and the boy had been told the news by Ellie, who usually took it upon herself to perform these melancholy chores. "The poor little toad is sunning himself out front now," Herries said. "Suppose you go and have a chat with him?"

"What could I say that Mrs. Herries hasn't already said?" David asked, and Herries said, airily, "Oh, I don't know . . . something about all the chaps who have gone on ahead, maybe. And perhaps what it's all in aid of," and at this David guessed Herries had heard, through the Bamfylde grapevine, of his 'Bolshie' chats with the Fourth and Fifth Forms, but was giving no clue as to whether he approved or disapproved.

He went out into the forecourt where Briarley sat on a seat under the huge cedar that spread itself across the headmaster's lawn. The boy looked stunned but more or less in control of himself. He sat very still, his hands on his knees, staring down across a field of rough pasture, part of which had been dug over for potatoes. Beyond the violet skyline granite outcrops of the Exmoor plateau winked and glistened in the pale sunshine, but nothing moved out there. The spring landscape looked as lonely and desolate as Briarley.

He sat down beside the boy, saying nothing for a moment, but then he saw Briarley's lip quiver and lifted his arm, resting it gently on the boy's shoulder. He said, at length, "Was he a professional, Briarley?" and when Briarley nodded, "We couldn't have held out this long without them, lad. They taught us everything we knew in the early days," and then, when the boy made no reply, "Do you care to tell me about him? I've served in the Lys sector twice. Maybe we met, spoke to one another."

He could not be sure whether his presence brought any real comfort but it must have eased Briarley's inner tensions to some extent for presently he said, "I didn't see a great deal of him, sir. When I was a kid he was mostly in India or Ireland. He came here once, on leave. Last autumn, it was. We . . . we sat here for a bit, waiting for the school boneshaker to take him to the station."

"Did he talk about the war, Briarley?"

"No, sir, not really. He only . . ."

"Well?"

"He said if anything did happen, and he was crocked and laid up for a time, I was to be sure and do all I could to look after the mater while he was away."

"Are you an only child, Briarley?"

"No, sir. I'm the only boy. I've got three sisters, one older, the others just kids."

"Well, then, you've got a job ahead of you. Your mother is going to need you badly. That's something to keep in mind, isn't it?"

"Yes, sir. I suppose so, but . . ."

He began to cry silently and with a curious dignity, so that David automatically tightened his grip on the slight shoulders. There was no point in saying anything more. They sat there for what seemed to David a long time and then, with a gulp or two, Briarley got up. "I'd better start packing, sir. Algy . . . I mean the headmaster said I was to go home today, ahead of the others. Matron's getting my trunk down from the covered playground . . ." And then, in what David thought of as an oddly impersonal tone, "The telegram said 'Killed in action', sir. What exactly—well, does that always mean what it says?"

"If it hadn't been that way it would have said 'Died of wounds', and there's a difference."

"Thank you, sir." He was a plucky kid and had himself in hand again. He nodded briefly and walked back towards the head's house. David would have liked to have followed him, letting himself be caught up in the swirl of end-of-term junketings, but he could not trust himself to move. His hands were shaking again and his head was tormented by the persistent buzzing that always seemed to assail him these days in moments of stress. He said, explosively, "God damn everybody! Where's the sense in it . . . ? Where's the bloody sense, for Christ's sake?" And then, like Briarley, he was granted the relief of tears.

2

There were plenty of moments during that period of initiation when he was able, to his own surprise, to put the war out of mind and find handholds that promised hope of a climb back to objectivity. Occasionally it was in class, when he was interested in some particular aspect of the syllabus, but more often it was in the common room, rubbing shoulders with the assortment of eccentrics that the arch-eccentric Herries had assembled round him to tide him through the war.

They were not a very likeable bunch but one had, David assumed, to make allowances. The older men were petrified in the Victorian mould, some of them so deeply rutted that they appeared to regard the war as a tedious and irrelevant interruption to their careers or well-earned retirement. Of the younger bunch, the C.3 men were almost pitiable, feeling themselves terribly handicapped as civilians in authority over four hundred boys, almost all of whom had fathers, brothers and uncles at the front. There was one among this latter group who was teetering on the edge of a nervous breakdown, Meredith, a twenty-five-year-old diabetic, with a sallow complexion and huge defenceless eyes. Meredith's classes, David learned, usually ended in a riot, and he was said to stand on the rostrum and let the tide of ribaldry sweep over him, bleating, "I *say* there . . . I *say*, you fellows . . . !"

Beyond that he would make no protest. Meredith had a curious sideways-sloping gait, moving over the ground with long strides, one shoulder raised an inch higher than the other. The boys had taken to mimicking him and some of them did it rather well, occasionally, it was alleged, lurching up to the blackboard in his actual presence and taking over, while Meredith stood helplessly, whimpering, "I *say* . . . I *say*, you fellows . . . !" Herries had done what he could to help and even advised Meredith to take a cane into class, but when the poor devil followed this advice even worse chaos resulted. Boyer and his ilk, pretending to be terrified of Meredith's ineffectual swipes, fled in all directions. When cornered they fell on their knees, shrieking for mercy.

The older masters showed no sympathy at all with the poor chap and frequently complained of the uproar resulting from his classes. Carter, the only younger master apart from David who had been in uniform, was the most persistent common-room nag, and David soon conceived an intense dislike for the man, whose conceit amounted to arrogance.

Carter was a stocky, rather florid man, with smooth red hair that he kept oiled so that it gleamed like wet rust. He had a long inquisitive nose, rimless glasses and no eyelashes to speak of. On the strength of six months' service as a Territorial officer, at a camp in Northumberland, he claimed David as a war comrade, explaining in great detail how a knee injury, received in a prewar football game, had been responsible for his discharge in 1915.

"Let me down with a bump, old man," he said, during one of his interminable reminiscences, that made David think of himself as a newly joined officer buttonholed by a patronising major. "Damn thing gave out the week my draft was due to leave for France. Most of them went west at Loos, of course. Damned awful show, Loos. Badly bungled, I gather."

David murmured that it was, and that he had seen some fighting in the area, but Carter was not interested in positive experience, preferring to talk of his triumphs on the drill ground outside Newcastle in the early days of Kitchener's army. He was still very much the martinet, with a small army of his own, the school O.T.C., and was extremely put out when David politely refused to join the Corps.

"Damn it, why not, old man? We could use a chap like you, someone with trench experience. I daresay you could teach us a few wrinkles if you cared to, and the top brass regard the O.T.C. as the nursery of subalterns, don't they?"

"If they do then God help the lot of us," said David, the Welsh lilt edging back into his voice as it often did under stress. "The average life of those kids out there is three weeks. Good God, man, they don't even have time to learn when to duck!" and at once regretted his testiness. He need not have bothered. Carter was exceptionally thick-skinned and said blandly, "Well, that's war, old chap. Can't win a war without losing a few. However, I'll not take no for an answer. The head tells me you're still convalescent. We'll talk about it again later, eh?"

He drifted off, unaware that the convalescent was having the greatest difficulty in restraining himself from committing assault upon his person, but the moment he was out of earshot Howarth, the senior English master, said, "Ignore the poopstick. Most of us do, whenever we can," and he at once felt cheered, for he was by no means sure, at this stage, whether Herries would expect him to take part in O.T.C. activities. He said, cautiously, "Is that true about his knee?" and Howarth, reluctantly laying aside his *Times*, said that everybody at Bamfylde took that knee on trust, as the medical board must have done, Carter being but thirty-one years old. He added, however, "The devil of it is it gives him the edge on all the civilians about here and being Carter he makes the utmost of it. Maybe somebody was lucky he was crocked on the football field. Shouldn't care to have him lead me into action, would you?"

"No, by God, I wouldn't," David said, and at once saw the testy, taciturn Howarth in a new light. Up to then he had been very wary of the man, a notable disciplinarian, with the reputation for possessing a bitter tongue. No one at Bamfylde, save Herries himself, had escaped Howarth's sarcasm, but he was recognised as a first-class teacher who had the respect, if not the affection, of the boys, even the wild ones in the Lower Fourth. When the other masters had drawn their dishwater coffee from the tarnished urn and moved off, David said, "You've been here a good many years, Mr. Howarth. How would you say it compares with other schools, schools of the same standing?" and Howarth said, for once without irony, "I can tell you that. It compares extremely well under Herries. It'll never be a Harrow, a Clifton or a Rugby. That chance passed us by when our numbers dropped in Bull's day.

But I think of it as a first-class second-rater. Or could be, when the wartime chaff is blown away, and the Governors spend some money on the fabric." He seemed to reflect a moment. "I stayed when I might have moved on and I've had my chances, especially in the last few years, when my age group has had it all their own way. But if you asked me why I don't think I could give you a specific answer. Maybe it's because I like and respect Herries. He's an original."

"You don't look for originality in this profession, do you?"

"You do here," Howarth said shortly, and abruptly terminated the conversation by picking up his *Times*, leaving David with the impression that Howarth was someone on whom it might be wiser to reserve judgment. He was right about Bamfylde as regards originality, however, as David soon discovered when he became better acquainted with the older men on the staff.

There was Cordwainer. There was Acton. And there was Gibbs, respectively known as 'Judy', 'Bouncer' and 'Rapper'. The Sixth called the trio 'The Magi', for each, in his different way, was a man of distinction. Judy Cordwainer taught geography as his main subject, and elementary mathematics to the juniors, but he did many other things. He played the organ at Stonecross Church, where the school worshipped on Sundays, marked out the cricket and football pitches with fanatical precision, presided over the school stationery cupboard and even taught woodwork. Judy came of the generation of school-teachers who practised before the age of specialisation and could turn hand and brain to anything once he was persuaded Bamfylde had need of his services. A tall, austere man, with cadaverous features, he was without a sense of humour, but his unswerving loyalty to boys and colleagues more than made up for this and, over the years, he had acquired a gratuitous popularity. Wags were fond of explaining how he came by his nickname, back in the nineties, when he had been housemaster of Outram's, a post he had relinquished in favour of Carter on his official retirement. It appeared that Outram's was cock-house that particular year and were expected to win the house cup for rugby, but their final game against Havelock's showed a lamentable lack of form. Cordwainer, disgusted by their poor performance, trotted up and down the touchline shouting encouragement to their rivals, who finally won both match and trophy. Cordwainer's own fifteen were so outraged by this treach-

ery that they styled him Judas, softened, over the years, to Judy.
A standard entertainment at Bamfylde was to crowd round the
stationery cupboard in the Remove in order to witness Judy issue
replacements. He would refuse to renew an exercise book unless
he was satisfied that every page of an old one was covered with
scrawl, and would sharpen an inch of pencil and uncross Waver-
ley nibs when boys presented evidence of spent equipment. He
had a high-pitched, honking voice, and despite his age could still
subdue a classroom, hurling a huge bunch of keys at inattentive
pupils and sometimes hitting the hot water pipes in a way that
sent an echoing clang through all the classrooms of Lower School.
He had a passion for neatness and precision. Later on David saw
him award marks to Third Formers with wrong answers, rejecting
correctly answered exercises that were decorated with blots. Cordwainer saw Bamfylde as a kind of rural Athens, and probably
thought of it as the centre of the cultural universe. Being as bald
as a tonsured monk (and looking like one in his voluminous
gown) he would wear his tweed cap in class on cold mornings
and stand honking there, a perfect prototype of the old-style
dominee, whose methods were unchanged since he came down
from Cambridge in the early seventies. Indeed, a parody of Judy
Cordwainer, one of the standard turns among the juniors who
could exactly reproduce his honking voice, usually began with one
or other of his favourite precepts—"I'll have *method* before speed,
d'ye hear?" or "Oh . . . *prince* of fools! Take it away, slovenly
numbskull!"

By contrast, Bouncer Acton was a hearty, excessively amiable
man, an ordained priest who ministered to a small parish north
of the school, where he occupied a rectory used as a spill-over for
new boys. Everyone liked Bouncer, who taught divinity throughout the school, and Latin to the juniors, but everyone took shameless advantage of his slight deafness and near-sightedness, and
the fact that he preferred to look over rather than through the
steel-rimmed spectacles perched on his pudgy little nose. It was
said that Bouncer had donned those useless spectacles while taking part in a charade as a boy, and had subsequently forgotten
them, leaving them perched there even when he went to bed.
The bolder boys were fond of asking Bouncer earnestly phrased
questions, concerning passages in the Bible relating to Lot's in-
cest, circumcision, concubines, how much the elders saw of

Susannah, and the Virgin birth, but he would always answer straightforwardly, seldom suspecting he was being hoaxed. On occasion, however, he could be savage. His standard punishment, for the few misdemeanours he detected, was a volley of four penal marks and this meant one hour's drill on Saturdays. As four was the limit allowed, and any penal marks in excess earned the delinquent a thrashing, this had the effect of keeping skylarkers in purdah for the remainder of the week. The wags were equally expert at mimicking Bouncer, who had pendulous cheeks that quivered when he bobbed up and down, the trick that had won him his nickname.

Rapper Gibbs was different again, a wizened insignificant-looking man, who taught music and accompanied the popular choral and operatic societies that Herries had founded on becoming headmaster. Rapper's soubriquet stemmed from the short pointer he used on the knuckles of blundering amateur pianists, but despite his asperity he was an excellent tutor and music, David discovered, played a prominent part in the cultural activities of the community.

There were some two dozen masters on the staff in the spring of 1918. Apart from outstanding characters, like Judy, Bouncer, Rapper and the sarcastic, withdrawn Howarth, there were several other oddities, some of whom David did not get to know until the following term. Ferguson, for instance, a volcano of a man who taught French, and would never utter a word of English during a class, ignoring boys who addressed him in their own tongue. His habit of prancing up and down the classroom, using his gown like a sail, had earned him the nickname of 'Bat'; Barnaby was an amiable, erudite man who taught Latin in Senior School, and was said to be inordinately fond of porridge, even the glutinous concoction ladled out in Hall every morning throughout the school year. There was the motherly Mrs. Parminter, who presided over the Second Form, and was so formidably corseted that her substantial bust projected like the flying buttress of a Gothic town hall. She was known, on this account, as 'Ma Fender', but the smaller boys, particularly those newly removed from home, were glad of her comfort and sympathy. There was only one other woman on the staff, Mrs. Gorman, the elderly Matron, who was inflexible and matter-of-fact with patients and malingerers alike. No one had coined a nickname for her until a returning Old Boy, happening to seek her out for relief of some minor ailment, emerged with a slip of paper marked 'M & D', that meant, so he told his audience, 'Medicine and Duty', thus establishing a legend that Mrs. Gorman had served in the R.A.M.C. in the Boer War. After that the boys referred to her as 'Kruger'.

They were, David decided, a very colourful lot, but apart from Herries himself he was unable, during those first weeks, to strike up a friendship with any one of them. It was as though he had joined a band of castaways on a desert island, the lone survivor of a subsequent wreck, and at first he was inclined to view his isolation as the inevitable result of his own mental confusion. In the end he took his problem to Herries.

"In a sense you *are* an outsider, my dear chap," he said, "and that's the reason I grabbed you the moment you showed up. You're the bridge, don't you see? A passage over a generation gap, and it isn't the conventional generation gap we all have to cross if we know our business properly. Your gap, caused by the war, is semi-permanent. It might take twenty years to close."

"But some of the chaps on the staff are only a year or so older than I am," David argued. "There's the C.3 men, and Carter."

"It's not a matter of years, but of experience, don't you see? What are our casualties to date? Not far short of three million, I'd say, and a third of them dead at eighteen-plus. No one who hasn't been out can imagine what it's like. Mentally a man like you must have aged about a year every month, and that makes you immeasurably senior to theorists like me, and faithful old buffers like Cordwainer, Acton and Gibbs. *Someone* has to tackle the job of nudging all those young rascals over the threshold into what I sincerely hope will be an entirely new world. *We* can't do it because we're even more adrift than they are and haven't a compass reading between us. In a year or so I daresay we can find you some help. Hang it all, everyone in his early twenties can't be dead or maimed or gassed. In the meantime you're on your own, lad."

He thought about this during his long tramps across the moors and his moochings around the silent and deserted buildings during the Easter holidays, when most of the staff and all the boys were gone save a dozen who lived in the head's house while their parents were abroad. It was a sombre thought but it represented the challenge that he, and Herries, and the Osborne neurologist thought of as therapy, and with the slow return of vitality, and a surer grip on his nerves, he began to respond to it in a way that revived his self-confidence.

The news from the front was bad but his infantryman's eye had taught him to read between the lines of press reports so that, alone among everyone he met in this backwater, he was able to assess the problems of the German vanguard, who had far outrun their supplies in the surging advance that began on March 21st. Right now they were crossing the old battlefields of 'fifteen, 'sixteen and 'seventeen, devastated country where the difficulties of the victors would be more formidable than those of divisions falling back on base areas. Eventually, he supposed, there would be a counter-attack, spearheaded by the Americans, so that on the whole he was optimistic of the eventual outcome.

By the last day of April, when the school reassembled, he was scanning the newspapers for signs of a large-scale holding operation and found his opinion eagerly solicited by boys whose fathers and brothers had been caught up in the spring débâcle.

"Will the Yanks attack, sir?"

"Is our own show under way, sir?"

"Do you suppose Jerry has shot his bolt, sir?"

It was curious, he thought, that even the fourteen-year-olds were more instinctively aware of what was at stake out there than men thirty, forty or even fifty years their senior. In a way, in a perverse way, it might even be hopeful.

Chapter Three

1

He was finding his way about, familiarising himself with the great, sprawling barn of a place that straggled halfway up the rise behind the grey-stone buildings of the original Bamfylde, built of imported materials that always seemed at odds with the honey-coloured local stone used for the extensions.

There were really two schools here, the tall squarish pile that reared itself four sides of the quad (and even after seventy years of Exmoor weathering, still looked like a baroque folly) and the utilitarian additions added over the years, that had already adapted themselves to the green-brown hillside, a straggle of farm buildings, and unfenced pastures bounded by the sports fields in the south and west, and plantation windbreak to the east, and the crest of the moor to the north. Herries and Howarth were right about the decaying fabric. It had needed extensive renovation long before the war began. Now it was beginning to look seedy, scarred and very shabby.

Most of the classrooms, together with Big School, and the headmaster's house that occupied the whole of the south side of the quad, were housed in the older block. Big Hall, the kitchens and all but one of the dormitories, were in the newer block. Long, stone-flagged passages connected these quarters with the quad.

Branching from it, one floor up, was a wainscoted passage known as the Rogues' Gallery. Here, in a sombre row, hung portraits of Bamfylde's five headmasters, including a younger, cherubic-looking Herries. Opposite them, posed in wide-eyed, dutiful groups, were football and cricket teams, reaching back to the earliest days of the school when nobody wore special clothing for games and everyone played cricket and football in workaday boots and shirtsleeves. There was a veritable warren of music rooms, laundry rooms, a boothole and a stray classroom or two about here, together with a school museum and, on the floor above, a range of attics used as storerooms. There was also a garret where, once a fortnight, the barber from Challacombe, the nearest market town, plied his clippers. One of Algy Herries' aversions was overlong hair and the boys, from the Fifth downwards, were shorn at frequent intervals. For a day or so after the appearance of Bastin, the barber, known and reviled as 'Sweeney' by the boys, everyone on the premises (the Sixth had won an exemption charter) went about with a whitish skull and Bastin was seen to drive away with a sack of clippings. The boys swore that he used them to make hairshirts that he sold to monks, but David later discovered that a condition of his contract was to dispose of his debris after a mass haircut, the school being desperately short of domestic staff.

Apart from the headmaster's house, which was spacious and comfortably furnished, and some of the quarters occupied by living-in masters, the premises were bleak and daunting to a newcomer. When he left the temporary refuge of the O.B.A. President's room, David was given a sitting-room and tiny bedroom in Havelock's House, ruled by Ferguson, the French master. Mrs. Ferguson was a Frenchwoman and reminded David of the black-draped madames he had seen counting their takings in estaminets behind the lines. The Fergusons were a staid, methodical couple, who left him to his own devices in his limited free time, and he grew to like his little sitting-room that looked south over a stretch of moor dotted with birchwoods and the rhododendron forest he had noted on his first walk from the station.

The aspect of the moor changed dramatically during his first few weeks up here. When he had arrived, in early March, the countryside had a wind-swept, breathless look, as though its hardihood had been taxed to the limit by winter gales and frosts, but even before the summer term opened, spring had enlarged its hold. All the beeches and elms in the two drives began to sprout new leaves, a sheen of bright green varying the mottled pattern of gold and russet, and a rash of primroses appeared in the breast-high banks, relieved every few yards by great plumes of cow-parsley and a scatter of scarlet campion. Soon, in the folds under the copses, where the little river Brent ran to join the Bray or the Barle (it seemed undecided which) acres of blue-bells dusted the margins, like early morning mist masking the shallow valley. The sky patterns changed minute by minute, now streaked and dappled with bluish trailers, now a jumble of plumped-up pillows, gashed by gusts of wind that came soughing down from the upper moor. This high land stretched away into the far distance, a series of brown and grey ridges, broken here and there by the blur of woods where pockets of ash, sycamore, thorn and elderberry had found some kind of refuge from the north-easterlies and south-westerlies that Herries said took turn and turn about from October to May.

The air and its landscape improved his health, soothing his ragged nerves and inducing a state of suspended dreaminess when he was not occupied in class, or with games, or dormitory super-vision. Slowly, week by week, the Western Front began to recede, an old wound he was learning to live with, and sometimes the war seemed so remote that it might have been fought by Welling-ton or Marlborough. He was helped in this by his growing rapport with the boys.

He had his favourites or, if not favourites, then his star-performers, whom he saw as he had once seen the section leaders of his platoon. There was a star-performer in every group and round him were gathered his acolytes. The mystique of leader-ship was as obvious here as in the trenches and he found he could soon spot the rankers marked down for a stripe. Boyer, of the Lower Fourth, was such a one, with Dobson as his runner-up. Blades, in the Upper Third, was another, a handsome boy who took the leadership of his group for granted and was said by Howarth to have an original mind. "Might even write some good verse when he matures," Howarth said, and then, as though un-willing to forgo the characteristic touch of acidity, "Poor devil!" Below Blades, in the Remove, was Bickford, a lumbering fourteen-year-old, lazy as a mastiff in the sun and attended, wherever he went, by his two henchmen, Rigby, a farmer's son, and Ford, whose father was said to be a bookmaker. Bickford, although indolent, was a bit of a bully, much feared by the urchins of the Lower Third and Second Form, over whom he held sway, a slothful, medieval despot, who could be mollified by tribute or subservience. The sort of boy, David thought, who needed watching, although his grin was infectious and he could sometimes exhibit a certain inventiveness. David discovered this one day when Bickford made use of a warped floorboard to set the stationery cupboard rocking without apparent agency, declaring that the manifestation was proof of the existence of the Remove ghost, a failed master of Bull's era who had, so the story ran, swallowed salts of lemon and been buried in Stonecross churchyard with a suicide's gravestone placed at a different angle from all the other monuments.

He grew to like some of the older boys in the Sixth, most of whom would be leaving to join one or other of the Services at the end of summer term. Cooper, Fosdyke and Scrubbs-Norton were typical of this cadre, boys who had come to Bamfylde in the last year of peace, and were now prefects and far better at keeping order than some of the younger masters. Their eagerness to get into uniform touched David as nothing else was able to. He already saw them in their Sam Brownes and British warms, seeking an opportunity to prove themselves as men, and while he was often tempted to introduce them to the stark realities out there, he never did. It would have been like telling five-year-olds that Father Christmas was a myth. He did get as far as accepting their shy invitations to take cocoa with them in their studies after prep, and would sit there discussing the war news with them, news that came to Bamfylde a day late in a bundle of papers from Challacombe. Luckily it was getting progressively more cheerful, with the successful British counter-attack at Villers Bretonneux, a unified Allied command and, in the first days of July, the beginning of the Le Hamel offensive. Farther south, in the Chemin des Dames area, the French were still taking a hammering and there were some spectacular German advances but these, David assured them, would soon peter out, as all offensives did in the non-stop slogging match. More and more Americans were landing in France, and the general pattern of the summer fighting was becoming clearer every day. "I think Ludendorff may have shot his bolt by the time you get back here in September," he said, cautiously, but then Cooper reminded him that most of the Sixth would not be returning for the autumn term, and all he could do was offer up a prayer that somehow these babies would be kept in training bases until the promised all-fronts counter-attack was launched.

The climax came, for David Powlett-Jones, on the eleventh day of August, just before he set off on his belated visit to his mother at Pontnewydd. Screaming headlines announced the breaching of the Hindenburg Line and unheard-of advances by the British in most of their sectors, places where, only a year ago, the gain of a few hundred yards of quagmire was won at the cost of a hundred thousand casualties.

He took Northcliffe's journal up to Herries' thinking post and read it very carefully, his heart-beats quickening when he came upon the familiar name of some devastated village where no building was more than a foot high, and the soil was rich with the bones of the dead of earlier battles. There could be no doubt about it now, surely? Cooper, Fosdyke and Scrubbs-Norton were reprieved. They would take their place in some office or factory, or perhaps spend a pleasant spell at one of the universities, after which, no doubt, they would marry some fluffy girl and have children of their own, earmarked for Bamfylde if they were boys.

He toyed with the fancy for a spell, visualising a subdued thirteen-year-old young Cooper, or a young Fosdyke, who would be coming here halfway through the nineteen-thirties, and the prospect must have caused him to smile, for suddenly he heard Herries' chirpy voice say, "Good news, P.J.? My stars, it would have to be to fool me! I've been inflated and deflated so many times by that rag that I've stopped reading it, apart from casualty lists."

David said, "It's real enough this time. We've broken the Hindenburg Line. I'd stopped believing that was possible. It'll be open warfare from here on and that's something positive."

"Was that worth grinning at?"

"In a way, sir." He could always talk uninhibitedly to Herries. "As a matter of fact, I was smiling at the prospect of Cooper's boy sitting under Mrs. Parminter in the Second in a dozen years or so," and he smiled again when Herries' tufted eyebrows shot up. "Pure speculation on my part, I'm afraid. What I mean is, the chances are that Cooper will live long enough to marry and have children. If he does he'd want to send his boys here, wouldn't he?"

"They all do," Herries said. "Without them we should wither, I'm afraid." He sat down on the shaft of the horse-roller, parked up here in obedience to his decree every time the roller-gangs finished a stint on the cricket pitch. "Haven't seen so much of you lately. Settling in?"

"I think so, sir. What do you think?"

"You'll do. You've frightened one or two of the old stagers, I'm told. Oh, don't let that bother you. It never did me. If you can't smuggle your own convictions into the curriculum you might as well go away somewhere, dig a hole and live in it." He lit his short pipe and puffed contentedly for a while. Then, cocking one eyebrow, "How do *we* look to you?"

"I've been very happy here, sir."

"I didn't mean that. How do we seem to be trundling along to someone from outside?"

David hesitated. It seemed a propitious time to make a point he was very eager to make.

"I can only answer that from an academic standpoint, Headmaster."

"Go ahead."

"It's the text-books I've inherited. Most of them were printed about the time of Victoria's first Jubilee. How much say does an unqualified man get in the choice of texts?"

"Depends on the man. You? I wouldn't pull on the bit unless I thought you were rushing your fences. You're a bit inclined to. Not that that's unusual in a chap your age. What kind of history were you taught as a boy?"

"Strings of dates and battles. The Treaty of Troyes and the War of Jenkins' Ear."

"Ah, that fellow Jenkins. I always thought that was a bit of liberty, passing his ear around Parliament like the plate at church. Still, it worked. They had their war, didn't they?"

It was always difficult to decide whether or not there was a coded message in Herries' puckish good-humoured talk and this time David decided to put it to the test. "I think we should have different text-books for different ages," he said. "The subject needs to be introduced with colour—Alfred's cakes, Bruce's spider and

42

so on, but it ought to progress from there without getting dull."

"What's your prescription?"

"To catch the interest in Lower School with the legends, move on to a more solid diet in Middle School, and then use half the periods for free discussion in the Fifth and Sixth. Especially the Fifth, when they're coming up to School Certificate and Matric. Discussion promotes original thought, doesn't it? And I believe most examiners like originality, even when it reads like heresy."

"Something in that. Maybe you'd like to work out a syllabus for next term. After all, you'll have more latitude then. I'll get someone else to take the Lower School in English. It won't be Howarth, of course. He likes his subject too much to reach down. Maybe one of the new chaps, there are a couple coming. Why the frown, P.J.?"

"If it's all the same to you, sir, I'd like to continue English with the Second and Third. I know I'll have to start reading for my own degree, but I can manage. The fact is . . . well, it might sound absurd, but those extra periods have helped. Helped me, I mean. In rediscovering Gray, Cowper, Tennyson and Goldsmith, and those excerpts from some of my old favourites, like *Silas Marner* and *Westward Ho!*. The mugging up enabled me to get things into a better focus."

"Well," Herries said slowly, "that sounds encouraging. If Gray's 'Elegy' still has relevance to you after all you experienced out there, then the sooner the young come to it the better." He relit his pipe and over the flaring match David saw he was smiling. He went on, "The jungle drum tells me you occasionally feed them something more up-to-date than Mr. Gray. Is it true you read the Sixth a poem by that chap Sassoon?"

"Yes, it's true. They're going out there, some of them. It seemed to me that someone ought to do something to counteract all the rubbish these chaps print," and he indicated the newspaper he had laid aside.

"What was it, exactly?"

"It was a poem called 'Memorial Tablet', that Sassoon published this year. I've got a copy of his later poems. Some of them are strong stuff but they have more relevance to what's actually occurring in Flanders than all the leading articles I've read on the war. I . . . er . . . I could lend you a copy, Headmaster."

"I'd be obliged," Herries said, without irony. "I like to keep up to date. Well, then, my compliments to your mother, and we'll expect you back a day or so before term begins."

"Yes, sir. Thank you."

They got up by mutual consent and went down the slope towards the nearest of the outbuildings, but when they drew level with the fives court Herries said, "I suppose you're aware of your nickname by now?" and David, suspecting it would be 'Bolshie', said he had certain suspicions but had thought it best not to pursue them.

"Oh, it's an amiable one," Herries said, "not like some of them. It stems from your . . . consultative methods in class." He stopped, taking his pipe from his mouth and extending his hand. "Well, goodbye, 'Pow-wow'. Have a good holiday!" and he wandered off towards the piggeries. David remained standing by the fives court for a moment, thinking, "I've had my share of luck, God knows, but running across him beats anything that happened to me."

He had a curious afterthought then, concerned with a squat, bowlegged, round-shouldered man, who had died underground in the summer of 1913, a man who, even then, had had unwavering faith in him and had never been diffident about showing it. It was as though his father, feeling the darkness pressing in, had called for help on his behalf, and Herries, walking his rounds on this high plateau, had heard him across the width of the Bristol Channel.

2

Just over a year had passed since he had visited the Valley on leave, a month or so before the Brandenburgers' mortar shell had blasted him out of the war. It seemed narrower and shabbier, a place of steep, huddled streets, fortress-like chapels, rundown corner shops with nothing much to sell, and the familiar tip overshadowing them all. The corporate spirit of the Valley, that had been its sturdiest plant ever since he was a boy, seemed also to have withered, translating itself into bitterness, a different kind of bitterness from that of front-line men, for it lacked the inevitable sardonic humour. There was no jingo stridency here, only a glowering sense of exploitation by politicians, by mine owners, by royalty leeches, by war profiteers. For the vicarious prosperity

44

that had come to other industrial areas seemed to have by-passed the coalfields. No one was encouraged to forsake the industry and enlist, or join in the scramble for high wages in the munitions factories. Instead they were expected, almost compelled, to go on dragging coal from the hillsides at twice the speed and without comparable rises in rates. There was an undertone of militancy and strikes, of demands to put the industry on a new and realistic basis, a war that had little to do with the war of the headlines. He sensed what was happening even before he talked to his brothers-in-law, both miners, and although this world was almost lost to him now, fenced off by an education that none of these men had had, and experiences at the Front they had been spared, he still thought as a miner's son and could identify with their grievances and fear for their future when the need for coal was not so desperate and their bargaining power had been removed.

For the first time he heard men of his own race openly champion the Russian Revolution, and Trotsky's separate peace at Brest-Litovsk, an act that many Welshmen in the line had regarded as a betrayal, but which miners here saw as a portent of enormous social significance. Ewart Griffiths, married to his elder sister Gwynneth, was the first to put this into words when he said, "There's a rumour we're going to be asked to dig coal and help turn the Bolshies out but I'm telling you, man, they'll get no bloody help from us down yer! Time we started our own bloody revolution, Davyboy."

His mother, miraculously, was untouched by bitterness. The tragedies of her life did not show in her round, smooth, unmistakably Welsh face, with its pink and white bloom, still there after sixty years in the valleys, and forty-odd years of making twopence do the work of a shilling. She still kept the little terrace house spotlessly clean, still spoiled her five grandchildren, still cooked an appetising meal from the cheapest ingredients, and glowed when he told her he was now teaching in a school of four hundred boys, a place she would surely think of as a Gentleman's College. To her this was a far greater achievement than surviving three years on the Western Front, scholarship representing maturity, warfare being a little boy's scuffle in the street outside. "Been that proud of you, Dadda would," she said, when he told her his post had been made permanent. "There's a wonder it is! That Dadda should know it all those years ago, and your brothers Hughie and Bryn too, for you were the only real book-worm of the litter. Are they feeding you well down there, boy? You could do with more flesh on your bones, but maybe that's on account of all those hospital slops they gave you when you were hurt in the fighting."

He reassured her as to his health, but as he did so a thought struck him. He said, "God knows, you've earned a rest, Mam. Why don't you pack your things and come back to Devon with me? It's beautiful country down there—like Wales in Grandfather's time —and we could rent half a cottage from old Mrs. Bastin, the wife of our lampman. He's got a splendid garden, chock full of vege-tables. You'd like it down there." But she said, sadly, "Nice to be asked it is, Davy, but my place is here, so long as I can give Gwynneth and Megan a hand with the children. Besides . . ." and she glanced through the gap between the freshly-laundered curtains of the tiny kitchen, contemplating a view of her lean-to shed and the uniform backs of the houses in Alma Street, "what-ever would I do with myself in a strange place among strange folk? I was born yer, and I'll die yer among my own people. It's different with you. You've moved on, as Dadda said you would."

He left it at that, but soon the stale, claustrophobic atmosphere of the little town began to oppress him so that he thought long-ingly of the miles of moorland he could see from his dormer window in Havelock's House. In the last week of August, when the newspapers were trumpeting the British advance on the Ancre and the capture of Bapaume, he slipped away, promising to return for Christmas. Late the same evening, he caught the Challacombe train for Taunton and got out at Bamfylde Bridge Halt, revelling in the two-mile tramp up the twisting roads to the sportsfield gate, still lacking a hinge and leaning outwards.

Dusk was settling in the highest folds of the moor and the scent of honeysuckle and thyme came to him, together with the pun-gent whiff of grass clippings where old Tapscott, the one grounds-man remaining to them, had been scything the grass on what would be the scene of the autumn house matches. The school buildings, from this angle, were silhouetted against a tangerine sky, where the sun was sliding down behind the sentinel beeches of the west drive. He thought, "It's the damnedest thing . . . I've been here six months but it's already more home to me than Pontnewydd. Can't imagine being anywhere else . . ." and vaulting the crippled gate he moved up towards the southern fringe of the Planty, as the boys always referred to it, then down past the cricket pavilion and swimming pool to Herries's thinking post and a blur of light showing in the headmaster's house. "It's a niche," he told himself, "and damned if I don't cling to it as long as I can!" It struck him, passing the Gothic arch into the empty quad, that niches, like most other things, were likely to be in short supply for ex-servicemen in the years ahead.

3

The world of school enfolded him. By half-term even the mounting relief that the war was nearly over was muted by the immediacy of Bamfylde's problems, by the trivia of existence within the periphery of his work and personal encounters. When Bulgaria sued for peace, in early October, he was very elated, but only for an hour or so. Beatty, the games coach (who also acted as assistant bursar) had persuaded him to replace Wilton, the running captain, as chief whipper-in for the fortnightly cross-country events and this was no sinecure for a man eight months out of hospital. Bamfylde took its runs seriously and in rough country like Exmoor, the post of whipper-in was equivalent to a rearguard command. Small boys, lagging a long way behind, and unfamiliar with the country, had been known to get lost. The job of whipper-in was to co-ordinate the efforts of the prefects who were not running colours and keep the laggards closed up over a five-mile course.

And then, on his very first run-in, Archer the Third had to go missing when call-over was held in the quad and the boys were about to disperse for high tea.

It was almost dark then and inclined to be foggy. With storm lanterns and a band of volunteers he headed back beyond Stone-cross, where Archer the Third was found snivelling in a gully, nursing a twisted ankle and the fear of death from exposure. They carried him home sedan-chair fashion and when he sat down to his pea-soup David was in worse state than Archer, and so stiff that he had to haul himself up to the staff bathroom and soak in soda. He had forgotten all about Bulgaria.

It was easy to see how ageing men like Cordwainer and Acton had become so barnacled, tending, as the seasons passed, to identify the universe with Bamfylde and Bamfylde's concerns. Decisions like the date of speech-day, which pitch should be used for the house semi-finals and crises like the influenza epidemic that filled the sanatorium in ten days, or the near-mutiny of the O.T.C. over threadbare puttees that kept unrolling during manoeuvres, had a way of enlarging themselves into events of tremendous importance. Who was the locker-pilferer in Outram's? Was he boy or domestic? Who was covering for Howarth, himself down with flu? What could be done to stem the overflow of the brook that flushed the latrines, inevitably known as the Bog?

Surprisingly, it was Algy Herries who restored to him his sense of proportion once a week when he announced, often with tears in his eyes, the death of yet another Old Bamfeldian in action, and spoke a few words about the boy's years at the school. It was a sombre, almost masochistic duty he inflicted upon himself but David, who was beginning to get the full measure of the man, understood why he performed this weekly penance. He would see it as an obligation, to speak aloud, possibly for the last time, the name of a youngster, or perhaps someone who was not so young, whose shouts had once been heard on the pitches beyond the pointed windows of Big School, a person who had taken away with him some tiny part of the ethos of the school, planted in his mind and muscle during his time here. It was on these occasions that David would get a glimpse of that multitude of khaki-clad figures who had disappeared in the slime of Passchendaele, or fallen on the chalky wilderness of the Somme. For casualties, despite the Allied surging advances almost as far as the battlefields of August, 1914, were still trickling in, four in August, three in September, two more in October, one of them Bristow Major, who had been head prefect the term before David joined the staff and whose younger brother, Bummy Bristow, was still in the Upper Fifth.

But then, like a thunderclap, it ended. Word came over the telephone—from Second Lieutenant Cooper, of all people, now training as a demolition expert in London—that he had it on the best authority (an uncle in Fleet Street) that a cease-fire was to be declared at eleven a.m. the following day, and although no newspapers confirming this stupendous news could be expected until late afternoon, Algy took a chance and announced a school holiday, with leave to go into Challacombe, if transport could be arranged. Local boys disappeared but a majority stayed on, pooling their pocket-money to empty the tuckshop, and Ellie Herries was set to work with other masters' wives to perform a prodigy of baking for a communal supper and sing-song in Big Hall instead of the usual prep.

The immediate effect upon David was to increase his popularity as the one member of the staff who had fought at First Ypres, Loos and Neuve Chapelle, and who was regarded, somewhat to his embarrassment, as the ultimate authority on all things martial. He was cheered when he made his way up to the dais, luckily a little in advance of the other masters save Bouncer, who was there to say grace, and found himself blushing, for although he felt an immense sense of gratitude he could feel no personal achievement in survival when nearly a hundred Old Boys had died.

He kept his gaze on the floor until Bouncer had subsided, but there was worse to come. When the school orchestra had assembled and the singing began, they chose numbers that the troops had sung so repetitiously down all the roads of Picardy and Artois, 'Tipperary', 'Who's Your Lady Friend?', 'Long, Long Trail' and the like. To someone who had heard these choruses sung in that setting it was unbearable and soon, but inconspicuously, he escaped, slipping out through the sculleries to the cinder path leading to the piggeries. And here, unashamedly, he wept, blundering through trailers of mist until he found the path to Herries's thinking post, and pausing there, gulping down the dank, night air but still within earshot of the uproar in the Hall. He thought, desperately, "For Christ's sake . . . what is there to sing about . . . ? Why does it have to be a celebration when it ought to be a wake?"

He lit a cigarette, inhaling deeply, and he was still there when he saw a match flare down by the fives court. Feeling the need to communicate, he made his way down, certain that he would discover that Algy Herries had excused himself under similar pressures.

It was not Algy, however, but that dry old stick Howarth, the English master who had once advised him to ignore Carter's appeal to join the O.T.C., still the basis of a feud between them. Howarth's pince-nez flashed in the glow of his Gold Flake. He smoked, they said, forty to fifty a day and this was not his only vice. Rumour had it that he also accounted for three bottles of gin each week in his cosy rooms at Nicolson's, where he was housemaster.

He said, greeting David, "Saw you slink off and decided to take the same route. Obliged to you for the hint." And then, in the friendliest tone he had so far employed, "I imagine you've even less stomach for it than a slacker like me, P.J. But I'm human, after all. Bristow Senior was one of the brightest boys I've ever taught. He wrote to me several times from France. Said he was going into publishing with his step-father and would have made a success of it, I daresay. But he had to die, at eighteen. For what? Can you tell me?"

"Not yet. I might, in a decade or so."

"You're another of the millennium boys, then?"

"Not necessarily. But something hopeful must emerge from it. If it doesn't it'll be our fault—yours, mine and Algy's. Even the fault of the old stagers, so long as they stay on the job!"

"The devil of it is," Howarth said, "I never did go along with all this hang-the-Kaiser balderdash. I've never been able to hate the Germans. Have you discovered Heine yet?"

"I'm afraid not."

"Try him, sometime. He's got a trick of suiting all kinds of moods. Tonight's for instance—'*Enfant Perdu*', Houghton's translation—

> *But war and justice have far different laws,*
> *And worthless acts are often done quite well;*
> *The rascal's shots were better than his cause,*
> *And I was hit—and hit again, and fell*

—appropriate, wouldn't you say?"

"It's appropriate to the whole generation."

Howarth said nothing and, more from a need to divert his own gloomy thoughts than his companion's, David added, "Didn't Heine write a lot about love?"

"Yes, he did.

> *The old dream comes again to me;*
> *With May-night stars above,*
> *We two sat under the Linden tree*
> *And swore eternal love.*
> *Again and again we plighted troth . . .*

Here, what the devil has got into me?" and Howarth hurled his cigarette across the gravel, as though its trail of sparks would purge him of sentimentality.

"Has Heine personal significance for you?"

"He did have, a long time ago."

"Were you ever married?"

"No." There was a pause. In the darkness David could sense Howarth doing battle with himself, trying to break through the home-baked crust of reserve that he wore like a breastplate wherever he went. Finally he said, "I was to have been, when I was about your age. But she made the right decision. She married a stockbroker. It wasn't the financial aspect,"—he said this almost defensively—"she just couldn't see herself as a schoolmaster's wife, and I don't blame her when I look at some of the old birds roosting about here. Besides, this is a job for a bachelor if you mean to make a go of it. Miserable pay, no real prospects unless you strike lucky, and a fresh family every four to five years. What woman in her senses would take that on?" He stood up, lighting another cigarette. "What the devil are we doing, sitting here in the fog and talking drivel? Come up to my rooms and let's do our celebrating in the warm," and without waiting for David's assent he stalked off, leading the way through the quadrangle arch and up the steep flight of slate steps to his quarters.

That was the beginning of his tacit alliance with Howarth and he was to be grateful for it, for Howarth, by far the prickliest pear of the common room, was a counterpoise to Carter and one or two of the older men who had already begun to identify him as a radical. He had a conviction that this was not so much on account of his discussions with senior boys on the war, or his championship of a poet like Siegfried Sassoon, who had bravely challenged the establishment the previous year, but because they saw him as someone better qualified than they were to communicate with a generation that had moved into adolescence in the last four years. Howarth, for his part, recognised and accepted this, as indeed did Herries himself. Their patronage probably encouraged men like Carter to think of him as an interloper currying special privileges on the strength of his war record.

Three other shifts in the pattern of his life at Bamfylde occurred before the anniversary of his arrival came round. One was distressing, one reassuring. The third was a compromise, made with the object of closing the breach between him and the commandant of the Officers' Training Corps.

The compromise was proposed by Algy Herries, an admitted past master at reconciling extreme points of view. Hearing of David's uncompromising refusal to take part in military exercises, he buttonholed him outside the tuckshop between periods one December morning and said, gaily, "You're a Welshman, Powlett-Jones, and all the Welsh are musical. How do you fancy yourself as a bandmaster?"

"A bandmaster, Headmaster? You mean a stand-in for Pym, as orchestra leader?"

"No, dear boy. As the organiser of a drum and fife band for the Corps. We've had a legacy. A consignment of instruments from an Old Boy, name of Cherriton. Before my time, but it seems he was a local Volunteer enthusiast up in Yorkshire, before the Volunteers were merged into the Territorials. They had a band and Cherriton stipulated in his will that the instruments should be sent on to us. They arrived yesterday, half a cartload of them. Do you play an instrument?"

His relationship with Herries was sufficiently relaxed to encourage him to slip back into the familiar idiom and he replied, smiling, "Play the piano by ear, I do Mister Herries. Blew the cornet too, as a boy in Chap-pel now," and Herries responded, "You see, I have second sight. We're not hoping to qualify for tattoo status, at the Tidworth annual camps. All Carter wants is something to jolly the company along on route marches." He glanced shrewdly at David under his tufted brows. "You and Carter don't hit it off, do you?"

"I wouldn't say that. He seems to resent my not taking an active part in the Corps but frankly, sir, I've had a bellyful of bullshine and brass. Did Carter actually propose me for bandmaster?"

"No, he didn't. As a matter of fact he doesn't yet know we've got the instruments, but he's put in several requests to the Governors for a band allocation over the years. It's my idea. I'm not putting any pressure on you to join the Corps. It's run on a purely voluntary basis, even for the boys, and this job is unofficial. You wouldn't have to appear in uniform, or even turn up on parade. Just supervise the practices."

It was as close to an order as Algy Herries ever issued concerning extra-scholastic pursuits. Put like this David did not see how he could refuse without seeming churlish, so he said, "I'll take a crack at it, until somebody more qualified turns up," and Herries said, "Splendid! I'll get that tip over the armoury cleared out and you can use it as a bandroom. I'll also post a notice, announcing auditions."

Before the last day of term David had mustered a band and Herries was correct in his assumption that this would re-establish a working relationship with Carter. It was impossible to like the man. He was too sure of himself and inclined to be testy if his prejudices were challenged, but he saw a band as something likely to enhance the prestige of his beloved Corps. Luckily he was tone deaf and unlikely on this account to challenge the dispositions of any bandmaster.

There were those whose steps led them past the bandroom in the early days of the Lent term who would have regarded tone deafness as a boon. Of the sixteen boys selected only three were familiar with instruments, that included four bugles, as well as six fifes, a bass drum, two sidedrums, two kettledrums, and a pair of cymbals. A seventeenth volunteer, Boyer, was chosen for drum-major on account of his stature, imposing for a boy of sixteen.

From the first session David enjoyed the extra chore thrust upon him and arranged rehearsals three times a week, fitting them in between tea and prep and sometimes consulting Rapper Gibbs on technical points. Rapper advised him to discard the bugles but the embryo buglers made such an outcry that David improvised fanfares at stipulated intervals, wedging them into tortured renderings of 'The British Grenadiers' and some of Sousa's marches.

The Corps band was soon an institution and a great joke for those unconnected with it. The bandsmen did not mind, aware that there were a dozen volunteers waiting to take advantage of one resignation, as was proved when fourteen sent in their names after the inexpert cymbalist had clipped a piece from his thumb. David gave the job to Briarley, the boy he had tried to console the day news came that his father was lost on the Lys. He had kept his eyes on Briarley, noticing that the boy was slow to shake off his depression and inclined to walk alone, daydreaming on an old log up at the Planty, or on the seat under the fives court where every Bamfeldian seemed to drift when he was in the dumps. The cymbals did the trick. After a rehearsal or two Briarley became an ornament of the band, whirling the polished discs in a way that spilled sunlight over them like a gyrating halo. Boyer made a spectacular drum-major in his pipe-clayed collarette and spent hours in a secluded corner of the rugby field, practising his extravagant flourishes, including one that sent the staff spinning twenty feet into the air. The fife players soon learned to read notes marked out on cards by Rapper, who was unaware that he was thus identified with a group known, at first, as 'The Boys' Brigade', then as 'The Cacophoneers' but finally, through the agency of Barnaby, the classics master, as 'The Orpheans'.

Barnaby was a good jester, but he liked to send his jokes out to work. It happened that he was presiding over a construe in the Lower Third, who occupied the nearest classroom to the band-room, on a day when the band had been granted a free period to rehearse for the drill competition. Intermittent snatches of 'The British Grenadiers', graced by the shrill blasts on the bugles, reached the juniors and Barnaby ignored the chortles until he happened upon a passage from Horace and invited Taylor, the most promising Latinist in the class, to try a free translation. Taylor began, " 'Dapibus supremi—Grata testudo Jovis . . .'—'The lyre is welcome—at the feasts of supreme Jupiter . . .' " The general titter was enlarged into a gale of laughter as Barnaby slammed the window, saying, "We are not feasting, gentlemen. And Orpheus, alas, has lost his touch!"

The band provided everybody with light relief during a season of hard frost that reduced football to a minimum but somehow persuaded the diligent Carter that he was training a company of Alpine troops. The band, all members of the Corps, slogged ahead wherever the rank and file went but were relieved of the necessity of humping kit and rifle, a privilege won for them by David. Thus, in a curious way, they formed a nucleus of boys who were disposed to champion unorthodox views on tradition and soon, without in the least wishing it, he found that he was regarded as the standard-bearer of dissenters.

Some of the boys in Middle School, David noticed, had reduced cribbing to a fine art. Everyone in the common room knew it went on, and punished it on the rare occasions when a culprit was caught, but they seemed to draw no distinction in cribbing during examinations for removes, and cribbing during Lent term examinations, when undeserved prizes sometimes went to accomplished practitioners of the art.

By keeping his eyes and ears open, yet without identifying specific culprits, David became familiar with methods employed during his own periods and those of the short-sighted 'Bouncer'. There was the time-honoured blotting paper memoranda, the strategic positioning (with or without complicity) of the more advanced boys during tests, the cautious raising of a sheaf of notes through the cracked lid of a desk, and the more sophisticated method of attaching notes to a shred of elastic fastened to the shirt cuff. He had still not succeeded in catching anyone, but by the end of term he could have assembled a black museum of cribbing apparatus. What dismayed him was the startling result of an examination paper set for the history prize in that citadel of the work-shy, the Lower Fourth. Youings, by far the best scholar in the class, was placed seventh, whereas the position of some of the leading six could only have meant cribbing on an organised scale.

He let the result pass without comment, however, until he had had a chat with Youings on the questions set, and satisfied himself that the boy had answered all but one correctly. Then, after the list had been pinned to the school notice board, he fired a range-finder at the class, announcing that "the standard of work exhibited in the examination was encouragingly high, so high, in fact, as to pass the limits of credibility". He let this sink in for a minute before adding, "I'm not actually accusing anyone in the first six of—shall we say—jogging their memory a little, or pulling themselves up by their bootstraps. Why should I? I didn't catch them at it, any more than I can explain poor performances on the part of those same experts in the weekly tests. Perhaps the questions were happily chosen. Perhaps some of you may have done some . . . er . . . late mugging-up," and at this the class relaxed and there was a subdued chuckle.

He did not react to it, as he generally did, for chuckles were by no means unknown during his periods. Instead he stepped down off the rostrum and sauntered up the central aisle, pausing beside Dobson, who had been placed fourteenth in test averages but who had scored ninety-six out of a possible hundred in the exam and qualified for the form prize. The chuckle died before it had properly begun and Dobson, flushing a little, avoided his eye. He went on, keeping his tone level and jocular, "There's something of a moral problem here, however. This particular exam wasn't for a place in form, or a comment on the reports you'll

55

take home at the end of term. It wasn't for outside examiners either. It was for a specific gain, a prize with the prizewinner's name on the flyleaf, and there's a difference. To my mind at any rate. Think about it."

The bell sounded then and he left abruptly, wondering if he had made a fool of himself and feeling somehow that he had. It bothered him so much that he finally took the problem to Howarth, giving it as his opinion that Youings was the only boy in the first seven who had written an honest paper, and recounting as much as he recalled of his sermon. "Was that the right way of going about it?" he asked. "I mean, having failed to spot anyone cribbing, wouldn't I have been wiser to keep my mouth shut?" and Howarth replied surprisingly, "You know a damned sight better than that. As to whether your pi-jaw did any good I can check on that tomorrow."

"How, without actually accusing anyone?"

"Oh, by means unknown to the beginner, old man," and he left it at that.

He was as good as his word. Just before prep bell the following evening Howarth accosted him as he was reading the exam lists of the Lower Fifth on the quad notice board.

"Thought you might care to know you scored a bull's-eye with the Lower Fourth yesterday. They've had a public soul-searching and that half-blind ass Acton has been reaping your harvest. You see those Lower Fourth Divinity prize-list results? They represent today's sitting, and the reverend gentleman has assured me they are a very accurate reflection of his preliminary tests."

"How can either of you be sure of that?"

"How? For God's sake, man, don't you know me well enough yet to realise I haven't taken a damned thing on trust since I left kindergarten? I asked Acton to play a little game with me. He wrote down his forecast of the first ten in the exam today and here it is. Compare the two lists and draw your own conclusions." David took the list and held it alongside the list on the board. It was almost identical. He said, wonderingly, "Does that mean those young devils have decided to stop cribbing?"

"Only when there's a prize at the end of it, I'm afraid, and you have Boyer to thank for the mass conversion. Don't ask me how I know that either. When you've been at this job as long as I have you develop a sixth sense in these matters. However, you appear to be developing satisfactory techniques of your own," and with that he drifted away, the inevitable between-periods Gold Flake stuck between his lips.

As it happened, David had to wait until prize-giving for confirmation. Dobson, to the accompaniment of ironic Middle School cheers, marched up and collected his history prize, a leather-bound copy of Prescott's *Conquest of Peru*, and David glowered as he shook hands with Countess Hopgood, the guest of honour. His resentment was premature. A day later a puzzled Youings hung about after second bell and seemed to want a word with him. When everyone had left Big School, he laid the copy of *Conquest of Peru* on the desk, open at the presentation page. Dobson's name had been blocked out and above it, in anonymous script, was the legend, *'Presented to Edward Youings, in appreciation of his unfailing assistance in history periods. By his grateful comrades in the Lower Fourth!'*

Youings said, "Is it . . . er . . . some kind of practical joke, sir? I mean, should I keep it? I found it in my desk this morning."

"It's not a joke, Youings," David said, "more of a peace-offering. The kind an errant husband brings home in the form of flowers when he's been out on the beer."

"Sir?" Youings, like many academics, was not very quick on the uptake.

"Keep it," he said, "it's yours anyway," and went in to lunch with a sense of elation and a sharp awareness of Howarth's sagacity.

He extracted no elation from another episode that occurred on the last Sunday of the Lent term but once again it taught him something.

He was in the library returning books when he happened to glance through the window that gave on the quad. A group of boys were skylarking under the Founder's statue and prominent among them was 'Bull' Bickford, and his two henchmen, Rigby and Ford, all three engaged in forcing the head of a struggling Second Former into the fountain that ran around the plinth. To further the work Bickford was methodically rooting at the victim's buttocks. David, through the open window, bawled, "Stop that, Bickford, and come up here! You too, Rigby—Ford. Look sharp about it!"

The Second Former, unaware of the source of his reprieve,

scuttled away as his tormentors slouched across the quad and up the steps to the library. Presently they appeared dishevelled, but not particularly apprehensive.

"What was that about, Bickford?"

"Oh, really nothing, sir. We were only teaching Skidmore how to make his bow. It's the last Sunday of all, you see, and Skidmore's a first-termer. He's a bit bucky, sir, and we gave him the chance of doing it on his own. When he wouldn't we had to make him."

"Make him half-drown himself?"

"Yes, sir, just as it says—'Last day but five, new kids take a dive.' Maybe you don't know how it goes, sir?"

David knew how it went. It was part of a string of doggerel devised, over the years, as an initiation rite for new boys. When Sundays fell on certain days, measured in relation to the days left in the term, rhyming couplets decreed that they perform certain idiotic procedures. One or two came to mind—'Last Sunday but six, new kids pick up sticks', 'Last Sunday but two, new kids feel my shoe', and so on. Towards the end of term, with only a few days to run, the nonsense proliferated, for the programme of work and games began to run down, and boys like Bickford had time on their hands to flush victims from the limited security of the Bog, and subject them to the rough and ready dictates of the tradition. There was no real harm in it, he supposed, except when they picked on a very sensitive boy, or when the ritual made a sadistic appeal to a natural despot like Bickford. He said, "Well, I don't give a fig for that kind of tradition. It's no more than a flimsy excuse for bullying. The next time I see you rough-housing a new boy I'll devise some doggerel of my own and you'll be at the receiving end of it. Is that clear?"

"Yes, sir," from all three, but he knew what they were thinking—"Who the hell is he to stick his nose in? He's only a third-termer himself!" The devil of it was that all the rest of the staff, even Herries himself, tolerated this kind of thing, so long as it was kept within limits, but who could say where those limits ran? He wondered briefly what made him so squeamish about it. Was it the orgy of bloodletting he had witnessed in Flanders, or the thought that there was already too much gratuitous cruelty in the world?

He went off in search of Skidmore, finding him, as he had half-

expected, barricaded in a cubicle in the Bog, the one relatively
safe retreat throughout a 'last day but five', or a 'last Sunday but
six'. He called, "Come on out, Skidmore, I want a word with you,"
and Skidmore emerged, a pallid little wretch, with a crumpled
Eton collar a size too large for him and a tear-streaked face. He
said, "All right, it's nothing to worry about. I only wanted to know
why you stood out against Bickford. Wouldn't it have been easier
to make your bow to the Founder? All the other new boys have,"
but Skidmore replied, "No, sir, it's an image."

"An image? What's an image?"

"That statue. You don't bow to images. It's in the Bible, sir."

He was taken aback. It seemed astounding that, in this day
and age, a child like Skidmore should be animated by the spirit
of Christian martyrs facing circus lions. He said, wonderingly, "Is
that why you preferred to be rooted? You're not pulling my leg?"
and Skidmore assured him gravely that he was not, and that there
was a hymn they sang in chapel that ran, 'the heathen in his
blindness, bows down to wood and stone'. He thought, dolefully,
"Good God, when do you stop learning about boys . . . ?" and
just stopped himself laughing.

"What's your father, Skidmore?"

"A minister, sir."

"Really? What denomination?"

"Wesleyan Methodist, sir."

"Will you tell him about this when you get home?"

"No, sir."

"You'd see that as sneaking?"

"Wouldn't it be, sir?"

Like himself, Skidmore was learning. You made your point,
where you could, but you didn't brag about it.

"All right, Skidmore. Run along and keep out of Bickford's way
if you can," but then, as the boy turned to go, "How are you
liking it here? In spite of today's business?", and Skidmore said,
"Well . . . all right, sir. I daresay I'll get used to it by next term."

"Me too," said David, grinning, and turned away from the boy's
surprised look.

PART

TWO

Catalyst in a Beret

Chapter One

1

The hat plummeted down out of nowhere, brushing his nose and pitching at his feet where it settled like a grey bird making a clumsy landing on the shingle. It was an altogether unremarkable hat, not a beret exactly, and not quite a tam o' shanter, but something in between, slightly larger than the hats French peasants had worn in the fields behind the line and with a tassel like a stalk.

Seconds passed before he realised the hat must have an owner and then glanced up, to discover he had been on the point of walking under the pier when the beret fell. A girl was looking down at him from a height of about twenty feet and the moment he saw her she began to wave, pointing to her head, then down at her beret. He smiled and picked it up, joining her in her dumb show by pointing to himself and then the pier, whereupon she nodded eagerly and put her hand to her mouth, masking a laugh. It was a trick the Second Form practised whenever he made one of his small jokes.

He climbed the shingle bank and vaulted the iron rail on to the promenade, moving along to the turnstile and paying his twopence to pass the barrier. The girl was awaiting him on the far side and he noticed now that she was less sure of herself and looked, indeed, a little shamefaced, again like one of the Second Form caught out in a piece of mischief. But then he noticed something else. She was a very pretty girl, with dark brown hair parted in the middle. She had large brown eyes with long, curling lashes, and small hands and feet that seemed no larger than a child's the way she was standing, feet close together, hands drooping and half-hidden in the folds of a tartan skirt. He said, diffidently, "It is yours, I suppose?", and she replied, breathlessly, "Yes . . . thank you very much . . . it was a silly thing to do! I was leaning out too far and I grabbed but missed. I say . . ." as she took the hat and began fumbling in her little handbag, "I owe you two-pence!" but at that he laughed and she did too as he said, "It isn't every day of the week a girl throws her cap at me." And then, for want of an idea as to how the conversation could be prolonged, he looked over her shoulder and saw the word 'Teas' on the shore side of the pier pavilion. "Couldn't we have some tea? Or coffee? Are you with anyone?"

She smiled, implying that she was more expert at this game than he was. "No, I'm not 'with anybody', and I'd love some coffee. I was just going in for some. They make good coffee here. For a pier pavilion, that is," and they walked along the echoing planks to a café that was almost empty. "Here," she said, "my favourite table. You can see the sea," and indicated a table looking over the western section of the bay.

He was so disarmed by her assurance that he forgot his manners and sat down without waiting for her. She said, trying to coax him out of his shyness, "What a nice thing to happen on the first day of the holiday. Yes, I know, you'll be wondering why I said this was my favourite table. I've been here four years running, you see. My sister and brother-in-law live here. He's a dairyman, and I come up on my unpaid week each spring. The paid week, in September, I'm expected to spend at home, and that isn't nearly so much fun. My name is Marwood, Elizabeth Marwood. What's yours?"

"Powlett-Jones," he said. "David," and was surprised when she brought her hands together, like a child expressing glee. "Why, that's better still!" she cried. "David is my favourite boy's name. It used to be Paul, until I had a fresh look at the Acts. Then I had second thoughts. Paul was a killjoy, don't you think? But

David was a proper old rake and much more human, if you see what I mean."

There was absolutely no resisting her. She had the charm and ebullience of a pretty child of about eight, reared by a pair of indulgent parents, and yet this assumption was not supported by her clothes. They were obviously off-the-peg clothes, chosen by someone who had to watch pennies. The tartan skirt, ending halfway up the calf, was all the rage that year, and the white silk blouse was almost certainly run-up by a home-plied needle. Hers or her mother's, he wondered? Shoes and handbag were of cheap imitation leather, and the heart-shaped cameo brooch at her breast was what his mother would have called a 'gee-gaw'. She had strong views about gee-gaws, dismissing them as an indication of extravagance in a woman.

A waitress arrived with a pot of coffee and Elizabeth poured, after asking him if he liked it black or white, and this surprised him a little. It was not until he became a member of the mess, in 1917, that he had known the difference or, indeed, so much as the taste of coffee. In Pontnewydd everybody drank tea.

He had an opportunity to look at her closely while she was pouring, deciding that she was one of the prettiest girls he had ever seen, although his experience was limited. Up to the outbreak of war he had been too busy with his studies to join his elder brothers in skirmishes at choir practice, and Eisteddfod rehearsal that led, in most cases, to walking out, and a wedding at one of the innumerable chapels. Then, during his years in the army, he had rarely seen a woman, except the hard-faced daughters of estaminet madames, or nurses of all ages, who had no time to spare for skylarking with wards full of the wreckage swept from one battlefield or another. And, on top of that, with most of his youth spent, he had chosen to live in another male preserve, so that he was not surprised to find himself tongue-tied in the presence of an attractive, talkative girl. Her friendliness, however, encouraged him to make an effort, and he said, "You pour like an expert. Do you work in a restaurant or hotel?" and she said he was getting warm, for she worked in 'a sort of hotel'.

"An orphanage?"

"A hospital, in Swansea."

She did not fit his idea of a nurse. Most of the older nurses, he recalled, had been martinets, sharp with their tongues, bossy and always in a hurry, and now that he thought about it they had all seemed mature, whereas she was hardly more than a girl, no more than nineteen, he would say. He wondered about her involvement in the war, for he had learned to tell at a glance those who had been scarred by the bloody business. Usually it showed in the faces of the young and middle-aged but there was no hint of it here. She was fresh, eager, unspoiled, chock-full of vitality.

He heard her say, "A penny for them?" and hastily he refocussed his mind. "Eh? I'm sorry . . . I was wondering . . . you being a nurse, I mean. Did you nurse soldiers?"

"No, worse luck," she said, "the staff nurses always hogged the men's wards. I was still a probationer while the war was on, and was fobbed off with the pensioners. The matron never encouraged probationers to nurse younger men. She seemed to think it might make them sit up and take notice too quickly!"

He laughed, responding gratefully to her sparkle. She said, "Were you in the army? You were, weren't you? I can tell, somehow. All the men who were in the trenches have that same look, as though . . ." but she checked herself, stirring her coffee so vigorously that it slopped into the saucer.

"What were you going to say?"

"It doesn't matter. Men who were out there don't want to talk about it."

She was not only pretty and forthcoming, he decided, but discerning for a youngster of her age. He said, "That's so, but I've been far luckier than most. Not only coming through more or less intact, but having something to take my mind off it when I was discharged."

"When was that?"

"Over a year ago. I got a Blighty, in the autumn of 1917, and started teaching as soon as I was boarded. It's amazing how it helped. The war already seems something that happened when I was a kid."

"Well, don't make it sound as if you were in your dotage," she said cheerfully. "How old are you, Mr. Powlett-Jones?"

"Twenty-two. And you?"

She blushed and then threw her head up, smiling. He noticed her white, even teeth, and her elfin prettiness touched him again, so that he was aware of the sense of renewal he derived from the juniors at Bamfylde. "I'm nineteen today," she said, and for some reason the news disposed of the last of his reserve.

"You are? Well, we can't celebrate on coffee. Wouldn't you like an ice or something?"

"No, thank you," she said, laughing, "but if you're free and on your own we might . . . well, we could have lunch. Not here. I know a café in the town where the food isn't at all bad," but then her irrepressible high spirits hitched on a small snag of modesty and she said, "I say, this is awful! I'm absolutely throwing myself at you. First the beret, then asking myself out to lunch. For all I know you've got a girl somewhere. You might even be married!"

"I'd be lucky where I work. There's four hundred boys, twenty-odd masters, most of them bald and grey, and two women. One is like your matron, the other a middle-aged widow. How's that for credentials?"

"Couldn't be better. Tell me about it. Is it a boarding school, one of those famous ones? And what do you teach? No, let me guess." She put a finger in her mouth. "French or Latin, isn't it?"

"You're not much good at guessing, Miss Marwood. History. And a little English to the juniors."

"You don't look like a schoolmaster."

"I'm very glad to hear it, especially from someone nineteen today. All right, I'll tell you about it if you like, but let's go out along the prom so far as Rhos. Then we'll have lunch, as you suggest, and after that . . . well, I was thinking of taking one of those afternoon charabanc trips to Conway Castle. I haven't been there since I was a kid. You'd be very welcome if you'd like to come along, but I'll almost certainly bore you if you do. Edward the First is one of my favourites. And me a good Welshman! How's that for heresy?"

That was how it began, effortlessly and casually, yet the most exciting thing that had ever happened to him, beginning with the drop of a beret from the head of a saucy girl, leaning over the rail of the pier at Colwyn Bay and ending in an involvement that was to shape the course of his life as surely and permanently as his arrival at Bamfylde, when he was still in a state of shock and nervous and physical exhaustion. Bamfylde had been a kind of staircase that he was obliged to ascend falteringly, grabbing at handholds and footholds represented by individuals like Algy Herries and Howarth, and by experiences like the first confrontation with the Lower Fourth and his attempt to console Briarley. Elizabeth Marwood offered herself as a smooth, level stretch, one he could pass without stress of any kind, someone who, in herself, was the very essence of hope, sanity, sweetness and promise, someone of his own generation who was able to convince him that, despite all that had happened out there under the growling bombardments, innocence survived, and was already throwing up new, green shoots. He sensed this much that first day and within a week he was gloriously certain of it. But by then, of course, he was hopelessly in love.

2

He never forgot the smallest particular of their first day together, their encounter on the pier, the walk along the promenade, lunch at a café called The Lantern, the chara trip to Conway and the almost comic deference she had shown him when he linked the valerian-sown ruins with events that had occurred there. And after that there was the visit to the churchyard to see the seven-spiked grave, featured in Wordsworth's poem, the row up the river, tea at a cottage on the quay next door to the Smallest House in the World, and then back to Colwyn Bay to meet her dairyman brother-in-law, Griff, and her sister Esther, who welcomed him into their flat over the shop as though he had been an old friend they had unexpectedly re-encountered.

But even that was not the end of it. In the evening he took Elizabeth to a variety concert in the pier pavilion and afterwards, when he saw her home, he kissed her at the gate. A very shy, restrained kiss it was, his first since party days in the Valley, a thousand years ago. Yet it did something to him, reviving, deep within him, a sense of being and existing, that snapped the final cord attaching him to the dried-out husk of a man he had been in the rejuvenating months at Osborne, a restoration of youth that he had come to accept as dead and buried, along with his generation, a quickening of ambition passing into his bloodstream like a powerful stimulant. It was too vitalising a mood to waste in sleep, so, instead of returning to the Y.M.C.A. where he was staying, he went back to the pierhead and leaned on the rail, looking out across the whispering bay and watching a sliver of moon ride the piled-up masses of blue-black clouds. He caught himself murmuring her name, catching and savouring its six syllables, and on its utterance the memory of her soft, eager lips returned to him, the final bonus of what he saw as the most exhilarating day of his life. He remained there a long time until he recalled he had no key and there was no night porter at the hotel. Then he moved on, smiling at the prospect of rousing the hotel at one in the morning but not caring a damn, for he saw himself then as a wandering drunk who, against all probability, had found his way home.

In the morning, the moment the shops were open, he went out to buy her a birthday gift and ended by buying three, an early nineteenth-century print of Conway Castle, a small bottle of perfume and a great bunch of narcissi, daffodils and tulips, taking them down to the pierhead where they met by appointment, not caring whether she thought him naïve. She was overwhelmed, and when his parcels had been opened, and the bouquet laid aside, she threw her arms round his neck and kissed him, exclaiming, "You know just how to impress, don't you, David? I believe you've had hundreds of girls and years of experience," but he said, shaking his head, "I've had far less experience than you—or rather, you couldn't have had less. I wanted to pay you back for that wonderful day we had yesterday. Where would you like to go today?"

"Somewhere less expensive," she said, laughing. "A walk up to Blackberry mountain, where you can't spend any more money."

"Oh, to blazes with that. I haven't touched my gratuity yet, and there's absolutely no way of spending money at school. The nearest real shop is at Challacombe, miles away. Why don't we book a round trip and explore all the castles? Unless you're fed up with conducted tours, that is. I've never seen Harlech and Beaumaris, although I've been to Caernarvon, and along the Straits as far as Telford's bridge."

"I'll go if you let me pay my share. That all-day tour is ten-and-six."

"I don't care if it's ten guineas. I came up here to enjoy myself and I don't fancy doing it alone any more. When are you due back at the hospital?"

"Sunday," she said. "What an awful thought. You've got a month, haven't you?"

"Not really," he said. "I've got to put in the last fortnight swotting for a degree. I should have done it last year but there was so much to learn about the job and, anyway, I wasn't really fit then."

"You are now, though?"

"Never felt better in my life. Partly Exmoor air but mostly you."

It surprised him that he could talk to a girl this way, easily and naturally, as he was learning to communicate with the Sixth, and some of his favourites, like Boyer and Briarley. But then, he supposed, she was easy to get to know, having none of the artfulness his memory associated with girls that the newspapers were beginning to call 'Flappers' for some curious reason. She laughed easily, said the first thing that came into her head, and flattered him a little by listening very carefully to everything he had to say about the castles, the men who built them, and the men who garrisoned them before they were made obsolete by gunpowder.

"My stars!" she exclaimed, when he told her about the Roman invasion of Mona, and the last stand of the Druids in Anglesey, "where on earth do you *put* it all, David? I mean, you don't have to look it up! You hardly glanced at that guide we bought," and he replied, chuckling, "You'd be astonished how much I have to mug up when I'm taking the Upper School in a period I'm not familiar with. It never does to let them see you at it, of course. They have to be bluffed. Like you."

"But you must have read a tremendous amount, in spite of all those years in the war when reading couldn't have been easy. Don't you ever want to write?"

Unconsciously she had touched on an ambition dormant in him since he was a child, something unfulfilled in his personal awareness that had surfaced from time to time in the years leading up to the summer of 1914, and again, but infrequently, in rest periods behind the lines, when he was looking for an escape from ennui.

"It's odd you should ask me that. No one else ever has. It's something I've often felt I could do, within limits."

"What kind of limits?"

"I don't think I could write fiction or verse. Maybe I could have, if things had been different, but any creative impulses I might have had were shelled out of me long ago."

"But soldiers did write poems, didn't they? I remember one of our staff-nurses was engaged to a boy who sent poems to her. Poems about the war, I mean."

"Yes, some of them did, and marvellous poems they were too. Sassoon and Owen and Rosenberg were three, and I've already introduced their work to the seniors. But they were articulate. With me it was always as if I was experiencing it secondhand. Maybe that's why I survived. Owen and Rosenberg didn't."

She must have noticed the change in his tone and expression for she said, quickly, "I'm sorry, David. I didn't mean to make you remember," but he said, taking her hand, "I don't mind talking about it to you. In a way it helps. It's not good, keeping it bottled up, the way I have to with the boys. They always seem so terribly young to me. Babies almost."

"But I don't?"

"No, and that's curious too, for you're only a year older than Simmonds, our head boy. Can you explain that?"

"The job, maybe. A nurse, even a pro', is always in charge. She's mobile and her patients aren't. It makes us seem bossy."

She would be a wonderful person to have around in the common room at Bamfylde, he thought, poised to puncture all those balloons of complacency and pomposity. He said, thankfully, "No man in his senses would mind being bossed by you, Elizabeth," and kissed the top of her head, but she was not to be dismissed in this way and said, "Save that, Davy, and go on with what you were saying. If you did write *what* would you write. Would it be plays?"

"Good Lord, no. Plays require a very special technique, and most playwrights serve an apprenticeship as actors. I'd write historical biography, but in a different way from academics. Most studies of the past are written by professional scholars, and dry as dust unless you've done your homework on the background. The ordinary reader has got to see historical characters as flesh and blood."

"But how would you discover human touches after all this time?"

"I suppose by putting two and two together. Fashions and attitudes change every generation but people don't."

She seemed to ponder this. Finally she said, "I think you'd do it splendidly, David. Who would you like to write *about?*"

For possibly the first time in his life he gave his potential subject matter serious consideration. "Well, now that you raise the
question, the royal tigress for one."

"Who on earth was she? Boadicea?"

"Someone much nearer our own time. Margaret of Anjou, the
French wife of Henry VI."

"Never heard of her. Tell me about her."

He gave her a potted history of Margaret of Anjou, as the
charabanc bounced along the road from Caernarvon to Menai
Bridge, then round the tortuous coast road to Beaumaris. She
listened attentively and it reminded him that he was becoming
as didactic as old Judy Cordwainer and he broke off, saying, "Look
here, that's enough of that. I'm beginning to talk like a schoolmaster off duty and that's a sobering thought."

"Why? After all, you are one."

"I don't care to be recognised as one wherever I go. You'd see
what I mean if you met some of the codgers in our common room,"
and that, he thought dolefully, was unlikely.

But was it? For a moment his imagination conjured with the
wholly delightful prospect of absorbing her into the Bamfylde
scene, so that he saw her, fleetingly, as someone always on hand
to encourage and sustain him. But then common sense caught
up with him as he thought, "What the hell have I got to offer a
girl like her? Two hundred a year, Mam to help out, and a life
removed from everyone but boys and old trouts, who would tut-
tut at the powder she dabs on her nose!" and he recalled the
opinion expressed by Howarth under the fives court on Armistice
Night, concerning the unwisdom of trying to combine marriage
with a job requiring so much dedication and monastic seclusion.

The fancy remained, however, and unconsciously she kept it
glowing, particularly when they said good night after tea and bread
and cheese at her brother-in-law's. She came out with him into
the backway that ran behind the shop and it seemed to him that
she was just as reluctant as he to bring another gloriously fulfilled
day to a close. When he kissed her, as gently as he had the previous night, she said, with her delightful lack of inhibition, "Here,
let me show you! I won't break, Davy!" and threw her arms round
his neck, kissing him in a way he had never been kissed and leaving him breathless with gratification but also a trifle dismayed at
such irrefutable evidence of a far wider experience than he pos-

sessed. He said, still holding her close, "Have you had lots of boy friends? You must have, a girl as pretty as you."

"I've had my share," she admitted gaily, "but never one the least like you, Davy."

"How am I supposed to regard that?"

"As a compliment, of course. No, I *mean* that! Most men don't need much encouragement, I can tell you."

"But I do?"

"Yes, but you don't have to apologise for it. All the boys I've known would have taken full advantage of the way I threw myself at you and I can't say as I'd blame them. By now I would have been fighting them off."

"I'd back you to take care of yourself, Elizabeth. You seem to me to be pretty well equipped to stand on your own feet in all kinds of ways."

"Not that way always." She was silent a moment. Then she went on, "Two or three of the boys who took me out the first year I was nursing tried it on, and made me feel a bit of a prude for holding out. There was always the chance of the war going on indefinitely, and them being sucked back into it. I don't think it was squeamishness on my part. It was a thought, in the back of my mind, of bringing a poor little beggar into the world whom nobody wanted, who would probably end up in an orphanage. So there you are, Davy. I'm still a virgin. Like you."

Her perception diminished him a little and she was quick to sense as much. "What's wrong with that? You're not the kind of person who would go looking for a prostitute. You're too fastidious for one thing. I daresay that's what kept you clear of the brothels out there."

"Good God! You know about that kind of thing?"

"David," she said, chuckling, "use your head, lad. I've been nursing for two years!"

"But not servicemen."

"What do you think nurses talk about in their free time? Crocheting?"

He laughed. "You're a very surprising person, Elizabeth. What old Algy Herries, my headmaster, would call 'A bit of a card'. Same time tomorrow?"

"Yes, *please!*"

He kissed her again, but as the week sped by he began to be

aware of a sense of desperation that was not moderated by her promise to write once a week, 'no matter how rushed we are'. Her train to Chester, where she was catching her connection to Swansea, left at midday on Sunday, and his spirits were at low ebb as he accompanied her to the station. It was no good telling himself he was exaggerating the terrible need he had for her gaiety and warmth, that something positive might develop from their correspondence, that they had made tentative arrangements to meet in London where her parents lived when she took her paid holiday next September. September was a long way off, and all kinds of things could happen before then. She might get bored writing. She might meet someone far more eligible in that hospital, probably crammed with young men with gratuities to spend, and four years' lost youth to make up.

They hung about waiting for the whistle to blow and when it did the blast hit him in the belly like the signal for an attack. The train began to move and he watched it slide away with a terrible finality, carrying with it all his hopes and certainties. It had moved about ten yards when he responded to an irresistible urge to stop it and sprinted along the platform until he was level with her compartment where she stood framed in the window. "Stand away!" he shouted, clutching the brass handle, "Coming with you!" and at that the guard, lower down the platform, roared his disapproval. A second later the heavy door was swinging free and he was inside the carriage on his hands and knees, and she had reached over him and slammed it and they were alone, Elizabeth looking at him with a stunned expression as he scrambled up, dusting himself.

"What on earth—Davy—you've no luggage . . ." and then she threw back her head and laughed and he caught her in his arms, so that they lost their balance and collapsed as the train gathered speed.

"To hell with luggage," he said, "I'll catch a train back from Chester, pick up my stuff and go on home to Bamfylde. It won't be any fun here without you. Besides, there's something I've got to know, and it can't wait on letters. Will you marry me, Beth? I'm very much in love with you, and if you wouldn't mind being the only wife under forty at a school miles from anywhere . . ."

He got no further. She caught his arm, pressing his hand fervently against her breast, crying, "Why, of course I'll marry you!

74

Just as soon as you like. And as for living on the moors in Devon, with all those boys and funny characters you've told me about, I can't think of anything nicer! I'll tell you something else too. I'm jolly glad you didn't propose to me solemnly, by letter. This is much more romantic, the first really romantic thing that's ever happened to me. There!" and she kissed him, first on the ear, then on both cheeks and finally on the mouth, so enthusiastically that a smudge of dust, gathered in his headlong fall into the compartment, transferred itself from his forehead to hers.

3

They had planned to be married in August, a week or so after the school broke up, and he had had a chance to make the half-ruinous cottage in Stonecross Bottom habitable after sub-leasing it from Farmer Brewer, the taciturn tenant, for fifty pounds a year. "A typical peasant-robbery", old Howarth called it, especially as neither landlord nor chief tenant was prepared to contribute a penny-piece towards rethatching, reflooring and generally renovating the place. It was not the outlay of capital that bothered him, however, but the shortage of skilled labour during that first, brilliant summer of the peace, when the sun shone from early morning until late evening, as though trying to make amends for the unremitting drizzle of successive Flanders summers.

Nobody recalled a summer as hot and dry as this, not even the long period of unbroken sunshine that preceded the outbreak of the war in 1914. The streams went dry and the grass withered. Cow-parsley, heavy with white dust, drooped in the hedges, and a special meeting of the Governors had to be called to do something about the drainage system. Everyone turned as brown as a longshoreman and the cricket pitches were bumpy and sun-slippery. "A damned menace to batsmen," Carter, himself an enthusiastic cricketer, declared after Simmonds, the head boy, had returned to the pavilion with a bump over his eye that would not have disgraced a prize-fighter. But for all the drought, and the euphoria the long sunny days produced in class, Bamfylde revelled in the heat, and Sports Day, the first dry Sports Day since 1914, according to Herries, was a tremendous success. So many of the parents seemed to have acquired expensive-looking motors that the sports field looked like Lords, as scores of fashionably dressed mothers and pretty sisters nibbled their ices, and God alone knew how many war profiteers sat around smoking cigars and practising refined vowel sounds. All this from the sardonic Howarth, who stood throughout the afternoon at the finishing line, with stop-watch in his hand, an inevitable Gold Flake in his mouth. There were plenty of Old Boys, too, some of them, including Cooper and Fosdyke, in khaki, and a few others on crutches.

"There's a whiff of national recovery about," Algy Herries remarked, watching Cooper win the Old Boys' 880-yards at a canter. "Something tells me we're getting back on course and, if *we* are, here in the wilderness, then everyone else must be, my friend. We've got a healthy waiting-list already, and when the post-war crop of babies grow up—a majority of them boys, please God— we'll have to tackle the Governors about the new wing behind Outram's. I doubt if I'll be here to see it full, P.J., but you will, since you've burned your boats by taking a wife! She's a fetching gel, I hope. We could do with a little uplift in that direction, although Irvine seems to be setting a spanking pace."

Irvine was the first of the reinforcements Herries had promised him, a genial, bullheaded, heavy-shouldered young man, almost exactly his own age, who arrived via a shortened ex-subaltern's course to teach geography to all but the Second and Third Forms, where Judy Cordwainer still campaigned for neatness in preference to speed and accuracy.

David soon made a friend of Irvine, despite the fact that he was a breezy extrovert, with limited imagination. Alone among the staff Irvine had an active service record, a year and a half spent in Palestine, where he received a foot injury severe enough to get him shipped home and discharged a year before the Armistice. The wound had healed satisfactorily but one of his great toes had been amputated, leaving him with a curious, bobbing walk, as though, at any moment, he would over-balance and turn a neat somersault. He had a good Army and Varsity sports record, despite his slight disability, and promised to prove very useful when the rugby season began. In the meantime, before even settling in, he produced a blonde wife, a pretty, talkative girl with a pink and white complexion, violet eyes and a quick smile, who was no sooner introduced to the Saturday night dancing class than the senior boys were queueing for foxtrots and one-steps.

Phyllis Irvine's tremendous popularity among the boys was a source of uproarious amusement to Irvine, a cheerful fellow who would laugh his head off recounting the circumstances under which he lost his toe. "Damnedest thing you ever saw," he said, telling the story to David over a gin and lime, in the tiny sitting-room at Havelock's. "We were lobbing five-nines from lorry to battery in a chain, and I happened to sneeze just as I laid hold of one of 'em. I dropped it, and didn't feel a thing until I came to after the anaesthetic, and saw my foot slung up to a gantry, swathed in bloody great bandages. Then I knew about it all right, and reckoned myself damned lucky it was one of ours and not one of theirs. Slice of plum cake really, since I missed the draft when we were pulled out and went in at St. Quentin, just in time for the Big Push. My battery was wiped out on March 21st. Jerry went through it like a dose of salts. Chum of mine defused my five-nine and sent me the case before he went west, poor devil. Phyl and I intend to use it for an umbrella stand."

That was Irvine, whom the war seemed to have touched very lightly, but he was honest enough to draw a sharp distinction between his eighteen months in the Near East, and David's three years on the Western Front. "Damned if I know how any of you chaps stuck it out without going loco, old man. Bloody shambles, they tell me. Don't wonder you holed up here the moment you got the chance, but I had second thoughts myself when I climbed aboard the old buggy down at the station. Reminds me a bit of Sinai—with vegetation, of course. I'm a bit worried about Phyl sticking it out in winter. Everyone except you and Carter are practically superannuated, aren't they?"

"You'll get used to it after a term or two," David said, "and if I was you I wouldn't be in too much of a hurry to move on. You might get a better social life but you won't find a more easy-going head and even some of the old stagers grow on you after a bit."

"Well, maybe you're right, but Phyl says she'll be relieved when your missus arrives. She says it's a bit like going back to school herself, with old Mother Kruger searching her desk for lipstick and letters from boys. The kids themselves seem a decent lot, taken all round. Is that your experience?"

David admitted that it was, adding that every time he moved among the seniors he had to remind himself that they were not so much sausage meat, queueing for Haig's mincing-machine.

By now, however, he was adjusting to all grades, enjoying teaching in a way he would not have thought possible a year ago. He had his own methods with the syllabus and had already introduced a range of new text-books.

His formula for teaching history seemed to produce good results, simple stuff up to Middle School, with the emphasis on personalities rather than text-book landmarks, and from then on any amount of free discussion on topics likely to crop up in the question papers of the junior and senior Cambridge exams. In the Second and Third Forms he instituted a question-and-answer system of oral tests, taught him by Howarth, who did not trust written work. "Like to find out on the spot how much has sunk in before I waste too much breath," he said. "When I'm sure I concentrate on the odd plant or two, where a modest crop can be expected. Damned waste of time marking all those bloody little test-papers, half of them cribbed. Nobody can hide ignorance at an oral round. Line the little beggars up, number 'em off, and throw spot questions at them. Give 'em three seconds before they pass and the first boy who comes up with the answer moves up to where it all started. Let 'em try and play fast and loose with that box of tricks."

It worked, as David soon discovered, but so did an innovation of his own that he employed not only in the Second and Third Forms but also in Middle School, and just occasionally in the Fifth. This was to capture the attention of the class by a whiff of scandal, or a bizarre episode that the academics would have dismissed as trivial or apocryphal.

His first real success was with the story of Owen Tudor's siege of the widow of Henry V, giving him licence to draw a lively picture not only of court life as it was lived in the mid-fifteenth century, but also of Newgate, and the administration of justice. He scored again in the blood-and-thunder-loving Third Form with a blow-by-blow description of Colonel Blood's attempt to steal the Crown jewels, an incident that led him to a general assessment of Charles II's character and policies. He sometimes started a class on a new period by plunging straight into an account of a particularly colourful incident, usually one with cliff-hanger aspects, like the flight of the Young Pretender after Culloden. All the time, with whatever period he was dealing, and whatever the age and standard of his audience, he strove to make history come alive, and would compare statesmen of the Tudor and Stuart periods with men like Lloyd George, whose antics featured in the daily headlines.

Sometimes, if he was lucky, or dealing with one of his favourite eras or characters, the lesson would fly, and both he and his class would be surprised by the five-minute bell, warning them that it was time to put away books and forage in their desks for the next period, or disperse to the dining-room.

For the rest, he was pretty well extended supervising sports, performing roster duties in the dining hall and dormitories, and helping out with activities connected with the Old Boys' Association, of which Cordwainer had been secretary for twenty-five years.

It was in this area that he began to perceive hidden qualities in the meticulous, unsmiling Judy, among them a fanatical loyalty to the school, that showed itself in endless letter-writing and formidable documentation. Judy had a phenomenal memory. He could tell you the age, occupation and address of every paid-up member—and there were many hundreds of them—but Judy's approach to Old Boys was never moderated by the passage of time. He still addressed distinguished members of the Governing Board (or such of them who had been boys at Bamfylde) as though they were thirteen-year-olds, presenting a botched exercise, whereas the Old Boys, for their part, treated him with tolerant amusement, and never resented his honking dismissal of what he sometimes denounced as a slovenly approach to problems of patronage and administration. Even when suggestions were put forward by Sir John Riscoe, who had been responsible for all troop movements in the northern command during the war, or Brigadier Cooper, who had been on the staff of General Plumer throughout the battle for Passchendaele Ridge, he would still honk them down if they trespassed on his preserves, and David would not have been surprised to learn he had hurled his keys at them into the bargain.

David also accepted the chairmanship of the Sixth Form 'Owl' Society, a group that specialised in debates on current topics, and played an important part in the social and cultural functions of the school, but all this was only his outward, visible life. Beneath it was a pulsating glow centred on Beth Marwood, and stimulated by her letters, helter-skelter outpourings of hospital gossip, preparations for their August wedding, and quaintly expressed endearments. Sometimes, musing over her letters for the fourth or fifth time, he would see her again as a lively, lovable child, living in constant anticipation of a stupendous treat.

In her actual presence he had never been conscious of his relative maturity, of the small gap in years, only the great gulf of experience brought about by his experiences in Flanders. But when he read her letters, or studied her photograph in nurse's uniform that stood on his bedside table, he began to see her in the context of boys about two-thirds of the way up the school, colts bursting with animal high spirits almost ready for the responsibilities thrust upon them by Algy Herries (a great advocate of the prefectorial system) the moment they reached the Sixth.

He wondered about her a great deal. What she would make of life in this remote but surging community; how his dour old mother would view her; whether she would make allowances for the terrible ageing process, forced upon every member of his generation who had survived the trenches but, above all, how they would adjust to one another as lovers. For here, he suspected, she would be far more knowledgeable than he was.

He became so apprehensive about this that he ultimately confided in Willoughby, the ex-R.A.M.C. doctor in his mid-fifties, who lived at Stoke Steps, the nearest village to Bamfylde, and was regarded as the school doctor.

Willoughby was a brusque, hardworking man, with a severely practical approach to his patients, and a sharp eye for malingerers. David would have thought of him as a typical ex-army doctor had not Howarth, whose standards were impossibly high, spoken of him as a man thoroughly up to his job. He made an appointment with Willoughby on the excuse of a general checkup demanded by an insurance company but when the doctor pronounced him one hundred per cent fit, he raised the subject uppermost in his mind. To his relief Willoughby shed his brusqueness and became almost sympathetic.

"Don't think your misgivings are singular," he said. "Quite the contrary. 'Veldt-starvation', we used to call it in South Africa—any number of men came to me after we had rounded up the last of De Wet's commandos over there. Same thing cropped up in P.O.W. camps this time. Fellows seemed to think they'd lost all interest, and capability into the bargain!" He smiled, as though recalling something out of his own youth. "I've known men ask for aphrodisiacs, along with their demobilisation kit, but it's all poppy-cock. The fact is, most males adjust to deprivation after a time. Damned good job they do, or every single one of you chaps would have come home with a roaring dose, and passed it on to the first decent woman he met. But why should you worry, seeing you've found yourself a filly you fancy? That speaks for itself, doesn't it? I hear you didn't take long to make up your mind about the girl."

"No, I didn't," David told him, "and Beth being a trained nurse ought to help, but . . . well, the fact is, before running into her I never had the slightest inclination to go out and find myself a woman. Isn't that unusual, a virgin at twenty-three?"

"Not in your case, old chap. Nonconformist upbringing, for one thing, and I've met plenty of Nonconformists who regard sex as the ultimate sin. Sensitive nature too, I daresay, but above all, pitchforked into that bloody holocaust, before your eighteenth birthday. The wonder is you can bring yourself to discuss it with a stranger. Oh, I could use a lot of long words, and sound off like a medical dictionary, but it isn't in the least necessary in your case. You're fit now. You've got the moor and that place up there to thank for that, and you've had the luck to meet a girl who re-vived your natural instincts. My advice to you, old man, is to let well alone and give those instincts free rein. And for God's sake, don't go into a solemn conclave with the poor girl when you're supposed to be enjoying your honeymoon. Don't plough through any of these well-meaning tracts my fellow witch-doctors are al-ways bringing out, either. The world's been going a long time, and the population is still rising, despite our attempts to kill one another off for the sheer hell of it! Do you want children?"

"I don't think I've thought about it."

"Well, don't. If they come, they come. When they like rather than when you like. At all events, that's my experience. Family planning, my good right foot!" His face clouded for a moment. "Had two myself. Boy and a girl. The boy was killed at Vimy. Fine young chap. Made up his mind to go for surgery, like his grand-father, but a Jerry hand-grenade put paid to that. Daughter's mar-ried to a chap about your age. He came out of it with a bad whiff of gas and they're living in Scotland. He had to take a forestry job, although he was trained as an accountant. Six months in an office would kill him. Told him so and he took my tip. Got a photograph of your fiancée?"

David showed him a snap of Elizabeth, taken with her Brownie camera on the walls of Caernarvon Castle and Willoughby studied it, objectively. "Looks a bonnie lass," he said. "Should be very good for you." And then, incuriously, "How are you liking it up there?"

"I like it fine, mostly because Herries knows what he's about."

"Aye, he does. But he's had his troubles, converting the traditionalists to his peculiar style of government. Well, proof of the pudding, they say. He's getting results, and it was a Dotheboys Hall when I remember it, in Wesker's time. Couldn't stand the man, neither could the boys. Here, what the devil am I doing gossiping to you? I've got a baby due over at Barrowhead Farm," and he grabbed his bag and hat and hurried out to a high-slung gig that his man had brought round from the stable. "I'll trade this in for a car as soon as they improve the roads about here," he called from the driving seat, and cracking his whip went off at a spanking trot, leaving David with the impression that Howarth was an excellent judge of character.

And suddenly it was here, the end of term with no time for any more private misgivings. Shouted good wishes from departing boys—"Have a good hols, sir!" "Make the most of it, sir!" and a daring parting shot from the irrepressible Boyer, who had got to hear of the approaching wedding, "Don't be good, be careful, sir!"

Watching Carter's spick and span Corps march off behind his band, to entrain for its annual camp at Tidworth, he thought, "Hanged if I don't belong here, almost as much as Herries and the old fogies. And me what Bull Bickford would dismiss as 'only a fourth-termer'." Suddenly he made up his mind to ask Howarth to be his best man and Howarth surprised him by being the slightest bit flattered. "You really want an old shellback like me? I haven't worn striped pants in twenty years, man."

"It's not going to be a dressy occasion. I persuaded Beth and her father to save money on the ceremony. There's only one bridesmaid, and about twenty of us at the reception. No one from my side, except my mother and younger sister. Almost everyone else I knew is either dead, or can't afford a trip to town."

"Very well, then, but I hope your wife won't judge Bamfylde

on your best man. She'll get the impression she's being sold into bondage. You're sure an ordinary suit will do?"

"Of course it will, it'll be a very simple affair."

But it wasn't as simple as all that. Waiting in the front pew of the little church at Elmer's End, where Beth's father had a clerical job with the South Eastern and Chatham Railway, David was surprised to see twenty to thirty onlookers file in, sober-looking, blue-suited men, for the most part, with hearty, shapeless wives, who he guessed were railway colleagues of Mr. Marwood, but also three youngsters in their teens, whom he recognised as Beth's younger sisters. The sight of them interested him, for he had forgotten he was acquiring a string of in-laws as well as a wife. But then a duty-conscious Howarth nudged him and he stopped looking over his shoulder, and sat waiting for the minutes to tick by, more diminished than at any time in his life, including the occasion he had first appeared in the mess on arrival from the commissioning course. His collar was fiendishly tight and his mouth and throat were parched. The organ began to play, and everybody stood up, himself in response to another nudge by Howarth, and suddenly there was Beth on the arm of her dapper little father, a cool, utterly composed vision in billowing white but with a very reassuring half-smile lighting up her brown eyes as he took his place.

Chapter Two

Whenever he recalled that day he could never reconstruct it in ordered sequence. It had that much in common with the early days of his spell in hospital, a series of fitful flashes, mostly unrelated, involving not so much himself as those about him. Beth's clear, almost defiant responses; his own nervous fumble with the ring, causing the rigid expression of Howarth to relax; the eager faces of Beth's three sisters, Margery, Beulah and Anne, as they left the church; the shower of confetti, a handful of which hit Howarth, inducing such a stare of outrage that David laughed out loud just as the photographer snapped them all in the porch.

And back at the semi-detached of his new father-in-law, with Beth's stepmother (who embarrassed him because she somehow conveyed the impression that Beth had captured an Oxford professor) piping her eye during the speeches. The latter were brief and banal including his own, but there was one exception. Howarth, charged with proposing the health of the bridesmaid, used the opportunity to deliver a blushmaking account of the groom's war service, and his arrival in Bamfylde where, Howarth declared, ". . . he is surprising everybody, because he is that rare phenomenon, a schoolteacher more anxious to learn than to teach". The company were inclined to accept this as a joke and began to laugh, but Howarth silenced them with one of his bleak stares, that must have killed ten thousand laughs over the past thirty years. "I don't say that in any spirit of levity," he went on, rubbing it in, and ignoring David's agonised look, "but on the strength of a close acquaintanceship of eighteen months. On behalf of Bamfylde School I welcome Mrs. Powlett-Jones," (it seemed odd to hear Howarth refer to Beth as that) "because new blood is badly needed in all our institutions nowadays, and none more so than in educational establishments. I should know. I've gone a distinguished shade of grey in the service."

It was permissible to laugh at that and Howarth implied as much by giving one of his rare, wintry smiles. They applauded enthusiastically and David got the impression that all those dour old railwaymen and their wives, and all the in-laws he hardly knew, and even his glum-faced mother toying with a glass of untasted port wine, wished them well—partly no doubt, on Beth's account for she looked breathtakingly pretty—but also, in some devious way, because of old Howarth, and the way he had spoken up for a groom few of those present had heard of a week or so ago.

He would have been worried about leaving his mother in town for the night but Esther, Beth's elder sister, the one married to the Colwyn Bay dairyman, promised to look after the old lady. So the couple were given a rousing send off at about three-thirty, and set out for Waterloo in a beribboned taxi, arriving just in time to catch the four-twenty for Portsmouth, en route for Shanklin, Isle of Wight.

*   *   *

The ability to think coherently returned to him when they were sitting facing one another over tea in the restaurant car, but a crippling shyness now seemed to have overtaken her as well as him. Their conversational exchanges had a hollow ring and neither one of them, it seemed, could think of anything worth saying. He continued to fight against it and, so it appeared, did she, but presently she excused herself abruptly on the grounds of disposing of confetti that she declared was still clogging her hair, although he could not see any from where he sat. After a few minutes he paid for the tea and went back to their compartment, expecting to find her there, but it was empty. She had been back, however, for her big attaché case had been opened and closed hurriedly, leaving the shoulder strap of a slip showing. A long time seemed to pass before she emerged looking, he thought, not merely distrait but tense.

He began to panic a little then, casting about for some phrase that might help to put her at ease, for the tight-lipped girl in the opposite corner, in her smart little two-piece, tan gloves, and blue straw hat, was a stranger to him and from the nineteen-year-old in whose company he had explored Welsh castles, and equally so from the confident bride who had smiled a welcome at him at the altar. He told himself, "It's reaction, I suppose. It's caught up with her and she's regretting it already! Why the devil was I in such a hurry? We should have waited and got to know one another properly in this hols, and over Christmas, then arranged a wedding in the spring . . ." But suddenly he saw, from her hardening expression, that she was on the point of saying something important and anticipated her, saying eagerly, "What *is* it, Beth? Tell me what you're scared of? It can't be me because . . ."

She relaxed somewhat and he smiled as she said, "Because you're scared enough for both of us? No, Davy, it's not that. Nothing to do with you, really. It's just . . ." and to his dismay her face turned scarlet, and her teeth clamped down on her lip.

"Tell me."

"I . . . I can't tell you, Davy."

"But you must. You were so sure of yourself at the church, far more so than me."

She said, desperately, "All *right*, then. If it stops you thinking I'm scared of being married, and that I regret anything . . ." He did not recall anyone ever looking so embarrassed but she pressed on; "You've . . . you've got sisters, thank God. You grew up in a little house just like ours . . ."

"What on earth has that got to do with it?"

"Everything, Davy. You see . . . well, something awful has happened—oh, no, nothing so out of the ordinary, just—just horribly embarrassing and very annoying, particularly now. That's why I dashed off. *Now* . . . of all times! Maybe it's the excitement, maybe I miscalculated . . . I don't know . . ."

Suddenly, and with a tremendous surge of relief, he understood what she was trying to say and what had caused her plunge from serenity to near-panic. And then, on the heels of relief, came a sense of the ridiculous, so that without pausing to think whether or not it would add to her embarrassment, he shouted with laughter, dived across the compartment and threw his arms about her.

. She looked momentarily bewildered but then, with urgency, "Pull the blinds!"

"The blinds? But won't it be obvious to anyone passing down the corridor?"

"I don't care about that! Pull them."

He did as she asked and while his back was turned he heard her giggle and then laugh outright. Her laughter was the most welcome sound he had ever heard and it encouraged him to laugh again.

"I feel such a fool," she said, presently. "I mean, any girl getting married *thinks* of that . . . if she's got any sense, that is. I know I did, but there it is, and it's really nothing to laugh at, is it?"

But it was, because the fact that they could laugh, and that she could blurt it out in that way, seemed to him of the greatest significance. It meant that they were in accord, to a degree that not so many newly-weds could be, and he saw it all as a tremendously encouraging portent for the future. He said, "Well, *I* think it's damned funny. And so do you really. I suppose, in some circumstances, a bride might be relieved," but she said, quickly, "Not since Victoria's reign, and even then the groom would be entitled to feel diddled," and they both laughed again, and were still laughing when the ticket-collector looked in to clip their tickets and said, as David pocketed them, "Sorry, sir . . . madam . . . got to be done. But the best of luck and I'll lock you in if you like?" and Beth said, when they had declined his offer and he had pottered off, "Now *what* a considerate man! That's just the kind of thing you would have said if you had been a railway guard clipping honeymooners' tickets! There, that's for being so understanding!" and she kissed him in that special way of hers, absentmindedly at first but then, on second thoughts as it were, enlarging the kiss and afterwards dabbing his mouth to remove a smear of lipstick.

It set the tone for the fortnight that followed, a time of laughter, discovery and great tenderness, so that as he lay awake listening to her regular breathing, and sometimes reaching out to touch the dark hair spread on the pillow, he thought, "Time was when

I had to get by on nothing but comradeship . . . comradeship of poor devils in the same boat, and it was enough when every minute might be your last . . . but now . . . well, she stands for hope, in the way kids like Boyer and Skidmore and Briarley do, and between 'em I daresay they can teach the left-overs to start out all over again . . ."

This notion of fusion, between Beth and his boys, enlarged itself in other ways during the honeymoon. It enabled him to see resurrection in others about him, at the little private hotel where they were staying, especially in the ebullience of a middle-aged Cockney with an empty sleeve and the placidity of his fat, amiable wife, and their tribe of children. "Two nippers the results o' two leaves from the front," the man told him, after a brief exercise in telepathy that was the language of all who had served time in hell. It was there also in the brassy summer sunshine, when it seemed that all the rain in the world had been absorbed into the Flanders sponge and there was none left in the sky; in the shouts of children, splashing in the shallows down at the beach; in the cheerful, vulgar postcards on the revolving display stand of a stationer's near their hotel, three of which he sent to Herries, Howarth and Judy Cordwainer, and a fourth (inscribed *'Giving my instincts full rein—damned good prescription!'*) to Willoughby. But, above all, he looked for and found it in Beth, who came to him gaily and gladly, who seemed to understand better than he did what was needed to erase the past, for she said, unexpectedly, "I hope I have a child right away, Davy. For both our sakes. For me because I'd like to be young enough to enjoy watching children grow up. For you because I think you'd see a son of your own as some kind of answer to what you and all those others had to put up with all those years. I mean, you'd be even more determined to make certain nothing like it ever happened again."

It was very perceptive of her, he thought, to say a thing like that, but then her perception, revealed by her intuitive grasp of the male ego, was one of her most surprising characteristics, as he discovered within a week or two of their return to Bamfylde, and the opening of the new term bringing a clutch of new boys fresh from home and prep school. They needed a little mothering, she said, when she proposed the first of her new boys' tea-parties at the cottage.

At first he was inclined to think that she was overdoing it a little. Mrs. Ferguson, who had been a housemaster's wife for years, never gave tea-parties, not even for the prefects of Havelock's, and he suspected that some of the other wives of senior masters would click their teeth over the innovation. But she soon infected him with enthusiasm for the idea. Seven crop-eared newcomers showed up that warm September afternoon, to scoff tea and chudleys—a Devon dainty, dripping with strawberry jam and yellow cream—on their tiny lawn, where tea was spread under their one tree, a windblown horse-chestnut that had weathered fifty Exmoor winters in the relative shelter of the Coombe.

The party, a little slow at first, was an unqualified success. Once their shyness had worn off the boys opened up to her, as they would to a cheerful elder sister, and he was very amused when Graves-Jones, the most forward of them, gave her a Prussian heel-click when he shook hands and thanked her gravely.

She said, when they had taken themselves off, "Well, did I strike the right note? I don't want them thinking all of us are as old as God and twice as high and mighty!" and he said, kissing her, "You were marvellous! I believe that saucy little devil Graves-Jones is hopelessly infatuated. He was looking at you over his last chudley as though you were Mary Pickford in the flesh."

"Very proper," she said, "for it's time someone did something to offset the monastic seclusion of this institution. The poor little beggars don't get a glimpse of a bit of fluff from the moment they board the train at the nearest junction, until they get back there the first day of the holidays. You can't count Matron, and that nice Mrs. Parminter. One's a dragon and the other treats them all as though they were still in the nursery."

"I'm not sure we should expect them to speculate on bits of fluff at thirteen," he said, but she replied, sharply for her, "Why ever not? They're just coming up to the age when the sex taboos are so impossibly complex that they have to be translated into dirty jokes. That's one of the mistakes about places like this. Oh, it's unavoidable, I see that well enough, but if they've got to have fantasies—and all the normal ones always will—then let them be romantic ones. I was madly in love with the All Angels choirmaster at their age."

"What was he like?"

"Like Lewis Carroll in temperament, but a little more positive.

Much given to patting and pinching. He tried hard to get the vicar and churchwardens to include girls in the choir, and even designed fetching little caps for them, but they warned him off, poor little man."

That was the way of her, from the very first. Unafraid, relaxed, perfectly at ease with the establishment, but never worrying overmuch about saying or doing the wrong thing in a world where, despite all Algy Herries' innovations, tradition still rose about them like a wall patrolled by an older generation suspicious of post-war freedoms and assuming that the Edwardian *status quo* had been restored by the armistice.

She got along very well with Herries, who at once enrolled both Beth and Phyl Irvine in his operatic society, allotting them principal roles in the forthcoming production of *The Mikado* as Yum-Yum and Pitti-Sing respectively. Rehearsals in Big Hall, with Herries himself as Ko-Ko, and old Rapper Gibbs at the piano, gave her an opportunity to mix with the boys from all grades, and she formed very definite conclusions about some of them, but did not necessarily confide her conclusions to him, or not yet.

Secretly she was hard at work sorting them into their various type-categories and the exercise afforded her a good deal of amusement. There was the dashing type, like the young heel-clicking Graves-Jones, and his well-grown prototypes, like Boyer, Dobson and Letherett, now wearing double-breasted lounge suits and narrow collars after moving up to Senior School. None of these were the least shy in her presence, but all treated her with exaggerated courtesy, as if they were rehearsing an approach to the flappers they would partner at dances in a year or so, and embrace if they could prevail on them to step outside.

Then there was the blushing, gawky type, mostly in the Sixth, almost fully adult now but having a hard time of it adjusting to the presence of two pretty girls in their midst, and not in the least sure how to approach them without seeming presumptuous. Bristow, who had followed his dead brother as head prefect and captain of the First Fifteen, was such a one. Invariably he began to stammer when he played Nanky-Poo to her Yum-Yum, so that she had to cast about for a means of putting him at ease and found one by getting him to tell her about his trainee manager's post in a rubber plantation he intended to take on leaving at the end of the summer term. And here and there she came across the arty type, like Archer the Second, who played the violin well, and Blades who, at fifteen, wrote poetry, and the brash beefy extrovert types like Rigby and Bickford, who needed slapping down, she thought, before they grew too big for their boots. There was yet another type that interested her and even puzzled her a little, the boy who walked alone, not as a romantic, like the musician Archer, or the poet Blades, but dourly, as if they were repelled by the gregariousness of school life. Briarley, whom David had told her about, was such a one, and she entirely approved David's efforts to develop the slender bridge between them, begun the day the news came that Briarley's father had been killed in France.

There were one or two others she felt very sorry for and mentioned to David, but tentatively, for it seemed to her easy, in this male world, to jump to facile conclusions. Young Skidmore, the idol-hater, was one of them, for David was right about him, in that he did seem hell-bent on martyrdom. Whatmore was another, whose parents had just been divorced, imposing all the stresses that would bring to a thirteen-year-old. She said, learning that Whatmore was taking it badly, "I've nothing against divorce if a marriage is intolerable to man and wife but why the hell can't they pretend to rub along until their children are old enough to acquire a little philosophy? I think I would even if I hated the sight of you, Davy!" and as always, when she showed storming indignation over something, she made him laugh.

All kinds of boys. Fat ones, thin ones, handsome ones, homely ones. Boys with plausible excuses, boys with lame ones, boys who never bothered to offer an excuse. Boys who excelled in class but were weeds on the playing field, amiable oaks who were lions on the field and played games inside their heads through four periods in succession. Integrated boys, like Nipper Shawe, the school bell-ringer, high-principled boys like Skidmore. Intelligent extroverts, with a bubbling sense of humour like Boyer, and boys who were having a very hard time of it, like little Whatmore. One would never have thought it possible to find so many varieties in one school and there were still others waiting to present themselves as term followed term. It was very exhilarating, however, to have so many male eyes on one at church and school concerts, and to have five eighteen-year-olds competing with one another at the Owl Debating Society to bring one cup of watery coffee during an

interval in the motion, 'That we support Home Rule for Ireland!'
Occasionally she heard something she was not meant to hear but
when that happened she was unrepentant. In a world where
women were out-numbered a hundred to one, a chance to eaves-
drop was a bonus.

The cottage hedge adjoined the long stone wall of Ricketts'
Farm, where the boys flocked between the end of afternoon school
and high tea to buy hot pasties and apple tarts, baked by old Mrs.
Ricketts, universally known as Ma Midden, on account of the
permanent slush pools in her yard. Towards dusk one October
evening Beth was in the roadside corner of the garden, screened
by the overgrown hedge, planting a rowan tree in a cleared patch
of ground when she heard the cheerful voices of Boyer, Dobson
and Letherett approaching the farm gate.

She had not lit the oil-lamps and they must have judged the
cottage empty, for Dobson said, "Old Pow-Wow's a lucky dog and
no mistake. His wife isn't the kind of lulu you'd expect to bury
herself alive in a dump like this. After all, she's not twenty yet,
and with her face and figure she could have married ackers,
couldn't she?" She only just stopped herself exclaiming at the
implied slight on David overshadowing Dobson's compliment, but
curiosity won and she remained bent over her spade as Letherett
said, "Betsy's a corker and no mistake. I'd sooner go to bed with
her than you, old sport. But don't get the idea she isn't stuck on
him. Anyone could spot that a mile off." And then, mercifully
before they passed out of earshot, she heard Boyer say, "And why
the hell not? Pow-Wow's a damned good sort, and more on top
of his job than any of them, bar the Old Man, and Howarth maybe.
Jolly good luck to 'em, I say. Tumbler's blonde is easy on the eye,
but a bit of a nag, I'd say . . ." and then Mrs. Ricketts' gate clicked
and she heard them bawling for Ma Midden, and scampered back
to the house to compose herself before Davy got home.

She didn't know quite what to make of that conversation, even
though she was already sufficiently familiar with school slang to
translate it without much difficulty. 'Ackers' meant money, a Birmingham word that had strayed into the Bamfylde glossary, and
Davy's nickname, of course, was acknowledged by all. 'Corker'
signified sex-appeal, and Herries was 'the Old Man' to everyone
who did not use 'Algy', whereas Irvine had acquired the soubriquet of 'Tumbler' on account of his bobbing gait. She was a little

shocked by the trio's genial contemplation of her as a bedmate, but decided adolescent boys talked the same language as hospital probationers, particularly here, where women were in such short supply. What intrigued her far more, however, was Boyer's championship of Davy, and his emphatic blessing on their marriage. It meant that Boyer at least, and perhaps most of the senior boys, had considered marriage, and her particular marriage, in the abstract and that, she supposed, was evidence that it was regarded as a success. She thought of it as such, of course, and so, she was sure, did Davy, but they were prejudiced. It was something else to have it blessed by a boy of sixteen, and she would have liked to have told Davy about it but knew, instinctively, that this wouldn't do at all. Instead she lit the lamps and gave the Irish stew a vigorous stir as it simmered on the old iron stove. 'A dump' Dobson had called the cottage, but to her it was very far from that. It was a home already, a cosier and more rewarding home than she had ever hoped to possess, notwithstanding Dobson's optimistic assessment of her chances in the marriage market. Dobson was in error anyway. Men of marriageable age were scarce, with a million dead and two million maimed and incapacitated and men of Davy's temperament were scarcer still. She had made up her mind as to that months ago.

He would have been surprised to have learned the real reason prompting her display of demonstrative affection the moment he loomed out of the dusk, and its sequel initiated by her the moment they turned out the lamp and climbed into bed. Up to his job, was he? Well, she was up to hers too, she hoped, and in the moment before she slept she raised his hand to her breast and held it there, thinking, "Dear God, how lucky I was to lean over that pier-rail that time and fish Davy up from the beach . . . !" and the random quality of life made her shiver a little, so that she tucked herself into him, as though fearing he might be snatched away and swallowed up with the rest of his generation, with all the boys she had flirted with in the middle years of the war, boys who had been there one day and photographs on their mothers' mantelshelves the next.

2

Her luck was set fair. She was granted her honeymoon wish. By late October she was so sure that she was carrying his child that a call on Dr. Willoughby for confirmation was a formality. She was amused by Davy's fussy concern, however, and even more by his immediate association of pregnancy with her forthcoming appearance in the star role of *The Mikado*.

"Good Lord!" he said, when she told him Willoughby had confirmed her hopes, "that'll put Algy Herries in a frightful fix! Who can he get to replace you at this stage?" and she said, through her laughter, "Why should he get anyone? I'll be less than four months on. Do you imagine I'm spending the next six months in a wheel-chair?"

"I wasn't thinking of that, Beth. Just the . . . well . . . the look of the thing. I mean, won't you feel damned silly, standing up there singing to an audience of four hundred boys in those circumstances?"

"Not in the least," she said, "for I shan't show much. At least, I hope not, and even if I did why should I be embarrassed? Good heavens, Davy, it's not as though the youngest of them doesn't know the facts of life. I'll wager some of them know more than me," and she remembered the conversation heard through the hedge.

"Well," he said, doubtfully, "if you don't care I don't see why I should. Look, do you mind if I tell Ellie? I'm sure she'll be delighted. The great sorrow of her life is that she and the Old Man never had any kids and I'd like her to stand godmother."

"Tell whoever you like," she told him gaily. "I'm already feeling insufferably smug about it, especially as Phyl Irvine's no-go turned out to be a false alarm." And then, squeezing his arm, "We haven't wasted much time, have we?"

"Who would, with you around?" he said, and although he said it as a joke she had a serene impression that he meant it.

As it turned out she was over-optimistic concerning the risks of a public display. In the straight, loose-fitting frocks of the current fashion it didn't show at all but it was a different matter when she came to tie the tight kimono sash of Yum-Yum, in the attic dressing-room she shared with Phyl Irvine at the top of the head's house. Inspecting her, Phyl succumbed to a fit of the giggles.

"I must say you look a very enterprising little maid from a ladies' seminary in that outfit," but Beth said, "It's all over the school by now anyway. Things like that are relayed by the jungle

94

drums. I expect poor Driscoe will be more embarrassed than either of us."

Driscoe, a fourteen-year-old with an excellent treble voice, was the third member of the trio, but if he did notice he didn't give himself away and the number went off very merrily, as indeed did the whole show, playing three nights to packed houses, that included several carloads of visiting parents. Algy Herries declared that it was the best opera yet, and booked Beth and Phyl a year in advance for *H.M.S. Pinafore*.

The predictability of a place like Bamfylde struck both David and Beth that winter and each of them pondered it in different ways. David saw it as a kind of sheet anchor, something to be prized in a world that he had come to accept, up to the time of his coming here, as disintegrating in volleys of thunder and deadly flashes of lightning, a place where one could be sure of nothing. She saw it, and welcomed it, in a more subdued light, part of a pleasant rhythm that was at one with her new life and the child in her womb. It was a reversion to sanity, where people were born, passed through infancy to childhood and adolescence, and then out into the world beyond Bamfylde to earn their bread. David she saw as a conscientious overseer, poised by the conveyor belt, adding a touch here and there as the products trundled by.

She enjoyed her first term immensely, with its nonstop hilarity and avalanche of tiny events, but to David's astonishment she also enjoyed the silence of the place when all the boys and most of the staff had departed, and those few remaining drew closer together, the rump of an enormous family getting its second wind after a long, rackety party.

It was then, when the north-easterlies came flailing over the moor bringing flurries of snow, and plateau temperatures dropped below zero, that she began to think of his immediate future and made an important decision on his behalf. He said one night, when they were sitting drowsily by a big log fire in the open hearth, "Look here, Beth, this won't do at all. I shall have to use this break to set about doing something practical about my degree. Damn it, I'm the only man on the staff without one. I can't expect Algy to regard me as a permanent wartime stopgap. There's always so much happening term time. Would you mind much if I spent the afternoon up at the school, cramming?"

She said, "Why up at school? Why not here, over in the window

95

alcove? We could get a desk and put some shelves up between the window and chimney breast. I wouldn't get under your feet, would I?"

"No," he said, "not in that sense, but I daresay you'd distract a man from the Reform Bills and Henry VIII's foreign policy from time to time. So far I've lived almost wholly in the past, even during my first year here. I don't mean the recent past, the war and all the bloody misery chaps went through over there, but the distant past, particularly the Middle Ages. But not any longer, or not in the way I did. It's the present that counts, and the future. I even find myself getting damned impatient with text-books that stop at Gladstone's first Government and the Corn Laws. I want the kids to concern themselves more with their own times, with living history."

"I've heard you say more than once history is all of a piece."

"So it is, if it's taught properly. But the exam syllabuses don't even acknowledge the twentieth century. There wasn't a single damned question on it in last summer's Cambridge senior papers."

"I daresay all those old buffers who set them regard what happened between 1914 and 1918 as another Crimea. They'll get around to it in time."

"But that's the point," he said, "there isn't time, at least, not if we waste it, the way those bloody politicians did at Versailles last summer. That treaty is an absolute shambles. Jerry was saddled with the entire responsibility for the war, and any chance of a just peace was lost in a sordid haggle for territory and reparations. There must be some way of putting that over."

"In a text-book, you mean?"

"No, but in a book written in language an intelligent seventeen-year-old could follow without yawning."

She had a mild inspiration then, arising out of one of the first conversations they had had when he introduced her to Margaret of Anjou. She said, "If you feel it that deeply you're the person to write it, Davy. Start tomorrow!", and he replied, looking at her with his head on one side, "*Me?* Oh, go easy, Beth. It's a job for a political journalist, based on London, with access to state papers and inside contacts."

"Why is it? You went through the war and you were born and raised in a Welsh valley, where your father and two brothers died for somebody's greed. I think you've got better qualifications than any journalist or academic. Besides, you're a born teacher. Anyone spending a day in your company would concede that."

He lounged over and sat on the hearthrug, leaning his weight against her knees. "Get along with you, you think I'm capable of anything, Beth."

"So you are. And I'm not the only one."

"Who else, apart from Mam, over at Pontnewydd?"

"The head, and Howarth. Both of them are much older than you but that doesn't stop them looking to you for a lead sometimes."

"A lead? In what cause, for God's sake?"

"Against the diehards, the people who think the clock was put back four years the day the war ended. But not only them. They're no problem really because they'll soon die off. It's the group around Carter I mean, people who escaped the war but are already looking on the job in an entirely different way from you or Algy, or even dear old stick-in-the-muds like Cordwainer. This place seems united enough on the surface but it isn't really, you know. Different people are trying to steer it different ways. You believe in real education, in letting boys develop their individuality, but Carter and some of the others don't. They're only interested in exam results. There's a conflict here. Even I can see that, after four months. In fact, I can probably see it more clearly than you because I'm outside, looking in on all but the frolics."

It struck him that she was extraordinarily bright for a girl not yet twenty. Sometimes it puzzled him a little. Where did her perception and natural intelligence come from? Not from her stolid old father, certainly, and a couple of years as a hospital probationer wouldn't account for it. He said, unconsciously expressing his line of thought, "How old were you when your mother died, Beth?"

"Seven. Why?"

"Remember much about her?"

"Not a lot. I remember she wore the trousers in our house. Father was quite helpless when she died. Esther and I didn't blame him marrying the first eligible woman who caught his eye, and Nell and I have always got along. She was a good stepmother, as stepmothers go. Why, what are you driving at?"

"You. Your way of looking at things, and seeing more than the average person would see. I think your mother must have been quite a person. How about your grandparents on her side?"

"He was a Methodist minister, and gran was a school teacher in one of the first elementary schools, but I don't remember either of them clearly. Longevity isn't a strong suit in the McLeods."

He had forgotten she had Scots ancestry and this might account for all manner of things. Her earnestness, for instance, her forthrightness and preoccupation with abstract ideas, watered down by the Cockney strain on her father's side, and a Cockney upbringing that would develop a latent sense of humour. Her directness flashed out again now as she said, "You're side tracking. It's a weakness of antiquarians and you're particularly prone to it. We're talking about *you*, Davy, not my family tree. Didn't I hear Algy or Howarth say something about you doing a thesis for your degree?"

"Not for my B.A. I'd have to get that first and turn in a thesis for Master of Arts."

"Right. We'll take it from there. I'll get that corner fixed up as a study as soon as the snow lets up. You start swotting for your B.A. and you've already got a theme for your thesis—'The Gaderene Rush' or 'How-we-got-into-the-pickle-in-the-First-Place'. I'll keep you at it. I want to be a helpmate, not just a bedmate and a brood mare. Pull me up and rake those ashes down."

They left it there for the time being but she held to her purpose and the new year saw him installed in his inglenook, where he could get the benefit of the fire in a room of persistent draughts. It took him a little time to get used to working there, with her rustling about in the background, unconsciously diverting him by her over-solicitous efforts to do everything quietly so that he said, chuckling, "You don't have to walk on tiptoe and practise controlled breathing. My first two terms I taught a class adjoining that poor devil Meredith, before he got his marching orders. It was like teaching in the crater of a volcano."

After that she relaxed and he was able to lose himself in study and analysis, working steadily until the little French clock her stepmother had given them chimed nine thirty, when she came in with the cocoa and the bread and cheese.

But then, in the third week of January, Bamfylde erupted again, and what old Howarth called the 'tight-rope term' began, meaning the cold, blustery period between late January and mid-

March, when inches of rain could fall in twenty-four hours, and the school was often shrouded in seeping mist. Sometimes the weather was so vile that the football field became a quagmire and matches had to be cancelled, but the runs went on. Nobody minded getting plastered with black Exmoor mud if it meant an afternoon's change of scene.

By that time, of course, Beth, in her own phrase, was beginning to look more and more like a penguin, and kept to the house, fearing a fall and disastrous consequences. But she remained very cheerful and knitted, he thought, enough tiny garments to supply a city orphanage, an occupation that seemed to bring a repose that by-passed him. For, towards the end of term, his mind was switched from her, and the winter discomforts of the cottage, by a confrontation that he was reluctant to confide in her. It was another and more serious clash with the Carter faction, highlighting her feeling that Bamfylde was indeed being pulled in opposing directions.

3

It was a deeper quarrel than the initial one, arising from his refusal to join the Corps, and left him with a sense of unease that augured badly for the future. It became known, in Bamfylde history, as 'The War Memorial Spuddle', 'spuddle' being a local word signifying a dispute between two rival parties.

It began on a relatively civilised level but quickly deteriorated into a sour, ding-dong battle, with himself and Howarth ranged on one side, Carter and the traditionalists on the other, and Algy Herries poised in a position of uncomfortable neutrality.

The controversy stemmed from the offer of Alderman Blunt, of Challacombe, to donate five hundred pounds for the setting up of a memorial to Bamfylde's war dead, an offer that was accepted by the Governors without prior conditions. Blunt was a local war profiteer, a timber merchant who, as Howarth put it, had been a twopenny-ha'penny supplier of builders' materials before August, 1914, but had burgeoned, in a matter of six years, into a magnate, with a yard, a country house set in a forty-acre country estate, an enormous Rolls-Royce, and a grand manner, far more impressive than that of old Hopgood, head of the Bamfylde landowning family with roots in the Middle Ages. Carter had

99

spent a great deal of time and patience cultivating Blunt, and enlisting him as a patron of the school. He was therefore inclined to take upon himself the credit of finding the finance for a splendid memorial to the Old Boys and in making the gesture public somehow implied that he, personally, was giving the money.

Ordinarily it would have been a matter for the headmaster and Governors alone, but a special committee had been set up to consider the provision of a memorial, and both Carter and David had been co-opted on to it, the one representing the housemasters, the other the Old Boys' Association.

At its first meeting the committee were asked to consider three designs submitted by Blunt's tame architect. They were conventional monuments, a plain stone cross, to be erected at the head of the east drive, a bronze statue of an infantryman in battle order, and a more pretentious design featuring an angel poised on a globe representing the embattled world. David, already nursing a profound prejudice against the rash of memorials sweeping the country, spoke out against all of them.

"As an ex-serviceman," he said, "I'm qualified to express an opinion on this. These things are meaningless. If five hundred pounds is going to be spent on a memorial to the dead why can't we spend it on something practical?"

"Such as what?" demanded Carter, sharply.

David was ready for this. "A gymnasium to replace the old covered playground. The installation of modern cooking equipment in the kitchen. Even a dynamo down by the piggeries, to provide us with our own electricity."

Algy Herries seemed impressed by the alternatives. "What do you say to that, Carter? Seems worth considering, doesn't it?"

"With respect, no, Headmaster," Carter said, "because it's out of step with the sentiment behind the gift. Mr. Blunt wouldn't favour it, I'm quite sure of that."

"You could consult him on the matter," David suggested, and Carter, seeing the head undecided, said he would do this, but was obviously delighted to inform the next meeting of the committee that his forecast had been correct.

Alderman Blunt, he reported, had now expressed a preference for the stone cross, inscribed with the eighty-odd names.

"Well, that's that," Herries said, philosophically, but David, nettled, said one aspect had been overlooked. "I think we should get the views of Old Boys before we accept," he said. "Nearly a hundred fell but six times that number served and survived. I propose we put it to the O.B.A. general meeting at Whitsun and get their views."

At this point old Bouncer, representing the church, rose to his feet and surveyed the meeting benignly under his useless spectacles. "Offer might be withdrawn by then," he said. "Settle for the bird in hand. That's my notion. Eh, eh, Carter?"

"My sentiments exactly," Carter said. "We don't want to give Mr. Blunt the idea we're looking a gift horse in the mouth. I'll move an amendment that we accept the money now and get the work in hand right away."

The amendment was put and carried, four votes to one, Herries as chairman, abstaining, and that should have been that, and would have been had David accepted his defeat gracefully. He would not, however, and sought the advice of Howarth, who said, sourly, "Since you seem determined to put a spoke in Carter's wheel, I'll give you some free advice, P.J. Can't stand the little squirt. Never could, although, for my part, I don't care a damn whether a gift from a man of Blunt's reputation is a stone cross or a supply of gold inkwells. His money's tainted and I wouldn't want it to feed starving children. The fellow's a frightful bounder!" and in a few acid phrases he outlined, for David's edification, Blunt's spectacular rise in the world. "Your best bet is to contact the Old Boys personally. Get out a circular letter on the duplicator, and ask for replies within the week. Then, if a majority support your view, throw the statistics at them." And this is what David did, sending out more than four hundred and fifty letters, and enclosing stamped addressed envelopes.

The response was gratifying. Within a week he received nearly four hundred replies. Eighty-seven per cent of them backed his proposal, favouring a memorial of some practical value to the school.

Armed with his figures he asked Herries to call a special meeting of the sub-committee and made his circular public, but Carter, forewarned, produced an ace from his sleeve in the person of Blunt himself, a florid, ponderous man, who struck David as a truculent peasant using his unexpected wealth to whip the shoulders of all the locals who remembered his hand-to-mouth days. Faced with the result of the postal poll Blunt said, without preamble, that when he proposed a memorial he meant a memorial, not an addition to the school that would lose its identity as soon as it was built or installed. There was nothing David could do but back down and if Carter had left it there the whole thing would have been forgotten by the time the cross was unveiled at the dedication service Herries had planned.

That was not Carter's way, however. Determined to savour his triumph he buttonholed David in the quad on the first day of the summer term, and said, with counterfeit affability, "Word in your ear, Powlett-Jones, and I hope you'll take it the way it's meant. You're comparatively new here, so you can't be expected to know how to handle the locals like Blunt. It so happens I do, not because I've spent ten years of my life here—aside from that spell in the army, of course—but because I'm West Country born. I know these chaps, believe me. Played the right way they can be damned useful to us. Blunt is rolling in money, and he loves kudos like a cat loves cream. Fine, let's humour him. Let's get all we can out of him. He'll end by endowing us handsomely if he's left to me."

"You want his kind of money that much?"

"Why the devil not? It's as good as anyone else's money, isn't it?"

"No, it isn't," David growled, "it's come from soaking the Government when they had no alternative but to pay anything men like Blunt had the nerve to demand. I hate the bastards who sat tight and made fortunes in the war. I've got a hell of a sight more time for the conscientious objectors."

Carter blinked at him. His eyes, David noticed for the first time, were angry, ferrety eyes, red-rimmed, as though to match his rust-coloured hair. Suddenly, inexplicably if he had been able to contemplate it in a rational mood, David discovered that he hated him.

"That's a high moral tone to take at your age," Carter said, in the voice he used to subdue mutinous spirits of the Fifth. "Why not go down to Blunt's bank and ask the manager if you can sniff his pennies one by one? Just in order to satisfy yourself none of them are tainted?"

"I don't have to, I know they are. I slept in barrack huts men like Blunt provided. They were built of unseasoned timber that worked out at about five bob a foot. The men who inhabited those rabbit-hutches—when they were lucky, that is—were getting a shilling a day, for keeping Blunt and his like from being walked over by Prussian jackboots. To hell with Blunt and everybody like Blunt! I feel like spitting every time I pass his bloody memorial, and you can tell him so if you care to!"

"But I don't, old man," Carter said, easily, "I've better manners," and drifted off, clearly quite unruffled.

It soon got around, as everything of that kind always did in a place like Bamfylde. A garbled version too, as David realised when Howarth drawled, "Hear you're likely to be running short on saliva as soon as that shroud comes off the war memorial, Powlett-Jones. Not wise, I think, to empty your chamber at a tyke like Carter. Better to leave a shot or two in reserve. You'll have more trouble with him, so take a tip from a veteran common room skirmisher like myself."

"How the hell *is* one to handle a man like Carter?" asked David, thoroughly exasperated. "He knows it all, doesn't he?"

"He doesn't know me," Howarth said, "and that's encouraged him to keep out of my way for years. In a place like this you don't fight with drawn swords, my boy. You find a nice little spot behind a chimney pot and snipe. Imagine me telling you about sniping! However, you're not a fool and you'll learn. Providing you stay long enough, that is."

It was odd how persistently his defeat at the hands of Carter nagged at him, and it wasn't long before Beth dragged it out in the open, demanding to hear the full story. She said, when he declared that he intended looking for a new situation the moment he had taken his degree, "That's silly, Davy, and if you think about it you'll see it is. There'll be a Carter in every school, and if you mean to stay in the profession you'd better face the fact. Howarth's right. It's your tactics that are amateur. You never want to give the Carters of this world an opening. I wish you'd told me about this before."

"Do you think I wanted to worry you at a time like this?"

"Pooh," she said, "a time like what? Life has to go on, doesn't it? But, in any case, I've news that should take your mind off Carter and Mr. Blunt for a spell. Doc Willoughby was here this afternoon and brought a friend of his. A gynaecologist from Bristol."

His jaw dropped and he looked so dismayed that she yelped with laughter. "Oh, David, don't keel over! It's not that bad; at least, *I* don't think it is. Tell me, are there any twins in your family?"

"*Twins!* Good God . . . are you sure? . . . Is Willoughby and that Bristol chap?"

"More or less, I think, but doing well so they tell me. No wonder I was such a size. I was beginning to think of discarding the name 'David' for 'Goliath'. Now it'll have to be David and Jonathan."

He said, wonderingly, "You . . . you don't *mind?* You're not scared?"

"Not in the least. No, honestly I'm not, I'm . . . well . . . rather excited if anything. But Willoughby says I can't have the baby—babies—here, as planned, with Nurse Arscott standing by. I'll have to go into a Challacombe nursing home a few days in advance. Can we afford it? It'll cost about eight guineas a week, they say."

"Good Lord, of course we can afford it if it's necessary. But are you sure it doesn't entail complications? I mean, why did he bring that chap here in the first place?"

"Just to make sure," Beth said, but nothing would do but that he should go hurrying over to the village the minute prep was over, to pursue his own line of enquiry. Willoughby satisfied him, or at least moderated his anxiety, assuring him that Beth was a good, healthy girl and unlikely to run into trouble. "At the least hint of it I'd plump for a Caesarian," he said, "but I don't advise it. Go on home, and let her calm you down, old man."

And David went, walking ruefully across the little strip of moor that gave access to the junior pitches and then, through a gap in the hedge, down the road to the cottage. As he passed the angle of the buildings housing the prefects' studies, however, his ear caught the lilting whine of Carrington's portable gramophone, playing one of his favourite jazz numbers. Part of the refrain, sung in a high nasal tone, came to him in the fading light,

> *Yes, I'm goin',*
> *Yes, I'm goin',*
> *And soon I'll be hallo-ing*
> *To that coal-black Mammy o' mine . . .*

It soothed his nerves somehow, so that he grinned, remembering that Carrington was jazz mad, and played the saxophone at school dances, familiarising everybody with the latest wave of song-hits from the U.S.A. He thought, "Two of them, eh? Well, if they're boys, and she swears they are, I'll have two Carringtons here about seventeen years from now. I wonder what they'll be playing then?"

He looked back over his shoulder as he vaulted the lane gate at the corner of the cricket field, seeing a violet glow moving like a slowly drawn curtain across the last rays of the sun. In the uncertain light the huddle of buildings no longer seemed incongruous up there on the lower edge of the plateau and he thought, glancing back at them, "Well, that's home, all right, and I'm damned if I let a twirp like Carter turn me out of it," and he went down the incline to Stonecross thinking of Blunt and his war memorial as very small beer indeed.

Chapter Three

1

He was down at the long-jump pit when little Stratton-Forbes brought him the news. Stratton-Forbes of all people. The smallest boy in the school, with round, cherubic face and snub nose supporting professorial, steel-framed spectacles, for Stratton-Forbes had a squint they were trying to correct—"Before it grows on me," as he had remarked, quite innocently, to would-be tormentors, completely disarming them.

Sports Day was upon them again by then and some of the junior events were scheduled to be run off in advance. Irvine, who had appropriated to himself the role of sportsmaster, asked David's help in measuring the cinder track leading to the pit, but Irvine was not the only one at work on the jump. Carrington, the Sixth Form jazz enthusiast was there, and with him two or three other seniors engaged in spreading the cinders, when a breathless Stratton-Forbes appeared and shrieked, at the top of his voice, "Please-sir-message-from-the-Head-sir! Head-said-to-say-two-girls-sir-both-doing-well-sir!"

The entire group, David excepted, exploded with laughter and Stratton-Forbes blinked, wondering what was so funny, so that the incident passed straightaway into Bamfylde legend and Barnaby, that master-coiner of nicknames, bestowed upon Stratton-

Forbes the title of 'Annunciator', soon shortened to 'Nun'. Years were to pass before Stratton-Forbes, a very serious-minded boy, fully understood how he came by his soubriquet.

But David did not hear about this until much later. The annunciation projected him through the beech hedge behind the jump-pit, up the east drive and across the threshold of the head's house in twelve seconds flat. Carrington, seeing him go, afterwards declared that Pow-Wow had beaten the world's sprint record, without even trying.

Algy Herries was standing beside the telephone in the hall, the receiver in his hand, a beaming smile on his face, so that David had no need to seek corroboration before grabbing the phone and bellowing, "Powlett-Jones here! That you, Doc? Is she all right?" and Willoughby assured him that she was as right as rain, except that the lady seemed a little put out they were girls, but had come to terms with her poor showing as a sex-determinator as soon as she was shown the twins. "She's tired, naturally," he went on, "but who wouldn't be? The first little monster turns the scale to six-three, her sister at just under the six mark. Faultless performance. Congratulations, old man. Will you put me back to the head?"

"Hold on a minute . . . when can I see her . . . them . . . ? Some time tomorrow, first thing? I can get Irvine to cover my periods. To hell with his hurdle course!" and at that both Herries and Willoughby laughed, and the doctor said, "Why not this evening? Say around seven. She's asleep now but they'll wake her for supper," and David turned to Herries, who nodded, and said, thankfully, "Seven sharp then. Thanks, Doc. I'll get there somehow."

"All in a day's drudgery," Willoughby said and had his word with the head, leaving David standing to one side and feeling extraordinarily foolish. He said, when Herries hooked up the phone, "Er . . . thank you for sending Stratton-Forbes, sir . . ."

"He got it right, then?"

"Word perfect. A little too perfect. He blurted it out in front of everyone. Shall we go in and tell Mrs. Herries?"

But there was no need. Ellie, concealed in the archway at the entrance to the study passage, had been present all the time and now came forward.

"Congratulations, dear boy. It's splendid, isn't it, Algy? The first Bamfylde twins I can remember."

"The first ever," Herries said, "but it would have been better if Powlett-Jones had had a house, and the brats had been born on the premises. Wonderful headline there. 'Girl twins born in boys' school'," and he chuckled, as he usually did at his own jokes.

"Don't tease the poor boy," Ellie said, "try and be serious for a moment, do! What will you christen them? Was it fixed in advance?"

"No, it wasn't, Mrs. Herries, for Beth would have it they were boys. They were going to be David and Jonathan, but now . . . well . . . have you any ideas?"

"*I* have," Herries said, unexpectedly. "Have you seen yesterday's papers? They're canonising Joan of Arc today. There was a lot about it in yesterday's *Times*. Your subject's history. Won't Joan do for one of them? I've always liked the name myself."

"I'll certainly put it up to Beth. Joan. Yes, I rather like 'Joan' myself."

"And how about the other?" asked Ellie. "Joan of Arc was unique, wasn't she? You could choose another saint of course . . . Ursula, Veronica, Mary . . . they're all nice names," but Herries cut in, impatiently, saying, "Pish, my dear! You're missing the point. People will never see Joan of Arc as a saint, no matter how much Rome puts out about the poor girl. She'll always be associated with simple heroics. What we need now is another heroine. An English one, for preference. Any ideas, P.J.?"

It seemed absurd to be standing here in the tiled hall, discussing his children's given names with Herries and his wife. Absurd but very cosy and reassuring, almost as if the rubicund, white-maned old chap had really assumed the personality of that earnest bow-legged miner, who had gone into the lower workings of the Pontnewydd pit one summer morning and never been seen again. And thinking this David felt an impulse to humour Herries at all costs and said, "How about 'Grace'? Grace Darling, of course! Or 'Emily', after the suffragette, Emily Davison, who comes from the same part of the world?"

"I'll plump for Grace, if you don't mind," Herries said. "We've had about all we can stand from the suffragettes."

" 'Grace' will do very nicely," said Ellie, "but for heaven's sake don't let him bully you into using those names if your wife doesn't care for them. He's always been very silly about names, and that's nonsense, of course. He's never liked my sister Maud, simply because he had a nagging aunt of the same name. But here, what am I thinking of? We should be drinking your health, shouldn't we? Wetting the baby's head, isn't that what it's called?" and she led them into the drawing-room where Algy unearthed a fine pale sherry that he kept for himself and a few chosen friends. "I never waste this on parents," he said. "Sweet does for them. For the Governors, too, except one or two Old Boys, sharp enough to hang about until the others have gone."

They drank to him and then to Beth and the twins, and by four o'clock that afternoon, having skipped his last period, he was halfway to Challacombe by the lower road, the longer but faster route on account of its surface and gradients.

It was years since he had sat a motorcycle. The last, he recalled was a Brough Superior he rode in the Salient while doing a spell of despatch-carrying. This one chugged along at an uncertain twenty-five miles per hour, giving him time to bask in his own serenity, that merged with the flowering May countryside and made him want to express his glee in song. And soon he did, keeping time with the stuttering beats of the Douglas engine, crooning snatches of 'Coal Black Mammy', Carrington's favourite dance-tune,

> Not a cent, not a cent,
> And my clothes are only lent . . .
> But I know she'll think I'm just fine . . .

His high spirits expressed itself in other ways, in cheery waves at farmhands he passed, and in squeezing the bulb horn at every bend in the road, and in this way, with two hours to spare, he chut-chutted into Challacombe and stopped outside Gorman's the florists, to buy an enormous bunch of flowers, remembering as he did that huge bouquet he had bought her the day after her nineteenth birthday.

*   *   *

She looked prettier and more radiant than he ever recalled, with colour in her cheeks and a triumphant sparkle in her brown eyes. Clearly she was tremendously pleased with herself and said, when he kissed her with the restraint he had shown that first time outside her sister's dairy, "Oh, come *on*, Davy! Don't travel backwards! You can do better than that, can't you?" and she kissed him, with no nonsense about it, and said she was quite reconciled to the girls because they were unbelievably pretty— "Far prettier than I ever was, and prettier than Esther was as a baby and she was the flower of the flock, so Father says. You can't actually see them but you can nip into the corridor and peep through that glass-panelled door. The staff nurse there is a frightful dragon. You'd think she'd given birth, and I'd tidied up afterwards!" and as much to humour her as satisfy his own curiosity he slipped out and glanced through the glass panel of a door marked 'Maternity', and was rather taken aback by what he saw, a row of half a dozen cots, each, presumably, containing a baby, although he couldn't be sure because some of the canopies were raised.

He was still craning his neck there, trying to identify his own children, when a pleasant voice at his elbow said, "Mr. Powlett-Jones, I presume?" and he turned, blushing, to confront a slim, blonde woman wearing a red-lined cloak of matron.

"Yes," he said, "I'm Mrs. Powlett-Jones's husband. I was trying . . . er . . . er which two *are* mine, exactly?" and the matron smiled and edged him over the threshold, saying, "Just a peep. They're sleeping and, anyway, you mustn't stay long. We don't usually allow visitors the same day but Dr. Willoughby said you were rather special. Are you, Mr. Powlett-Jones?"

"Every father of twin girls is special," he said, quickly getting the measure of her, in the manner boys like Boyer and Dobson had taught him. "These two?" and when she nodded, "Well, Beth's right! They are pretty, the pair of them, but I suppose all the fathers say that, don't they?"

"No," she said, "mostly they stammer and goggle, and don't say anything intelligible. I suppose you don't because you're accustomed to infants."

"Not this age, and certainly not this sex," he said, taking a sudden liking to her. Then a door at the far end of the little ward banged open and a buxom nurse cruised in like a Whippet Tank, and sensing her extreme indignation both he and the matron made a strategic withdrawal to the passage where she went about her business. He returned to Beth's room, announcing that he had not only seen Joan and Grace but compromised the matron in the eyes of her underling.

"You're absolutely right," he went on, "they're a couple of . . ." but she cried, "You *named* them! You called them by name! And I've been lying here cudgelling my brains ever since I was told David and Jonathan were out. Joan and Grace! Why, that suits them exactly, Davy! How clever of you."

"I can't take credit for it. Algy and Ellie agreed the names between themselves, and presented me with a *fait accompli*. Seriously, though, I'd like to call them that, if only to please the old couple. Algy's been splendid all the time you've been gone, and I've been pigging it up in the President's room. Since they heard it was twins they've begun to think of them as grandchildren."

"Joan and Grace it is then . . ." but then she yawned, so that he said, "I'd better take myself off. I can look in tomorrow, it's a special half-day for the Devonshire Dumplings match. I'll borrow Barnaby's Douglas again. He's umpiring, I think."

"Please," she said, but sleepily, so he kissed her and stole away, walking down the hill into the evening sunshine and feeling slightly less excited than when he climbed it but more certain, somehow, of the unfolding pattern of his life and hers.

2

There was no doubt about it. The twins and their presence in the crowded little cottage at Stonecross increased his confidence in himself in a way that everyone about him noticed, not only Herries and Howarth, but the more discerning of his boys, especially those that he had begun to think of as friends. Boyer put it into words when David's name cropped up during one of those desultory conversational exchanges the old hands indulged in concerning members of the staff who had joined the family after themselves, thus giving them licence to patronise.

"Y'know, history periods were a crashing bore before Pow-Wow showed up but now they're a high spot. You never quite know what line he's going to take, in or out of the syllabus. Carrington told me he introduced another book of war poems to the Sixth yesterday. By a chap called Wilfred Owen. Bolshie, of course, but that's Pow-Wow, isn't it?"

But no one could accuse him of Bolshevising history in the junior forms although, judged by his own standards, he was prone to revert to old-fashioned methods. The truth was he would use any means to brighten a period, to leaven it with anecdotes, speculations and sometimes doggerel rhymes that he recalled from his elementary school days.

There was a great favourite, designed to jog the memory concerning the string of battles in the Wars of the Roses, dull enough in themselves, maybe, but not the way Pow-Wow presented them, for he used them as a means of teaching the Second and Third Forms the art of war in the fifteenth century, and would even turn aside to sketch bills, glaives, body armour and the early ancestors of the trench mortar on the blackboard. As regards the doggerel, he felt it contributed a little to Irvine's geography lessons, whisking the boys all over England in the wake of the Yorkist and Lancastrian armies. 'All-Boys-Naughty-Won't-Memorise-All-Those-Horrid-Hateful-Battles-To-Bosworth' the Second Form would chant, thus, by identifying the capitals with place names, recalling battles at St. Albans, Bloreheath, Northampton, Wakefield, Mortimer's Cross, St. Albans again, Towton, Hedgley, Hexham, Barnet, Tewkesbury and Bosworth.

It was a great success, as was the old saw to remind them (God alone knew *why* they should be reminded) of the fate of Henry VIII's wives, viz:

> *Divorced, beheaded, she died;*
> *Divorced, beheaded, survived.*

He sometimes invented new ones to raise a laugh, as when he fixed the sequence of the Stuart kings in their minds with—

> *James was nearly blown sky-high,*
> *Charles, his son, knelt down to die.*
> *Charles-the-next hid in the oak,*
> *James-the-next was a bigoted bloke.*

It was all very juvenile, he supposed, but it added to his popularity, for the boys loved to feed upon staff eccentricities and this was one of his. The broad effect of his free-ranging and highly improvised methods had more important results, however, introducing a fruity generality into his periods, and enabling a class to break free of the cast of history text-books and cruise down what he thought of as the mainstream of time.

He had always seen history as the Clapham Junction of education. It opened doors on so many other subjects, not only geography, but English prose and poetry, economics, law, religious knowledge and any number of fringe subjects. A brief study of Edward I's administrative reforms, for instance, whetted the appetite of some—just a few, here and there—interested in the British jury system. An hour or two spent with Lord Shaftesbury's industrial crusades shed some light on the Trades Union movement, and the strikes headlined in the newspapers. In the Fifth and Sixth Forms it was sometimes possible, in his view, to humanise history to a point where he had seventeen- and eighteen-year-olds questioning accepted attitudes concerning the structure of democracy, and the lessons that were to be learned (but rarely were) from the long stalemate on the Western Front.

Here and there, of course, he was challenged. Gilbert, a Tory M.P.'s son, boldly disputed his over-facile analysis of the Russian Revolution, but he dealt with him gently, content to point out that the Czarist regime had been overthrown by the abysmal folly of the ruling class, stoking the fire century by century without once opening a valve to siphon off the steam.

"But surely that's no justification for slaughtering the entire royal family, is it, sir?" Gilbert had argued, and he said, mildly, that it was not, but one rarely looked for justification in human affairs, only the merciless logic of cause and effect. "If the Czar, or rather that neurotic wife of his, had bent a little in 1916, she wouldn't have been murdered in 1918. Over here, thank God, our royal family had more sense, or perhaps more regard for their own skins. Victoria was the most revered monarch in the world when she died in 1901, but as to real political power, she exercised virtually none compared with her uncle, in 1837. That's what I mean by bending, and as a nation we're very good at it, Gilbert. You ask your father if you don't believe me."

Fortunately for David Gilbert *père* was a left-wing Tory, with a heavy build-up of unemployment in his own industrial constituency. "Like to meet that chap," he told his son during the holidays. "He sounds original for a schoolmaster," and Gilbert Junior obliged, introducing them at the subsequent Speech Day, when they had an amicable discussion on the wisdom of national-ising the coal mines.

This was the way of it, and all that summer and autumn, while Beth was fully occupied coping with the twins in a four-roomed cottage lacking piped water, electricity or even an indoor privy, he was growing into the ethos of the school, so that sometimes it seemed to him he had been here ten years instead of just over three.

It was often difficult, under the circumstances, to continue studying for his degree, but he achieved slow progress and made tentative arrangements to sit for his B.A. at Exeter University College of the South-West during the forthcoming Easter break. He hated the idea of leaving Beth to cope with two twelve-month-old babies but there was no help for it. Exeter couldn't give him a degree but it was the nearest centre available for sitting the exam. Long before he went, however, something occurred that entrenched him even more deeply at Bamfylde, enabling him to throw down roots that would take a great deal to dislodge.

*   *   *

They were passing through one of their tiresome periods, as-sailed by snow, then by ceaseless downpours, and finally towards the fag end of the Christmas term, by another sharp spell of frost that caused havoc with Bamfylde's antediluvian water supply. On the last day of February Bat Ferguson approached him with news that his aged French mother-in-law had died in Beauvais, and he was obliged to cross the Channel, attend the funeral and clear up her affairs. He would be away a week, he said, and would be greatly indebted to David if he would live in as resident house-master of Havelock's during his absence.

It was a confounded nuisance but, having lived there prior to his marriage, he was more familiar with the routines of Have-lock's than any of the younger men, and Ferguson invited him to bring Beth and the twins up from the cottage and occupy his quarters for the week. David accepted the chore but Beth declined the invitation to move into the school.

"It'll be an awful upheaval, with all the children's things," she said, "and not worth it for a few days. You sleep up there and come home for lunch every day. I'll be perfectly all right down here, and I can always send a message by Mrs. Ricketts' boy if I need to. You ought to help out, oughtn't you? You always told me the Fergusons were kind to you in their old-fashioned way when you lived with them."

She packed him off with a bag and he took up quarters in his old room, with its view over the rolling moor. Nothing much was to be seen there now, apart from wan glimpses of frozen stubble and a desolate hillside whenever the wind tore rents in the prevailing mists. Shouts, scuffles and the impact of boots on the setts of the quadrangle below were muffled, and even the clamorous notes of Nipper Shawe's bell-ringing seemed to come from far out on the moor.

He called the roll, went the rounds, exchanged a joke with Boyer and Dobson who were Havelock boys, and supervised 'Silence', the five minutes dedicated to private prayer by the bedsides. It was a duty he performed with secret amusement, being absolutely certain that young Skidmore, the Methodist parson's son, was the only boy there who used the interval to commune with the Almighty. After that he followed Ferguson's Airedale, Towser, into the housemaster's study, where he built up the fire and spent a couple of hours brushing up on Central European history as far as Charlemagne's death.

It was a period that had always confused him and his mind kept wandering from the page, isolating irrelevant incidents from his own past rather than that of Charlemagne's. He saw himself fishing with his father in the then untainted stream a mile or so above Pontnewydd. He mused for a moment on the chubby face and clear blue eyes of a girl called Olwen Thomas, who had attracted him when he was at the Grammar School. Errant thoughts of Olwen's smile led him, naturally enough, to a sleepy awareness of Beth and the twins, sleeping as soundly, no doubt, as the seventy-odd boys in the two dormitories overhead. When he heard the duty prefect's step pass on the stairs he roused himself and, telling himself he was entitled to a whisky for leading a bachelor's life for a week, poured a stiff tot from Ferguson's decanter, afterwards re-addressing himself to Charlemagne.

It was no use. Apart from Beth's spell in hospital, this was the first night they had spent apart since their marriage, more than two years ago, and already his body hungered for her, so urgently that he could laugh at himself as he thought, "My God, I wouldn't

care to live celibate again in this place . . . I wonder if she's missing me?" and then the unaccustomed whisky (he was a gin or beer
drinker when he drank at all) had its effect and he nodded off,
the heavy book slipping from his knees and falling with a soft
thud beside the indifferent Airedale.

Outside the wind got up, whooping down from the moor like
a foray mounted by savage hill-tribes but it did not wake him.
What did, some twenty minutes after midnight, was Towser's
long, spine-chilling howls, projecting him from the arm chair at
a bound.

The dog was crouching over by the door, feet braced, head
thrown back, every hair on his body standing out like the coat of a
hell-hound in a Nordic folk-tale. He shouted, "What *is* it, Towser?
What's up, for God's sake?" and the dog stopped howling and
began to whine, weaving his muzzle to and fro, as if terror was
communicating itself to him by the scent of something gross and
evil.

David felt his own flesh crawl as his bemused senses grappled
with various possibilities. A ghost? Was Havelock's haunted? If so
he had heard nothing of the story, and it would be common currency in Bamfylde, where legends were hoarded like miser's gold.
Boys, perhaps, out on the prowl? That was more likely, and glancing at his watch David reached the door in three strides and flung
it open.

The stench and unmistakable sounds that assailed him were
far more frightening than any ghost. Something was burning
and, to judge by the volume of smoke billowing in the strong
draught on the stairs, it was well alight. Standing there, momentarily paralysed by dismay, he could see a small rosy glow pulsing
behind the pall, and hear the soft, menacing crackle of burning
woodwork. It was the sound that prompted reflex action, of the
kind he had learned over three years of kill-or-be-killed at the
Front. Leaping down the stone stairs, with the terrified dog at his
heels, he tore open the heavy door of the linen-passage leading
to the western arcade of the quad, grabbed Nipper Shawe's bell
that stood on a niche beside the post-box, and swung it. Seconds
later he was halfway up the second flight leading to the dormitories, where a stream of boys collided with him, some in their
dressing gowns, some in their pyjamas, all pouring down the steps

in a flood so that he had to grab the iron rail to prevent himself being carried away with the rush.

He managed to grab Dobson, somewhere in the middle of the bunch, and bellowed, "Junior dorm . . . boys beyond? Are they all out?" and Dobson shouted, "Yes, sir! Think so! Ridgeway was there counting them . . .", and then Dobson was swept away as Ridgeway, the duty prefect, appeared just above him bawling, "*Steady*, there! . . . Take it *easy!* The bloody stairs can't burn, you idiots."

He fought his way up level with Ridgeway, a tall, pallid boy, wearing fancy check pyjamas. Odd the things that struck you at a moment like this for he recalled, even as he grabbed Ridgeway by the shoulders, that Ridgeway was the dandy of the Sixth, with his locker full of fancy ties and purple socks. He shouted, "Counted the juniors? They're *all* out?" and Ridgeway wincing, said, "Counted eighteen, sir! That's the lot in there, but the annexe . . . !"

"Who sleeps in the annexe?"

"I . . . I'm not sure, sir!"

"*Think*, man, *think!*"

"The two Kassavas, sir . . ."

"They didn't pass you?"

"No, sir, I'm almost sure they didn't . . . it was one hell of a rush, can't be sure."

He said, between his teeth, "Take the bell. Go on down and line 'em up in the quad. Count 'em again, double-check 'em and send someone over to the head's house to phone the Brigade."

"Yes, sir," and Ridgeway was gone, leaving him alone two-thirds of the way up the stairs, with the smoke thickening, the glow beyond it spreading, and a sound like ten thousand dry sticks being snapped over in the boarded passage on the left of the landing.

He identified this at once as the heart of the fire, a draught funnel running immediately above the linen rooms below, but the identification seemed unimportant. What obsessed him now was the thought of the two Kassava brothers, almost surely cut off in the little annexe just beyond the junior dormitory, two first-termers from India, the sons of a rajah's physician so they said, who slept in Havelock's as spillovers from Outram's, very short of bedspace that term. He thought, with a sickening fatality,

"They probably don't even know the geography of the bloody house, but there's nowhere they *could* have gone, except through the junior dorm and past Ridgeway," and clapping a handkerchief to his face he dashed into the disordered senior dorm and down its length to the connecting door. But here, to his amazement, he was checked. There was no hope of going beyond it for the fire seemed to have run along under the floor and burst out of the pipe vents beside the washstands. The junior dorm was blazing from end to end, the fire concentrating at the extreme end, where the annexe lay.

He could not go on but he was terribly unwilling to leave. He stood there dithering a moment, the iron clamour of the bell reaching him from below, a background rhythm to the swelling tumult down there. Then somebody coughed at his elbow and in the light of the flames he saw Boyer, who gasped, "They're out on the roof, sir! Between the two gables . . . Ridgeway's shouting to them to move along . . . Better go, sir . . . before the floor caves in!"

They ran back through the senior dormitory, across the landing and down the two flights of stone stairs to the quad, and as they went Boyer said breathlessly, "Roused the head, sir. Mrs. Herries phoned Stoke Steps and Challacombe. The village team shouldn't be long . . . Head's taking a roll-call . . ." and then they were in the quad and Ridgeway was pointing up at a steep 'V' between the two gables at the north-west angle of the quad. In the rosy glare outlining the roof he could see two small figures, peering down into the surging quad, and right below them Irvine, chivvying a squad of about a dozen senior boys, ranged around the tarpaulin that covered the cricket pitch on rainy days in summer.

It seemed to him astounding that the tarpaulin could have been located so quickly, and even more so that everybody but the Kassava brothers were right here in the quad, ignoring Ridgeway's shrill commands to go down the passage to Big Hall for a call-over, but staring upward at the two little figures crouched behind the guttering. He understood then, however, that the Kassava brothers would never jump, that they would have to be pushed, or shown some safer way down, and once again his trench reflexes came to his aid, and he grabbed Boyer by the arm, saying, "That rope in the covered playground—the one with the hook . . . And the *lighter* rope, holding it to the wall . . . we'll have to get them!"

They crossed the quad at a run, elbowing boys out of their way, and in ninety seconds were back with the ropes, a thick one fitted with a brass hook, part of the makeshift gymnasium equipment, and a long coil of clothes-line rope, used for fastening it back when it was not in use. Boyer said, "We could fasten one to the other and throw it up . . . But even if they grab it they'll be too scared to make fast and slide down . . .", and he saw Boyer was right, and that someone would have to carry the lighter coil up to them.

He said, "I could make it from the Remove window . . . There's all that creeper and the drainpipe. Find the head, tell him what I'm at, and keep that tarpaulin team in position. Never mind the bloody roll-call, the fire's confined to Havelock's, no other house is involved yet."

He thought Boyer said, "Come with you, sir," or something like it, but he could not be sure. He was gone by then, pounding up to the steps to the Remove that was situated immediately below the gable ends one storey down. There was plenty of light here, not only from the glare above but from the quad lamps. It took him no more than seconds to join the ropes, force open the tall window and scramble through on to a tiny, lead-covered platform surrounding the braces of the drainpipe.

There was just enough room here to pause and regain his breath. Looking up he saw he was now about sixteen feet from the ridge between the gable ends but the fire beyond the inner gable was spreading rapidly. From this angle it seemed to be on the point of engulfing the gables. He lifted one foot and wedged it into a clutch of creeper, then hoisted himself up another foot or two, the lighter rope gripped between his teeth. He had a curiously intense feeling of isolation up here, as though he was separated from the sea of upturned faces below not by some thirty feet but by the height of a mountain. It was oddly silent, too, despite the steady crackle of the flames and the soughing gusts of wind fanning them. The drainpipe was rusty under his palms but the creeper seemed tough and fibrous, sufficiently so to support his weight, so that he went steadily upward until he could have reached out and touched the two white faces peering over the edge of the guttering.

It would have been simple enough if he could have called to the boys, telling them to stretch out an arm and take the rope but this was impossible with the rope clamped between his teeth and in any case they seemed immobile, wedged there like a couple of gargoyles. So he pushed on over the gutter, its rough edge tearing at his jacket and his outflung hand found a leaded ridge to give him a final purchase. With the rope entangled in his legs he rolled on to the platform, sat back and began to haul, looking over his shoulder for a crevice or leading edge where he could fix the hook when he had drawn it up.

Kassava Major came alive then, moving forward a few inches to help him pull, and between them they hauled in the full length of the lighter rope, and then the hook and a few feet of the heavier rope. It would be too short by a couple of yards, he would judge, but with so many below this was nothing to worry about. The immediate problem, having wedged the hook under the inner window ledge of the annexe, was to persuade the boys to trust themselves to the rope. He said, addressing the elder Kassava, "It's the rope from the gym, strong enough to support a horse. Can you shin down it? If you slip there's a tarpaulin to catch you." Kassava Major's voice seemed steady enough as he said, "I'll do it, sir . . . but the kid . . ." and he left the sentence in the air, spreading his hands outward in what struck David as an oriental gesture of resignation.

He was right, of course. Kassava Minor, rigid with terror, was a child of eleven. Nothing would induce him to project himself over the edge of the drop. He made up his mind on the spot. "We'll have to lower him . . . Explain what he has to do . . . he'll take it better from you," and he hauled on the heavy rope until he drew it in and made a loop of the loose end.

The elder boy seemed to have completely recovered his nerve. Above the roar of the flames he could hear Kassava Major repeating over and over again, "It'll be all *right*, Jimmy . . . Do what Sir says . . . Just *do* what he says," and between them they managed to slip the loop over the child's shoulders and tighten it round his waist, but once that was done they were no farther on, for Kassava Minor clung to the guttering with both hands, and with his full weight braced to the rope David could take no part in prising them loose. He saw Kassava Major's right arm move then, just once and very swiftly, up and then down, and suddenly the rope went taut, and Kassava Minor was suspended below the guttering and he was able to pay out, a few inches at a time, until suddenly the rope went slack and he could haul it up again, finding that in that tiny interval someone below, with their wits about them, had climbed on to the tuckshop roof and untied the cradle, giving him another three or four feet to spare.

There was no time, and no need to peer down to satisfy himself that the younger boy had made a safe landing. Showers of sparks shot from the windows of the annexe and smoke was thickening, masking everything about them but the stark silhouette of the gables and the roof of the head's house immediately opposite. They had little chance of surviving. The orange flames, shooting horizontally from the annexe window, would blast them from the crevice at any minute and send them plummeting down to the quad. He could not see Kassava now, despite the glare, and might not have realised he was alone up here had not the roar from the crowd announced the plucky kid's safe arrival thirty feet below. Then he saw that he must shift for himself and rolled on his belly, testing the anchorage of the rope before projecting himself backwards and outwards, over the gutter. His jacket caught again, ripping clear down the front and he seemed an interminable time going down. Then, inexplicably to him, Irvine was there, and Howarth wearing a bright plum-coloured dressing gown, and old Algy Herries shouting, "Take him inside! Take him across to my house . . ." and he felt himself half-lifted and swept clear of the press and the next moment he was sharing a sofa with Kassava Major, who was grinning and rubbing the knuckles of his right hand. He said, vaguely, "Where's your brother, Kassava?" and the boy said, almost apologetically, "He's still out cold, sir. I had to do it. He was like . . . like a limpet, sir!" and grinned again, holding up his bruised knuckles for inspection.

3

He played no part in subsequent events, in containing the fire to the top storey by a human chain of bucketeers, senior as far as the first landing, staff and domestics on the flight of steps beyond. He did not see the arrival of the village handpump team, or, some twenty minutes later, the crashing descent of the Challacombe brigade, in their new Merryweather engine. Between them they got it under control by dawn, sending their jets arching across the quad and stopping the spread of flames south to the Fifth form room and his old bachelor's quarters, or north to the Outram dormitories the covered playground and the labs. The damage was extensive, two dormitories and the linen room gutted, Ferguson's living quarters flooded and all its ceilings down, but it might have been much worse and surely would have been but for so many factors that, looking back, made a pattern of his disorganised memories. The Airedale's spine-chilling howl. Ridgeway's cool performance at the door of the junior dormitory. Boyer's timely appearance through the smoke. Kassava Senior's pluck and resource in knocking his brother cold when he was clinging to the ledge. Carter's cool lead in evacuating the Outram dormitories, and the Herculean performance of the amateur fire-fighters and their antiquated equipment from the village. But he saw and evaluated none of these things at the time, for the nervous reaction was swift and salutary and he was back again, physically at least, to a time nearly three years before when a single tiresome incident would cause his hands to shake uncontrollably and the nerves in his cheek to twitch. He spent the rest of the night with the Herries; and Beth, leaving the twins in the care of Ma Midden at the farm, came to claim him in the morning. With her on the scene he quietened down and began to come to himself but slowly and uncertainly, like a man snatched from the sea at his last gasp.

He certainly did not see himself as a hero but there were others, it seemed, who did, and he was made aware of this under circumstances of hideous embarrassment when, on the final evening of term, he went into Big School to take prep for the Lower and Middle School. On the instant of his setting foot on the dais everyone stood up and began cheering, so that he gazed around as if everyone there had lost his wits. After a moment or two, however, he understood that the ovation was for him, and that it was completely spontaneous, touched off by some hidden spring of emotion in the hearts of the boys who had stared up at him and the Kassava boys on that niche. He raised his hand then and when they did not stop he roared, "Sit *down!* Everybody *sit!* Where the hell do you think you are? At a Cup Final?" and at that they laughed and resumed their seats, and he too sat and pretended to read but found himself listening to the pounding of his own heart as he thought, presently, "I couldn't leave here after this . . . This is the end of the road for me, and for Beth too. I thought I was home and dry a long time ago, when I brought Beth here and she liked it, when the twins were born. But they were only stages and this isn't. It's a terminus."

But even that wasn't quite the end of the affair. Towards the end of the holidays, when he was spending an hour with Algy Herries on the timetable, Ellie looked in with tea and said, "The post is in. There's a parcel for you, dear boy!" and while he was asking himself who on earth would be likely to send him a parcel, and why it should come to the school rather than the cottage, he saw Algy and Ellie exchange the kind of look parents exchange over a Christmas tree when the family are opening gifts, and fumbled with a small, carefully wrapped package bearing a Delhi postmark that only increased his mystification. Then Algy said, impatiently, "Here, give it to me! You'll let the tea go cold!" and took it, stripping away the wrapping to reveal a square cardboard box. Inside, bedded in blue velvet, was a slim, very elegant gold cigarette case, inscribed with his initials.

He stared at it uncomprehendingly until Algy said, with a chuckle, "Go on, open the wretched thing. Touch the spring and tell us who's playing Father Christmas in April." He touched the spring and inside was a visiting card bearing the name S. E. Kassava, M.D. (Edin.) F.R.C.S., and when he lifted the card there was an inscription above the hinged clip that read, "In deepest appreciation", and underneath it the date of the fire.

He said, wonderingly, "It's magnificent . . . ! But he didn't have to do that . . . Why, young Boyer would have shinned up that drainpipe if I'd let him. So would Irvine or Ridgeway or anyone else if they'd thought of it."

"But that's the point, dear boy," Ellie said, her Adam's apple sliding up and down with emotion, "they didn't. Or not so quickly. Now, Algy, put that horribly complicated-looking timetable aside and have tea. We're supposed to be on holiday, aren't we?"

Chapter Four

1

1922, 1923, 1924. The years unfolded, season by season, term by term, with a pleasant, almost timeless rhythm, as though Bamfylde, tucked away under a fold of the high plateau, was a planet in its own right, only marginally involved in the rest of the solar system.

Ordinarily, sometimes for months at a time, the planet spun an unremarkable orbit, within the ageless succession of spring, summer, autumn and winter, changeless or so it seemed to David, with its traditional sequences marked off in the school calendar issued to every boy on the first day of a new term.

In the Lent term there were the house matches, the second half of the cross-country season, the Choral Society's Holy Week Concert, the confirmation classes conducted by Algy Herries, the end-of-term examinations for class prizes to be distributed at Speech Day, and the endless shuffle from class to class and period to period, a marathon that took him, in a matter of thirteen weeks, all the way from the Roman conquest to the murder of the Archduke Franz Ferdinand at Sarajevo, in June, 1914, and occasionally a little beyond, as when he asked of the Sixth what they made of the poems of Owen, Graves, Rosenburg and Siegfried Sassoon.

He was invading Howarth's territory here but old Howarth did not seem to mind and was, in fact, grateful for David's English periods in the Second and Third Form. He was glad these had been fitted into the timetable more or less permanently. An hour or so every week, he was able to commune with Goldsmith and Gray, Swift, Tennyson and Blake, airing the corridors of his mind and opening up rewarding cul-de-sacs on the eighteenth and nineteenth centuries. The same applied to trespasses on Irvine's subject, when he would draw a freehand map of Europe on the blackboard of Big School and illustrate, with a cluster of sweeping, south-easterly curves, the dramatic switch of Napoleon's Grande Armée from the Boulogne camps to Ulm and the defeat of the Coalition at Austerlitz in the winter of Trafalgar.

Of his incidental efforts in these directions both Howarth and Irvine would sometimes make common-room jests, as when Howarth said, referring to his introduction of the Middle Third to Goldsmith's 'Deserted Village', "Keep 'em hard at it, old man! With you clearing the ground in that Lower School desert there's that much less sod-breaking for me when The Lump gravitates to Middle School! Not all that much less, of course. Most of The Lump doze through *Hamlet* and Marlowe, damn their churlish souls. But every now and again I find an uncut diamond where I least expect it. Blades is a case in point. Two years ago you started him on mere doggerel, like 'The Ballad of Patrick Spens'. Now he plagiarises Robert Herrick!"

'The Lump' was the staff name for the inevitable group in every new cadre of boys, those odd dozen or so, who clung together in a sullen, unleavened mass, moving up the school at the rate of one shift a year, and finally coming to anchor in the Lower Fifth, where they grew downy moustaches while making successive stabs at school-leaving certificate.

"Autrefois Le Lump, toujours Le Lump," as Ferguson put it, but this wasn't strictly true. Now and again, about halfway up the school, a boy's interest in a subject would quicken, so that he broke free of The Lump and set an individual course. The Lump, incidentally, contributed all the regulars to Saturday penal drill, where they applied the same tactics dodging punishment as they displayed work-dodging in class. It was years before David, who occasionally took the penal squad, discovered why boys like Bickford, and his henchman, Rigby, seemed so fresh, and in good heart, after a double round the buildings. The command was always, 'Rear rank to the left, front rank to the right, round the buildings—*Double!*' Old lags like Bickford would tear round the first corner and wait there until the greenhorns came puffing past the fives court. They would then rise from the seat and join the leaders, nobody having observed to which rank they had attached themselves at the start of the drill. The Lump, however, invariably included many of the most amiable boys in the school, so that David continued to see them as a latter-day equivalent of the old sweats in the platoon, men who were always being promoted and then reduced to the ranks for minor crimes.

The summer term was quite different. For one thing the weather was much better. For another the thirteen weeks were starred with a variety of red-letter days. These included Sports Day, Speech Day, the visit of a field officer from the War Office to judge the O.T.C. drill competition, and a variety of other functions, including several important cricket matches. But the summer event David always enjoyed most was the Whitsun Old Boys' Reunion, when as many as three hundred Old Boys, a few of whom he taught in his first two years, would descend on the school and indulge in an orgy of reminiscence in the old army hut bar provided for them.

He always felt rather sorry for their young wives and fiancées, many of them shy and pretty, who drove up with the impression that Bamfvlde was a compromise between Sandhurst and Blenheim Palace. Once there, however, they were abandoned by their menfolk and could be seen wandering about rather forlornly, searching for the lavatory, or somewhere where they could sit and take tea.

It was Beth who spotted this unchivalrous deficiency in the O.B.A. programme and tackled Judy Cordwainer's wife about it, so that she found herself appointed hostess to the visitors and persuaded David, as Assistant Secretary of the Association, to give her ten pounds from O.B.A. funds, to be spent on fitting up an old linen room in Nicolson's house as an oasis for bored brides and disconsolate brides-in-waiting.

The Michaelmas term was different again, for it brought a spate of new boys, who were duly invited to the new boys' teas in the cottage garden. The Michaelmas term, in its opening weeks at least, was a time of renewal, with almost everyone settling to a new routine in a different part of the school, with the autumnal running season and rugby football season and, above all, rehearsals for the Christmas Gilbert and Sullivan opera.

Beth was now a regular in the dramatis personae, having already starred in *The Mikado*, *H.M.S. Pinafore*, *The Gondoliers* and *The Yeomen of the Guard*. David never succeeded in making more than the chorus but was sometimes called upon to deputise for Rapper Gibbs at the piano, having learned to play by ear in recreational centres and the officers' mess at Blandford and later, behind the lines in the Ypres sector.

November 11th saw the parade round the War Memorial, where Algy would read the names of the fallen before the two minutes' silence, followed by the sounding of 'The Last Post' and 'Reveille'. David's sour tussle with Carter over the stone cross was forgotten during that first service, in 1920, after watching Algy stumble through the long list of names with tears streaming down his cheeks. So the years slipped away but not without the occasional crisis that would highlight a day, or a week, or sometimes a term.

From the personal standpoint they rarely deserved to be called crises. Once the twins went down with measles. Another time part of the cottage thatch was stripped off in a tearing southwesterly. And twice, during the years when Joan and Grace were toddlers, Beth gleefully announced that she was pregnant again and he made frantic efforts to stake a claim on one of the new bungalows that were being built on an extension of the football field, fifty yards south of the plantation.

He was never able to get one. There was always a queue of men senior to him but in the end it did not matter, for Beth's news turned out to be premature and for a week or two she was down in the dumps. "I so wanted a *son*," she said, when he tried to console her saying they could not really cope with five in the cottage. "I want a son and I'm jolly well going to have one, so just you get used to the idea! It'll soon sort itself out when there are five of us, and there had better be before you spoil those girls to death!"

It was a just accusation, as he was always ready to admit to himself, if to nobody else. For him, and many of the boys, there never had been two children like the twins. They were pretty, biddable, and sharp as a couple of pins, and apart from the fact that Beth insisted on dressing them individually ("I'll not have anyone thinking I'm stage-managing a showpiece wherever we go!") only their intimates, like Ma Midden and her arthritic husband Ben, or Ellie, up at school, could tell them apart. They reminded him more of his elder sister Gwynneth than of himself or Beth, for they were all Celt, with round chubby faces, dark curls and creamy complexions. He even declared he could detect the Welsh lilt on their tongues, especially when they were excited. "That'll be your doing," Beth told him, "but maybe it's just as well. Growing up in this rural wilderness they'll soon be talking broad Devon and we shall have a job finding them anything but pigmen for husbands."

She took this matter-of-fact line with him whenever they discussed the children and subconsciously he understood why. Not only did he spoil them but everyone up at the school did the same, and so did his old mother and Beth's father whenever they got the chance. In this sense, he supposed, it was important they did have another child and they never went out of their way to avoid having one. This in itself was a bonus, as she would sometimes admit in the heavy silence of the moorland night, when they lay still in one another's arms in the main bedroom of the cottage.

"I think we're very lucky this way, Davy," she said, on an occasion quite early in their marriage. "It must be absolutely awful to have to go through a chemist's shop drill every time you want to make love. I suppose people get used to it but I don't think I could."

"You might have to eventually," he said, grinnning at the moonlight patch of plaster above the bed. "If I can't bully Algy into giving us married quarters someone will be roughing it in the outhouse and it's not going to be me. I've too much on my plate and need my sleep."

He had, too, for his long-term plans were beginning to mature. They had altered since the days Beth and he had planned how to go about getting his degree. Various opportunities had opened up for ex-servicemen who could claim a spell of teaching experience at a reputable school. He was now working hard for an external London degree, using an Oxford correspondence course that required of the student a minimum of eight hours' work a week. In fact, David was able to put in more, mostly by reading while supervising in class or prep. He was covering British and European history from earliest times to 1900, social and economic history over the same span, one special subject—he chose his favourite fifteenth century—and political theory. There was one other paper, translating a historical extract from two modern languages out of a choice of five, and this required special cramming. His French was adequate, but he knew very little German and had to be coached by Ferguson, a fluent German speaker although he did not teach it. His intermediate was behind him now, taken at Exeter in 1921, when he sailed through in four subjects, including English and European combined history, English literature (coached by Howarth) and Latin, in which he gained a poor pass after some steady coaching by Barnaby.

As the time for taking his finals approached he sometimes wondered whether he would use all this effort as a means of moving on, perhaps applying for a more important post at a better-known school, but it seemed unlikely so long as Herries was around. Even before the incident of the fire he had acquired a special relationship with Algy, whose unconventional approach to education made a direct appeal to him, whereas Beth seemed happy enough, despite social isolation.

Against all probability, she had integrated into the school and come to share his love of the untamed countryside, even in its savage moods. Yet it was not her humour and unswerving devotion alone that played their parts in banishing the final traces of shell-shock, in healing a mind and body that had survived three years on the Western Front. The cure, to his way of thinking at least, had been wrought mainly by regular access to a woman whose approach to him was maternal, in that she was equipped to ease the tensions that had built up inside him, simply by being herself and absorbing him with a directness and merry-hearted innocence. Simply to lie there and watch her undress in the lamplight was a kind of therapy. The sight of her young, supple body, glowing with health and redolent with mystery, even when she was naked, was a demonstration of wholesomeness and flawlessness to a man who had been in such close contact with everything foul and shattered.

He would watch the lamplight play on her breasts and move, like a sensuous lover, over her thighs and buttocks. Sometimes, by way of a laughing glance over her shoulder, she would assess the intentness of his fond scrutiny before pursuing her unhurried way to bed and bestowing on him a few brief moments of ecstasy that would leave him speechless with gratitude for her presence and for her being.

This was her unique contribution, but the other, broader road back to vigour and full mental health was signposted by boys. Boys of all ages and all temperaments, boys who came to represent for him a world of rich and varied promise, that he had assumed lost for all time in hurricane bombardments under Aubers Ridge and Polygon Wood.

They were signposts of variable aspect. Humour was there, and sometimes pathos, and two incidents stood out during that period, so that he thought of them, in after years, as important crossroads.

The funny one, that had the undertones of an outside world's tribulations, was the affair of Paddy McNaughton, the Irish boy who staged a spectacular and convincing show of running amok one wet half-holiday, when games were cancelled, and a group of his peers in the Upper Fourth were passing an idle hour tormenting him about his championship of the Irish Free State. That was in the winter of 1921–22 shortly after Bloody Sunday brought about a final crisis in Irish affairs, and Michael Collins, the Sinn Fein hero, made a clean sweep of British Intelligence officers and Scotland Yard men assembled in Dublin to arrest a number of rebel leaders.

Nobody really resented Paddy's chauvinism. By then it was an accepted fact of the Bamfylde scene, particularly as it was generally known that Paddy's father had been badly wounded serving with the Munsters, in France. But on this particular afternoon Lower Fourth banter over-reached itself and Paddy was collared and thrust into the Big School dust-hole, a relic of the Victorian era, that still absorbed dust and rubbish under the rostrum and was reached by a small trap door.

They got him down there easily enough, egged on by Bickford, Rigby, and several other members of The Lump, but their high spirits turned to panic when Paddy re-emerged via a wormeaten section of wainscoting flourishing a large Smith and Wesson revolver, that he used to corner all but one of his persecutors, yelling that he would show them that one Irishman was the equal of a dozen Englishmen.

Half-mad with fright, Bickford and his associates were backed the full length of Big School but Rigby managed to slip away, dashing into the quad and flinging himself upon David, who happened to be crossing the quad on his way to the bandroom.

"Please, sir, come quickly, sir! He'll shoot 'em all, sir! He's in there now, with a damn great gun. Clean off his rocker, sir . . . !" and David hurried in the direction indicated, too late to rescue the hostages but in time to see them herded over the slushy ground in the direction of the swimming pool. He ran after them, a crowd of whipping boys in his wake, but seeing Boyer, now a Sixth Former and trainee prefect, he shouted to him to keep the others back.

He was twenty yards short of the cricket pavilion when he heard a confused outcry, terminated by a series of splashes, and when he burst into the enclosure there stood McNaughton, enjoying the prospect of Bickford and five of his cronies floundering in the deep end.

He walked up to the boy with his hand extended and McNaughton, breathless and grinning, lobbed the revolver in his direction. He caught it and saw at a glance that it was far from being a lethal weapon. It was hammerless and corroded by rust, the relic, no doubt, of a discarded war issue rescued from a rubbish dump.

"What the devil possessed you to play such a tomfool trick?" he demanded, and McNaughton said, cheerfully, "I had to do something, sir. There's a limit to the ragging a man can take. I'll take a beating and no complaints at all, sir. It was worth it, to see 'em cooling off in there, and this no weather at all for a swim, sir!"

He snapped, "Wait here, McNaughton, I'll deal with you in a moment," and leaving the boy by the firing platforms of the miniature range he hurried down to the bedraggled group climbing out of the pool and looking, he thought, extraordinarily foolish as they shook the water from their clothes.

Bickford said, breathlessly, "He's raving mad, sir! He would have drilled us if we hadn't done what he said and jumped . . ." but David said, holding up the rusting antique, "With this?" and the pistol passed from hand to hand with cries of indignation. Bickford said, uncertainly, "He kept telling us it was loaded, sir. He said he'd brought it back from Dublin, and kept it specially for us. We didn't get a chance to get a close look at it. It's . . . it's a real one, isn't it, sir?"

"It was. About the time of the Phoenix Park murders over there. Run on back, strip off and give yourselves a good rub down. Then go down to the kitchen and tell Ned Priddis I said you were to have a pint of hot cocoa apiece. Off with you and don't hang about," and they went, making a cautious circle round the impassive McNaughton as they filed through the gate.

He sauntered back, balancing the weapon in his hand and said, curiously, "Where did you find this, McNaughton? And how did it come to be so handy in that dust-hole?"

"I've had it since I was a kid, sir. I found it on a Liffey dump years ago and brought it back after last hols."

"Why, exactly?"

McNaughton hesitated. "Nothing to do with them. The Black and Tans were making house-to-house searches at the time. I didn't want to give them an excuse to shoot the Governor. Even an antique like that could cause trouble over there, sir."

"Ah, so I've heard," David said, and the boy looked at him carefully, as though trying to decide whether the remark was ironic or conciliatory. He said, finally, "My people are neutral actually. My Governor fought for the British and won the M.C. at Cambrai," and then, defiantly, "But the Tans were right bastards, sir!"

"Do you really feel steamed up about asses like Bickford and Rigby?"

"Och, no, sir. Bull Bickford's dim, but there's nothing personal, sir. And the others, well, they just go along. It all began as a lark, sir."

"But got out of hand?"

"Well, yes, sir. But like I said, they asked for it, so they did." Then, doggedly, "I'll shake hands, sir, if Bull and the others will, but there's sure to be a rare shindig now. It'll be all over the school by tea-bell."

"That won't matter, so long as it's handled properly."

"You're saying you'll speak to the head, sir? Tell him my side of it?"

"Wouldn't you prefer to tell him yourself?"

"No, sir. You see—well, I reckon you know about Ireland and the Irish. You must have been in the trenches with people like my Governor. Maybe you could make him see why I blew my top?"

"Very well, leave it to me. As to this gun, what shall we do about it?"

"Throw it away I'd say, sir."

"Good idea. I've seen all I want to see of guns, antique and otherwise."

He nodded and went off towards the plantation, finding a fox earth, stuffing the pistol into it and ramming it home with his boot. He had no intention of punishing McNaughton for what he saw as a justifiable explosion of wrath, and he did not think Herries or Howarth, McNaughton's housemaster, would overrule him. And anyway, by now Paddy McNaughton, with his cool truculence, and his disposition to fight his own battles in his own way, had joined the company of Bamfeldians who had succeeded in forming a strong, personal contact with him, a group that already included Cooper and the Sixth Form volunteers of his first term, Boyer, Ridgeway and the Kassava boys, on account of the shared adventure of the fire, Skidmore, now known as 'Preacher', on account of his prolonged bedside prayers, Briarley, the boy he had tried to comfort back in the days of the Big Push, and one or two others, whom chance had singled out for eligibility. There was to be one other before that integration period ended, the boy who now featured in what he would recall as the curious affair of Blades and Julia Darbyshire.

2

Like most of the episodes that passed as peaks in the terminal graphs it came about by chance, one hot afternoon in late May, when he was taking the long way home over the plank bridge of the stream that ran between two folds of the moor above Stone Cross.

The First Eleven were playing Christow Manor and there had been two free periods after lunch. It was an important match but he had cramming to do and after watching the visitors' innings, he left the field and cut through the plantation to the slope that led down to the Coombe. He had a purpose in mind. A rivulet ran through the cottage garden and Beth had made a water-garden there, planting wild flowers on the margins and hoping for the best. She was now in search of marsh marigolds and he remembered having seen them growing in the river bottom when he had passed this way during the last of the Lent term runs. He borrowed a trowel and a carton from Westacott, the gardener, and decided to see what he could find on his way home.

He had reached the head of a steep path leading to the bridge, half-aware of the distant sounds from the cricket-field that carried all the way over here when the wind was in the west, the faint but distant *sn'ack* of a ball hit for a four and the scattered applause, pleasant, summery sounds he thought them and very English in that setting. Perhaps this was why he paused a moment to listen, his back to the school, his eyes on the valley below, a riot of brown and russet, shot through with the vivid green of new growth and, on more open ground, the gleam of celandine showing among the softer hues of lingering primroses and columbine. Rashes of campion grew there and a few sparse patches of bluebells at the top of the wooded slope, a complex that utterly transformed the aspect of this same Coombe once summer was at hand.

He was standing there, about twenty yards from the stream, when he heard a woman's laugh and swinging round detected a slight movement among the waist-high ferns. There was no reason why he should investigate. The village women went there to mushroom and collect wood but the sound did not strike him as a local's laugh. It had a light, musical quality that told him whoever was down there was what the moor folk would call a 'foggy-dew' or foreigner. Something else, too. The laugh was associated with dalliance. He thought, shrugging, "Well, I'm no spoil-sport. Nobody tips his hat to a Peeping Tom," and was already turning away when the laugh was repeated, followed by a few indistinguishable words in the voice of a boy, almost certainly a Bamfylde boy, judging by the vowels. He thought, dismally, "Well, that does it. Now I'll have to stick my silly nose in," and moved a few yards lower down, walking on brindled turf, to a point where he could see through a gap in the young foliage to the bank of the stream.

What he saw made him recoil. Sitting against the bole of an ash, her thick chestnut hair unpinned and half-screening her face, was Julia Darbyshire, the new Second Form mistress, who had recently replaced Mrs. Parminter, the motherly soul everybody knew as 'Ma Fender'. And reclining full length, his head on Julia's lap, was Blades, plagiarising the poet Herrick in a somewhat different sense from that implied in Howarth's comment.

There was nothing really startling in the little tableau, framed in the hawthorn and sycamore leaves. On the contrary, if one could have regarded the couple anonymously, it was an idyllic glimpse of a man and his maid, at peace with the world, at one with their pastoral surroundings, oblivious of everything but each other. As he stood there gaping, he was able to identify the source of Julia's laughter, for she leaned forward so that her hair brushed his lips, then drew back with another chuckle but at this Blades roused himself and grabbed a double handful, pressing them to his face in a way that succeeded in checking Julia Darbyshire's merriment. Her face clouded and she said, rather desperately, "No, Keith, you promised!"

It was as much as David could stand. He turned and retreated swiftly up the slope, not pausing until he was on the eastern side of the plantation and here, cursing the chance that had involved him in such a ridiculous situation, he took the shortest way home, hurrying along at such a pace that he was sweating when he reached the cottage gate.

Beth called, from the kitchen, "Tea now, or will you wait until Ben brings the twins in?" and he called back, "Now!" and slumped down on the bagged-out armchair, dabbing his temples.

She was beside him in a couple of minutes and even before she set the tray down she realised something was wrong. She said, "Well, what is it? Why the scowl on a lovely day like this?"

"I'm not sure I should tell you, Beth."

"That means you'd rather, so out with it. What's happened up there?"

"The twins are in the farmyard?"

"Having their pony ride. Well?"

"It was something I saw, almost stepped on. On my way home."

"Another adder?"

"No, not an adder. I wish to God it had been." He thought for a moment, aware of needing, if not her advice, then certainly her reassurance.

"It was Julia Darbyshire and young Blades. They were necking, down in the Coombe. They didn't see me. I backtracked and came home by the road. I went that way to get your blasted marsh marigolds."

She said, slowly, "Necking? How do you mean, exactly? You'd best tell me all you saw, if you want my opinion, that is. If not, we'll leave it there."

"I want your opinion. I'm damned if I know who else's I can

seek, or not without starting one hell of an uproar. Blades is in Carter's house."

He described what he had seen and when he finished she was silent. Finally she said, "In your view, are they lovers?"

"I don't think so. Not from the way it looked, nor from her tone of voice, come to that. My guess is that he's making the running and she's holding back. For his sake more than her own."

"Why do you say that?"

"I don't know. Just a hunch. I saw them and you didn't."

"How old is Blades?"

"Seventeen."

"And Julia?"

"How would I know? About twenty-four, I'd say. I hardly know the woman. Algy appointed a spinster who had been a matron at a school up north but she let us down at the last minute and the agency sent Mrs. Darbyshire."

"She's married?"

"She might be a war widow, I don't even know that. She seems to have made a hit with the Second Form. You've seen her, haven't you?"

"Once or twice, at a distance. Is she pretty?"

"Not pretty but attractive in an odd sort of way. She's got a kind of stillness, not the kind of face at all that goes with playing the fool like this. God damn it, if she was a kid in her teens I could understand it. We had trouble of that kind two years ago with Manners and one of the maids."

"What happened then?"

He grinned. "Old Judy Cordwainer caught them in the shrubbery behind the piggeries. Nearly gave the old boy a seizure. They took a very dim view of it. Manners was sacked, the week before he was due to take Cambridge Senior and the girl was packed off back to Challacombe. But this is worse. I mean, how the devil can one leave a woman like that in charge of twelve-year-olds? I'll have to tell Algy."

"I wouldn't."

"But damn it, I have to. You must see that."

"Not until you've talked to her and to Blades, if necessary."

He looked exasperated and ran his hand through his hair. "But that's poppycock! I'm a junior master, I can't accept responsibility for a thing like this."

"You can find out more about it before a nice boy like Blades gets kicked out at seventeen. And the woman is put in a position where she couldn't hope for another job."

"She doesn't deserve one, does she? And as for Blades, he's one of the brightest chaps we've ever had. He must have known what he was about."

"He might have, but then again, he might not. How can you know what led up to this, unless you talk to them, separately, and let them know you saw them down there? You owe them that much. I think you do, anyway."

He considered, checked by her earnestness but by no means converted to her point of view. He said, at length, "I'm not certain that's loyal to Algy. What makes you so sure there's more in it than meets the eye?"

"Living here. Being a part of it for four years."

"How do you mean, exactly?"

"Look, I'm flesh and blood, and so are you. So is everybody else up there, except one or two who have fossilised, like Ferguson. You've got to make allowances for four hundred boys cooped up in a place like this throughout their entire adolescence, without any contact with women, of the kind boys have in a day school. If half of what you've told me is true there's far worse than this goes on in some of those famous schools. At least this is straightforward, a bright boy, his head stuffed full of romantic poetry, and a lonely woman, plumped down among God knows how many attractive young males. It can't go on, I'll grant you that. But if you take it to Algy Herries and Carter it will end in something that will do harm out of all proportion to the harm that's been done. Providing any has."

Her logic began to make sense, or better sense than emerged from his own reactions. He said, "I'll sleep on it. Pour me some tea, I'm parched."

3

He took her advice, as he had known he would. Julia Darbyshire's quarters were two rooms on the second floor of Outram's, over the quadrangle arch and he knew, more or less, when he could slip in there unobserved, for the Second Form had a woodwork class towards the end of morning school that coincided with

137

his one free period of the day. He waited until they had trooped in and then followed Mrs. Darbyshire up the stone steps to her sitting-room, pausing outside for a moment, summoning enough nerve to knock. Her "Who is it?" from the far side of the door, told him a little more about her. She had a very pleasant voice, low-keyed and as musical as the laugh he had heard in the Coombe.

"Powlett-Jones. Could I have a word with you, Mrs. Darbyshire?"

She opened the door and stood there smiling at him, a petite woman, with good features and rather sad grey eyes. Her hair was her most attractive feature. It was a particularly fine shade of chestnut, almost auburn, and she wore it coiled in what they were now calling 'earphones'. She had a presence that he found difficult to relate to the woman he had seen teasing a bewitched boy in the Coombe. It was as though he was looking across the threshold at two women, with nothing in common except a wealth of soft, chestnut hair. She said, still smiling, "Well, and what can I do for you?"

He said, falteringly, "Could I . . . er . . . step inside for a moment?" and at once the sad eyes betrayed uncertainty as she said, stepping back, "Certainly," and then, her fugitive smile returned, "Have you come to give me good advice, like Mr. Carter?"

"Has Carter been here today?"

"Not today, every other day for the first month of term. Until I told him I'd prefer to learn from my own mistakes."

It was awkward, her saying that, and in that tone of voice. He floundered a moment and then made an opening of the chink she had offered saying, "I'm giving advice of a kind, Mrs. Darbyshire, but I'm not sure you'll relish it," and she replied, seriously, "I will if it's well meant. You're a very different kettle of fish to Carter."

Her unexpected coolness made it even more difficult than he had imagined and silently he cursed Beth for putting him into such a ridiculous situation. Suppose she laughed in his face? Suppose she denied she had ever been in the Coombe? Blades would almost surely support her story, and that left his word against the two of them. Algy would believe him, of course, but Carter wouldn't, or would pretend not to, if only to make a score. He said, measuring his words as in the witness box, "I'm here at the insistence of my wife, Mrs. Darbyshire. Before I talked it over with her I had made up my mind to go to the head, and let him cope with it the best way he could. I say that because I want you to understand from the first I don't like saying what I came to say. As a matter of fact, I find it horribly embarrassing. I was on my way home across the Coombe yesterday afternoon. I saw you and Blades down by the stream."

She flushed, the colour of her cheeks at odds with the shade of her hair but, apart from that, showed no particular response. He went on, hurriedly, "You must realise a thing like that can't go on. Sooner or later someone else would see you and if it was one of the boys he wouldn't report it, simply pass it on. From that moment both you and Blades would be in an impossible position . . ." He broke off because she had moved away, across to the little dormer window overlooking the quad. It was very quiet down there at this hour, with everybody in class. The noon sun flooded the room with golden light, revealing its shabby paintwork and plaster, despite pathetic efforts she had made with chintzes and a few reproductions, among them Millais's 'The Order of Release'. He noticed something else, a silver-framed picture of a second lieutenant on the mantelshelf and recognised the cap badge as that of the Hampshires. Her voice, when she spoke, was very small, the voice of a child.

"You say your wife advised you to come to me? Does that mean you don't intend making it public?"

"I suppose that depends."

"On what?"

"On all kinds of things."

"On one thing really. Whether we've been lovers." She faced him, bracing herself, as though for a blow. "Well, you can set your mind at rest as to that. We haven't, and wouldn't have been. On my honour, for what that's worth in your eyes."

Suddenly he felt disarmed and very much on the defensive, as though he was at pains to explain to her he wasn't here to pry into her private life. He said, "I believe you."

"Why should you?"

"Partly because I overheard a word or two you said before I backed away. I didn't follow you there. It was pure chance I saw you, and chance again that you didn't hear me coming down the path. But my job, as I see it, is to consider Blades, and I suppose that's why I'm here. The head would have to sack him the moment he knew."

"And you wouldn't want that?"

"No, I wouldn't. I've always liked Blades. He's not . . ."

"Not the type you'd expect to imagine himself deeply in love with a woman eight years his senior?"

"I don't know. I've been at this job since I came out of the army five years ago. You learn something new every day. He's the starry-eyed kind, I suppose, but the bright ones often are."

"Is that frowned upon in a place like this?"

"Not necessarily. The point is . . . I . . . I don't see how it could have started, how someone as adult as you could have let it begin, and develop to the stage it had up to yesterday. You don't have to tell me. I've the right to question him, I suppose, or Carter has, as his housemaster."

"*No!*" The word was flung at him, more of command than an appeal. "Not Carter! Anyone but Carter. I can imagine how he would go about it . . ." And then, with a gesture of helplessness, "Give me a minute or two. Sit down. Let me think, just for a moment."

He lowered himself carefully into a small, cane-bottomed chair. She stood quite still for thirty seconds, then crossed over to a bureau, opened a drawer and took out some papers. He said, "If they're his letters I don't want to read them. God knows, this is complicated enough as it is."

"It's not a letter," she said, extracting two sheets of paper, "but you asked me how it began. Read that. Then I'll do what I can to explain. After that we might, conceivably, come to some kind of . . . well . . . arrangement. But that would be up to you."

He took the sheets and saw at a glance that the top one was half-filled with a couple of verses by Herrick, copied in Blades' precise handwriting. It was entirely deficient of the flourish of a seventeen-year-old, whose hand was not yet formed. He was familiar with the poem, one called *Upon Julia's Clothes.*

> *When as in silks my Julia goes,*
> *Then, then, methinks, how sweetly flows*
> *The liquefaction of her clothes!*

> *Next, when I cast mine eyes and see*
> *That brave vibration each way free,*
> *O how that glittering taketh me!*

He glanced up, not yet taking her point despite the obvious one as regards her Christian name.

"Read the other page."

He took the second sheet and read:

> *How easily from there to take*
> *My Julia's hand, and for her sake*
> *Forswear all sleep and lie awake*
> *The long night through,*
>
> *And conjure with a fancy fine*
> *Of making gentle Julia mine*
> *Of seeing in her eyes the shine*
> *Of her love too.*

*   *   *

> *O, I could dream by day and night*
> *Of consummating my delight*
> *At Julia's entrancing shrine.*
> *But how could such reward be mine*
> *For dusting off some musty book?*
> *I've been well paid—by one sweet look.*

"This is his? He gave it to you?"

"He sent it through the post."

"Those last two lines, what's behind them?"

"Nothing very subtle. It was just his way of making sure I identified him."

"You mean this arrived out of the blue?"

"No, I'd been here a fortnight and almost made up my mind to leave. I'll tell you why later if you're interested. I was on my way up here one wet morning when my attaché case burst open and some books fell out. Keith . . . Blades appeared out of nowhere, and scooped them up. When he saw they were muddy he insisted on carrying them up here and cleaning them off with his handkerchief. It would have seemed churlish not to let him."

"And then?"

"He stayed about ten minutes. I had the kettle on and gave him a cup of tea. He began telling me about himself, the way any boy of his age might. What he liked. What he hated. What he wanted to do when he left school. I suppose I encouraged him, partly because he struck me from the first as being a very charming boy. But that wasn't the sole reason."

He looked up at her, but seeing her lip quiver looked down again at Blades' verses. She went on, "I hadn't spoken two words to anyone real for months. Before I came here I'd gone weeks without talking much to anyone at all. I see now how much he read into my eagerness to listen. The next day the poem came."

"You could have ignored it. Wouldn't that have been simpler for everybody?"

"Simpler? Yes, it would have been simpler. But it seemed to me, at that time, that it would have been callous too. At least, that's what I told myself. I realised later it wasn't the truth."

"What was the truth, Mrs. Darbyshire?"

"That I was nearer the end of my tether than I realised. Or anyone else realised. I asked him up here. I honestly meant to tell him he had been stupid and, well a little presumptuous, but to do it as kindly as I could. But then I realised he hadn't written the verses as a joke or a try-on. He intended them to be taken at face value."

"You're sure of that?"

"I'm sure. I daresay you find it difficult to believe, Blades being one of the white hopes at Bamfylde, but it's true. He *is* intelligent. Very. But he's also highly strung and seventeen. Didn't you fancy yourself in love at that age, with the first woman who looked at you as if you were a man?"

"I was seventeen in August, 1914, Mrs. Darbyshire."

"Well, that makes it a little easier. For me, I mean."

She went across the room and lifted the photograph from the mantelshelf. "That was my husband. I say 'was' because the man there is just as dead as the million others in France, even though I'm still married to him. I only had one week with Arthur. What's left of him is still at Netley, and likely to stay there so long as the law regards euthanasia a crime instead of a duty. Maybe you're wondering what all this has to do with Keith Blades?"

He wasn't. Something of Beth's intuitive awareness of the complexity of the situation stirred in him, at least enough to make him glad he had followed her advice.

"Well, there is a link, but Blades didn't forge it. I did, by giving myself away."

"How, exactly?"

"I said my piece. It had a hollow ring but I said it. Blades just stood there, waiting politely for me to finish. Finally I did, in a flood of tears."

Somehow it wasn't improbable. Blades being lectured on his forwardness but sensing, behind the rebuke, the pent-up wretchedness of a lonely, distracted woman, deeply touched by his approach, and not knowing how to deal with it.

"It was all he needed. He put his arms round me and kissed me. Just once, and on the head. He held me but he didn't say anything. He'll make some girl a wonderful husband one day. I hope it's soon and that she appreciates him. It took me a longish time to pull myself together and everything emerged when I did, all the wretchedness and strain of the last few years, neatly bottled and corked since 1919, when they first showed me the man they said was my husband. Everything else developed from that, you might say."

He got up, not wanting to hear any more. Suddenly he did not give a damn about Blades' involvement. Only hers, and the savage wounds the war had inflicted on her, more pitiless, he would say, than on him and his like. He said, "You don't have to go on, Mrs. Darbyshire. I served three years out there and was pretty well used up myself when I came here, in 1918." A thought occurred to him. "What made you take this job in the first place?"

"I thought it might be a way back."

"It was, for me."

"It wouldn't have been, if you hadn't taken out insurance on a happy marriage. I've not met your wife but she must be an intelligent, compassionate woman. Well, it's that much easier for a man, especially with men in such short supply." She paused for a moment as he stood hesitantly by the door. "I'll tell you something else. That's how I came to see Keith, young as he is—one of the few whole men left on earth. It wasn't easy to keep it on its original level, tenderness on his part, overwhelming gratitude on mine. Sometimes it was all I could manage to stop myself begging him to take me and he knew it. If it hadn't been for his essential decency you might have had a real mess to sort out. After all, I'm still human, in spite of feeling like a dried-out husk for so long. And it's not as if I've never held a man in my arms. I did, that one week, before Arthur was recalled for the March offensive. Then I had to do a crazy thing like this, surround myself by hundreds of healthy male animals. I should have known myself better."

He was able to smile. "That's asking a lot at our age, Mrs. Darbyshire. Mostly it doesn't happen till we reach the fifty mark."

She looked at him steadily, still holding the framed photograph of the young lieutenant in the Hampshires. "You've been very kind, the sort of man Keith led me to expect. Is it fair to ask you what you intend doing now?"

"Nothing," he said. "I'll leave that to you. You couldn't have been more frank, and I daresay Herries would understand. But Carter and the others wouldn't, and you wouldn't suffer alone."

She said, slowly, "Would you trust me to see Keith once again? I could tell him we had been seen, and that I'd received a friendly warning. Also that I was leaving at the end of term, having decided how utterly stupid it was from his point of view and mine?"

"Would he be likely to accept that as final?"

"He'd have to, the way I put it. I should tell him I'd had better news from the hospital, that my husband was on the mend, and I had to go to him."

"Very well, you do that. I'll go now, before the five-minute bell."

"Could we . . . would you . . . shake hands on it?"

"Why not?"

Her hand was cold, and small as a child's. He clasped it and turned away, trudging down the curving stairway to the quad. The sun was blazing out here but there was no warmth in it.

He was never quite sure how the strange affair worked itself out during the remaining seven weeks of summer term. Julia Darbyshire refused Beth's invitation to call at the cottage and he understood why. There is no comfort for the sick in taking tea with those who fancy themselves secure in their own immortality. But he did notice traces of her ultimatum in Blades, whom he found himself watching closely through the next week or so. Outwardly the boy gave no sign that he was in despair, a state of mind the very young sometimes find consoling. His work did not suffer and he had always been one of those who liked to walk alone. But one day, after Nipper Shawe's lunch-bell set everyone about him desk-banging and scurrying, he gave himself away to some extent. He sat on, hands deep in his pockets, looking directly at the dais in the Fifth Form but not seeing it. His eyes were clouded and his expression drained. For a moment David was tempted to descend to floor level and have a word with him but he thought better of it.

Instead he gathered up his books, nodded briefly and stalked out, leaving Blades the sole occupant of the big room and its ineradicable smell of apple cores, blotting paper, exercise books, chalk and dust.

PART
THREE

The Bell in the Brain

Chapter One

Bat Ferguson died early in the Lent term, 1925. He was getting on for seventy, years past retirement age, but had hung on, hating the notion of uprooting himself and seemingly very fit. Yet in the end Bat Ferguson literally flapped himself to death.

He had taught in Bamfylde classrooms for forty years and collapsed at the apex of one of those furious bouts of exasperated energy that were in the repertoire of every mimic in the school. According to the death certificate, simple heart-failure killed him, but the wits put another suspect in the dock, one Dixon, a day boy of the Lower Third. For Bat was in the very act of pouncing on him when he choked, and crashed his length against the blackboard.

Witnesses who tried to revive him affirmed the dramatic truth of Bat's last moments. He had just descended on Dixon, renowned throughout Lower School for his buzz-saw Devon brogue, demanding, at the top of his voice, to be told the colour of the pencil he flourished. Dixon, an attentive boy, knew the word and answered up promptly. *"Le crayon est vert, m'sieur!"* but because he was Dixon the word emerged as *'verrrrrert'* and sounded like a long, half-stifled belch.

It was too much for poor Ferguson, who pranced (this from

Archer the Third, who was within touching distance) exactly two feet in the air, descending like a thunder-cloud screaming, "Vair, idiot boy! Vairr!" It was his final word and Mrs. Ferguson, with Gallic stoicism, received him into her house, where he died ten minutes after Dr. Willoughby's arrival.

Mrs. Ferguson did not find his death incongruous and neither, for that matter, did Bamfylde. Everyone seemed to think of it as a very fitting end, thoroughly in character, a veteran Roman soldier, shouting defiance at a swarm of barbarians. Dixon was rather upset but he cheered up as soon as he realised that a little of the savage splendour of the occasion reflected upon him, a thirteen-year-old who had slain a grown man with a single word, and a foreign word at that. He was given the rest of the day off and cantered his pony home, arriving at his father's farm pale, proud and extremely hungry.

Behind him the machinery of a state Bamfylde funeral went slowly into action, with directives for black ties for all, and special armbands for the boys of Havelock's house. Ferguson, as a stripling, had enrolled in a Paris student corps for the 1870 war, and remembering this Carter moved in on the act and selected a Corps firing-party for the graveside. Mrs. Ferguson produced a tricolour for the coffin and this was thought equally proper, for although Bat had been born in Scotland, of good Scots parentage, he was always regarded as more than half a Frenchman. In steady Exmoor drizzle the long procession wound its way over the half-mile to Stone Cross churchyard where Bouncer, walking ahead in dripping surplice, recited the burial service. This was strictly according to the English prayer-book and some of the dead man's former pupils, remembering how a chance remark in their mother tongue had so often driven the dead man into a frenzy, thought it in poor taste. As Morgan-Smith put it, turning away from the grave and regretting that the solemn occasion prohibited a dash across to Ma Midden's yard in search of apple turnovers, "It was all I could do not to convert the final Amen into Fin."

Everybody regretted Bat Ferguson's passing but nobody save his wife mourned him in the real sense of the word. No one, that is, except Towser, his faithful Airedale, who made several careful tours of Havelock's dormitories, passages and linen rooms in search of his absent master. Unable to find him, he slumped in his basket in the Fergusons' living-room and refused to eat until

Madame Ferguson, with a French lack of sentimentality concerning animals, shrugged her shoulders and would have ignored him had not David, who came to pay his respects after the funeral, asked how the dog was taking it.

"Very foolishly," she told him. "Three suppers have been thrown away. It is a waste of good meat and my husband would have disapproved. What am I to do with a dog that will not eat, M'sieur Powlett-Jones? I am preparing to leave on Saturday. I am going home to Beauvais, to live with my sister and brother-in-law, and they do not approve of household pets. I shall take the dog to the vet to be destroyed."

"I say, you can't do that, Mrs. Ferguson," David protested, thoroughly outraged. "At the time of the fire Towser's howl saved us all."

"So? I did not hear of that and find it interesting. But what has it to do with a dog that will not eat?"

"Give him to me. I'll coax him to eat. He knows me and I'll soon pull him round."

"But you have a wife and two children in that small cottage of yours. There is no room for a big dog, M'sieur Powlett-Jones."

"We'll find room. We can't let him be put down. He's no more than three or four, is he?"

"I have no record of his age. However, take him, if you wish."

So Towser was led away, to the shrieking delight of the twins, and after a day of their sustained attention he abandoned his suicide bid. Within a week or two, however, Bamfylde received another grievous blow. Old Judy Cordwainer, also well past retiring age, followed his colleague to the churchyard, having caught a severe chill standing bareheaded in the rain throughout the service.

"Rectitude killed *him!*" commented the irrepressible Morgan-Smith, "so that day-kid now has two beaks on his conscience."

Once more the long, black-tied procession wound its way to Stone Cross and Algy Herries, quoting Marshal Soult, looked up at the sky as they were returning and said, "I'm beginning to hear the recall up there."

"Nonsense," said David, unable to visualise Bamfylde without Algy's cheery presence, "you're only sixty-two, and that gives you a minimum of another three years. Besides, you're the fittest over-sixty I ever saw. Won't you apply to the Governors for a stay when

TO SERVE THEM ALL MY DAYS

you reach official retirement age? We all hope you will. The place wouldn't seem the same with a new head. And, anyway, what would you do with yourself?"

"Oh, I'll apply for a small, comfortable living somewhere handy," Algy said. "This place will need a face lift by then and not only structurally, my boy. Educational processes are changing as rapidly as everything else. Ferguson and Cordwainer belonged to the old school and could never really adapt. I did, with all you youngsters pushing from behind, but a man can't change to that extent at my age. Hang it all, they taught practically nothing but Latin and Greek when I was a boy here. They welted it into you, too. None of this cosy uncle–nephew relationship that you and Irvine encourage."

"You too," said David, smiling, "so why not own up to it?"

"I've never been one hundred per cent sure," Herries said, thoughtfully. "The average boy has changed, along with every-thing else. The war did that, I suppose, with that queer chap, Kitchener, sweeping everybody into khaki, and putting them through the mincer out there. Much more individualism nowa-days. Don't tell me the Fifth and Sixth don't argue the toss with you every now and again for I know very well they do." He trudged on in silence for a moment. Then, lightly, "How would you feel about taking over Havelock's, P.J.?"

"*Me?* Getting a house at my age? And with an external degree?" He gave Herries a suspicious sidelong glance. "Are you pulling my leg, sir?"

"Of course I'm not," Herries said, grumpily. "What the devil has an external degree got to do with it? You're a born teacher, and I don't mean by that a man with the knack of imparting in-formation. You still have it in mind to move on, haven't you? Well, I daresay you could, and make a go of it in one of these big modern schools, but I don't know that you'd be any better off for it. Except financially, of course. You've come to know my methods, my eccentricities if you like, and you suit Bamfylde. At least, you suit my idea of Bamfylde's true function."

"Can you define that function?"

"Yes, I can. To select what's worth having from the green wood and hang on like grim death to the best of the seasoned timber. I've never been a great advocate of exams, or dedicated scholarship, or even technical education. You know that. Everybody knows it.

I've always been more interested in turning out well-adjusted human beings and I imagine you go along with that. Think it over. Discuss it with that nice gel of yours, and let me know by the end of term. For if you don't take it I'll have to advertise for a man around forty, and my guess is I'll have the devil's own job finding someone who suits me."

It was curious that the day of Judy Cordwainer's funeral should prove such a red-letter day for them. There was no question in Beth's mind but that he should accept the offer. Not merely for financial and prestigial reasons—the post carried another hundred a year, plus free living accommodation—but because, much as she had grown to love the cottage, life there in winter left a good deal to be desired. She said, excitedly, "Havelock's is the newest house in the school, isn't it? I'll have much more room over there, and you'll be right in the centre of things. Don't think I haven't realised how difficult it has been to divide your time and energy between the school and us, Davy. And I'll like it too, although I can't really see myself as a housemaster's wife."

"You're better qualified than any woman for miles around," he said, but she laughed, saying, "That isn't the compliment it sounds. There's only about eight of us all told. Seriously, though, I'm absolutely convinced, Davy. You'll be a huge success, you see if you aren't. Not that you don't deserve it. You've worked harder than any of them up there. Won't some of the younger men be jealous?"

"Irvine won't. He doesn't want a house, at least Phyllis doesn't. Too much a tie, she told me, only the other day. Besides, I don't think they'll stay long. She's a town girl, really."

"So am I," she said, but he caught her round the waist, saying, "Ah, but you're different. You threw your cap at a schoolmaster, remember?" and he kissed her, his mind ranging on the vagaries of luck that never seemed to have permanent favourites but played the field, a man-hungry jade. Ferguson had seemed lucky up to now. And Cordwainer, too, in his staid settled way. Both of them too old to get caught up in the war and sticking it out down here, where they were not even obliged to go short of butter. But every now and again your luck ran out, as his had seemed to in the last months of 1917, when he had wished that mortar shell had finished him off, along with all the others in the traverse. Mostly it was a matter of holding on, as Algy Herries had held when he saw an entire generation of his boys killed off in their prime. He was not Anglicised beyond the point where he had ceased to think as a Welshman and caught himself contemplating Bamfylde from a Celtic standpoint, almost as his sisters or brothers-in-law might; "Funny that . . . used to think of places like this as proper old snob-factories . . . laugh at 'em behind their back, I would. But these hills are as old as ours and the folk holding them are as obstinate as the people of the Valleys . . ." And then, as it were, he translated himself, thinking, "If I can emerge as human as Algy in late middle-age, then I'll count myself lucky. He must have had his doubts, pulling this place together when he first came here, but he won through in the end, against the fuddy-duddies, the die-hards, God knows how many cheeseparing Governors, and the percentage of failures chaps in our line of business have to accept."

They spent the entire Easter break moving house and settling in, counting themselves lucky that her father and stepmother took the twins off their hands while they did it. For him it was easy enough to adapt, having lived in Havelock's during his first four terms, and later seen large sections of the house rebuilt after the fire. That, Beth said, had been a blessing in disguise, for now she had a modern kitchen with piped water, and the new dynamo they were installing promised electric light. The two rebuilt dormitories had been fitted with a fire escape, a novelty the boys of the other houses professed to despise. Morgan-Smith gave it as his opinion that any potential arsonist among new intakes would naturally gravitate to Havelock's, where they catered for such specialists.

The rest of the staff took it philosophically when news leaked that he was to replace Ferguson. Barnaby, senior to David by several terms, was a little put out, and honest enough to admit it, but he was far too amiable to nurse a grievance, whereas Irvine had been conditioned by his wife to leave his options open. He said, "Best of luck, old man, but it'll bog you down. Phyllis is always nagging me to move on, but it'll bog you down. I've already been on a couple of short-lists. She fancies a prep school of our own, in a seaside town where there's a bit more social life. But we'd need capital for that and I can't see us getting it until her Aunt Faith kicks the bucket. Phyl's her favourite niece and god-daughter, so we've expectations, but there's a snag. We have to spend every Christmas with the old girl, and her parrots and cats, and I can't stand bloody cats."

When Barnaby got over his pique he said, "Old Howarth is delighted, of course, but he's always regarded you as his protégé, ever since you stood up to Carter. They've hated one another's guts for years. By the way, has Carter brought himself to congratulate you?"

"No, he hasn't, and I don't imagine he will. Doesn't it strike you as bloody silly, Barnaby, that we wage our little feuds in a place like this, where we've all got to live and work together?"

"It's damned silly but inevitable, old man. The smaller and more isolated the place, the sharper the clash of personalities. You'd find it no different in a firm, a hospital, or government office. Wasn't it the same in a regiment?"

"Not once we came under fire."

"Ah, well, there you have it. Consult your Ovid, old boy! 'Fortuna miserrima tuta est; Nam timor eventus deterioris abest.' Look it up. I took you over it last year," and he floated off, hunching his gown about him in a way that enhanced his counterfeit inscrutability.

David did look it up, finding it in his notes on Ovid's elegies, written during his banishment. 'Tuta petant alii. Fortuna miserrima . . .' 'Let others seek what is safe. Safe is the worst of fortune; for the fear of any worse event is taken away.' Like all Barnaby's tags it was apt. Every succeeding generation had to learn from its own experiences. The wonderful comradeship of the trenches, the only solid gain of the war to those who fought it, rested on Ovid's dictum. It was perfect because it was practised by men who had reached a point where they had nothing else to lose. Under those circumstances most human failings fell away. But once the pressure was removed people reverted to what they were and he and Carter were alike in this respect. He thought, "Howarth's wrong and I'm wrong, to persist in this game of 'you-did-I-didn't' with Carter. We're level pegs now, and he can't patronise me as a housemaster. I'll find some way of holding out the olive branch once we're all back for summer term . . ." and he meant to consult with Beth about it but it slipped his mind in the whirl of end-of-term activities.

* * *

Looking back on that final period of unclouded happiness he could not recall much but laughter. Laughter, welling from small, insignificant sources, like the ultimate sally of Bickford, in Bouncer's divinity period, one that earned the culprit the standard four penal marks, plus several more on his leathery backside from Bouncer's ill-directed cane, but passed into Bamfylde legend and changed his name to 'Ruby'.

It was a very small joke really, but good enough to be re-told over common-room coffee—how Bouncer, spouting Proverbs to an indifferent Fifth, quoted, 'Who can find a virtuous woman? for her price is far above rubies', whereupon Bickford raised his hand and asked, blandly, "Please, sir, what *was* Ruby's?"

There was laughter among the Orpheans, when Baines Minor, drumming away for dear life one damp morning, drove both sticks through his soggy drumskin. Laughter in the Second Form, when Gilroy, a new boy, lacking a nickname, earned one by pausing at the unfamiliar word 'apostrophe' while reading aloud and finally made a gallant try with 'Apos . . . apos . . . apos-TROPHY-sir' and was afterwards known as 'Strofe' Gilroy. Small, asinine incidents that yet added something to the texture of life on the plateau. Nipper Shawe (now launched into the world and said to be doing well in marine insurance) had surrendered his job as bell-ringer to a pallid boy called Fogaty, innocuous at work and play but, given his bell, someone who took on the gravity and dignity of a town-crier. It was thus a joke to be relished when someone in the Lower Fifth, whose quarters were situated immediately above the niche where the bell was kept, bored a hole through the floorboards and attached a strand of fine wire to the handle, pulling it up the moment Fogaty reached out to grasp it, so that it began to ring itself. Then there was Vernon, the amateur ventriloquist, who threw the entire Corps into disarray issuing orders in Carter's testy voice; Nixon Minor, who got hold of a noxious dye, and stained the water in the swimming bath the colour of blood, and Boyer's swan-song as a practical joker, that led to a confrontation neither Boyer nor David ever forgot, for it struck a new balance in their relationship and presented David with his first major decision as master of Havelock's.

Boyer had sobered over the years but every now and again his extravagant sense of humour shot through the crust of Sixth Form sobriety like a geyser. His ultimate escapade was to borrow an

Old Boy's motorcycle, disguise himself in a smock, felt hat and false beard, and ride into the village where, for a bet, he drank half a pint of beer in the presence of Barnaby. Barnaby far too much of a sportsman to identify him on the spot, none the less told David, who sent for Boyer, demanding to know what had prompted such an idiotic performance. Boyer said, quite seriously, "I . . . er . . . don't really know, sir. Exhibitionism, perhaps."

"Exhibitionism, my good right boot!" bellowed David. "Don't quote any of those fancy Freudian words at me! I could get you sacked for a thing like that. Kicked out, after how long here?"

"I'm in my ninth year, sir."

"Nearly two more than me, and you in the Sixth. It's the maddest thing you've ever done and by God, that's saying something! Here I was, hoping you'd help play me in as house prefect for my first year."

He was relieved to see Boyer frown as he said, "Does that mean I've been passed over, sir?" and David said, irritably, "I'm hanged if I know! You've got more potential than any other senior in Havelock's. But how the devil can I trust you with responsibility for younger kids when you act as if you were still in the Lower Third?"

"Couldn't we make a bargain, sir?"

"What kind of bargain?"

"Well, sir, you forget my jaunt to the Maltster's Arms, and I'll back you to the hilt until I leave here next spring. The fact is, sir, I've played the fool for so long it's difficult to stop overnight. The chaps . . ." and here he stopped, avoiding David's eye.

"What about the chaps, Boyer?"

"Well, they expect it of you, if you know what I mean, sir."

David knew but was not prepared to admit it. Boyer was the exact equivalent of the daredevil subaltern, the sort who went out into no-man's-land for the hell of it, and finally got himself killed establishing he had guts and initiative. He wondered, fitfully, at his propensity to equate almost everything that happened here with his experiences in the trenches, yet he did, almost as though his time out there had been an apprenticeship for the job.

He said, finally, "Look here, Boyer, against my better judgment I'll take a chance on you. I'll recommend you to take Brandon's place. He's leaving in a week or so, to take that job he wrote after in Rhodesia. But if you let me down, I'll see you don't forget it.

I ought to give you a damn good hiding but you know I don't even approve of thrashing juniors, let alone a great lout of your age. All I can do is to appeal to you for help, the way I did the night of the fire. I'll keep this last idiocy to myself, and ask Mr. Barnaby to do the same. But it's the last, you understand?"

Boyer, looking more thoughtful than David had ever seen him look, slipped away and that same night David asked Herries to make the appointment. Algy, who had always been slightly bewildered by Boyer's explosive high spirits, said, "Boyer, eh? Well, I hope you know what you're doing, P.J. He's a wild one and no mistake. Sort of chap who might land himself in real trouble one of these days. And without meaning to, for he's got his points. I've always seen him as a chap who took on too much too quickly and went bankrupt. Or a cat-burglar, who only robbed the rich. Nothing the slightest bit vicious about the boy, mind you, just someone who has to let off steam every now and again. What's he got in mind when he leaves here?"

"I don't think he knows himself, sir. That'll depend on the exams at the end of next term, won't it?" but Herries smiled. "Not on your life. Examinations are for the conformists, as I've told many an anxious parent in my time. And nobody could call Boyer a conformist."

They dispersed the next day and holiday stillness descended on the place. In the lull that followed, David, recalling that he and Beth were approaching the sixth anniversary of their encounter on the pier at Colwyn Bay, posted off to Challacombe on the excuse of seeing his bank manager and collecting some curtain materials Beth had ordered. With these errands accomplished he made for Merriweather's, the Challacombe jeweller. He had intended buying her an oval wristwatch as a birthday gift but on entering Market Street he paused outside Marty Lile's car mart, spotting a three-wheeler, with '*For Sale—Bargain*' scrawled on its windshield. Marty, seeing him, waddled out, chafing his hands, in a way exactly mimicked by two generations of Bamfylde boys.

He said, in his broad Devon burr, "Top o' the mamin' to 'ee Mr. Powlett-Jones! That there motor is a praper ole steal. No more'n dree thousand on the clock. Why dorn 'ee try her out?" and when David said he was in no mind to buy a car, especially a three-wheeler, Marty said, "Giddon, you and the missus need transport outalong, dorn 'ee? Youm stuck fast half the year round.

Woulden it be nice to have your orn means o' poppin' inalong for a visit to the pictures every now and again?"

It would at that, thought David, remembering the long winter evenings, and reminding himself that the twins were due to start nursery school at the village primary in a month or two. "How much, Mr. Lile?"

"Thirty pounds to you, and I'd ask thirty-five to anyone who wasn't up at skuel. Try her, there's petrol in the tank."

He said, taking his seat behind the wheel, "I've never been sold on three-wheelers. They're so easily overset," but Marty denied this, declaring that it only held good when there were two wheels at the front. "Tiz like a triangle, you see," he went on. "Knock un from the apex an' 'er lifts an' stays put. But youm out looking for trouble. How much traffic do 'ee pass tween yer an' skuel?"

He drove down to the quay and back, finding the car handled very easily, so that he thought, "Beth would get more use out of this than a watch. I could teach her to drive on the level stretch outside the cottage in a day or two . . ." and after a little bargaining he dragged Marty down to twenty-seven pounds ten, and drove back to Bamfylde in high spirits.

Beth, exasperated with her efforts to adapt the cottage curtains to the tall windows of Havelock's, was delighted. In the first flush of enthusiasm he coaxed her out into the drive and gave her her first lesson, finding that she was a quick learner once she had mastered the gears. "At least we'll be mobile," he said, congratulating her, "and not dependent on bikes. You can pack the twins into the dickey seat, drop them off at school, and then do your shopping in Challacombe. I made it home in twenty minutes and she took Quarry Hill like a bird. I'll give her a good going over when I get time."

But he was short on time just then. Overnight, it seemed, the school was full of boys again, swapping holiday yarns, and Beth was preparing for the first of her new boys' teas in Havelock's, and there were a thousand things to attend to as he began his first full term as housemaster, with a complement of eighty boys, including four first-termers.

And then, just as he was getting into his stride, the Winterbourne divorce had to blow up out of a clear sky, and all his nervous energy was directed towards ensuring that Winterbourne survived what promised to be an extremely unpleasant term and an experience that could, if it wasn't carefully handled, scar a sensitive boy's mind.

2

The news of Viola Winterbourne's divorce reached the school via the Sunday papers, about a fortnight before half-term.

Everybody knew the celebrated Viola Winterbourne, a popular musical comedy actress, currently starring in *Under My Balcony* in the West End. She had, in fact, shown herself at Bamfylde from time to time, queening it over all the other visitors on Sports Days and Speech Days, for Winterbourne (nicknamed 'Spats' on account of his sartorial elegance) was in his second year, and currently in the Lower Fourth.

David had met her, and not been over-impressed, seeing her as a gossipy, vapid woman, obsessed by her own elegance and popularity, and much given to stage chit-chat that always headed listeners back to Viola Winterbourne's career. He had to admit, however, that she was a very dashing woman and a handsome one too, in yards of flowered silk and a close-fitting cloche hat, that emphasised the good bone-structure of her face and brought a sparkle into her cornflower-blue eyes. She was regarded as the principal showpiece at Bamfylde functions, whenever she bothered to attend one, and usually succeeded in relegating most other mothers to the status of peasants. He did not know much about the relationship of mother and son but guessed that Winterbourne, a neat, self-contained boy of fourteen, was embarrassed by her style and scintillating personality. Mothers had to be extremely judicious whenever they appeared at school, striking an exact balance between elegance and frumpishness. Many boys preferred their parents to keep their distance or, if they did come, to remain in the background. Cookson's father, a war profiteer, owned a Rolls-Royce, but Cookson saw to it, after one visit, that he left it at home when he called to take his son out for the day and arrived in a sedate Austin. At the other end of the scale was Gilroy, whose father, a Challacombe grocer, sometimes showed up on Sports Day wearing a large, cloth cap, vintage 1903, and pepper and salt knicker-bockers, garments that made Gilroy blush for shame, especially as Gilroy *père* was an excitable little man, prone to rush from behind the ropes and thump his son on the back whenever he won a race.

David was aware that young Winterbourne, a member of his house, was a target for the wags of Middle School, and this was understandable, for Viola Winterbourne was more likely to be in the news than out of it. She had been seen dancing with the Prince of Wales at a nightclub. She wrote chic fashion articles, almost certainly ghosted, in women's magazines. She had campaigned for her Conservative candidate and kissed electors in public. She was always ready to pronounce upon any subject, from the Black Bottom and birth-control, to survival after death. Ordinarily a well-conducted boy, Winterbourne had been known to hit out at those who made jovial references to his mother, and there had been rumours of a stand-up fight between Winterbourne and Curtiss, after the latter had pasted a picture of Viola in a bathing suit inside his desk, along with a page torn from *London Life,* featuring the *Folies Bergère* star, Josephine Baker.

Hints of the approaching divorce bothered David a little, though not seriously. Divorces, nowadays, were common enough, and almost everyday occurrences among stage-folk. Winterbourne would just have to ride it out, like anyone else with a personal problem. But then the unexpected happened. News came, via the midweek papers, that Viola Winterbourne's divorce promised to be a particularly spicy affair, and David at once took steps to prevent the more sensational papers from being circulated that week. This was not too difficult to achieve. The papers were always late, anyway, and were distributed, one to a class, by the school bursar. On Sundays, when no train stopped at Bamfylde Bridge Halt, no papers were delivered. David went so far as to take Boyer into his confidence, telling him to keep an eye on what the Middle School were discussing over the weekend. There was always a chance that a boy on day leave, or a servant returning from a Sunday off in Challacombe, would introduce a popular paper into the school. There was not much to be feared from Upper School, where a majority would be likely to exercise tact, or indeed from Lower School, where papers like the *News of the World* were not in great demand, but instinct told him boys of the Fourth and Lower Fifth Forms were alerted as to the possibility of a Sunday spread and would keep a sharp lookout for reports of proceedings.

To be on his guard David arranged with one of the domestics

to get a copy of the *News of the World* from Challacombe and a single glance at its contents dismayed him. On an inside page was a headline reading ' *"Farmyard Morals!" Scathing Comment by Divorce Judge,*' and below it '*Musical Comedy Star Cited in Divorce Proceedings*'.

The report itself spared nobody's blushes. It was before the passing of the Domestic Proceedings Act, limiting what could be printed concerning cases of this kind, and Viola's private life was hung on the line, the story of her involvement with Victor Manners-Smith, her co-star, being told in detail. There was mention of champagne parties in Paris, and nude bathing parties in the villa of an impresario at Cannes. Even passages from her wildly indiscreet letters were quoted, one describing her feelings about the co-respondent the first time she got into bed with him. Her husband, whom David had never met, had been granted a decree nisi, with costs amounting to over two thousand pounds.

He said, after Beth had read the story, "We've got to keep this from circulating somehow. That kid's life won't be worth living if this is bandied around Big School."

Boyer came to him after the dormitory bell had gone and said that no Sunday papers had been passed around Middle School and that Winterbourne, whom he had been watching closely, seemed to be taking the scandal in his stride. "I even had a word with him before prep," Boyer said, "and he seems to have himself well in hand. I didn't mention the divorce, of course, but told him he was picked for wicket-keeper in the house match on Wednesday. That seemed to cheer him up no end. Anything else I can do, sir?"

"Not for the moment," David told him, "but keep your eye open for Sunday papers in tomorrow's distribution. I'll warn the bursar and if any show up whip 'em out of circulation," and he left it at that, more or less satisfied that his strategy had succeeded.

It had not, apparently. At precisely six-forty on Monday, about an hour before rising bell when he and Beth were still in bed, there was an urgent rapping on the door and Beth shook him by the shoulder, struggling into her dressing gown. He said, sleepily, "Who the devil would that be at this hour? Get rid of him, whoever he is," and he rolled out of bed yawning and pulled

162

the curtains aside, looking down on the empty quad as Beth crossed to the door calling, "Who is it?"

"It's me, Mrs. Powlett-Jones. Boyer. I'd like to speak to the housemaster at once, ma'am!"

David said, briefly, "Go into the bathroom," and he threw open the door to find Boyer on the threshold looking distraught.

"I'm sorry about the time, sir, but you had to know as soon as possible. Winterbourne's gone, sir. I don't think his bed was slept in, although it was rumpled a bit. I was up early to do an hour's cramming for the exam and I noticed he'd gone. He must have slipped down the fire escape in the night. Do you imagine he's run off to his father, sir?"

"I can check on that, his father's on the phone. That's the likeliest bet, but he wouldn't be able to get a train to Taunton on Sunday night, would he?"

"There's the milk train from Challacombe, sir. It stops at all the halts to pick up churns. That's about three-thirty a.m. If he hopped it he could be in Taunton by five and catch the fast to London. I've looked at the timetable, sir. There's one gets into Paddington at nine-ten."

He thought, "Thank God for Boyer . . . I was right about him after all . . . !" and said, "Did you think to look in his locker?"

"Yes, sir. It's difficult to be sure but I think he's taken sweater, slacks and stinkers. His two suits are there."

"Why the devil should he run away in plimsolls?"

"He might have planned on covering the distance between here and the next halt, at Crosshayes, sir. I would, knowing I'd be recognised and stopped by Walrus Tapscott down at the station. No one would question him buying a ticket at Crosshayes."

"Thank you, Boyer," David said. "Keep it as quiet as possible. He won't be missed for a bit. Everyone will assume he went out early for a training run. I'll tell the head and do some phoning. I'll let you know what happens."

"Thank you, sir," Boyer said gravely and withdrew as Beth emerged from the bathroom. "I heard," she said. "He can't have gone far, can he? And if he goes home to his father there's nothing to worry about, is there?"

"In that case, no, but it's something we've got to check at once." He threw on some clothes and went down into the quad and across to Herries's house. Ellie, he knew, was an early riser, and he found her making tea in the kitchen. She said anxiously, "I'll fetch Algy. You can find Mr. Winterbourne's telephone number in his address book. It's in the top, right-hand drawer in the study desk."

He got through to Winterbourne Senior with surprising speed. The Winterbourne house seemed to be a high-powered ménage, with any number of lackeys about, even at this hour. 'Spats' had not shown up but his father did not seem ruffled by his son's disappearance in the middle of the night.

"Probably taken it into his head to go off somewhere he had fun in the holidays," he said, as though Spats had been a man in his mid-twenties, with a particularly independent disposition. "Impulsive kid. Always was. Haven't you noticed that?"

"No," said David, grimly, "I can't say that I have," taking a dislike to the flat, impersonal voice. "To be perfectly frank, Mr. Winterbourne, I've got the impression he's very upset about the publicity Mrs. Winterbourne's been getting."

This seemed to jolt him a little but not much. He said, carefully, "Really? Surprised to hear that. She's made headlines of one sort or another all his life."

Herries bustled in, buttoning his trousers, and David offered him the receiver. The head said, in a whisper, "You deal with it, P.J. The boy's not arrived, has he?" and when David shook his head he frowned. It was not often that Algy Herries frowned and his face seemed to resent it.

"Are you still on the line?" enquired the bored clubman's voice.

"Yes, Mr. Winterbourne. The headmaster and myself think it almost certain he'll come to you. Have you any idea where else he might go? To a relative, maybe?"

"I'll put my mind to it."

"Will you phone us at once if he does show up?"

"Of course."

"Good. Meantime we'll check the railway stations this end. Someone must have seen him. Can I get you on this number any time?"

"No. Ring City 7404 after nine-thirty. My secretary will put you through. I'll leave instructions if I'm in conference."

"Very well."

There seemed nothing more to say so he jotted down the number and rang off, saying, "He's a cool customer, isn't he?" and

Herries grunted, "So would you be if your income was twenty thousand a year plus. I've never been able to decide what made a chap like Winterbourne send his boy here. Couldn't trust his wife at Eton or Harrow, I wouldn't wonder."

"I'm beginning to understand Winterbourne's problem," David said. "That chap might have been discussing a lost dog."

"Spats is a bit of a lost dog, P.J., and so would I be if I was his age, and had his home life. Do you know what I think? I don't think he'll go that far. He'll just hang around. Bamfylde has been more a home to him than anywhere else, I wager."

"Then why should he leave it?"

"To think things out, maybe. And let the dust settle."

"Where does that leave us, sir?"

"Under an obligation to go through the motions of the lost, stolen or strayed drill. Get Boyer and four or five of the sharpest seniors in Havelock's. I'll check the stations."

"Couldn't we enlist all the prefects, sir?"

"I wouldn't if I were you," Herries said, calmly. "It's your first term as housemaster. You don't want kindly patronage from all your colleagues at this stage, do you?"

"No, I don't. Thank you, sir," and he went back to Havelock's where Beth was brewing coffee, having first sent for Boyer and four seniors of his choice. They joined him before he had finished his first cup. Boyer said, doubtfully, "We've . . . er . . . got a clue, sir. Not where he is but why he cleared off."

"Well?"

"It came from Johnson Major, sir. He was out with his people yesterday and . . . well, he'll tell you himself, sir." He went to the top of the stairs and bawled Johnson's name and a moment later the boy sidled in, looking, David thought, shifty and ill at ease. He said, at a nod from Boyer, "If Spats . . . er . . . Winterbourne *has* gone off, sir, I might be the reason but I thought I was doing the right thing, sir. I mean, well, sir, he's a good sport, and I didn't want anyone to spring it on him. With that kind of stuff in the papers it was bound to get around sooner or later, wasn't it, sir?"

"What are you trying to tell me, Johnson?"

Johnson swallowed. "I . . . er . . . I saw the paper in the lounge of the Hopgood Arms, in Challacombe yesterday. I didn't want my people to see me reading it, and start asking questions, so I slipped it in my jacket and took it away."

"You're saying you showed it to Winterbourne?"

"Yes, sir. I took him on one side after prep and I waited around while he read it. He asked if he could keep the paper and I said he could. After all, it wasn't mine, sir."

"How did he take it?"

"He was sick, sir."

"Sick? You mean really sick?"

"Yes, sir, there and then, behind the bandroom. I told him to go to matron, sir, and he promised he would, but he made me swear on the Bible not to let on to anyone. I wouldn't have, if Boyer hadn't explained."

"No one else knows, sir." This from Boyer, who looked a little sick himself. "This is the first Dobson and the others have heard about it. Does it mean anything?"

"I think it does." He pondered a moment and then, out of the corner of his eye, he saw the wretched Johnson eyeing him. He said, "Look here, Johnson, nobody holds this against you. I'm not sure you did the right thing but who the devil knows what the right thing is under these circumstances? Clear off now and don't breathe a word of it to anyone, you understand?"

"Yes, sir. Thank you, sir," and Johnson shot away, relieved to be out of it so cheaply.

Herries appeared with one of his half-inch ordnance maps and once again David had a fleeting trench memory, this time of an old, grey-haired brigadier, mounting a company-strength raid on the Boche line. He said, calmly, "I've mapped out the likely routes. He didn't get the train at Bamfylde Bridge and he didn't get it at Crosshayes. Before we start half a dozen hares we'll check the locals. I'll drive over to the Crosshayes area myself and call in one or two of the farms. You take that three-wheeler of yours, P.J. and do the same as far as the Barrows. You others take the routes I've marked and check with any moorman you meet, but make it casual. Don't let them see we're much concerned, you understand?"

"Yes, sir."

"We'll rendezvous at midday under the Clump and pool what news we have. Hold on, you can't comb Exmoor on empty stomachs. Go and get breakfast first. I've told Priddis to serve you before the multitude descends."

They went out and Herries said, "I didn't tell 'em to keep mum, did I?"

"You didn't have to, sir," and he recounted what Johnson had told them. Herries said, "Poor little toad. It's young to have to stand up to that kind of fire, but my guess is he'll do it somehow."

"He's not likely to . . ."

"Do anything silly? Not a chance. Winterbourne isn't the hysterical type. Could that gel of yours spare me a cup of that coffee?"

"Of course," and he fidgeted while Herries sipped the coffee Beth handed him. Over the rim of his cup Herries's sharp eyes caught the movement. "It's all happened before," he said, "and it'll happen again. The important thing is to tread softly, my boy."

* * *

They met as arranged at the foot of the knoll, marked on the maps as the Clump, but none of them had anything to report. Winterbourne had vanished and Herries thought it likely that he might be home by now but he was not. There was no message from Winterbourne Senior and when Herries rang the City number he was told the boy had not yet appeared. Herries said, quietly, "We've searched a five-mile radius here and we'll extend it to ten or twelve before dark. If he's still in the district we'll find him, Mr. Winterbourne. Are you prepared to leave it at that, or would you prefer me to notify the police."

David, standing near the door, heard the calm voice rise to a crackle and saw Herries scowl. "Very well, that's your prerogative, Mr. Winterbourne," and he replaced the receiver.

"Damned codfish," he said. "That's what comes of making too much money, P.J. The word 'police' sent his blood pressure soaring, just as I knew it would. Still, he has a point. The police mean publicity and he's had a surfeit of that. Wouldn't do us much good, either. We'll keep it in the family for the time being."

After lunch they assembled all the prefects and sent them off in couples, nine pairs in all, covering all points of the compass ten miles afield. Those with farthest to go were given bicycles and instructions to phone in.

David pushed his own enquiries as far as Challacombe but when they all met again at dusk no one had seen or heard anything of Spats. Exmoor had swallowed him up.

Herries said, as they picked over a cold supper, "There's no help for it. Publicity or no publicity we'll have to report him missing and I daresay we'll get a wigging for not doing it earlier."

Beth said, unexpectedly, "But you're still not really worried, are you?" and Herries replied, "No, my dear, not to that extent. I'm irritated, and concerned as to his state of mind and my responsibilities. But when you've been at this as long as I have you learn to rely on the barometer in here," and he tapped his hard, round stomach. "Get a good sleep, both of you. We'll turn to again after breakfast tomorrow but I'll discuss it with Inspector Chawleigh at Challacombe before I go to bed."

"But you're worried sick, aren't you, Davy?" Beth said, as soon as Algy's steps had died away on the stairs, and he replied, "By God, I am! Who wouldn't be?"

"Why not trust Algy's instinct?"

"It's not only Winterbourne I'm concerned about," he admitted, with something of an effort. "It's us, you and me. A thing like this, to happen my first term here as housemaster. Damn that silly woman and her peccadilloes! Right now I could strangle her with one of her own silk stockings."

She said, "Come to bed, Davy," and he followed her, without much confidence that he would sleep.

And yet he did, a few minutes after she had taken him in her arms, and as he drifted off he thought, drowsily, "She's right . . . I can cope with anything so long as she's around . . . I've been feeling damned sorry for myself all day but I'm luckier than that chap Winterbourne, for all his investments and fancy trappings . . . If he'd had the sense to marry someone like Beth his boy wouldn't be out on the moor feeling the sky had fallen on him." His hold on her tightened, as though he was suddenly aware of the fragility of happiness, how chancy it was and how easily lost.

Chapter Two

1

It had leaked by rising bell the following morning, a heavy, sultry day, with a promise of sticky heat and thunderstorms before evening.

The wildest stories concerning Spats Winterbourne were circulating and there was no stopping them, as Boyer told him after the school had gone in to breakfast. Even Algy had lost some of his ebullience and drifted in to tell them Inspector Chawleigh would be making his own enquiries from Challacombe, and was sending a man over to get statements.

"None of these people seem to be able to do a thing without first putting it on paper," he grumbled. "One of these days the entire Western world will grind to a halt, its apparatus clogged with forms, files and memoranda. I had it in mind to comb the south-eastern area today, starting from farther out with Boyer, and one or two others. Will you stay here meantime and cope with that scrivener?"

"Anything you say," David said, feeling that he had lost control of the situation. "Beth planned to take the twins into Challacombe for their inoculations, so I won't have the car until she gets back. I could cancel it, of course."

"Don't do that," Herries said, "that diphtheria scare is still

169

on, I'm told. We had everyone jabbed the first week of term. I was an idiot not to tell Willoughby to do the infants then. I'll phone in around midday and we can exchange news. I daresay Mr. Moneybags will call again. Tell him the state of the poll."

David watched him drive off, his Austin Seven grossly overloaded with the Sixth Form posse. Ten minutes later Beth drove the Morgan round from the coach-house with the twins aboard, Joan in front with her, Grace perched in the dickey seat behind. He did not go down and reassure the children about the inoculation. In his present mood she was more qualified to do that, but he waved as they bumbled off down the west drive and Grace waved back. There was no point in going into class. For one thing he couldn't concentrate. For another he was likely to be fetched at any moment to deal with Inspector Chawleigh's man, so he asked matron to show him Winterbourne's locker, sorting through his belongings in the linen room, looking for some kind of clue as to the boy's whereabouts.

There was nothing of any consequence in the pockets and turning them out lowered his spirits a degree or two farther, for he remembered performing this same office for casualties behind Béthune, in the autumn of 1915. A cardboard folder caught his eye and he took it over to the window, surprised to find it contained about a dozen very creditable watercolours, all of Exmoor scenes and signed 'E. W. Winterbourne', with dates reaching back a couple of years.

The quality of the work astonished him. Spats could not have been more than thirteen when the first of them was painted and, so far as he knew, the boy had had no training. There was one that impressed him particularly, a limpid sketch in bronze, russet and green, of Chetsford Water, where it flows out of the middle moor and passes under an old stone bridge through a desolate area of upland. The autumnal tints of the moor had been trapped by the boy's brush. It had a soft, brooding quality, unrelieved by the width of a sky dappled with those long streamers of cloud that passed in endless procession over the scene at all seasons of the year.

He was still looking at it when Mrs. Gorman, the matron, presented herself. "The policeman is here now, Mr. Powlett-Jones. Mrs. Herries is showing him into the head's study. Will you be wanting any further help from me?" He told her no, tucking the folder under his arm and going down the slate steps to the quad. The light seemed very queer out here, overcast with a yellowish tinge as if, at any minute, the low clouds pressing on the school buildings would split and empty themselves. From the direction of Big School, where Bouncer was in session, he heard a burst of laughter, and turned in through the arched door leading to the head's kitchen quarters and thence to the study, where a young policeman, looking just as green and uncertain of himself as he had when he reported for his first interview there more than seven years ago, was thumbing his notebook.

2

Venn's lorry-driver, emerging from the quarry two-thirds of the way up Quarry Hill, was aware that something was amiss the moment he levelled out on the gradient, about one in six here but steeper beyond the ash coppices that grew on each side lower down the road. He braked as hard as he dared but the speed of the heavily-laden lorry increased so that he made a wild grab at the handbrake, throwing all his weight on it as the vehicle weaved the full width of the road, its speed increasing with every yard it covered. As he approached the bend he realised he could never make it and acted on impulse, swinging the wheel hard right, mounting the low bank and crashing into the little forest of saplings to cut the corner or, if he was lucky, snarl up on the tangled undergrowth there. His left hand still gripped the brake lever but his right was pressed on the horn, so that his blaring progress could have been heard a mile away.

Old Chuff Greenaway, Farmer Grover's part-time man, was the only witness to the lorry's crashing entry into the wood. He was hedging fifty yards lower down the hill, heard the horn and glanced up just in time to see the vehicle tear into the copse and plough on down the slope, its progress marked by the travelling tumult among the trees that tossed and whirled as though struck by a cyclone. The undergrowth slowed the lorry's progress somewhat but the weight of stone behind it was too much for the ten-year-old growth in the coppice. It shot out on to the road again at about thirty miles an hour, the driver still wrestling with the gears, the horn still trumpeting his terror.

Beth, changing gear to tackle the second stage of the hill, saw

it as a looming shadow, bursting out of the woods like a masto-
don on the rampage, but she had no real awareness of the impact
when the lorry tore into the nearside of the Morgan, crushed it,
caught it up upon its front fender, carried it fifty yards or more
down the hill and then discarded it before striking the far hedge
and overturning on its side. Nothing could have been more sudden, more unexpected or more final. One moment she was addressing a remark to the children about the blaring horn, the next
this great thing was looming over her, blotting everything out.
She felt no fear or even dismay, only an intense curiosity concerning its sudden eruption from the little green wood on her left.

Chuff Greenaway, panting hard, was on the scene in less than
a minute, and what he saw caused him to stand wheezing yards
short of the two piles of debris, one big, one small, his mouth
agape, his eyes starting from their sockets. Then, with a groan,
he turned and tottered back to the farm lane beyond the bend,
sobbing out his story to Martha Grover, who was hanging out
washing in the cobbled yard.

With a small part of his mind David heard the young policeman's intermittent rumble, something about a terrible accident
on Quarry Hill involving Venn's lorry, Beth and the children, but
the full portent of what he was saying was too obscene, too mon-
strous to be absorbed. The man went on mumbling, his big hands
fidgeting with his helmet on his knees, but soon David could make
no kind of sense at all out of what he was saying and gestured so
that he stopped, sitting immobile on the chair David had occupied that first spring day he came here and took tea with the
Herries. Then, but dimly, he was aware of several other things,
the presence of Ellie Herries who, for some inexplicable reason,
was pressing his head to her chest, and a sustained roaring sound
in his ears, like the sound of the pre-zero-hour Somme bombardment, and behind it a complex of inconsequential sounds, a distant roll of thunder, the five-minute bell signifying the end of a
period, the familiar clatter of boots on the quad flagstones outside, and the shrill voice of Rawlins—it was odd how easily he
identified the voice-shouting, "No! Find your own ruddy atlas!
You're always scrounging . . . !" as he scuttled past under the
window.

He got up, very stiffly, and moved out into the passage, through the arched door to Big School and into the forecourt, instinctively turning half-left and moving up towards the stump of the riven beech, Algy's thinking post. The roller was here again, parked where it should not have been by one of the chain-gangs, very active at this time of year, and he sat on it, grappling with the enormity of the news that the pink-cheeked young policeman had brought. Beth and one of the kids dead. The lorry driver dead. The other twin, he did not know whether it was Joan or Grace, badly injured and rushed by ambulance to Challacombe hospital.

The roaring in his ears increased in volume, blotting out other sounds although he could see, as through the wrong end of a telescope, some of the First Eleven at the nets below the pavilion, and even wonder why they played so soundlessly. One of the groundsmen was poking about the cricket pitch, searching for evidence of his implacable enemy, the mole. It astounded him that life, distorted into an unimaginable nightmare for him, continued to flow so smoothly and unremarkably elsewhere.

His brain was still three-parts numb. It was impossible to absorb a shock of this magnitude. And yet, below the area of numbness, was a terrible rawness that quivered and winced when partial consciousness invaded it. He sat there like a stone carving, hands on thighs, chin thrust forward, seeing without actually seeing, hearing nothing but that dull roaring and then, as unaccountably as Ellie had appeared, Howarth was there, feet planted astride, hands locked behind his back as he sometimes stood in class. He said, "Come up to my rooms, P.J. Come and have a stiff drink, man," and when David did not answer, "The police say someone will have to go to Challacombe. I'll come with you, as soon as the head gets back with transport." And then he did a strange thing, strange that is for Howarth, who had never, in the seven years he had known him, betrayed any emotion other than irritation. His tight little mouth twisted, the eyes behind the prim, pince-nez glasses glittered, and he reached out and placed his arm about David's shoulders, letting it rest there, lightly but firmly.

Away across the field the bell jangled for lunch and a muted clamour reached them. The sounds roused him somewhat. He said, hoarsely, "Do you suppose it's *true*, Howarth? I mean . . . couldn't it be some . . . some frightful mix-up?" and Howarth said, hoarsely, "We'll call in on Doc Willoughby's on the way to Challacombe, David. He'll give you something to help ride out the shock."

It was strange. His brain recorded the fact that Howarth had never before addressed him by his Christian name and this, improbably, touched some hidden spring behind his eyes, so that he began to weep, tears brimming over and coursing the length of his jawline. He even noted that one of them splashed down on the smooth shining surface of the roller, bursting like a starshell over the lines at night, so that it recalled violent deaths in the past, the very distant past, it seemed, although the wounds those deaths inflicted on him were not healed, as he had always assumed them to be. He said, brokenly, "Out there it was different. Everybody was going to die. It was only a matter of how and when."

"You got through that," Howarth said.

"Not this. *Not this!*"

"*Yes!* Here you've got something to hold on to, make something of. Out there it was just . . . just bloody waste!" Suddenly he became extraordinarily animated, putting both hands to David's shoulders swinging him round and shaking him. "The people round you aren't numbered for death, the way everyone was out there. You've got thirty to forty years of hard grind ahead of you, doing a job you're uniquely equipped to do and in a way no one else could do it! It won't make much difference for a month, a year maybe, but it will in the end, I promise. A clear purpose always does, and I'm qualified to tell you that."

Something of Howarth's urgency got through to him. Not much, but enough to bring him partially out of his stupor of grief and despair. He said, carefully, "I couldn't go to Challacombe, Howarth. I couldn't identify her. Someone else will have to do that. Killed outright, that policeman said. Crushed by a bloody great lorry, running wild . . ." He stood up. "I'm going across the moor. Alone. I can't fight it . . . can't accept it . . . here. Not where *she* was, not where that kid waved goodbye three hours ago. Tell Ellie. Tell Herries when he gets back."

"Let me come with you."

"No! I can only cope with it alone, but it must be away from here." He glanced down at the great sprawl of buildings, silent again for the lunch break. "This place was a part of her. She's too close here. So are the twins. Can you understand that?"

174

"Yes," Howarth said, "but for God's sake remember what I said, about using it to hold on to. The place itself, *all of us here.* For there isn't one soul down there who isn't grieving with you, or won't be the moment he knows. That's worth thinking on, David. It's the only thing worth a thought just now."

He stood and watched him go, up past the pavilion, along the fringe of the plantation, then left into the undergrowth. Sullenly he groped for his cigarettes and after three fumbled attempts lit a Gold Flake, inhaling the smoke deep into his lungs. He stood there watching until he saw the tall, spare figure emerge from the far side of the plantation and head for the Coombe. Then, with a grunt, he turned back towards the school buildings, walking swiftly and purposefully, but wondering just how he could explain his sanction of P.J.'s lunge off into the open country, with a more than even chance that he would never find his way back again.

3

David had no awareness of familiar landmarks, or not after crossing the plank bridge over the Coombe, where he had seen Blades and that woman Darbyshire last summer. He walked swiftly but blindly, vaulting stiles, scrambling up and down briar-sown banks, so that often he stumbled and sometimes fell. But he picked himself up with a kind of ferocity and pushed on over miles and miles of upland and across a dozen or more timbered gullies. As long as he could keep walking at this speed he was able to keep at bay the full impact of the blow, to stop it flattening him and leaving him as crushed and broken as Beth and the twins, wherever they were at this moment. His sole awareness of the landscape was the curious yellowish light he had noticed earlier that day and persisted even here, fifteen hundred feet above sea level. Every now and again thunder rolled but it was not until he paused gasping, on the crest of the long, heathery slope leading down to Chetsford Water, that the storm began to gather overhead and one or two heavy spots of rain fell on his sweating face. The soft, yellow glow in the sky dispersed then, replaced by a grey curtain of rain moving swiftly in from the east, a swaying, gently undulating curtain, immensely tall and hissing, coming to meet him like a vast, all-enveloping sheet of old canvas, the sail of some giant galleon torn loose by a cyclone and running free across the middle moor.

He had never seen its like before. Perhaps nobody had. Perhaps it was the forerunner of the Apocalypse.

He stood there watching it until it reached him, drenching him through in a matter of seconds. He was standing in a particularly open place, two hundred feet or more above the floor of the valley, where a great belt of brushwood grew both sides of the stream. There was something vaguely familiar about the landscape, as though he had seen it in a recent dream. He recognised the lie of the land, the long straggle of crouching timber down there, the strangely even ridges of the hills, like a choppy sea studded with flotsam represented by boulders and gorse patches. Great arteries of forked lightning lit it up in great detail, tearing jagged rents in the rain curtain and over all, in a succession of ear-splitting discharges, the thunder rolled.

It was only then that he became aware of the dog and its presence amazed him almost as much as the spectacle. It was Ferguson's Airedale, Towser, that must have attached itself to him the moment he left the plantation and followed at his heels over God knew how many miles of moorland. The dog was whining, terrified by the uproar, and at every fresh clap of thunder he gave a series of sharp, high-pitched yelps. Finally, getting no response from the man, he ran, still yelping, the full length of the slope to the cover of the brushwood. David did not follow. The cataclysm was a solace, the teeming rain beating over every square inch of his body, a balm. It was the end of the world. He saw it as a kind of climax to the horrors of the day, and, at a farther distance, to days of almost identical uproar in the Salient and the Somme.

And then, just as the dog reached the floor of the valley, he became aware of a figure blundering up the slope, head invisible, shoulders hunched under a yellow oilskin, and with a small part of his brain he wondered who the devil it could be, and what he was doing down there in such chaos. At that moment the whole sky blazed up and, a second or two later, an explosion of enormous weight burst over him, stunning his senses so that he was only vaguely aware of the arrival of the figure in the oilskin, who seized his hand and began dragging him down, down to the valley until, in the space of a lightning flash it seemed, they were threading a tunnel of dripping foliage leading to a shallow cave in the rock face beside the rushing stream. Inside it was quite dry and the place was clearly inhabited. An array of kit lay about, including blankets and a knapsack. A small fire smouldered under the overhang, obstinate tongues of flame holding out against the hissing downpour.

He sat down then, limp and exhausted, and as in a dream he saw the figure of a boy, tousled and laughing, emerge from beneath the folds of the oilskin and recognised Spats Winterbourne who seemed, for some obtuse reason, to be enjoying himself, for he said, shouting above the uproar, "It's a corker, isn't it, sir? Never seen one like this before!", and then, with concern, "I say, you're drenched through, sir! Peel off and rub yourself down. There's a towel here somewhere. It's a bit grubby, I'm afraid . . ." and David, hypnotised by the boy, obediently shed jacket and shirt, and began towelling himself.

It was extraordinarily cosy in here, a refuge not only from the storm but from the pitiless world outside, where women and children were crushed under lorries overloaded with building stone. Mutely he watched Winterbourne busy himself about the fire, putting a kettle on a grid and ladling cocoa from a tin into a thick earthenware mug. What astonished him far more than the coincidence of meeting Winterbourne here, of having directed his heedless steps to the very spot where the boy was hiding, was Winterbourne's identity with the moor, and the impression he gave of being an integral part of its wildness and remoteness. He had always thought of Winterbourne as a town-bred boy, dapper and clothes-conscious, even elegant in a slightly comical way, but here, in a cave beside a rushing stream, he was a gipsy, moving and doing for himself, as though this was his natural habitat. A sense of curiosity close to wonder invaded him, holding his own tragedy at bay, so that he grabbed at it, as though Winterbourne and Winterbourne's identification with the moor was a raft in an ocean of misery. He said, "You've been here all the time, haven't you?" and Winterbourne, with a self-effacing grin, replied, "Yes, sir. I suppose you were out looking for me."

"Everybody's looking for you. Including the police."

The boy's cheerful face clouded slightly but then he shrugged. "What does it matter? I'll be sacked, anyway, won't I?"

He sat crosslegged on his blanket, looking into the fire and presently he said, incuriously, "You were lost, weren't you, sir?"

"I was lost right enough," David thought, "but not in the way

177

he means," and said deliberately, "I hadn't the vaguest idea where I was or how I got here. I didn't even know the dog had followed me," and the boy looked quickly, his woman's eyes sharp with intelligence. He said, "Has . . . has anything happened? Something serious, sir?"

"Yes, but it has nothing to do with you. I'd forgotten you were missing. Forgotten you existed."

The bell in his brain began to toll then, slow, ponderous strokes with a repetitive message for him. *'Beth is dead . . . Beth is dead . . . The twins are dead . . . Everything's over . . .'* and he gave a kind of sob.

The boy was beside him in an instant. "What *is* it, sir? What's happened?"

"My wife . . . she was killed by one of Venn's lorries on Quarry Hill this morning."

He heard a long hiss of escaping breath as he bowed his head. He could not bear to talk to anyone who had seen her, gay, carefree and terribly alive. Not even a boy like Winterbourne, who could have known her but slightly.

Winterbourne said, brokenly, "That's . . . that's awful, sir. No wonder you . . ." and he stopped. When he spoke again there was a quaver in his voice. "Was she . . . was *she* out looking for me, sir?"

He raised his head. The boy, so heedless a moment since, now looked as scared as a recruit sitting on the forestep awaiting zero-hour. "No, she wasn't looking for you. It had nothing to do with you. She was driving the twins back from Challacombe."

"The . . . the children, sir?"

"One was killed, the other seriously injured. I daresay she's dead by now."

The rain continued to thresh down beyond the fringe of brushwood. The stream before the cave entrance boiled, rushing over the sloping stones in a cataract. Thunder still growled and occasional lightning flickered, but the centre of the storm was moving away to the north-east. The lid of Winterbourne's kettle began to dance and he got up in a single movement, lifted it from the fire, poured water into the mug, and stirred it with the deliberation that attended all his actions. "Drink this, sir. *Please*, you must!"

David took the mug and sipped. The scalding liquid warmed

his belly but his hands began to shake in the old familiar way and he had difficulty in holding the mug. The boy was beside him again, as solicitous as a mother nursing a sick child. "Take it easy, sir. Just a sip at a time. But get it down. All of it."

It was impossible to resist his gentle persuasiveness. He finished the cocoa and Winterbourne took the mug, setting it before the fire.

"Shouldn't you . . . we . . . start back, sir? It'll take two hours, even using short cuts, and some of the streams might be too wide to jump. That other little girl . . . you'll have to *know*, sir." He waited, and when David said nothing he went on, "We could make it to Withybridge across the shoulder. There's a phone there in the village store, sir. They could send transport and we could wait for it there."

David said, "You go to Withybridge and call in. Tell them to pick you up before dark. I'll stay here."

"You can't do that, sir."

"I'll do what I damned well like, boy."

"No, sir, I'm not leaving you. We could stay here but then everyone will start looking for you and they wouldn't find you, any more than they could me. They'll think . . . well, it just won't do, sir. You must see that."

After a moment he tried again, in the same insistent voice. "The other little girl. She may need you, sir."

It was a possibility that simply hadn't occurred to him but he gave it thought. A gleam of hope probed the farthest recesses of his mind, an eightpenny torchlight, of the kind boys used to read under the blankets, projecting its feeble beam across a vast belfry, where the one-note bell tolled and tolled in his brain. Was it remotely possible that something—anything—could be salvaged from the wreck of his life?

He reached out and groped for his sodden shirt but Winterbourne anticipated this. "Put this on, sir. It'll be tight but it doesn't matter if it rips," and he began to force a sweater over David's head, struggling with it until it had passed his chin, then smoothing it down so that it fitted like a skin. Out of the corner of his eye David saw a cardboard portfolio, a duplicate of the one he had found in Winterbourne's locker. His mind made the connection, telling why the valley had looked familiar from the crest.

He said, "Have you been here often? To paint watercolours?" and surprisingly Winterbourne blushed. "Yes, sir. I didn't think anyone knew. About the painting, I mean."

"Nobody does. I found some of your paintings in your locker. How long have you been coming here?"

"Whenever I could, sir. I found this place by accident, during the Middlemoor run my first term, sir. I didn't tell anyone about it. It was just somewhere to come when . . . well, when things got a bit much, sir."

'A bit much.' It was a strange typically English way of summarising the enormous pressures Winterbourne had been resisting, and resisting very successfully he would say, all the time he had been at Bamfylde. A boy with an exhibitionist mother and a cold fish of a father. A child who could never escape the harassment of the one and the inadequacy of the other. It was remarkable, really, how well he had weathered the long, stark terms, retreating into himself, his painting and his integration with the moor, that must have seemed a kind of refuge. Algy Herries had been absolutely correct about Winterbourne, as he was accurate in his assessment of nearly all the boys who passed through his hands. Winterbourne was not really a boy at all but a young and superbly adjusted adult, and somehow, understanding this, David felt the terrible weight pressing on him lift a fraction, as Howarth's words came back to him—"Here you've got something to hold on to, to live for, to make something of. It won't make much difference for a month or a year, but it will in the end, I promise."

Was there anything in that beyond conventional words of comfort? Howarth's astringent way of saying that time would heal, or something equally banal? Winterbourne's private battle seemed to insist that there was, that by submerging body and soul into the ethos of Bamfylde, or some other school with an identical function, he could, in the years left to him, find shape and cohesion in the way he had when he had emerged, equally battered, from an earlier ordeal. They were not the same, as he had protested to Howarth, but in their very difference there might be a chink of hope. For here, in Winterbourne's survival, was a ledge, a handhold that someone with more courage than he possessed, might use to haul himself out of the slough. He said, at length, "About the one in the hospital . . . you might be right . . . We'd better start back. Now, before the light goes. How long would it take us? To Withybridge, say?"

"Under the hour, sir."

He glanced at his watch, amazed to find that it was after eight o'clock. More than seven hours had passed since he turned his back on Howarth and struck into the plantation. Winterbourne said, "It'll stay overcast and there's no moon, sir, but we would make it the whole way by ten-thirty. It could be quicker that way, providing you don't mind wading, sir."

"Let's go."

He watched the boy pull on his oilskin, damp down the smouldering fire and take a last look round the little cave. He gave the impression of a man taking a final glance at home before emi-grating to the far side of the world. They went out, Winterbourne leading, and tackled the long, dripping slope to the crest. The Airedale, subdued now, trotted at their heels. It was still raining but the weight had gone from the downpour. Over in the west there was a small rift in the great banks of clouds and the glint of bronze light beyond reminded him of the glow of a dying fire, or perhaps a few chrysanthemums, glimpsed through a door left ajar. They walked in silence, one behind the other and even under his oilskin Winterbourne still looked dapper and self-contained. He had his mother's easy grace, and perhaps his father's sense of om-nipotence, conveyed to David over two hundred miles of telephone cable yesterday. As long as Winterbourne led the trek some kind of purpose attached itself to this silent squelch over miles of seep-ing moorland.

Chapter Three

There were periods during the three years he served at the Front that were lost to him. Weeks and even months, when his senses, dulled by physical exhaustion, anaesthetised by the thrum of shell-fire and the sheer boredom of active service in that morass, were expunged from the record of his years as though they had never been.

The period immediately succeeding the calamity on Quarry Hill was such a time, embracing, as it did the dismal aftermath of identification, inquest and double funeral at Stone Cross church-yard where, only a few months before, Beth had stood with him to watch the irascible Ferguson, and then that ageing perfection-ist, Cordwainer, laid in that part of the yard that was, albeit unof-ficially, a Bamfylde preserve.

The news that five-year-old Grace had survived the accident, despite terrible injuries, had no power to cheer just then, for he had to steel himself against tidings that she had followed the others. It did not seem credible that a mite her age could survive a compound fracture of the right leg, a shattered left arm, three broken ribs, severe concussion, and extensive lacerations to the right side of the face, the result of being flung clear from the dickey seat and half-buried by a cascade of stone from the overturned lorry. As yet, as the long, thundery spell continued throughout June, she held on, never fully conscious, and all but invisible in a cocoon of bandages that concealed the whole of her face save for the mouth and left eye. He was not allowed to see her for more than a week and when, at last, he looked down at her, lying there among a grotesque array of cradles and pulleys, he wished he had stayed away. There was something obscene seeing her in that fearful context when he remembered so vividly his final glimpse of her from the window of Havelock's first floor, as the Morgan trundled down the east drive at the start of that frightful day.

He asked Willoughby, liaising with the surgeon, for a frank estimate of her chances and Willoughby, accepting the fact that he was no stranger to violent death, did not hedge. He said that they were fifty-fifty, depending upon factors that could not be assessed at this stage. "She's getting first-class care," he added, "Harvey-Smith, who is in overall charge of the case, regards her as a challenge. If her condition improves in the weeks ahead, she'll have to undergo several more operations, then move on to a London hospital for a skin graft. But there's a chance, a very good one, I'd say. So try and keep that in the forefront of your mind."

It was some consolation, he supposed, or might become one as time went on, but it did not help him to tackle the task of picking up the ravelled threads of his life, and making some kind of attempt to adjust to the bleakness of the future.

He let Ellie persuade him not to attend the funeral. Alone he could contain his grief. He could not share it with four hundred others and there seemed no point in insisting on a private affair when Beth had been so popular with staff and boys all the time she had lived here.

There were two tiny sequels to the melancholy event, one on the evening of the funeral, when he was trying to occupy his mind replying to some of the fifty-odd letters sent him by Old Boys who remembered her, and two more from Cooper and Scrubbs-Norton, who did not. There came a discreet tap on the door and assuming it was Ellie, with some sleeping pills Willoughby had prescribed, he called, "Come in, Mrs. Herries." It was not Ellie but Boyer, carrying two tattered books.

He stood hesitantly beside the desk, sympathy distorting his mobile, amiable features into an unfamiliar and incongruous mould, as he said, with an apologetic cough, "Am I . . . er . . . disturbing you, sir? I can pop in later, I'm duty perk tonight," but David, glad of his company, pushed the correspondence aside and told him to sit down and help himself to a cigarette from a packet on the reading table. Boyer looked startled, as well he might. Smoking was high on what veteran Bamfeldians called the 'watch-it-list', drawn up by Algy Herries when he put into practice his Roman precept of 'Few Rules But Unbendables'. David said, noting the look, "I know you chaps get through ten a day when you can lay your hands on them. This is one occasion when you don't have to climb up among the stacked trunks for a smoke. Don't take it as general, however, or there'll be the devil to pay. For me as well as you."

So Boyer took a Player's from the packet and inhaled expertly, saying, with a fleeting grin, "Er . . . hadn't you better light up yourself, sir? In case someone else looks in?" and when David had stuck a cigarette between his lips, "I actually looked in to give you these, sir. I remembered you quoting from them in the Upper Fifth last year. You said you had them both out there, but lost them with the rest of your kit at Third Ypres."

He passed the books over and David recognised them as old favourites he had read and re-read many times in the last ten years. Fortescue's translation of *The Memoirs of Sergeant Bourgoyne*, and Butler's translation of *The Memoirs of Baron de Marbot*. Boyer went on, "I found them in the Charing Cross Road during the hols, sir. I was going to keep them as a leaving souvenir, but well . . . it occurred to me that you could do with a couple of old friends just now. I've written in them, sir."

David turned to the flyleaves and on each was an identical inscription in Boyer's devil-may-care hand, '*For David Powlett-Jones —In Friendship. Chadwick S. Boyer.*' He said, "That was a nice thought, Chad. I don't think many would have had it. Thank you very much. They were both books I've always been meaning to replace but never did." He sat musing a moment. "I'll tell you something that might sound odd. They were a comfort to me out there. I don't know why, unless it was the reflection that, bad as things were, they were sometimes worse for Marbot and Bourgoyne, soldiers at a time when field surgeons used hacksaws and a pint of raw spirit. No, 'comfort' isn't the word," he knitted his brows, trying to remember when he had last sat in a dugout, and read one or other of the journals by the light of a candle stuck in a bottle. "They had a personal message. Neither man would give up, or even contemplate giving up. They stuck it out and they came through on that account. I suppose I told myself that if they could, then I could. I'll treasure them, always."

Boyer said, with difficulty, "There was one other thing, sir. The perks wanted me to tell you how they felt about it. We all liked Mrs. Powlett-Jones very much. She . . . well . . . fitted in so well, sir, right from the start. I know talking doesn't do a da—doesn't help much, sir. But they wanted you to know. I'll go now, sir," and he crushed out his half-smoked cigarette and rose, abruptly.

David said, "Stay till Silence bell. God knows, I need company," and Boyer sat again, and when Ellie Herries came in with his coffee and pills, he fetched another cup and saucer from the kitchen and poured from the pot. He said, as soon as Ellie had gone, "This is going to take some weathering, Chad. Between ourselves I can't see myself making it."

"I'll bet you will, sir."

"Would you mind telling me why? Without the usual flannel. The way you might discuss it with Dobson, or some other chum, and I don't ask out of curiosity. I need to know if I'm to stay on and that's doubtful, I can assure you."

He was struck by the boy's crestfallen expression as he protested . . . "But that . . . that's *daft*, sir! I mean, it's not *you* at all . . . !"

It occurred to him that one never ceased to be taken unawares by boys. He had always thought of Boyer as an original. A boy who conceived the idea of epileptic fits to beguile a classroom had to be, and, to add to that, he had always seen him as enterprising and possessing above-average intelligence. But he had never thought of him as vulnerable, or having much of what he had come to regard as a boy's poignancy, something nearly all of them had in one way or another. Boyer's distraught look brought to mind earlier encounters. His talk with Briarley, the day Briarley learned of his father's death on the Lys. Skidmore's stiffnecked refusal to bow to the Founder's statue. Blades' lost expression, soon after Julia Darbyshire had warned him off. And, more recently Winterbourne's look when told of the accident. He said, quietly, "I'm not saying I shall end up cutting my throat. Just that

I might feel the need to get away from here, where we spent six happy years. Start again, maybe . . .", but he couldn't go on.

"I think you're absolutely wrong about that, sir."

"Why? Isn't it a natural impulse?"

"Maybe, but well . . . I don't know whether I've any right to stick my oar in."

"I'm asking you to."

"All right. You belong here. You have from the first day, sir, and that isn't flannel. It isn't because the chaps like you either, although they all do. It's because . . . well, because you get *through* to them, in a way older masters don't and can't. Particularly in your subject. I never gave a damn about history before you taught it. I mean, it was no more than a string of dates, and dead mutton to me and to most of the other chaps. But you made it . . . well, *mean* something. You showed us how it fits in with today, if you see what I mean?"

It was a queer kind of compliment but it warmed him. He said, however, "Couldn't I do that at any school?"

"No, sir. Or not so well."

"Why?"

"Because . . . well, because you learned the trick of it here, sir. You're part of the place now. The way you teach . . . well, it fits in with Alg . . . with the head's way, sir."

"Are you saying you fellows really understand the head's theories on education?"

"I think some of us do. By the time we get to the Sixth, that is. Some of the chaps have been to other schools, although I never have. I came here as a nipper. They all say the same thing, that this place is different, not just because of the head but because of where it is, up here on its own and with its own way of life. And lately because of you, and the way you try and put the head's ideas into practice. Do you get the message, sir. Or am I talking a lot of coc—er . . . rubbish?"

"I get the message, Chad."

"You'll think about it, then?"

"I'll think about it."

*   *   *

That was the first incident, but there was another a few hours later when, just before morning school, Graves-Jones poked his head round the corner of his sitting-room, holding a bunch of freesias, carnations and maidenhair fern.

Graves-Jones was not a boy one might expect to see presenting a bouquet. David remembered him vividly, from the first day they met in the garden of the cottage, when Beth gave her first new boys' tea-party, and how he clicked his heels, Prussian-fashion, when thanking his hostess. All the way up school—he was in the Sixth now—Graves-Jones had justified Beth's first impression of him, a suave, confident boy, with demonstrably good manners, a little at odds with his generation. He said, without a trace of embarrassment, "I was just going into class, sir, and thought these should go into water. Will you be going to the hospital this afternoon, sir?"

"I'm not sure. I might. Why?"

"Well, if you do, sir, I wondered if you'd take these along? We tipped Westacott to cut them from his patch, and we intended putting them with all the others in the churchyard. But then it seemed a bit silly, sir. I mean, they'll wilt down there, in this weather, and your . . . the little girl might like them in the ward. I know she can't see them yet but these freesias smell nice, sir."

He reached out and took the flowers wordlessly, too moved to do more than nod his thanks, but Graves-Jones didn't seem to expect thanks. He stepped back, gave one of his little bows from the waist, and withdrew, quietly closing the door. David went into the kitchen, filled a vase and put the flowers inside. His hands shook and his throat felt terribly constricted. He wept then and the relief was immediate. He thought, "Boyer's right, of course . . . bad enough here, but it would be a damn sight worse among strangers. I'll give it a go. At least until the end of term . . ." and he found his gown, shrugged himself into it, and went down the steps just as the bell signalled the start of morning school and his first period with the Lower Third.

2

That was the way of it, not only as far as end of term, and through the summer break, but on through the Michaelmas term to his first Christmas alone.

It was as though his existence, as a man with some useful part to play in life, was a shallow-rooted plant, dependent upon the strength of a cluster of root fibres that ran just below the surface, searching for points of anchorage; another, stronger root perhaps, or an angled rock, or a layer of heavier soil. Each tiny fibre was a part of his identity with the place and some ran deeper than others. One was little Grace's survival, of course, and her slow climb back to a point where hope was definite, corrective operations could be attempted, and she could move on to Great Ormond Street for a period of about six months, they said. Another was the close companionship of Herries and Ellie, backed by the unsentimental but solid comradeship of Howarth, and the sympathy of Barnaby, the two Irvines and even, in his bumbling way, dear old Bouncer. A third fibre was the prescribed rhythm of the school, with its succession of red-letter days and self-made entertainments, particularly the Gilbert and Sullivan opera, in which he featured as relief pianist. But much stronger than any of these was his closer integration with boys at all levels, not only old stagers like Chad Boyer, Dobson, Blades, Winterbourne, Skidmore, McNaughton, Graves-Jones and Ruby Bickford, but later arrivals, some of whom had not even known Beth and the twins.

He made the discovery, as the autumn mists closed in, that the ache in his own heart enabled him to take unexpectedly close-range peeps into the hearts of others, so that he began to mellow in a way that suited the new furrows on his face and the touch of grey in his hair. It was as though he had compressed a couple of decades in six months, converting himself into a more youthful edition of Judy Cordwainer, set in a groove before he was thirty. He was aware of this but did nothing to counteract it, or not mentally. Physically he made a supreme effort, refereeing and occasionally playing a practice game with the First Fifteen, and accompanying the cross-country runs as whipper-in. The season of the year helped to acclimatise him to the rapid change in his character, for the moor, in the late autumn, was at one with his prevailing mood. But what really enabled him to come to terms with his loss was a growing sense of usefulness that might, in time, resolve itself into a definite purpose, of the kind he had had when he and Beth moved into Havelock's last spring.

He might have resigned his housemastership, despite clamorous opposition to the proposal, had it not been for Herries' ruse in making him responsible during the holidays, for the group of boys known as 'The Sunsetters', a group nickname Barnaby had invented for the score or so boarders who lived permanently at the school because their parents were scattered about the dominions, the crown colonies and the protectorates. The label was a play on the imperial claim that Britain still ruled an empire on which the sun never set, and was in no sense a gibe, rather a good-natured joke, aimed at the separateness of boys who looked upon Bamfylde not as a school but as a home. About half of them were coloured, like the Kassava brothers, the remainder the sons of men with overseas posts who, for one reason or another, preferred to have their children educated in England.

For some years now this expanding group lived on the third floor of the head's house but in September, 1925, the second stage of the new building plan was started and their dormitory was converted into a sick-bay. Herries said, when the builders moved in, "My common sense tells me I ought to scatter them to their respective houses, P.J., but they're all very much against it. I suppose they think of themselves as a little house of their own, and don't care to lose their identities. Do you think you could make room for 'em? Take 'em over, lock, stock and barrel? Someone will have to when I put my feet up, a couple of years from now."

David said he would think about it and came up with a plan to extend the junior dormitory at Havelock's by cutting through into the old Remove and the music room beyond. The Remove he said, could be transferred to one end of the woodwork room. One less music room might annoy Rapper Gibbs but was unlikely to trouble anyone else. "I could get twenty beds in there if the builders went about it the right way," he said. "It wouldn't be much of a job. There's no stonework, only partitioning they should have ripped out at the time of the fire but didn't because it was costing so much."

Herries was enthusiastic and at once switched the builder's men from his third floor and set them at work on the new dormitory but before they were finished David had another thought. "Why don't we make a recreation room out of the music room?" he suggested. "The annexe and Remove will give us enough space for beds, and a room of their own will stop the Sunsetters making free with your quarters in the holidays. Besides, only the seniors among them have studies. They ought to have some stake in the place apart from a bed and a locker."

Herries agreed and the conversion was finished before the end of Michaelmas term, giving the Sunsetters a common room where they could keep their array of overseas journals and play their gramophone, a place where 'Massa' Heilbron, a tall West Indian and a very promising cricketer, could strum his ukelele, and little Kilroy, the fleetest runner in Junior School, could massage his calves, against the day when he would be awarded his running colours, and him only fourteen, the youngest colour on record.

Imperceptibly David found himself saddled with the post of holiday uncle to the Sunsetters but the job, demanding as it sometimes was, proved another fibre binding him to Bamfylde. Even so, when all the roots were down, there were still moments when the transplant seemed very insecure.

They would steal upon him treacherously, always taking him unawares. Sharp, poignant reminders, as when he looked up at the tall windows of Havelock's and saw a maid shaking a duster in the manner of Beth when they were settling in nine months before. Or when, coming out of church, he glanced down the road to the cottage, and saw snowdrops crowding the patch where she had planted her rowan tree. The long winter nights were the worst times, however, when the wind came shrieking down from Middlemoor, rattling the slates and searching out chinks in the old window frames, and he would awake and suddenly find himself harassed and sweating, with the sense of having escaped from a situation in which Beth and the twins were calling from behind a wall of quarry stones as high as the plantation. At times like this he would have to come to terms with the truth all over again.

He broke the habit of Willoughby's sleeping pills. They left him drowsy and not up to his work, but he found another antidote. In October, when the nights had closed in, he dug out his folder of notes on 'The Royal Tigress' and began arranging them into sections, and during the Christmas holidays he actually began to work, and was soon able to lose himself in the surge of Lancastrian and Yorkist armies the length and breadth of England, and the struggle for the crown that had given him yet another of his Second Form tags, viz.,

In the fight for England's head,
York was white, Lancaster red . . .

He did not think it would be a very original book but at least it kept his thoughts occupied throughout the small hours, and the sleep that followed a session was free of dreams.

He raised another barrier against introspection and self-pity. He had always been primarily interested in post-Conquest history but, via some construes he had made of Plutarch's *Lives* when mugging for his degree, he was led back to the Ancients and tackled, for the first time, Gibbon's massive work on the Roman Empire. Having whetted his appetite, so to speak, he began to study Persian history, from Cyrus the Great to the Alexandrian conquest, so that his small store of Latin was of real service to him and names like Darius, Xerxes and Zenophon emerged as something more than cardboard figures and supplied him with a new source of anecdotes that he could retell to the Third and Fourth Forms.

Barnaby was the first to note this extension into what he regarded as his field and said, when they were sharing a coffee break one morning, "I always took you for a bit of a Philistine, P.J., a chap who thought history began at the traditional starting point, 55 B.C. I was wrong it seems. Young Hilary, a duffer if ever there was one, came out with something I didn't know about Hannibal this morning during construe. Damned if I didn't think I was hearing Joan of Arc's voice for a minute. Then he admitted you gave them half an hour on the Punic Wars on Thursday."

The incident, trivial enough, had the effect of bringing him and Barnaby closer together. He had always liked the classics master, a very easygoing man, despite a touch of exhibitionism, but he had never quite succeeded in making a friend of him. Now they sometimes took long walks together, or shared a drink in Howarth's rooms, and the association helped, as did the tendency on the part of everyone save Carter, and Molyneux, who had replaced Ferguson in modern languages, to go out of their way to help. There were still two vaguely hostile camps in the common room. His own, that included the amiable Barnaby and was led from behind by Howarth, and Carter's, for Carter, although a stickler for discipline, had a talent for recruiting the younger, pushing men, often with pet theories on education, men who were slightly contemptuous of Algy's refurbished Arnoldian concepts. The rift was deeper than appeared on the surface, dividing those who thought of themselves as progressive-traditionalists, like Herries himself, and those Howarth labelled the Eager Beavers, committed to raising

Bamfylde's academic status and attracting a different kind of parent. There was, however, no danger of a flare-up so long as Algy remained in charge, for although he was careful not to flaunt his authority, it was he who charted the school's course and formulated its policies, and his influence with the Governors, some of whom shared Carter's outlook, was very strong after twenty years of steady progress and the lengthy waiting-list he had built up since the war. Sometimes David wondered what would happen when Herries retired, as he was scheduled to do after the summer term of 1927. He would be sixty-seven then, and had already made arrangements to take the living of Yatton-under-Edge, twenty miles nearer the coast.

He did not give it much thought, however, being fully occupied getting his second wind, and in the event it was not until May, 1926, when the shock waves of the General Strike rolled as far as the Exmoor plateau, that the breach was highlighted, not so much between the two factions as between himself and Carter, catalysts of opposing schools of thought.

3

It almost surely would not have occurred had not David chosen that particular week to pay his first visit to Greystoke, the Kent rehabilitation hospital to which Grace, now making very definite progress, had been transferred in April.

He found her in far better health and spirits than he had anticipated. The legacy of that avalanche of stones could still be traced down the dead side of her face, where plastic surgeons had been at work, and in a heavy limp caused, they told him, by the shortening of muscles in the left leg, where three operations on the bone had resulted in a contraction of half an inch. In all other respects, however, she seemed to have made an amazing recovery and Harvey-Smith, who had maintained his personal interest in the case despite the fact that he lived in Plymouth, told him the child would always limp but that the scars on her face would fade a little every year.

"If she had been a year or so older," he said, "say, around eight when it happened, we shouldn't have been so lucky and the limp would have been worse. As it is she'll climb to ninety-five per cent in six months. Apart from strenuous games there's no reason at all why she shouldn't lead a perfectly normal life."

It was a kind of miracle to watch her tackling her formidable exercises in the solarium. He had expected a pale, withdrawn child, heaving herself around on crutches but it was not like that at all. At first she was as shy with him as he was with her but after his third visit they adjusted very well and he was astonished, and a little touched, by her curiosity about the past, asking him all kinds of questions to supplement her fragmentary memories of the last year in the cottage and the few short weeks they had shared at Havelock's.

She said, almost gaily he thought, "I remember bits, Daddy, but mostly it's all mixed up, and there's a lot I don't remember at all."

"Do you remember the actual crash?" he asked, fearfully, and she said she did not, recalling nothing whatever of the final trip they made to Challacombe, not even the inoculation immediately preceding the accident. Her memories, it seemed, were concentrated on the last year at the cottage, leading up to the move to school and the Easter she and Joan had spent with Grandfather Marwood, at Elmer's End. She remembered the last new boys' tea-party Beth had given, in September, ". . . because it was the day a boy with glasses upset the tea-pot on Towser."

"Ah, that was Rowlandson," he said, "he remembers that too, and will laugh when I tell him you do. How much do you remember about Mummy and Joan?"

"I remember Mummy bathing us in front of the fire in a tub, and wrapping the towel round us to look like Indian girls. And her singing instead of reading a story when we went up to bed."

"Singing what, Grace?"

"A song with a lot of words, that all came out in a rush. About a queen it was."

It was like a dart and the impact made him catch his breath. It had been one of Beth's songs from *The Gondoliers*, that year's Gilbert and Sullivan, and the laughter behind her voice came to him now, as clearly as though she was serenading them from the terrace outside. He steered her away from memories after that, telling her of his plans for her when she was finally discharged from hospital, tentative as yet but sketched over the last few weeks after Harvey-Smith had said she could be home by the start of autumn term.

"You'll have my old room overlooking the moor," he said, "the one I slept in, and used as a study before you were born. The builders, who are working at school now, are going to fix it up and make it pretty and Mrs. Arscott, our new Second Form mistress, is going to give you private lessons for the time, to help you catch up. You'll have to look after me at Havelock's, because I'm all on my own there apart from the boys, and Mrs. Herries says she'll teach you to cook. Would you like that?"

"I'd like it very much," she said. "Could I give new boys' tea-parties?"

"Why, that's a splendid idea! So you shall, as soon as you're settled in. I've arranged with old Hodge to give you riding lessons too, on that pony of his, the one that used to scrape his hoof at the door for bread crusts. You'll be able to saddle up and ride down to see Ma Midden whenever you want, and over to the village to do the shopping. Granfer and Grandmummy Tilda ('Tilda' was Mrs. Marwood's collie, and the twins had used her to distinguish between their two grandmothers, ever since they were three) will come down here and see you, and take you out once in a while, and I'll come again at half-term. Keep at those exercises, won't you, love?" and he left her, a little hurriedly, reflecting thankfully that she was a cheerful, uncomplicated child, and likely to prove a great comfort to him in the years ahead.

Summer term had already begun when he paid his visit and he was due back on Monday but then, spending Sunday with his father-in-law, the strike was upon them, and there was no hope of returning by rail. He got through, with some difficulty, to the bursar's office, and was somewhat taken aback when the phone was answered by Carter, who happened to be in the office while the bursar was out. David explained the circumstances, asking Carter if he would tell the head he would be back at the earliest opportunity, and was puzzled rather than annoyed by Carter's breezy rejoinder, "Right, Powlett-Jones! Leave it to me." Then, "A case of hoist by your own petard, eh, old man?"

"How's that again?"

Carter said, in what David had learned to think of as his Sixth Form voice, "Nothing, old chap. Only a little dig on my part. After all, you're for the red flag, aren't you? No, that isn't fair, let's call it pink!"

He did not trust himself to answer, having learned something about the art of duelling with Carter over the years, but rang off, glowering through the kiosk panes at two special constables enjoying the brief authority vested in them by their armbands. Then, muttering "Bloody little swine . . ." he walked down the main road towards Clockhouse.

Carter's gibe, and his own instinctive sympathy with the miners, based on all he knew of the Valleys, conditioned his approach to the strike from the outset. Temporarily stranded, he passed the time talking to anyone who he thought might give him deeper insight into the cause and effect. This included not only members of the British public (as communicative during an emergency as they were uncommunicative when life ran smoothly) but local organisers, who were holding street-corner meetings to promote solidarity. He also read the *British Gazette*, Churchill's broadsheet, impatient with its stridency, and even probed the police point of view from a sergeant guarding a bus driven by an undergraduate.

What surprised him, dismayed him somewhat, was the apparent absence of acrimony on both sides and the inclination of the general public to regard the stoppage as an impromptu national spree. There seemed no way of communicating to the man in the street the reality of the miners' grievances and the unsentimental justice of their claim. As a miner's son he was unable to share the hilarity of the occasion. As a teacher of nineteenth-century history he was all too familiar with hidden factors contributing to the present confrontation. Long hours, backbreaking, primitive conditions above and under ground, miserly pay, the ever present threat of death or mutilation—these were things that men who hacked a subsistence living from the seams had taken for granted over two generations. What stuck in the craw was the underlying conviction in the heart and mind of the miner that, whereas an approach to some kind of equity was apparent in every other heavy industry since the Armistice, his own had got itself bogged down in a slough of bureaucratic wrangling, Governmental indifference and avarice on the part of the mine owners and drawers of dividends. And behind all was a threat that few ever voiced outside the coalfields, the prospect of technological advances hurrying the industry towards a date when the demand for coal dropped away, a little every year, leaving skilled men, now in their late twenties and early thirties, without such bargaining power as they held today, perhaps without a trade to ply. It was like a huge, ugly boil slowly coming to a head, with everyone watching and no one possessing the wit or the spirit to apply an internal remedy and frustration ultimately drove him to the public library to read some of the debates in Hansard preceding the stoppage.

He found little here he did not know already. There were thousands of words on pay, safety devices, pithead baths and the like, but no one seemed to have commented on the inborn pride in his craft that the miner carried underground every working day. Neither, for that matter, had anyone at Westminster seen fit to acknowledge the modesty of the Miners' Federation's claims made the previous year. It make him wonder, not for the first time, if he had made the most of such brains as he possessed by burying himself on a Devon moor all these years, when he might have played some part in the nation's affairs, either in politics, or as a professional organiser of the Workers' Education Association, that was striving so hard to improve the education of men and women who had left school at fourteen and younger. But, somehow, illogically, it all led back to Carter and Carter's type, lucky renegades as he thought of them, who had used their superior educations to infiltrate into the lower ranks of the bosses' class. He thought, "I've got to get back there somehow. I've got to see how Bamfylde is taking it and whether anyone down there is trying to see our side of it!" It reminded him how deeply rooted were his prejudices against monied interests, that had succeeded in killing his father and brothers, and an entire generation in the years that followed.

"I'll bloody well get there if I have to walk," he told his railwayman father-in-law. "There's no damned sense in what I'm doing, unless I can say my piece at places like Bamfylde," and he went out and bought a knapsack, begging a lift on a milk lorry as far as the Great West Road, where he got another lift in an army lorry returning to Aldershot for more troops.

He walked nearly twenty miles the next day before putting up at a cyclists' hostel and the day after that, following a succession of lifts and tramps, he came down over the moor near Dulverton, riding a market cart. He made short work of the last leg, arriving at school just after dusk on Sunday, May 9th. The strike still had three days to run.

*   *   *

He was surprised to learn from Herries that school routine had not been disturbed by more than a ripple or two. They produced their own bacon and vegetables and their milk came from local farms. They had had no newspapers, of course, and Herries was intrigued to hear David's first-hand account, but said, "I appreciate you taking all this trouble to get back here on the job, P.J., but surely you know me better than to have expected it in the circumstances?"

"It was a chance remark that Carter made over the phone that encouraged me to make the effort," and he repeated, word for word, what Carter had said.

Herries said, thoughtfully, "You're very prickly where Carter's concerned, P.J. Too prickly, if you ask me, but that, off the record, applies equally to him. Do you mind telling me why? I wouldn't ask if it wasn't important."

"It isn't important."

"Oh, but it is. To me and to Bamfylde. My guess is that both of you are pretty well entrenched and disinclined to move now that you each have a house. Why the devil do you let him rub you up the wrong way so easily?"

"It's his general attitude. Not to me personally—you can't expect to make a friend of everyone in an enclosed community like this—but he always gives me the impression he's cockahoop at practising a profession, instead of following a trade or craft. That approach is pretty general among men on the way up from nowhere. What bothers me about post-war Britain is that it's getting worse all the time."

"Can you be a little more explicit, old chap?"

"Yes. The gap between the collarless and the fancy-tie brigade keeps on widening and it shouldn't, not after the comradeship they shared in the trenches. I was born into the working class and come from a long line of miners. I'm proud of it. Why the hell should I have to apologise for it to a chap like Carter?"

"But, my dear chap, you don't have to," Herries said, with one of his cherubic smiles. "And it isn't your background that bothers him."

"Then what does?"

"Your war record. He hasn't got one to speak of, and he was quick to notice the difference it made to you when you started here."

"But the war's been over nearly eight years! Nobody here gives it a thought any more."

"Except you," Herries said.

"I find it hard to forget. Is that so wrong?"

"It's neither right nor wrong, old son. It's inevitable. You witnessed those eighty-odd Old Boys of mine blown to bits, and you won't ever forget and forgive."

David said, with some difficulty, "Does that imply you don't approve of me keeping it in front of the boys? You saw those boys die, too. You knew nearly all them by their nicknames. I'd say they were still very fresh in your memory."

"One has to strike a balance," Herries said. "That's what education is about. Rationality, tolerance, give and take, call it what you like. Carter has his faults. So have you, and all the rest of us. But he's a first-class man at his subject, and very sound as a housemaster. He's exam mad, of course, and almost certainly thinks me an old fool for not being, but he has a point. Life *is* getting more competitive and we have to have a modern side here and might do worse than Carter, judging by some of the science men I've interviewed in my time. This is what it boils down to. I'll be gone in just over a year and some new man will move in. My bet is the Governors will appoint a modern man, but whoever he is he'll have to learn to lean hard on you and Carter. So my advice to you is to call a truce."

He took Algy's advice. His first impulse had been to buttonhole Carter and challenge him about the phone jibe, but he thought better of it. A few days after his return he was approached by Bamfylde's sole Free Stater, Paddy McNaughton, now a leading light of the Sixth. "I'm in a rare fix, sir," he said, with the conspiratorial grin that had been common currency between them since the incident with the pistol. "I volunteered to present the T.U.C. case at the Society's debate tomorrow and I don't know the first thing about it. Can you brief me, sir? The proposition is, 'That the Trade Unions were justified in supporting the Miners' Federation in recent strike action'."

David grinned. "You're backing a lame horse, aren't you?"

"Oh, sure I am, sir," said McNaughton, "but why not? It's a chance to take another crack at The Oppressors. You know the drill, sir. Anyone heaving a bomb at Westminster is welcome in

Ireland. I only volunteered for devilment, but now I'm stuck with it."

"Who's opposing?"

"Sanders, sir. He's hot stuff, and does his homework."

"I'll brief you," David said, "and it's lucky you came to me. I was in London last week, and Sanders isn't the only one who does his homework."

He gave McNaughton several lines of argument to pursue and when the boy had jotted them down he said, "Er . . . would it be asking too much to get you to second, sir? We could pull the pants off 'em, between us."

David had taken part in several Sixth Form debates but never on a controversial subject. He said, doubtfully, "Would that be fair on Sanders?" and McNaughton replied, "Sure it would, sir. The seconder only has five minutes. All you need do is sum up."

There seemed no harm in it and secretly he relished an opportunity of speaking up for the miners.

"Very well, then, but only in support of the arguments you put forward, so don't go off at the tangent. You Irish have been doing that for centuries!"

The debate was a cheerful, innocuous affair. Sanders, son of a Conservative candidate in a Liberal-held constituency, was Bamfylde's most accomplished public speaker and had obviously had a briefing from his father. He trotted out all the old saws in reply to McNaughton's passionate defence of the workers, loss of trade, breach of working contracts, readiness to put the nation in jeopardy for a shilling, and so on, but coming from a pleasant chap like Sanders the arguments sounded harmless and David saw them as no more than an exercise in schoolboy polemics. His own speech was brief and to the point. He stressed that the mining community was defenceless against the owners and that their work, vital to the nation, deserved a good working wage and better working conditions. The strike was the only weapon they had against exploitation. He or Paddy or both must have converted some among the audience. The motion was lost, certainly, but by the narrow margin of four votes and Paddy claimed this as a victory.

The sequel was not slow in coming. The next day, entering class to take the Sixth on the Reform Bills of the eighteen-thirties, David found a newspaper cartoon pinned to the blackboard with a thumb tack. It was a particularly lurid one, depicting a leering

Bolshevik fishing in British industrial waters, using a bag of bait ticketed '£400,000 Bolshevik subsidy'. The sea in the drawing was marked 'British Coal Dispute'.

It was the kind of prank that he, and every other master at Bamfylde (with the exception of Howarth and Carter) was expected to take in good part, but somehow, in his present mood, that was asking too much. He said, "Who owns this sheet of toilet paper? I'm not asking who put it there. Who owns it?"

Sanders rose, looking a little apprehensive. "It was mine, sir."

"Where did you get it?"

"Where?"

"Yes, where? It's a simple question, isn't it?"

"My . . . er . . . my father sent it. With some other newsclippings. After I'd written home for material on the debate, sir."

Boyer rose from the back, looking, David thought, very glum. "Nothing personal, sir. Just a joke and we were all in on it, even the chaps who voted with you and McNaughton last night."

The flicker of anger that had stirred in him subsided but the ember glowed. He waited, getting himself in hand, before crumpling the cartoon and tossing it into the wastepaper basket. "Right. I don't find it all that much of a joke but I suppose I'm expected to make allowances in the Sixth and I will. However, while we're on the subject let's jump a couple of generations from the Reform Bills and I'll tell you something you might not know. As far as I'm concerned very few here do know, for I've never made a parade of it, and I wouldn't now if you hadn't sat up and begged for it. I'm a miner's son. I was born and grew up in a Welsh mining community. I saw, at first hand, the kind of deal those chaps get, and have been getting, ever since the English moved in and made a midden out of their valleys. Most of them bring home fifty shillings a week for a five-and-a-half-day week underground, where they might die at any moment. From a fall, from fire-damp, from flooding. There are no pithead baths in most of the pits. The absentee owners drawing royalties on seams thousands of feet below the surface are too damned miserly to instal them. So the men wash in tin baths before the fire, scrubbed by their womenfolk. Think about that. Fifty shillings a week, for a man with a wife and family and it costs around four-ten a week to keep one of you fellows here for eight months of the year. But that isn't all, not by a long chalk. When I was a kid younger than anyone here I went off to school one morning leaving behind a father and two brothers, working early shift—four a.m. to midday. When I got home that same night my father and brothers were dead. Their bodies were never recovered. Ewan, my younger brother was sixteen at the time. Now let's get back to the syllabus."

They were silent and attentive during the remainder of the period. Nobody approached him afterwards, as he half-expected they would, but he felt much better for having blown his top, as he described the outburst to Howarth that evening.

Howarth was mildly amused and said, at length, "You got quite a kick out of that, didn't you, P.J.?"

"Yes, I did. But I don't fool myself I got through to anyone."

"You might have. One or two. But I'll give you yet another piece of advice if you care to have it."

"To work a bit harder at cultivating the Englishman's stiff upper lip?"

"On the contrary. To blow your top more often, and give the Celt an airing every now and again. You'll feel the better for it and it won't do them any harm. Or the rest of us either for that matter. Have a drink."

It was over and done with as far as David was concerned, but there was an unlooked-for sequel that made nonsense of his outburst in class. A day or so later he was standing before the open window of his own kitchen quarters, looking out on the quad, when he saw a Third Former, Watson Minor, emerge from the arch with a tuck parcel and call across the quad to Vosper, one of his boys. "I say, Voss! . . . There's been a balls-up in parcel handout. This isn't an Outram parcel, it's for Kidbrooke. He's in the Kremlin, isn't he?" Vosper, taking the parcel, made no comment except, "I'll give it to him," and disappeared into the main entrance to Havelock's.

David called across, sharply, "Hi! You there! Come over here, will you?" and Watson turned on his way back through the arch and sauntered over. "Me, sir?"

"You used a certain word just now, in respect of Havelock's. What was it again?"

Watson looked bewildered for a moment but then he grinned. "A certain word? You mean . . . er . . . 'balls-up', sir?"

"No, I don't mean that, although that isn't King's English according to Mr. Howarth. I meant 'Kremlin'. It *was* 'Kremlin', wasn't it?"

"Oh . . . yes, sir."

"That's new, isn't it? I've never heard Havelock's called 'Kremlin' before."

"Well, no, sir, but it is now, sir. In Outram's that is, and in some of the other houses I think. Is there anything wrong with it, sir?"

Watson, not a particularly bright boy, had already enlisted in The Lump. It would take him four more years to get as far as the Fifth, if he ever did. "Just what do you know about the Kremlin Watson?"

"I don't know anything about it, sir."

"Then why did you say it just now?"

"Well, it . . . it sort of came out, sir. Like I say, the chaps are calling Havelock's the Kremlin."

"All right, that's all, Watson. Mere curiosity on my part," and Watson, relieved of the tiresome necessity to rack his brain, trotted off.

After prep that evening David found Boyer and told him of the encounter. "Did Sanders coin the phrase, Chad?"

"No, sir. It wasn't Sanders."

"I didn't think it would be. Who did originate it?"

"You're asking me, sir?"

"I'm asking you."

"Well, as a matter of fact, it wasn't a boy at all. I heard it was one of Mr. Carter's. It cropped up when someone in the Lower Fourth made a mess of something they were doing in the lab and caused a fearful stink. Mr. Carter said something about 'Stink-bombs being the prerogative of Havelock's, otherwise known as the Kremlin'. I thought it was a bit thick, sir, but it was just a joke and seems to have stuck, the way some of them do. Like nick-names."

"That's about it," David said, "a nickname. Well, thanks for telling me, and for your information I'm going to follow it to source right now. Don't worry, I won't involve you," and he strode off through the quad arch and up the short flight of steps into Outram's.

*   *   *

Carter was just dismissing Sanders, his head prefect, with laundry lists and other notices for the board. David waited until the prefect was out of earshot before saying, "Can you spare a minute, Carter?"

"Certainly. About Saturday's house match? Come inside, old man," and he led the way into his ground-floor study. His affability, as always, was deceiving. He was the kind of man who used forms of address like 'old man' and 'my dear chap' as camouflage. David followed him inside and closed the door.

"It's about a remark you made in the lab a day or so ago. You referred to my house as the Kremlin."

Carter's red-rimmed eyes blinked rapidly. For a moment he seemed baulked but he made a quick recovery.

"I did? Well, what of it? Don't you make jokes in class sometimes?"

"Not that kind of joke, Carter."

"What the devil are you driving at?"

"You know bloody well what I'm driving at. It was a personal gibe at me, on account of the part I took in the Upper School debate. Or maybe what I told the Sixth two days ago."

It was being challenged in his own den that nettled Carter, so much so that David saw him as he had never seen him during all the years they had sparred together. His jauntiness fell away and with it that shrewd command of tongue that usually enabled him to get the better of their skirmishes. He jumped up, red in the face, stuttering and shouting, "How *dare* you bully me in my own house! I've always thought you a bounder, Powlett-Jones, but there are limits—*limits*, you hear? And you're exceeding them!"

"Doesn't it occur to you that you did just that in the lab? You as good as accused me of being in Russian pay. And within the hearing of boys I have to teach!"

"I did *no* such thing! I made a small joke at your expense. How many have you made at mine since you came here? I . . . I won't continue this discussion, d'you hear?"

"I can hear. They can hear you across the quad, I daresay. But you will continue it, until I get an apology. Just what is it about me that makes you behave like a police stooge?"

He had never thought to see a man so beside himself with rage and the streak of malice he had always nurtured for this one man at Bamfylde enjoyed the spectacle, one that would have embarrassed him in different circumstances. "God bless my soul, you're the right one to come in here talking like that, I must say! Ever since you set foot in the school you've tried to foist your filthy principles and . . . and disloyalty on the boys. I'm not alone in thinking so, either!"

"Who else, Carter?"

"Alderman Blunt, for one, and other Governors and parents I've talked to. I'm hanged if I know why you haven't been asked to resign before this! You wouldn't stay here ten minutes if I had my say!"

"So long as you haven't I'm in no danger. But at last we seem to be getting somewhere. 'Filthy principles' you said. And 'disloyalty'. Disloyalty to whom, Carter?"

"Why, to the country, to the type of parent who sends his son here to get an education. Your entire approach to your work is . . . is slanted, twisted in favour of class hatreds and destructive forces. But I'll not stand here and . . ."

"You'll stay until we've had this out, Carter. You'll do it if I have to pin you down in that tinpot throne of yours. Disloyalty, is it, eh? Was it disloyal on my part to spend three years in those bloody trenches, fighting for trench-dodgers with gammy knees? That knee of yours came in handy, didn't it? It enabled you to play soldiers when there was a real war on your doorstep."

He hadn't meant to go that far and regretted it the moment it was out. It was not that he failed to view Carter in this light. He had heard too much about 'gammy knees' and 'faulty tickers' to believe Carter's explanation of his discharge on the eve of his draft crossing to France, but it was a cheap, easy gibe, of the kind he would have despised in the mouth of another opponent. It lit another fuse under Carter, however, who began to dance with rage, his little tripping movements bringing him closer to David, who was standing with his back to the door. And then, to add to the absurdity of the scene, Carter began pushing and he pushed back, so that neither of them heard or saw the door open and close again. When they circled, however, there stood Herries, watching them from just over the threshold, and it seemed to David that he had materialised through the ceiling or floorboards.

"For God's sake! Pull yourselves together both of you! I heard you from the Founder's statue and I daresay others did too, apart from the boys in your house, Carter!"

They separated, a couple of admonished Second Formers,

caught scuffling in the dormitory after silence bell. Then Carter began to bleat, and it seemed to David he was very close to tears.

"It was Powlett-Jones, Headmaster . . . he came in here making the vilest accusations . . . I told him to go but he wouldn't . . . wouldn't . . ." and suddenly, to David's dismay, he did crumple, slumping down in his chair, whipping off his pince-nez glasses and pretending to polish them with a piece of tissue.

Herries said, "Take yourself off, Powlett-Jones. We'll go into this later," and David went, out of the study, down the passage and into the quad that was empty, so that he guessed prep bell had gone, although he did not remember hearing it.

As a housemaster he was exempt from prep-taking, unless deputising for a colleague, so he went straight upstairs to his living-room and poured himself a whisky. He was pouring another, and wondering wretchedly about the outcome of this extraordinary scene, when there was a tap on the door and Herries entered in response to his gruff invitation. Algy said, bitterly, "I'll take one myself if you're making free with them," and sat heavily on the padded window seat. David poured the drink, adding a touch of soda.

"You don't have to tell me," he said. "I know it if Carter doesn't. We both made damned fools of ourselves and if he'll accept an apology I'll offer one," and when Herries, sipping slowly, made no reply, "Did he tell you his version of it?"

"About that crack in the lab? Yes, he did, and made the same offer as you in that respect."

"It was about even," David said, glumly. "We both behaved like Second Formers. Did anyone else hear us?"

"If anybody did you can wager it will be all over the school by dormitory bell." He looked up, knitting his shaggy eyebrows. "Not so good for discipline, is it?"

"Not good at all," David said, resisting an insane impulse to chuckle.

"It was that final taunt of yours that did the damage. You hit him where it hurt like the devil, and you had no excuse for it. I warned you about that the night you came back from town."

"He made some pretty wild accusations himself."

"Why the devil didn't you go when he asked you? Why didn't you write him? Or come to me? How is either one of you going to bury the hatchet after this? I'm hanged if I know why I should be that concerned, I've only a year or so to go."

"But you are concerned."

"Good God, man, of course I am! This place is my life. I've put twenty-three years into it. Given it all I've got! Do you think I can turn off my love for it like . . . like a tap?"

"I know you can't, sir. What's to be done then? Do you want my resignation? Or his? Or a matched pair, maybe?"

"You know better than that," growled Herries. "Any other bright suggestions?"

"I could apologise in writing. Admit I lost my temper, and make no reference to the Kremlin business. That would smooth his feathers, if I know Carter."

"It would still leave yours ruffled."

"Yes, it would. But I'd do that much for you after all you've done for me. And mine."

He saw the older man's expression brighten a little as he said, "Well, that would be a start. Seems to me a bit one-sided but you're young enough not to bother about that. Yes, I know, Carter's only a few years older, but he's always seemed to belong to my generation more than yours. I don't know why, but he has. You write that letter, and send a boy straight over with it. Then we'll see what happens." He sighed. "It's all so childish when you think about it. People say schoolmasters end up by treating all adults like Third Formers, and dim-witted ones at that, but it isn't really so. The truth is, most of 'em revert to Third Formers in their forties. Sometimes they don't even wait that long."

"Suppose I took the letter over myself?"

"You'd probably find Outram's out of bounds and sentinels posted. He's not so resilient as you, P.J."

He got up, nodded and drifted out in that soft, floating way of his. David sat for a long time looking out on the orange sunset over the moor but without appreciating it. Presently, he got up and went across to his desk. On a sheet of Bamfylde paper he wrote,

My dear Carter, I behaved like an ass and present my apologies. We could have talked this out like adults. The fact that we didn't was my responsibility, not yours. Very sincerely, David Powlett-Jones.

As soon as end-of-prep bell rang he went out on to the landing and caught little Hobson scurrying up to the junior dormitory, telling him to give the letter to Carter personally but not wait for an answer. Then he went down and out across the cricket-field, half-shrouded in violet dusk, and heady with the scent of grass cuttings, wondering if Beth would have approved his backdown, or merely laughed at them both, saving her sympathy for Algy Herries. It was imponderable, but he did recall what she had said on the occasion of a previous quarrel, about 'there being a Carter in every school, office or factory, from here to Land's End'.

By the time he got back for supper Carter's reply lay on his desk. It was as brief as his own but more guarded. It said:

My dear Powlett-Jones, I accept your apology. I should not have lost my temper, in that fashion. It was unprofessional on my part, as was my remark in the laboratory. Sincerely, Trevor S. Carter.

Unprofessional. It was a curious word to use in the circumstances. He stood by the window, watching summer darkness fall across the moor. It was not a reconciliation on either man's part. More of a truce, each agreeing to stay within his own lines.

Chapter Four

1

The bell in his brain, tolling an intermittent knell for some sixteen months now, was stilled by Grace's homecoming, in the first week of the Michaelmas term, 1926.

The intervals between its clamour had been lengthening all summer, not because he missed her the less, but because there was always so much to do, so many claims upon his attention, so that he saw the wisdom of Herries's insistence he stayed on as housemaster, and even enlarged his responsibilities by adding the Sunsetters to the Havelock roll.

Grace's return took priority over everything that September, when summer lingered on into autumn, and a record number of thirty-eight boys arrived, eight of them coming to Havelock's, but there were partings as well as greetings. He would miss Chad Boyer badly. Of all the links he had formed with boys who had come and gone in the last eight-and-a-half years, Boyer had forged the strongest, and would be the most difficult to replace after he went up to University to read modern history and economics.

"I'll keep in touch, I promise," he said, when he marched off to summer camp at Tidworth Pennings with the Corps, on the final day of term, and David hoped he would. It might prove useful to get Boyer's private opinion of any innovation he had in mind. Having spent nine years on the moor, Boyer was as dedicated a Bamfeldian as Herries himself.

Helen Arscott, the businesslike Second Form mistress who had replaced Julia Darbyshire, took a fancy to Grace on sight and Grace responded, perhaps because, in the child's mind, her manner matched so many 'let's-brush-our-teeth' sisters and nurses of the last sixteen months. She still limped, and was under orders to persist in her exercises, but the surgeon's prophecy regarding her facial scars was fulfilled. They were hardly noticeable now, no more than a flattish area of tissue, spreading from below the eye to the sweep of the chin—Beth's chin, as he noted, swinging her joyously out of the station taxi and hugging her close.

Ellie Herries wept, as he knew she would, and they all trooped in procession up to his old bachelor quarters, overlooking the forecourt, where Grace was ceremoniously installed. She seemed a little overawed by her reception, but soon settled down under the sharp, no-favourites eye of Helen Arscott, who promised her seven hours' tuition each week.

David found the child's gravity very appealing. Months of dragging pain, and a longer period of convalescence, had left its mark on her, but in a way that one soon came to accept. Somewhere along the line she had acquired the patience of a serious-minded child twice her age, offset by a rather comic dignity, that showed in her determination to do everything for herself and break out of the invalid cocoon. Her approach to him was almost maternal, as though someone had coached her in the need to fill the gap in his life and sometimes, watching her slyly, David was reminded of a string of Victorian heroines: Beth in *Little Women*, Little Nell, in *The Old Curiosity Shop* and Eva, in *Uncle Tom's Cabin*. She was going to be pretty, despite the terrible mauling she had received in the accident. Her hair was a glossy black, curling at the ends, and her eyes as large and brown as Beth's, with identical high cheekbones and dimpled chin. And yet, in another way, she reminded him of his Rhondda nieces, for she was Celt in complexion and build. She had a Celtic imagination too, with a whiff of Beth's Cockney humour added, not the irreverent humour of her mother, but what Herries called 'the stand-off-and-chuckle' brand. "That's the Welsh in her," he added. "You Taffys can laugh at yourselves more than most, even when you're singing."

In no time at all she became a tremendous favourite with the boys. Paddy McNaughton, the Irish boy, was a friend of hers because he treated her as an equal, but of all the boys in Havelock's she seemed to favour Winterbourne, perhaps because Winterbourne took such an active interest in her, dating from a premonition in the cave beside Chetsford Water, that she had survived and needed help.

The first time David became aware of this relationship was one evening when he looked in to say goodnight, and found her sitting up in her dressing gown, sketching. She was hard at work on a crayon sketch of old Hodge's pony, the one selected for her first riding lessons in their cottage days. The background of the drawing was recognisably Hodge's broken-down stables, on the eastern shoulder of Stone Cross Hill, and he exclaimed, "Hi, where did you learn to draw as well as that? In hospital?"

No, she told him, shading industriously, Winterbourne had taught her one wet afternoon, when a house match was cancelled and he called in search of David.

"I always thought Spats buried his talents. He's very good at it but I got the impression he thinks it's something a boy shouldn't do at a place like this."

"I think that's silly," Grace said, "for he ought to be proud of it. I would be, if I was a genius like him."

"Well, he's got a genius for teaching," David said, and later sought out Winterbourne, thanking him for giving the child a new interest, for time hung heavily on her hands when everyone was in class. Winterbourne said, unexpectedly, "But she's got a gift, sir. I saw that at once. She sees all the stronger lines in her head, before she starts scribbling, the way all kids do. Er . . . could I make a suggestion, sir?"

"Of course."

"Get her a really good box of paints, an old easel, and some of this paper, sir. She'll never be bored then and she'll teach herself far more than I could teach her." He produced a roll of stiff cartridge paper from his desk and David noted that its sticker bore the name of a Challacombe stationer. "It comes in largish blocks, sir, but be sure and get Marker to sell you a professional watercolourist's outfit. Don't tell him it's for a little girl or he'll fob you off with rubbish."

"I've got a better idea," David said. "How much would such an outfit cost, together with the paper?"

"Oh, around fifty bob, sir."

"Well, here's three pounds. When you go into Challacombe, for the match on Saturday, buy it for me. If there's an easel small enough for her to cope with order that too. Would you do that?"

"I'd like to, sir." And then, shyly, looking over David's shoulder in that self-contained way David had noticed the day he got to know the boy out on the moor, "She seems bonnie enough now, sir. Will she . . . grow out of that limp?"

"I rather doubt it, Spats. It'll certainly become less pronounced but it'll always show."

"Does she mind it all that much, sir?"

Did she? He had no idea as yet but he imagined she might come to mind it as time went on, and she mixed with other girls at school. "I just can't say, Spats. She's intelligent enough to learn to live with it. More than that who can tell?"

Winterbourne said, "Would you mind if I spent a bit of time working with her when she gets her kit? You can't teach anyone painting, sir, but well . . . I think she's a real tonic, and that's a fact! I mean, most kids that something as bad as that had happened to would be floored, wouldn't they? Or the smart ones would start trading on it."

Not for the first time he found Winterbourne an uncomfortably perceptive boy but it was clear that Grace had struck some chord in him. On the following Saturday evening he appeared with an impressive-looking paint-box, ten blocks of paper and an easel. "I've paid for the easel, sir, and I'd like very much to make her a present of it. I left the blackboard behind. She'll see more than enough blackboards round here, won't she, sir?"

It was the first time that he had ever heard Winterbourne make the smallest joke, so he let him pay the extra and give Grace another lesson before prep. He thought, seeing their heads draw together over the paper, "She's got her mother's way with men. I wonder how her sister would have turned out? Would she have been a contrast, in spite of them being twins?" It was odd, his memories of Beth were sharp and clear but he was finding it difficult to remember anything distinctive about the child who had died with her. Somehow he had never seen them as two people, not since the moment Stratton-Forbes had panted up to the long-jump pit, shouting news of their arrival and qualifying on the spot for the nickname, 'Nun'. And thinking of Stratton-Forbes,

David made a decision he had been putting off for days, the choice of a head house prefect to replace Boyer.

Stratton-Forbes was no longer the smallest boy in the school. He was now the fattest; a droll, cumbersome figure with all that flesh, and the squint they had never been able to correct. He was nearly eighteen now, and the most promising Latin scholar Bamfylde had ever had, according to Barnaby. The classics master used him as a junior master in the Second and Third Forms whenever he could be spared from his effortless studies. But despite his reputation as a swot, despite his flabbiness and malevolent squint, Nun was well-liked, enjoying that gratuitous popularity often granted a butt. Far too overweight for any active game, he had brought his impressive powers of concentration to bear on musketry, down at the long range, and had twice captained Bamfylde's team at Bisley. The squint, that had so worried his parents when he first arrived at Bamfylde, did not inhibit him as a marksman. Discarding unnecessary glasses he practised shooting with the single-minded fanaticism he brought to the classics and was soon the pride and joy of his fellow enthusiasts. For all that David hesitated to appoint him Boyer's successor. Popular or not, he was still a butt, even with Lower School boys, and a job of that kind sometimes demanded a strong hand.

He took his problem to Howarth, an acknowledged expert in these fields, who decreed that the appointment be made without delay. "A boy as self-disciplined as that will suit your book admirably," he said. "Stands to reason, doesn't it? Anything Stratton-Forbes sets his hand to he accomplishes and the same will apply to any responsibility he's given. He'll keep far better order than Boyer, you see if he doesn't! Besides, I hear he's staying on for extra cramming, and that'll save you the trouble of replacing him next year."

David took his advice and Stratton-Forbes was appointed head of the house, proving his worth at once, for he came to David within the week with a problem that a less conscientious boy would have shelved.

It concerned the perennial nuisance of bed-wetters in the Junior dormitory, where Havelock's had two, Lowther Minor and Grindling. Persistent bed-wetters were not uncommon and all the usual expedients were resorted to, but with the pair berthed side by side at the far end of the dormitory the problem was seemingly aggravated.

Stratton-Forbes appeared in David's study one night looking more than usually serious. Not being given to finesse he went straight to the point. "It's about Lowther Minor and Grindling, sir. I think something will have to be done before one of the others writes home on the subject."

"Why on earth should they do that?" asked David, innocently, and Nun said, without a flicker of a smile, "They are calling the space between their beds the Hellishponk, sir!" and David, turning away, muttered, "Ask a damn silly question . . ." But there was nothing funny about it to the boys concerned, as he well knew, "Tell them to come and have a talk with me in the morning," he said. "Lowther before morning school, Grindling immediately after, but Nun . . ."

"Sir?"

"Let 'em know in advance I'm taking the medical approach. I don't want either of them upset. Do you think you could manage that?"

"Well, in a way I already have, sir. I read it up, and then asked around a bit."

"*You read it up?* Bed-wetting? Where?"

"There's a book in the library that goes into it very fully, sir. I don't know how it got there and it isn't catalogued, but it's there, sir. It's in my study now."

He looked at Stratton-Forbes with reverence. "Drop it in on your way to bed, will you? What conclusions did you reach, if any?"

"Well, sir, it's generally recognised now as a psychological problem. In most cases, that is. There were quite a few words I had to look up in a medical encyclopaedia, but I decided that both our cases come under the heading of emotional stress, sir."

"They do?"

"Yes, sir. In Lowther's case it's the old story of divorced parents, but in Grindling's case it's pure funk, sir, this being his first term. I daresay we could iron them out in time but it might be as well to check up with Dr. Willoughby first, wouldn't you say, sir?"

"It would indeed, Nun, and I'm uncommonly obliged to you for the research. On second thoughts, don't mention the matter to either of them. I'll read that book myself, and check up with the doctor in case we go off on a wrong tack."

"Yes, sir," and Stratton-Forbes left, with the polite unconcern of a gardener who had been discussing early tomatoes with an attentive but ill-informed employer.

He read the book and had a long telephone conversation with Willoughby on the subject, after which he sent for Lowther's elder brother, currently one of the bloods in the Upper Fifth. Lowther Major, vice-captain of the Bamfylde First Fifteen, was aggrieved when David broached the subject. He said, dismally, "The kid's been that way for long enough, sir. It's a frightful bore, isn't it? I mean, it lets a fellow down, wouldn't you say?"

"I didn't bring you in here to cry on my shoulder, Lowther. What's behind it? When did it start?"

"When? Well, about the time the pater took himself off, sir. The kid was about ten then."

"Can't you be more explicit? I don't want to pry into family matters but it's very important to your brother. If we can do anything to help it might save him a lot of grief."

"Well, sir, he was closer to pater than me. They were both a bit—well, highbrow, sir. My Governor is nuts on Shakespeare and that kind of stuff. He used to take the kid to the theatre a lot."

He implied, somehow, that father and brother had conspired to go to the devil in consort. "Then the pater got a job abroad and breezed off to Canada and the kid started brooding. Mater seemed to think that coming here early would take him out of it."

It struck him then, by no means for the first time, how damnably unfair life could be, how effortlessly cheerful oafs like Lowther Major could coast along when weaker, more sensitive vessels were caught up in cross-currents and thrown about like matchboxes. He said, "Look, Lowther, you ought to help out in this. That kid needs encouragement and you're the best one to give it. I'll do what I can, and so will Stratton-Forbes, but you've got to back us up, do you understand?"

Lowther Major blinked, "Well . . . yes, sir, but how exactly? I mean—well—he's seen doctors before and we all assumed it was just a leaking tap—a weak bladder, sir."

"Dammit, boy, it's very little to do with his bladder! Once he gets over the shock of being separated from the one person in life who meant anything to him, he'll stop wetting his bed. You can take my word for it. And Doc Willoughby's. In the meantime look out for him, spend time with him if necessary and that's an order."

"Yes, sir," and Lowther Major left, about as puzzled as he could be.

Grindling was something else again. David had him in after Willoughby, on the excuse of a routine chest examination, had had a talk with the boy.

"What did the doctor have to say, Grindling? You're not going into a decline, are you?"

"He said I've got an above-average expansion, sir. He had me go up the ropes in the gym and I did it in nine seconds."

"Nine seconds, eh? That's very lively. Keen on gym?"

"Yes, sir."

"What else are you good at?"

The boy hesitated. "I like playing the piano, sir. I've started with Mr. Gibbs, but it's difficult to practise properly here. I mean, there's generally a queue for the music rooms, and you don't get time off as it's an extra subject."

"Oh, I think we could fix that if you're really keen, Grindling. Would you like me to have a word with Mr. Gibbs?"

The boy relaxed a little. His head went up and his mouth, pressed in a nervous, downward curve, straightened out. "I'd like that very much, sir."

"Then take it as done. How's your voice? Can you sing?"

"A little, sir. My father . . ." and he stopped, his crestfallen expression returning.

"Well, what about your father?"

"He's a pro . . . professional, sir. He's singing baritone, in an opera company touring South Africa, sir."

"How would you like a tryout for this year's opera? We're doing *Pinafore* again."

The boy hesitated. "I'm still treble, sir."

"Half the chorus is treble. The head likes to rope in everyone he can get for the girls. It's a lot of fun, believe me."

"Very well, sir."

He forced himself to come to the point. "Look here, Grindling. I know you're finding it a bit difficult to settle but there's nothing odd about that. Most first-termers do. Did myself, for that matter, but it soon wears off, once you start taking part in things. As to that bed-wetting business, the important thing is to stop worrying about it. A lot of kids your age go through that stage, for one reason or another and you'll shake it off in no time, providing you don't see it as—well, put it like this—as a permanent handicap you're lumbered with, like a wooden leg. Do you follow me?"

"I . . . I'm not sure, sir."

"Well, think it over and if you have any other problems, go to Stratton-Forbes about them. That's what he's there for. And if he can't sort 'em out, I can."

"Thank you, sir," and Grindling slipped out, glad to be gone no doubt but very relieved, David thought, judging by the way he tackled the stairs and dived across the quad to scrutinise the day's parcel list. The campaign must have had some effect for around about half-term Stratton-Forbes reported a great improvement in both cases, even though, from then on, the far end of the junior dormitory was stuck with the name, 'Hellishponk'.

2

The new boys' tea, presided over by Grace, was a tremendous success, reminding David a little of a stylised gavotte, with everyone present on their dignity. His own thirtieth birthday fell on St. Luke's Day, so Grace decided to combine tea and party in one event, and decorated the cake baked for him by Ellie Herries with thirty candles.

She went about her preparations so seriously that David, fearing an anti-climax, summoned all the new boys an hour or so in advance and laid his cards on the table.

"Now, listen here, you chaps. This tea is an old custom at Havelock's, but it's very special this year and I'll tell you why. My daughter, Grace, just out of hospital, remembers her mother giving these teas, and although she's only six, and you might find it all a bit solemn, you'll have to play along, you understand?"

Bristow, boldest of the new boys, spoke for all of them. "How do you mean, sir? Help her pour out?"

"No, by George! Quite the reverse. Let *her* do the pouring. *And* all the passing round. That's her job as hostess. Just keep the conversation going and don't laugh, whatever you do. If she thinks any of you find it funny she'll be very upset and I don't want her upset. She's been through a very rotten time." He hesitated a moment, then took the plunge. "Do any of you here know what happened a year or so ago?"

Most of them looked blank but Bristow spoke up again. "I do, sir. There was a motor-smash on Quarry Hill and Mrs. Powlett-Jones was killed, sir."

"My wife and Grace's little sister. Grace was badly knocked about but she pulled through."

They stared at him with embarrassed sympathy. Then Grindling said, with an effort, "Er . . . just leave it to us, sir."

And he did, to such good effect that, ever afterwards, he had a particularly soft spot for the Michaelmas intake of 1926. Grace sat at the head of the table and poured, looking like a tiny grandmother entertaining a flock of grandchildren on their very best behaviour, but then, Bristow, already qualifying for the role of Second Form humourist, made everybody laugh describing an adventure he had in Boulogne that summer, when he had lost his way and talked French to a gendarme. Then Grindling played 'Autumn Ride' on the upright piano Mrs. Ferguson had left behind, and made them laugh again by declaring that the piano needed tuning, and Grace limped around the circle with a bowl of crystallised fruits and everybody seemed genuinely reluctant to leave when the prep bell went. Bristow, he noted with approval, bowed from the waist in Grace's direction, and thanked her very politely on everyone's behalf, and they all went off with a slice of his cake wrapped in paper napkins.

"That was absolutely splendid!" he said, as soon as the door had closed on them. "You did it just as well as your mother. I'm only sorry Winterbourne wasn't here to see it," and she replied, mildly, "Oh, he would have felt silly among boys that age." She said it as if Winterbourne would soon be up here celebrating his own thirtieth birthday.

* * *

So the days sped along, to half-term and onward to the Michaelmas climax, the opera, staged in Big Hall two days before break-up. A rather sad occasion this, for it was Algy Herries's last. "Twenty-three in a row!" he crowed, as they were wedging him into his First Lord's uniform. "That's a run, if you like! Only D'Oyly Carte can equal that and this role is my second favourite. I've always had a weakness for Ko-Ko."

David, sitting in as understudy for Rapper Gibbs at dress-rehearsal, had a surprise in store for him, however. At the given moment in marched four marines, sent to their stations down-stage by a piping command of a midshipman, and it was as well he wasn't accompanying at the time for, from under the band of the flat white cap, peeped Grace's dark curls and the try-it-on-the-dog-audience cheered, presumably all in on the secret. Young Masters, it seems, cast as the midshipman, had gone down with a feverish cold, and Algy, taking Helen Arscott into his confidence, had coached Grace to take his place. She had no words to learn, other than the command, and among all those white bell-bottomed trousers her limp did not show. But David had a bad moment, remembering Beth as Buttercup, in 1921, and it took him a minute or two to recover. It was reckoned a great joke to play on a member of the staff and Algy, apologising afterwards, said, "I daresay it gave you a jolt but it tickled her no end and the audience too, as you noticed. She's a great favourite, they tell me."

She was too, more of a favourite than even Algy knew, for be-sides having Winterbourne to teach her to paint in watercolours, she now had 'Sax' Hoskins teaching her the Charleston and the lyrics of all the dance hits that were crossing the Atlantic in a flood just then.

'Sax' was the current Bamfylde jazz enthusiast. His five-piece band played at all the weekly dances, and there were even rumours that he would begin training as a professional when he left. He was a noisy, uninhibited chap, with no other interests or attain-ments to his credit, and approached David one day after seeing Grace at her exercises.

"Excuse me, sir. It might sound daft but couldn't we make that drill of hers a bit more interesting? I mean, if she is supposed to exercise the muscles in that way, wouldn't dancing help?"

"Dancing? What kind of dancing? Folk dancing of some kind?", but at this Hoskins looked outraged. "Good Lord, *no*, sir! *Real* dancing. Modern steps. The foxtrot, two-step and waltz. Even the Charleston, if she's up to it!"

David said, chuckling, "Well, I don't see why not, so long as she doesn't overdo it," and Hoskins said, "I'll watch that, sir. Af-ter all, she'll want to learn ballroom dancing in a year or so. They all do, sir. My kid sisters are absolute dabsters, and they're not much older than Grace."

So it was done. Hoskins carried his portable gramophone up to the living-room at Havelock's and put on a number he described as 'just the job'. It was called 'Crazy Words, Crazy Tune', and David looked on as Hoskins taught Grace how to shuffle her feet this way and that, and cross over, and perform all manner of ritual hand gestures while doing it. She seemed extraordinarily quick to catch on so that Hoskins pronounced her 'a natural'. "She's quicker on the uptake than my sister Margaret," he said, "and Miggs won a box of chocolates for shimmying at a concert."

One way and another it was a memorable, rollicking term, and for once he was sorry to see them depart six days before Christmas when, in the period between first light and nine a.m. the place emptied and then, magically, was still.

The next day the station taxi called to take him and Grace to catch the Bristol train for Wales, where they were spending Christmas, this being 'Granmam Powlett-Jones's turn'. Some of the Sunsetters helped load their bags and as the battered old Belsize ran over the frosty surface of the east drive, and swung left to pass along under the playing-field hedge, Grace voiced a thought that had occurred to him while he was making the early morning tea. She said, "It'll be fun seeing Granmam and Auntie Gwynneth, and Uncle Ewart and Auntie Megan. But I'll miss everyone here, won't you, Daddy?"

"Well, let's say I shall by the day they all descend on us again," he said. "Let's see, when *is* that exactly?"

"January the nineteenth," she said. " 'New boys arrive the day before'."

You could never catch Grace out on any Bamfylde milestones.

PART

FOUR

Ave et Cave

Chapter One

Few among those acclimatised to Howarth's glacial classroom expression would have spotted anything amiss with him that particular morning, some halfway through the tight-rope term, that is to say, towards the end of February. But David, who looked upon the dry old stick as friend and counsellor, noticed it as he helped himself to his bacon and eggs from the side-table in Big Hall.

It was not that Howarth looked more disdainful than usual, or more likely to erupt in the quiet, deadly way he reserved for the fool and the chatterer. He picked at his food with his customary air of distaste, and crumbled his toast with the air of a man disposing of an unpopular relative's ashes, and all the time kept his deceptively neutral gaze on his customary focal point, namely the kitchen hatch at the far end of the hall. Yet David noted something particularly wary about him, and something supremely world-weary too, as he raised his coffee cup and sipped as though sampling hemlock, then set it down again, noiselessly, for Howarth hated racket above all Bamfylde's shortcomings.

David's eyes rested for a moment on a buff, typewritten envelope, neatly slit, lying at Howarth's elbow and presently, speaking very quietly, he said, "Not bad news, I hope?" Howarth's bleak gaze turned on him and he saw that he was right. The face of the man under its frigid mask was deeply troubled as he muttered, "Doing anything tonight?" and when David shook his head, "Come up and take a gill then. After prep bell," and got up abruptly, striding down the centre aisle between the massed tables and out. He took the letter with him but left a barely tasted cup of coffee and most of his rasher and toast.

He was in command of himself again several hours later, and had the tray of drinks and his usual box of Gold Flake set before the fire when David joined him at eight. "Must have given myself away. Wouldn't have said so but evidently I did."

"Not to anyone but me. What's up?"

Howarth got up and crossed to his tidy desk, opening a drawer and taking out a large silver-framed photograph, of the type usually kept on a piano or mantelshelf. It was a studio photograph of a girl about twenty, wearing a style of dress popular about twenty-five years before. The features were very delicate and the small, slightly prim mouth sensitive. The hair was fluffy and looked very fair. David studied the photograph, recalling a chilly confidence on the bench under the fives court more than eight years before, when Howarth had mentioned the girl who turned him down for a stockbroker. He had never referred to her since and was not a man one questioned on personal matters.

"Was the letter from her?"

"It was about her. She died, six months ago."

"You didn't know?"

He said, petulantly, "I haven't kept in touch with her. She had a son nearly as old as you!"

It was curious how certain David was of the closeness of the link between news from some matter-of-fact executor, and Howarth's ravaged look at breakfast and somehow the circumstances were uncharacteristic. He had always thought of Howarth as a man proof against deep feelings. Yet here was evidence of another kind. Clearly there had never been any other woman for Ian Howarth.

"I'm sorry. It's hit you pretty badly."

"Like the very devil, but don't ask me why. Haven't set eyes on Amy Crispin since the spring of nineteen-hundred and six."

"You keep her photograph handy."

"Out of sight. You've never seen it before, and nobody else ever will. Not until they poke around my things and wonder what the hell to do with it. Keep me company, P.J.," and he poured two more pink gins, larger ones than usual.

David said, carefully, "You want to talk about her?"

"I don't know. There isn't a day when I haven't thought about her. But talking, that's different. As you must know to your cost."

It drew them closer somehow. Not much but a little. Himself nursing a half-healed wound, with its unpredictable ache and Howarth, outwardly the eternal bachelor, mourning a certain Amy Crispin, lost to him a quarter-century ago. Howarth said, at length, "What the devil can it be to you, anyway; a man at the receiving end of a real tragedy?"

"Beth and I had six years together. They were very happy years."

"That's a point of view," Howarth said. "I wonder if Amy or I could have said the same."

"Were you engaged?"

"For more than a year. Do you know what they paid an usher in '03? And you think we're underpaid now! I was getting a hundred and thirty a year at Beckworth Grammar School, and I was twenty-four. It was late to change horses and in any case I had no mind to, then or later. If I have a vocation it's teaching. Like you, my friend."

"I daresay she could have waited."

"For how long? Five years? Ten? She wanted children and went elsewhere for them. I never held that against her."

"Was she happy?"

"I always assumed so." He sat thinking a moment and then, with a grunt expressing protest at his own sentimentality, he took out the letter and passed it across the table. It was the lawyer's letter, but its content was arresting, perhaps on that account. Howarth had been left the sum of eight thousand pounds by the late Amy Hodgson, née Crispin, together with his pick of the library at a house called Clearwood Court in Sussex. There was a brief footnote to the letter. Seemingly in an agony of embarrassment the lawyer had added, in his own handwriting,

"I feel it my duty to quote the relevant passage from my client's codicil, relating to the bequest, viz. 'To Ian Howarth, whom I remember with the greatest affection'."

It explained, David thought, so many things. Not merely Howarth's bleak and hurried exit from the dining-hall that morning but the threads that made up his entire personality. It was as though, somewhere around 1903, eleven years before the world went raving mad, a young, love-sick schoolteacher in a provincial grammar school, had sentenced himself to self-petrification, a penance that had, in the end, transformed him from an eager, dedicated youngster, into a wry, ironic husk of a man, racing towards middle age and the ultimate pedantry that awaits all but a very few of the profession. It was a personal tragedy, in its way as much a tragedy as the loss of Howarth's generation in Flanders, and yet, as David acknowledged at once, the petrification had never been wholly achieved. Somewhere, under the ice of the simulated personality, the original Howarth was still there, trying hard to get out, and once in a while almost succeeding.

"Eight thousand pounds! That's a small fortune. What will you do now?"

"What should I do but leave it in the bank? Money never interested me. If it had, I shouldn't be here, any more than you."

"But, damn it, man, you could retire now if you cared to. Properly invested that would provide an income double the pension you can expect."

"I don't give a damn about the money," Howarth said, savagely. "It's discovering, this late, that I could have married the girl if I'd had the nerve. You can't buy back the fruits of your own folly and cowardice with eight thousand pounds! She must have been miserable with that bloody stockbroker!"

He took another drink and his gin began to mellow him. "Let this be a lesson to you, P.J.! Get married again if you can. Don't play the little gentleman, as I did."

"I'm not looking for two lucky breaks, Howarth. Most men don't get one. You didn't, it seems."

"Well, then, what will you do with your life? Don't fancy you can live celibate, my friend. Or not without corroding your personality. Some could, but you aren't made that way and it's my opinion you know it."

He wondered if this was true. In the last twenty-two months he had not been aware of physical yearnings, of the kind Beth had satisfied so gaily and so graciously, but who could say whether this was permanent? A time might be approaching when enforced celibacy developed an itch, to be scratched at all costs, or bottled up until it began to warp him, the way he had noticed among ageing bachelors and long-term widowers. In the strictly personal sense the prospect of holding a stranger in his arms was vaguely repugnant to him but would it always be so? He was only just thirty; all things being equal he had another forty years ahead of him. Curiosity nagged him, encouraging him to risk a formidable snub. "What did you do about women all these years, Howarth?" and Howarth, draining his gin, got up and crossed over to his bureau again where he extracted another photograph. From a different drawer, David noticed. It was an enlarged snapshot, featuring a very different woman, a big, blowsy, cheerful girl about twenty-five, with bold eyes and a wide mouth daubed with too much lipstick.

"I know her, don't I?"

"You should. She keeps the Unicorn, over in Challacombe. She didn't when that photograph was taken. It was partly my money that set her up. Before that she was the barmaid for ten years."

"You still call on her?"

"No, but I could do. She's a generous soul. She probably wouldn't charge me nowadays."

On the face of it it seemed incredible. Howarth, the dry, irascible symbol of rectitude, utterly dedicated to his job, feared and respected by almost everyone at Bamfylde, slipping away to a chintzy bedroom at the Unicorn every now and again and paying cash down for a few moments' frolic. It occurred to him that Howarth was tacitly offering him solace if he needed it. Not in a spirit of leeriness, like two men drinking and talking women in a pub, but as a sincere gesture of friendship.

He said, deciding to make a joke of it, "Well, thanks for the tip. I'll bear it in mind," but Howarth replied seriously, "There's something more important you should think about. If you mean to spend your life here, and not move on if you get the chance, then it's time you began planning, my friend. Herries will be gone in a few months, and so far there's been no serious attempt on the part of those idiots on the Board to replace him. Why not put in for the job?"

"For Algy's job? As headmaster here? You can't be serious, man."

"I assure you I am. You've taken to this place and it seems

to have taken to you. The most hopeful sections of it, that is. Well then, since you've committed yourself to soldier on to the point of no return why not try to ensure it's run your way, and not the way of some other officious new broom. Replacing Herries won't be easy. Whatever this place is it's his creation and he's stayed too long to give it flexibility. Someone who had worked under him would have a flying start."

"But good God, Howarth, you're senior to me by twenty years. Why not you?"

"Can you see me assuring mothers that their little darlings won't be corrupted by the writing on the lavatory walls? Or that Bloggs Minor, solid from the neck up, is a future Cabinet Minister? Don't talk bloody nonsense, P.J."

"Well, then, Carter, although God forbid. Or Barnaby, for that matter. He was upset when Algy gave me Havelock's after Ferguson died."

"Barnaby's a pleasant chap but he isn't headmaster material. He's too amiable and too close to his subject. Administration and real authority would send him out of his mind. How does communion with the Ancients qualify a man for the job of modernising this place, without converting it into a factory, of the kind Carter and his ilk regard as essential? And speaking of Carter, he's already backing himself for the job."

David had heard a vague rumour to this effect but Howarth's positive statement shocked him into reassessing his own future. He could never work here under Carter, or anyone like Carter. Their methods, theory and practice were too opposed, and suddenly what had so far proved a fireside chat with an intimate ran him into an impasse. He said, sullenly, "If Carter was appointed I'd resign. I wouldn't even wait until I found another billet."

"You don't have to tell me that. Well?"

"What are his chances?"

"Only fair. He's got Alderman Blunt in his pocket, and can probably win over one or two of the fence-squatters, men too timid to jump down until Herries is out of the way."

"Suppose he got it, what would be his line?"

"Overnight modernisation, with the emphasis on science and technical education. New labs, I daresay, and men like yourself replaced with nonentities. History and the classics don't cut much ice with Carter."

"But Bamfylde isn't that kind of school."

"A school is what a headmaster makes it."

"But there are several Old Boys on the governing board. They wouldn't stand for a complete reversal of policy."

"They mightn't see it as that. Who knows? Maybe Carter is right. This is 1927, and Herries's conception of the place is 1907, or earlier. Don't forget he was a year old when Prince Albert died."

"Bamfylde could be brought up to date without making a bonfire of everything Algy brought to it."

"By someone like you, someone with imagination plus drive. Not otherwise."

"I've been here eight years, and I'm five years younger than the most junior headmaster in the country, discounting day-schools. What chance would I stand?"

"About the same chance as Carter. I'd say you were about even at the moment. It would mean canvassing, of course."

"You mean soliciting votes among the Governors?"

"In the nicest possible way."

"I don't think I could do that."

"You'd have to, old boy. And you jolly well would if it meant keeping Carter out. You could begin on Brigadier Cooper. He's very partial to you, I hear. Converted by that son of his, no doubt."

"Will Herries have any say in it?"

"Officially, no. Unofficially, quite a lot."

He sat pondering a moment, his thoughts centring on the likely reaction of both Brigadier Cooper, 'Warrior' as older Bamfeldians thought of him, and Algy Herries. Headmaster at thirty. Headmaster of Bamfylde. In authority over men like Howarth, old Bouncer Acton, Rapper Gibbs, Barnaby and even Carter if he didn't resign. It was preposterous and yet, if it meant a choice between him and Carter, he couldn't stand aside without a fight, even if it was only a token fight. He said, "I'll think about it. No more than that, Howarth," and then, with a slightly baffled expression, "You'd serve under me?"

Howarth permitted himself the luxury of one wintry smile. "What choice would I have, so long as I stayed on the job? I'm well past the point of no return. Besides, I daresay you'd need your Eminence Grise!"

Down in the quad the end-of-prep bell jangled. On its final, jarring notes, the hum of the manumitted rose to a subdued up-roar. David got up. "Thanks for the gin, Howarth. And thanks for your trust. I'll think about it, I really will."

In fact, he did rather more than think, broaching the matter to Brigadier Cooper when he saw him emerge from Algy's house one afternoon a week later.

Howarth must have been a shrewd judge of character. The Warrior was surprised but delighted, making no bones at all about his dislike of Carter or, for that matter, his apprehension con-cerning the appointment of anyone likely to change the style of the school. In fact, his extreme conservatism left David a little doubtful of his choice of patron. "We don't want a Clever Dick prancing about here with God knows how many damn silly modern theories," he growled. "All I ask of the place is to turn out chaps who can speak up, play up and look anyone straight in the eye. Some of the Governors have been naggin' poor old Algy for years. 'Get the scholarship level up and never mind Kipling's "If",' they kept telling him, but he never took a dam' bit of notice, bless him. He knew what he was about and kept the flag flying, didn't he? As to that feller Carter, he's not the type either. We used to regard chaps like him as oddities in my time here. Called 'em 'Stinks' and they were very small beer then, I assure you. Not say-ing we haven't got to watch the science side, mind you, but he'll do well enough right where he is for my money. Have a crack at it, young feller-me-lad. Why not? What have you got to lose?"

"My job, sir. I couldn't serve under Carter. We'd be after one another's scalps from the word go and no matter who won the school wouldn't."

It was a situation the Warrior obviously relished. He said, rub-bing his long nose with a nut-brown forefinger, "Tell you what you do. Leave the reccy to me. I'll sniff around and flush some-thing out before the next monthly meeting. Carter's application is in, and they're already whittling the first batch down. Nothing definite yet, of course. They'll leave it all to the last minute, if I know 'em. Wish to God I'd had a few of 'em under me in S.A. and Mespot."

He went off, growling to himself, the traditional Blimp and a Godsend to the cartoonists but still a man to be reckoned with. He had won his V.C. at the Modder River more than a quarter-century ago, and later served four sweltering years in Mesopotamia, Palestine and Salonika when he was recalled from retirement. David had intended asking his advice on approaching Algy if he hadn't marched off so abruptly. As it was, he decided to delay that until he got some idea of the amount of support he was likely to receive.

He did not see the brigadier again before the end of term but on the first day of the holidays the old chap wrote saying David could be sure of three votes, including his own. Three wasn't many out of a Governing body of eighteen, but it insured him against ignominy. The brigadier added that the short list was now almost complete, and that it included at least one headmaster, of a school roughly equivalent with Bamfylde. The passing of information, he supposed, was very unethical but Cooper was not a man to worry on that score. It had the effect, however, of preventing David from confiding in Algy. The approach would now have to come from him, as soon as the news leaked that he had applied. In the interval David took Grace off to London to spend the Easter holiday with Beth's people. It would provide a change for her, Beth's sisters having daughters about her age. "She'll grow into a boy if I don't change her diet now and again," he told Ellie. It did not occur to him, as the Taunton–Paddington express pulled in, that he had reached a point where he needed a change himself.

2

He had almost outgrown cities and city amusements but he liked to visit the theatre when the opportunity offered and with Grace in good company took himself off to the West End one afternoon to see a matinée at the Globe, in Shaftesbury Avenue. The play did not impress him overmuch and he was emerging into the crowd of teatime shoppers, heading for the Coventry Street Corner House, when he heard his name called and turned to see a smartly dressed woman waving excitedly in his direction. At first he could not be sure and hesitated but then, with pleasurable surprise, he identified her as Julia Darbyshire, who came up very much out of breath, saying, "You always were one for stepping out! I saw you in the foyer and almost lost you . . ." then stood back, letting her glance run over him as she said, "You're looking well, P.J.! Better than I expected. Wuthering Heights must agree with you. All I really wanted to say was . . . well . . . how terribly sorry I was when I heard what happened, and how many times I thought about writing but didn't. Why? Does one ever know whether letters of that kind are welcome?"

She stopped, looking a little confused, so he came to her rescue, telling her he would have liked to have heard from her, and was pleased to see her looking so pretty and cheerful. She coloured at this, but then smiled and said things had taken a turn for the better. Her husband had died a year ago and it would be hypocrisy to regard that as anything but a mercy. Later she had landed a job as manageress of a fashionable teashop, in Old Bond Street. "The pay is a lot better than Bamfylde's," she added, "and the waitresses are a nice bunch of kids. I get a free hand running it and every now and again celebrities drop in and that gives me the illusion I'm back in the swim. The wide open spaces were never for me, P.J. I was an idiot to ever imagine they were. As for Arthur, well, to be frank, I was relieved when he died under an operation. Glad for both of us but especially for him. There was absolutely no hope and he was never free from pain. Your loss was very different. I couldn't get you out of my mind, and you've no idea how glad I am to see you looking fit and . . . well, more or less yourself again. Not surprised, though. You always had plenty of guts."

"Don't let's stand here," he said, embarrassed by her directness. "I was popping into Lyons' for tea. Won't you join me?" and she said she would be delighted for it was her day off, and everybody she knew in town was at work. He said, as soon as the Nippy had taken their order, "How did you come to hear about it, Mrs. Darbyshire? I had no idea you kept in touch with Bamfylde. I always had the impression you were thankful to scrape the mud from your shoes."

"Keith Blades wrote. Don't worry. Just once, and only about you." She hesitated a moment. "You see, I told him about your part in it. I thought I owed it to both of you, but don't worry, he's a very discreet boy. I'm quite sure he's never mentioned it to anyone and probably won't until he finds a nice girl, marries her, and lays his murky past on the table, the way men do once they've sown their wild oats."

He had always respected her for her courage and integrity but now he found himself enjoying her company, partly as a fellow traveller but also as a smart and attractive woman, who had faced her troubles and side-stepped self-pity. Everything about her indicated a cheerful ability to get up and try again, and again after that if need be. She had taken great pains with her appearance, and although he knew she was the same age as himself she could have passed for a woman in her early twenties. She had what he thought of as 'the West End look', and her forthrightness was much at odds with the Julia Darbyshire he had confronted in that shabby little sitting-room above the quad. He could see now how entirely possible it was that an imaginative boy like Blades had persuaded himself that he was madly in love with her. She had charm and high spirits, as well as good looks, but more than enough femininity to captivate an adolescent romantic, especially one isolated in a male community. Algy, he thought, should have had more sense than select her, even as a stop-gap. There was magnetism here, and promise too. It was a wonder there hadn't been a dozen boys mooning after her during her brief spell as Second Form mistress.

He told her the facts of the accident, then how he had succeeded in adjusting to it, partly on account of Grace's survival, partly because of the stimulus and comradeship offered by the staff and boys. He told her how the boys competed to spoil the kid, how Winterbourne was teaching her to paint, and Hoskins to dance. "It seemed to me I owed it to everybody to make the effort," he admitted. "It was like being at the receiving end of trench comradeship, with everyone in the unit reaching back to give you a hand. Does that sound fanciful?"

"Not from you it doesn't. I don't suppose I'm telling you anything you don't know when I say you're so *right* for that place. It wouldn't surprise me, thirty years from now, to hear you had spent your entire life down there, and enjoyed every moment of it, even your feud with Carter."

Her mention of Carter reminded him of their present rivalry and he was surprised to note how even the remote possibility of him replacing Herries excited her. "Why, that's perfectly splendid, P.J.! I can't think of anyone who would make a better job of it and the boys will be rooting for you. Is it likely? I mean, you're very young for the job, aren't you? Or they'll think so, won't they?"

"I'm only a few years younger than Carter," he said, "and he's applying. He's down there right now, canvassing like mad if I know him."

"Oh, they'll never give it to *him*," she said, so emphatically that he felt encouraged. "If it isn't you it will be a stranger, someone in his late forties, you see if it isn't. Would you be terribly disappointed?"

"No," he said, "as a matter of fact I think I'd be relieved, providing he was the right chap, of course, and didn't play merry hell with Algy's legacy. It's a very special kind of school, Mrs. Darbyshire. It's difficult to say why or how, but it *is*, you know. It's got so many of the good things about the old-style public school, a kind of steadiness, continuity, and a touch of genuine idealism, but it also has—how the devil can I put it?—post-war optimism, and a broadening of outlook that's been achieved in all kinds of ways since people got the war into perspective. Put it this way, it's a kind of launching platform for kids moving out into a world that's still doing precisely what you and I have been doing this last year or so."

"And what's that?" she asked, smiling.

"Licking our wounds, and preparing for another go. That's Algy's doing, of course. He's a bit of a genius really, especially when you consider he was born at a time when they were still hanging people in public and schools like Bamfylde were a cross between a gaol and a four-ale bar! We'll all miss him but we'll survive, given half a chance. Mind you, the setting has something to do with it. It's so . . . so permanent, so English if you like. But the best of England."

He broke off, laughing at his own enthusiasm, but she said, "Go on, P.J."

"Well, Algy and the surrounding countryside complement one another. There's Exmoor, looking just as it did when your tribe and mine were wearing skins and painting themselves blue, and there's the grab-your-girl-grab-your-cash world outside. And smack in the middle, like an adjudicator, is old Algy, doing a weighing-out act to make sure one doesn't swamp the other."

"That's a pocket sermon," she said, "with the smack of the Welsh about it, but then . . ." and she stopped, smiling.

"Well?"

"I was only going to say that every time you get enthusiastic about anything, I remember you're a Taffy who has decided to throw in his lot with the English. Do you ever regret doing it?"

"No," he said, chuckling. "The English have got their points. An ability to organise is one of 'em that we lack. The truth is I had my faith in the future handed back to me at Bamfylde. The place saved my sanity, so naturally I'm prejudiced."

She said, with conviction, "You're one of the sanest people I've ever met, P.J. You'd have steadied up somewhere but I see what you mean, nevertheless. Well, here's hoping those Governors see it too, and give you the chance you deserve. Why don't we drink to that somewhere? I might be the very first to wet the new headmaster's head."

They went out and she piloted him expertly through crowded side streets to a pub she knew, where they drank three gins and he listened to her for a change.

After leaving Bamfylde, she had gone to Southampton, taking an office job in a solicitor's to be near her husband. After his death she had been lucky enough to land the managerial job at the Old Bond Street teashop. It was an American firm, and paid above average for good executives. The owner, who spent half his time over here, was a genial middle-aged New Jerseyman called Sprockman—"Hiram Ulysses Sprockman, believe it or not," she told him, "and a real sweetie, in a ponderous, teddy-bear way. He takes me out to dinner sometimes, and even asks my advice on buying pictures and Regency furniture. He's a terrific Anglophile, all set on becoming a New England squire when he's tired of making money, but that won't be until he's in his dotage if I'm any judge. Once Arthur's estate was cleared I could afford a flat to myself in Camden Town. It's very handy and I've furnished it myself with pieces my mother-in-law left me." She paused a moment. "Look, why not come back and let me cook dinner for you? I'm far better at cooking than teaching."

"Let me buy you dinner in Soho," he suggested, but she shook her head. "Not on your life, P.J. Their menus look appetising but I've seen the inside of some of their kitchens and prefer to poison myself. Are they expecting you back early?"

"No," he said, excited at the prospect of being entertained by her. "Grace is sleeping out at her aunt's tonight and I said I'd be late back. I thought about taking in another show. The Aldwych, perhaps."

"Nothing worth seeing," she said, "and I've had a look at most of them. Come back to my place and let me cook you something. Time somebody fussed you a bit. The way your wife did when you'd been fussing over those boys all day. Or is that taking things too much for granted, P.J.?"

"Don't you believe it. I can't think of a better way of rounding off a very pleasant reunion."

*   *   *

She was better than her word. It was a long time since anyone had pampered him and she prepared a very appetising meal, carrying on a conversation with him through the door of the kitchen while he sat before the fire. She was much more relaxed in a house, reminding him more of Beth coping with the unpredictabilities of the cottage stove, but there was nothing of that kind here. Someone, Julia or her parents-in-law, had excellent taste. All the furniture was antique and well-cared for, each individual piece being the work of an eighteenth- or early nineteenth-century craftsman. There were one or two valuable paintings, among them a Chrome, and a display of Rockingham china in a china cabinet. The neighbourhood outside was rackety but the flat was in a cul-de-sac, backed by a high wall beyond which, she said, was a market, unused at this time of day.

After the meal he helped her wash up and she brought coffee into the big living-room, where he felt so relaxed that he had no inclination to leave and make his way via tube to Charing Cross. Here, on her own ground, she was very easy to talk to and when dusk fell outside, with an accompanying drizzle, she drew the curtains and came and sat beside him on the sofa, kicking off her shoes and shooting her legs towards the fire so that once again he had a sense of renewal, as if they had known one another intimately, had been separated for a long time, and met again under congenial circumstances.

He said, after praising her cooking, "This is the most enjoyable afternoon and evening I've spent since it fell on me, Julia," and as he said it he became sharply aware of her nearness and her easygoing approach to him ever since her initial hail encouraged him to take her hand. He would have thought he had outgrown his early shyness with women but he had not, or not entirely. When she turned her head he felt as young and inexperienced as young Blades must have done, and then, as though to explain away his impulsive gesture, he said, "I haven't touched a woman since it happened . . . was hardly aware of them again until lately."

"And now?"

"Now? I'd be a prize-hypocrite if I said I didn't want to kiss you, Julia."

She said, evenly, "I'd be a worse hypocrite if I didn't admit I was rather hoping you would," and took the initiative by kissing him, gently but assertively, as though she was experimenting, and he was encouraged to take her in his arms and kiss her properly, not as he recalled kissing Beth, on that last occasion he had held her in his arms the night after Winterbourne went missing, but as they had kissed in the earliest days of their association.

He was not disposed to let her go then and there was no occasion to, for she seemed content to stay with her head on his shoulder, looking into the shifting coals. They sat like that for what seemed to him a long time before she said, "Two years, David. It's a long time, for a man as lively and imaginative as you. Beth was a very affectionate girl, wasn't she?"

"Very," he told her, "from the very beginning. It's not that I haven't begun to think of women again, particularly in the last few weeks. Sometimes I had half a mind to go out and look for one. But with me . . . well, it sounds damnably stuffy, but there has to be a personal relationship of some kind. The fact is, I had very little experience with women before I married and it wasn't wholly on account of the war. Somehow a casual relationship, after Beth died that is, would have seemed . . . well . . . too damned clinical for my taste." He had to laugh at himself then, adding, "By God, I sound as pious as Skidmore, the parson's son, telling me why he wouldn't make the new boys' bow to Founder's statue in the quad."

He wondered if she would remember Skidmore but she made no comment and seemed, in fact, to be pondering memories of her own. Presently she said, "Listen, David, I'm going to take a big risk. Big, because I've got a hell of a lot of respect for you, and I wouldn't care to have you leave here with the wrong impression. If you hadn't said what you said just now it wouldn't have occurred to me but here it is, without a lot of fancy talk. You're very welcome to stay the night if it would help. I wasn't in love with

Arthur, not in the way you and your wife were in love. I didn't have time to discover whether or not we would have made a go of it after the war. Frankly I doubt it. I was very young then, and as full of silly ideas about love and marriage as most girls growing up with a war on. When we married Arthur was very much the extrovert, keen on games, and making a good impression on people who didn't matter. When he did come back he wasn't anything at all. Just a hulk, and that was that, for both of us."

"And since then?"

"Since then I haven't been Goody Two Shoes. I tried now and again, wanting very much to be a real woman, instead of something and nothing, the way it had to be all that time, but . . . well, nothing sparked. The few men I met wanted to use me, and I soon came to the conclusion that I would be using them, and that wasn't me, for roughly the same reasons as you held off."

"You mean it might be different with me?"

"I know it would be. You don't need me in particular but you need affection even more than I do, and that's saying a hell of a lot. Well, there it is, except that you can say 'Thanks very much but . . .' and walk right out of here, with no hard feelings."

He noticed then something that touched him deeply. Her voice was very level but the hand clasping his as his arm rested on her shoulder, shook in a way that was painfully familiar to him, the tremor betraying the careful flatness of her voice. He said, kissing her cropped hair, "I should like to stay very much, Julia. And I wasn't fishing for it, if you can believe that."

The hand stopped shaking, and she lifted her face to him, laughing like a girl. "You never went fishing in the whole of your life. You wouldn't know how. Give me five minutes," and she got up, turned off all but the centre light, and put the guard in front of the fire.

He gave her ten minutes, then went across to the bedroom and knocked. She was sitting up in bed, the pinkish light of the bedside lamp glowed on her white shoulders and neck, throwing a shadow across her full breasts in a way that made him catch his breath. He said, standing looking down at her, "Why did you get your hair shingled? You had lovely hair. It was one of your best features. The first thing I noticed about you."

"You didn't notice me at all until you convinced yourself I was seducing one of your ewe lambs."

"That's what you think. Well?"

"It was the fashion. Up here you have to stay in the fashion. It cost me a pang or two, until I got used to it. Shall I turn off this light?"

"No," he said, "not for a minute," and he sat on the edge of the bed, took her face between his hands and kissed her gently on the lips. He noticed aspects of her that seemed new to him, the clearness of skin, the vivid flecks in the grey eyes, the regularity and delicacy of her features that added up to a stillness and dignity that was singular and striking. There was character behind her prettiness, but warmth, too, and fleetingly he remembered his wife but without guilt.

She reached out and extinguished the bedside light and he undressed in the glow of the street lamp outside but when he laid himself down beside her and ran his hand across her breasts, she seemed to hesitate a second and said, turning to him, "You're sure, David . . . ?" and he said, impatiently, "I'm sure. We've both had more loneliness than anyone deserves," and then her arms went round him and she came to him not merely joyously but with a spontaneity that confirmed his guess about her desperate loneliness over the years. He said, when they were still, "You've been through as tough a time as me and learned more."

"Tough, David. But not as tough as yours."

"With me there was always someone around to lend a hand," and the admission had the effect of redoubling the tenderness he felt for her at that moment.

*   *   *

It was a bright day when he awoke to find her smiling down at him, with a breakfast tray resting on her forearm. She was wearing an Oriental dressing gown, embroidered with dragons and pagodas. "What time is it?" he asked, sitting up.

"Why should you care what time it is? That dreadful bell is out of earshot." She gave him the tray and sat on the bed. "God, how I hated that damned bell! I always thought of it as the equivalent of a prison siren," and he laughed, saying one got used to it in time.

"I don't think I would, not in a century. But then, you like a well-regulated life, don't you?"

He considered, stirring the excellent coffee she had brewed for him. "I suppose I do. I hadn't thought of it but I like predictability and you get plenty of that at a place like Bamfylde. Within a framework of chaos, of course."

"By God, they'll be fools if they don't grab you while they have the chance, Davy! Dr. Arnold, in the splendour of his youth! What more could they ask?"

"Arnold died getting on for a century ago," he said. "All his disciples are dead too, and I sometimes wonder if there's any place in the post-war world for their gospel."

She leaned back on her hands, relaxed and smiling. They might have been lovers for years instead of hours. "What exactly *was* that gospel? Was it the academic version of Victorian muscular Christianity?"

"No," he said, "that's only how the cynics think of it . . . Carter, and all the other modern pushers. It was more fundamental than that. Algy Herries both understood and practised it, and he laid it out for me, the first day I met him. The war was still on then."

"But what *was* it exactly?"

"In its day it was an entirely fresh approach to the word 'education'. Or a rediscovery, maybe. Two thousand five hundred years ago the Greeks had the golden key, but it was lost, somehow, when their civilisation crumbled. I suppose it concerned itself with a search for truth. Not simply truth about the universe but about us—ourselves. To see things and ourselves as they and we really are, not as fashionable trends and fashions project them, generation by generation. Get that across to kids in their formative years and there's hope for everybody. It always was important but now more than ever."

"Why now particularly?"

"You ask me that? After what the war did to you?"

"Then it's teaching the young how to learn from the mistakes of the past?"

"That's part of it, an important part, but you can't begin searching out truth until you know yourself, and getting to know yourself demands a reasonable amount of self-discipline."

She was laughing at him now but not in a way that he resented.

"You shouldn't have much difficulty in that respect, Davy."

"As much as anyone else. That's why professionals have to lean heavily on a system, symbolised by that bell you hated. There's got to be a system, an organisation, a chain of command. Like the army, the church or a well-run business, come to that. And you have to work within that system, even though it's far from perfect and needs adjustment all the time. Here, what the devil am I doing. Pontificating at this time of day, and with you sitting there half-naked? You aren't thinking of taking another teaching job, are you?"

"God forbid!" she said, and got up, hitching her dressing gown.

"Take the tray and come back to bed," but she said, "I'm sorry, Davy. I'd like to very much but I can't. I'm off to work as soon as I'm dressed and I'm late now. How about you?"

"I'd better go home, I suppose. They'll wonder what I'm up to and fear the worst. But I can see you again, can't I? I'm here for another ten days."

"Do you want to?"

"When are you going to get it through your head that my bones aren't chalk and there's no watered-down ink in my veins?"

"Oh, I never did suppose that," she said, kissing him swiftly and relieving him of his tray, "even before you accepted my invitation last night." She laughed again. "I say, I really have seduced Bam-fylde this time, haven't I?"

"Never mind that. Where do we go from here, Julia?"

"That's up to you, Davy. I'd love to see you again, so long as you're on the run from that gaol on the moor. But how about your little girl?"

"I planned to take her to Hampton Court on Sunday. Why not come with us? I'd like you to meet her, and you'll find she's very easy, growing up among all those ruffians. In any case, I have all my evenings free and we could do a few shows. You don't have to catch up on what's happening in the outside world, but I do. What are your hours at that teashop?"

"Nine-thirty to six, with Wednesday afternoons off. Look in and have tea about five today and I'll go through the theatre guide and find something you'd like. I'll take you up on that Hampton Court invitation too; in fact, we could strike a bargain. You pilot me round the tourist spots, guide services thrown in, and I'll show you post-war Gomorrah."

"It's a deal," he said, climbing out of bed. "See you at five. What's the place called?"

"The Maypole," she said. "Very significant, don't you think? I'll have to fly now. Bathroom's over there but watch the geyser, it's temperamental. Let yourself out. I'll be gone by the time you're ready."

He caught her by the arm as she turned, whisking her clothes from the dressing-table stool.

"Julia!"

"Well?"

"No regrets?"

"None at all. Quite the contrary. And you?"

"That's a silly question."

"No sillier than yours, sir!" and she plumped herself down before the mirror, applying make-up at what seemed to him phenomenal speed.

3

It was one of the gayest intervals of his life, certainly the most carefree since the time he and Beth and the twins had moved into Havelock's, after Ferguson's death.

Julia and Grace got along splendidly, and he was quick to notice that Julia adjusted almost at once to the maturity of the child and did not make the mistake of talking down to her, as some of his relatives were inclined to do. He enjoyed himself so much that he spent the entire Easter holiday in town. Every Wednesday and Sunday the three of them made excursions, to Hampton Court, the Tower, down the Thames to Greenwich on a launch, and to St. Paul's for morning service. Every evening, save for an odd one or two he spent with Beth's folks, he took her out somewhere, and on several occasions he called in at her sedate teashop where, on one occasion, he met the owner, Hiram Ulysses Sprockman, taking an immediate liking to the breezy, outward-looking man of about forty-five, with his genial approach to all his employees, even the junior waitresses, but what seemed to David a steady admiration for his manageress, whom he treated with elaborate courtesy. On one occasion he took Sprockman to Westminster Abbey to show him the Coronation Chair, and the tomb of Elizabeth, renowned for the superbly modelled hands on the effigy. Sprockman had an enthusiastic approach to all things English and said he had half a mind to retire here. "My part of the States has a past," he said, ruefully, "but not beyond the late sixteen-hundreds. I never forget what that guy Rupert Brooke said, when he paid his first visit to the American continent."

"What did he say?" David asked, and Sprockman seemed mildly shocked that he had to ask. To him Rupert Brooke epitomised England. He quoted, " 'The breezes have nothing to remember and everything to promise. There walk, as yet, no ghosts of lovers in Canadian lanes . . . It is possible, at a pinch, to do without gods. But one misses the dead.' "

"That's pretty good," David said. "I'll try it on the Upper School when I get back. We've got two Canadian boys in the Sixth." It was easy to see why Julia Darbyshire liked Sprockman, and why she had found security and repose in her job.

They were lovers on several other occasions, rather dismally on her part the night before he was due back to Bamfylde for Algy's last term, but by then he had quite made up his mind, remembering Howarth's advice on the subject of remarriage. Physically she attracted him very strongly but he knew himself well enough to admit that he was not in love with her, that he could never love as he had loved Beth. But he had no doubts about their compatibility, and tremendous respect for her courage and fundamental honesty, towards himself and everyone else. His one lingering doubt, involving Grace, was erased by the pleasant, undemanding relationship they formed during their jaunts about town. Grace, for that matter, could adjust to anyone who gave her half a chance. Growing up among four hundred boys, all of whom she knew by their Christian names and nicknames, she was the most adaptable seven-year-old in his experience.

They were half-dozing in front of the fire when he proposed, very soberly in the circumstances, for they had been in one another's arms a few moments before and this time, aware that there was no prospect of seeing him until July at the earliest, she seemed as fully committed as himself. It was this that helped as he said, "Julia, suppose I land that headship. Or if I don't, and aim higher at some bigger school, would you like to think about marrying me? I don't expect you to decide right away, of course. You've made your own life here, and it's a very pleasant one, so long as you work for Sprockman. But you've made all the difference in the world to me and I'm sure you and Grace would get along fine." But, to his dismay, she did not even wait for him to finish, saying sharply, "No, Davy, my dear! That's something I don't have to think about. I'm very fond of you, and always will be, but marriage . . . that simply wouldn't work, not for us."

"But why not? I'm not saying it would ever be quite the same for me again. I'd look after you though, and I daresay we'd have a lot of fun together. Children, too, if you wanted them. And neither of us are beginners, so we'd each make allowances. At least think about it until I come up again at the end of the term."

She said, with shattering finality, "As I say, Davy, there's no point in that. For two reasons. In the first place, you're not in love with me . . . and bed isn't the kind of love that's essential to you."

"What's the other reason?"

"I couldn't come back to Bamfylde and you'll realise that if you think about it."

He was harassed enough to misunderstand her. "Good God, woman—that nonsense with Blades? Nobody knows about it except the three of us. And even if they did what the hell does it matter now? Knowing you, I see it wasn't even important at the time."

"I wasn't meaning that. Something else that's very important to both of us, if we were stupid enough to confuse our physical needs with all the other essentials."

"But I could leave Bamfylde and get another school . . ."

"Any school, no matter where it was, would be the same for me and the same for you. You're as dedicated a man as I ever saw. But me . . . ? A job is a job, a means of getting the things I want, and keeping boredom at bay. No matter how much I cared for you or you for me I wouldn't make out as a housemaster's wife, still less as wife of a headmaster. I'm the wrong material, Davy. I'd hold you back and you wouldn't be held back and we'd fight. We'd fight like hell. The job, and the boys, would always take precedence with you, and I might come to accept that. But I'd fall down on what was expected of me and in the end you'd have a straight choice—hating the sight of me or compromising, as most husbands have to when they've made a bad choice and are wrapped up in their jobs. That would be damnably unfair and I'll have no part in it."

She was so explicit that there seemed no point in arguing with her just then, so he said something about writing as soon as he got back, and of putting it all on paper, but this only made her laugh. She said, kissing him, "Now don't go off down to that barrack on the moor looking like the wrath of God. Everyone will think the cares of headship have settled on you in advance. And don't spoil our last evening, either."

"You don't know me if you think I'll give up that easily. I'll see how that application of mine fares and if I'm lucky I'll pop up in that teashop of yours when you least expect it."

"You do that, Davy," she said, equably, "but face the risk of wasting your railway fare. I mightn't be there towards mid-summer."

"You're not thinking of switching jobs again?"

"Sprockman has been talking about sending me to the States. He's hoping to open a chain of Ye Olde English Tea-Shoppes in New Jersey, Maine and Connecticut."

"You mean you might be gone permanently?"

"No. He just wants me to survey the towns and report on sites and locations. And why not? Do you know, I've never been abroad in my life? Not even across the Channel. I thought it might be fun."

"How long would you be gone?"

"Oh, not all that long, five to six weeks, maybe."

He tried to extract more information but failed. There were areas of Julia Darbyshire she preferred to keep fenced off and he left her with a sense of complete bafflement. But then he took a more philosophical line, thinking how much good she had done him in the last four weeks, and telling himself that one had to make allowances. Bamfylde was not an ideal place for a woman like her, city-bred, and earning good money (more than he earned, he suspected), at the hub of affairs. Clearly Julia Darbyshire and Bamfylde, as it existed, would not mix, but this was not an insurmountable obstacle to marriage. If he got the headship he could do a great deal to improve Bamfylde's image in her eyes, refurnishing and redecorating Algy's quarters, and buying a car that would give them local mobility and easy access to the tourist areas in the West. If he was rejected, as he felt certain he would be, then he would assault the agencies for a post in a more civilised area, and wait until she was disenchanted with a five-and-a-half-day week in the West End. Such a time would come with a woman as mercurial as Julia and there were advantages in delay. He had no doubts but that she approved of him as a lover, and could also evaluate the security he offered as a husband. She was not the kind of woman who could do without a man for long, the little she had told him concerning her previous relationships indicated that. As for himself, he was more and more certain as the days passed, and he picked up the rhythm of his life, that he stood in sore need of her cheerfulness and brisk common sense. The memory of her lying in his arms unsettled him and made him impatient with fools, and the guerilla tactics of The Lump in Middle School, so that the more observant boys began to notice a tetchiness about him that had not been there in the past.

It was Winterbourne, who missed very little, who reassured them all concerning Pow-Wow's uncertain temper as the term got into its stride, saying, "Go easy on him. He's tensed up these days, on account of Algy leaving and a new man taking over. They're all on edge, he and Carter more than the others, seeing they're both lined up for the job."

For it was now common knowledge that there was a possibility of Algy being succeeded by the housemaster of Outram's or Have-lock's and, to a degree, the tension spread downwards as far as the Lower Fifth, where Collier, a barrister's son with a penchant for colourful metaphors, said, "This bloody place is like Pompeii this term. Everyone is waiting around for the lid to blow off. Even Algy's lost some of his bounce. He's trotting around looking as if he might run into the Press Gang behind the piggeries."

The Governors seemed to take an interminable time to come to a decision, and it was Howarth who, for all his air of detach-ment, was invariably the best informed of the staff, who advanced sound reasons for the delay. He told David one evening, when they were taking their constitutional round the cricketfield, "There's something of a deadlock, I understand. Short list of six, and you and Carter both on it. Of the other four only two are in the running. A man from Repton, and the former head of a school in Cape Town, who retired and settled over here last year. They're both highly qualified, both around the fifty mark. Actually, I be-lieve everybody's waiting for Sir Rufus Creighton to show up."

David had heard a good deal about Sir Rufus Creighton but had never met him. He was an ex-Indian judge, a County Councillor and notable educationalist, who owed his seat on the Board to Bamfylde's status as a direct grant school. Having taken it into his head to go on a world cruise, none of the other Governors felt disposed to make the appointment without his guidance. On Howarth's advice, David stayed clear of his sponsor, Brigadier Cooper. "Won't do to compromise him," he said. "He's tamed tribesmen on the North-West Frontier and knows more than you and I about in-fighting."

And so, for David, time stood still. May passed, and half of June, long, sunny days that ordinarily he would have enjoyed but in the circumstances, and for the first time since settling here, seemed flat and stale. Apart from one letter in reply to his four Julia had not written and was incommunicado, for her trip to the States had materialised and she was living a life of rapid movement up and down the eastern seaboard. He read and re-read her letter until he knew it by heart. It was breezy and friendly but gave no hint that she had changed her mind, or was likely to, only that she was finding America an exciting, stimulating place, that parts of New England reminded her of Devon, and that she had resorted to remote hypnotism of the Bamfylde Governors in order to influence their choice of candidate. She was likely to be home in early August if everything went according to plan. She addressed him as 'Dearest Davy', and concluded 'All my love to you, dear'. He recalled then that the odd letter from Beth had always been starred with crosses, schoolgirl fashion, but there were no crosses here and the impersonality of the letter bothered him a little. At a deeper level, however, he did not devote a great deal of thought to Julia. The looming possibility of triumph or failure absorbed most of his nervous energy.

And then, catching him offguard after weeks of suspense, the summons came. All short-listed candidates were to be interviewed on the following morning by a specially convened meeting of the Governors in the school library, that had done duty for a Board Room ever since it was built in the first years of Herries's reign. Both he and Carter were spared the embarrassment of a waiting period, in the company of the other four applicants, who were interviewed swiftly, one after the other, the last of them during morning coffee break. The two local men were asked to present themselves at eleven-thirty a.m., when the others had been taken to the head's house for refreshment. On the way across the quad, David caught a glimpse of two of them, a tall, slightly stooping man, some twenty years his senior, with a high-domed head and thick, greying hair, and a much younger man with quick, nervous movements, who looked as though he was convinced he had missed the boat, for he scowled at the Founder's statue as though he entertained the same feelings for it as Skidmore. David thought, "One down and one to go, but I don't like the look of that beetling chap. The old place is in for a shake-up if they settle on him . . ." But then, surprisingly, Carter touched his elbow, betraying his own extreme nervousness by saying, "I say, Powlett-Jones, this is a bit of an ordeal, isn't it? I mean, being quizzed by the whole bunch of them on our own ground. I've got the most appalling indigestion, damn it!" The brief encounter did a little to resuscitate his own confidence as they went up the steps together and took two of six empty chairs ranged along the wall of the duty-librarian's office, reminding him of a row of chairs in a dentist's waiting-room, a dentist who wasn't doing so well.

He said, gritting his teeth, "Well, good luck, Carter. Don't let 'em rattle you!" and Carter, blinking nervously, made his first and only joke in David's presence, saying, "When I get in there I know just how I shall feel. Like that smug little brute in the picture, 'When Did You Last See Your Father?' "

There was no chance to cap Carter's joke. The head's part-time secretary, Miss Rowlandson, from the Old Rectory in the village, appeared and said, in a hushed voice, "You now, Mr. Carter . . . !" and Carter rose, straightening his tie, smoothing his wet-rust hair and lurching towards the door like a felon summoned by the hangman.

It seemed very strange sitting there alone, in a room that was as familiar as his own bedroom. His thoughts ranged back nine years, to the days he had first poked his head into the library, finding it a hotchpotch of books, most of them tattered legacies from Old Boys and including, surprisingly, a full set of G. A. Henty's. He tried to concentrate on something inconsequential, the gable end of the roof where Havelock's met Outram's, the perch where the Kassava brothers had taken refuge on the night of the fire. It seemed a very long time ago, an incident in his childhood, like the day he came home from school to be told that his father and two brothers had died in the pit, or that bright summer dawn on July 1st, 1916, when he had waited, mouth parched and heart hammering, for the second hand of his watch to move up to zero-hour. But then he tried to think of something more cheerful, selecting Julia Darbyshire at random—Julia Darbyshire, stark naked in the faint glow of the street lamp the night they became lovers in her flat, and this focal point was more rewarding, for at least it stopped him trying to make sense of the indistinct murmur beyond the door. He thought, gloomily, "I wouldn't give a damn if she had been here, or even accessible. I could have put through a trunk call tonight and laughed it off, but the only one handy to serve as a buffer is old Carter. Queer him being so nervous, and coming out with that joke. Not such a bad joke, either. Howarth will swear I've made it up when I tell him . . . By God, they need some new linoleum in here—this is shredding away . . . hasn't been renewed since Queen Victoria died . . . What the devil am I yawning about? Haven't yammered like that since I was in a dugout under bombardment . . ." And then, his nerves taut as trip wires, "I was an absolute bloody fool to let Howarth talk me into this, curse him! He made sure he kept well clear of it himself. Damned if I can recall having been more embarrassed in my life . . ." But he was more resilient than he realised. A moment later his thoughts took a new turn; "To hell with them all, boyo, Julia included! If I miss out, as I'm certain to, I'll drift, and give the new man a sporting chance . . . Grace is settled here and so am I in normal circumstances . . . Wouldn't care to start all over again, and lose touch with young Cooper, Chad Boyer, Skidmore, the Kassavas, Briarley, Keith Blades and all the others . . . I already feel as if I'd attained my century. What you need right now, Davy, is a good stiff gin, so damned if you don't go looking for Howarth the minute we're finished in here . . ."

And then the door opened and Carter came out, so red in the face that he looked almost apoplectic, but before he could say a word Miss Rowlandson appeared again and said, in the same empty-church voice, "Mr. Powlett-Jones?" and he tried to grin at Carter and slipped past him across the threshold.

Chapter Two

1

He remembered reading somewhere that a man awaiting a verdict on a capital charge could assess his chances the moment a jury returned to the court. If they looked at him he was acquitted. If they avoided his eyes he was guilty.

There must be something in it, he decided, for the same applied here. His known sponsors, Brigadier Cooper, and his two converts, Birley, the Challacombe grocer and Newsom, another Old Boy, glanced up and smiled. The brigadier might be said to have winked. About half the remaining fourteen kept their eyes on the blotters, Carter's backers no doubt, but the Chairman, a little brown nut of a man, looked at him quite impersonally when inviting him to take a seat.

There was a little shuffling and throat-clearing and then Sir Rufus took him gently through a formal application check—full name, age, degree, and so on, until David began to wonder whether the whole thing was rigged, either in favour of Carter or one of the other candidates, and that his presence here was no more than a polite ritual. Then Sir Rufus asked him about his war service, what regiment he had served in, and where, and what part of the line he was occupying when he was buried by a mortar shell. He answered briefly, almost impatiently, until the brigadier said,

"You were awarded the M.C., Powlett-Jones. Would you care to tell us about it?"

"I'd prefer not, Brigadier Cooper. You were out there, and you know how many chaps earned decorations and didn't get them," and Brigadier Cooper twinkled again, implying that this was a perfectly satisfactory answer and one he had expected.

Newsom, an apple-cheeked man in his fifties, said, vaguely, "You've . . . er . . . been happy here, Mr. Powlett-Jones? Apart from that dreadful business on Quarry Hill, of course," and then chewed his moustache, as though he regretted raising the matter.

"Very happy," David said, "and that's mainly why I applied. I realise there are men senior to me, of course, but I made sure none of them wanted the post before I filed an application."

This seemed to nonplus them a little but the brigadier rallied and mentioned the fire, addressing his colleagues as though David wasn't present.

"Dam' fine show he put up on that occasion," he said. "Been a shambles if he hadn't been up to the mark," and he glared around as though others were denying the fact.

There was an awkward pause then until Sir Rufus said, "I understand you took an external degree while serving on the staff, Mr. Powlett-Jones. Wouldn't it have been more satisfactory to take advantage of the shortened University course for ex-officers?"

"Possibly, sir. But it would have meant a two-year break with Bamfylde. I was married then, with two children to support, and would have had to chance getting back here." He wondered if this was the real reason and decided it was not. "The fact is, Sir Rufus, Bamfylde was rehabilitating *me* at the time. I wanted to take full advantage of it."

The qualified answer interested the little man. He screwed up his face so that eyes and mouth were all but lost in a maze of wrinkles. "Would you care to elaborate on that a little?"

"Sharp as a damned needle, he is," David thought, checked for a moment, but then he said, deliberately, "I was in very bad shape when I came here, in 1918. The hospital specialist decided a job would be the best therapy. I didn't take him seriously at the time. I did later, as soon as I'd met Mr. and Mrs. Herries, and made friends with some of the staff."

"Weren't the boys something of a strain in the circumstances?"

"No," he flashed out. "No! . . . Not once I'd let them see I wasn't to be fooled around with. I got the measure of them in less than a week."

There was another awkward silence. Still nobody else spoke, and the interview seemed likely to resolve itself into a wary dialogue between himself and the little Indian judge. Sir Rufus said, carefully, "To sum up, Mr. Powlett-Jones, what, in your view, is the most essential factor of a school like Bamfylde?" and David heard himself say, "I can answer that straight out. A happy atmosphere. If that's there everything else falls into place."

That, at least, resulted in a shift of glances of the committed and neutral groups. Fourteen pairs of eyes moved as one to his level, then half of them were lowered to the doodle-starred blotters on the table.

Sir Rufus said, quietly, "Thank you, Mr. Powlett-Jones. That's all, I think, unless any other member of the Governing Body would like to ask a question." There were no questions and after a lapse of a few seconds he got up, bowed towards the chair and walked out.

Back in the little lobby he found he was sweating freely. He said, aloud, "By God, I need that drink!" and went in search of Howarth and his decanter.

Hoskins, whom he thought of as Grace's dancing professional, came up to the living-room a few minutes after lunch and David, brooding in his study with the door open, heard Grace's squeal of delight as he said, "New one here, real hot number, Tuppence! You must have heard it on the wireless but this is the first recording to reach the Outback!"

"Put it on! Put it on, Sax," he heard 'Tuppence' exclaim but Hoskins, briefed in these casual visits, said, "I'll have to ask your father first. Is he around?"

"I'm in here," David called. "Play the damned thing. I shan't get any peace if you don't," and Hoskins called back, "Thank *you*, sir! Just the one side," and in a moment later the half-familiar rhythm of ''Bye, 'Bye, Blackbird' grinding out of the portable, followed by the thuds and squeals that invariably accompanied a 'lesson' in the latest ballroom craze.

It was not by any means soothing music but it helped and he found himself humming the lively refrain.

. . . So, make my bed and light the light,
I'll be home, late tonight,
Blackbird, 'bye, 'bye!

There was a small oval mirror immediately above the desk and David watched his own grin, thinking, "Do I really give a damn whether they turn me down or not? What the hell does it matter on what terms I stay? I belong here. Grace belongs here. Beth and Joan are still around somewhere, and so are all the names on that war memorial outside . . ." and then he heard the gramophone needle screech to an abrupt halt and Hoskins say, "I'm sorry, sir, just trying out a new one. Yes, he's in the study . . ." and after that whispering and the sound of the door closing on Tuppence and her instructor.

Algy's white head showed round the door. He looked like an elderly, pink-eyed rabbit, tufted and slightly scared, as he said, "They're through, P.J. I volunteered to come up with the news." He came in, shut the door, and stood with his back against it.

"Well?"

"It's . . . er . . . good and bad, though I shouldn't say it, not to someone with his hat in the ring. I wouldn't either, if I hadn't started packing and that lets me out. You and Carter broke exactly even. No one would budge an inch. That's why they've been closeted up there for nearly three hours. Haven't even lunched. Scared someone would get at them, no doubt."

"Who is it, then?"

"Neither of you. Sir Rufus gave his casting vote for Alcock. He wouldn't have, or so he hinted, but for the long-term risk of having either of you serving under the other, and he has a point there. Suppose you or Carter had got it, and the other had decided to soldier on? It wouldn't have worked, would it? School would have been split down the middle in no time at all. As it is, you're both level pegs under a new man, with impressive qualifications. He'll have to lean equally on the pair of you."

He felt no real pang of disappointment. Rather relief that Carter had not succeeded in pipping him. He had not exchanged a word with Alcock, the bowed, beetling man from Cape Town, so he could form no opinion how he was likely to set about following an institution like Algy Herries. 'Better the devil you know . . .' they said, but it wasn't true in this case. Carter would have made

253

a shambles of Algy's carefully erected edifice and as things had turned out Carter wasn't getting the chance to monkey with the place. That was a gain, he supposed, and his mind raced ahead to a point when, conceivably, today's ordeal might be repeated, for somehow he couldn't see himself leaving Bamfylde now.

He said, "How old is Alcock, sir?" and Herries said, "Fifty-three. Late for it, I'd say. He could stay seven or twelve years, depending how he feels, or how well off he is. I think he's pretty well fixed for cash and will likely put his feet up at sixty. There's one other thing. Nothing to do with today's business."

"Yes, sir."

"For Heaven's sake call me 'Algy' to my face from here on. I've always had a very soft spot for you, P.J. So has Ellie."

David turned away, looking down on to the forecourt through the window he had last seen Beth drive off in the three-wheeler, and had raised his hand in response to Grace's wave. He said, at length, "I'll never have another friend like you, Algy. That goes for most of us here, I imagine," but Herries said, fruitily, "Oh, come now, old sport, don't talk as if I was tucked away at Stone Cross, with Ferguson and Cordwainer. I'm only in the next parish but one, and I'll be over here at least once a month, I promise you."

"Well, I'm glad to hear that," and then, "What sort of chap *is* he, Algy?"

"Alcock? Difficult to say. An activist, judged on his record. He could have done much better than Bamfylde if he'd been ten years younger. Very quiet. No nonsense about him. Not much sense of humour, either, and that'll hinder him unless he develops one. However, we might have done worse. As for you, I'll risk offence by telling you something no one else would, not even Howarth. I admire your pluck for trying but you weren't ready for it. It would have been a gamble, and Bamfylde isn't something I'd care to stake in a lottery, even with the dice loaded in my favour. Can you take that, David?"

"Why not? It's true."

"Then come on down and I'll introduce you. The others have gone off in high dudgeon, all sharing a taxi. Carter's already made his bow. The king is dead. Long live the king!"

They went out, passing the side table where Hoskins' new record, arrested in the middle of a chorus, still lay on the portable.

" ' 'Bye, 'bye, blackbird',"' David said, and when Algy muttered "What?" he said it was nothing, just a private joke for Sax Hoskins and Tuppence.

"In a place like this, distinguished for nicknames, you ought to find a more dignified one for that mite," said Algy.

2

The letter came by the afternoon post, an innovation since the Challacombe sorting office had acquired a van for its country round.

He saw it lying on the tray on the landing when he came up from afternoon classes to make himself a pot of tea before devoting an hour or two to the final chapter of 'The Royal Tigress', now standing in a foot-high pile on his desk and crowding all his other correspondence to one side.

He saw at first glance that it was from Julia and that she was still in America. With a feeling of elation he carried it into the living-room, and settled to read it slowly, relishing every line. But then, his eye leaping down the page and catching a phrase, he read swiftly, imbibing its contents like a draught of bitter medicine:

. . . They tell me it takes about eight days door to door for a letter to cross The Pond, Davy. So, by the time you get this, I will have been married. Mrs. Hiram Ulysses Sprockman, no less. Sonorous but . . . well . . . rather sweet once you get used to it. This will come as a shock to you, but I'm not apologising for that. I'd apologise to a little man but you're not a little man. Given a few years you'll be the biggest one Bamfylde has ever seen. Everything I said to you the night you asked me to marry you still holds good. I would have been a terrible flop as a schoolmaster's wife, worse even than as a parson's wife, for parsons, these days, are often anxious to get in on the act and keep up with the latest fads and fashions. A good schoolmaster isn't so daft. He tends to adapt with more dignity. I'll always remember your proposal as the greatest compliment anyone ever paid me. Much greater than Arthur's and Hiram's, for neither really knew me as you did. But that wouldn't make it right in anything but the purely physical sense and as regards that I give you full marks. Ten out of ten, for loving. It would do for most men but again, not for you, not since you've matured and distilled all you learned and suffered in France into a kind of— how can I put it?—a rejuvenating elixir. For the exclusive benefit of generations of Bamfeldians.

That elixir would have been watered down if I had been around when it was being mixed, stirred and seasoned, and I don't mean by this you shouldn't ever think of marrying again. You should. Given the kind of luck you once had, and deserve again, you'll make some lucky wench a wonderful husband, providing she has the sense to give you your head, and not go for the old impossible—changing a man into her image of what she thinks he ought to be.

As to me marrying Hiram, well, I'm not pretending I'm in love with him and I've told him so, over and over again. I didn't tell you but he had already proposed twice when we met again by chance that time. But Hiram doesn't need your kind of wife. He's been married to commerce ever since he discovered what fun it was to make money. What he needs—what he is getting —is a mistress-cum-manageress. Apart from that, he's kind and considerate and intelligent, as you were quick to notice.

Well, there we are, Davy. I've cut the knot for you and left you free to push on and I still don't know whether or not the Governors gambled on you or kept you in cold storage. Touching that, will you let me give you one last piece of advice? *Stay where you are, no matter what.* I couldn't say why but I *know* Bamfylde is right for you, and whilst you'd do a good, conscientious job elsewhere it wouldn't be an inspired one.

My best love to little Grace. I adored her. She'll grow up to be a credit and a solace to you.

My love to you, too, Davy. I'll never forget you and if you care to write and keep in touch I'd always be happy about that, although I leave this entirely to you.

Very, very affectionately,
Julia.

He drifted across to his study and sat down at his littered desk, trying hard to come to terms with the new situation. Julia married. Julia's cheerfulness and stimulus denied him. And this, on a day when he had to begin all over again and practise his trade under the cold eye of a stranger.

His first reaction was one of bitterness but almost at once resentment was reduced to indignation that she could have been so damned secretive and left him half-hoping, despite her unqualified refusal of marriage. But then, looking out on the moor, shimmering in the heat haze as far as the lip of the plateau where he had walked into the thunderstorm the day another woman was lost to him, a spring of common sense welled out of his resentment. It wasn't really ruthlessness on her part. Behind it was discernment, of a kind not vouchsafed to many women, with their eye on the main chance. As man and wife they might have made it but not as consorts, for a woman like her would never have been able to get Bamfylde into his kind of focus. In the end, she would have lost patience, first with it and then with him, and there would have been, as she had warned him, compromise on an ever-enlarging scale. A man shouldn't compromise with his search for personal fulfilment. He could only compromise with a creed, Carter's kind of creed, that was really no more than a set of prejudices.

Well, that was that. Now, all that remained, he supposed, was to decide on an approach to their relationship in the future and he found the answer to that almost at once. What was the point of keeping up an intermittent correspondence? Where was there sense in torturing oneself with sensual images of a vigorous, clear-skinned body stretched on a bed, the kind that would come to mind every time he sat down to write to her? Howarth had probably done that with the memory of Amy Crispin and what had it brought him but hardening of the emotional arteries, and a constant reminder of wasted years? He cleared a space on his desk and wrote, on a sheet of Bamfylde notepaper:

My Dear, I didn't get the headship. We have a new man . . . not Carter, thank God. I'm staying on here indefinitely, partly because I can't be bothered to change, but mostly, I think, because I still have a notion I owe the place something. Congratulations to both of you. You made a neater, swifter job of pulling out of the Sargasso Sea than I did, and you're clear-headed enough to stay out. Good luck always, Julia dear. Very affectionately, Davy.

PART

FIVE

Impasse

Chapter One

1

Looking back on the period of his life that he came to think of as 'the impasse years', Powlett-Jones could never be sure of the precise moment when the shadow first touched them, when he and the rest of the rump became unpleasantly aware that one era had ended and another, stormy and cheerless, had begun.

It must have been during the last few weeks of Algy's reign, between his first formal handshake with Alcock on the day of the appointment and the final night of term, when he sat below the dais in Big Hall helping Skidmore with the presentations at Algy's farewell supper.

It was then, looking directly up at the new man sitting on Algy's right hand, and noting his impassivity during the farewell address, that he finally acknowledged Alcock's implacability, for no man, he reasoned, could be completely unmoved (as Alcock obviously was) by Algy's valediction, a subtle and wholly unselfconscious blend of pathos, humour, gallantry and profound resignation. But there might have been earlier indications of what lay ahead, for he recalled a curious incident in Barnaby's study, a day or two after he and Carter had finally buried the hatchet—'a couple of rejects here to console one another' as Carter had put it, and very handsomely David thought, considering the bitterness of their feud over a stretch of more than eight years.

Both had accepted Barnaby's invitation to partake of 'real' coffee in his quarters, at Nicolson's on a day that school ended at eleven a.m., in honour of the match with the Devonshire Dumplings. Barnaby, a ritual coffee-maker, scowled down at the common room brew and said, "With important visitors about the place other ranks can be moderately sure of a bubble-and-squeak lunch. Come and fortify yourselves. Everyone invited."

Irvine and Howarth had joined them, and all five sat around talking shop before Carter raised the subject that was in everybody's mind.

"What do you make of this chap, Alcock? Oughtn't we to begin trimming our sails?" An innocent-enough remark one would have thought, hardly calling for Howarth's testy, "Trimming is more in your line than mine, Carter!" whereupon, anxious to demonstrate that their peace treaty was more than a gesture, David said, "No, Howarth. Carter's right. We ought to have sized him up by now, he's been mooching about the place ever since he was appointed. Has anyone exchanged more than a word with him?"

Nobody had, not even Carter who, as they all recalled, had been the first to congratulate the incoming head. Irvine said, with an uncharacteristic touch of malice, "He's been living with Algy. P.J. is the only one with a direct line to the Gaffer. Hasn't the Old Man leaked anything to his protégé, Davy?"

"He hinted that Alcock was short on humour. Nothing more. I'd say he was a pedant, and will act like one until the place takes him over," whereupon Carter said, flatly, "It'll never do that, old man. Never!"

He sounded so emphatic that Barnaby raised an eyebrow. "What makes you so sure of that? It managed to mellow everyone here, didn't it? Not much but somewhat. Even Howarth," but then rendered the gibe harmless by winking very solemnly and refilling Howarth's cup.

"Call it a hunch," said Carter and then, with a nod at Barnaby, that might or might not have been an acknowledgment of his hospitality, he slammed down his cup and stalked out.

"Hallo, hallo, hallo? What brought that on?"

This, from Irvine, whereupon Howarth growled, "Pique. Plain, unadulterated pique. The little man has been given the cold shoulder and wants us to restore circulation."

It was not often that David ran counter to Howarth and never had on Carter's behalf. He said, carefully, "You might as well know, all three of you, that Carter and I have settled our account."

"You might have settled yours, my friend," Howarth said sourly, "but don't bank on Carter paying up. You should have learned by now that common room feuds never heal. Invariably they fester."

"Well, this one won't," David said, and went on to give an account of his meeting with Carter in the library annexe on the day of the Governors' meeting. "As for Carter being the first to shake hands with Alcock, why read anything into that? I'd have done it myself if I'd thought of it. My impression is Alcock is difficult to classify."

Howarth yawned, indicating that the subject bored him, but it was one of these infelicitous occasions when everyone makes the wrong remark at the wrong moment. Irvine, always baffled by abstracts, said, "Tell you something else. There'll be no more bonus free periods like today's, for cricket or rugger. Man isn't interested in games. Probably never played anything but croquet in his whole life."

"That raises him a notch in my estimation," said Howarth, and went out before Irvine could protest, and although Howarth's contempt for games was a long-established school joke, David could see that the bull-necked Irvine, whose tireless coaching had made Bamfylde the most formidable school side in the West, was upset.

He said nothing, however, but followed Howarth out, so that David had an uncomfortable suspicion that the arrival of Alcock might mean a reshuffling of common room alliances. For a moment he was tempted to explore this thought with Barnaby but thought better of it, remembering that Barnaby made a point of never quarrelling with anyone and would explain why when he could find anyone to listen. Trudging across the moor on one of their hikes he had once said, "A man can't teach Horace and Cicero all day and fall to bickering between times. It's all been said before, P.J. A long, long time ago."

He continued to think about it from time to time, however, inclined to dismiss the notion that a stranger, not yet in office, could introduce new tensions into the place, and yet, it did occur to him, as the last weeks of term ran out, that the Lent tight-rope was making an unseasonal appearance in high summer. It could only be, he reasoned, the impending departure of Algy, whom everybody liked, and most of them revered. Halfway through the head's farewell speech he changed his mind again.

Algy was not rated high as a speechmaker, an after-dinner speaker that is, where the neatly turned phrase, and the gilded platitude, is almost obligatory. He was, however, a breezy chatter-up and today, somewhat to everybody's surprise, he excelled himself. He seemed, almost, to be voicing stray thoughts and deductions rather than saying his official goodbyes, or acknowledging the gift of silver tableware, inscribed with his name and dates. Instead of addressing himself to a rambling tour of something over sixty years of Bamfylde history (a speech that everyone present felt his due) he preferred to present a potted *raison d'être* of the profession, illustrating his theme with all manner of sly jokes at the expense of boys, staff, Governing Body and himself. Mostly himself, for Algy appreciated a joke against himself above all others.

". . . Occasions like these are free gifts to the professional windbag . . . I could keep you here until rising bell, telling you Bamfylde stories, most of which would qualify as thrice-baked chestnuts . . . Things I have seen and experienced, since I came here as a scared little toad of eleven. By Christopher, I *was* scared too, now that I think of it! Oblige me by passing that on to the smallest and scruffiest of your September intake, Mr. Alcock. Who knows? It might cheer him up a bit."

But Alcock, legs neatly crossed, arms carefully folded, did not so much as blink.

". . . I could spin yarns of long ago, when anyone with more than six mistakes in Sunday dictation was flogged by that brute Wesker. God, in His supreme mercy, endowed me with an ability to spell. But I was caught on 'rhododendron' and had them rooted out when I came here as head. I could spin yarns of Wesker's time and yarns of the day before yesterday, when I overheard something to my advantage while seated on Mount Olympus, otherwise known as Spyglass Hill . . ."

For half a minute he paused to allow the laughter to subside. Almost alone, among those crowding the hall as far as the kitchen hatches, Alcock was ignorant of the fact that Mount Olympus, otherwise known as Spyglass Hill, was not to be found on any local ordnance map but was the head's privy, with its stained-glass Judas window, opening on to the quad. The man could be forgiven, perhaps, for looking bewildered at the immoderate reception accorded this innocent-sounding remark but not, David thought, for withholding a token smile when Algy went on to say that he overheard one boy tell another how he had managed to gouge ten shillings from his father to add his name to the farewell gift subscribers' list. "He then contributed a mere five and was gracefully complimented by the head boy for his extreme generosity.

"No matter . . ." and here Algy picked up the silver teapot, lifted its lid and glanced inside, ". . . I wouldn't like to give anyone the impression that I'm complaining. It is indeed a very handsome reminder of my twenty-three years here as headmaster, and the subscriber in question—no names, no penal drill—can always salve his conscience by slipping across the parish boundary on the first Sunday of Michaelmas term and dropping the missing coins into my offertory plate."

Not a muscle of Alcock's face twitched. He might, David thought, have been listening to a lecture on bimetallism, so that Carter's remark—what was it?—the man's inability to identify with Bamfylde, suddenly had relevance, and the laughter, renewed and prolonged had no power to cheer.

He had missed a quip or two by then but Algy was now ambling towards his climax, with his audience silent again as he tried to explain what he saw, what he had always seen, as the true function of a headmaster. "It isn't an instructor. Any reasonably staffed school should have plenty of trained instructors on hand. And it isn't an administrator, either, or never has been in my case. Anyone here will tell you that, judged on my paperwork alone, I wouldn't qualify for a remove every other year. No, no, I've seen myself, latterly at all events, as a kind of co-ordinator of all the aims and impulses that keep a place like Bamfylde alive and useful. Education, in the generally accepted sense of the word, has never rated very high on my list of priorities. All that the best of us can do is to teach boys how to educate themselves between their time of leaving here, and their time of crossing that Rubicon, that comes, for most of us, at about twenty-five, when the memory sponge is getting soggy and we tend to read and forget.

"I've had plenty of first-class scholars through my hands since

1904, but I can't claim much credit for their academic successes. They would have been achieved at any school, given the same material. But helping to equip two generations of predatory males with the qualities of patience, tolerance, good fellowship and the ability to see someone else's point of view—qualities I see as the keystones of democracy—that's something else. I'll pipe down now —did I catch a gusty sigh of relief from the back? But let me close with a final anecdote, one that came to mind when I was riffling through the Old Boys' register this morning, in search of inspiration for this interminable valediction.

"It was a very trivial incident but it must have impressed me at the time. Why else should it have stayed in the mind for nearly twenty years? It concerned two boys, Petherick and 'Chuff' Rodgers, who accompanied me over to Barcombe by train, when we were giving a charity performance of that year's opera. It was Christmas time, of course, and the train was very full. We finally secured seats in a compartment where a young woman was nursing a baby. Within minutes of starting out the baby was dramatically sick . . . I remember poor Petherick's expression well, as he took refuge behind my copy of *The Times*. Upside down it was, but a thing like that wouldn't bother Petherick. He was one of our sky-rockets, and went on to become president of a famous insurance company, and collect the O.B.E., or whatever they give the cream of insurance brokers. But I wasn't thinking so much of Petherick but of Chuff. Always unlucky, he had been sitting alongside the mother, and was thus on the receiving end of the business. I didn't know what to do but Chuff did. He whipped out a handkerchief—the only clean handkerchief I'd ever seen him sport— leaned across, wiped the baby's face and then the mother's lap. And when I say 'wiped' I mean wiped. It wasn't a dab. It was more of a general tidy-up, all round. After that we had a tolerably uneventful journey, with Rodgers making soothing noises all the way to the junction.

"Now some of you might think that is a very damp squib to conclude the regular fireworks display we have had here tonight, with so many kind speeches, and the giving of such splendid farewell gifts, but it isn't, you know. It's very relevant, to me at any rate, relevant to what we've all been engaged in up here on the moor all these years. For Chuff Rodgers, bless his thick skull, never won a prize or a race in his life. Neither did he find time to do the only thing he was equipped to do—raise a family. He was killed at First Ypres, but I still remember him. Rather better than I remember Petherick. As a matter of fact, when I came across his name this morning, I thought of him as one of our outstanding successes."

He may have intended saying more but nobody gave him the chance. After a dithering moment he sat down and reached for the beaker of water. Because the story was so typical of Algy it touched an emotional spring in his audience that could only find surface in applause of the magnitude no one had ever heard in the Big Hall. David, joining in, forgot to notice if the armour of Alcock's implacability had been dented but then, suddenly remembering him, he glanced that way again, and was momentarily certain that Chuff Rodgers' handkerchief had achieved what all Algy's jokes and nudges had failed to achieve. Very deliberately Alcock unfolded his arms, uncrossed his legs and bent towards the floor. It was only when he straightened up that David realised he had been fooled. Alcock's head came up like a stork's, neatly and tidily, as he replaced the table napkin that had fallen when Algy lifted the water beaker. His long fingers busied themselves straightening the creases and then, as he refolded his arms, his expressionless eyes resumed their neutral scrutiny of the middle distance.

David thought, with an inward qualm, "Carter was right. He'll never identify," and wondered what the near future had in store for everyone cheering the tubby little man in the centre of the stage.

2

Before half-term he had acquired a variety of nicknames. It was held at Bamfylde that a nickname, even when the bestowal was derisory, none the less implied absorption into the family. Alcock was the exception to this rule. The very nature of his nicknames signified his separateness, rare even for an instant failure, or a boy or master who had never rated a nickname.

Howarth, the one member of the staff who did not appear to be rattled by the man's remoteness, called him The Mandarin. Barnaby, paying his usual tribute to the classics, called him The Stoic. "A Stoic of the woods, a man without a tear," he quoted, and

there was something stoical about Alcock's detachment, as though
he had set himself a task that absorbed the last dregs of his nervous energy, leaving absolutely nothing to spare on the units of
the school as people rather than pieces of a jigsaw puzzle to be
contemplated from above and ultimately, one hoped, allotted
their proper place in his neat, tidy mind. Always, they came to
realise, his mind. Never his heart, providing he had one under
the trim alpaca waistcoats he wore.

He had been widowed, it was said many years ago in Africa, but
no one could be sure of this or, indeed, of anything out of his past.
Alcock's personal life was double-padlocked against them all. His
degrees, which were impressive, and his educational achievements
in the Dominions, were there for all to see. Beyond this nothing.
Nothing at all, so that communication with him, from the first
day of his first term was reduced to a kind of sign language. "Of
the kind," jested Barnaby, "that a cautious trader might use to
barter with a native despot of unbelievable taciturnity."

Grudgingly, as the weeks passed, they conceded his few good
points. Under him, in a matter of days, the administrative machinery of the school achieved the smoothness and impersonality of a
heavy turbine engine, tended by a dedicated engineer, who had
identified every nut, bolt and piston of its composition. He had
the knack, also, of maintaining an awed and hushed discipline,
without raising his voice, and he achieved this with his eyes,
quite expressionless unless he had occasion to stare anybody down.
When this happened, as it frequently did, the eyes were those of
a man fanatically involved in himself. Steady, penetrating and
terribly chilling. His face, if one happened to study it without meeting his gaze, was at odds with his personality, in that it was
slightly puckish, with deep creases on either side of the prim, contained mouth, topped by a clipped moustache. But instead of
softening his eyes the creases had the reverse effect, converting
what might have been sardonic humour into an icy impatience, so
that one was left with the impression that Alcock believed himself to be living in a world peopled exclusively by fools of one kind
or another.

His administrative expertise was effortless, that of a Trappist
monk with a high spiritual reputation. He seemed to solve day-
to-day problems without giving them a fleeting thought, but although his decisions were effective, inasmuch as the problem was

solved on the spot, there was about these snap decisions the neutrality of a mathematical equation. One had a feeling that all they need in the way of a signature were the letters 'Q.E.D.'.

This first became apparent in his marginal involvement in games. It seemed that he approved games, always providing that they were pursued as a means of exercising bodies. No more and no less, deserving no more prominence in the curriculum than, say, a bi-weekly hour of Swedish drill. His first time-table was a masterpiece of precision, with not a minute of anyone's day wasted. His review of the school diet and reorganisation of the kitchens produced startling gastronomic improvements, welcomed alike by staff and boys, who had muddled along for years on lumpy porridge, burned toast, tough beef, doubtful stews, semolina puddings and strips of treacle tart that the boys called dry-dock wedges. Under Alcock even the fabric of the old place took heart. Surfaces, dull and scarred for a generation, began to glow, and the sun found its way into long-forgotten corners. Scuffed coconut matting was banished from the central aisles of the dormitories, replaced with fibrous material that looked exactly like congealed oatmeal. The boys soon found a name for it, calling it 'Donkey's Breakfast'. Out-of-the-way windows, some of which had not seen a leather in months, lost their ribald slogans, written in ancient dust, and down at the church scores of laboriously carved initials disappeared overnight under thick coats of pew varnish, the smell of which was capable of materialising the new headmaster the moment a head bowed in prayer.

For that was Alcock's way. He was never once present as the actual agent of these changes and transformations. Nobody ever saw him perform or initiate them. They simply happened, and whenever they did one or other of the senses proclaimed that Alcock had been there. Alcock had heard, seen and decreed.

He took the modern Sixth for advanced maths and here, it was claimed, he occasionally emerged, if fleetingly, as a man rather than a force, using symbols as a lesser mortal might use a quotation, or a piece of apparatus in the laboratory. But once the bell had clanged he withdrew into himself before he had so much as stepped down from the dais and they were left with the familiar enigmas; who was he, and why? What secret forces kept his batteries charged? What did he think of them as people and of Bamfylde as an institution? Was he dismayed or satisfied with his results so far? Was his withdrawal due to a terrible shyness, or was it a personal preference? Did he like the job or did he regard it as a penance, stoically performed? Nobody knew the answer to any one of these questions.

Here and there, as the term unrolled, he left a clue, as in the case of his silent assault upon the sanitary system, and the clue indicated that he was a fastidious man who had been appalled (justifiably, some thought) by prevailing conditions down at the Bog.

Nothing effective had ever been done about the Bog. Under Algy, as under his predecessor, it had remained medieval until, presumably, Alcock had stumbled upon it by chance, at once summoning an army of plumbers who transformed it overnight. Under its heavy coats of whitewash, and sporting its shining array of copper cisterns and pipes, it suddenly assumed the aspect of a twentieth-century privy in a small, well-administered township. There was no question now of flushing fugitive new boys into the open by the time-honoured ruse of a 'fireship', that is to say, a bunched-up newspaper, set alight and launched downstream. The cubicle partitions were raised by more than a foot and, as was inevitable, all the entertainment value of the walls disappeared under the whitewash. It was now a sterile, featureless place, and even the sanitary-minded regretted its passing.

It was the transformation of the Bog that brought about David's first brush with the new man, touching off a series of smouldering rows that had the effect of changing the system by which David had measured time over the last decade.

In Algy's day every season had a focal point, some of them disagreeable, but a majority associated with sparkle of some kind. Now this was changed utterly. Weeks merged into one another, starred only with head-on collisions, and he could never be sure when one of these confrontations would occur, or even how some of them began. They were bracketed, in his mind, as a series of 'times'. The Time of the Missing Edict. The Time of 'Stoker' Monk's Pipe. The Time of the Stoic's Statute of Limitations, and so on, a long period of ding-dong strife, ending in an eruption that tested his staying power to the utmost, and set him examining and re-examining all the underlying reasons for withholding his resignation.

The very first of these clashes stemmed directly from the face-lift at the Bog. As usual, it came out of an indifferent sky.

The boys, they learned in the common room, had yet another nickname for the new head, a tag that puzzled everyone, even Barnaby, mintmaster of nicknames. They called him 'Noble', and the word was so much at odds with Alcock's image that the staff pondered its origins unceasingly, Barnaby claiming that it cost him sleep. Questions in the form of hints produced no satisfactory answers from the boys. The boldest evaded the query, the timid declared it was outside their experience. David stumbled on the answer one lunch-hour when, on his way up to the pavilion, he popped into the Bog when all its official patrons were in Big Hall.

The first thing that attracted his attention, aside from the transformation, was a large official notice, presumably prepared by the headmaster's secretary, Miss Rowlandson, for it was professionally typed on foolscap and pasted on the angle of the wall sub-dividing the building into two unequal halves. It was a typical Alcockian decree. Boys would refrain from clogging the drain with refuse. Every effort would be made to trace culprits who persisted in this disgusting practice, and so on, and David glanced down it until his eye stopped at a pencilled addendum to the typed surname under the signature. Someone had printed, in bold capitals, 'AND NO BALLS', after the world 'ALCOCK', so that it was clear how the nickname had originated. It was obviously a codeword for the addendum. He removed the notice and hastened to put Barnaby out of his misery.

Barnaby was very impressed. "It shows a certain dignity, don't you think? It makes its point, while masking its basic vulgarity. There's logic in it too."

"Logic?"

"Yes. I imagine they think of him as a eunuch. I'm not suggesting he is, of course, but you might look for that terrible separateness in someone who has been castrated, wouldn't you say?"

"Are you implying that Alcock is psychologically frustrated, and that accounts for his detachment?"

"How do we know? What do any of us know of his childhood, boyhood or ancestry for that matter?"

"Freudian cock," David said, "and you know it, Barnaby. You're just playing with words."

"But of course," replied Barnaby, swiftly. "Do I ever do anything else?"

"No, you don't," growled David, "and apart from Carter—of all people—no one here seems alive to what might happen to us all under that bloody cipher."

"Cipher? Well, that fits too, but I see him more as an eccentric, an eccentric with a strange knack of getting things done, P.J."

"Howarth made the same point but it doesn't console me." He tore the notice into small pieces and dropped them into Barnaby's wastepaper basket. "Fine. He gets things done. The grub improves. The Bog is rebuilt. The church pews are revarnished. But what's happening to the *tone* of the place? The real Bamfylde, *Algy's* Bamfylde? This used to be a lively, noisy, happy school. Alcock has subdued it in a matter of weeks. What might he do in a year or two, sitting up there on his bloody private Olympus? All right, maybe Carter and I are especially anti because we were passed over, but I for one never expected to land that job. Damn it, Barnaby, you're a pretty discerning chap most times. Can't you *sense* a creeping paralysis?"

"I can smell dust raised by a brisk new broom. I wouldn't put it higher than that. And, even if you're right, institutions of this kind aren't frozen. They like to prattle about tradition but change is at work all the time, and the pace has speeded up appreciably since the war. You'll join me for coffee, I hope?"

"Not today, thanks," David said, for the man's neutrality irritated him, equating, as it did, with Howarth's on the same topic. Only two days previously he had had an almost identical discussion with Howarth, and had been surprised to discover that Howarth had drawn up a balance sheet as regards the new man's innovations, deciding that Alcock emerged with a small credit balance. He had said something else, too, doubtless aimed at dispelling David's misgivings. "Why worry? He'll spend himself in a term or two. That kind of chap always does. Bamfylde isn't an old foundation, as schools go in Britain, but it's old enough to slow his gallop," and when David denied this Howarth said, spitefully, "Then go and mull it over with Carter, your new friend. You and he are in cahoots now."

It was an overt display of jealousy on Howarth's part. A little of the cordiality that had developed between them during his feud with the Outram housemaster had been dissipated by the armistice and this retort proved that Howarth was no more proof against the occupational hazard of schoolmasters than the next man. As for the feud, it struck him as absurd that he could have maintained it for so long, for now they were on the best of terms, drawn together less by their shared failure on the day Alcock was appointed, than by a common distrust of the new man and his methods. Twenty-four hours later David had a chance to assess Alcock's uncanny grasp of the minutiae of school life.

When the boys assembled by houses after morning school, preparatory to dispersal to Big Hall for their midday meal, the head emerged from his quarters through the door opening on the quad and took over the parade from Heffling, the duty prefect. He said, in his quiet, carrying voice, "Before you disperse—a small matter, but one I require to be cleared up before lights out. A day or so ago I caused a notice to be posted in the latrines, regarding the disposal of litter. This notice has been removed by some unauthorised person. I require whoever removed it to return it, with a written apology. He will be admonished, no more. If he has insufficient moral courage he may return it to me anonymously. That is all. Carry on, Heffling."

Heffling, somewhat taken aback by the terms of the ultimatum, called the parade to attention, and dismissed it. The boys streamed off into the corridor and over them, like a swarm of bees, buzzed a cloud of speculative guesses. For here was an unusual use of the traditional code of honour that was supposed to apply to a situation of this kind. It had, in effect, been turned inside out, for while, from time to time, appeals for culprits to own up and face the consequences had been made by authority, it was only resorted to in cases of grave breaches of discipline, usually involving clashes with outside personnel, farmers, tradesmen and the like. Judy Cordwainer, David recalled, had been a great believer in extracting confessions by a threat of collective punishment, but Algy rarely employed the device. David could even recall what he had once said of it: "Germanic! Don't care for it. Has the smack of the hostage system, and it's damned lazy too. Our job to catch the burglars, without holding a pistol to their wives and families."

Forty-eight hours passed before Alcock launched his second ultimatum, appearing through the same door at the same moment in the school day. This time Winterbourne was duty prefect, and David could have sworn he winked in the direction of the knot of housemasters, waiting, as by custom, for parade dismissal before going in to their own lunch.

Alcock said, in the same reasonable tone, "Er . . . pertaining to that missing notice. No one has come forward. No one has returned the document anonymously. I have therefore no alternative but to take steps that will involve the innocent. Unless that notice reaches me by lights out today Saturday's half-term holiday will be cancelled."

There was an involuntary buzz at this, loud enough to cause Alcock to call for silence, before handing the parade back to Winterbourne. Barnaby said, as they passed through Fifth Form arch, "Here's a how-de-do, P.J. What now, I wonder? Do you keep mum, and inflict injustice on the least of us, or volunteer for six of the best from the Noble Stoic?" but David, profoundly irritated, derived no compensating humour from the situation. "All that, over a damned litter warning! Doesn't that highlight the idiot's inability to communicate? Algy would have made a joke about it, posted another notice, and threatened the hide of the next boy who removed it."

"Ah, so," said Barnaby, "but Algy was twenty years threatening to rebuild those latrines. It was fortunate I concealed the source of my information concerning the euphemistic 'Noble'. As it is, what the devil can you do, without sacrificing your dignity?"

"You let me worry about my dignity," and he moved up to the staff dining table, choosing a seat between Bouncer, who had not been present when the ultimatums were issued, and old Rapper Gibbs, who never spoke at mealtimes. Fifteen minutes before the bell signalled the first of the afternoon periods he made his way to Alcock's study.

He had not been in here since Algy left and was stunned by the changes. The place had always looked a regular tip, with papers spilling from every chair, books from every shelf, and every inch of wall-space covered with group photographs of Bamfeldians in operatic or athletic costume. Now, he mused, it looked like a specialist's waiting-room. Every book and paper was in its proper place, and the walls, freshly distempered, were quite bare. He wondered what Alcock had done with all those yellowing groups, including the one Algy had pointed out the first afternoon he stood here—Bamfylde's Fifteen of the 1913/14 season, the names of all but two inscribed on the cross outside. Alcock was at his desk, writing. He even had the look of a specialist, an exclusive and very expensive specialist, very scrubbed, very clinical. His manner, without being friendly, was polite.

"Do take a seat, Powlett-Jones. I won't keep you a moment," and he wrote an address on an envelope and used a sponge to seal it. "He would," David thought, "licking would be out for him," and as Alcock raised his head he said, "It's about that litter notice, Headmaster. There's no occasion to cancel the holiday."

"You have identified the culprit?"

"In a sense I have. It was me."

"*You* removed that notice?"

"I had a good reason."

"Of course. What was it?"

"It was defaced."

"You mean you caught someone defacing it?"

"No. Everyone was at lunch when I found it."

"I see. You kept it, I hope?"

"No, I didn't. It was scrawled over and if I could make a suggestion, Headmaster, I should advise replacing it and leaving the matter there. It won't be interfered with again, they've had their warning."

"I rather think that's a matter for me to decide, Powlett-Jones."

"Yes, of course. I was offering a suggestion."

"It's good of you." There was a moment's silence, Alcock occupied in lifting and clasping his hands, as if in prayer. "Damn it, the man doesn't even doodle," David thought, "he probably did once and cured himself of the habit." Then, from Alcock: "I made my first appeal two days ago. You seem to have been reluctant to tell me. Was there a reason for that? Possibly you suspect a boy from your house?"

"I haven't the least idea who it was. In the circumstances, however, I think you'll agree that any member of the staff would hesitate to admit that he had removed a notice posted up by the headmaster."

"I really can't see why."

"You don't think he would have found it embarrassing?"

"That depends on the nature of the defacement. Just how was it defaced?"

For a moment David was almost inclined to tell him, and see

what he made of it, but he thought better of it. He said, "Nothing particularly obscene, if that's what you're thinking. Just a piece of schoolboy mischief."

"In other words, you refuse to tell me in what way the notice was interfered with?"

"Yes, I do. The main thing is that you now know that a boy didn't remove it."

"I don't think that's relevant, Powlett-Jones. The main factor is surely that one of my staff, and a housemaster at that, refuses to co-operate with me in the maintenance of discipline."

"I'm sorry, Headmaster, I still think it's best forgotten."

He had expected some reaction but there was none. Alcock had himself completely in hand. The familiar empty expression had returned to his oddly puckish face. He said, standing, "Well, then, we shall have to leave it there, won't we? Regretfully, on my part, I may add."

He nodded and David moved out into the corridor, leading to Big School. He had a strong sensation of having been dismissed, or having narrowly escaped a thrashing for some silly prank, of the kind Boyer had perpetrated when he was in the Lower Fourth. There was no victory here for either of them, just stalemate, leaving their relationship, an important one for Bamfylde he would say, precisely where it had been before he tampered with that damned notice. He mooched off to take the Upper Fifth in his favourite nineteenth century but there was neither pleasure nor profit in the period. Gilroy, still stuck with the name 'Strofe', on account of his mispronunciation of 'apostrophe' years ago, remarked to Fogaty, as second bell rang and David moved off, "What's eating old Pow-Wow these days? He's been moody all term, hasn't he?" and Fogaty, who missed very little, replied, "He isn't hitting it off with Noble. Wouldn't surprise me if he didn't pack it in after a term or two."

"I hope to God not," Gilroy said. "We could do a lot worse than Pow-Wow. At least he can make a period pass quicker than some of them."

3

It did, in fact, occur to him to start hunting up another job during the Christmas break, when he and Grace went to Wales for a fortnight, and afterwards spent a long weekend in town with Beth's folk, but then he realised that resignation, at this stage, would be an empty gesture he would live to regret. He had small hopes of learning to live with Alcock, as all but he and Carter seemed able to do, and apart from that silly business of the notice there had been no open conflict between them, only a dragging sense of impermanence and disarray that hung over the school, as though he and everyone else were experiencing everything second-hand. It astonished him that only Carter, whom he had always regarded as a very insensitive man, shared this sense of strain.

Then, towards the end of the Lent term, the 'Stoker' Monk crisis was upon them, reducing the litter-notice tiff to insignificance.

*   *   *

Monk was a seventeen-year-old in the Upper Fifth, whose addiction to pipe tobacco had earned him his nickname as a Third Former. Returning from a visit to Austria he startled the hard core of Bamfylde's smokers by squatting on a trunk in the hideout above the covered playground (the smokers' favourite retreat) and puffing away at a huge, ungainly pipe, with a bowl carved in the shape of a Tyrolean peasant's head.

The addicts had laid bets that Monk would throw up in something under three minutes, but he did not. On the contrary, he seemed proof against the fumes of the strong Longshoreman's Flake he was using, and henceforth refused anything less lethal, declaring that a cigarette was a little lad's smoke. Soon it was rumoured that Stoker got through two ounces of pipe tobacco every week. He was caught on three occasions, twice by prefects, who beat him, and once by Carter, his housemaster, who lectured him for the better part of forty minutes and beat him into the bargain, but at least Carter refrained from carrying out his threat to write to Monk Senior. Stoker, a quick-witted boy, pleaded that Monk Senior had a serious heart condition, and hinted that a letter home might lay Carter open to a charge of manslaughter.

Beating and lectures notwithstanding, however, Stoker refused to be parted from his pipe, replacing the three that were confiscated by a fourth of equally extravagant design. Apart from his incurable smoking habits, he was an amiable, law-abiding boy, and his

academic progress better than average. Somewhere along the line
he had acquired the habitual pipe-smoker's habit of cool reflection,
and could digest everything he imbibed in class. He thus sailed
through exams and trick questions held no terrors for him. He
could sniff them out, he said, in the phraseology they employed.

His end-of-term reports were spattered with commendations.
He was living proof, his contemporaries declared, that the warning
alleging the habit caused dire shortness of wind was a load of
codswallop. Monk made the Junior Fifteen while he was still in
the Upper Third, and the First Fifteen a year later, where he
played as scrum-leader throughout the season Bamfylde never lost
a game. He was also a long-distance runner, and came close to
winning his running colours last season, so that Carter, himself a
non-smoker, was baffled by Monk and through bafflement came
to conceive a deep respect for the boy. Perhaps he saw him as a
medical phenomenon, to whom ordinary rules of health did not
apply. At all events, he made him a house prefect and looked the
other way if he had reason to believe that yet another pipe had
replaced the one with the negro's head, now reposing in the Outram repository of confiscated items. He was heard to say, on the
last occasion Stoker's name came up over common room coffee,
"He's going to have quite a collection of keepsakes when he leaves.
As well as three pipes, all made in appalling taste, there are two
catapults and an air-pistol, dating from his pre-smoking days. I
suppose we should rejoice that the Stoker took to the weed. Harm-
ful it may be but only to Stoker." They deduced from this that
Monk qualified as one of Carter's favourites.

David's first knowledge of the crisis at Outram's came when
Carter stopped him in the quad after morning school one gusty
March day. He seemed extremely agitated and the signs were so
obvious that David enquired if he was ill. "Not ill," Carter said,
breathlessly, "but more upset than I can remember being since
the day those asses appointed that brute over both our heads.
Will you oblige me by stepping inside a moment, P.J.?"

David, mystified, followed him up the steps into Outram's, remembering the occasion he had gone there to complain of
Carter's snide comment on his political sympathies. It seemed a
long time ago. Already the benign reign of Herries was receding
into history. Carter closed the door and stood with his back to it,
still breathing very heavily, and looking dazed and distraught.

"You won't believe it, P.J.," he spluttered at length, "nobody would who really *knew* the old Stoker. It's clear against the rules. Everybody knows that. But in every other way Stoker's a brick, an absolute brick! Besides, he's due to sit for matric in June. Why the devil did he have to do it *there*, of all places? Why didn't the idiot stick to the plantation? That's where they go since we rooted them out of the covered playground, isn't it?"

"You aren't making much sense. Do I gather Alcock caught Monk smoking one of his gaudy pipes?"

"In the coke-hole, after prep. He should have known the wretched man is always poking about in premises that were always left to the maintenance staff. And now he's been sacked. Sacked, you hear? And without so much as a reference to me, if you please! I wouldn't have known a thing about it if the boy hadn't made a direct approach to me."

"Alcock sacked Monk for smoking? Is that what you're telling me?"

"I said you wouldn't believe it. Hang it, if every boy caught smoking had been expelled over the time I've been here, we should have been reduced to a handful of prep school boys by now. You know it and I know it! Everybody knows it except that . . . that iceberg over there!"

"Have you tried to talk him out of it?"

"Good God, man, of course I have but I didn't make the slightest impression. I pointed out that Stoker was a splendid type in every other respect, and that no one had ever been expelled for smoking, but he kept insisting that Monk was a previous offender and he was going to make an example of him. I begged and I pleaded. Practically grovelled before him, but the man has no human feelings, P.J. I even suggested a compromise, that we let Stoker stay on, take the exam in June, and leave in July, but he didn't take kindly to that either. Now old Stoker is packing and that brute is putting him on the four o'clock train. How did he know Stoker had been caught once or twice in Herries's time?"

"He probably keeps a dossier on everyone, us included. But what did you think I could do about it, beyond sympathising?"

Carter looked evasive, then said, with a rush, "You're . . . you're very popular here, P.J. More popular than any of us, I'd say. You get along with people in a way I never could."

"Good of you to say that, Carter, but I'm less popular with the

Noble Stoic than anybody. If you want someone to intercede, and I don't think it would do any good, why not approach Barnaby, Howarth or both?"

"I mean to," Carter said, knitting his sandy brows, "but . . . er . . . *through* you, if you follow me, P.J."

"I don't, but I'll do anything I can to help."

"Well, then, suppose *you* tackle Barnaby, Howarth and some of the others, and get them to add their names to this. They'd do it for you. I don't think they would for me," and he took a paper from his 'in' tray and thrust it under David's nose.

It was a sheet of letterheaded Bamfylde notepaper, rubber stamped 'Outram's', and closely written in Carter's neat, legible hand. It said:

Sir, we, the undersigned, respectfully request a reprieve on behalf of C. J. Monk. We do this in the hope that you will reconsider three factors, all of which we regard as extenuating, viz:

(a) We have all known Monk since he first came here four years ago and can testify, (corroborating the opinion of his housemaster) that he has proved a great asset to the school; socially, academically, athletically.

(b) No previous warning has been issued to the effect that smoking carries a mandatory penalty of expulsion. We feel one such warning should be given.

(c) Monk is due to sit for University Entrance in June. In our view he is certain to gain exemption from matriculation. Dismissal now would have a disastrous effect upon his career.

Signed,
T. S. CARTER, M.A. (London).

"Good God," David exclaimed, "this is a bit of a belly-crawl, isn't it?"

"Yes, it is," said Carter, readily, "but that's the point. An appeal like that, signed by all the old hands, will be a feather in Alcock's cap, even if it means him climbing down. If that petition is in his hands before Monk's train leaves, I've got a feeling he'll act on it, in his own interests. It isn't blather, either. The old Stoker is aiming for the F.O., and expulsion would put paid to that, unless he could bring some powerful influence to bear. I happen to know he couldn't. His father is an ironmonger. Will you do it, P.J.? For him, and for me? I can't tell you how much I'd appreciate it."

It was not only Carter's pitiful earnestness that prevailed but David's curiosity concerning the reaction of Alcock and the staff to his extraordinary petition. Especially, now that he came to think about it, that of men who had been his own and Carter's colleagues for more than ten years. One assumed that one got to know people very well in these confined circumstances, but clearly this was taking too much for granted. Why if Howarth, Barnaby and old Rapper Gibbs were friends, was he quite unable to predict in advance how any one of them would respond to a move that would diminish them in the eyes of Alcock. There were several unknown factors here. How much loyalty and comradeship existed between them, now that Algy had retired? How many would be likely to put themselves in Carter's place? Or in Stoker Monk's place? How much dignity would, say, Howarth, be prepared to sacrifice in the cause of Carter and Monk? Answers to these imponderables might be interesting.

Tucking the letter into his jacket pocket he said, "I'll give it a try, Carter. I haven't got much faith in it working but you'd probably do the same for me."

"I would, I would, P.J."

"Maybe you'll have to, if things don't take a turn for the better," and to by-pass Carter's gush of gratitude he hurried out, crossing the quad and making his way up the staircase over the Fifth to Barnaby's quarters.

*　　*　　*

It would be best, he thought, to start with an easy one, and Barnaby was by far the most congenial man on the staff. Aware of the need to cut corners he explained the situation in a few sentences, then produced Carter's plea, having added his own signature before knocking on Barnaby's door. At least one man was predictable. Barnaby, regarding the thing as a huge joke, signed without hesitation.

"We seek tears from the Noble Stoic of the woods? I think the hope is vain, P.J., but I should be delighted to be proved wrong. Whom will you tackle next? Howarth? He'll refuse, shooting quills in all directions. Come to think of it, I doubt if he'd sign a bleat like that for you, much less Carter."

Bouncer and Rapper both signed, the one gladly, because he agreed with Carter that the sack for smoking was 'a bit much'. His standard punishment, four penal marks, would have been more seemly, he thought. Rapper Gibbs, the music master signed reluctantly, and after a good deal of persuasion on David's part.

"I'm not doing it for Carter or Monk," he grunted, "but because you've got yourself mixed up in it. Seems to me I owe you a favour or two, Powlett-Jones, but maybe you've forgotten."

"I'm afraid I have. What favour do you owe me?" Rapper sniffed and rubbed his long nose, a habit he had picked up from Algy during the countless operatic rehearsals they had shared over the years. "Well, not you, exactly," he said, "your wife."

"Beth?"

"I was very fond of her, did you know that? Best leading lady we ever had, and the easiest to coach. No sulks and no temperament, just hard graft, ending in a rattling good performance, even when she was carrying those twins of yours." He looked glum for a moment. "They were the salad-days, Powlett-Jones. We aren't likely to see their like again under him. This is the first year since 1904 we haven't produced a Gilbert and Sullivan. *He* thinks they're frivolous, you know. So what did we have to cheer us along last Christmas?"

"Excerpts from Molière."

"Ah, yes. Lot of piffle. Who the devil wants to listen to a lot of French gibberish? Nobody, save that rackety chap, Molyneux. Place isn't what it was, is it?"

"If it was I wouldn't be standing here asking you to put your name to a document of this kind," David said, and Gibbs signed, advising him to try Molyneux next, for Molyneux and Carter had 'once been thick, hadn't they?'

If they had the relationship must have cooled, David had never been close to the man who took Ferguson's place as French master. He was well up to his work, they said, but difficult to know, another who seemed unable to identify with Bamfylde, in the way the Old Guard had before and throughout David's time. He had private means and drove a red sports car to and from his lodgings in the village. He was also reckoned a highbrow, on account of regular visits to town and Bristol where he patronised obscure productions in club theatres. Molyneux got along reasonably well with the new man and now confirmed as much, refusing to co-operate in any way. "Ridiculous gesture," he said, returning the petition. "Damned surprised at Carter going to these lengths, and even more surprised at you and the others abetting him. Kind of thing that belongs in the Lower Third, doesn't it?"

"We don't think so. Carter has a point about the effect it might have on Monk's career."

"Monk is Outram's pigeon. He certainly isn't mine. Try How-arth, and see what change you get from him."

But David went first to Irvine, where another shock awaited him. Irvine also refused to sign, on the grounds that Alcock would interpret his signature as a climb-down regarding the disputes between them concerning the amount of emphasis to be placed on games.

"But that's ridiculous," David argued. "This has damn all to do with games."

"Indirectly it has. I've stood up to him about free periods for training, and I mean to tackle him again when the cricket season opens. This would give him the edge on me and, in any case, what the devil has Carter ever done for any of us? He's always had his eye on the main chance."

David left him and made his way up to Howarth's study, where Howarth heard him out, his expression even bleaker than usual. He said, "Can't understand why you're trotting about the place pulling Carter's chestnuts out of the fire. I realise you and he had signed articles, but Carter is still Carter, isn't he?"

"I don't think he is," David said, voicing a persistent thought that had kept recurring to him since he quitted Carter's study. "Something odd is happening to Carter. He seemed to me almost hysterical. He's been brooding a lot about Alcock over the last two terms, mostly about Alcock taking house decisions out of his hands, but he's not had a direct confrontation as I have. Or not until now."

"Let me see that silly petition again."

Howarth took it, adjusted his pince-nez, and read it very care-fully. "Well, there's a hint of hysteria here," he said, and then, shrewdly, "I hope to God it isn't rubbing off on you, P.J."

"I'll survive it," David said. "And survive Alcock too, I wouldn't wonder. I suppose the truth is we all had it pretty soft under Algy. He was my sole experience of a head."

"He wasn't mine, and there's no tyranny like it if you happen to strike it unlucky." He pondered a moment. "I'll sign the damned thing. Monk has potential, and who the devil am I to penalise a boy for smoking? If you denied me my forty a day they'd soon be calling for me in a plain van."

He took a pen and signed with a kind of snarl and David thanked him and withdrew. "What the devil is happening to us?" he asked himself, moving down the steps and recrossing the quad to Outram's. "In spite of occasional bickering we used to be a team. Now everybody's pulling a different way."

4

Carter's hunch was correct. Within an hour of receiving the petition, signed by Carter, David, Barnaby, Acton, Gibbs and Howarth, Alcock relented, if that was the word. The reprieve was granted on two conditions, both, to Carter's way of thinking, harsh. Monk would be allowed to sit the examination and finish the school year but there could be no question of his staying on after that. He was also required to submit himself to a public dressing-down in Big School that night and concerning this Carter had misgivings.

"Even Alcock can't beat a man in the Upper Fifth," he told David, and when David suggested that he might make an exception, Carter shook his head. "He's against corporal punishment. I know that from something he said during our discussion."

"Well, that's at least one thing we have in common," David said, "for you all know my views on it. It's always seemed to me a miserable confession of failure on our part. So what else can Alcock do but jaw?"

"I don't know," Carter said, gloomily. "We'll soon find out."

They soon did. Immediately before prep bell all the boys, including the juniors, were crammed into Big School, and Alcock swept in with Monk in tow. There was just the faintest suggestion of a sigh when they appeared, prompted perhaps by the tacit implication that the old Stoker was seen as a heretic about to be burned at the stake. David noticed then that Alcock was carrying the Stoker's fourth pipe, the usual monstrosity, with a curved stem and a bowl of impressive proportions, again carved in the likeness of a negro's head. He held the ungainly thing between his finger and thumb, so that Howarth muttered, "Looks as if the dam' fellow is handling a rattlesnake. Why the devil doesn't he throw it in the wastepaper basket and be done with it?" But Alcock had more ceremonial intentions. Standing well forward on the rostrum, with the abject Monk slightly behind him, he held the pipe aloft for everyone to see, and began: "I am probably correct in assuming everyone present knows why we are assembled. It is to draw your attention to a disgusting habit practised by the wretched boy you see beside me, a boy I happened to catch indulging himself on school premises, with this so-called symbol of manhood in his hand. You are aware, of course, that every school has strict rules against smoking. Apart from a health hazard, it is generally regarded as a grave infraction of discipline. Yet Monk saw fit— indeed, has seen fit on previous occasions—to set the rule at defiance."

He paused for a moment, an actor getting the feel of his audience. Then he continued, "It had been my intention to expel Monk forthwith. The fact that I had second thoughts is due, solely, to an urgent intercession on the part of his housemaster and some of that housemaster's colleagues. All stressed the fact that I had issued no specific warning concerning the automatic penalty for smoking, adding that Monk was due to sit an important examination in June. Those reasons, although not strictly relevant, had validity. I was moved by them. I took them into account. However, you may take it as read that *no* extenuating circumstances will influence me in the future. Any boy caught smoking, or found in possession of a pipe, or cigars, or cigarettes, will be sent home within the hour, notwithstanding his age or the circumstances. In the meantime, however, in order to underline this example, I propose to destroy this implement in your presence," and to the amazement of everyone present, including Monk, he reached into the folds of his gown and produced a claw-hammer.

David had the impression then that Alcock had quietly gone mad and was about to use his hammer on Monk as well as the pipe, but then his attention was deflected by a movement of the head's right hand, as he laid the hammer aside, raised his left arm high above his head and snapped his fingers twice. At the signal, Potter, one of the junior kitchen staff, made a self-conscious entry carrying a tin tray, of the kind in daily use in the dining-hall. Setting it down on the desk he retreated wordlessly, stepping down from the rostrum and disappearing as unobtrusively as he had appeared. Alcock placed the pipe on the tray, picked up the hammer, tried it for balance, and then delivered his first shattering blow on the bowl, smashing it so effectively that fragments shot across the dais and ricocheted from the panelling. Five other blows followed until the pipe was in small splinters, the clang of each impact shattering the silence of the big room. As the final clang died away a loud buzz of exclamation arose and under its cover David murmured, "He's dotty! He must be . . . !" but Howarth said, "Not in the least. In his way he's an artist. It will add flavour to every cigarette I light from here on . . ." But by then Alcock was calling sharply for silence and at once a sense of anti-climax descended on them all. From the rear of the big room somebody was heard to smother a laugh and the sound was so distinct that everyone's head turned, trying to identify the culprit. Alcock said, crisply, but still without raising his voice, "Will the boy who finds this amusing step forward?" and there was a stir among the two ranks representing the Sixth as Sax Hoskins moved out into the central aisle and stood there, nearly six feet in height and not, David would have said, as shamefaced as he should have been.

"You, Hoskins?"

"Yes, sir."

"Would you mind telling us all what prompted you to laugh?"

"I . . . er . . . couldn't help it, sir."

"I see. You couldn't help it. That is *all* you have to say?"

"Yes, sir. I'm sorry, sir."

"I'm glad to hear it. You're a prefect, I believe."

"Yes, sir."

"Next term, under normal circumstances, you would have become head boy of the school?"

"Well . . . yes, sir."

"You are no longer a prefect, Hoskins. Prefects are expected to co-operate with the headmaster in the maintenance of discipline. That is all. You may dismiss."

They rose as Alcock descended the two steps to floor level and swept out. There was no point in anybody making the least attempt to stifle the loud buzz that followed his exit. Everyone, masters as well as boys, contributed to it, and the only two present

who had nothing to say were Carter and Monk. The first sat beside the radiator looking stunned. The other moved closer to the
desk and looked down at the small heap of debris in the tray. The
rest of the staff moved out in a body, turning, by common consent,
into the quad where Maxton, the third official bell-ringer David
could recall, was already swinging his handbell for prep.

Barnaby said, "I like to think we have just witnessed the compulsive act of a throwback. That was almost an exact reproduction of a medieval book-burning, the kind of thing Tyndale might
have been called upon to witness before being burned at the
stake. Interesting, don't you think?"

"No, I don't," snarled Rapper Gibbs. "It was the silliest piece
of cheap melodrama I've ever had to witness. The man is a complete ass."

"Howarth doesn't agree," David said. "You don't, do you,
Howarth?"

"Not entirely," said Howarth, ostentatiously lighting a Gold
Flake, and inhaling deeply. "You don't have to like him in order
to concede his originality."

But Gibbs had drifted off, and Barnaby began to elaborate his
throwback theory, so David turned back towards Big School and
was just in time to see Monk cross the quad with Carter. The
housemaster's gait was jerky and in the half-light it looked almost
as if Monk was assisting him. He hurried across and caught them
as they were mounting the steps to Outram's and Monk, turning
aside, said, "Mr. Carter told me, sir. I'd like to say thank you, if
I may."

"It was your housemaster's idea, Monk. I didn't have much
confidence in it." And then, "For God's sake, man, stay well clear
of the head until the end of next term. I wouldn't like to see that
little scene repeated, would you?"

"No sir," said the Stoker, seriously, "it was a very good pipe,
sir," and David felt a tide of profound irritation rising in him,
not merely with Alcock but with youth and youth's ability to
slough off emotional involvement in all manner of things, not
merely an idiotic pipe-smashing ceremony but the stupidity of the
entire human race. It was a very disquieting sensation, carrying
him all the way back to a time when boys not much older than
Monk were exchanging facetious jokes within minutes of walking
into a curtain of shell-fire. He said, curtly, "Cut off, Monk, and

try and stay out of trouble," and as the boy withdrew he glanced through the open door of Outram's, wondering whether he should go in and console Carter. He decided against it. The episode was finished and already, he supposed, absorbed into Bamfylde legend, to be passed from generation to generation until it became apocryphal with Alcock portrayed as a mountebank, chasing Monk up and down Big School with a hammer in one hand and a gaudy pipe in the other.

He climbed the stairs to his own quarters, wondering how Grace would take the summary demotion of Hoskins, perhaps the only one among them with a true sense of proportion, and was not surprised to see Sax awaiting him on the threshold, holding a record in its cardboard sleeve. Sax said, cheerily, "Evening, sir. I was on the list as duty perk to take prep, but as I'm reduced to ranks that'll be out, won't it? The head does like us to keep to the letter of the law, doesn't he?"

"I believe he does, Hoskins," David said, and suddenly felt immensely grateful to the boy. He thought, "Maybe we can all learn something from him," and said, "Is that a record for Grace?"

"Yes, sir, came this morning by post. A peaches and creamy number, sir—'Carolina Moon'. Good rhythm, tho'. Harry Roy's orchestra, playing 'Button up your Overcoat' on the reverse side. Would you give it to her, sir?"

"Give it to her yourself," he heard himself say, "we all need a bit of cheering up, Sax." And then, as they went in, he called to Grace that Hoskins was here. "Did anyone else laugh, Sax?"

"No, sir. They were all too concerned for poor old Stoker. I think it rattled 'em a little, sir."

"It obviously didn't rattle you."

"No, sir. To be honest, it just struck me as . . . well . . . the funniest thing I had ever seen happen here. I mean, walloping away at poor old Stoker's pipe with a hammer. And that bit of stage-dressing—Potter coming in bang on cue, with the tray. I don't mind about the demotion, sir. In a way it was worth it. I mean, you could wait around a long time before you saw anything as funny as that."

The near-despair he had experienced a few minutes ago turned itself inside out, so that now he saw youth's resilience as a miraculous restorative, capable of reducing everything to a laugh. He thought, "That's how it's been from the very beginning, since the day I first came here, looking and feeling a total wreck. Self-pity was out from the moment Algy collared that boy on the way in from the playing fields . . . Who was it again? I remember, Daffy Jones, with news of a last-minute recovery by Nicolson's. And then Nipper Shawe appeared, swinging that bell, and I felt . . . renewed somehow. I hope to God that's how it'll always be, with someone like Sax Hoskins around to remind us that nothing matters much. Except the ability to laugh at ourselves now and again."

Grace had dashed out of her room, welcoming an opportunity to abandon her homework, and in a moment they had the record turning. Sax was right about 'Carolina Moon'. It was a peaches and creamy number, but soothing to the nerves in an odd sort of way. He smiled across at them and went into his study, closing the door on Alcock and all his works.

Chapter Two

1

He saw it, throughout the summer and autumn of that year, as a cross-country ride on a half-broken mount, a succession of jolts, swerves, slitherings and punishing jog-trots, interspersed, every now and again, with a head-on collision, incidents like the lavatory notice row, and the last-minute reprieve of Stoker Monk.

Looking back on his ten years under Algy, his life seemed, in retrospect, to have been unbelievably smooth, even allowing for occasions like the Havelock's dormitory fire, the Carter feud, Winterbourne's disappearance, and his own personal tragedy. Now, with the staff divided and distrustful, the boys bored and bemused, and everyone isolated from the methods and policies Alcock adopted, he was more often out of the saddle than in it, usually, he would have said, just about holding on in hope that some dramatic improvement was around the corner. And yet, for all his misgivings, he never thought seriously of throwing in the sponge and leaving Bamfylde to run itself into the ground.

The summer up here had always been especially welcome after the frost, wind and rain of the Lent term. Year after year the weather was predictable in May and June, although it sometimes deteriorated towards the end of the term. It seemed settled enough now, after their reassembly in late April, and he made a resolve to enjoy it in spite of Alcock, immersing himself in his day-to-day schedule, and dividing his spare time between work on 'The Royal Tigress', and excursions beyond the school boundaries, where he could put the school out of mind.

But then, confronting him in much the same way as the two previous eruptions, the Hislop crisis loomed up and within a few weeks of that the certainty of Carter's withdrawal and almost total isolation. And after that, towards the end of the succeeding Michaelmas term, an uncompromising declaration of war, that could only end in outright victory for one man or the other.

*　　*　　*

Hislop was the leader of The Lump, a cadre now trapped in that traditional repository of rascals, the Lower Fourth, where one always looked for the originals and (providing one was lucky and patient) promise of better things to come once the natural leaders had moved to the Fifth. Boyer, Winterbourne and Sax Hoskins had been of this ilk, incorrigible at fifteen and sixteen, but worth their weight in gold once they had sobered down and been given responsibility.

Hislop was a boy who could go one way or the other; towards a modest fulfilment, or to perdition, like Ruby Bickford, now, it was said, spending his father's money in the Argentine, and living the life of Old Reilly according to ill-spelled letters to former contemporaries.

Hislop's father was a publican, a heavy, florid man, with a sharp little wife, said to bully him unmercifully. Hislop got up to all the usual pranks, including the placing of a plaster cast of Aphrodite in Barnaby's bed when he was absent, then spreading a rumour that there was a corpse on the premises. He had averaged, in Algy's time, about one hiding a week, but he never minded that, viewing authority, and authority's visitations, much as the old lag regards arrest and an occasional stretch in gaol. It was this attitude in mind, of which David and other old hands were well aware, that made his admission so surprising. One would have thought that, given the circumstances, he would have swallowed his loss, and gone about his business, without taking a course that was bound to lead to one hell of a row.

Havelock's had been troubled, of late, by an outbreak of petty thieving, not unique in David's experience, for once or twice, in Algy's day, there had been trouble of the same kind. Small, personal items had disappeared from lockers, rarely anything of value but enough to promote an orgy of padlocking, enquiry and surveillance, involving domestic staff as well as boys. Then, one day towards the end of May, Hislop presented himself at the door of David's study and reported the theft of twelve pounds, fifteen shillings.

It was the size of the haul that staggered David and he questioned Hislop closely as regards the source of money that had been stolen, according to Hislop, from a bedroom slipper kept in the laundry basket that lived under every boy's bed.

He said, appalled, "Nearly thirteen pounds? Taken from a slipper in the senior dorm? But that's ridiculous, Hislop. Apart from having that much money, what on earth possessed you to hide it in a slipper?"

"I thought it would be safer there than in my locker, sir. Anyone can open those padlocks on the dormitory lockers. Gage's was opened a week ago and a fountain pen stolen."

"I know all about Gage's fountain pen. He reported it at the time. But that was worth five shillings. What were you doing with twelve pounds, fifteen, anyway?"

Hislop looked evasive. Unlike most of The Lump he had never been a good liar and David's experience told him at once that he was hoping to gloss over the source of the money.

"Well? You'll have to tell me now you're here."

"It was from my aunt," Hislop said. "She was going to live abroad and gave my Guv'nor fifteen pounds for me when he came over for Sports Day. I was supposed to bank it in my Post Office account but I didn't. I spent some on a binge at Ma Midden's, and was saving the rest towards a motorbike."

"And you were daft enough, knowing that there was a thief around, to hide it in your slipper?"

"Yes, sir. I see now it was crazy but it seemed a good idea at the time. I thought he wouldn't be likely to look there, among stuff awaiting to be collected for the wash. I stuffed it into the toe and kept it there with a ball of newspaper. It was there last night, sir, and it couldn't have gone during the night."

"Why not?"

"Because I put the slipper under my mattress and took it out again in the morning. I didn't check then but I'm certain it was still there."

"And then?"

"I nipped up during break to get five bob to blue at the tuck-shop. The ball of newspaper was still in the toe but the money was gone."

"Well, that seems to be that. Unless you have any bright ideas."

"I know who took it, sir."

"You *what?*"

"It was Cricklade. That new chap, who cleans up in Havelock's."

"You saw him take it?"

"No, I didn't see him, sir, but I've got proof. I asked around, and Trubshawe, in the kitchen, said Cricklade was the only one who had been up there since breakfast. So I . . . well . . . took a chance, sir."

"You challenged him?"

"No, sir. I knew that wouldn't do any good. I got Gower to tip him to go into the village for cigarettes. While he was gone Gage and I went through his room, sir."

"My God, that was a risky thing to do. Did you find the money?"

"Thirty bob of it, sir. He must have the rest on him. We found Gage's pen, too, sir, and Harper's postal order that he hadn't cashed."

"Apart from the postal order and the pen how do you know his thirty bob was part of your money?"

"It was three ten-bob notes, sir. One had been ripped across and stuck with transparent paper. Another had an ink blotch on it, shaped a bit like a thistle. I know they were two of mine, sir, but . . . well, I would have kept mum about it if it hadn't been for the postal order."

"What do you mean by that?"

"Well, sir, it was that that decided Gage and me to go through his room. Gage didn't care about the pen, and I wasn't that worried about losing the money, but Harper's just a kid, and that four-and-six meant a lot to him. He hasn't got a father and his mater's pretty skint—not so well off, sir. He doesn't even have tuck money, just the Wednesday sixpence for pocket-money. Losing that postal order worried him. He was blubbing about it."

It seemed conclusive. Two identifiable ten-shilling notes, Gage's pen and Harper's birthday postal order, lost five days ago. He said, thoughtfully, "Cricklade is new here, isn't he?" and Hislop confirmed that he had been taken on during the Easter break. "Couldn't we—just, well, collar him, Gage and me, sir? He's only a little squirt and we could give him a going over between us. Maybe he'd cough up the rest."

"Don't you do any such thing! This is a matter for the police, or if the head wants to keep it inside the school, something he and the bursar can attend to. The head will have to know right away in any case."

Hislop looked alarmed at this. "We didn't reckon on that, sir. We reckoned it was Havelock's business, and that you'd tackle it on your own."

"I can't. Cricklade will have to be sacked, and I can't sack him."

"You could frighten him into leaving, couldn't you, sir?"

"Not even that. He's obviously a cool customer, and if it came out that you and Gage had searched his room God knows what counter-charge he might bring. I'm sorry, Hislop, I'm glad you came to me, and even more so that you made a clean breast of it because of the thieving element but I've no alternative but to tell the head. You see that, don't you?"

"I suppose so, sir," he said, glumly. Then, "Are we likely to catch it hot, sir?"

"Not if I can help it. In a way you've done us all a service, as I see it. But you have to admit you went about it very unconventionally, and I daresay the head won't care for that part of it. How about Harper's four-and-six?"

"You don't have to bring him into it, sir. I made it up to him and kept the postal order. I've got it here, sir," and he handed it over.

"I'm afraid I'll have to borrow those ten-shilling notes, Hislop."

Hislop shrugged and groped in his pocket, coming up with three notes, two of them disfigured as he had described. Lunchbell sounded then and they went down together, parting in the quad where David said, "Both you and Gage will be wanted after lunch. In the meantime, keep your mouth shut about this. That's an order, understand?"

"Yes, sir."

He slouched off and David spared him a sympathetic thought. It was interesting, that reason he had given for searching Cricklade's room, and not all that improbable either. Hislop, although a young ruffian in many ways, was popular among the Lower School urchins, possibly on account of his openhandedness and reckless attitude to authority. He decided to see Alcock at once, letting himself into the head's house by the quad door and catching Alcock just as he was going to his own lunch.

"Could I have a word with you, Headmaster?"

Alcock glanced at his watch. "Now? I was about to have my lunch."

"I'm sure you'll agree it's urgent."

"Very well."

He turned and led the way back to his featureless study, motioning David inside and taking his customary place behind the desk. That was one of the many irritating things about Alcock, his way of reducing every interview to a confrontation between headmaster and erring pupil. David told his story factually, exactly as he had heard it from Hislop, and Alcock, his eyes on the strip of moor seen through the narrow window, heard him in complete silence.

"Is that everything, Powlett-Jones?"

"Everything I learned from Hislop, and I've no reason to suppose he was holding anything back."

"I'm afraid we differ there."

"I don't follow you, Headmaster."

"You don't? I think you should, after eleven years as a schoolmaster and, what is it, five as a housemaster? Wouldn't you say it was extremely unusual for a boy to possess that much money? Even a senior boy, and Hislop is not a senior."

"It is unusual, but not unique. Some of the parents are generous about pocket money and Hislop's father is that kind of man. Breezy, and a little . . . well . . . loud. Apart from that Hislop is an only child."

"You're telling me you believe that story of his about his aunt?"

"Not entirely. It's probably a cover story."

" 'Cover story?' What is that, exactly?"

"A half-truth."

"Concealing what?"

"I don't know. How could I know? Some personal transaction, conducted during the holidays, possibly. He's saving for a motorbike. He might have made a sale that he wouldn't want his people to know about. Frankly, sir, I don't see the source of the money as important. Surely the important thing is that Cricklade should be seen and questioned."

"That will occur, naturally."

"You intend reporting the matter to the police?"

"I might. Then again I might not. I'm afraid that's a decision you must leave to me."

"Of course. But it happened in my house, and naturally I'm very concerned."

"I should be surprised if you were not. Kindly ask both boys to report to me immediately after lunch. That's all, I think."

It was another of his curt dismissals. Not for the first time David restrained an impulse to insult the man, to shake him, pinch him, anything calculated to smash through the glacial screen of his self-sufficiency. There was nothing to be done, however, so he nodded and went out, wondering why successive events continually contrived to bring him into collision with a man of Alcock's disposition.

He told Hislop and Gage to report and noticed they were still absent from class when he took the Lower Fourth for last period. By the time tea was over he could endure the suspense no longer and went in search of them. Neither was to be found, so he entered the headmaster's house from Big School passage and knocked on the study door. He was still there, awaiting the summons to enter, when Rigby, the aged butler Alcock had inherited from Algy, came out of the kitchen and said, in response to David's question, "The headmaster isn't back from the station yet, sir."

"What's he doing down there, Rigby?"

"I'm afraid I couldn't say, sir. He went off about an hour ago, with two boys."

"Hislop and Gage?"

"I couldn't be sure, sir. My eyesight isn't what it was. I only caught a glimpse of the car moving off. He's sure to be back for dinner. Any message, sir?"

"No message." He went through the tiled hall into the forecourt, standing at the junction of the twin drives and wondering what Alcock and the two amateur detectives could be doing down at the station. It seemed likely they had gone there to catch and confront an absconding Cricklade.

He was conjuring with this and other possibilities when Alcock's Morris Oxford swung in the east drive and ran between

the beeches at its statutory twenty-five miles an hour. Alcock had
a reputation for excessively careful driving, a subject for the school
wits to work on. Hoskins had laid a wager that he could beat
him to Stone Cross and back on foot, providing he cut across the
cricket-field. Rockingham Major, who owned a Douglas motorcycle
that he rode in the holidays, said the Noble Stoic had never
learned the difference between the accelerator and the footbrake,
and drove by Braille, using his big toes. The car drove up, made
a cautious half-circle, and was backed carefully into the parking alcove. Alcock and Gage got out but Hislop was nowhere to be seen.
With mounting curiosity David followed them through Big School
arch and into the quad, where they parted, the head going across
to the bursar's office, Gage making for Outram's.

There was no point in asking for developments in front of the
bursar so David went after Gage, catching him halfway up the
steps to Carter's house.

"Hi, there! Gage!" and the boy turned. He looked, David
thought, as though he had been undergoing considerable strain.

"Sir?"

"Where's Hislop?"

"Hislop?"

"Yes, Hislop, man. He went with you, didn't he? To the station
in the head's car?"

"Yes, sir, but . . . well, he caught his train, sir."

"Train? What train?"

"The train home, sir."

"Are you telling me Hislop has been sent home, Gage?"

The boy now looked completely bewildered. "Yes, I am, sir
. . . I thought . . . Hislop thought . . . well, that you must know,
sir."

"Know what?"

"That he's been sacked."

"*Expelled*? Look here, Gage, are you pulling my leg?"

"No, of course not, sir. I was there when he went. His things
are being sent on and I've got to tell Matron. But first I've got
to report to Mr. Carter, sir."

"But why? For heaven's sake, what did Hislop do or say to get
himself expelled? If it was for searching Cricklade's room that's
an outrage and how is it that you're still here? You were with
him, weren't you?"

"Yes, sir, but it wasn't for that. It all came out when the head telephoned Hislop's pater, sir. About the money, I mean, how he got it in the first place."

"How did he get it?"

"By . . . by making a book, sir. On Sports Day. He cleaned up, especially on the steeplechase."

"Hislop got that fifteen pounds making a book?"

"Yes, sir."

"Laying odds on the races?"

"Yes, sir."

"And the head found out about it?"

"Yes, sir. Mostly the senior events. The head phoned and Hislop's pater blew the ga . . . told him it didn't come from an aunt, sir."

It took him so long to absorb this that Gage began to fidget. "I . . . er . . . have to report to Mr. Carter straight away, sir. I'm not even allowed to go into prep tonight. Can I go now, sir?"

"Yes, yes . . . and I'll see you don't get into more trouble for telling me. Tell Mr. Carter I'd be obliged if he'd come over to Havelock's after prep."

"Yes, sir," and Gage scuttled off just as the prep bell began to clang and the half-empty quad erupted with boys hurrying to and fro under the arcades.

He pushed his way through them, too stunned to notice the occasional collision, or heed the lighthearted apologies. Hislop sacked. For making a book on Sports Day. In other words, sacked because he had been sharp enough to use his wits about tracking down a persistent thief, then honest enough to report his loss to his housemaster. Blind, unreasoning fury rose in him as the probable sequence of events took shape in his mind. Alcock's relentless questions concerning the money. Hislop's reliance on a fictitious aunt and a telephone exchange that had disposed of her. And then, his alibi in ruins, a confession resulting in a second phone call to Hislop Senior, and a final trip to the station.

"Good God!" he blurted out, reaching his own quarters, "that bastard didn't mean me to know until I missed Hislop at callover, and came running to him! Damned if I don't deny him that little triumph . . . !" but standing there he heard his phone ringing and force of habit projected him across the room to the study.

Grace was already answering it and said, "He's here now. It's one of the parents, Daddy. I didn't catch the name . . ."

"I'll take it. Go out and shut the door, Grace."

She slipped out and he heard Hislop Senior's gravelly voice say, "Powlett-Jones? That you? My boy's housemaster?"

"Yes, this is Powlett-Jones. I've only just this moment heard about it. I'm going down to see the head now. Do you mind if I ring you back?"

"Wait—listen—this is a damned outrage! The boy explained everything, tells me he was robbed . . ."

"So he was, and reported to me at once. I repeat, I've only just heard what happened. The head didn't see fit to consult me. Is your boy with you now?"

"Yes, he is, but . . ."

"Would you put him on, Mr. Hislop?"

"What good would that do?"

"I want to explain my side of it. Then I'll see the head, ring back and tell you what happens."

There was a pause. David heard himself breathing hard. Hislop Junior spoke into the phone. "You, sir?"

"Listen, Hislop. I got the story from Gage and I'm going down to see the head right away, but I thought you ought to know this is the very first I've heard about you being sent home. I think the head is seeing the bursar about the servant in question. Don't mention the name on the telephone and try not to worry too much. I mean to do everything I can. And, as I said at the time, I very much appreciate you coming to me in the first place."

"Yes, sir. Thank you, sir."

He rang off and helped himself to a drink, a stiff one. Then, leaving a message with Grace where he was likely to be, he went down and marched along the passage to Alcock's study.

Alcock must have recognised his step on the flags for he called, clearly, "Is that you, Powlett-Jones?" and David went straight in without answering. This time he was standing by the window, perusing a small file of carbons. He said, absently, "Cricklade's references. They seem in order. Probably wrote them himself."

"Hislop's father has just telephoned me!"

"Indeed?"

"He's very angry and I think he has a right to be."

"He'll cool down when he gets my letter. So will you, no doubt, when you know the facts."

Resentment at the man's majestic calm rose up and almost choked him. He made a tremendous effort and succeeded to some extent in controlling himself. "I don't understand . . . it can't be right to take advantage of the boy's straightforwardness . . . in his coming forward, voluntarily."

"His straightforwardness? That's a curious word to use regarding a boy who sets himself up as a bookmaker on the precincts of his own sports field. I assume Hislop Senior told you why I sent him home, as soon as I had confirmed the source of that money?"

"But don't you see none of us would have known about the bookmaking if he hadn't reported the theft. Most boys wouldn't have. They would have realised straightaway that it was certain to get them into serious trouble."

He had at last succeeded in astonishing the man. Alcock's head came up slowly. "What on earth has that to do with it? You don't seem to appreciate the enormity of his offence. *Bookmaking!* Taking bets from other boys, on school premises! It's the most reprehensible thing I've ever heard of."

"More reprehensible than breaking into lockers and stealing money and goods?"

"They are virtually one and the same, aren't they? Both acts of complete irresponsibility."

"What Hislop did was wrong but it was really no more than an extravagant lark—he's that kind of boy and always has been. And what about all the boys who placed bets with him? Are they exempt? Half the school must have wagered if he showed a profit of fifteen pounds."

"I should be equally severe with them if I could trace them. Obviously I cannot, so I must make an example of the one I have caught. Apart from that, do I take it you approve of boys breaking into a servant's quarters and searching his belongings?"

"In Cricklade's case? Yes, I do. If it had been left to us Cricklade wouldn't have been caught. Or not until we had a real problem on our hands. But even that isn't the whole of it. Hislop's action was disinterested."

"You say that? With all his money stolen?"

"He didn't care about his own money. He told me, and I believe him, that he was encouraged to do what he did on account of young Harper's money. Doesn't that put the whole thing in a different light?"

"I find it irrelevant. Even if it's true, which I beg leave to doubt."

"Very well. Let me try and explain it from a personal angle. I came to you within minutes of Hislop coming to me. I came in confidence and trust. But you dealt with the matter summarily, without even consulting me, making nonsense of the tutorial system we've practised here since the school was founded. Boys are encouraged to trust their housemasters. What kind of trust will they have when it gets about that I was the means of Hislop implicating himself? Even Cricklade, if you catch him, will be warned that anything he says might be used in evidence against him. Try and put yourself in my place, Headmaster."

Alcock was silent for a moment, drifting over to his customary vantage-point behind the desk, so that David thought, "He needs that barricade . . . without it he's just one of us . . ." and the thought encouraged him to add, "Under these circumstances we might just as well abolish the house system."

It seemed then that he had scored a point, an insignificant one perhaps, but at least Alcock paused to consider. Then he said abruptly, "I agree. It has occurred to me more than once that it serves no useful purpose. An institution can only have one source of directive. It is sometimes confusing to have half a dozen. However, that's something else, and I would want to give it a serious thought before I introduced an alternative system."

David stirred but Alcock raised his hand, indicating he had more to say. "You asked me just now to regard this on a personal level. I'm very willing to, Powlett-Jones. Sometimes I ask myself if you and I can ever hope to work as colleagues. Why? It's quite clear you resent me, have set yourself against me time and again, and you encouraged Mr. Carter to make me act against my better judgment as regards that boy Monk. Now you seem determined to provoke an open quarrel over another flagrant breach of discipline. It won't do, will it? Am I to expect your resignation?"

He said it almost casually, as if he had been talking about a laundry list or a parcel notice, but in a way this helped.

"My resignation? No, Headmaster, you may not. Not now, not any time."

"You don't agree we are likely to prove incompatible?"

"I think that's so, but it's not going to scare me into resigning.

You can try and get rid of me, as you got rid of Hislop, and tried to get rid of Monk, but I'll fight and I'm in a position to fight hard. I'll fight like the very devil. I've put years of my life into Bamfylde, and it owes me as much as I owe it. I don't mind you knowing I disagree with your entire policy here, and I'm at a grave disadvantage, but while making things very uncomfortable for me it doesn't frighten me. Tell the Governors anything you like, Headmaster. Then I'll give them my side of it and leave them to judge. Neither of us would come out of it with much credit but that can't be helped, can it?"

He was encouraged to note that Alcock seemed the tiniest bit rattled. He was toying with his paperknife, and even this was a concession. Perhaps twenty seconds ticked by. Then Alcock said, in the same infinitely restrained voice, "Very well, Powlett-Jones. We'll leave it there, shall we? I don't think we can have anything more to say to one another just now."

"Is it too much to ask you to reconsider Hislop's case? To suspend him until the end of term and give him a fresh start next term?"

"Altogether too much, I'm afraid." He got up, crossed to the door and opened it. David went out, wondering who had had the best of it this time and thinking, possibly, that it was honours even.

2

Carter was waiting for him, unable, it seemed, to contain himself until the end of prep. It was a very different Carter, however, from the semi-hysterical man who begged his help over Monk in March. He seemed confident, almost jaunty, having, it appeared, had time to absorb Gage's story, but he raised his eyebrows when David told him about Alcock's mention of a resignation.

"I'm glad he didn't put the same hint to me," he said. "I should have been very tempted to throw the damned job in his face and that would have been a little premature on my part."

"You're thinking of resigning?"

"Well, let's say I'm thinking of promoting myself. I've got a bit put by, quite a bit as it happens, for I've been careful, and lucky with my investments. I want my own school and I mean to get it. As a matter of fact, I've got my eye on one, and if I made an offer I should want a partner. We behaved like a couple of bloody fools for long enough but that's all behind us. I'll never forget your attitude over Stoker Monk last term, and we seem to be the only two here who have faced up to the fact that Alcock is in a fair way to ruining this place. Suppose I come up with a proposition, would you be interested in buying in?"

"That depends on all kinds of things. What sort of school, what sort of money you'd want."

"It's a good-class prep school, in Kent. About a hundred boys so far, but we could soon double that. I believe we could work together and, frankly, I'd sooner take the gamble with someone I know and trust than a stranger. As to the money, you could give me a hint. How much, in round figures, could you raise if you had to?"

"Not more than a couple of thousand, and I should have a job raising that. I've saved, and I've never touched my gratuity, but I'm still responsible for my mother and I've Grace to think of."

Carter tapped his teeth, a habit of his. "Well, no point in pushing it further now, but this last business has helped me to make up my mind. You didn't persuade that bastard to give Hislop another chance, I suppose?"

"No, and there's no point in another round robin. That worked once but it wouldn't work again. I've promised to phone Hislop's father now."

"Then I'll shove off, for there's nothing I can offer but sympathy, old man. You know that, I imagine?"

"Yes, I do. And thanks, Carter."

They shook hands and Carter let himself out. For a long time David sat looking at the phone. It required a considerable effort to pick it up and ask for Hislop's number. When he did Hislop's wife answered and her voice had a cutting edge to it.

"You're *sure* he won't have second thoughts?"

"Quite sure. He never has second thoughts about anything."

"There's the possibility of legal proceedings. It wouldn't do the school much good, would it?"

"No, Mrs. Hislop, but it wouldn't do your lad any good, either. He'll be going on to another school, won't he?"

"If we can find him one, after this."

"I think I could help there."

"How?"

"By setting out the facts as his housemaster, and presenting a case in writing that any intelligent headmaster would take into consideration."

"You'd do that?"

"I'd be glad to. Your boy isn't a bad boy. He's very popular here, especially with the juniors. How does he feel about it?"

Her voice had mellowed a little. "Well, naturally he's shocked, but in a way he's also relieved. To be out of the man's reach, I mean. He tells me things aren't at all the same since Mr. Herries retired. Is that true?"

"Quite true, unfortunately. All the decisions are taken out of our hands. The new man is a law unto himself and I'm only saying that because I feel I don't owe him loyalty."

There was a pause, then she said, "Will you write that letter? Something I could enclose in an application to a headmaster?"

"I'll write it now. Tonight."

"Good. Then I don't think you need worry about legal proceedings. Don't tell that awful man as much, however."

"Madam," said David, "I wouldn't tell Alcock the time of day," and it was a pleasure to hear her laugh.

He replaced the receiver and was surprised at his own calmness. Whatever it was something had been resolved, and that was an improvement. He took a pen and began to write, reflecting as he did that he had never improved on 'Moderate' in any report he had compiled in respect of Hislop, king of The Lump.

Chapter Three

It arrived in the form of a housemaster's circular, a few days before the end of summer term. A brief crisply worded directive, couched in terms that were, David decided, so typically Alcockian as to qualify as a self-parody. It was more of an edict than a statement of policy. There was nothing in the least consultative about it and it had the surprise side-effect of rallying them, temporarily at least, under a single banner. Barnaby, mulling it over, said it would have looked well under the signature of the Emperor Caligula. In their long association David had never seen the amiable Barnaby show that much resentment.

The edict announced: "It has come to my notice that a number of sentimental friendships appear to exist between senior and junior boys. I do not think I need be explicit as to what this presages. I have therefore decided that steps must be taken to suppress such friendships as, at best, undignified and, at worst, extremely unhealthy. I look to all housemasters to co-operate. Signed, J. D. Alcock, M.A. (Lond.)"

It referred, of course, to the custom recognised as 'ninging', and it was manifestly clear from Alcock's tone that he had completely misunderstood the traditional Bamfylde approach to the practice. David did not blame him for this. He himself had taken time to adjust to it and it was to be expected, he supposed, that a new man, with little or no experience of British schools, should take a very prejudiced view of an association between boys of different age and status. It was one more example of Alcock's failure to communicate.

'Ninging' was a verb that Bamfylde appeared to have appropriated to itself round about the turn of the century. In the view of Algy, and other old hands, it had its approximate equivalent in every public school in the country. In general terms it was no more than a personal attachment between a boy in Upper School, and a boy who was working his way through the Lower School. What Alcock overlooked at Bamfylde was its comparative innocence.

In his very earliest days on the moor David had half-concluded that ninging was a polite euphemism for a positive homosexual relationship, of the kind common enough in the army. Soon after settling in, however, and guided by the prescient Algy Herries, he had seen it for what it was, a combination of hero worship on the part of the younger boys and what he could only describe as a status charade on the part of a senior boy, advertising his improved position in the school, a traditional, if bizarre, example of throwing his weight about, much in the way he might flaunt newly acquired school colours. Sometimes it showed itself in nothing more than a beefy patronage towards his fag, or some other junior. Occasionally it progressed to the stage where the younger boy was the recipient of teatime extras or minor privileges.

In his Grammar School days he had heard very sinister rumours of the kind of friendships said to exist between seniors and juniors in all English boarding schools, and had thought of them as yet another instance of English decadence. But under Algy, and particularly when he had a house of his own, he had seen these associations for what they were, at least on the spot. In Wesker's time, again according to Algy, he might have had good grounds for suspecting the worst but as the tone of the school improved in the decade leading up to the war, Algy's policy of tolerance had paid an unexpected dividend. Algy's approach to ninging, like his approach to many aspects of school life, had been unconventional. David recalled him saying, on one occasion, "Drive this sentimentality underground and every now and again you'll encourage it to develop into something positive and dangerous. Let the nippers have their hero and the seniors their sounding board and admiring private audience and you take the steam out of it in ninety-nine cases out of a hundred."

David had asked him what he did in the hundredth case and Algy said, with a shrug, "You sit on it within the hour. Not forgetting that it was slackness on a housemaster's part for not spotting it from the beginning."

He had never had occasion to question Algy's precepts. Not once, in his time as housemaster, had a friendship of this kind merited intervention on his part.

It seemed, however, that Alcock had other views. Possibly his experience in schools overseas was that much wider but if this was so why didn't he say so?

"That's asking altogether too much of the idiot," Carter announced, when the matter was being discussed over coffee in the common room. "We should have learned by now that the man is constitutionally incapable of communicating."

But Alcock wasn't, or not altogether. To everyone's amazement he suddenly presented himself in the common room and addressed them as a body, just as if they had been a group of monitors training for promotion to positions of full prefectship.

He said, distantly, "Touching that letter I sent to housemasters. It occurred to me later that I should have addressed a copy to every member of the staff. I take it you have had time to discuss it among yourselves?"

Irvine, not a housemaster, growled that they had, and went on to demand, with his usual bluntness, what, if anything, he was expected to do about it.

Alcock said, mildly, "Why, sever it, Irvine. On the spot. And then report to me, in order that it can be fully investigated."

Barnaby spoke up. It was the first time he had ever challenged the new man but he did it without preamble.

"There's nothing of that kind in my house, I can assure you of that. Friendships, yes, but perfectly harmless ones, believe me."

Alcock lifted one shoulder. "I should like to, Barnaby, but none of us can be sure, can we?"

"I can," Barnaby huffed. "I don't speak for anyone else."

Alcock seemed to consider this for a moment and then, when nobody followed it up, nodded and withdrew. Barely was he clear of the threshold when the bull-headed Irvine exploded.

"Bloody man's a nut-case! First he cancels free periods to watch important matches, then he starts sacking left, right and centre, now he confronts us with a thing like this! How the hell is a man supposed to investigate a ning without risking a snub? Aye, and a bloody-minded parent's letter into the bargain! Bound to make a fool of yourself, however you tackle it," and he went on to provide them with what David thought a very fair illustration of his point. "I see Skelton, pacing round the plantation boundary with young Grattan, deep in conversation with him. Now *I* happen to know that Skelton regards Grattan as the likeliest kid among the juniors to captain that new Colt's Eleven I'm bringing on. Boy's going to make a first-class bowler, providing he keeps at it, and where the hell would he look for coaching if he's got a ha'porth o' sense? To the captain of the First Eleven, wouldn't he? And that man would have us believe they were madly in love with one another, when the damn fool has never watched a match in his life!"

Barnaby, having recovered his equanimity somewhat, resumed his favourite role of verbal *agent provocateur*. "They might, of course, be using cricket as an emotional bridge, Irvine."

"Cock!" roared Irvine, who had never adapted to Barnaby's gentle leg-pulls. "I *told* Skelton to coach the kid! What does that make me? A pimp?"

It became known, when discussions on the subject widened, as the Stoic's 'Statute of Limitations', an attempt to draw an arbitrary line between seniors and juniors. Among the boys it acquired a less dignified title. They called it 'Noble's Three N's, or Non-Ninging Notice', and this is how it was referred to years later, when Old Boys reminisced round the bar at Whitsuntide reunions.

But at the time it soon ceased to be a joke, especially after Alcock launched his follow-up, demanding of each housemaster the imposition of a virtual ban in association between the two groups. It was then that Howarth scored for the staff, following a demand for a personal report on two of his boys transgressing the Statute of Limitations. Replying to Alcock's enquiry concerning the relationship between Dobson, an Upper Fifth rugby colour, and Vesey, a first-termer in the Lower Third, he produced a letter written from Vesey's father, then serving in the R.A.M.C. in India alongside Dobson's father, whom he happened to outrank. The relevant quotation was passed from hand to hand as proof that even the Stoic was vulnerable to Howarth's irony. Vesey *père* had written,

> The kid is sure to feel a bit low, seeing that this is his first trip home, but Captain Dobson happened to mention his younger boy is in his fourth year and asks me to ask you to put in a word with young Dobson on the kid's behalf. I don't want him coddled, mind you, but it was a great relief to his mother to learn that Dobson's boy is still with you . . .

"You see the supreme wisdom of keeping files," Howarth said, savouring his triumph, "for I've come to believe that chap takes nothing on trust." Then, glancing around the common room he added, "Not that I blame him altogether when I regard you lot."

They conceded Howarth his gibe for by then the Statute of Limitations had crystallised the opposition in a way that no previous act on Alcock's part had. Yet it proved something of a false dawn for David, who soon found himself in a position of virtual isolation. By the end of the following term wickets were falling fast. Howarth had once again withdrawn into himself, Irvine and Rapper Gibbs had resigned, and Carter had made his move.

* * *

Rapper's retirement came as no surprise to anyone. He was sixty-four but had let it be known that he was prepared to soldier on indefinitely. He was a widower without children, and Bamfylde had been his life since before Herries's time. He had no stomach for a man who was not only tone deaf but seemed to regard housemasters as palace spies. For him the Three N's was the final straw. He gave in his notice and shuffled off to do for himself, and his two Siamese cats, in a cottage adjoining Gatwick's farm north of the village.

Surprisingly, Alcock offered Irvine Gibbs's house, Campbell's, and even more surprisingly Irvine rejected the offer. Even in Algy's day Irvine and his attractive wife had been restless, Irvine seeking a more prestigious school, where his talents as a rugby and cricket coach could expect greater scope, and his wife Phyl could look for more sophisticated leisure. Secretly, it seemed, they had gone about their prospecting, and Irvine had finally landed a new post in a well-known Eastbourne prep school.

David was sorry to see them go. Among them all Irvine was the only man on the staff who had shared his army experiences in a time that sometimes seemed as distant as the Crimea, and both man and wife had been close to Beth. The time was approaching when no boy, and few among the staff, would remember her. Irvine, breaking the news, urged him to join them in a move, but David said, "I'll stick it out a while yet. It can only get better or worse. If it doesn't improve then I'll take your advice. Meantime, Carter is still around and since Howarth went back in his shell he and I have been getting along extremely well."

Phyl Irvine said, shrewdly, "Is it Bamfylde or Beth that keeps you here, Davy?" and he replied with a smile, that it was a little of both, plus the occasional visits of young men whom he had taught in the Second and Third Forms. There was a grain of truth in this. Almost every week one or other of them zoomed up the east drive in a jazzy sports car, or astride a powerful motorcycle. The trio he always thought of as The Reprieved—Cooper, Fosdyke and Scrubbs-Norton, boys who had been in the Sixth when he came here early in 1918, and were saved by the Armistice the following November, were frequent visitors. All doing very well, he noted, for two of them were married, and Cooper was the father of the boy he had visualised that summer day when Algy had surprised him reading the news of the breaching of the Hindenburg Line.

Another regular visitor was Boyer, who was up at Cambridge and had decided to teach if he got a good degree. Taylor, the Latinist, was making his mark at Oxford, and Dobson I, who once won a history prize by cribbing, had struck oil in an expanding radio firm and appeared at the Whitsuntide reunion driving a Rolls-Royce. Of the others he had come to like, Skidmore, embryo martyr, the two Kassava brothers, Nun Stratton-Forbes, who had brought him news of Beth's twins, Ruby Bickford, broke and home in disgrace from Brazil, and many others, some put in an occasional appearance, others wrote. Possibly his most regular correspondent (and an unlikely one at that) was Paddy McNaughton, the gunman, who had a tourist office in Dublin, and was assembling material for a documentary film of the Irish troubles. He kept in touch with more than a hundred of them all told, and a very few of the cream, like Spats Winterbourne and Sax Hoskins, were still here, so that he was able to salvage something of the family spirit of happier days, sensing that their loyalty was to him rather than the school. Whether this would survive the departure of the very last of the boys here under Algy he was not sure. Probably not, in which case he might well take Irvine's advice and make a change.

A fortnight before Christmas it got around that old Bouncer, the last survivor of the veteran quartet that had included Judy Cordwainer, Rapper Gibbs and Ferguson, had been pressured into resigning, ostensibly, Doc Willoughby told him, on account of deafness, but this was not the real reason. Ever since David could remember Bouncer had been deaf, but he could still teach, and even keep order with his volleys of penal marks. It was rumoured that Alcock had overcome Bouncer's reluctance to resign by getting at the Governors.

That left only Howarth, Barnaby and Carter of the originals, and on the final day of term, when everybody's mind was on Christmas, Carter cut another link, appearing in his quarters while he was helping Grace to pack for their biennial trip to the Valley, and announcing that he had something important to say.

David left the rest of the packing to Grace and took Carter and the whisky decanter into the study. Carter was buoyed up, he noticed, more like the man he remembered from their feuding days than the jaded housemaster of recent terms. He said, accepting a whisky, "Fill your glass, P.J. This might be to us."

"You've decided to go ahead with that prep school idea?"

"All settled," said Carter, beaming. "Got a phone call from the agent in the lunch hour. Now it's up to you."

"Come again?"

"You said you could chip in two thousand, remember? Well that still goes as far as I'm concerned."

"You mean, it depends on my putting up money and coming in as a partner?"

"Well, no, not exactly. I mean the offer is still open if you want to accept." He looked, David thought, slightly embarrassed but then, swallowing half his drink he added, "I won't hedge with you P.J. I've got all the money I need. As a matter of fact, I can raise two thousand by private loan if you turn me down. I . . . er . . .

prefer not to disclose the source at this stage. What's it to be?"

"Let's get this straight. If I join you, and bring in two thousand, we're partners. If I don't, then you can still go ahead by borrowing the amount I should contribute?"

"That's the picture, old man."

"Not quite, or not what I would think a fair arrangement, Carter. You told me some time back you would be paying five thousand plus for fabric alone. That would make you the senior partner, wouldn't it?"

There was a rather uncomfortable pause. Finally Carter said, carefully, "That was my idea when I proposed it, back in the summer. But, as I said then, I think we could work well together, and I wouldn't lay down any conditions about seniority. Regardless of stake we should start out level pegs."

"That's damned generous of you, Carter."

"No, it isn't. To my way of thinking it would be the only way to ensure harmony. Well?"

"I couldn't accept in those circumstances. I don't doubt your good faith for an instant, but if I came in now it would have to be on the basis of a junior, with a possible option to buy equality later, if and when I could afford it."

"And that doesn't appeal to you?"

"No. To be honest, I can't see myself ever possessing five thousand pounds, but neither could I work under anybody."

"Damn it, you're having to work under that brute, aren't you?"

"Yes, I am, but on ground I know much better than the brute. It makes a difference. You must see that."

"Yes," Carter said, thoughtfully, "I see it, partly because I like to think I've come to know you pretty well, P.J. What you're really saying is, as regards Bamfylde you still hope?"

"Yes. And I'm backing myself to hold on, even with you and most of the others gone."

"Then it's 'no', old man?"

"Regretfully. Have another drink. Let me drink to your school. What's it called?"

"St. Magnus. Bloody awful, don't you think? It's got a bloody awful motto, too. 'Facta Non Verba.' I intend to change that, however."

"It would suit the Stoic. He performs all the deeds and we have to get along on his words. No matter, here's to you, Carter, and to St. Magnus, and I'll add something to that. One of the more intelligent things you and I ever did during our time was to bury the hatchet."

"Yes, it was," Carter said, "but it makes leaving you in the lurch that much more difficult."

"I'll cope."

"I bet you will."

They finished their drinks and shook hands, David seeing Carter down the steps and across the quad to Outram's, where they shook hands again.

When he retraced his steps he heard the whine of Grace's gramophone, backed by thumps and squeals of glee. She and Hoskins were dancing to the rhythm of Sax's latest record, a convivial number called 'Happy Days are Here Again'. He thought, sourly, "Not for me, they aren't. With Carter gone, I'm more or less alone, for I can't look for much support from Howarth and Barnaby. One seems to be going stale, and the other has no real feelings for the old place." He went in and Sax grinned at him over Grace's dark, bobbing curls. "And there's another of them," he thought, crossing to the study, and glaring down at the pile of manuscript representing the latest draft of 'The Royal Tigress'. "Old Sax will be leaving at the end of next term. I'm beginning to feel like Crusoe up here."

2

He was on the point of leaving the following morning when Howarth appeared, the inevitable Gold Flake between his lips, and an expression of bafflement that David recognised as the forerunner of a confidence of some kind. Howarth found every confidence a great embarrassment, irrespective of whether it was given or received, so that David thought, "I hope to God *he* isn't packing it in! He's been more than usually crusty of late but I'd miss him more than any of them." He said, "Is it about keeping the Sunsetters occupied?", and Howarth said no, he could cope with the Sunsetters for a week or so, and was here to confirm that Carter had not talked him into that prep school venture.

"You knew about that?"

"Good God, of course I knew about it. Have you ever known anyone pull wool over my eyes?"

"No," David said, grinning, "I don't think I have. I turned him down, although I must say he made me a very generous offer."

"I'm glad you showed that much sense. If you hadn't my little backstairs strategy would have gone for nothing. Have you got a minute or two?"

"Half an hour. The taxi is due here at eleven. Will you have a drink?"

"Not at this hour of the day." He drifted over to the gramophone table, picked up the record Hoskins had left in the turntable, scanned the title, grimaced and put it down again. "Funny thing, that," he said, "I got it into my head you'd welsh on us. Must be slipping."

"You haven't exactly given me the impression you were overconcerned who stayed and who left. I'd come to believe you'd opted out."

"Sidestepped that guerilla war you and Carter have been waging with Alcock? Well, you're right. It irritated me. I never thought Alcock was worth it. However, we owe the fellow one thing. He got Carter out of the way."

"What are you driving at, Howarth?"

"What's in it for you—and the school. That's what I'm driving at. I know you and Carter formed an unholy alliance, and that annoyed me, for I never did trust the chap. He'd have let you down in the end, you know. If you had gone in with him you would have lived to regret it."

"Is there much to regret at the moment?"

Howarth gave him one of his bleakest looks, of the kind he reserved for boys who shattered the silence of a classroom by dropping a desk-lid. "The present has very little to do with it. This place has had bad men in the past. That sadist Wesker was one of them, if you believe everything Herries told you. But Herries pulled it up in no time at all and you could do the same if you had to. One thing is for sure. You wouldn't have had the chance if you had sunk every penny you possess in that venture with Carter. Why don't you look ahead a little? Alcock isn't forever. He's older than I am, and looks to me like a man who drives himself. Anything could happen in the next year or so and if it does, who will those fools on the Board look to for a rescue operation? Don't tell me you haven't thought of that."

"Oh, I've thought of it, but I can't see myself sticking it indefinitely with Alcock breathing down my neck. He could easily stay on as long as Algy did."

"I can promise you he won't," Howarth said.

"How can you possibly say that? You're not in his confidence any more than I am."

"I can promise it, none the less. I give him two years. Probably less. How old will you be at, say, Christmas, 1932?"

"Thirty-six."

"Just right. So my advice is to stick it out, and do what you can to chasten that damned Welsh pride of yours in the meantime. You and Carter and Gibbs, and even Barnaby, have all been behaving like Second Formers lately. I say nothing of Irvine. He was always poised for flight, with that flipperty-gibbet wife of his."

"Damn it, Howarth, you can't say we haven't been provoked."

"Not madly provoked. Show me any job without stress. Pinpricks shouldn't induce hysteria in a man who stuck it out three years in the trenches. As to Alcock's ultimate impact on the school, I think it'll be negligible. A new head, who had his finger on the pulse of the place, could achieve a turnabout in a month."

"Then secretly you've sided with us all the time?"

"As regards him? Up to a point. He's not interested in the school as a school, only as a source of power, and a stage for his ego. Somewhere to strut, like a ham actor. He'd behave in exactly the same way if you put him in charge of the regional gas board. That shows you how much degrees are worth. Most people, including parents, still regard schoolmasters as desiccated imparters of fifth-hand information, but you know and I know that they're more than that if they're any good. What applies to one school doesn't necessarily apply to another. You wouldn't administer a Crown Colony the way you run the London County Council, would you? Besides, we've got something out of the silly ass. He's improved the fabric, and his window-dressing isn't so bad. We needed a spring clean and an academic hoist. And the numbers have remained fairly steady, haven't they?"

"The tone isn't the same and on your own admission that's what is important."

"You can adjust a tone. Those new latrines of his will last us a generation. I wouldn't be talking this way if our waiting-list had suffered but it hasn't and it won't, until the blight sets in."

"What blight?"

Howarth glared at him again. "What blight? Great God, man, I thought you were a political animal! Can't you see where we're all heading?"

"You mean the Wall Street crash?"

"Among other things. The 'thirties are going to be a bloody difficult time for all of us, especially for places like this, that aren't buttressed by inherited wealth and a snob reputation. By this time next year numbers will have fallen by ten per cent. And by the year after that by thirty per cent. Many of the parents we rely on won't have the cash to keep boys here, and as soon as the barometer falls Alcock will go, you see if I'm not right."

It was a point of view, and one he had never thought about, perhaps because his continual collisions with Alcock had obscured what was happening outside, where the unemployment figures were mounting month by month, a minority government was running the country, and a gale was blowing through the treasuries of the world. He wondered if Howarth's prophecies were relevant and decided that they were. Alcock was not a man who was equal to a challenge of that kind. He was too dedicated to rule of thumb, too self-assured, too set in his ways. He said, "What was that you said about your backstairs strategy, Howarth?"

"Oh, that?" He gave one of his thin smiles. "That was masterly, though I do say it myself. Did you wonder where Carter got that private loan he talked about? It was from me. I advanced him three thousand, at a rate of interest he wouldn't get from any bank in the land. Almost interest free, you could say."

"You did that? To prevent him roping me in?"

"Why not? I can afford it, as you well know. Buying the man off seemed the best way to go about it, although I misjudged him in one respect. I didn't really suppose he would offer to take you in on equal terms. I suppose even Carter has his own interpretation of the word 'loyalty'. Well, I'm not here to apologise for it. Go off and enjoy yourself over Christmas. I daresay you'll find things seething in the Valleys, and come back here with a crated guillotine. That could lead to another display of fireworks, I suppose, but I never minded fireworks, providing a professional was lighting the fuses." He nodded and stalked off. Grace appeared from the bedroom, saying, "Will you fasten the straps, Daddy? The trunk is too full for me to manage," and he said, absently, "Yes, dear, right away. Go down and watch for the taxi. We've cut it fine if we're after that eleven-thirty train."

Chapter Four

1

Howarth was right about the mood of the Valleys. David could not recall a time when there had been no talk of militant action and when the names of families drawing royalties from deep and dangerous seams were mentioned without a curse. But now, with a sense of crisis that recalled the long dragging strike of 1925/6, the mood of the mining communities was one of blazing anger and frustration. "A Socialist government is in, isn't it? A Socialist Prime Minister has plumped his arse down in Number Ten, hasn't he, boyo? Then why the hell doesn't he do something about unemployment and nationalise the whole bloody industry?" All the miners he met, including his brothers-in-law, Ewart and Bryn, talked this way, rejecting the argument that MacDonald was only holding on to power by the skin of his teeth, and could do little without Liberal support. For years now they had seen their own salvation in Labour's promise that the industry would be taken over by the government, and the fact that Ramsay's victory, in the spring of 1929, had not achieved this by December, implied that they were going to be betrayed yet again.

Some of the older men, pillars of the local constituency parties since pre-war days, were already toying with Communism, and a majority of the youngsters were casting around for Communist

317

candidates, swearing that nothing would improve until capitalism was confronted with the demand of a majority to wrest power from the hands of the few.

He was able, nowadays, to regard pit politics objectively, and it struck him at once that the miners were being unfair to men like MacDonald, Snowden and Jimmy Thomas, the jovial ex-railwayman. Against every forecast, and with the minimum funds at their disposal, they had emerged from the last general election as the majority party. It seemed to David uncharacteristic of the long-suffering Welsh to expect an instant solution of tormented domestic problems in the face of international depression. Local Labour stalwarts were fighting back, however, and he attended one of their meetings, addressed by a fiery Doncaster speaker, called Routledge, whose co-speaker was a young woman, a lucid platform speaker and clearly a person of education. Enquiries established that she was an Economics graduate, with an Honours degree gained in Manchester.

She received a good, if ironic hand from the men when she sat down, after talking for twenty minutes on the Labour government's present difficulties, and when the meeting dissolved into a dozen argumentative groups, and tea was served by the women workers, Ewart, the husband of his sister Gwynneth, offered to introduce him. Routledge, the Doncaster man, had spoken at previous meetings in the area, and Ewart knew him well. The girl, he said, was travelling about to gain experience for a bid at the next election, and her name was Forster, Christine Forster, a Yorkshire lass well in with the party executive. "Not that I give her a dog's chance whereffer she stands," Ewart added. "She's sharp enough, and can talk the hind legs off a donkey, but why waste deposits on a lass at places where even a man like Routledge couldn't dent the Tory majority?"

He introduced Davy, using the reverent voice the uneducated miner habitually reserves for someone wearing an educational halo. "My wife's brother, Davy Powlett-Jones—schoolmaster he is, at a big college, in England. But he hasn't forgotten where he comes from, have you, boyo?" After which, slapping David's shoulder, moved off and joined the group surrounding Routledge.

Ewart's implied dismissal of her was not lost upon Miss Forster, who smiled and said, "Your brother-in-law is very proud of you, Mr. Powlett-Jones. But he doesn't give a slice of streaky bacon for my chance of getting elected. Neither does anyone else in the Valleys."

She looked far more personable down here on floor level, away from the yellow glare of the footlight bulbs. She had thick brown hair, lighter than Beth's, sharp green eyes and an exceptionally clear complexion, as fresh and pleasing as a flower. She had a long, thinnish nose, that some would have said spoiled her looks, but David decided suited her figure, the exact opposite to Beth's figure, he found himself thinking, with no well-defined curves but long, elegant legs. Her accent was what these people would call 'posh', but he could detect a trace of Yorkshire in the broad vowels and clipped consonants. She seemed to know what she was about, and had come to terms with the prejudice against all women candidates among constituency workers.

She said, politely, "A college, he said. What kind of college, Mr. Powlett-Jones?" and he replied, smiling, "Every school bar a red-brick council school is a 'college' to Ewart. He has the Celt's veneration of all educational establishments. My place isn't much to write home about, a small public school, called Bamfylde."

"Bamfylde? In North Devon?"

"Why, yes. You've actually heard of it?"

"Heard of it? I've visited it! One Sports Day, several years ago, when I was still at school myself. One of my cousins went there. His name was Ridgeway, my mother's sister's eldest boy."

"The Ridgeway who was there in 1925. A tall boy? A first-class miler?"

"He did win the mile that year."

"But of course I know him. He was head boy of my house, just before I took over. He put up a first-rate show the night we had a bad fire, and helped me get the boys out. I'm delighted to meet you, Miss Forster. How and where is he? I don't think I've had word of him since he left. That would be in 1926," and as he spoke he realised why the girl's strong features had seemed familiar as she had advanced downstage to speak. With so many faces imprinted in the memory, however, it was difficult to compare one with another when a coincidence like this occurred. Now that he had a chance to look at her closely he could see a resemblance to Ridgeway's bone structure, particularly as regards the nose and jaw.

"I believe he's in tea-planting in Malaya," she said, "but I can't be sure. We've lost touch lately. All the older members of the family are true-blue Tories, so I'm cut off from family chit-chat. A case of 'Turn-Christine's-face-to-the-wall', you could say."

He laughed, liking her wry sense of humour, and remembering how it would have appealed to Beth. Whenever he met a young woman he caught himself comparing her to Beth, and measuring her by Beth's standards. It was morbid, he supposed, after four-and-a-half years, but there it was, an instinctive reflex that time was transforming into a habit.

He said, offering her sugar, "I think it's encouraging, a person like you, with a good degree, coming over to us," but she replied, "Nonsense! No one who thinks and observes, could do anything else in present circumstances. The majority of my University set vote Labour, and two are nursing constituencies in the North. I took my time waking up to what was going on. Five years ago I was a snooty little bitch from a *nouveau riche* family, who regarded myself as a cut above most folk."

"I can't believe it, but what changed you?"

"The General Strike. That was in my second year at Manchester and Manchester is a good place to see what goes on below stairs. Almost as good as here. The textile industry up there is in a terrible way, and unemployment is even higher than in the northeast. But I suppose Bamfylde is true blue, isn't it?"

"I'm afraid it is," he admitted, cheerfully, "but I'm chipping away at it. My subject is history and that gives me an advantage."

"In what way?"

"Well, think of the ammunition at my disposal. The Peasants' Revolt, the Civil War, the Industrial Revolution, the Chartists. Not to mention the Tolpuddle Martyrs, Peterloo and the Mutiny at the Nore. What chance does a Tory philosophy stand among young animals who spend their entire lives looking for ways to overthrow authority?"

"Do you know, Mr. Powlett-Jones," she said, "you're putting heart into me. I can't recall meeting a schoolmaster of your type. Certainly not one from 'an English gents' college'. Look, I'm speaking at an afternoon rally in Newport, on Saturday. Could I persuade you to attend, and sit in the front row? I should like one sympathetic face in a dozen rows of blanks."

He said that he would come gladly and meant it. Her enthusiasm reminded him vividly of Beth when she was riding a hobby-horse, but when, later, he told Ewart of his promise, the miner echoed Christine Forster's own doubts about her ability to help Labour in a way beyond service behind a tea-urn, or selling raffle tickets.

"Pretty little thing, she is, and means well, I daresay. But women and politics don't mix, Davyboy. No woman elector will cotton on to a lass, in the way she will to a pair o' breeks. Besides, folk in the Valleys don't trust anyone outside their own class. If she was a scholarship lass she might cut some ice but she's not. According to Routledge her folk are stinking rich, boy. Doesn't add up, to my mind."

"That's the most prejudiced summing up I've ever heard in these parts, Ewart, and that's saying a hell of a lot. She's got a quick brain and the party ought to be able to use young women with her qualifications, who cross the floor on account of deep, personal convictions!" But Ewart only grinned at David's sister, Gwynneth, saying, "Sounds like Davy's started looking for consolation in his old age. She's bonnie enough, I'll grant you, but too skinny for my taste," and to illustrate his preference he slid a great horny hand over his wife's behind. "What did you think of Routledge?"

"Not much. He's too platform-conscious. It was like listening to someone reading from a radical pamphlet and an out-of-date one at that. It's time you chaps dropped your nineteenth-century slogans and started persuading the floating voter that a Socialist isn't a home-grown Bolshie. I'll go over to Newport and tell you what line they're taking in a city. I hope it's a bit more sophisticated than here."

*   *   *

He found a seat in the middle of a row of empty chairs in the fifth row, although even here he was well exposed, for the meeting, so close to Christmas, was thinly attended and that by the converted, judging from the ritual 'hear-hears'! every time a speaker made a point.

He found himself studying Christine Forster objectively, not merely as a speaker, or even as prospective Labour candidate, but as an attractive woman, with a pair of shapely legs that tended to get between her and her theme. When the speeches were finished he joined her in the committee room behind the stage and, without giving the invitation a previous thought, "Why don't we go in search of something stiffer than stewed tea? Would you care for a drink before you catch the train to Cardiff?"

"I certainly would," she said, without hesitation, "but I'm not much of a drinker. Two ports and lemon have me giggling. Three are enough to start me singing 'The Red Flag' solo."

"Try beer or shandy," he said, and she told him, smiling, that she wouldn't, for the smell of beer made her sick. "It must be an ancestral hangover," she said, "I come from a long line of chapel teetotallers. Even port, in our house, was always called 'medicinal', so I came to that in stages."

She arranged to meet Routledge and other speakers at the station at seven o'clock, and they found a pub called the Prince of Wales that looked less seedy than its neighbours. He ordered port and lemon for her and gin and tonic for himself, and they carried the drinks over to a table under the frosted window of the saloon bar. She was the only woman present and one or two early drinkers gave her disapproving glances.

"I'm sure they take me for a tart chatting up a client," she said. "Wales has that much in common with the North. Women aren't any more welcome in the pubs than they are in the pulpits."

"Tell me a bit more about the North," he said, "your area particularly. I've never been there, except to pass through in my army days."

"You were in the war? You were old enough?"

"Don't I look it?"

"No, you don't, David. You mean, you actually *fought* in that awful business?"

"Yes," he said, "but as we've only an hour I don't intend boring you with trench stories. Tell me about Sheffield. That's where you come from, isn't it?"

"It's where I was born, but my people moved out when I was fifteen. Father could afford to by then. He cleaned up during the war, though we were terrace-house before that. He had a tiny foundry, employing two men, in 1914. By 1917 he had seventy on the pay-roll and was turning out shell-casings at about a hundred pounds a shift. Profit, I mean. It still sticks in my gullet."

"I don't see why it should. Somebody had to make shells to throw back at Jerry."

322

"Not at that price. It's odd, really, I never thought of myself as lucky in those days, just special, in the way second-generation Victorians thought of themselves if their fathers made a pot of money in a mill or a factory. It never occurred to me that, if the cards had fallen differently, I would have been one of those kids whose fathers were killed out there, and whose mothers were left to bring them up on a pittance. When I did realise it, I felt guilty. I even used to tell girls at school my father 'worked for the government', implying that he was in the Foreign Office, or something of that kind. Later I decided to do something to . . . well, pay back if you like, using the education his money had provided to even things out a bit. It sounds frightfully smug put like that but I don't know how else to put it. As a matter of fact, I've never admitted that much to anyone else."

It was good, he thought, to hear her say that. Like Christine Forster, at this stage of his life, he was in need of encouragement and somehow she did encourage him. He said, "I don't think it's smug. Honest, maybe, and the kind of thinking that's rare these days. What are your plans now?"

"I'm on the roster for a candidature, but that doesn't mean much. The party needs candidates, God knows, but a constituency would have to be pretty hard up to choose a woman of twenty-six. I've been on a short-list once or twice, and there's another in the offing, but I haven't much hope of being selected ahead of an eligible male. Deaf and dumb he'd stand a better chance than me."

"Now it's you who are letting prejudice take over. The party will soon get around to shedding its sex bias. It'll have to, to ride out the weather we're headed into."

She said, hesitantly, "There's another thing."

"Well?"

"Technically I'm a Roman. I'm married, you see. Separated from my husband, but still married. And because he's R.C. likely to stay that way."

He could think of no reason why this totally unexpected piece of information should hit him like an umbrella handle, jabbed in his stomach, but it did, and the fact that it did made him so nervous that he stuttered.

"M-m-mmarried! But when? . . . I mean, you only got your degree a year or so back, didn't you?"

"I met Rowley at University. He was a don, frightfully brainy, and the youngest member of the faculty at the time. I imagined I was in love. I probably was and still might be if he hadn't been the person he was, and I hadn't been the person I was; or became. Oh, I'm not blaming him. He was born a Roman, and their values are different from ours. Not better or worse, just different. It was a disaster almost from the beginning." She stopped, swallowed what was left of her port, and said, "I'll risk another, if you want me to go on."

"You don't have to."

"I'd like to. It's too long since I talked about it to anyone."

He bought her another drink and returned to the table. She was applying lipstick with the aid of a tiny handbag mirror and he found himself noting the movements of the long, supple fingers shaping the cupid's bow. Her hands were as elegant as her legs, with finely tapered fingers, and perfectly formed fingernails. He also noticed, for the first time, her backward-curving thumb, an invariable sign, in his experience, of a strongly independent nature.

"Rowley was thirty-three when I met him. He was what my mother would have called 'gentry', before she began to think of herself as belonging in the same class and moved to Harrogate. That, in a Yorkshire terrace-house, means class. Yorkshire folk aren't taken in by second, or even third-generation wealth. His father owned a big estate in Northumberland. I still can't figure out why he married me. It might have been to forestall his father marrying him to a neighbour's daughter, with legs like those on that billiards table over there. He was a rebel in those days but first-class at his job. We were lovers for nearly a year before we married, but I didn't put pressure on him. Maybe someone else did. Somebody senior to him might have found out he was bedding one of the students, and passed it on to the vice-chancellor. I never did find out, and now I never will. Anyway, he proposed and I jumped at it. We were married in his church—he's a very good Catholic—and naturally I was expected to go along with it all the way. Before and after marriage. It was the after bit that we came unstuck on."

"Children?"

"The certainty of having a string of them. I lost the first, still-born, and it was his attitude to that that produced the first drip of acid. He wouldn't even discuss using any form of contraceptive, or practise birth-control other than their rhythm system. Not even the first time we made love, a few days after I came out of the clinic. We began rowing over that, and it soon led to other rows, over all kinds of things, silly things mostly. We said unforgivable things to one another and after a final, blistering row, we parted. He took the initiative, actually, and went to Quebec. He must have planned it in advance, for he'd not only given notice at the University but made arrangement for my allowance to be paid through his family lawyer. He wasn't mean about money. That was one of his good points, and he didn't have many when I came to reckon them up. I've never set eyes on him since. All that was two years ago."

"You wouldn't ever consider giving it another chance? Over there, in a new country?"

"Quebec wouldn't be a new country to him. It's more Catholic than the Pope from what I hear. Not that I've a thing against Catholics as Catholics. Sometimes I envy them very much. They've got something to hang on to, and that's more than you can say of us heretics. Besides, his people were kind, in spite of the fact that they were opposed to the marriage. I can go there any time, and be sure of a welcome, but I don't take his money. It's still accumulating at the lawyers for all I know."

"What did you do after that?"

"Your job. Teaching at a girls' school in Lancashire, but I was no better at that than keeping a man. I know what I want to do now and nothing is going to stop me. I'm hoping to get into that male club at Westminster and say my piece. On behalf of the working-class in the North, and on behalf of so-called liberated females everywhere. I don't care if it takes me twenty years. Or maybe that's just the port and lemon talking."

She jumped up, pointing to the clock that stood at ten minutes to seven. "What's special about you, Davy? I'm a very punctual person and you almost made me miss my train. Are you going to walk me to the station after confessional?"

They went out into the street, meeting a light flurry of snow that was beginning to lie on ice below. She took his arm, explaining, half-seriously, that she was obliged to with two-inch heels and a glacial pavement. She said, as the station lights came in view, "All that, and you haven't told me a thing about yourself. All I know is your name, your profession and the fact that you taught a cousin of mine who took off for Malaya."

"We'll have another chance, I hope."

"I don't know when. I'm not likely to get to Devon, except on a charabanc trip, taking in Clovelly and the Doone Valley."

"You will," he said, with a strong inward conviction, "and before the tourist season begins. Your platform is five, isn't it? Mine's two. I can catch a local five minutes after your train." They stopped at the barrier. Beyond it he could see the stocky figure of Routledge, beckoning. She said, "Wait, Davy . . . can you tell me one good reason why I should unload to that extent on someone I've only met twice?"

"Yes," he said. "It's a fallacy that professional schoolteachers are just talkers. If they're interested in the job, as I am, they have to learn how to listen. I must be progressing."

2

The letter came when he stood in most need of it, when he had reached a new low, despite his good resolutions on returning to Bamfylde at the start of the tight-rope term.

He had renewed his resolve to concentrate on his subject, and on his book, with the intention of keeping well clear of Alcock, and going out of his way to avoid a clash. He saw himself as a kind of Perrin, in the schoolmaster's cautionary tale by Walpole, *Mr. Perrin and Mr. Traill*, that had been a subject for common-room jokes since it had passed from hand to hand in the early 'twenties. Like the wretched Perrin he had found himself repeating, 'It *will* be better this term . . . it might be different this term.'

But it was not. He did succeed in finishing the book to his satisfaction but by late February, when the moor looked its dreariest he came to the conclusion that Bamfylde, Algy's Bamfylde that is, was dying on its feet. Not academically, and not from a numerical or economic standpoint, but inwardly, as though Alcock had petrified it.

The rhythms within rhythms that had been such a comforting feature of the place were shattered and he doubted if anyone would ever be capable of restoring them. Something of the national mood of flatness and political stalemate had invaded its draughty corridors. The Choral Society was all but defunct. Carter's beloved O.T.C. was a ritual exercise, performed every Wednesday afternoon. The Debating Society had wilted under rigorous censorship. Entertainments, uninhibited in Algy's day, were now limited to classical plays that even Howarth thought a crashing bore. The emphasis was on work and exam-passing, so that the gulf widened between the clever boys and the slackers, one group exulting in their exemption from compulsory games, the other becoming bored and listless, so that even the occasional flash of mutiny showed as no more than a ripple. The rugby and cross-country enthusiasts missed Irvine's stimulus. Molyneux, who lived off the premises, was no substitute as games master, and David had not been offered the job, although he still went out on the runs as whipper-in, and played an occasional game in the senior scrum. Alcock kept mostly to himself, the remote, austere abbot of a monastery where all the monks were at odds with themselves.

It was difficult to put one's finger on the major cause of the decline and Howarth, Barnaby and himself, who clung together these days ('Like three old drunks going home in a storm', Barnaby jested) occasionally searched for it over a bottle of gin in Howarth's quarters. Barnaby may have touched on a root cause when he said, "Place reminds me of a Regency rake who has undergone religious conversion. He's much more likely to pass the Golden Gate but he's damnably poor company at home." Howarth had another analogy: "It's getting to *smell* like a grammar school in a red-brick town. Well-scrubbed and antiseptic, but me? God help me, I'm nostalgic for the smell of damp-rot and boiled greens, of Herries's days."

Then, one dull overcast morning, he found the letter on his hall table, the envelope addressed in strange, flowing handwriting very legible despite the fact that it looked as if it had been dashed off in a hurry. The postmark was 'Taunton' and he opened it unsuspectingly, thinking it must be from someone's mother, making enquiries about a new boy's winter cough or a supply of underclothes.

It was from Christine Forster, announcing triumphantly that she had been adopted as prospective candidate for the South Mendips division, a rural constituency where Somerset, Wiltshire and Gloucestershire merged, for the most part agricultural but with several small industrial pockets, including one small coal mine, a glove factory, and several leather-processing centres. "It really is a forlorn hope," she said. "The Tory majority here is over fifteen thousand, and they've never even elected a Liberal, although one came close in 1911. It means starting from scratch, because they've never had a Socialist candidate, but the Trade Unions have got their foot in the door at two or three of the factories and there's potential in the farm labourer's vote. The Liberal candidate seems a colourless chap and his vote has been dropping steadily since the 1918 election. We could even run second, if we put our backs into it, and that would encourage the party to field more women candidates. What I really want to know is, will you be a dear and come over and support me on the platform at my adoption meeting next Saturday? It'll be a very modest affair in the Church Institute, at Bilhampton, the constituency capital (pop. 2,301) but you wouldn't have to speak if you didn't want to, although I'd be very flattered if you gave us a blessing. Wire me if you can come. If you can't, I'll understand and write again, sending on press cuttings, providing the press bother to report it. One other thing that I thought you might like to tell Bamfylde. My cousin *is* in Malaya, up-country on a rubber plantation. (I said 'tea', didn't I?) The poor boy lost an eye a year or so ago in a hunting accident but the other wasn't impaired and now he has a glass eye that he turns to unique advantage. He has persuaded the poor devils who work under him that the eye can see them whether or not he has it in. He puts it in a glass of water and leaves it on the bungalow steps when he goes off for a drink, declaring that it keeps the helots at work when his back is turned. The feudal tricks you Bamfeldians practise in far-flung outposts!"

She signed it, 'Affectionately', as Julia Darbyshire had signed her letters. Warmed, and excited at the prospect of seeing her again, he dashed off a reply saying she was to look out for him on Saturday and ran down to broadcast the story of Ridgeway's glass eye. It might cheer the old hands who remembered him. There were still four or five of his contemporaries, and a story like that was certain of a place in Bamfeldian lore.

He told Howarth and Barnaby about Christine that same night, mentioning that he was attending the adoption meeting, but saying nothing of her invitation to sit on the platform. He knew that Howarth despised all politicians, and that Barnaby had voted

Liberal all his life, but they had all grown accustomed to his party loyalties by now. Barnaby agreed to stand in for his one Saturday period.

He set off in high spirits early Saturday morning and soon after midday caught the branch line train to Bilhampton, a pretty, sleepy, red-roofed little market-town at a junction of two sluggish rivers. He had not expected to be met at the station but there she was, looking very spruce in a navy two-piece, and a short ocelot coat, a scarf over her brown hair. She called, gaily, "Welcome to Rotten Borough!" and kissed him on the cheek, and then, smiling, "I know precisely what you are thinking—that this ensemble doesn't fit the party image—but you're wrong, you know. Cloth caps are fine for the lads, but this place needs a boost. The Member's wife is a frightful frump, despite her husband's seat on God knows how many boards, and the Liberal is a bachelor who trots around in tweeds and a pork-pie hat. It was nice of you to come, Davy. I appreciate it very much. Now let me give you lunch at the Bull. It's a nice old pub and you can meet the troops."

It was, he reflected, a very different Christine Forster from the disconsolate girl he had met in Wales two months before. Selection, over the heads of three young men, had boosted her self-respect and it seemed to have done something for her appearance too, for she had obviously made a favourable impression on the middle-aged men composing the constituency committee. More than that, there was no question but that she meant to be boss down here, and was unlikely to let herself be regarded as a kind of mascot, the impression he had got watching her in the company of Routledge and the Valley stalwarts.

The adoption meeting was a great success. Unlike so many of these occasions it had dignity, and a sense of purpose, and perhaps it was this that encouraged him to call her aside during the coffee-break and take her up on the offer to speak.

She said, eagerly, "You mean it? Well, that's fine, Davy! But will you let me give you a hint? Cut the flannel and say something factual, on the lines of what you said to me that first time we met. About your job as you see it, and the ammunition you feed boys."

"But that's ridiculous," he said, laughing, "this meeting is about you. You're the star here tonight."

"Maybe, but I've got my reasons. This is Monmouth country.

In that market-place out there nine local weavers were hanged for their share in that uprising."

"But it wasn't a popular uprising in that sense. Monmouth was a royal bastard, and a feeble one at that."

"It was a case of the people versus the others, and that's good enough for me. Moreover, it's a local banner, so why can't we wave it?"

He had a conviction that she was hedging, that her insistence on reference to a local revolt two-and-a-half centuries ago was based on instinct, an instinct that rested on something more subtle than an attempt to highlight Bilhampton. It was a woman's attempt to establish that the Socialist cause was attracting intellectuals and here was proof of it, a schoolmaster, who taught at a public school, but was ready to champion her in public.

He took her advice. Years of dominating The Lump, on its long haul from Second Form to Sixth, had disposed of any inhibitions he might have had addressing an audience. He spoke authoritatively and lucidly, giving the town its place in the history of the Englishman's struggle to wrest power from the hands of narrow, sectarian interests, and prepare the ground for real democracy, and because the Bilhampton victims of Jeffries' Bloody Assizes were local, whose family surnames were still familiar to his audience, he made his impact. "They died in what we should think of as a poor cause," he concluded, "but it wasn't as poor as all that. The men who came out to fight for Monmouth, in that wet summer so long ago, were responding to an impulse that has brought the Englishman into conflict with local tyrants down to this day, a determination to have a say in how he is taxed and governed. Sometimes, his leaders have been demagogues, or opportunists, but that did not keep him at home, making do on the leavings tossed him by entrenched privilege. He came out, generation after generation, often dying for a principle, and today we are privileged to hold the torch. Not only with a vote but under trained leaders, of the calibre of this young woman, whose educational qualifications could earn her a thousand a year if she had an eye on the main chance. My advice, for what it is worth, is lend her a hand. And when the time comes to vote for her, in the certainty that she cares deeply for the descendants of men Kirke's dragoons hanged from the end of a rope, at the command of a pedant in Whitehall."

The weight of applause astonished and embarrassed him, so much so that he took small heed of the rest of the proceedings, not excluding the speech of a minor Cabinet figure Transport House had sent from London. But afterwards the politician set the seal on his success by singling him out saying, "Ever thought of politics as a career, Powlett-Jones? You might do worse, with your natural feel for an audience. I've no doubt we could find a constituency for you to nurse," and while David was wondering how to reply to this, he caught a glimpse of Christine's flushed, smiling face over the politician's shoulder, and she answered for him, saying, "Leave him be, sir. He's far more help to us where he is, preaching the gospel in the tents of the Philistines. Isn't that so, Davy?"

"It's what I'm better qualified to do, enjoy it or not," David said, and momentarily his mind returned to Bamfylde under Alcock, and he wondered if, since Algy's departure, he could claim to have preached the gospel in the way she claimed on his behalf.

3

He stayed overnight and on Sunday morning, having borrowed the local Secretary's Austin Seven, she drove him round the constituency. About noon they stopped at the summit of Coverdale Beacon, dominating the plain and giving a view, in clear weather, of the three counties.

It was a fitfully sunny day, with the very first hint of spring in the wind, and great masses of cloud casting shadows as they drove across the lightly wooded landscape.

"I haven't thanked you properly, Davy. You can't have the least idea how much you being there meant to me. You were the jam on what looked like being a stodgy helping of rice pudding. Do you mind if I kiss you?"

"Mind? Damn it, I've been wondering ever since I saw you on the platform how I could get your mind off politics for a few minutes."

Her lips were as warm and responsive as they had promised to be. There were aspects of her, temperamental aspects that, until then, had reminded him a little of Julia but now, letting his fingertips trace the length of her cheek, he had a very poignant memory of his wife, lying in his arms in the winter half-light of the cottage bedroom at Stone Cross. It was odd, he thought, that she should choose that moment to say, "I know what happened to you, Davy. I was curious, and asked around when I went back to the Valley after Christmas. You've come through it with more credit than you give yourself, do you know that?" He said nothing, testing the strength of the affirmation, so she went on, "It would have embittered most men, coming on top of that pounding you had in France. You're still very much a lonely person, however, and that shows too."

"Only away from Bamfylde."

"It means that much to you?"

"Pretty well everything."

"That invitation you had last night—politics, and the power to work in a wider field—it makes no appeal at all to you?"

"Why do you ask?"

"I don't know. Maybe it was because it struck me that if it did we could do it together. It would be more fun with you around. You're a rare bucker-upper or didn't you know?"

"I seem to have lost the trick of boosting myself lately."

He told her something of the changed situation at school, of its cheerfulness under Algy Herries and its decline, in all but material ways, under Alcock. She said, "He sounds an absolute horror but you don't have to suffer him. You're young enough to make a shift, aren't you?"

"It isn't so simple. A school is a tribe. You can't switch tribes as if you were getting on and off a bus."

"You can if you're going in the wrong direction."

"There are all kind of factors. Loyalty to the boys, old and new. Loyalty to the rump of the original staff, to the school servants even. Some of them have been there since before Algy's time."

She said, smiling, "Down under all that smouldering Celtic banner-waving you're a bit of a Tory, Davy. The very nicest kind of Tory and they do exist." Then, with a sincerity that he found uplifting, "You will keep in touch? Come over whenever you can, as soon as I find permanent digs in the constituency, and write to me when you can't. I say, I'm making all the running this afternoon, aren't I?"

"I'll help you out when we've got a bigger car. Or when the ground isn't so soggy."

That made her laugh and she kissed him again, switched on

and drove off down the hill. They said little until she had bought her platform ticket, and accompanied him over the bridge to the down-line. Then, as he found a seat in the little train, "Would I be welcome if I ran myself over to Bamfylde as soon as I get myself a car? I've got my eye on a third-hand sports."

"Why don't you pick up some of your separation money and buy yourself a new one?"

"You know better than to ask that. Well?"

"You know better than to ask if you'd be welcome."

The guard, slamming doors with the flourish obligatory to all official door-slammers at small stations in the shires, blew his whistle. She lifted her hand and, as the train pulled away, he had an even more vivid memory of Beth, standing where he was standing now, framed in the window of a third-class compartment, with himself where Christine stood. It was the moment prior to surrendering to that impulse on Colwyn Bay Station, nearly twelve years ago, followed by the leap on to a moving train that had had such bitter-sweet consequences.

The comparison was so poignant that he almost cried out to her to hurry but then, as the train gathered speed, she disappeared behind a cloud of smoke.

Chapter Five

1

He was taking Lower Third history when Christopherson Major arrived. Beguiling thirteen-year-olds with Owen Tudor's dalliance with the widowed Queen Catherine, a favourite of theirs and his, for somehow, the way David told the story, the knowing impudence of the philanderer reached out to them over more than five centuries.

Christopherson Major, duty monitor of the headmaster, arrived on the crest of a ripple of laughter, David having quoted Tudor as saying, "Madame, since you can't understand a word of my spoken Welsh, I will sing everything I say, in the hope of conveying my regard for you in music." He often clowned his way through a Lower School period in this way, improvising dialogue and dialect to match it. His justification, had he been asked for one, would have been that it was the only way to capture the laggards' attention for the red meat of history later on.

The appointment of headmaster's monitors was another of Alcock's innovations. Each week a trainee prefect was employed as his errand boy and the job was popular in the Upper Fifth, for it meant, among other minor privileges, a week of sanctioned idleness and plenty of fresh air. Christopherson, however, was a studious boy, who took his duties seriously.

"The headmaster's compliments, sir. Would you please step across for a word with him?"

The laugh died, killed, no doubt, by the expression of irritation that crossed David's face. It was not unknown for members of the staff to be summoned to the presence in the middle of a period, but it was unusual. He said, "Right, Christopherson, take over here, while I'm gone, I won't be more than a jiffy, page one-o-six in the text-book, the minority of Henry VI," and dusting chalk from his gown he went out across the quad, entering the head's house through Big School passage.

Alcock, as he expected, was seated behind his rampart, frowning down at a neat, taped file, the kind of file, David thought, one might associate with an old-fashioned solicitor or a civil servant in the Ministry of Agriculture. He knew enough of Alcock, however, to be certain it was a file with his name on it, possibly in private code.

"You wanted me, Headmaster?"

"Yes, please be seated. This may occupy us some little time. You were taking the Lower Third, I believe."

"He knows damn well I was," David reflected, "since he memorises the timetable every new term . . ." but said, briefly, "I left Christopherson in charge. You won't want him while I'm here, will you?"

"Er . . . no," murmured Alcock vaguely, and his rare uncertainty alerted David at once. It was not often that Alcock showed vagueness in the presence of anyone he summoned.

"Well?"

"It's about this. I thought it only fair to ask for an explanation at once, for there may well be some unfortunate misunderstanding. The press is notoriously inaccurate in these matters."

He passed over a news-clipping, a single column report, cut from a provincial paper, and dealing with Christine Forster's adoption meeting. David was surprised to see it, and even more surprised to notice that the introduction, set in heavy type, concerned his own contribution to the evening's speeches. It was headed 'SCHOOLMASTER SUPPORTS LABOUR CANDIDATE', and below, in smaller type, 'Reference to Local Hangings—"Martyrs to Freedom's Cause" Claim'. A few lines of the introduction were linked to a summarised version of his speech on the Monmouth weavers, executed in Bilhampton Market Place, in 1685, and the closing section of the speech itself was given verbatim. He said, carefully, "I don't think there's any misunderstanding. This is a pretty fair report of what I said."

"You actually appeared at the meeting, and spoke from the platform?"

"Of course I did. It says I did. What's unusual about that?"

"It doesn't strike you, not even on reflection, as a very impulsive act on your part?"

"No, it doesn't. I know the candidate. She's related to a boy who was head prefect of Havelock's, before your time. She asked me to speak and I did. Members of the staff aren't banned from making political speeches, are they? For if they are it's the first I've heard about it. Mr. Herries once presided over a Liberal rally at Challacombe to my certain knowledge, and Mr. Carter signed the Conservative candidate's nomination papers last election. I had no idea the speech would be reported, and I'm surprised that it was, but I'm not going to apologise for it. Did you expect me to?"

"No," Alcock said, "knowing your headstrong character, I didn't, Powlett-Jones. But I would anticipate a certain reluctance on your part to appear on a public platform at a political meeting of that kind. You note that the name of the school is quoted."

David glanced at the cutting again and saw that this was true. He had no recollection of having mentioned the school to anyone save Christine and could only assume the reporter had got the information from the local secretary, who might have had his address. It still did not seem important, however, and despite his knowledge of Alcock, he remained puzzled by the man's obvious concern. "Would you like to elaborate your own views, Headmaster?"

"I need to do that?"

"I think you do. You summon me in the middle of a period, and put a newspaper cutting into my hand, implying that I have overstepped the mark in some way. I should like to know what way. We live in a democracy, and the Labour Party is at present in office. Are you suggesting schoolmasters don't enjoy the same political liberty as other people—doctors, clergymen and so on?"

"In a sense I am. How a schoolmaster casts his vote is, of course, his own concern. How he conducts himself in public is not. It never has been. Do you take my point?"

"No, and to make it you'll have to do better than that, Headmaster. If I had been drunk, and caused a public disturbance, or appeared before magistrates on a charge of bothering women in cinemas, you would have every justification for summoning me here, and even asking for my resignation. You could hardly do that on the strength of an innocuous speech I made at a public meeting in another county. Or in this county, for that matter." He got up. "Is that all?"

For the second time he noticed that Alcock was fidgeting, his fingers unlocking and the knuckles gleaming as his right hand closed and unclosed on an ivory paper-knife, shaped like a scimitar. Then, as though catching himself giving ground, he pushed the knife out of reach and made a 'steeple' with his hands.

"It can't be all, can it? As a matter of fact, I think it essential, Powlett-Jones, that we . . . er . . . er come to some kind of understanding, here and now. I see that newspaper cutting as important. You don't. No matter, let us shelve that for the moment, and concentrate on your attitude towards me ever since I was installed. You have made it manifestly plain that you dislike me, and dislike my methods even more. I am not interested in knowing why. Within certain limits any member of the staff is free to exercise personal preferences, providing they do not affect his loyalty to a colleague. But I think even you will admit that our relationship has reached something of an impasse, that it can no longer be subjected to strain without rupture of the discipline I try and maintain here. I did not mention resignation but you did. Perhaps it *is* something you would like to think on for the remainder of the term."

David sat down again. He was red in the face but not from embarrassment. Alcock was no longer capable of embarrassing him but he could still make him almost incoherent with rage. Knowing this, he gave himself a full half-minute before saying, "You're *asking* me to resign? On account of that newspaper report?"

"I'm asking you to think about making a change. And not on account of that newspaper report. Rather on the impossibility of us arriving at, shall we say, a working compromise. Carter and Gibbs reached the same conclusion, I imagine, but they . . . er . . . acted on it."

He had himself in hand now. The rage in him cooled and in its place came a sense of release, of having suddenly seen a rift in the wall Alcock and Alcock's methods had raised between them, brick by brick, over the last few terms. He braced himself, leaning forward and staring the man down in a way that anyone but Alcock would have found embarrassing. Instead he only looked mildly astonished as David said, emphatically, "I'll be damned if you're going to bully me into resigning. And I wouldn't advise you to try on this issue. It could land you, rather than me, in a very embarrassing situation. Do I have to explain what I mean by that?"

"Not necessarily," Alcock hedged, "and I can only repeat I'm *not* asking you to resign. Only to ask yourself if a change wouldn't be the wisest course in what remains of the term. We could come to some arrangements about the usual notice."

David got up again. Suddenly, and to a degree that astonished him, he was composed, almost jaunty. Declaration of open war came as a relief.

"Well," he said, "suppose we leave it like this. Here's your clipping. Show it to whom you like. And show them the contents of that file too, providing you send me a duplicate of any allegations it contains. If it came to a show-down I could demand that. Or my solicitor could. But it need not go as far as that. I only want to make two things clear. Resignation on my part—the dignified version you're seeking—is out of the question. And I reserve the right to appear on any public platform I choose, so long as I am convinced, in my own mind, that such appearances don't reflect on the school's reputation. You can try and force me to resign, but if you do I'll fight. I'll fight every inch of the way, inside and outside Bamfylde. I've disagreed with you, yes, in all manner of things, but I've never been disloyal to you in the way you imply and I never would be. I'm far too attached to the school to act the fool in that respect. My . . . er . . . compliments, Headmaster. I'd best get back to the class now."

He went out, shutting the door carefully behind him, and was relieved, as he crossed the quad and started up the steps to the Lower Third, to hear the bell announce the end of afternoon school. Before he reached the landing the Third Form had erupted and Christopherson slipped out, descending the stairs quickly and pretending not to notice him. He thought, grimly, "Is that because he has a pretty good idea the Stoic and I have just had a God Almighty row? Or is it because the class was out of hand before the bell?"

He turned left and cut through the Rogues Gallery to the linen room, thence to his own quarters, glancing sideways at a cherubic Algy Herries, beaming down from the panelling. "I won that round on points, Algy," he said aloud, and little Burnett-Jones, emerging from the linen room with a newly darned pair of socks, scuttled off to tell the Second Form that Pow-Wow was beginning to talk to himself, a certain sign of onrushing lunacy. He was a little crestfallen when this piece of intelligence caused no stir at all. Venn, from the lofty peak of a third-termer, hardly looked up from a count of grimed cigarette cards as he said, "Queen Anne's dead. They all do that. You'll get used to it in a term or two, new kid."

2

He had won on points, he claimed, but Howarth wasn't so sure, and neither, it seemed, was Barnaby, usually so sanguine.

"He'll carry it farther," Howarth said, glumly. "Don't you see that he has to? His position here is untenable if he doesn't."

"You could say it's untenable if he does," said Barnaby. "For one or the other of them, that is."

"You think he'll be stupid enough to lay that cutting before the Governors?"

"A careful selection of the Governors. And not the cutting alone, you can be sure of that. It will be a door opener and inside will be a long-winded report embracing your stand on that smoking incident, and your fight to save Hislop."

"If he confines himself to those issues the Governors can't do a thing," Barnaby said, perking up a little. "Any housemaster worth his salt would fight for one of his boys, and that's all Carter and P.J. did. No, it's the cutting that bothers me. How many Socialists occupy seats on that board, P.J.? Frankly, I can't see why you're so cocksure, can you, Howarth?"

"Knowing our boy, I can," Howarth said, lighting one Gold Flake from another, "but I don't expect him to unmask his batteries for our edification. Watch and wait, Barnaby!"

"I will," said Barnaby, "and I won't forget to pray while I'm at it."

*　　*　　*

He found the two letters on his hall table, assuming they had come by the late afternoon post, that rarely yielded anything of interest. One, from Christine, was a crackling account of her first week's canvass in the constituency, enclosing a duplicate of the cutting Alcock had just shown him. It was overscored, '*Look who is stealing my headlines! Not to say a cabinet minister's!*'

He opened the other letter, bearing the imprint of the literary agent he had chosen at random from the *Artists' and Writers' Year Book*. He read it at first without taking in the contents but then, re-reading it, he uttered a shout of glee. The agents had found a publisher for 'The Royal Tigress', Millards, a firm specialising in educational books, and were offering an advance of one hundred pounds, on a royalty of six per cent on the first five thousand copies and ten per cent thereafter. The agent enclosed the publisher's offer, and the letter quoted from a reader's report in what David regarded as flattering terms. 'A neglected period extremely well researched . . . readability one seldom finds in work of this kind . . . human insight into characters usually seen as pasteboard figures in a text-book . . . exciting blow by blow descriptions of the major battles . . . a firm grasp of military strategy, particularly that of Edward IV . . .' and so on. He sat in the embrasure of his study window, looking out over a moor touched by the first kiss of spring, savouring his personal triumph and a sense of achievement that reduced Alcock and all his works to insignificance. He had never really imagined a reputable publisher would pay good money for the book. In the far-off days when he had begun it, he saw it as a kind of private joke between himself and Beth and later, after her death, he had resumed it as a means of keeping gloomy night-thoughts at bay. Later, when the theme and the period took hold of him, he had enjoyed writing and rewriting the battle scenes, and making fresh guesses at the principal actors in the long drama. Now, with the offer of a hundred pounds in his hands, the stack of manuscript that had occupied an undusted corner of his desk for so long had a real place in the pattern of his life and he picked up the carbon copy of the dedication page and read, '*To My Wife, Beth, who never ceased to urge me to write this book*'. He thought, "By God, I should have liked her to have shared this moment . . . but she will in a way, for young Grace will be madly excited. I'll tell her, of course, but the others . . . Howarth, Barnaby and so on, they can wait until the printed version actually appears." There was one exception, however, and he sat down and wrote a brief letter to Chad Boyer, now in his final year at Cambridge, saying nothing of his recent confrontation with Alcock but telling him about 'The Royal Tigress', and adding that he would be delighted to see him if he could get down during the vacation.

3

Knowledge that the book was in the pipeline (earliest date of publication was September) kept him cheerful for the remainder of the term. For the first time in more than eighteen months Bamfylde saw Pow-Wow Jones as the older hands among them recalled him in Algy's time, a jester who yet managed to convey to them something of the grandeur of British history, who scratched among the trivia of text-book names and treaties for something that could link dry-as-dust facts to today's headlines in the press, who was not above telling the Fifth and Sixth Forms risqué stories of Lord Melbourne, and Madame du Barry, and resorted, in Lower School periods, to a repertoire of jingles and tag-lines, in order to fix a date or an event in the memories of boys who might otherwise have made their minds a blank until the first clang of the dismissal bell. He still infiltrated current affairs into his Upper School lessons, sometimes spending an entire period discussing the League of Nations, the seven-and-a-half-hour working day laid down under the Coal Mines Act, or the end of the Allied occupation of Germany. He had, that year, a particularly bright Sixth and an unusually quiescent Lower Fourth, so that he was able, almost effortlessly, to lose himself in work and outdoor activities, such as O.T.C. band-practice and the tail end of the cross-country season. Havelock's, inspired perhaps by his own keen interest in running, won the cross-country shield that term for the first time in school history, and this, in its small way, was another personal triumph. He also began to take a desultory interest in the work of young Renshaw-Smith, the music master who had replaced Rapper Gibbs, an aesthetic-looking twenty-four-year-old, devoted to his subject but inclined to be nervous and obviously terrified by Alcock's occasional appearance, at a choral society or church choir rehearsal. David did what he could to pump confidence into the man, telling him he was just in time to prevent the virtual extinction of musical interests in the school, a sparetime activity that Algy had done so much to foster. David went along to one or two choral society rehearsals himself, and was moved, as he always was, by the sexless voices of the juniors singing traditional songs, like 'Greensleeves' and 'Gaudeamus', always among his favourites.

Howarth and Barnaby, noticing his cheerfulness, made characteristic comments. Howarth said, "Glad to see you perking up again, P.J. Must be Carter's absence," and when David denied this, saying that old Carter wasn't half bad once you got to know him, Howarth smiled his wry smile and added, "Well, then, it's probably the relief that accompanies a burst boil, old son. You've thrown down the gauntlet and that bounder hasn't the guts to pick it up."

"That's nearer the mark," David conceded, but he was able to improve on this when Barnaby, marking the same rise in spirits, quoted his favourite Horace—'The beardless youth, his tutor being dismissed, delights in horses, dogs and the sunny expanse of turf.'

"Not strictly applicable," David said, "but Horace can probably tell you how I'm disposed towards the Noble Stoic, now that I've told him to jump in the river—how about 'Ignem gladio scrutare'? Do I have to translate?"

"No," Barnaby said, mildly, "but I could quote back at you in the same context. 'Sometimes it is folly to poke the fire with the sword'—a proverbial phrase, I believe, don't ask me the source. If I were you, P.J., I'd let things ride for a term, and give us all a much-needed breather."

Barnaby got his wish, at least through the fag-end of the tight-rope term, and up to the time he went off, with half a dozen Sun-setters, on a walk along Hadrian's Wall. David would have liked to accompany him but it would have meant leaving Grace alone, for they had made no arrangements to go into Wales, or up to town to visit Beth's folk. He remained Bamfylde-based, therefore, spending his time riding and walking with her over the plateau.

Sometimes, when they were mounted, they pushed as far as Chetsford Water, where he told her, for the first time, of his despairing tramp through the storm the day her mother and her twin sister were killed, and how young Winterbourne, no more than fourteen then, had taken charge of him and piloted him back across the sodden moor to learn that she herself had a sporting chance.

The story touched her deeply, for she had always been close to Winterbourne, and had never ceased to acknowledge the part he had played in helping her to adjust after a year in hospital. "Spats and Sax Hoskins are the very nicest boys we've ever had at Bamfylde," she said, and he replied, smiling, "Well, let's settle for the fact that they're among the most original. It's a funny thing, but the originals are usually the easiest to get along with."

He gave her a shrewd, sidelong glance, as she kicked her pony into a trot and passed him on the down-slope to the river bottom, a healthy-looking eleven-year-old, or coming up to eleven in a week or so, with a ruddy complexion and no sign of a handicap as she sat her pony. A year or so ago she had continued to remind him poignantly of Beth, but lately he had begun to see her more as a miniature of his own sister, Megan, when she was flitting up and down the steep streets of the Valley, before the war. Living here, growing up among so many boys, she had a quality of self-confidence not given to many girls of her age, and it might stand her in good stead when she reached the proverbial awkward age. She would never, so long as she lived, show embarrassment in the presence of the male animal, and that was something he supposed, for even his tomboyish sisters had blushed on occasion. "Somebody," he pondered, "has done a good job on Grace, and I can't really believe it was me. It took me all my time to ride out of the shock of that bloody awful day . . . Maybe she's right, and it was Winterbourne, with his painting, and Sax Hoskins, with his foxtrots, and any number of others who went out of their way to help at the time."

They got back to school about five o'clock, having left the horses at Stone Cross Farm, and walked up, and there, framed in Big School arch, was Brigadier Cooper, his personal champion on the Governing Board. He noticed at once that the old warrior looked bothered, as though planning a foray across the North-West Frontier that might cost the lives of men.

He said, briefly, "Been hanging around waiting for you since early afternoon. Like a word if you're free. Where can we go?" and when David suggested his quarters he said firmly, "No, your little lass and the butler will be there fussing with tea. It's a private word I want. How about the planty?"

"Suit yourself, Briggy," David said, and they went off across the football field, past Algy's thinking post, to the coppice marking the school's north-eastern border, now showing green where larches and the odd horse-chestnut broke the phalanx of Scots firs.

"Thought you might like to know what's going on," mumbled the Brigadier. "That chap is after your scalp and means to get it!"

"Jolly good luck to him, but somehow I don't think he will."

The brigadier's salt-and-pepper brows knitted. "Not so sure, P.J. He's a devious devil, and he's going to work in what I consider a thoroughly under-handed way. That's why I'm here, d'ye follow?"

"No," David said, "but I'd like to. You mean he's approached some of the more conservative Governors, I imagine?"

"He's got at that dry old stick, Sir Rufus, for one. And that tyke, Blunt, who still seems to have it in for you over that memorial rumpus. The hard core that never really took to Algy or to Algy's way of running the show."

"Is he still flying that damned silly kite about my right to air political opinions on a public platform?"

"No, he's played that down so far but he'll bring it forward. It's his strongest card with that bunch. Matter o' fact, I did a reccy as soon as I discovered what was afoot. Got the results here," and he fumbled in his Norfolk jacket, producing a crumpled scrap of paper on which he had written some notes under alphabetical headings. "Here it is—(a) Claims you spearhead staff opposition to everything he attempts. (b) You yourself commit acts of indiscipline."

"Such as?"

"You got up that petition about Carter's boy, the one he intended to sack. Dam' lot o' nonsense, sacking a boy for smoking in the bushes. Standard punishment for getting caught has been six of the best for time out of mind. Then there was that Hislop business—he made hay of that, implying you were encouraging gambling."

"Anything else?"

"Yes, the most serious allegation to my mind. He says your teaching methods are eccentric, that you don't stick to the syllabus, and refuse to base your teaching on previous exam papers, thus prejudicing boys sitting for school-leaving cert. For good measure, he claims you use historical doggerel that was out of date when he was a boy. What the hell did he mean by that, P.J.?"

"Aide-memoires I use in Lower School," said David, and quoted the famous 'All-Boys-Naughty-Won't-Memorise-All-Those-Horrid-Hateful-Battles-to-Bosworth', explaining to a baffled brigadier its use as a reminder of a string of fifteenth-century battles.

"But that's damned good!" exclaimed Cooper. "If someone had taught me that when I was a nipper I'd have soon had those bloody battles off pat! Fact is, I can't recall any of 'em but Hedgeley and Hexham. They stuck in the mind somehow."

"How did you get all this?" David asked, steering him back to the point, and Cooper said, winking, that 'he had put the ferret in', his usual practice when he wanted to prod rumours into the open. Alcock, it seemed, hadn't tackled a single Old Boy on the Board, and had been careful in his general approach, but had inevitably made one or two blunders, so that information of the backstairs campaign had leaked.

In spite of maintaining a casual front David was more worried than he was prepared to admit, even to himself. Championship of Hislop was one thing, and so, to an extent, was his loyalty to Carter over the smoking incident, but it was humiliating to learn that Alcock was calling his teaching to account. He saw, too, that the references to his free-ranging current affairs sessions was merely a lead-in to a direct attack on his political opinions, opinions that Tory Governors would almost surely regard as subversion of the young. He decided, therefore, to test this outright and said, "Regarding my public support of a Labour candidate, how do you feel about that personally, Briggy?"

"Bound to be frank. Don't care for it," Cooper said. "All the same, I'm not such an ass as to think we can proscribe a man's politics in his free time. Neither is Alcock, I imagine, and that's why he's played it down while the Socialists are in office. There'd be one hell of a row if Fleet Street got hold of a story you were being pressured to resign on that account. Wouldn't do any of us a dam' bit o' good, would it?"

"No," David said, "and I told him that." They stopped to retrace their steps at the point where the plantation turned a right-hand angle. "How do you regard it, then? He couldn't get me kicked out, could he? Not on this kind of evidence?"

"It's possible," Cooper said, thoughtfully, "but even if he failed you'd have trouble living it down. I've had a lot of experience of committee work, and learned enough to realise that all this is doing you real harm. What you do about it is your affair. My responsibility stops at letting you in on what's being said behind your back. You could confront the bounder, I suppose."

"That wouldn't be the slightest use. I've already confronted him, on three separate occasions."

"You might frighten him with a solicitor's letter."

"Without anything but hearsay to back it?"

"That's a point. All I know is you can't let it go on. Talk it over with one of the old hands, Howarth or Barnaby, maybe. What I'm really driving at, I imagine, is that if he can whip up a sufficient body of opinion against you he could offer his resignation unless you submitted yours."

"Would that be best for Bamfylde in the long run?"

"No, it damned well wouldn't! I told you I know more about committees than you do and here's proof of it. If he tendered his resignation on those terms they'd be obliged to ask him to withdraw it, then put the pressure on you. His seniority assures him of that. Can't go above the head of a C.O. on behalf of a sub. Throws the whole damned system out o' gear. The Old Boys would back you, of course, and so, I daresay, would some of those who voted for you, but there are the neutrals, the Any-Way-For-A-Pinters, to think of. In the end they'd come down on Alcock's side, leavin' you high and dry."

"Then it looks as if I've got to mount a counter-offensive and I think I know how to do it. Isn't that a maxim you professionals favour? The thing to do when your retreat is cut off is to advance?"

"I daresay," Cooper said, gloomily, "but damned if I can see how you'll go about it. Keep me in touch when you do, however."

"You can be sure of that. Could I have that scruffy bit of paper of yours? I'll copy it out and destroy it and I won't quote you, not even with my back against the wall."

"If I hadn't been sure of that, young feller-me-lad, I'd have kept mum and let things take their course." He stood looking down across the field at the buildings, etched in the clear evening light. "Place means a lot to me, P.J."

"More than Alcock or Powlett-Jones, I imagine."

"Yes, if I'm honest, but that's how it should be with a man's school. I spent six happy years here. Dam' place taught me everything I know. Funny thing, I often used to picture it in this light

346

when I was sweating it out in temperatures of a hundred plus, on the far side of the world. Always cheered me up somehow."

4

He had had an inkling of what to do while the brigadier had been listing his shortcomings, according to Alcock. Now, as twilight stole down from the moor, he sought out Molyneux, who he knew was living in school for the holidays while his lodging in the village was being decorated. He did not want Molyneux's advice but he needed his motorcycle, a heavy Brough Superior, that the French master kept in the cycle shed when he was on duty. Molyneux said he wouldn't need the machine until the following day, so David thanked him and called Algy Herries's rectory at Yatton-under-edge, the far side of the moor, catching Algy just as he was leaving to take confirmation class. "How long will that keep you, Algy?"

"No more than an hour if you're thinking of coming over. Haven't seen much of you this winter but I realise why. The weather's been foul."

"It's not that," David said, "I didn't want to involve you. But now I've no option if I'm to survive."

"You sound worried, P.J."

"I am. May I come right over?"

"Of course, I'll warn Ellie. She'll be delighted. We don't get much company until the warm weather sets in."

Algy's rectory was a large, tile-hung house, built in the era when church attendance was obligatory among a larger population, most of whom had now moved off, the young to the cities, and the middle-aged to places like Lynmouth and Ilfracombe, where the tourist pickings were good. Ellie used no more than half the house but what she called the snuggery was a very cosy room, already beginning to reek of Algy's tobacco.

He told his story simply, guessing that both Algy and Ellie already knew most of it, either from village gossip, Old Boys who had visited them and the one or two conversations he had already had with them on the subject of Alcock. He said, "I'm not asking you to take sides, Algy. That wouldn't be fair now that you're out of it. It wouldn't be fair on Alcock, either, although he isn't so squeamish by the sound of things. All I want is a straight 'Yes' or

'Nay' to a course of action I propose taking. After that I'll ask a question or two as to tactics and leave you to await results. Is that understood?"

"Are you lecturing me or asking me how to hit back, P.J.?" but when Ellie exclaimed, "I think it's *disgraceful* . . . !" he silenced her with what was, for him, a savage gesture. "Keep out of this, woman, it's a man's business," and she tightened her lips, looking quite unhappy. "Right, now let's hear what you propose doing."

"Going over to the offensive before Alcock does. I'm going to write to the brigadier in formal terms, saying it has come to my knowledge that Alcock is slandering me, and request a special meeting of the Governing Body to lay down a directive concerning how much liberty a man has or has not to engage in political activity while serving on the staff."

"Well, that would certainly stir 'em up, but it would also have a very predictable side effect as regards your future, P.J."

"In what way, Algy?"

"I really have to tell you that?"

"I came here for advice."

"Very well, I'll give you more than you bargained for. Point one, write to the Governors by all means, but not to one of them known to be predisposed in your favour. Write to Sir Rufus, the Chairman, and do it officially, through the bursar."

"But Briggy hinted that Sir Rufus was one of those Alcock had approached."

"Precisely, and made a bad error of judgment when he did it. Why? Because Sir Rufus has been a judge and is the only man on that Board trained to keep an open mind. Dry as a fossil, no doubt, but entirely free of prejudice, take it from me. Make sense?"

"Good sense, Algy. And point two?"

"The crucial one. Don't be the first to introduce that political angle. If it is raised let Alcock be the one to raise it, thereby taking upon himself the risk of involving Bamfylde in a national how-de-do. I went astray there myself during the war. Burnt my fingers defending an Old Boy who claimed exemption as a conscientious objector. Never again. Some of the mud thrown takes years to scrape off. No, no, my boy, your strategy is professional, but your tactics are amateur. Believe me, I've been dealing with Governors the better part of my working life, and if I don't know how many beans make five, nobody does."

"But surely, that's the main point at issue, isn't it? The one where I can fall back on democratic principle."

"Democratic fiddlesticks! Do I have to tell you, a crusader in the cause, that only the theory of democracy holds any attraction for the majority? And only then when it suits their book. Face the facts, man. How many headmasters or school Governors in Britain today wear a red tie? Two per cent? I doubt it, for even the Liberals don't muster a handful. The row would flare up. It would have to if you alleged political persecution. The press would get hold of it, there would be questions in Parliament, God help us all, and I daresay you'd be vindicated in the end—famous, maybe, for twenty-four hours. After that your life would be made so damned uncomfortable you'd be glad to leave, Alcock or no Alcock. There's a much craftier approach than that, my lad, and you're lucky. You have a weapon in your armoury you don't even know about and he put it there!"

"You mean his allegations of disloyalty and indiscipline?"

Herries sighed and said, as an aside to Ellie, "Bring the brown sherry, m'dear. Several terms under that fool has dulled the man's intellect," and Ellie rose and crossed to the cupboard where she kept what she still called her 'Old Boys' Decanter'. Herries spread his knees, re-addressing himself to David. "He's impugned your teaching methods, hasn't he? He's claimed they are eccentric and old-fashioned. Fair enough. So tell me, in terms of round figures, how many boys got a history pass last June?"

"Nineteen. Three distinctions."

"Out of?"

"I'm not sure, without checking. Twenty-eight or twenty-nine, maybe."

"You haven't even done your homework, P.J. But you'll have to set about it, quicksticks. In that letter to Sir Rufus you'll enclose a summarised table of pass percentages and distinctions in your subject over all the years you've taught at Bamfylde. They should be impressive, especially when set against those of preceding years. Norrington, the fellow you followed when you came in, like a dog out of the rain, averaged under a dozen a year, I believe. Less in his last three years. I have a flair for remembering these things. I didn't spend all my time sitting on Spyglass Hill, listening to quad gossip." He got up and moved over to one of his leaving presents, a black-oak Bible box, converted into a desk. In less than a minute he was back again with a file entitled '*Examination Results, 1911–17*'. Opening it he did a quick cast, then beamed at David over the top of the file. "Better than I thought," he said. "Norrington's history passes averaged nine a year, over seven years. Making allowances for the smaller numbers we had in the Fifth throughout the war, that gives you a substantial margin. Around double, I'd say. Something to be said for historical jingles, eh?"

The sherry warmed his belly, and Algy's lively handling of the situation gave him a foretaste of victory. He said, "I've always thought of you as the best friend I ever had, Algy . . . you and Ellie. The best Beth ever had too, and she often said as much. It was different when you were around . . . we all missed you, but I missed you more than most, perhaps because the others were established when you got to them whereas in my case—it was as you said, a dog coming in out of the rain. And pretty sorry for himself into the bargain. I had no idea how closely you were watching us. I suppose I'd come to think of you as disengaged."

"It doesn't say a lot for your powers of deduction, boy. Do you imagine Ellie and I could spend half a lifetime building something, then never look at it again? Even from a distance?"

"I've felt damned lonely, particularly since Carter left."

"Well, I gave you a hint there but you didn't profit from it. Like everyone else you had to learn from experience."

"Don't we all?"

"Yes, I suppose we do," Herries conceded, "even in a backstairs business such as this, but there's no sense in turning up your proud Celtic nose at a short cut, is there?"

"No sense at all. Thank you, Algy, more than I can say. I'll hurry off now, for I mean to get that letter off tonight."

"Ah, you can't do that, I'm afraid. It's been a long day. A wedding, three christenings, a funeral and a confirmation class. Frankly, I don't feel up to it."

"You don't feel up to what?"

"Do you think I'd trust you to write that letter without an edited draft? What's on the diary for tomorrow, Ellie?"

"Tomorrow is Sunday," Ellie said, primly.

"My God, so it is! Well, that's a bore. You'll just have to contain yourself until Tuesday, won't you. Afternoon post probably. And tell me all about that book of yours. Ellie was very impressed to hear it was being published at last."

"You know about 'The Royal Tigress'? But I only told Grace!"

"I have a very long telescope," Algy said. "It can range freely over three parishes, yours, mine and the one in between." Somewhere, deep in the recesses of the rambling house, a small bell tinkled.

"That," said Ellie, "will be Mrs. Shawe, telling us dinner is served. Imagine ringing a bell for cold pheasant and pickles? I've always thought it silly but she will do it."

"It came to her ears," Algy said, "that for years and years and years our lives had been regulated by bells, my dear."

"Ah, but that was a real bell, Algy. Hers is an Alpine tinkle, half-heard among the edelweiss."

"I say, that's rather neat," Algy said, cocking his head like a robin, " 'Half-heard among the edelweiss'. Yatton-under-Edge has reawakened the muse in you. Perhaps you can go back to composing your greeting verses thus augmenting our pitiful stipend." He turned to David. "Did I ever tell you that family secret, P.J.? Before we married Ellie earned pinmoney writing verses for birthday and anniversary cards. What did they pay you, m'dear?"

"A guinea a gross," Ellie said, "and it was very hard work, I can tell you."

"Sweated labour, I'd say. P.J. will get somebody at Westminster to look into it."

They were now, he decided, well launched on one of their time-honoured pursuits, an elaborate leg-pull that had, as its unspoken object, the disarming of an audience and a general relaxation of tension. Over the years he had watched them at it. With boys, with parents, with visiting notabilities, all manner of people who drifted in through Big School arch with their problems and grouses. They were very, very good at it, so good indeed that it was impossible not to humour them.

He got up, and Algy led the way into the austere dining-room across the hall. Three places were laid at the Sheraton table. Presentation silver winked from the sideboard. Above it, hanging three degrees out of true, was an oval portrait of a rotund little man in the frock coat and punishing cravat of the early nineteenth century, Ellie's grandfather, he believed, who had been a vintner with a prosperous business in Tunbridge Wells. The vintner looked very much at home here, far more so than when he had sat peering down between framed photographs of First Elevens in what was now Alcock's monastic parlour at Bamfylde.

* * *

It was coming up to eleven o'clock when he set out on his return journey over the broad shoulder of the west plateau and down the narrow flint roads where the headlight beam made a tunnel of the high arching hedgerows, rich with the scent of honeysuckle and the riot of hedge flowers that grew there. He heard Yatton Church clock strike the hour as he crossed the Bray at the packhorse bridge and began the gentle climb towards Stone Cross, three miles away on the rim of a fold bathed in moonlight. He drove carefully, for the surface was loose and the bends very sharp, and by the time he had chugged past the church the moon was sailing free of cloud wisps and the playing-fields and buildings were in clear view, so that he stopped by the old, unmended gate, straddling the machine and looking at the place from the angle he had first seen it the day the Osborne specialist sent him here on what he had thought of as a fool's errand.

It hadn't changed much but by moonlight, with the rearward part of the buildings in shadow, it looked smaller and more compact. A thought came to him, the tailpiece of an anecdote he had told the Lower Third a day or two before the end of term, relating to Charles II's final look at England at the end of his long flight from Worcester. Legend had it that the king, an hour or so before joining the collier that was to take him to France, had reined in and said to a companion, "It's worth fighting for . . ." It was too, and he felt a closer affinity with a monarch he had always admired for his common sense and humour, rare qualities in a Stuart. He said, aloud, "Well, you'll get your fight, Alcock, old sport. And it'll be a bonny one, I'm telling you!" and then restarted the machine and drove the last two hundred yards home.

Cut and Come Again

Chapter One

David began to see himself as a trial balloon for national weather, a tiny unit released to test the force of the unending series of storms and gales that had blown across the country since the long, Edwardian lull, when he was growing up in the Valleys. In an almost predictable way his personal fortunes seemed to coincide with those of the country, ever since that day he came home from school to be told his father and brothers were dead in the pit disaster. For that had been shortly before a few shots in a Balkan town had heralded the storm that engulfed everybody.

Then, again running almost parallel with what was happening in the world outside, came the death of Beth and little Joan, coinciding with the start of the long, dragging strike in the coal mines, and its climax in the General Strike of May, 1926, when the national mood had matched his own despondency. He emerged from it during the tail end of the 'twenties but soon, with the coming of Alcock, it came on to blow again, and here they were approaching crisis point, both he and the nation, in the spring of 1931, and MacDonald's government as beset by problems in Westminster as he was at Bamfylde.

Algy's draft letter arrived on Tuesday, as promised. By Wednesday night, a day or two before the start of summer term, he had written his own letter, and posted it to Sir Rufus Creighton, in spite of a warning that the old chap was off on yet another of his tours, this time to India, and was not expected back until June. He could afford to wait, however. His batteries were still masked and if Alcock challenged him in the meantime, so much the better.

Christine wrote twice a week, keeping him up to date with her progress in the constituency, and they met occasionally in Taunton. She was settling down thereabouts, having taken a part-time secretarial job, and gone back on her obstinate decision to leave her husband's allowance untouched. "I can use the money for things I plan to do between now and the next election," she said. "There's to be one soon enough, for Ramsay is floundering. The whole world is going broke, they say. There's even talk of a Coalition."

"Would your people stand for that?" he asked, and she said the party stalwarts would not, but it was possible Ramsay Mac, Snowden and Jimmy Thomas might. "They're proving a frightful disappointment," she admitted. "Power seems to have watered their beer. I don't mean Ramsay's grand manner, and all that rubbish they print about him kissing duchesses. It's more serious than that. The leaders aren't in touch any longer, especially with the unemployed."

"I don't see what the poor devils can do with nearly three million on the dole. This crisis is international, isn't it?"

"They could keep faith with the people who voted for them," she said, "even if it meant going into opposition again."

"What good would that do?"

"I don't know. I only know I prefer the Labour Party when it's attacking."

He sympathised with her but was more concerned with his own situation than that of a harassed Prime Minister and Chancellor of the Exchequer. The weeks drifted by, just as they had when he was nursing a tiny flame of hope that he would succeed Algy Herries. He confided, to a degree, in her, and to a greater degree in Howarth and Barnaby, but in no one else on the staff. Howarth was taciturn about the possible results of his counter-attack but Barnaby was encouraging. "You're a bonnie fighter, man," he told David, when the latter explained what he had done, and as usual he had an appropriate tag for the occasion—'*In rebus dubiis plurimi est audacia.*'

In the second week of June Sir Rufus sent a bleak reply to his letter. It contained little but a promise that he would 'take counsel with certain of the Governors' and 'consider the possibility of calling a special meeting'. He gave no hint as to whether any direct approach had been made to him by Alcock, and none as to when the meeting, if there was one, would be called, or what the terms of reference were likely to be. He did add, however, that he could rest assured the matter would be investigated and should hold himself in readiness to answer any questions put to him. David showed the letter to Howarth who grunted, "Typical bureaucratic response. So guarded and qualified it might be addressed to a blackmailer. But then, come to think of it, I suppose that's what Alcock is making us in his quaint, original way."

One of the few breaks in the rhythm of the term was Christine's visit on Sports Day, accompanied by her cousin, the one-eyed Ridgeway, home on leave from Malaya. Ridgeway found it difficult to accept his former housemaster's close friendship with someone he had been taught to regard as the family black sheep and while Christine was being shown over the kitchens, he said, half-apologetically, "She was always a bit of a Bolshie, sir, if you know what I mean." David, much amused, said, "Alas, Ridgeway, I'm a 'bit of a Bolshie' myself. That was accepted here, even in your time, but you never held it against me, did you?" to which Ridgeway replied, with terrible earnestness, "Of course not, sir, but she's a woman!"

It was no good reminding Ridgeway that even the flapper had been eligible to vote since 1928. It still seemed to him indefensible that a female relative of his should enlist under a Socialist banner, likely to shame him publicly if she ever got into Parliament, an event he considered slightly less probable than a landing on the moon. "I mean, after all, sir, politics are still a man's business, aren't they? The very idea of her standing on a platform, and spouting about the Means Test and whatnot, is a pretty bad show, taken all round. I can quite understand Uncle Willie cutting her out of his will. The pity of it is, of course, that she's not old, only a year or so older than I am. I mean, if she was a middle-aged frump it might be different."

He gave it up after that but relayed the exchange to Christine, as soon as Ridgeway was off hobnobbing with his cronies in the Old Boys' bar. It kept her amused for the rest of the day.

There was one result of her visit, however, that inclined him to agree with Ridgeway that Christine Forster was a little odd when you came to think about it. She declared herself daunted by the Spartan aspects of Bamfylde and said, "It's so frightfully austere, isn't it? Aren't there any home comforts at *all*? I mean, hasn't anyone ever heard of soft furnishings, and carpets? Or kitchen implements superseding those used in a baron's hall at the time of the Conquest?" And when he explained that the one gain of Alcock's stay among them had been an improvement in fabric, she exclaimed, "My God! What was it *before* he arrived? A Dickensian workhouse? Why does a public school have to look like a penitents' monastery as well as act like one? I never was much of a one for tradition, but I've never had anything against stainless steel, floor coverings, curtains, modern plumbing and the odd incinerator, instead of that stinking bonfire you keep burning down at the piggeries."

"The place isn't very well endowed," he argued, much on the defensive, "it needs money spending on it to bring it up to date but we don't cater for satraps, just chaps equipped to work for their living, and stand on their own two feet when they leave here."

"Well, you don't even succeed in that if my cousin's story about his glass eye is to be believed. The general picture I get of him and his type is a layabout in a wicker chair, knocking back whiskies and sodas and watching the black, browns and yellows do the hard graft. Oh, I admit that boys brought up in these cheerless barns do seem to have much more confidence than the ones in day schools, but I can't help feeling you need a few women around the place to cushion the corners. Is it true that nearly all the masters are bachelors? Or widowers like you?"

"Not always from choice," he said, thinking of Howarth, and the girl who had turned him down for a stockbroker. "You don't go into this for money, Chris. However, talking of feminine touches, come and meet Grace. She's over by the finishing tape, offering up a prayer for one of her two favourites to win the steeplechase."

They crossed behind the east drive beeches and he introduced them, noting that Grace had made an immediate impact on

Christine. They chatted amiably for five minutes or so, then Grace forgot them both in the excitement of the run-in, as the leaders of the field came streaming through the gap behind the plantation, to cover the last quarter-mile of the course. Christine whispered, in an aside, "She's delightful, Davy, and does you credit! She'll break hearts in another few years."

"I doubt it," he said, glancing across at the tape, and making his almost daily comparison between the child and Beth, "but she'll be pretty, I think, in a Romneyish kind of way."

Hoskins, whose wind seemed to have thrived on all the practice he put in on the saxophone, passed the favourite Collier, within two yards of the post, and leaving Christine he crossed to the finishing post and joined Grace prancing up and down with delight as everyone crowded round the winner to congratulate him. Then, feeling a little foolish at his own display of glee, he rejoined Christine on the far side of the spectators' rope. She said, smiling, "You're really rather sweet, all of you. I'm glad I came, for at least you can rely on me going into the Tory lobby when Labour gets around to abolishing these archaic institutions. Now let's have tea, and after tea take me down to that little church you told me about, and show me where you and Beth lived when you were first married. If you don't mind, that is."

"I don't mind," he said, "and for a special reason. You and Beth are two of a kind in some ways."

He took her arm and they moved off across the forecourt. Watching them, from a discreet distance, stood Ridgeway, and with him Simmonds, an old friend of his period. Both recalled Beth Powlett-Jones and Simmonds said, "Old Pow-Wow never married again, did he?"

"No," said Ridgeway, hastily heading him off. "How about a couple of jars, Sim?" but Simmonds said, thoughtfully, "That bit of skirt he's squiring, she's not a bad-looker, is she? Know her?"

"Never seen her in my life," Ridgeway answered and if he thought of Simon called Peter, the apostle could have counted on his heartfelt sympathy.

2

He wondered whether he should show her Beth's grave but thought better of it, passing round the tower and entering the church by the west door. There was still more than two hours' life in the day but inside it was already dusk. Sniffing the faint whiff of incense, and glancing up at the Stations of the Cross, she said, "Is that new head of yours a would-be Catholic?"

"No, just 'high'. We were very 'low' in Algy's time, but Stone Cross has always been part of Bamfylde and adjusts." He ran his hand along the smooth varnish of the pew, feeling the ridges of obliterated initials carved there by three generations of boys, and it struck him then that Alcock's spring-clean could be interpreted as a kind of vandalism, symptomatic of so many changes that had occurred over the last three years. She must have sensed his disquiet for she said, quietly, "It's beginning to show, Davy. The battle with the new man. How will it end?"

"In his departure, or mine, and soon, I imagine."

"Why's that?"

He summarised the situation to date, even telling her about Alcock's clean sweep of the pew initials, and she said, after a moment, "I think you'll win, Davy."

"Why?"

"Feel there, just above that hassock," and she took his hand, guiding it to the limit of the pew-back, where his fingertips brushed against some raw indentations.

"They're already at it again. Flick your lighter."

He humoured her, producing a small flame and bending low, where he made out a freshly carved name, executed in letters about half an inch high.

It must have required a deal of patience, he thought, to chip away down there during brief intervals of prayer, but Hislop had made a fair enough job of it. He had even scooped out three full stops, one after each initial, one after the final letter. He said, chuckling, "Good old Hislop. He left his mark, after all. I suppose you could call that a sign. Not from Heaven, however."

"Was Hislop the boy you told me about, the one who was sacked for bookmaking?"

"Yes, but I'll wager he wasn't the only one to counter-attack." He moved the full length of the church, glancing at the half-seen pew-supports. Bristow, Hoskins and Collier were represented, and in the rearmost pew Winterbourne had got as far as 'B'. He drifted back to the front pew, thinking how pretty she looked, sitting there in her pink cloche hat, with the slanting light of the rose window converting the tip of a stray curl from chestnut to bronze. "You're very good for me, Chris," he said, kissing her.

"We're good for each other," she said, and then, smiling, "Now I wonder if that's ever happened before?"

"The carving?"

"No, a front pew kiss."

"They've had the occasional wedding here."

"Ah, but that's not the same. It would be done standing, there by the altar. And a chaste kiss at that." Then she added, "If the cards don't fall your way, if they back Alcock and put the pressure on you, would you make a fresh start, at another school?"

"No."

"What then?"

"I'd take that tip given me in Bilhampton and have a crack at politics."

"Could you afford to?"

"I've got a bit put by, and could use it to keep me going while I nursed a constituency. It would have to be one with real prospects."

"Not like mine, you mean?"

"You'll get promoted, as soon as they've had a chance to assess your worth. One good fight at Bilhampton and you'll be nominated for an industrial seat up North . . ." but she wasn't listening. Presently she said, "I suppose I ought to be hoping those Governors do come down on Alcock's side. That way I'd have a sporting chance."

"I don't follow. What has the Governing Board got to do with your chances?"

"You can be very thick, Davy. Put it like this. If you win then that's it, so far as I'm concerned. Oh, I daresay we'd go on seeing one another occasionally, but it would be a case of me trotting down here, and soon enough, wallowing in Bamfylde, you'd regard everything happening outside as trivial. Not yet, maybe, while you're still in your thirties, but later, when you're 'over the hill' as they say. Now look at the other side of the coin. If Alcock wins you'll prise yourself loose and it's possible we'd make a formidable team."

"As a pair of candidates?"

She looked at him steadily. "No, with you as candidate and me loading for you."

He saw it as a graceful compliment. Of all her associates only he understood how deeply she was committed and how passionately she needed to justify herself in her chosen field. That she was ready, eager even, to step down on his account, and put her enthusiasm to work on his behalf, struck him as a very positive expression of faith in him.

"You'd do that? For me?"

"Why not? One of my rare qualities is that of knowing my own mind and having the nerve to act on it. You're very fond of me, Davy. But I'm very much in love with you."

It didn't really astonish him. By now he was growing used to her devastating honesty. She went on, "That doesn't obligate you in any way, and I wouldn't have owned up to it without the special circumstances."

"You mean Rowley's refusal to make separation final? Because if that's so I've got a say in it now, considering what you've just said. 'Fond' was your word and it's an understatement, Chris. There have been plenty of times since we met . . ."

She said, gently, "Hold it, Davy! Don't say more than you need. This came from me, and the circumstances I mentioned have nothing to do with Rowley. It concerns you and how you feel about me and about women in general. You were very deeply in love with Beth. That's my impression anyway, and there's never much wrong with my instincts. You could make do, and put up a pretty good show of loving, but there would always be a big slice of you that no other woman could possess. You can protest as much as you like but it's true, and deep down you know it."

It was all but dusk in here now but light enough to see her eyes searching his, and she was not the kind of person who would settle for anything short of the whole truth, or the truth as she saw it.

"It wouldn't be the same and you're right about a very special relationship. But don't most couples feel that in the first years of marriage? Beth was only twenty-five when she died. I'll say this, however." He took her hand, gloveless and passive, "With a person like you it would be the nearest I could ever come to starting all over again, and that's more than enough for me. Is it enough for you?"

She shrugged. "What point is there in answering that? I'm not even in a position to try."

"I'm not so sure about that. He's been abroad for years, hasn't he? If he stays over there indefinitely I daresay you could get a divorce on grounds of desertion. He might change his mind, might even want to marry again himself. So far as I know you haven't even corresponded with him, except through lawyers."

"I made enquiries, though, and it's a dead end. Knowing Rowley, it's likely to stay one. I said his family behaved well towards me but as regards divorce they'd range themselves with him. Catholics of their kind take their religion much more seriously than we do. It isn't something they put on and off like an overcoat. They wouldn't lift a finger to help, and told me so when I raised the matter a year back."

"Then to blazes with him. We owe ourselves some consideration, don't we? I'm not that stuffy."

"You mightn't be and I'm not. But, as I said in the first place, it doesn't depend on us, does it? If you still have any hope of qualifying for a headship you've more sense than to pursue that line of thought, Davy. The odd weekend is one thing. A permanent relationship, with you in the running for a post of that kind, is quite another. Besides, I might want children. Have you ever thought of that?"

He saw himself trapped in a web of conflicting loyalties and her availability, implicit in her honesty, was an entirely new factor in their relationship up to that moment. It had about it the inevitability of a Greek tragedy, with a dash of French farce thrown in for good measure. It had progressed, at a bound, from the camaraderie of their first encounters, to a stage where he was more than half in love with her and she was avowedly in love with him. Yet it promised little. They were trapped, not only by her situation but by his. It represented an equation. Rowley, plus Chris, equals stalemate; Powlett-Jones, plus Bamfylde minus Chris, equals celibacy. And there were any number of incidental factors, among them Alcock, Alcock's impact on his future, Chris's involvement with politics, and that hint of hers about children.

He gave it up. It was too much to conjure with without isolating every factor and examining them individually. He said, "Well, I'm a free agent right now, and likely to be until those damned Governors get around to sorting the muddle out. Let's get out of here, and go back to my quarters. You don't have to drive back tonight, do you? I could get you a room in Challacombe for a few days and come over every evening."

"On your home ground? Under everybody's nose? Use your head, Davy!"

"Where, then? And when?"

"Are the Governors likely to meet before you break up for the holidays?"

"I don't know. I wouldn't think they'd make a final decision. There's only a couple of weeks to go, and they don't usually meet in August."

"Well then, we'll find some neutral ground. It's time I took a holiday anyway. Until then, just hold me a little."

They sat on in the pew for another hour or so, until, carried faintly on the evening breeze, they heard the sound that had regulated his life for more than twelve years now, the far-off clang of Bamfylde's handbell, swung by the latest successor of Nipper Shawe, going his rounds as far as Algy's thinking post. Then, silently acknowledging the summons, they walked the half-mile back to school.

3

Alcock went out of his way to avoid him, or so it seemed through the fag-end of the term. Whatever Sir Rufus Creighton was about he confided in no one, yet Algy Herries, who dropped in for a chat one evening during the final week of term, was convinced something was stirring out there. "Don't ask me for evidence," he said, "for I couldn't produce any. I can only tell you I know those stone-faced arbiters of our destinies and if I don't, who should? There are probably the same three sets of plotters hard at work. The liberals, chivvied along by Brigadier Cooper. The conservatives, rallying to that bounder Blunt. And the uncommitted or, as Cooper would put it, the Any-Way-For-A-Pinters. They're a majority, I'd say. They hate decisions, and are prepared to go to extraordinary lengths to avoid making one."

"And Sir Rufus?"

"Ah, that joker is out on his lonesome, and prefers it that way. You mightn't believe it to look at him, but he's a slave to the pursuit of power."

"Then it's Creighton I should concentrate on, isn't it?"

"You leave him alone," warned Algy, severely. "Believe me, I

364

know what's best for you. The pressure has eased, hasn't it. Since you despatched that letter?"

"Alcock and I haven't exchanged two consecutive sentences this term, if that's what you mean."

"So much the better. We all talk too much."

"But in God's name, Algy, it ought to be possible for adults to run a place like this without resorting to petty intrigue. Damn it, I sometimes think I'm back at school myself, and nursery school at that—'He was my friend before he was your friend, so there'!"

"You should have learned, my boy, that only the rare spirits grow in mental stature after the age of, say, five-and-a-half. Whenever one does he qualifies as an Immortal. I'm off now. The confounded parochial church council is meeting at seven-thirty, and I'm in for another stint of smoothing ruffled plumes. My advice to you is to get right away from here for a bit. Go somewhere anonymous. Have you any plans for the long break?"

He was obliged to lie. "Grace is spending a month with her aunts in Kent, then another week at the seaside with cousins. I thought I might go north, after I've paid a duty visit to the Valley."

"Good. Well, write if you have to but meantime, put it out of mind. I'll keep in touch with the brigadier by phone. He's our only source of news."

A day or so later the thirteen-week turmoil reached its brief climax. Homesick boys crossed the final day from their pocket calendars. Trunks came tumbling down from the platform over the covered playground. The Corps, headed by its band, marched off to entrain for a week's camp at Tidworth Pennings.

"Have a good hols, sir!"

"Can I move into the Senior dorm next term, sir?"

"Cookson's leaving, sir. Who'll be Havelock's house perk, sir?"

And from the departing Cookson, "Keep me in touch, sir. I'd like to know if Havelock's hold on to that shield."

The staff scattered. Barnaby to his beloved Greece, Howarth to town for his annual spree (what did he do up there alone at the Strand Palace, David wondered?), others to the seaside. All save Molyneux who appeared, burdened with kit, to announce that he was attempting a new climb in the French Alps. "Always the chance he might fall into a very deep crevice," Howarth said, never having caught on to Ferguson's successor. "Is there any likelihood of us meeting in town, P.J.?"

"Not until early September."

"By early September," Howarth grunted, "I shall be back here, getting ready for another three months' purgatory. Enlivened, I hope, by a display of fireworks."

"That's very likely," David said, and was surprised, and even a little embarrassed, when Howarth shook his hand and said, in a rare moment of expansiveness, "Well, I don't have to tell you where my money is going, P.J. Take Herries's advice. Get clear away and forget the whole damned lot of us for a month," after which he withdrew hastily, as he invariably did after a display of human feeling.

*　　*　　*

They met, by appointment, at Exchange Station, Manchester, half an hour or so before the train to Windermere pulled out. She arrived by taxi from London Road Station, a breathless, carefree Christine Forster, who somehow reminded him of an overgrown schoolgirl who had given her chaperon the slip.

They had exchanged letters as regards the locality of her 'neutral ground'. He had favoured Anglesey but she said Anglesey was Welsh, and not neutral enough, and had suggested they should go to Skye, Mull, or another of the Western Isles. She had had second thoughts about this, however, reasoning that the Hebrides, at this time of year, was almost always wet, and she was badly in need of sunshine.

"It's different for you," she said, over the phone, "you're country-based. I've spent the last six months drinking tepid tea in terrace houses and my evenings in committee rooms that haven't seen soap and water since the election of 1918. I've found a place for us at Windermere."

"Are you absolutely sure you want to leave your constituency at a time like this?" he said, when he met her. "They say things are hotting up at Westminster, and there might be a snap election any moment," but she said, coolly, "Have I ever tried to teach you your business? Pipe down, Davy. Let's try a little cheerful sin for a change," and held up her left hand, displaying what looked like a new wedding ring.

He said, sharply, "Is that Rowley's? Because if so, take the damned thing off."

"It isn't Rowley's. I popped his long ago. It's the Christmas cracker variety," and she kissed him, at an awkward moment as far as an oncoming porter was concerned, for the three of them collided and the porter scattered his burdens on the platform.

It would take time, he thought, to adjust to this high-spirited girl, who seemed to find in him a source of release denied her for a long, long time, but before their first twenty-four hours together had elapsed he was attuned to her gaiety and lack of inhibition, seeing her as an unlikely amalgam of Beth, in what he thought of as their middle period, Julia Darbyshire, before he made the mistake of committing himself, and a dash of the extroverts in the Lower Fourth.

He was particularly aware of this early that first morning, when he opened his eyes and heard her humming to herself in the little kitchen of the wooden chalet they occupied on the deserted western shore of the lake, under High Dale Peak. It was a particularly isolated spot, with its own tiny beach, south of the little river Cunsey. Over on the Bowness shore the summer season was in full swing and boats were constantly coming and going, the voices of their passengers reaching them across the flat expanse of lake, like the echo of a junior football game played on the higher pitch under the planty. But nobody seemed to want to explore the south-western tip of the lake, and very few cars passed along the road behind the chalet.

She had been very clever to find it, he told her, when the taxi dropped them off, but she said it was luck mostly. A cousin of her father's had stayed here last summer when Segrave had made his fatal attempt on the water-speed record higher up the lake. She had remembered the name of the firm who hired out the chalets and a reference book had supplied her with its phone number. It was no more than a simply furnished shack, with a window looking eastwards across the water but as a hideout, she said, it had a lot to recommend it. Her father's cousin, who drove an Alvis, had taken a dislike to the place when he ran out of petrol here the day Segrave's boat had capsized, missing, as he had put it, all the fun.

It was getting dusk before they finished unpacking, and eating eggs and bacon she fried on the oil-stove, and when he proposed a walk as far as the island opposite she said, in that frank way of hers, "Is that proposal made out of regard for my modesty, Davy? I mean, waiting until the light fades?" and when he admitted that it was, she said, lightly, "Then don't bother, lad. I've waited a long time. Almost as long as you. We'll go for a walk if you need the exercise but not otherwise."

She had a way, he discovered, of sloughing off her earnestness, and her tendency to view most things from what she herself described as 'the Yorkshire common-sense angle', emerging as an altogether different personality. It was the one, he imagined, that had prompted her to dance naked on the college precincts when she was an undergraduate, a prank that reached the ears of her father and precipitated the first of many family rows. As a bedmate she was equally spirited and would have taken the initiative if he had given her the chance, for her gaiety, he discovered, was infectious. It had not been difficult to adjust to what he accepted as a final commitment, for he had learned something useful from the brief Julia Darbyshire incident.

They lay still on the rumpled bed, using the first few moments of the aftermath to assess both each other and themselves as lovers, admittedly out of practice, but then, turning to him, she raised herself on her elbow and studied him in a way that invited mutual laughter, for it was so transparently clear that each was engaged in the business of reappraisal.

"You weren't disappointed, then?"

"Did you think I might be?"

"No, not really, but as I said, it's been a long time. God knows I wanted a man often enough but I'm glad now that I obeyed my instinct to hang on and wait."

He smiled, reaching up to pull her down, saying, "I always said we're good for one another. I didn't know how good until now. It's tempting to make a virtue out of deprivation but I have. Sometimes I've come close to making a cult of the dead."

"There never was anyone else? Before or after Beth?"

"There was one, but all that Julia did, looking back, was to add a shaving or two to the chip I was carrying around."

"Tell me about Julia."

He told her the story of Julia Darbyshire, and how he had seen intense physical relief as a permanent cure for loneliness that had led to his proposal.

"Would it be so very different with me?"

"I think it would."

She looked thoughtful for a moment. Then she said, "I

wouldn't commit myself, Davy, or not yet. Let's take it a step at a time. I had a special reason for asking the question."

"I can guess the reason."

"I'll wager you can't."

"It has to do with your marriage going on the rocks, and whether it was caused by inadequacy on your part. Right there?"

She sat up. "Hey! You can be sharp when you try, can't you? I suppose that comes from listening to so many excuses, then writing those awful school reports—'Could do better'—'Doesn't concentrate'—are you going to write me one? I'd love to read it."

"If I did you'd frame it and hang it over the bed."

She eased herself back, clasping her hands behind her head, stretching out her long, graceful legs and wriggling her toes. Her long, contemplative silence implied that she was still in need of reassurance.

"Well, what's your problem? Don't hedge. I didn't hedge about Julia."

"I don't mind telling you, Davy. I went into that marriage full of girlish confidence. All my problems were solved. This was IT, and Rowley was the knight in shining armour. When things began to drift from bad to worse, I kept telling myself that it was all his fault and I still think it was, mainly. But later, after we broke up, I got to wondering whether it mightn't have been fifty-fifty. Maybe I wasn't patient enough. Or clever enough. This way, I mean, flat on my back. I don't know. It's hard to tell after all this time."

"You don't have to worry about it any more."

"But I do, if I'm to learn the truth about myself. I only know that I did try. I tried damned hard, Davy."

"Hasn't it occurred to you that neither of you was to blame? That you weren't the least bit in love with one another?"

"It's possible. I was flattered to be singled out from all those other girls, most of them much prettier, and all of them more sophisticated than I was. Maybe he needed sophistication, and felt cheated when he didn't find any. Do you suppose that was . . . what's so funny about that?"

"You are! Lying there without a stitch on, trying to make one guinea pig out of me and another out of yourself. All right, I'll humour you. Most men don't look for sophistication. They think that's their prerogative. What they like to find in a woman is generosity and you'll never run short of that. So cut the inquest on imaginary shortcomings. Ever hear what Napoleon said to his valet, Constant, after his first night with Marie Louise?"

"You mean that Austrian girl he married? The one who could wiggle her ears, and had never been allowed to own a male animal?"

"That's her. He said, 'My friend, marry a German. They are the best of all women, sweet, gentle, fresh and innocent as roses!' In your case, for 'German' read 'Yorkshire'."

"That's nice of you but it was boorish of him. To come down rubbing his hands and discuss the bride with his valet, I mean."

"Well, he was feeling smug, and had to discuss it with someone. Constant was the only one around at that time."

She turned impulsively and her arms went round him. He sensed, somehow, that he had succeeded in dispelling some of her doubts, and it may have been this that set the tone of their relationship as lovers all the days they spent alone by the lake. And because of an overwhelming tenderness, that multiplied in him day by day, he came at length to prize her in a way that would have seemed extravagant a week ago, when he was still subconsciously comparing her to Beth. What intrigued him, what sometimes amazed him, was the range of her personality, only now fully extended, with good humour as its base, and variants all the way from a gentle withdrawal to a gaiety capable of enveloping them both in a sense of release that was balm to a man scarred by war, by a deep personal tragedy and currently holding anxiety at bay.

As the time passed it seemed to him foolish that she could have ever doubted her capacity to induce anything but restorative peace in a man, any man, that is, with his wits about him. In her arms he found an enlarged confidence in himself, and beyond this a depth of relationship in another human being that had eluded him ever since the day Beth had died.

This sense of attainment reached him from many sources. From her effervescent sense of humour, seldom absent from their most intimate moments, from a freely offered body that he came to venerate, but mostly from her ability to communicate. He had no doubts now but that he returned her love, that she could, in essentials, fill the gap left by Beth. In her arms, in her company even, Bamfylde and Bamfylde's concerns moved a great way off, a place where he had suffered and learned, but he did not believe Bamfylde alone would ever satisfy him now. It would have to go about the task with Christine as the bridge between him and personal fulfilment. Time, a wide variety of interests, physical fitness, stemming from the active life he led up there, these things and the obsessive problems of his housemastership, had healed the last of his trench scars, but his emotional reawakening, within the embrace of this girl, went a good way beyond that. It was a process of rejuvenation, stimulating the nerves and quickening the imagination, so that what lay ahead for him seemed unimportant unless it was linked to her. He had thought himself deeply in love with Beth through that first, peacetime spring more than twelve years before, but Beth had grown on him, season by season, so that he had no clear memory of an onrush of affection such as this, a tumult of the senses that sometimes seemed too violent to last.

One afternoon, when they were lying on the bed watching the curtain of rain move across the lake, he voiced this doubt.

"It's an ideal, Davy, and something to be fought for, but face it, lad, it won't sustain us for the rest of our lives."

"Now that's a depressing thought!" he grumbled, but she went on, "It's a statement of fact, no more and no less. We'll need luck, and a lot of patience, so don't ever forget it."

"Patience, maybe, but what kind of luck, other than finding a way of getting the divorce? And that isn't the moon. Knowing our own minds is the vital factor, and I know mine as regards you. I'd be very happy to take Bamfylde plus you, but you take precedence."

"Over-simplification, Davy. Follow that through and what am I left with? Half of David Powlett-Jones, and that barn of a place on my conscience, where it would sit more heavily than Rowley. No thanks, Davy. I like you very well as you are, doing a job you enjoy."

"That's a different line from the one you took in the church less than a month ago."

"Yes it is, but I know you much better now, *really* know you. You'd never be happy or fulfilled in politics, or doing anything but what you are doing, so let's plan ahead from there."

It did not seem worth an argument. The important thing was

they both had direction and this seemed enough to be going on with. He said, lazily, "That's the trouble with the Welsh."

"What is?"

"Love of discourse, especially on abstracts and imponderables. What could happen if something else happened. We run up the pulpit steps at the drop of a hat—

> Myself when young did eagerly frequent
> Doctor and Saint, and heard great argument . . .

Trust a Welshman to indulge in great argument, even when he's in bed with a girl like you."

"Even a Welshman needs a breather now and again."

He laughed and kissed her. It was easy enough to set imponderables aside with a woman like her in his arms. The future could take care of itself for a change. He was more than satisfied with the present.

Chapter Two

1

The blow fell on the day of their first expedition across the lake to Bowness, indeed, to anywhere save the fells, Lodore Falls, or the village where they bought stores. Three weeks had elapsed since they had read a daily paper and there was no wireless set in the chalet. "We might," she said, "be living on Juan Fernandez. I'm sure my constituency wouldn't approve of me being in purdah this long. Why don't we hire a skiff, pull over, and find out what's going on, if you can row that far after your frightful exertions," and when he suggested that they might leave well alone until it was time to collect Grace and go home, she said, "We won't stay. Just an hour's shopping, lunch somewhere and back here for tea."

They tied up to the jetty about eleven and the first reminder that they were back in circulation was a newspaper contents bill, clamped to a billboard outside a tobacconist's shop. It announced, 'MACDONALD TO HEAD NATIONAL GOVERNMENT'.

The starkness of the statement precluded exclamation or comment. They stood quite still, backs to the kerb, mouthing the words once, twice, three times, as though neither had the courage to acknowledge what it could mean in terms of their future. Then, releasing her hand, he went in and bought a paper, re-emerging to find her standing in the same stunned position outside the

shop door. He read the headlines aloud. 'MACDONALD HEADS NA-
TIONAL GOVERNMENT', 'LABOUR PARTY SPLIT'—'PROSPECT OF OCTO-
BER ELECTION', and other double-column headlines, all concerned
with cataclysmic occurrences that had, it seemed, been piling one
upon the other during the twenty days they had spent three miles
east of this same, steep street.

She said, "You know what this means, Davy?", and he replied,
doubling the paper, "To everyone or to us?"

"I must go back at once. You surely see that."

The abrupt end of their idyll outraged him. "No, I don't! Or
not until we've had time to digest it, to . . . plan something about
what happens from here."

"How could we plan, with this hanging over us? I'm an adopted
candidate. Dedicated people have put their money on me. Give me
the paper."

"We could have lunch, talk things over . . . you don't even
know about trains, when you can start . . ."

He was talking to himself. Already, reading as she walked, she
was retracing her steps down the hill to the boat and he followed,
pausing to light a cigarette when she plumped herself down in the
stern of the skiff and went on reading. He said, at length, "Well,
what's it to be? A private airplane? Or would a hire car do?"

She folded the paper and slipped it into her handbag. Her expression told him that he had lost her, temporarily at all events.
"He's sold us all out," she said. "He and Snowden. Traitors, the
pair of them! Jimmy Thomas, too, and who knows how many
others?"

"But if he's going to the country . . ."

"You don't understand," she shouted at him, "this is the worst
thing that could happen to us as a party, worse than being beaten
at the polls ten times in a row! Ramsay Mac, the first Socialist
Prime Minister. The man who stood out against everybody, when
men like you were up to their necks in mud and blood. He's sold
out lock, stock and barrel. Don't ask me why he did it. To keep
office, I imagine, but it makes nonsense of everything we've believed since the war."

"But you always agreed you couldn't survive long as a minority
government. You must have suspected something like this would
happen, sooner or later."

"I thought he would resign, and try for a real majority."

"He'd never get one, with the country's finances in the state they are. You've said that too."

"It wouldn't have mattered. It was the honourable thing to do, wasn't it?"

"You don't look for scruples among politicians, Chris."

"I do. How will this look to the electorate? Leading Socialists, who can be bought and sold."

"You intend to throw in with the backbenchers?"

"Good heavens, of course I do. You've learned that much about me, haven't you? Is a National government, overweighted with Tories, likely to do a damned thing for the unemployed. You've only glanced at that paper. There's talk of a ten per cent cut in unemployment benefits. There'll be hell to pay everywhere."

"If Ramsay and some of the others are still in office they'll block unfair economies."

"As prisoners of bankers and industrialists? Don't be naïve, Davy. And anyway, we're wasting time. I'm going to phone my Chairman. Go over to the station and find out about trains."

"You intend going back today?"

"Of course I do. With an election in the offing I can't waste an hour. I'll head for London and try and catch the paper train out of Paddington early tomorrow."

She climbed out of the skiff and moved towards a telephone kiosk outside the harbourmaster's, opening her bag as she went. He watched her for a moment, then went off to the station to study a timetable pasted to a hoarding in the yard. There was a London train via Kendal and Birmingham at twelve-thirty. It would give her plenty of time to cross to Paddington and catch a late evening train for Taunton, then on to Bilhampton. She could, with luck, be back in her constituency by breakfast time tomorrow.

She was still in the kiosk when he returned, talking earnestly, one elbow propped on the bracket, one leg raised and resting on the ledge. She seemed smaller and remote somehow, a serious, animated girl, but removed from him, deep in her own concerns. The sudden change in their relationship made his heart ache.

She rang off at last and came out, flushed and distant. When he gave her the times of alternative trains, she said, "I'll catch that twelve-thirty. You go back, collect our things, lock up, and give the key to Witherby's clerk."

"But you haven't even got a toothbrush, woman. Besides, it'll be damned cold travelling all night down to that Godforsaken place."

"I've got a mac. How much money have you on you?"

"About three pounds." He gave it to her. He knew her well enough to know that a protest would only mean they parted with acrimony and this he was determined to avoid. "Could you bring my things on? Leave them in the left-luggage office at Taunton, then send me the ticket? There's no mad hurry in that respect. I've got a change at the digs."

"I can bring your bags to you on my way back with Grace."

Her expression softened. For the first time since she had read the poster she looked at him as a friend and not a stranger who happened to be standing around. "No, Davy. It's sweet of you, and I'm terribly sorry it had to happen like this, but you don't get yourself mixed up in this election. Not until you see how things work out at Bamfylde."

"But that's silly. Term doesn't begin for a fortnight. I'll have time on my hands once I've parked Grace."

"No, Davy. This is my show. You've got a battle on yourself, remember? Don't give them ammunition to fire at you. This election is going to be very bitter indeed. All kinds of smears are going to be laid on, all kinds of abuse thrown about, so stay clear of it until you straighten things out back there. If they make life impossible for you, and you decide to pack it in, I'd be very glad of your help. But not otherwise."

He made one last effort. "Look here, you know you can't possibly win that seat now. Everyone will be waving the Union Jack like mad in Tory-held constituencies. Is there any point in it, really? I mean, why don't we concentrate on getting Rowley off our backs and marrying as soon as possible?"

She said, slowly, "We'll marry, Davy. Some time, some place. That much I promise you, providing you don't find someone else. And if you did I wouldn't blame you. I'd always remember you with love, and a lot of respect. But in the meantime I owe it to myself to make a fight. I owe it to those people down there, who backed me against male candidates, but even more to myself. You've achieved something, but I haven't. Not a damn thing so far and here's what might be my last chance to have another go. Don't deny it me."

There was no kind of answer to that. They walked to the station, hand in hand, and when the train came in he saw her aboard, buying her an armful of papers and journals to enable her to get up to date en route. He said, as the whistle blew, "I'm beginning to hate railway platforms. You won't object to me phoning from town, will you?"

"Phone every night if you can afford it," she said. "I'll need that where I'm going."

He kissed her and held her hand after the train had begun to move. Then, releasing it, he watched her face until it was blotted out by smoke, just as it had been on most of the occasions they had met since he walked her to the station at Cardiff after that Christmas confessional in a pub.

2

The showdown, for him, came within a week of the commencement of the Michaelmas term.

The old Warrior rang late at night, a few moments after he had had his talk with Christine, battling it out against frightful odds at South Mendips. The brigadier said, testily, "Been trying to raise you for nearly an hour. They said you were engaged speaking."

"So I was, Briggy. Long-distance."

"Well, it's happened. There was a special meeting of the Executive yesterday, and there's a full meeting in the library tomorrow. More than half the Board have promised to attend and they'll hear you both. One at a time of course. You first, I understand. Thought you might like to go over your brief. I'd be kicked off the Board if anyone knew I'd tipped you off!"

"I know that, Briggy. You've been a brick, all the way through. Can you give me a hint how it might go?"

"No, I can't. Might go any way. No precedent for a dam' silly confrontation like this. But if it means anything at all I'd say it was a point in your favour, them agreeing to meet in this way, I mean. Damn it, you don't carpet a headmaster every day of the week, do you, and that's what it amounts to! You'll get a fair hearing, both of you. That dry old stick, Sir Rufus, will make sure of that. It'll depend on him in the end. The O.B.s will stand with you but there's only three of us on the committee. God knows how the odds and sods will react. Depends on the sort of case you put up, I imagine. I've only got one more piece of advice and it's the same as I've given you time and again since this blew up. Stick to the point. Don't lambast him or his policy. Keep to the personal issue, my boy."

"Sure. And thanks again, Briggy."

"Been a pleasure. Can't stand that fellow. Too bloody pernickety. Best o' luck."

"Thank you."

The phone clicked and David slowly replaced his own receiver, pouring himself a drink and carrying it to the armchair that faced the window. In the summer, and throughout the earliest weeks of the Michaelmas term if the weather was fine, he kept his armchair here, facing south-east across the moor. The moon was full and silver light lay on the pastures, silhouetting the beeches in the drive, trees still wearing their full spread of leaves, for the earliest south-westerlies were still a week or two away.

It was very still and empty out there. An owl hooted in Algy's thinking post, his favourite perch because it was within easy killing-range of vermin in the planty. He tried to marshal his thoughts, but instead of rehearsing his brief found his mind ranging over random incidents of the past, back to the night he first sat here as Bat Ferguson's lodger, a callow, inexperienced youth, beginning to get the feel of the place. Towser, Ferguson's dog, now twelve by his reckoning, was the only Havelock survivor of that time, apart from himself. He ran his hand over the dog's head, recalling how his barks had averted what might so easily have been a terrible tragedy the night of the fire. Other memories stole upon him, smoke from a bonfire that had never burned itself out. Beth's laughter as, five months gone, she had waddled up and down in Yum-Yum's costume; Stratton-Forbes, earnestly discussing the root causes of bed-wetting in the Junior dorm; Chad Boyer, making his final call, with the gift of Bourgoyne's and Marbot's memoirs; Carter, offering him a partnership with no strings, Chris's one visit here last Sports Day, and her light-hearted remark, "It's the only room in the entire place that doesn't *smell* like a barracks. It's got another smell. It smells of bachelors."

He thought, "I wish to God she was here now, to hold my hand. This time tomorrow it'll be over, one way or the other, and I don't know whether to be relieved or not. If they come down on Alcock's side it's curtains for me, as far as Bamfylde is concerned.

And if they don't it can only mean an indefinite period of 'passed to you, Stoic', and 'passed to you, Powlett-Jones . . .' Do I really want that? Won't it rob us all of what dignity we've got left?"

The owl hooted again and he got up to put the fireguard over the grate. Fire was an ever-present hazard here. If he stayed on he would find a way to bully the Governors into installing a fire-escape in every house, but would he ever have his way in decisions of that kind? He doubted it. He doubted it very much. He carried his whisky glass into the kitchen, washed it and went to bed.

* * *

It was like a playback of his vigil here more than four years ago, when he had sat waiting for his interview on the outside chance they would select him in preference to Carter, or the man who would be asked to submit a full report on him, perhaps within minutes of his own dismissal. It was a repeat performance, played to a mildly hostile house, so that he felt slightly sick and had recourse, for the second time since breakfast, to the brand of indigestion tablets Carter had always carried about. He was not too familiar with the men closeted behind that door. He could count on Briggy, of course, and his two Old Boy allies, whereas Alderman Blunt, still throwing his weight about as a Governor, would surely see this as a second chance of getting his revenge for the bust-up about the War Memorial business all that time ago. Of the others he barely knew them by sight, had never spoken to two of the latest additions. All he could count on, apart from Cooper's championship, was Sir Rufus Creighton's neutrality, until the full facts were before him.

They seemed to enjoy keeping him on tenterhooks in this dusty little lobby, one of the few school backwaters Alcock's spring-cleaning mania had by-passed. He had sat here, biting his fingernails and sucking his indigestion tablets, for twenty minutes now, and Miss Rowlandson, the head's secretary, had still not appeared. Down in the quad the bell rang for luncheon parade and the familiar buzz and scuffle of assembly reached him, a sound inseparable from any gathering down there. Then he heard Heffling's raucous voice calling them to attention—"Paraa*aaaade*—shun! *Leeeeft*-turn! Disssss-*miss!*"—and another clatter of shoes on gravel and stone, and after that a heavy silence that lasted another five minutes. The library door opened and Miss Rowland-son bobbed out—"Mr. Powlett-Jones?" He got up stiffly, flexing his fingers, a surge of devil-may-care fatalism routing his extreme nervousness and went in, anticipating the Chairman's wordless offer of a chair.

*   *   *

They were ranged in their familiar horseshoe and again they re-minded him of Roundhead inquisitors in that picture Carter had mentioned—'When Did You Last See Your Father?' He avoided the brigadier's eye, knowing it would be too sympathetic. Some-body coughed. Someone else rustled papers. Sir Rufus Creighton sat in the Chairman's seat, looking like a Venetian Doge in a fifteenth-century Italian painting, small, compact, infinitely old and wrinkled, but terrifyingly alert. He said, impersonally, "We have considered all your correspondence, Mr. Powlett-Jones. At two earlier meetings, and again this morning. You will agree, I think, that this is a somewhat unpleasant business for everyone. Yourself included."

"Yes, Sir Rufus. But it seemed to me I owed it to the Governors and myself to put my case last term. I had a choice of doing that or letting things drift until . . . well, until something occurred that might reflect on the school as a whole."

"What kind of occurrence did you envisage, Mr. Powlett-Jones?"

"An open quarrel, with everybody taking sides. With respect, it's not uncommon in a school crisis, sir."

"Do you wish to express your view of the headmaster's policy as a whole? That isn't usual, of course, but it seemed to me criti-cism was implicit in your original letter to me. Whatever is said here will be said in confidence."

"No, Sir Rufus. That isn't my right, and I'm sorry if I implied it in my letter. I'm sure I did not intend to. I wrote on a purely personal basis."

"Regarding your alleged attempt to influence the boys politically?"

"Yes, sir. That mainly, but also a statement he made alleging disloyalty, and wilful non-co-operation on my part."

"Come now, you won't deny that you have challenged his deci-sions on a number of occasions?"

"Yes, I have, but I challenged them in the capacity of a house-master. I've put forward strong views, as I think any housemaster is entitled to do, particularly as regards his own boys. Nothing more than that."

There was a moment's silence. He could sense the Warrior's approval of his answers so far. Then Blunt said, "Mr. Chairman, I'd like a word. Do I have your permission?"

"Of course."

"Right." He faced David squarely. "It doesn't do to have a head-master and a housemaster hammering away at one another. You won't deny that, Powlett-Jones?"

"No, Alderman Blunt, I won't because I can't. But it hasn't been a case of 'hammering away at one another', as you say. We've had disagreements, as I've already admitted, but in private, with no other person present. And I've kept my own counsel about them."

"Not always. Carter told me . . ."

Sir Rufus lifted his hand and David saw it as a beautifully judged gesture. "I'm sorry, Alderman, no hearsay, evidence, please. Mr. Carter is not present and not available."

"I think I know what Alderman Blunt is referring to, sir, and I don't mind it being raised. Carter asked me to plead for him, when one of his boys was threatened with expulsion. I did what he asked, and several of the staff joined the appeal. Later on, when one of my boys was sent home, I naturally sought advice from Carter as to what I should do."

"On a point of order," said Brigadier Cooper. "All this is past history and irrelevant."

"I agree," Sir Rufus said, "and tried to indicate as much." He turned to David. In his brown, freckled hand was the breakdown of examination results Algy Herries had advised him to submit. "We've been over these figures," he said. "Personally, I think they do you credit, Mr. Powlett-Jones."

"Thank you, sir."

"There is nothing you would like to add, then?"

"No, sir, except perhaps that the last time we had a private talk the headmaster as good as asked me to resign."

"How do you mean, 'as good as'? Did he or didn't he?" This from Blunt, in a tone of voice that suggested he considered himself on losing ground.

"It was a broad hint. Mr. Alcock said I 'might like to think about it'. I told him it was out of the question."

"You still feel that way?"

"Yes, I do. I'm very attached to the school. I always have been, from the first week I arrived here, in 1918."

"Thank you, Mr. Powlett-Jones."

It was dismissal. He rose, without catching anyone's eye, but Sir Rufus Creighton's husky voice stopped him as he reached for the doorknob.

"No need to wait about, Mr. Powlett-Jones. We shall be writing an official answer to your letter, of course."

He went out. The last of the indigestion tablets had left a sour taste in his mouth. He thought, "And what the devil am I supposed to deduce from all that, I wonder?" and although he reminded himself of Sir Rufus's comment on the examination results, he still felt baffled and irritated. In a way the long-awaited confrontation had been an anti-climax.

It remained so for the rest of the day, and on into the night. No one rang and all the others somewhat pointedly he thought, left him to himself, perhaps out of courtesy. In the meantime, however, it was impossible to settle to anything. He tried proofreading the final edition of the printer's proofs of *The Royal Tigress*, but the prose seemed turgid, the slow build-up to the first battle at St. Albans dull and diffuse.

At eleven he tried to get through to Chris but there was no reply. With the election looming she would almost surely be out canvassing, or addressing a meeting in the outback of the constituency. He said, aloud, "This won't do! Must think things through properly," and he made a tremendous effort to project his mind into the library, where Sir Rufus and the others had presumably quizzed Alcock shortly after they had quizzed him. Did they sympathise with Alcock for having a near-mutinous housemaster on his hands? Did they wave those examination results under his nose, and tell him to stop behaving like a stuffy, overweening ass? Had the matter of his public appearance on a political platform been raised? He had no means of knowing the answer to these questions and was on the point of giving them up, and going to bed, when the door opened and Grace glided in, wearing her blue woollen dressing gown. "It's Towser, Daddy," she said, frowning with the effort of concentration, as he remembered her mother had been given to doing. "He's snorting in a funny way and I don't think he's well. Will you look at him?"

It was a relief to have one's mind switched to a practical issue, so he followed her into the kitchen, where Towser slept in a laundry basket beside the stove. "He woke me up twice," Grace said, and when he knelt beside the basket he saw at once that the grizzled old dog was in a bad way. His breath was laboured, and every few moments he tried, unsuccessfully to shift his position. He offered the dog a drink but he could not raise his head to the bowl. He said, "Towser's getting on, Grace. Only last night I reckoned his age as twelve. That's old for a dog."

"Eighty-four," she said, and knelt, stroking Towser's head. "Is he dying, do you think?"

"I don't know. He might be. All I can do is to try and get him to take a Bob Martin's and get the vet over first thing in the morning. You'd best go to bed now, my love."

"Couldn't I make tea and watch him? I don't feel a bit sleepy. Besides, I couldn't sleep with him snorting like that."

"I could shift him to the study."

"I'd sooner watch him, Daddy. Honestly. I mean, he's a very special dog, isn't he? You think so yourself."

"Yes, I do. Very well then, for a little while. It's Saturday tomorrow, and you can sleep on. Make a cup for me while you're at it. We'll have it in here."

She skipped over to the gas-stove and put the kettle on. He watched her absently, thinking how much she meant to him, and what a permanent reminder she was of Beth and her twin sister. Their relationship was very close on this account, and he wondered, fleetingly, how she would react to the prospect of a stepmother. Then, reminding himself of Christine's husband, and the complex situation they were in at the moment, he thought, "No sense in bothering about that yet. She'll be in her mid-teens before we get around to marrying, and then it won't matter so much." The kettle began to steam and she made the tea, deftly, the way she did most things. They were sipping their second cup when they heard the discreet knock on the outer door.

He glanced up at the kitchen clock and it told him it wanted a few minutes to midnight. "Who the devil can that be at this time of night? Probably Matron, about one of the boys in the sick-bay."

"There aren't any in the sick-bay," Grace said. "Vesey, the last one, went out today."

"I'll go and see. Meantime, get that pill from the medicine chest and see if Towser will take it hidden in a bit of cake."

He went out across the living-room to the landing door and opened it. Old Rigby, the head's butler, was standing there, looking like a stage butler in a bad play. Old and shuffling but very dignified.

"Excuse me, sir. Sorry to knock you up at this time of night, but I saw the study light from the forecourt and I'm puzzled, sir. It's the headmaster, and I . . . er . . . wondered if you could advise me."

"About what, Rigby?"

"Well, sir, you know he's such a regular about turning in. I've never known him stay up a minute after ten-thirty, no matter what, but he's still in his study, the door's locked, and he won't answer when I knock. I was turning in myself but saw his light under the door. It struck me he was working late and might like another of his hot lemon drinks. He has one about nine every night but he didn't ring for it tonight, and that's strange too, come to think on it. I knocked several times but he didn't answer, so I went round and tried to peep through the window but the curtains are drawn tight, sir."

"He obviously doesn't want to be disturbed, Rigby."

"That's what I thought, sir, but it struck me that . . . well, he might have been taken bad, sir. I mean, I've never known that door locked since Mr. Bull's time, sir."

On the face of it, David decided, it was very odd. Bull had preceded Herries, and Rigby had been Bull's butler more than thirty years ago. He said, "I'll gladly come down and knock myself, Rigby, if that's what you'd like."

"I would, sir, if it's not too much trouble. I'd sleep easier if you did."

He followed Rigby down to the quad and turned in through the head's door. Light was still showing under the threshold. He knocked three times and when there was no response he called, "Headmaster? It's me, Powlett-Jones," but there was no reply. He said, "I think you must be right, Rigby. Have you got a duplicate key to this door?"

"No, sir, but I can open it. With your permission, sir."

"How?"

"The way I've opened many doors about the place in my time, sir. Mr. Bull was a rare locker-up. Sometimes he turned a key here and there, then went out the front door or quad door and closed 'em on a spring. One moment, sir." He went to his pantry, re-emerging with a square sheet of zinc that he used on his stove. Slipping the zinc under the study door he took a button-hook from the drawer of the hallstand and inserted it in the large, old-fashioned keyhole. There was a sharp metallic sound from the other side of the door as the key fell on to the zinc. Rigby drew it out, modestly triumphant.

David said, thoughtfully, "Listen here, Rigby . . . I happen to know the headmaster has had a particularly trying day. If he's dropped off in there he'll be very embarrassed being disturbed in this way. Take yourself off, and let me deal with this. I'll explain that you were anxious about him."

"Thank you, sir," and Rigby shuffled off, gratefully it seemed to David, although he couldn't be sure. Rigby's long service at Bamfylde had brought him into close contact with so many eccentrics that he probably found nothing unusual about Alcock's frigid manner. He opened the door quietly and peeped in. The desk light was burning and Alcock was, as he had suspected, inert in his swivel chair, legs fully extended, head thrown back, mouth half-open. David coughed twice but Alcock did not stir. He moved forward and prodded his forearm and Alcock slumped sideways and would have fallen if David had not grabbed him by the hand and shoulder. The hand was chillingly cold. He realised then that the man was dead.

His first impulse was to shout for Rigby but then, as he braced himself to ease the body back in the chair, his glance fell on a sheet of paper on the desk, an unfinished letter addressed to the Chairman of the Governing Body, and beginning, "Dear Sir Rufus . . ." At the same time, his eye travelling rapidly down the few lines of closely written handwriting, his own name jumped at him, and instinct inclined him to steady Alcock with his right hand and lift the sheet of paper with his left. He acted purely on impulse, aware that, before the place erupted, it was very necessary that he should know what was written on that paper. He

385

read, still holding Alcock firmly with his right hand, one completed paragraph and another half finished. Alcock had written,

"Touching the private conversation we had, following my full statement to the Governing Body this a.m., I can only deduce from it that a majority of the Governors, headed by yourself, see fit to regard my submissions concerning Mr. Powlett-Jones as irrelevant, and prompted by my personal dislike of him.

"I made what I consider to be a frank and full assessment of the facts, and made them entirely without prejudice. You have since explained to me your reasons for ruling the substance of that statement out of order. That, of course, is your privilege, and I bow to it. At the same time it makes my position here untenable and I hereby proffer my . . ."

He had been unable, it appeared, to write the word 'resignation'. Something, choking rage, an excess of bile, or even an interruption wholly unconnected with what he was doing, had broken the smooth flow of words and he had died here in his chair. Of what, only a medical man could determine. Awkwardly he pushed the letter into his jacket pocket and called aloud for Rigby, at the same time stooping to lift Alcock bodily from the chair.

It required considerable effort, but once the burden was adjusted he weighed surprisingly little for someone approaching six feet. Rigby appeared almost at once and David heard his sharp intake of breath. "Unconscious, sir?"

"He's dead, Rigby. He's been dead two hours, probably longer. Hold the door and switch on the landing light. Then get through to Dr. Willoughby and if he doesn't answer keep ringing."

"Yes, sir . . . at once. But . . . what was it, sir? A sudden illness or . . ." He left the sentence unfinished, but David understood what had prompted it. Rigby's unswerving loyalty to the school reached all the way back to Bull's time, when he had arrived here as a kitchen servant in the last years of Victoria's reign. He said, quietly, "It was almost certainly a heart attack, but I can't be sure." Then, "I've had more experience in this field than most people, Rigby. There's no question of it being anything but illness."

The old chap dodged in front of him and switched on the landing light, then back again to address himself to the telephone. David knew his way about the house as well as Rigby and went slowly up the curving stone staircase to the front bedroom that Algy had shared with Ellie for twenty-three years. It was not quite as Spartan as the study or parlour. Over the single cot was a reproduction of Botticelli's *Venus Rising From the Sea*, an improbable picture, he thought, to occupy pride of place in the bedroom of a man of Alcock's temperament. On the facing wall was an enlarged photograph of Alcock's educational college in Cape Town, and framed in silver on the dressing-table was a studio portrait of a jaundiced-looking woman about forty, wearing an evening gown fashionable just before the war. He noticed all this as he crossed the room and laid Alcock on the bed, straightening his limbs and closing the jaws and eyes. As he did this he had a sharp memory of trying to perform the same office for Nick Austin, who had died on the wire opposite Delville Wood. But in Nick's case it had proved impossible. He had been out there a day and a night.

He stood breathing heavily beside the bed. The folly and incongruity of the long, smouldering quarrel settled about him like a cloud of marsh gas, poisoning his nostrils and drying out his mouth. For more than four years now they had been at it, just as Alderman Blunt had alleged, hammer and tongs, tit-for-tat, so that in the end they had arrived at a point where arbitrators had to be summoned to patch up a peace between two men charged with the education of four hundred boys, and both behaving like the youngest of them. Alcock's death, he supposed, in the very act of conceding defeat, would be seen as a great stroke of luck by some, but not by anyone who valued his self-respect. Victory, at this price, was a kind of defeat, and as he thought this he understood what had prompted him to slip that letter into his pocket. Everybody concerned was likely to accept it as the token of Alcock's surrender, Powlett-Jones's legitimate prize as a trophy of war, and the prospect of this made him feel meaner and shabbier than ever, so that he put off thinking about it. He drew the spotless coverlet over Alcock's face and stole away, meeting Rigby on the stairs.

The butler said, in a hoarse whisper, "I got him, sir. He's coming right over."

For some reason the prospect of Willoughby arriving with his bag reminded him of Towser, snorting his life away in his basket, watched over by Grace. He said, "Would you do something, Rigby? Pop up to my daughter, tell her I'm likely to be some time, and that she's to leave the dog and go to bed?"

"Yes, sir. Certainly, sir," but he hesitated.

"Well?"

"About Mr. Alcock, sir . . . I don't know as it's any of my business, but he had a sort of attack halfway through last term. It had been a very hot day, during that long dry spell, sir. I found him gasping and a very bad colour in the parlour. He wasn't unconscious. He could tell me where he kept his pills, and I got him two, with a glass of water. They seemed to have a very strong effect, sir. He was himself again almost at once, and sharp enough to warn me to say nothing about it to anybody. It was some kind of tropical illness, according to him."

"Thank you, Rigby. Do you remember where those pills are?"

"Yes, sir. He kept them in the small drawer of the sideboard. I took the liberty of getting them. Thought Dr. Willoughby might want to see them," and he handed over a small red pillbox, containing about a dozen yellow tablets the size of aspirins.

"That was very helpful of you, Rigby. Thank you again, and I'll pass them on. You can go up to bed if you want to, but if I were you I'd first help myself to a drink if Mr. Alcock kept any about the place. If not use my whisky. My daughter will show you where it is."

"Kind of you, sir," and the courteous old chap shuffled off, letting himself into the quad and closing the heavy door with exaggerated care.

David went back into the study and re-read the letter, trying to decide whether or not to replace it where he found it but then Willoughby's car lights swept round the bend of the west drive, and he heard the car pass and stop, and Willoughby's brisk steps on the gravel.

He said, opening the door to him, "Were you treating Alcock for anything, Doc? A tropical illness of some kind?" and Willoughby said he had never spoken more than a dozen sentences to him since he had come here and went quickly upstairs, with David behind him.

He made an examination, pausing to look attentively at the bluish lips. "Tropical illness, my eye," he said. "It's angina, just as I suspected the moment Rigby told me. Had a feeling about the chap the first time I met him. You do about some people. Just a few and he was one of them. He held himself in, didn't he? Kept the lid screwed down in case it blew off at the wrong moment."

"That's one way of putting it. Nobody could get close to him, but I never saw him lose his temper, not even when he was in a quiet fury, and he usually was when I had words with him."

"It fits. Did he take anything?", and when David gave him the pills he glanced at them, then pocketed them. "I'll hang on to these, P.J. There's a possibility of an inquest but it isn't likely. He's bound to have a medical record somewhere, and the bursar could look into it first thing. Will you notify his next-of-kin?"

"I haven't the faintest notion who his next-of-kin is, or even if he has one. The bursar might help there."

"It'll keep until morning. Nothing more I can do. Bit of a shock for everyone. Lucky job you and Rigby had the sense to break in. I'll write the certificate downstairs."

David said, when Willoughby had finished his writing, "Do you notify the coroner or do we?"

"Me. He wasn't a patient but Bamfylde is. You'd better get on to the Governors tomorrow. As you were the one who found him they'll expect that." Then, with a shrewd look, "You didn't hit it off at all, did you? Not from the word go."

"Nobody hit it off. It was all a ghastly mistake, due, in a way, to that idiotic quarrel between Carter and me four years ago."

"What'll happen now, P.J.?"

"I'm damned if I know. We were both up before the Governors only this afternoon. He was alleging slackness and insubordination, so I got my oar in first. On Algy's advice, I might add. But if I had dreamed it could have led to this . . ."

"It didn't. Man's been living on borrowed time for years in my opinion. His papers should clarify that, unless he carried secrecy to the point of self-destruction, and I don't think he did. Too careful. Then there are these pills, they must have been supplied by somebody qualified. For God's sake, don't start reproaching yourself. You've no cause to at all."

"Doctors don't know the lot. How about this?"

He took out the letter and passed it to Willoughby who read it slowly, then went back to read it a second time.

"He was writing this at the time?"

"It was on the desk."

"I stick to my point. This fits too. Severe emotional strain, self-induced, and I stress that, mind. You Celts and your damned guilt-complexes! Sometimes I think guilt is a Celtic sport, a variant of masturbation. All his life that chap has been driving himself, and in the last few years he's had his foot slammed down on the accelerator. Every man needs to blow his top now and again, especially a man in authority, but he never did, you say. Probably never so much as raised his voice. Well, this is the result, and it would have happened anywhere, anywhere at all, provided his job entailed responsibility." When David made no reply he went on, "Listen, P.J., he scared some of the others off, but not you. You hung on, another Celtic characteristic. Well, who was right about that? Carter, who packed it in, or you, who stuck it for the sake of the place as a whole?"

"Was it worth a man's life?"

"Who knows? It might be, in the long run. You've got thirty years ahead of you. He had about one, I'd say. Let things drift awhile. Let the Governors and the bursar sort it out."

He strode off, a big, bustling, hard case of a man, that nothing could rattle. David let himself out and went up to his quarters, passing through to the kitchen, his senses alerted by the silence reigning there. Towser was dead, curled in his basket and looking, somehow, as if he had died without much distress. He thought, "Funny that. Two eras closed in an hour. The Old Guard's, represented by Bat Ferguson, and Alcock's. Grace will be upset if she wasn't here when it happened, but I hope it was after Rigby sent her to bed." He sat looking down at the basket, remembering the fire of eight years before, an ordeal that was much closer to the war, but in those days he had never shirked issues the way he was inclined to shirk them now. The older a man grew the less sure he was about anything. In the end, perhaps, he came face to face with the fact that he was still looking through a crack in a door, wondering at the things he saw within. What had Alcock's fifty-odd years taught him about handling people? Or Howarth's? Or Barnaby's? They were all amateurs at the game, himself included. He wondered whether to ring Chris again but decided against it. She had enough on her plate at the moment and the new situation wouldn't do anything to aid her concentration. There seemed even less point in rousting out Howarth or Barnaby at two o'clock in the morning. Technically Howarth was senior master, and would be saddled with the job of making the announcement at morning parade. Suddenly he felt drained of energy, too confused and dispirited to devote a single thought as to where Alcock was likely to be buried, and whether or not his funeral would rank as a Bamfylde ceremony. He reeled off to bed and within minutes, against all expectation, he was asleep.

Chapter Three

1

Alcock was not buried at Stone Cross, beside such classroom warriors as Judy Cordwainer and Bat Ferguson. His London lawyers had received specific instructions concerning his disposal. He was to be cremated, and his ashes conveyed to Cape Town.

He had a family after all, two sons, both living abroad, but the bursar dealt with the family and the lawyers. All David was required to do was to write a detailed report of what had occurred, sending one copy to the Governors, another to Dr. Willoughby, who took it upon himself to superintend the medical aspects, notwithstanding the fact that Alcock had never been his patient. There was no inquest. It emerged, in a matter of hours, that Alcock had been under a London heart specialist, a man of repute, according to Willoughby. "He couldn't have given the chap very good advice," Willoughby said, "or maybe he did and it was ignored. I thought you might like to know that I was right in my spot diagnosis. He left Africa for health reasons, and I suppose that accounts, to some extent, for him concealing it so successfully. They wouldn't have appointed him if it had got about he was a heart risk."

It was queer, David thought, how rapidly and completely Alcock had effaced himself. He had seemed so brooding a presence but now, in a matter of days, there was hardly a trace of him, if one excepted the new bog and his other renovations, like the donkey's breakfast floor coverings in the dormitories, and the revarnished pew-backs at Stone Cross Church. He appeared as a brief visitation. No more and no less. Algy Herries, four years absent, was a far more active ghost, and it was Algy who came to their rescue, slipping back as acting-head until the end of the term and spending four days a week at the school. He did not live in but motored home to his parish every night, so that it was not like having Algy actually restored to them but rather helping out, like Rawson, the honorary football coach, now on four months' leave from Rhodesia.

David heard nothing from the Governors concerning a replacement. They would delay it, he imagined, until the new year. There was no immediate hurry, with Algy on the doorstep, and when Brigadier Cooper rang, hinting at a renewed application, he steered him away from the subject. It was something he preferred not to think about for the time being. Willoughby had kept that letter but what use he had made of it, if any, David had no idea. He was aware of the effects of shock in the days that followed, and this in itself was strange, in view of the hundreds of deaths he had witnessed, and all the corpses he had handled between 1914 and 1917. The others, Grace included, found him very subdued, and there was the minimum of conversation on the subject in the common room. It was as though Alcock, who had divided them in life, continued to isolate them in death. Only Howarth spoke out, growling to David, as they stood watching the hearse drive off, "That's that, and I hope to God nobody asks me to comment. If there's one form of hypocrisy I can't tolerate it's sentimental regard for the dead, simply because they *are* dead. To hear some people talk at a funeral one would suppose dying was limited to the chosen few."

As it happened, however, there was a funeral at Bamfylde that same week. Towser was buried on the edge of the planty by David and Grace, just beyond the bank where the first of the trees grew. Grace marked the spot with two white stones and it was not until two days later that Coxe Minor presented himself at David's door, asking, very politely, if he might have a word with his housemaster.

Coxe was a fresh-faced thirteen-year-old, lumbering his way through Lower School. A dreamy, inoffensive little chap, no good at games or work but with a consuming passion for wild life that made him, while still in the Upper Third, Bamfylde's authority on ornithology.

Coxe was said to run a kind of birds' hospital up in the planty, a hedge-hide where he collected not merely birds but stoats, weasels and other creatures, all reputably charmed by his various whistles and calls. One of his owls, wounded in some affray, had been nursed back to health in a hut down at the piggeries and later set free. Barnaby christened him Frankie, after St. Francis, as soon as this story got about and the name stuck. David, inviting him inside, asked, "What's bothering you, Coxe?" and Coxe said he was there to make a request on behalf of himself and Davidson. Davidson, a local farmer's son, was his special crony, also serving time in the Upper Third.

"It's about Towser, sir. Davidson is hot stuff at carpentry and he's made a headstone—well, head*board*. He asked me if he should and I told him to go ahead, seeing that Grace's dog had been about the place so long, sir. I've got it outside, and I wondered if she could tell us where Towser is buried, so as we could put it up, and whether it would be right to do it, sir."

Without waiting for reassurance, he slipped outside, reappearing almost at once with a board about two feet by one foot, shaped to a gothic apex, and with a smoothly planed oblong enclosed within deeply scored lines. The lettering on the oblong was neat and clear: *Towser Powlett-Jones, died Sept. 30, 1931, aged about twelve. R.I.P.*

He saw it not as a tribute to Towser but as a graceful compliment to Grace, who was popular with everyone about the place. Each of them, apparently, thought of Towser as Grace's dog, not his, or something inherited from the Fergusons. He said, "I think that's very kind of you and Davidson, Coxe. Do thank him for me. Take the board to the planty, and I'll send Grace along to show you exactly where to put it." He paused, pondering a moment. "It's a pity you didn't add something about the fire we had here. Towser saved us all by waking me up. We always had a very special regard for him on that account."

"You mean the Havelock fire, sir?"

"Yes, long before you came here."

Coxe considered, his head on one side. "Davidson could add a bit if we gave him an hour or so. Would Grace like that, sir?"

"I'm sure she would, if Davidson felt equal to it. Upper Third's first period is history this afternoon, isn't it? Tell Davidson he needn't come in if he wants the time to work in the shop. Then I'll come up with my daughter after final period bell."

Coxe scuttled off with his headboard and David went in search of Grace who was, as he suspected, infinitely touched by the gesture.

"Frankie Coxe is a very nice boy," she said. "He wants to be a vet when he leaves."

"I'll wager a term's salary he will be, even if only half they say about him is true." Then, thoughtfully, "You don't think, in the circumstances, that it's pushing things a bit far. Marking a dog's grave, I mean, with Mr. Alcock dying here only a few days ago?"

"No, I don't. The two things aren't to do with one another, Daddy. Everybody liked old Towser and I never liked the new head."

"Why do you say that?"

She looked at him steadily, another trick inherited from her mother. "Because he wasn't nice to you," she said, simply. "You never said he wasn't but I know just the same. I'm sorry he died, but that doesn't mean I have to pretend to like him, does it?"

"No, I suppose not," he said, thinking of Howarth's comment on graveside hypocrisy. "Very well, pick me up after the final bell outside the Fifth and we'll go up and see what Davidson makes of it."

They met them at five minutes after four, waiting a hundred yards or so south of the cricket pavilion, and Grace led the way over the bank to the stones marking Towser's grave. The autumn light was already fading inside the wood hut beyond the trees, the clear sky was flooded with molten brass where the sun slipped down beyond the school buildings. Coxe displayed Davidson's additional handiwork, a single sentence, carved low on the board, 'This dog saved life when Havelock's ct. fire. He barked.' As an epitaph, David thought, it had a smack of eighteenth-century forthrightness, and that was just the way a stolid boy like Davidson would think of it. 'He barked.' Nothing gaudy or flowery but the whole essence of Towser's spectacular feat in two words.

Coxe acted as a kind of interpreter. "Davidson's sorry about shortening the word 'caught', sir. There wasn't room, you see. Will it do, sir?" Coxe, usually a very untidy boy, had clearly smartened himself for the ceremony. With his eager eyes, his black hair neatly parted and his shiny black mackintosh turned up at the collar, he reminded David of a rook.

"It'll do splendidly," David said. "Thank you for taking so much trouble, Davidson," but Davidson blushed and stared hard at his boots.

Coxe used a trowel on the ground just beyond the line of stones and carefully inserted the board, afterwards producing a tent mallet from his mackintosh pocket to hammer it firm. Then he and Davidson heeled in the loose soil round the base and stood back. Grace said, a little tearfully, "Thank you, Coxe. Thank you, Davidson. It was *jolly* nice of you to think of it," and they all moved off in response to the clamour of the tea-bell, Coxe, Davidson and Grace moving ahead in a group.

The thought occurred to him, as he crossed the forecourt and passed under the windows of the head's house, "Funny a dog should make more impact on all three of them than a man dying of heart failure within shouting distance of where they slept," but then, partly on account of the incident, he was able to get Alcock and Alcock's reign into some kind of perspective. "I'll talk it over with Algy, then put it out of mind," he promised himself, as he turned down the flagged corridor to supervise tea.

2

The Saturday before the election he begged a loan of Molyneux's car and ran over to Bilhampton. It did not seem to matter now whether or not he involved himself in politics but Christine, drawn and exhausted after six weeks' nonstop campaigning, would not hear of him speaking at either of the two meetings he attended. "Your field is wide open again," she said, "and what sort of selfish bitch would I be to stand in your way a second time?" When he told her he was not disposed to play the field again, and that it was extremely unlikely, after the row preceding Alcock's death, that the Governors would short-list him for the job, she said this was no time at all for a professional man of any kind to enlist with so-called Bolshies. "It's like rolling a boulder up Snowdon," she said. "There's a kind of hysteria running loose, as if the country was waging some kind of patriotic war. The National Government is seen as a lifeboat, and whoever won't jump aboard and give thanks to God is off their rocker. One would have thought, with nearly three million on the dole, and wage cuts all round, the tide would be running for us, not them! Not on your life. You should hear the gibes I've had thrown at me, and from people living on pittances! 'You're the bastards who have landed us in the mess!' someone shouted at me on Thursday, as if the British Labour Party had engineered the Wall Street crash, back in '29. It's absolutely incredible what people will believe if it's told them often enough. There are chaps about here wearing blue rosettes and taking home thirty-five shillings a week to a tied cottage they can be evicted from at any moment. Talk about a working-class Tory being too green to burn, that's an understatement. You can dry green wood but how the hell do you light a fire with solid ivory?"

He sympathised with her but could have wished she was equipped to take things more philosophically. People were scared, he said, scared stiff of losing even that thirty-five shillings a week, and probably saw a national government as the only solution. Moreover, who could blame them, with men of MacDonald's stature, and Snowden's famed integrity, leaving the ranks? "Don't mention those names to me," she snapped, "and as for that word 'national', for heaven's sake, get it straight, Davy. It *isn't* national, it's *Tory!* How long will it be before they drop the pretence and that charlatan with it? What happened to Lloyd George when he did a deal with the Tories in 1916?"

"Lloyd George probably wishes he could back-pedal right now. So will Ramsay when things have gone off the boil."

"Do you think we'd have him back after this? The one thing that cheers me up is the prospect of him losing his seat and having to ask the Tories to find him another. Look, I can't waste any more time, Davy. I have to go over my speech for this afternoon."

It was a very different Christine Forster, he reflected, from the girl who had lain in his arms beside Windermere two short months ago. She was strong, and very dedicated, but she would need all her strength and dedication to maintain the pace for long. The afternoon meeting was thinly attended, and depressing apart from the interruption of a few hecklers, but there was serious trouble at the evening rally, with constant interruptions, a spate of abuse, and, at one time, the prospect of a general scrimmage. No warm-up speaker could make himself heard and Christine was greeted by the slow handclap and backrow jeers of "Find yourself a man and get yourself a couple of kids!" "Chuck it, love, and come and give us a cuddle!" and a few mild obscenities. It was all he could do to stop himself getting up and fighting his way over to one lout who bawled, "Yer ol' man run orf, didn't he, ducks? And buggered if I blame him!" a sally that was greeted by a gale of laughter and another scuffle in the aisle.

She was in tears when he called for her in the committee room behind the stage. The sheer weight and ruthlessness of the opposition was beginning to tell, not only upon her but on her few steadfast supporters. All her committee men looked sullen and despairing, so that David said, for their benefit as much as hers, "You've made your gesture. That's all that really matters. People will remember it when things drift from bad to worse. With a majority of over twelve thousand, and a three-cornered contest under these conditions, you can't expect to get a fair hearing. My advice is to cut out meetings and concentrate on door-to-door canvassing in the factories and working-class districts. Hold an open-air meeting beside every dole queue in the division. Then move on, speaking in every street where there's a concentration of unemployed. They won't vote Tory."

She said very little during the walk home but at the gate, where he was prepared to leave her, she said, "Come upstairs. I'd made up my mind not to ask you in. For my sake, as well as yours, for you must have heard what that swine shouted about me being a married woman, living apart from her husband. They only need a whiff of scandal to put paid to me here, but to hell with all of them!"

He followed her up a staircase lit by a 25-watt bulb to a front-room bedsitter in the ugly, Londonbrick villa she occupied, near the station. It was a cheerless, anonymous room, with bagged-out furniture, bilious-green tiles in a grate fitted with a small gas-fire, and dun-coloured curtains screening the bed. She did her own cooking here on a primus stove, she told him, and the smell of paraffin did battle with the reek of lino polish and bacon fat.

He said, "Do you have to live in a place like this, Chris? You said something about making use of Rowley's allowance."

"I do make use of it. It goes into the funds. We've hardly any money to fight the election."

"Well," he said, "you're a game one to be sure. Keep reminding yourself of that. It might help."

"It did once," she said, throwing her off-the-peg coat on the bed, and filling the kettle. "It doesn't now."

"Because of a bunch of hecklers?"

"Not just them. I didn't come into this expecting miracles. I knew that at best it would be a long, uphill fight to build a party organisation. No, it was you, I imagine."

"*Me?*"

"Being cut off from you in this way, feeling as guilty as hell every time I'm alone with you, because of what happened the last time you stood up for me in public."

"But Alcock's dead. Algy is deputy head now, and Howarth will probably succeed him. Neither would dream of trying to control what I did in my spare time."

"You're kidding yourself, Davy."

"How? I know Algy. He's a democrat and he's been teaching democracy all his life."

"It's the mood of the country. Nonconformist Socialists are seen as revolutionaries, people who want to drag the whole shooting match down. I know, I'm much closer to this than you, and I *know*. And as if that wasn't enough there's the moral aspect—a man like you, supposed to set an example, tagging along with a married woman."

"But damn it, you aren't married in the proper sense. You haven't set eyes on that damned Rowley for nearly three years."

"It's still a stick to beat you with, a smear that can stop you getting what you're after, what you've set your heart on getting, being Gaffer of that place. It's a very worthwhile objective and a practical one too, for I've seen the way all those boys look at you and address you. You'll make it, but only if I let go of your coat-tails."

"But can't you see, I don't want to make it at the price of losing you? I'm in love with you. More than ever now I see you bruised and battered and still on your feet. What kind of man would that make me, to turn my back on you now?"

"A sane one, with the right priorities in view. You can do untold good at a place like Bamfylde. Not just for the boys who go there, but for all of us."

"Good God, are you suggesting we should break up on that account?"

"Yes, I am. And don't imagine it's a pretty gesture on my part. It hurts like hell, even the thought of it."

"Then don't think of it. Because I won't go along with it. Not now, not ever."

"What does that mean? We go on meeting and mating in anonymous places? We make love once every six weeks standing up in alleys, or in the back of a car on a moor? No, thank you, Davy. You deserve better than that and so do I. The fact that I was having an affair with that schoolmaster who made the famous Monmouth speech at my adoption meeting wouldn't only ruin you, it would ruin my candidature. We're up a dead end, Davy."

Something warned him to stop arguing with her now, with her so tired and dispirited, with the echo of that heckler's gibe ringing in her ears. It was wiser to sheer away and wait for the feverish atmosphere to spend itself, to wait patiently, if that was possible, for some kind of break that would offer hope. Away in the back of his mind was the thought that perhaps this baptism of fire would prove too much for her, that she would emerge so ignominiously from the polls that she would swing away from politics, and if she did that they could soon find a way to get married and put both Rowley and politics out of mind. To his way of thinking, there was not much prospect of him being encouraged to take up the fight again. Even Howarth had as good as conceded that, when he and Barnaby had been speculating idly about Alcock's successor. The best he could hope for was another stopgap man, and a chance to persuade the Governors, over a long period of time, that he was something more than a born trouble-maker, who had quarrelled with Alderman Blunt, Carter and his headmaster in rapid succession. That might take a decade and by then he would be in his mid-forties, and as set in his ways as old Judy Cordwainer.

She made tea and they sipped it in silence. He noticed the colour had gone from her cheeks and the sparkle from her eyes. For the first time he understood why she persisted in regarding her nose as a feature that spoiled her looks. The heat and turmoil of the meeting had made it glow in the light of the Woolworth's shade. She had lost weight, too, a surprising amount of weight, in a few weeks. He had reason to know that her breasts were round and full but tonight she looked flat-chested. Only her elegant legs reminded him of the Chris Forster of Windermere, and earlier.

He said, earnestly, "Listen, Chris, you've got to ease up a little. What's an election, anyway? There'll be other, luckier elections, with the tide of events on your side. It won't help to tax yourself this way. You look as if you haven't had a square meal since we parted in August."

A flicker of her independence showed.

"I look anaemic? I'm losing my sex-appeal?"

He said, taking her cup, "Who lives here? Who is your land-lady?"

"Dora Beavis," she said, "a widow with three cats called Shad-rach, Meshach and Abednego. She's a strict Methodist. However, we're in luck tonight. She and her blasted cats have gone to Lang-port to stay with a sister."

"I've got to drive back tonight. I'm on duty tomorrow, and Molyneux wants his car. But I'm staying here until the small hours. I'll make sure I get away well before daylight."

She made no protest. The temperature of the dismal room was rising a little, now that the curtains were drawn, and the gas-fire had been singing for half an hour. He turned off the overhead light and the outlines of the cheerless place were softened. "Go to bed," he said, "God knows, you look as if you need some sleep," and she replied, "That's gallant of you, after a hundred-mile drive, and the prospect of another in slashing rain." Then, forlornly, "I need you right now more than sleep, Davy."

He took her at her word. There was not much room in the nar-row bed but in one another's arms they found at least a temporary solution to their problems. She might be tired out, he thought, but she still had reserves of vitality and enfolded him with desper-ate eagerness, too impatient and too much in need of solace to give a thought to contraceptives.

She said, before she drifted into sleep, "That would just about put the tin lid on it, wouldn't it? A candidate, separated from her husband, and several months gone." But there was a trace of laugh-ter in her voice.

3

She must have been as tired as she looked. About five o'clock, long before it was light, he relit the gas-fire, slipping a shilling into the meter and glancing over his shoulder to see if the click had disturbed her. It had not, so he dressed quickly in the feeble orange glow, determined to let her sleep on until one or other of her supporters roused her. She looked more or less herself again, with colour in her cheeks. Deep sleep had brought a total relaxation of her face so that he was able to see her less as a woman than one of his first-termers, relieved by sleep of the strain of keeping up appearances during the day. He thought of himself as having loved Beth to the limit of his experience but it had never quite reached the pitch of intensity he felt for her at this particular moment. He and Beth had achieved what he thought of as a supremely successful partnership, but Beth had never stood in such terrible need of his protection, had never once appeared to him so defenceless and spent. In the last few years Chris had taken any amount of hard knocks, and the passage between her awakening at university, and last night's rowdiness in a small-town drill hall, was marking her spirit, now masked in sleep that would sustain her for another day or so. After that, he would say, it would be touch and go, depending upon how she fared at the polls. He was sure of one thing. She was not capable of absorbing humiliation on a grossly wounding scale.

He had seen himself, up to that time, as a committed radical, but he understood now that he was really no more than a dilettante. Bamfylde had replaced his hunger for social justice, quickening in him since his schooldays in the Valley. He was much tougher, too, and far more resilient. Trench warfare had seen to that long before he had come of age. It was something she would have to work out for herself, win or lose. Nobody could help her much, except maybe by the odd word of encouragement at the right time and place. He took one of her leaflets from the bamboo plant-table in the window and wrote, in the glow of the fire, "You needed sleep. Good luck and God bless. I love you very much, so bear this in mind, no matter what happens on Thursday. God knows, dearest, love is what it's all about really. If it isn't, does it matter who runs the show? One other thing—you look younger, prettier, and more desirable than ever at this moment. Davy."

He put the leaflet, written side up, on the chair where she had thrown her clothes and tiptoed out, groping his way down the steep stairs to the front door and striking a match to help him grapple with its fastenings. The doorknob felt greasy under his hand and the narrow hall smelled unpleasantly of cats.

4

The furore of the Governors' meeting, followed by Alcock's death, and Chris's dilemma, had banished all thought of his book from his mind. Perhaps he was beginning to see it, in retrospect, as a mere time-consuming enterprise over the ups and downs, mostly downs, of the last few years. A means of escaping, for an hour or so, first from the pressures of grief, then Alcock's nagging presence. At all events he had forgotten it completely, so that he stared at Barnaby uncomprehendingly when, soon after noon that same Sunday, he saw him waving a newspaper as he passed under the front of Nicolson's on his way to confer with Heffling, head prefect, about the prep roster for the ensuing week. Barnaby shouted, "Hi, there! You're being very modest, aren't you? I knew we had a literary presence about the place, but I was under the impression he was a cub, not a lion!"

"What the hell are you waffling about?" he called back, but then he saw that the newspaper in Barnaby's hand was yesterday's *Times* open at the book page. The Sunday papers would not get here until late afternoon, so that they had formed a habit of saving Saturday's papers to combat ennui between Saturday night and Monday morning.

He said, excitedly, "There's a review of my book in there?"

"There is, my dear chap, and a regular corker! It's either a first-class book, or you've struck uncommonly lucky with a critic." Then, bleakly, "Are you telling me you didn't look for it yesterday?"

"I was travelling," David said. "Would you lend me that paper, Barnaby. You can have it back."

"I don't want it back. You can mutilate it as far as I'm concerned. Everyone else has read it, but you can't expect anyone but me or Howarth to glance at the book reviews on the way to the sports pages. Take it, and congratulations, and I mean that, P.J."

"Thanks very much, Barnaby. Will . . . er . . . has Howarth seen it?"

"Probably not. He was off duty yesterday and over at Algy's. And the old bird doesn't usually surface until Sunday afternoons if he can help it. Were you supposed to be taking lunch today?"

"Yes, I'm duty wallah."

"I'll take it for you. We can't expect bona fide authors to sit watching boys stuff themselves with boiled cabbage and beetroot on occasions like this."

David thanked him and set off across the playing field to Algy's thinking post where, in the two winter terms, the roller was parked under its tarpaulin. There were a few boys about but just then the lunch-bell rang and within minutes the field was empty. He sat on the shaft of the roller and read the review from start to finish. Then he went back and read it again, letting his eye rove up and down the column in search of phrases that pleased him most, those in which the reviewer, who signed himself 'John Ellicott', had used to emphasise an overall theme that here was someone who could make an absorbing narrative out of the confused canvas of fifteenth-century England.

Ellicott made his first point (or perhaps his literary editor made it for him) with the headlines: "FRESH SPARKLE ON DULLED SURFACES—HIGHLY READABLE ACCOUNT OF WARS OF THE ROSES", and on the same theme—

Amateurs interested in English history, in the middle decades of the fifteenth century, approach it with a certain knowledge that they will soon lose their way in a welter of warring dynasties. Until now, that is, for an unknown biographer (this is his first published book) has shown that patience plus enthusiasm can crop something very palatable from these pastures. The book is *The Royal Tigress*, a study in depth of Margaret of Anjou and her period, and the author is David Powlett-Jones, a West Country schoolmaster, a man with an obvious passion for the bloody struggle of York and Lancaster from first St. Albans to Bosworth Field . . .

Here followed a summary of the narrative that was more than a busy journalist's rehash of the publisher's blurb.

It requires more than a detailed knowledge of the period to convert shadowy figures like the saintly Henry VI, his vitriolic French wife, the Duke of York, Warwick the Kingmaker and others into the flesh-and-blood portraits Mr. Powlett-Jones has drawn for us. He has brought to this thinly chronicled period a searchlight that reveals some of the motives and methods of power-hungry men, of the kind frequently encountered in later centuries. It is this that makes the book unique. As well as being as exciting as a well-constructed thriller, it is a warning to all men in high positions who allow personal ambition and pride to dominate their lives. Most of them, as we know, came to a very sticky end and Tudor England was the richer for their demise. But, apart from being a cautionary tale, this book is a romance set in the twilight of feudalism. The author is, I suspect, a romantic, who began writing *The Royal Tigress* biased in favour of Lancaster. He ended a dedicated Yorkist. Edward IV, that genial, womanising giant, is seen here as the first modern sovereign of England, and his brother, the much-maligned Richard of Gloucester, as its last warrior king. Between them, the one consciously, the other unconsciously, they prepared the way for modern England.

In addition are portraits of many colourful characters: Margaret herself, indomitable, cruel and always unlucky; Tiptoft, the sadistic scholar, who said to his executioner 'Behead me with three strokes, in honour of the Trinity'; the Kingmaker, playing for high stakes all his life and dying like a gladiator at Barnet and many others. Mr. Powlett-Jones has also taken the trouble to make a study of the military strategy and tactics of the period, supplying us with comprehensive maps of the campaigns. Altogether an extremely readable book and one that can be recommended to student and layman.

Nobody, he thought, could be anything but flattered by Mr. Ellicott's review, and he wondered if he could hope for equally encouraging notices from other papers. It occurred to him then that here, if he was looking for it, was an alternative livelihood. A modest one, perhaps (the agent had warned him he would be very lucky to make four hundred a year from historical biography), but a living on a par with the one he was getting now, and this might mean he could abandon teaching if he felt inclined. It occurred to him also that it was strange he had not yet received advance copies of the book, and thought it possible that the parcel had arrived and was unclaimed in the parcels room.

The mere prospect of touching the book, of feeling it under his hand, sent him down the field at a trot to seek out Heffling, head prefect, and ask for the key of the parcels room. Heffling said, at once, "Sorry about yours, sir . . . it came Friday afternoon and was on Saturday's list, but you were away, so I asked Taylor to leave it at Havelock's. It must have slipped his memory, sir."

"Come along with me and get it, Heffling, for this is a magic moment I must share with somebody. Unless I'm mistaken it's my author's copies, copies of the book I've published on the Wars of the Roses," and Heffling, taken slightly aback, said, "You've actually written a book, sir? A real book?" and David laughed and said, "Real enough in that it represents quarts of midnight oil. I began it before you arrived here in the winter of '25."

It was the books right enough, six of them, clean, crisp and emitting that singular bookish smell everyone here associated with the start of the new school year, when all classes were issued with new exercise books. It was a fatter, heavier book than David had imagined, and the maps and illustrations had reproduced extremely well. Heffling turned the leaves reverently, almost as though he was handling the Book of Kells.

"Gosh, sir," he said, at length, "this'll put Bamfylde on the map, won't it? I mean, the chaps will be tickled to death. Even chaps who think history is a bit of a bore."

It slipped out, a virtual confession that Heffling spent most of David's periods planning the tactics of the next game with Blundell's or Queen's School, Taunton, but Ellicott's review had worked wonders on his goodwill. He said, "Look here, Heffling, you were the first in on this, apart from Mr. Barnaby, who had to remind me I'd written the book at all. Would you like that copy as a keepsake?"

"Me, sir? I'd like that very much, sir!" and then, shyly, "Would you . . . could you *autograph* it, sir?"

"Delighted. Never had the honour before. Here . . ." and he took out his fountain pen and wrote on the flyleaf, "*For George Heffling, presented by the author on the day of publication,*" and signed his name with a flourish. "It isn't strictly true. Official publication day is tomorrow, but what's in a day? Hand me those others. I'm going to autograph copies for Mr. Howarth and Mr. Barnaby, who read it in proof form."

He left Heffling clutching his windfall and carried the books up to his quarters, wishing Grace was around to share his triumph, but she was pony riding on the moor and lunching at Ma Midden's. He signed copies for Barnaby and Howarth, and a third for his mother, who would never read it but would take it up and down the street. Then, just as he was going to seek Howarth, Chris rang, calling from 'The Mitre', the Bilhampton pub.

"Davy? I'm so glad I caught you. I've only got a minute before they pick me up for the motorcade. Motorcade! One Morris, one Austin Seven, and two tradesmen's vans. I just wanted to say thank you . . . thank you for everything, Davy darling, but especially the note you left. I feel much better, honestly. I don't know how I would have coped last night if you hadn't been there. But when I woke up and found you gone, then read your note and had a cup of tea and a serious talk with myself, things seemed different. I'll show these baskets what I'm made of yet!"

It sent his spirits soaring even higher to hear her talk that way. "All you needed was a good sleep."

"Ah," she said, chuckling, "but I wouldn't have had that if it hadn't been for you. They always say it's the best soporific in the world, don't they?"

"No hangover?"

"None. I love you, remember?"

"Good. Then here's something that might send your mercury up another point, as it has mine," and he told her about the review in *The Times*, and the early copies of *The Royal Tigress*.

Her enthusiasm crackled over the line as she said, "But that's wonderful! And to think I never asked about it."

"Don't let that bother you. I'd completely forgotten it myself. Hi, you read all the papers. Will you keep an eye open for other reviews?"

"I'll do better. There are papers right here on the hotel table," and he heard her slam out of the booth and a moment later her voice saying, "I won't have time to read them but I've got the *Chronicle* here, and some others . . . hold on," and he listened, grinning, to a prolonged rustling, ending in a shout, "There's one here! In the *Empire News*, of all papers . . . 'When Knights Were Bold!' What an awful heading! . . . But it's nice. The man seems quite taken by it, says it reads like a thriller."

"That's what Father Times says."

"You'll be famous by tomorrow!"

"Nonsense!" he laughed, "but I must say I'm bowled over by them reviewing it at all. After all, I'm not a professional historian."

"Of course you're a pro if you teach history, then go on to sell it between hard covers. Will you make a lot of money?"

"The publisher says around four hundred if it sells out. A bit more on a reprint."

"This will send your stock soaring at Bamfylde, won't it?"

"I don't quite know, they've never had an author before. But there's another aspect of it, Chris. If I go on to write other books, and I'm sure I could, couldn't I think about doing it full-time? Who gives a damn whether an author is married, single or living in sin?"

She said, in an incisive voice, "Cut that out, Davy! Write as much as you like. Make as much money as you can, and jolly good luck to you. But stay with what you're doing. I know you far better than you know yourself, and you wouldn't enjoy doing anything else, no matter how successful you were. They're paging me now, darling. I can't stay, except to say thank you over and over again, and how terribly pleased I am for you. Goodbye, darling, darling Davy."

She rang off and he sat there with one hand holding the receiver, the other resting on the small pile of books, considering the unequivocality of her advice, and wondering how she could be so sure of his vocation when she was not in the least sure of her own. She had predecessors in this field. Both Beth and Julia Darbyshire had given him the same advice, and usually, when the ride was smooth, he found himself in agreement with them. But four years under Alcock had gone some way towards undermining his confidence. Now he was not at all sure. It would depend, he supposed, on how Bamfylde lurched into the new year, when the Governors met again to fill the vacuum. Until then there seemed no profit in seeking a hard decision. It was a time, surely, to drift along with the tide.

He went over to the bookcase and pulled out a copy of *Who's Who*, thumbing through the flimsy leaves until he located 'Ellicott, John Ernest; historian and author . . .' with a long list of books to his credit. He even recognised the title of one that he had read and enjoyed. "So much for chaps who write books," he said aloud. "I didn't even remember the author's name," and for some reason this made him chuckle. He put two copies of the book in his bookcase between Oman and Macaulay, picked up those destined for Barnaby and Howarth, and went down the stairs whistling. "Queer that," he thought, as he crossed the empty quad on his way to relieve Barnaby. "I often used to whistle my way down these steps in Algy's day, but I stopped doing it when Alcock took over. Maybe it's the end of the tunnel."

Chapter Four

He had no difficulty in recognising the pattern. Ever since he climbed the winding road from Bamfylde Bridge Halt for the very first time, it had forever reasserted itself, a personal within a national cycle, so that he could always see Bamfylde and the outside world as reflections of one another, hope countering disappointment, slump following boom, pain giving way to pleasure, failure to modest triumph.

The term, after such a gloomy start, was settling down to a minor boom, with Bamfylde back on course under Algy's caretaker administration, with the surprising success of the book and the queer, quirkish satisfaction that it brought when he realised staff and boys took pride in his achievement. And after that, in mid-October, Chris's amazing rally in South Mendips, where she too made headlines, with her unexpectedly high turnout against impossible odds, the Liberal pushed into third place, and a total of eleven thousand, four hundred and two votes.

There had never been the slightest hope of victory. All over the country Labour strongholds were falling, as the electorate opted for business as usual (whatever that meant) and the economies of the 'National' government were approved by all who were not directly savaged by them. The Government was back with four hundred and ninety-nine seats, Labour losing a total of two hundred and thirteen, including those of thirty-four ex-ministers. Socialism was in retreat everywhere and yet, in South Mendips, that had returned a Tory by mammoth majorities ever since the earliest days of extended suffrage, a slip of a girl beat the Liberal by over a thousand votes and cut the overall Tory majority by fifteen hundred.

He phoned the day after the election to congratulate her, finding that she was naïvely proud of her achievement. "It's almost as good as being elected," she told him excitedly, and added that she had had a telegram of congratulations from Transport House, together with a promise that they would set about finding her a constituency where her chances of getting elected would be appreciably improved.

"Will you accept, after so much groundwork right where you are?" and she said she would think about it, for that, after all, was politics.

After that the term slipped by, with nothing much to distinguish it from any other term this time of year. The weather worsened. Flurries of sleet slashed down from the moor, and all the lanes following the river valleys became shin-deep in red porridge, making it impossible for leaders to maintain average times during the runs. David still went out with them, arriving back in the quad in the winter twilight wet through and plastered from head to foot with Exmoor mud. The area between the rugby posts became a quagmire, scrums slithering across in a mad, splashing frolic whenever the weaker side lost anchorage in the mire. Sometimes you could hardly follow a game through the curtain of mud and every other pass was fumbled as the threequarters dropped the soggy ball. Then the frost came, with every hedgerow hawthorn bush transformed into a chandelier, and a cloud of breath rising over the house warm-up runs like vapour over cattle, and everyone blowing on his hands and jostling for seats nearest to the defective hot-water pipes, that gurgled like a gourmand's belly, giving the professional time-wasters any amount of excuses to practise their craft.

Coxe, inspirer of Towser's headboard, found a half-frozen blackbird up in the planty and restored to it the power of flight. The sick-room was full, the matron irritably busy. Skelton, notable cricketer, left at very short notice to take a job in Christchurch,

New Zealand, embarrassing himself and everybody else by piping his eye at a farewell supper in Nicolson's. Barnaby sympathised. "Poor chap's been here since he was nine. As a Sunsetter, it's the only home he's ever known. Must be damned frightening being uprooted by a telegram, and sent halfway across the world to muddle along among strangers." Barnaby was more discerning, David thought, than most people would have you believe.

Heffling, poor wight, broke a wrist when tackled by the visiting full back on frozen ground far out on the touchline, and had to be driven to hospital over treacherous roads by Molyneux—the small change of a term, but the big pay-off was on its way so far as David was concerned. In the last week of term, while David was superintending the unblocking of a frozen drain in the forecourt, he saw Sir Rufus Creighton drive up in his Daimler and give him a distant nod, descending a moment later to make his way into the head's house without a backward glance.

He thought, "That old brown nut still has it in for me, despite his qualified support the day Alcock died—probably regards me as responsible for it, the way I did myself when it happened," but then Algy bobbed out, pink-cheeked and excited, saying, "Leave that infernal drain, P.J.! Let the outside staff see to it. Chairman wants a word with you. I'll get Rigby to bring in coffee at breaktime and rejoin you then."

"Hi, wait! What's this in aid off?" he demanded, but Algy was giving nothing away. "Not my pigeon," he said, "I'm only the caretaker here, old son!" and skipped away, moving, David thought, more like a first-termer trying to keep the blood circulating than a parson in his seventies.

*   *   *

Sir Rufus was seated in what Algy called 'The Privileged Culprit's Chair', at angles to the study desk. It was a chair covered with petit-point, used by parents, members of the staff being consulted, and seniors being lectured by the head. Junior or Middle School defaulters were never asked to sit in here. "They wouldn't know what to do with their hands and feet," Algy had once told him. "They much prefer to face the music standing." The old judge still looked like Buddha, his smooth brown flesh stretched tightly over his skull, his mottled hands tidily folded, as in prayer or meditation. The mark of his years in the East lurked in posture and sunken eyes. He said, quietly, "Take a seat, Powlett-Jones. Behind the desk, please." Then, surprisingly, "Do you smoke?"

"Yes, Sir Rufus."

"Try one of these? Burmese. I indulge once a day, after dinner. One now would give me heartburn. I have them sent, you know, in boxes of one hundred. All the way from Rangoon."

David accepted one of his cheroots and found it very strong. Sir Rufus, who seemed in no hurry, waited for it to draw. "Well?"

"It's . . . er . . . very good, Sir Rufus."

"I think so. Never could be bothered with whiffs. If you like to smoke then smoke the leaf, as God intended. Don't poison yourself with chemical products, hashed up in Nottingham or Bristol." He paused, looking down at his brown, wrinkled hands, splashed with age spots. Then, raising his head, "When Herries retired a few years ago you had hopes of succeeding him, I recall?"

"No real hope, sir."

"But you applied."

"I was talked into it."

"Indeed? By whom? By Herries?"

"Not really. By Brigadier Cooper for one, by Mr. Howarth for another. But I realise now that I applied against my better judgment."

"You wouldn't back yourself to take over here?"

It took him getting on for a minute to absorb the shock. Then he said, carefully, "It isn't that, sir. But I see, looking back, that my original application was a brash gesture on my part. I had only been teaching for nine years, and needed a great deal more experience."

"I see. And now?"

He smiled. "Well, I've had four years' more experience. And I'm that much older and wiser."

The little man pondered a moment. Then, with the greatest deliberation, he drew a folded sheet of paper from his inside pocket and spread it out on his knees. With a sense of shock David recognised it as Alcock's unfinished letter. Sir Rufus said, "Dr. Willoughby passed it to me. It was correct of you to give it to him. Some men, I think, would have hesitated to do that in the circumstances."

"I was tempted myself, sir."

"Ah, I daresay. However, it tells us a good deal, I think."

"Sir?"

"I don't see why I shouldn't be as frank with you as you have been with me. I consider we made a haphazard choice as regards Mr. Alcock. We shirked the issue. We owed it to everyone to take more time to probe a little deeper. Do you blame yourself for his death in any way?"

"A little. I was clearly a contributory factor."

"That's nonsense, Powlett-Jones, and I believe Dr. Willoughby told you so at the time."

"Yes, he did."

"Well, then, oblige me by putting it out of mind. Alcock was a very sick man and deliberately concealed the fact. The point is, how would you feel about taking over as deputy here? Until the next full meeting of the Board in March?"

"Deputy? You mean, take Mr. Herries's place for the time being?"

"Not exactly. To deputise with confirmation in mind. As a near-certainty, I should add."

It had come. After all this time. Right out of the blue, on a frosty December morning, getting on for fourteen years since he had first sat in this room, and shared Algy's sorrow over the slaughter of the 1913 Fifteen. He was lost for words. His hands shook a little, reminding him again of that first interview, half a lifetime ago it seemed. Before Beth. Before Chris. Before Alcock and the dragging weight of Alcock's corpse in his arms. He stammered, at last, "I . . . I'd like that more than anything in the world, Sir Rufus. It's extremely kind of you to make the offer."

"It isn't an offer in that sense. I can't make it official. You realise that, I hope?"

"Naturally, sir."

"It would have to have the full approval of the Governing Body. But . . ." he came as near to smiling as was possible with that taut, brown skin—"I have a feeling that could be managed. With tact and gentle persuasion. I'll go farther and risk getting myself into a scrape. In your place, Powlett-Jones, I would take it as read. Take over from today and see the term out. I'll accept full responsibility for that. But first, are there any conditions on your part?"

"Conditions?"

"Preferences, then?"

He suddenly realised there was one. "I'd like to go on teaching, sir, other obligations permitting. The Upper School at least. And perhaps one period a week in Middle and Lower Schools. I would confine myself to current affairs."

"That could be arranged. We should have to get a junior for history, of course. Anything else?"

"I . . . er . . . don't know exactly how to put this, sir, or not without seeming presumptuous. I'm sure you must be aware of my political outlook. I wouldn't preach it in class. I never have, or only in the very broadest sense, despite anything you might have heard to the contrary. But I do have to feel free as regards my deep personal convictions. I said nothing about them at the time because they seemed to me irrelevant, but there was friction concerning them between Mr. Alcock and myself, especially after I appeared on a Socialist platform a hundred miles from here."

Sir Rufus placed his finger-tips together. "I know about that. I wouldn't be much of a Chairman if I didn't, would I? But we're looking for someone who cares more deeply for the school than any segment or faction in the world outside. I have it in mind that is true of you. Isn't that so?"

"Yes, it is."

"I also happen to know how you came by those convictions, Powlett-Jones, and they seem relevant to me. In fact, I tell myself that had I been reared in a Welsh valley, and seen my father and brothers sacrificed to industrial greed, then I would have gone through life as a militant radical. More militant than you, probably. It's mostly a matter of milieu, and mine happened to be different. Cushioned . . . very conformist. But a judge learns to evaluate each factor objectively. Speaking personally, all I would require is a pledge that you don't embarrass us on home ground. What you do well beyond that, in the exercising of your democratic privilege, is entirely your own concern. You're a free-born Englishman—I beg your pardon, Welshman. Many good Welshmen have sacrificed their lives for the liberty of conscience you demand. Who am I to deny it?" He paused, as though to give David time to digest this, but went on, "I'm more than twice your age, Powlett-Jones. I'm older even than Herries, and I've seen a great deal in my time. Tyrannies overthrown, new ones set up. The ebb and flow of reforms and repressions in many parts of the world. I have few real convictions left, but I can think of one.

415

This country, although it still has a great deal to learn, is the flower of the flock as regards the theory and practice of maintaining a free society. Its party politics, to me, are a charade. They have a part to play in the democratic process but they remain a charade. This is going to be a stormy decade, and will almost certainly end in a drawing together of all shades of political opinion, here in Britain at least. At a time like this we need flexibility, particularly if our work takes us among growing boys, with their way to make in the world. I think you're flexible enough. More flexible than most. There's the bell. I believe Herries promised us some coffee."

"Rigby is brewing it now, sir."

"Good. Then I think I'll break my rule and smoke one of those cheroots of mine," and he took out his worn leather cigar-case, snipped the end with a cutter and lit up, blowing a thin stream of smoke towards Alcock's freshly distempered ceiling. "This is a pleasant room," he said. "I've always thought so. But its original atmosphere needs replacing, wouldn't you say?"

"Yes, Sir Rufus, and I have plans for it."

Algy bustled in after a perfunctory knock, carrying the coffee tray. On his heels came Rigby, with a bottle of Old Boys' sherry, miraculously restored to the cellarette in the parlour. "Had a notion we should want to drink a toast," he said. "Pour it, Rigby, there's a good chap. Do you remember that toast we drank in the parlour to your twins, P.J.? My word, that was a turn-up for the Bamfylde book! Won't happen again in my lifetime."

With a kind of wonder David watched him hand round the coffee while Rigby, ceremonious as a small-town mayor, filled the sherry glasses.

2

There was a price, of course. He was under no illusions regarding that, and was called upon to pay the first instalment only a week or two later, when, on Christmas Eve, he met Chris by appointment outside Piccadilly Underground, and took her to dinner at a restaurant Howarth had introduced to him years ago, a quiet place off Leicester Square, renowned for its cuisine.

It had been a hectic eight days, with the school breaking up, the Sunsetters' Christmas to be arranged, Grace to convey to

Elmer's End (it was Grannie Marwood's 'turn' that year), and all manner of plans sketched out pending his return to school the day after Boxing Day, for he wanted plenty of time to work on his blueprints.

It was a notable end-of-term, one of the liveliest he remembered, as he stood on the steps of the head's house in the forecourt, and watched the school bone-shaker take its final load down to the station at the tail of a procession of private cars, driven by parents who had called to collect their sons. Trunks and hand luggage were trundled out, roped and labelled, the turmoil beginning before it was light, with any number of mufflered boys coming and going, shouting their usual farewell quips.

"Have a good hols, sir!"

"Don't forget matron's present, sir!" Matron was getting married, late in life, and the boys had collected for a leaving present she was unable to accept in person.

"I'm going to miss Grace like nobody's business, sir!"—this from Sax Hoskins, who was also leaving them, and finally Heffling, shaking hands with his left because of his plastered wrist, "I've persuaded the pater to let me stay on until July, sir. Wrote the day I heard what had happened. I had to bluff. He thinks I'm dead set on having another go at the Cambridge but it's the cricket really, sir."

It was touching, he thought, how they had all seemed to come alive again and that within an hour of the news leaking that he would be taking over, and he wondered, a little anxiously, if he would be able to justify their ebullience and goodwill, or whether, once they had adapted to his headship, they would begin to keep their distance, as they always had with Alcock. Well, that was up to him, he supposed, and it might be a good idea to regard the term ahead as a honeymoon period. He had his own innovations in mind and not all of them would be popular. Besides, it was well known that he was not yet officially appointed, so they had every right to regard him as a caretaker's caretaker, standing in for Algy, whom many would not recall as the resident occupier of the house at his back.

Grace came down, looking very pretty, he thought, in her Red Riding Hood cape, trimmed with fur. She seemed to have shot from childhood to full girlhood in a term and was growing more like Beth every day. Her limp was almost unnoticeable now, unless you studied her walk from a distance. Sax swore that she could out-foxtrot any of his holiday partners, whereas Winterbourne, who had offered to collect her, and bring her back from Elmer's End on January 14th, the day of reassembly, was enthusiastic concerning her ability to capture a mood of the moor with her brush. "Especially in spring," he told David one night, when they were glancing through her sketches. "You see, she's a spring painter. There's absolute honesty in every sketch she makes between March and June, but after that . . . I don't know . . . she loses the trick. They might be anyone's watercolours."

There was significance here, he supposed. Grace had always seemed a springtime person, ever since he had lifted her from the taxi that brought her back from that Kentish convalescent home five years ago. For him, as for Winterbourne, Hoskins, and even for young Coxe, the embryo vet, she carried the promise of the primrose and the daffodil whenever she moved among all these boisterous young ruffians, indeed, she introduced a little extra fragrance into the place at all seasons of the year, and although he knew it was time she became a weekly boarder over at Challacombe, he still delayed making the change. One of the things he had looked forward to most was a crumpet tea with Grace, when winter dusk was closing in on the moor. He made a rapid check of her exact age as she ran down the steps, carrying a book of patterns she had been inspecting, prior to replacing Alcock's neutral curtains. Eleven years, eight months, from the day he dashed up these same steps in response to Stratton-Forbes' annunciation of her arrival, down at the long-jump pit. She looked older. Around thirteen, he would say, but then, she had always seemed mentally and physically mature after that tight-rope walk between life and death when she was a mite of five.

She said, in between his farewells of boys, "Never mind them a minute, Daddy. This is most important. Rigby is going to order the curtains for us when he goes into Challacombe tomorrow. Which do you prefer? I've pinned back the two I like best, the rose pink and the primrose yellow."

"Primrose yellow," he said without hesitation. "It's you, Grace."

She ran up the steps again and he resumed his farewells. It was going to take a lot of getting used to, this ordering and rearranging of what he never ceased to think of as Algy Herries's house. The last car sped away, its tyres scattering gravel. A few Sunsetters (they always looked forlorn at this moment of term) emerged from Big School arch with a ball for a puntabout, and he spared them a sympathetic thought, boys with parents at the ends of the earth, thinking of them no doubt at this time of year. Then he remembered that Barnaby, who was spending Christmas at school, had promised to take them all into Challacombe to see a gangster picture at the Capitol Cinema this afternoon, and bent his mind to his own affairs. They promised to keep him pretty well occupied until he left for town on the twenty-third.

*   *   *

She looked her usual, pert self as she emerged from the Regent Street exit at six o'clock sharp on Christmas Eve. She had bought herself a pair of Russian calf boots and they looked very fetching on her long, pretty legs. She had matched them with a Cossack-type hat, perched at an angle, so that he thought, "She looks more like a well-heeled Tory's wife than the only Socialist candidate to emerge with credit from that shambles", and told her so, as soon as she had kissed him.

"Thank you, sir. Very civil of you, sir! I've never actually kissed a headmaster before, although I had my bottom pinched by one in Yorkshire. 'The Octopus' we used to call him at Chapel. You look pretty spry yourself, Davy darling. Where do we celebrate? I'm going to drink half a bottle of champagne tonight, I promise you!"

They walked along Coventry Street to Leicester Square and all the way she held his arm, her touch giving their relationship a permanence it had not had on earlier occasions. Her conversation was sustained but brittle, a shade too chirpy, he thought, and this was confirmed two hours later, when the cadaverous waiter, who had been hovering about them all evening, bustled away to attend to a stage party in the far corner of the room.

"You've got something to tell me yourself," he said. "You've been saving it for the right moment," and suddenly she looked disconcerted and said, staring hard at her glass, "Yes, I have, but I should have known one can't keep guilty secrets from old Pow-Wow. It's a plan, at least, you could think of it as that. It might help. I don't know. It'll depend on you, I suppose. Like everything else in the end."

He said, dismally, "Let's hear it. At least we've wined and dined."

"It's two things, really, one hinging on the other. One is an offer I've had—no, not of a good constituency, but an exchange, under a Labour Party Educational Trust, the Jesmond Foundation. I've been selected as the likeliest young hopeful to take advantage of a year at Montreal University. They have very advanced syllabuses over there—far wider in scope than most of ours. I'm told I could get a Canadian degree in a year. Not that that means much in academic terms, but from the practical viewpoint it could do me a lot of good, and give me the edge on most candidates. Providing I emerged with credit."

The prospect of not seeing her for a year dismayed him. In the months ahead he was going to need her as much as she had needed him before the election.

"How do *you* feel about it? Honestly. No hedging."

"I should enjoy it, if I could separate it from you, Davy."

"But we can't separate it, can we?"

"It might be wise to try. At least for a year."

"Say exactly what's in your mind."

"You know what's in my mind. What's been in my mind concerning you for long enough. The plain truth is, Davy, you simply can't risk an affair with me. I believe you know that but won't face it. Not that I blame you. I have enough trouble doing it myself."

"Hasn't it occurred to you that you might be exaggerating the risks?"

"No. It hasn't and it won't. Listen here, Davy. I'll draw a picture for you. We go on seeing one another—not as close friends, that's quite another thing, but as lovers. Okay, we're careful. We keep a sharp lookout. We only meet in out-of-the-way places. That's a dreary enough prospect, but we'd cope, I daresay, until the unlucky moment. Don't say it mightn't come because it would. Hundreds of boys pass through your hands. Sooner or later we'd run into one and he'd talk. 'Hi, Porky, what do you know? I ran into old Pow-Wow with that cousin of Ridgeway's. He's doing okay. They were staying as man and wife at the same hotel!' The snippet is relayed and sooner or later a parent comes to hear of it. She passes it on, and it gets expanded a little. 'But I *know* her! A married girl, with a husband somewhere, the one who turned her back on her family to stand as a Socialist. Of course, Powlett-

Jones is that way himself, isn't he?' From there it's anybody's guess. All I know is that it would damage you, might even bring you down, seeing that all Bamfylde parents are Tories. Do you want me to let my imagination run ahead?"

"No," he said, "there's something in what you say. I'd be a fool to deny it."

"Well, then . . ."

"That's the rub, Chris, the 'Well, then . . . ?' What are you really saying? That now I'm acting head of Bamfylde, with every prospect of it being made official, we should stop seeing one another? Break it off? Finish?"

She said, tracing a pattern in breadcrumbs, "I'm saying we should give this break we've both had a fair chance. For a year at any rate. You won't miss me nearly as much as you think you will. You'll be fully stretched in that job."

"And you?"

"I'll get by."

"And a year from now?"

"All kinds of things can happen in a year. A year ago we hadn't even met."

"You said something about a plan."

"A sort of plan. It's sheer coincidence this offer leads to Canada. Rowley was still in Canada the last time I heard."

"Where does that take us? Assuming he's still there, and assuming you get to see him and talk to him?"

"I don't know, Davy. How could I know? It's getting on for three years since I set eyes on him."

"I know, Chris. You could sue him after seven. That's four years from now, and God knows how long after that the divorce comes along. I'll be forty and you'll be over thirty. You once mentioned children."

"Don't make it harder, Davy."

"Is that possible?"

"Yes, it is possible. You've got what you've always wanted and worked for, and I'm making progress. How many can say as much in their mid-thirties and late twenties?"

"It isn't enough. Not for me."

"It'll have to be, Davy. At least for the time being. Deep down you know that."

The sparkle had gone from the evening. Across the restaurant the stage party was erupting. Jokes and laughter emerged from it and the place was filling with customers, most of them oiled with Christmas cheer. Gloominess invaded him, making objective thought and discussion all but impossible. First Beth, then Alcock and now this. And away behind that a serious-eyed boy coming home with his satchel, to be told at a street corner that his father and two brothers had died underground. And after that the trenches. Three unspeakable years of trudging to and fro across a desolate swamp, three years of seeing friends torn and mutilated. When the hell did life settle and lie on an even keel? When could a man hope to enjoy the fruits of personal fulfilment, of the kind he had glimpsed so briefly, in the early days of his marriage? He said, beckoning the waiter, "What choice do I have? What choice do I ever have?" and she said, "How about me, Davy?"

"You're making the decision."

"No, I'm not, circumstances are. All I'm doing is facing them. Or trying to, and you aren't helping much. It isn't like you. I always took you for a fighter."

"I'm bloody well sick of fighting. Sick to death of it. Some way this has to be resolved. If it isn't we'll drift apart." He remembered Howarth, husked and emotionally sterile at fifty, showing him that photograph of Amy Crispin, the day he received her legacy. Well, he could level with Howarth at around forty. He, too, would have photographs tucked away in a drawer, one of Beth, one of her. Three, if you counted Julia Darbyshire.

"I'll write," she said, "often, and telling you everything. It's the best of a bad job."

"Yes, it is," he said, "but you've got more guts than I have. Or maybe less need."

"Need? No, Davy, we're even on that score. God knows, there have been times lately when I would have risked everything to spend one night in your arms. That night before the election was only one of them."

"It's more than that with me. That way a man can manage. Howarth has, and Barnaby has or seems to. Even I did for a long time after Beth. It's sharing, unloading, talking things out with someone who matters, understands. I'm supposed to do all that on paper from here on. Indefinitely."

"Not indefinitely, Davy. Only until you've had a sporting chance

to concentrate on something you love. You think of me as important and so I am, but not so important as that."

They left it there. She was staying in the flat of a university
friend at Cricklewood. There was no question of them going there,
and none of taking her home to the Marwoods, at Elmer's End.
They could book in somewhere, but he did not fancy Grace waking on Christmas morning and asking where he was. She walked
him down to Charing Cross, saying she could get a bus or tube any
old time. In forty-eight hours he would be on his way back to
Bamfylde and she, he supposed, would be making ready for the
Canadian adventure. At the barrier he kissed her, noticing that
her cheeks were wet and that she had difficulty in speaking. Compassion, of the kind he had felt for her after that rowdy meeting,
returned to him.

"It's still a case of hanging on, of waiting for the next spin of
the wheel. I can't say any more just now. Will you be going back
to Bilhampton before you take off?"

"If I do I'll ring. I'll ring, anyway, wherever I am. I can cope
when you're at a distance."

He left her then, sensing that she preferred it, but knowing that
she was watching him move along the platform to catch yet
another train. Bamfylde, like Paris, he had once told her, was worth
a mass. But was it, now that he had it under his hand?

* * *

He was able, to his own surprise, to keep thoughts of her at a
safe distance during the next few weeks. Bamfylde engulfed him
like a long, rumbling avalanche, a clamorous torrent of letters, decisions, long- and short-term plans, the least of which was that
perennial bugbear of the schoolmaster, the timetable.

Throughout the early part of January he worked alone, spending
long hours in Algy's old study. When he could escape he set out on
tours that took him into every nook and cranny of the great sprawling place, noting down its deficiencies, conjuring with changes,
adjustments and adaptations, and getting an inspiration now and
again from all he saw and remembered.

One came when he turned out the contents of Alcock's study
cupboard and came across the cane he had inherited from Algy.
He tossed it aside, with a pile of other rubbish. There would be

no question of him beating mischief out of Bamfeldians. He made up his mind as to that long ago. Neither Algy nor Alcock, to do them justice, had been floggers, in the old tradition of headmasters and towards the end of his long reign Algy had all but discarded corporal punishment, but the right to beat Junior and Middle School boys was still reserved by senior prefects. Alcock had preferred outright expulsion for what he regarded as major crimes, and subtle humiliations for minor infringements.

David, over the years, had given a good deal of thought to the maintenance of discipline, accepting the fact that it wasn't something to which spot decisions could be applied. Every boy varied as did every offence to some extent. What he aimed at—an ideal, he supposed—was the maximum use of the average boy's response to fair play, to seeing authority's point of view, accepting reproof and apologising with good grace. But every now and again one ran across a boy totally unresponsive to this approach. Then, if one ruled out corporal punishment, what did one do? How did one safeguard the system?

He came up with an experimental idea, one that seemed worth exploring. The institution of a forum of peers, based on where the culprit was lodged. Several such committees might be set up, with jurors voted in, term by term, by boys themselves, sitting under the chairmanship of the current house prefect. As to penalties, here again he opposed the principle of boy beating boy, any boy. In a majority of cases it didn't matter a jot but if the boy at the receiving end was sensitive, or the prefect at the distributing end a bully, it could do untold harm. The whole thing was too fallible and in its place there would have to be a range of sanctions, all the way from the withdrawal of privileges to a vote of censure, expressing disapproval of the majority. It was an idea that Barnaby, with his easy access to the wisdom of the Ancients, might find workable and he made a note of it in his memoranda book.

Scores of random thoughts were finding their way into what Grace was already calling The-Book-From-Which-There's-No-Rubbing-Out. A resolve to tap Old Boys' funds for a gymnasium to replace the old covered playground. An additional classroom block, abutting Big School, that would, in itself, greatly simplify the timetable. Concrete litter disposal units designed to put an end to those stinking bonfires Westacott was always building down by the piggeries. Revival of the Choral Society, that had languished under Alcock. Upgrading of the Owl Society into a Sixth Form Club. Studies, if they could be squeezed in somewhere, for the Upper Fifth. A thorough turnout and restocking of the library. And, with Algy's help, revival of the annual Gilbert and Sullivan opera, an event that had never failed to fill a vacuum in the Michaelmas term, when the days were at their shortest and the evenings not wholly devoted to prep.

Prep was another aspect of the system he hoped to revise. He had unpleasant memories of homework in his Grammar School days, of sitting hunched in the fireless parlour with a mountain of work to get through, and organised periods of evening prep such as existed in the routine of most boarding schools, had been an improvement on this. It had its faults, however, especially in summer term. It might be an improvement to introduce a period-length spell of early morning prep, between April and July, and possibly through the first weeks of the Michaelmas term. Thus evening prep would be shortened, and boys freed for communal activities, not necessarily aligned with sport.

There were, he soon discovered, whole new vistas to be explored, and much would depend on available funds, no doubt. He had no more than a working knowledge of the school's finances, and a a talk with Redcliffe, the bursar, proved depressing.

"We've always run on a tight budget," Redcliffe said. "So tight that I confess I was frightened when I took over from Mr. Shawn, early last year. The fees are too low, if you want my opinion, Headmaster."

It would take time, he thought, to adjust to this form of address. Somehow he was unable to rid himself of the notion that his leg was being pulled. He said, "There's no need to call me 'Headmaster' when we're alone, Redcliffe. I know Alcock insisted on it but I don't. Will you pass that around? It's embarrassing to have to tell everyone separately."

Redcliffe, a young, eager man, looked flustered but said, with a smile, "Er . . . what exactly do we call you, sir?"

"Well, it can hardly be what every boy from the Second Form up calls me behind my back and the Old Boys to my face, Pow-Wow, that is. How about taking a tip from Barnaby and Howarth? They've settled for P.J. and it looks to me as if you and I have got a lot of conspiratorial work ahead of us. Do you think the majority of parents would stand for a hoist in fees?"

"Yes, I do," Redcliffe said, unequivocally. "It would be a matter for the Governors and would need the approval of the Ministry, of course, but there wouldn't be much difficulty. I could prepare a case for you."

"You do that," David said, "and we'll try it on the dog later in the term. Let me have a look at the waiting-list."

The waiting-list was even more depressing, the lowest, according to Redcliffe's summary, since 1921. The graph had risen steadily up to a peak in 1929, the second year of Alcock's administration, but then, just as Howarth had predicted, Bamfylde had begun to feel the pinch of the Depression. There had been a slow falling off in 1930, and a steep plunge in 1931. This would have to be considered in relation to any proposed increase in fees.

Already he had learned the trick of dividing his problems into categories of the kind that encouraged the enlistment of one confidant, selected in advance. Thus, major changes such as those he was now discussing with Redcliffe, demanded the shrewdness and experience of Howarth, but what he thought of as climatic changes, like a new approach to discipline, demanded the more flexible approach of a mind like Barnaby's. He soon made a friend of the newly appointed music master, Renshaw-Smith, whom he tackled about the revitalisation of the Choral Society.

Renshaw-Smith, a young man with a narrow face, thinning hair and a sharp, predatory nose, always put him in mind of a fledgling sparrow-hawk, but although shy and inclined to be self-effacing, he responded to encouragement. When David told him of his intentions he said, eagerly, "That's good news, Headmaster. We've some very promising trebles and at least two good tenors. I was wondering, would you think it too ambitious to start training a choir for the Devon Musical Festival, in April? At my last school we won high placings, although of course, we had girls there, Melbourne House being co-ed. I really would like to try."

"Try by all means," David told him. "You'll have the whole of the Lent term to bring them on. Who is your best tenor, by the way?"

"Dobson, without a doubt, and keen to improve."

"Really? I would have said he was the hairy outdoor type but I'll tell you why I asked. I'm hoping to revive the annual Gilbert and Sullivan. We were famous for them in Mr. Herries's time. Would Gilbert and Sullivan be too lowbrow for you?"

Renshaw-Smith looked shocked. "No, indeed, Headmaster. Sullivan wrote some excellent light music, and I know about the Bamfylde operas. I've seen the photographs and old scores. Mr. Gibbs gave them to me."

"Would you enjoy getting some kind of orchestra together for a production next December? It's a chore, I warn you. We hold the auditions in summer, and rehearse every night throughout Michaelmas term."

"I should enjoy it. I found time hang rather heavily last term. You see, Melbourne House was close to Bristol, and I had most of my evenings free. I miss the opportunity of getting to a concert now and again and this place . . . well, it is something of a wilderness, isn't it?"

"It's seemed that way lately," David said, "but it never did in Herries's time. We made our own entertainment and a lot of it was very stimulating. I'm going to do my damnedest to start everything up again, but I should have to rely on your help, Renshaw-Smith."

"Oh, but you can," Renshaw-Smith said, seeming to peck with excitement, and David left him, wondering if he knew the boys referred to him as 'Pecker' and had done, since the day of his arrival.

He went next to Howarth to discuss finance in relation to building plans. "I don't intend to tinker, like the Stoic. I've always believed in Rothschild's dictum—'Buy on a falling market'. With a shrinking waiting-list we need to offer something extra, and get plans for an extension into the new prospectus. God knows, that old one needs rewriting. It always reminds one of a spa holiday guide, about the time of Victoria's Jubilee."

"And we thought of the Noble Stoic as a new broom," Howarth said, wryly. "Well, I'm with you by and large. You recall I foresaw this shortage of cash reacting on us, but don't talk to me about retrenchment. I never did trust that word. It's usually a sluggard's euphemism for parsimony and cowardice. Still, it all comes down to cash in the end, and how the devil do you hope to raise the ten thousand or more that a new classroom block and gymnasium will cost you?"

"From the Old Boys. There's a couple of thousand in the kitty.

It's been accumulating and I'm planning a big appeal next Whit-sun, when I can corner more than a hundred O.B.s at their annual meeting."

"You honestly believe you can squeeze eight thousand pounds out of Old Boys? Good God, man, half of them are still looking for jobs, or living on their parents' fat. Boyer, for instance, he's still on his uppers, isn't he?"

Boyer was, or more or less. He had come down with a good enough degree two years ago but had since had to make do with starveling appointments in private schools. He wrote, from time to time, but he had not revisited the school and David had the impression he would find it difficult to scrape together the rail fare from the far north. He said, "I'll get the money somehow but it would help if you took over as O.B. secretary. I've been doing it for six years now, and no complaints, but I don't see how I can combine it with the headship. After all, Howarth, who was it pushed me into this job in the first place?"

"Me," said Howarth, with one of his frosty smiles, "but my sponsorship went off at half-cock. I don't mind admitting I had nothing whatever to do with this latest turn-up. That was all Algy's doing, or Algy's and Doc Willoughby's."

"Willoughby got at Sir Rufus?"

"How do you think our respected Chairman came by that bit of evidence you pocketed from Alcock's desk, the night he died? Willoughby took it to Algy and they hatched the plot between them. They asked Sir Rufus over to dinner, filled him with old port, and set him to work on the waverers. But for God's sake don't let them know I told you and don't thank Willoughby your-self. He's like me that way. Feels a damned fool if he's caught out doing a good turn."

They began to fit together all the pieces of the jigsaw that had been assembling from the moment of Alcock's death, but it seemed unlikely now that he would ever know just how the final picture emerged as a likeness of himself. Howarth was right, how-ever, it would never do to probe too deeply. All the same, the in-formation made him glow a little. It meant that he had the full trust of at least two dedicated Bamfeldians apart from Howarth's steady patronage.

He said, "I always knew you approved, Howarth, but how does old Barnaby feel about it. After all, he's senior to me, and was piqued when I pipped him as housemaster?" but Howarth said, "Barnaby's purring, so leave him be. He's happy enough. A house is as much as he cares to handle. Besides, he's like me. Too idle to envy you your job. It wouldn't surprise me if, in a year or so, we didn't start wishing to God that you'd run out of steam."

"Will you take over that Old Boys' job *pro tem?*"

"Just long enough to tide you over. Then one of the younger chaps can have it, and I'll put my feet up until I retire. Only another four years, thank God."

"I can't imagine this place without your crustiness to give it savour. What will you do then, Howarth?"

"Go abroad and die in the sun," Howarth said. "I often ask myself why the devil a sane man, with money in the bank, should spend eight months of the year with his coat collar up and his toes to a gas-fire."

*   *   *

He shelved his forum idea for the time being. It needed more thought, and he was not yet ready to take either Barnaby or Howarth into his confidence. Instinct told him that he would need to win over some of the younger masters, especially Scott, a stern disciplinarian, who had come to them from a prestigious school to replace Carter on the science side and take his place as Outram's housemaster. Scott was forty-eight, and a cut above their usual replacements. He was here, it was said, because of his chest, that played him up in the damp Thames valley, and a somewhat prickly little man. The best approach to him, David thought, would be a juicy carrot in the form of an improved laboratory, and science was low on his list of priorities just now.

There was one other thing, however, concerning which he consulted nobody. The night before the new term began he checked through his records and traced Hislop's home number, for Hislop, penalised for straightforwardness over the loss of his illgotten gains as school bookmaker, was still on his conscience.

The shrewish voice of Mrs. Hislop answered the phone and he was glad it was her and not Hislop's father. He said, "Mrs. Hislop? It's Powlett-Jones, calling from Bamfylde. You remember me, I hope?"

"I remember you, Mr. Powlett-Jones. I remember everything about that disgraceful business."

"It's about your boy I'm ringing. It may sound presumptuous on my part, but is there any chance of him wanting to return here? He's still only sixteen plus, isn't he? Of course, if you've got him in elsewhere he'll probably be better off where he is, but I'm acting headmaster and I'd like to have him back, if he wants to come."

He heard her sharp intake of breath and waited, letting the prospect of a fresh start for Hislop make its impact. Then she said, "You mean that? You . . . *want* him back?"

"Yes, I do, Mrs. Hislop. You may remember I thought he had been very unfairly dealt with by Mr. Alcock but I could put that right now, providing he undertook to work, and toe the line generally. I always did believe in him."

"Thank you," she said, and then, after a long pause, "He's with a private tutor. He seems keen to study for a short-service commission in the Air Force. That awful business changed him. I don't mean for the worse, maybe the opposite, but well . . . he's never been quite the boy he was when it happened."

"Would you like to discuss it with him? He could go into the Lower Fifth, and I'd keep a sharp eye on him until he settled down. I know he was happy here."

"I don't need to discuss it with him," she said, "although of course I will. I know he would like to come back, particularly under you. He came to understand precisely how you were placed, and that things were very difficult for you at the time."

" 'Difficult' is an understatement, Mrs. Hislop. I came close to getting sacked myself more than once. Can I take it that he'll come then?"

"Yes. When exactly?"

"Right away if you can arrange it. It doesn't matter if he's a week or so late starting term. Bring him over yourself if you like, and we'll have tea."

"I'd like that. A week, you say? Sunday? That's the best day for me, on account of the business."

"Sunday will be fine. I'll look forward to it."

"Right." And then, with a little difficulty, "I very much appreciate this, Mr. Powlett-Jones, and I know Rex will. Mr. Hislop will stand on his dignity but leave him to me. Goodbye for now."

"Goodbye, Mrs. Hislop."

He rang off, reflecting that one did not always take the privileges of power into consideration, but they were there, as he was beginning to discover. He thought, "I daresay eyebrows will be raised when Hislop shows up but to hell with that. His reinstatement will make Chris chuckle but she at least will approve."

And within hours the shut-down Bamfylde dynamo went into action, with cars and attache-case-carrying railway arrivals, moving up both drives to converge on the grey buildings that sat so incongruously on the ridge, palisaded with leafless trees, moated by seeping fields where veils of mist deadened every sound, converting Bamfylde into a battleship alone in a vast, grey-green sea.

For him there had never been a first day of term like this. It was not merely an occasion for another new boys' tea but an entirely new beginning, with himself feeling rather like Keithley, smallest of the new arrivals, who drifted in at dusk, clutching his overnight case and a plaid rug, and looking as if, given the least excuse, he would drop everything on the study floor and flee across the moor. He said, calling to Grace, "Look after Keithley, Grace, while I check the last batch in. He's come a long way, haven't you, Keithley?"

"Y-yes, sir . . . from Manchester. Change at Bristol," he added, a little pompously.

"By George, that's a long journey for a chap your size! And you made it in one. Bravo! Don't be scared, you're going to like it here, they all do after a day or two, and my daughter will show you the ropes once you've had tea and a warm-up by the fire. He'll be going into Nicolson's, Grace."

"Well, that's a shame," she said. "We've only got three new ones this term, hardly enough for the cake, but Keithley could come, couldn't he?"

"My dear girl, they'll all have to come, not just the Havelock new boys. We can't have the head showing house favourites."

"Havelock's will always be my favourite," she said, but added, doubtless for Keithley's benefit, "Nicolson's is second-best."

He left her then, ministering to the encumbered Keithley, and went out through the quad door to take the first start-of-term callover by lamplight, for the school's generator batteries were not yet fully charged.

Standing there, on the plinth of the Founder's statue, where Keithley and his peers would soon be making their bow, he gripped the clipboard tighter than necessary, aware of an under-swell of emotion and hoping it passed unnoticed by the very few senior boys who would recall Algy Herries standing here, on the first evening of every new term. It was a memorable moment, one to be put under glass, alongside many others—the Kassava brothers, huddled under that dormer window three storeys up; the first overtures of peace between Carter and himself, in the library passage; Algy's white head emerging from the window under the arcade, to demand, of little Daffy Jones, who had won the house match that first spring afternoon, when Ludendorff was still attacking on the Western Front. These memories and many, many others, standing like pennants on a hard-fought battlefield and somehow adjusting to the rhythm of the roll-call, so that he seemed to be checking not merely on the present but also the past. It made him feel much older than thirty-five.

PART SEVEN

Island in a Torrent

Chapter One

1

David Powlett-Jones had always thought of himself as a political animal, and perhaps he was, up to the moment Sir Rufus Creighton offered him the acting headship. After that a streak of parochialism, that had been broadening within him ever since he had been absorbed into Bamfylde, began to spread until the men he had once jested about, stick-in-the-muds like Judy Cordwainer and Rapper Gibbs, became in a sense his prototypes. The overall effect upon him was curious. His personality both narrowed and deepened.

He did not see himself as inward-looking but was honest enough, in reflective moments beside Algy's thinking post, or sitting within earshot of the muted clamour of the quad, to acknowledge a definite shift in the centre of gravity. What happened here under his nose began to assume an importance that someone in close touch with the world outside would have mistaken for extreme insularity.

For a time he resisted it, telling himself that Bamfylde was not really the crossroads of human affairs, that casting round for some means to alleviate little Keithley's homesickness ought not to take precedence over, say, the state of the economy, or the Japanese invasion of Manchuria, but in the end, after a term or two, he had to admit that it did, and soon abandoned any attempt to keep abreast of national and international affairs. Running Bamfylde was a full-time job, even when the parent ship of state was on course. When it looked like foundering, as lately, it was comforting to address himself to the problems at hand and turn his back on the world beyond school bounds.

It was a conscious withdrawal, for the plight of Bamfylde, and the frightful disarray of the world outside, were inseparably linked. His acting headship began at a time when politicians had abandoned all serious attempts to solve the unemployment problem, when processions of sullen men trudged south to the capital to voice their grievances, when America, for so long a country said to be capable of achieving anything, was reeling under the blows dealt by the Wall Street crash of October, 1929, when bizarre adventurers like Ivar Kreuger, Swedish match king, were bankrupting governments, when the optimism of the 'twenties had spent itself and the League of Nations, hope of liberals the world over, was being scuttled by Japan.

These events, remote as most of them were, redounded on Bamfylde, destroying confidence in traditional values and inducing a general shortage of cash. Warned well in advance by the prescient Howarth, David had expected school numbers to fall but the steepness of the drop surprised and dismayed him.

In 1928, shortly after Algy had retired, they had mustered three hundred and ninety-one. By the spring of 1932 they were down to under three hundred, with a greatly reduced waiting-list. Parents, having a hard struggle to make ends meet, tended to encourage boys to leave at seventeen, or even sixteen, instead of letting them progress to the Sixth and move on to university. There were noticeably fewer majors and minors on the roll, for often a father whose eldest son had done well at Bamfylde left younger sons at their local grammar schools. The modest increase in fees was paid but the belt-tightening it produced could be seen in the waiting-list. Indeed, the only marginal advantage gained from the slump was the comparative ease in finding trained servants, or masters with academic qualifications that would have gained them more important appointments in better times.

For all this, he turned away from Baldwin's policy of retrenchment, and was aided and abetted by Algy Herries, to whom he went, in the Easter break of his first year.

It was not the first time he had sought Algy's advice. Often, during that first tight-rope term, he lured Algy into his quarters on the excuse of a glass of Old Boys' sherry, and put some problem to him, knowing he could rely on an opinion free of prejudice. He did not invariably follow the advice given but he was always influenced by it. In the case of an appeal to expand he was gratified to discover Algy's views coincided exactly with his own.

"I have always thought," the old man said, revolving sherry glass between forefinger and thumb, "that that chap Danton was the most positive windbag to emerge from the French Revolution. What was it he said, when things were at low ebb, and Brunswick and the emigrés were after his scalp?"

" 'The kings of Europe advance against us . . . !' " David prompted, but Algy exclaimed, "Don't tell me! I remember exactly. '. . . We throw at their feet, as gauge of battle, the head of a king!' Rather splendid, wasn't it? Reprehensible, of course, but what a gesture! What a pity his career was cut short by that frightful prig Robespierre."

"I didn't get you here to philosophise on the French Revolution, Algy, but to confirm my opinion that this is a time to attack rather than run for cover. If you agree then I'd be delighted to hear you say so. It's all I need."

"You don't need it at all, P.J., for I'm no more than your long-stop now and well you know it. You ask me back here out of sentiment, but don't think I fail to appreciate it."

"That's not true, Algy, but let it pass. I've discussed it with Howarth and Barnaby, and they both take a more cautious view. Howarth has been grousing about lack of classroom space for years, but now that our numbers have dropped, and we've got more elbow room, he counsels patience. As for Barnaby, he'll never make an important decision if he can avoid it. The Ancients have taught him to keep an open mind about everything. But you're different. In many ways you're still younger than any of us. All I really need to know is why you favour attacking instead of waiting for better times."

"When you've been sitting in that hot seat as long as I sat in it," Algy said, "you'll learn that the time is never ripe for advance on any one front, let alone all of 'em. Someone will always be around to shout 'Whoa!' to tell you to stay looking instead of leaping. If you pay the least heed to 'em you'll fossilise at fifty.

See here, we look at the place now and what do we find? Numbers down, waiting-list shortening, head-wagging all round. Very well, but aren't they very sound reasons for a special effort, and the right sort of advertising? Education in the public sector is improving and expanding all the time. We've got to give a parent something extra to tempt him to invest in us. I've always believed that although, as far as the fabric is concerned, I'm the wrong chap to be lecturing you. Alcock did more for the buildings in four years than I did in twenty-four, but I was here at a time when fabric didn't count for much. That's all behind us now. Parents think their little darlings are entitled to as much comfort in term as they get in the holidays, at 'Green Gables' and 'Windy Nook'. Can't have 'em warming their bottoms against the hot-water pipes, and giving themselves constipation, or finishing off Saturday's joint with shepherd's pie and bubble and squeak until Wednesday. They judge a school on its fabric and its menus. Why, if that cold fish Alcock hadn't seen to those latrines you would have had the County Sanitary Inspector breathing down your neck by now. Just go right ahead with your improvements, and use every trick in the book to raise the wherewithal. Get the Governors to sanction a big overdraft if necessary and, talking of Governors, I'll let you into a secret. I'm taking Blunt's place on the Board at the start of summer term."

It was excellent news and David greeted it with a schoolboy whoop. "Going on the Board? But that's marvellous! And here I've been biting my nails and wondering who would replace that old blockhead."

"Hush now," Algy said, holding out his glass for a refill, "the distinguished Alderman is hardly cold in his grave," but David said, "He was stone cold before he reached it. He blocked everything and in the end even Carter admitted we'd made a damned bad bargain enlisting him after the war. But with you in there, wheedling and cajoling . . ."

"Cajole I often do, but wheedle never. There's a difference, P.J. Always leave the options open on dignity. Well, now, to sum up, I take it you'll go for a gym, new science lab and three new classrooms. That demands a one-storey new wing, at right angles to Big School. The gymnasium? Simple matter of roofing over the space between present stables and fives court. Even I got as far as drawing up plans for that. But what about the concert hall?"

"Concert hall? Good Lord, suppose we could afford one, where would it go?"

"Cheapest way would be to make the new wing a two-storey block, with the hall on the ground floor and a flight of steps giving access to the labs and classrooms from the quad. Cost you half as much again, but you'd have a real focal point for entertainments. I won't tell you how sick I became of playing Gilbert and Sullivan to audiences soggy on the smell of boiled greens and pig-swill bins. And while you're at it you might as well give the kitchen a face-lift. Never did care to show mothers over *that*. Once had a big hotelier here who peeped in when I wasn't looking. We never saw him again. They tell me he kept all his sons at a secondary school until they were fifteen, then sent 'em to learn the trade in Switzerland."

"But, hold on, Algy," David protested, "where the devil are we to find money for renovations on that scale? I set our target on a modest ten thousand."

"Change it to twenty. Make a splash. We'll tap new sources that way. With Marie Stopes' contraceptive campaign catching on we can't rely on more than a hard core from the Old Boys in the future. When I started here the average family was five. Now it's two and a bit. Money shortage isn't the only acid eating into the waiting-list."

It was good to have such enthusiasm behind him and David launched his initial personal appeal at that year's Whitsuntide reunion.

It was a great occasion. So many familiar faces were there, ranged in rows in the library, and their presence assured him as to a general feeling of goodwill. At least a dozen covenants were forthcoming on the spot, a particularly generous one from the red-headed Letherett, one-time crony of Boyer in his wilder days, who had struck oil, so he said, in a large advertising business, inherited from an uncle who had died of drink. "Took a fancy to me, Pow-Wow," Letherett told him later. "My family is very strait-laced, and dropped him when he took to lifting his elbow too much, and buying fur coats for his typists. But I went to work for him, and used to get him home and put him to bed, and pass the typists off as my private harem. He changed his will in my favour a week before he snuffed it. Said I was the only relative he had who wasn't a snivelling Puritan and therefore the only one who could hope to succeed in advertising, lair of the accomplished liar. Put me down for £100 a year over seven years."

There were several equally refreshing encounters. The Gosse brothers, Archy and Starchy, were doing well in the paper-making business. David, accepting a covenant from Starchy, reminded him of the occasion when sitting on Algy's Mount Olympus, he had heard himself described as a Bolshie.

"You still are, according to whispers reaching me, Pow-Wow," Starchy told him, "but so what? This place needed a bit of fresh air after the war. Makes you think, doesn't it? I came here in 1916, when I was still wearing short pants, and look at me now. Not only shorter of wind, but pretty thin on top!"

Not all the re-encounters were breezy, however, and one in particular left him with a feeling that life was still very much a matter of pot-luck. After they had all gone, and plans were being drawn up for a rebuilding scheme, provisionally costed at sixteen thousand pounds, Boyer showed up, wan and a little threadbare, so that David did not have to ask how he was riding out the slump in the north. Over a beer in the living-room Chad confessed the real reason why he had not attended the annual reunion. "It wouldn't do much for my morale to admit to chaps like Letherett that I couldn't stand a round at the bar, Pow-Wow. The fact is, I earn well under two hundred a year at a private school in the north. The head and his missis are very kind but the place has to be run on a shoe-string, with the general shortage of cash up there. It's no good advising me to look for something better. I do, every time I nip around to the reading-room at the public library. It never struck me that jobs would be this hard to come by if I had a degree, but there are chaps with better degrees than mine who are on the skids. You need family money to tide you over something of this size and I never had any. Both my parents are dead and neither left me small change."

"What's this place of yours like, exactly?" David enquired, remembering the original Boyer, chockful of humour and boisterous high spirits. "It seems to have got you down more than somewhat and it isn't just shortage of cash, is it?"

"No, it's the general atmosphere of the area—defeated and played out. I don't mind cities all that much but cities are places to work in and half the population seems to be on the dole. We've got a little Scots skivvy up there, pretty kid from the Highlands,

mad keen to get an education. She sneaks up to my room whenever she can, not only for the obvious reasons but to cram. I don't
see much of her, mind. Her working day is around fourteen hours.
She gets her keep and about ten bob a week. Talk about sweated
labour, but cases like that are common in all the industrial areas
today."

He glanced out of the window across the moor, now touched
by the advance of spring. "I was very happy up here, Pow-Wow.
They really look like proving the happiest days of my life." And
then, with a touch of shyness that reminded David of the time he
had called on him the night of Beth's funeral, with the gift of
books to replace those lost in the trenches, "I almost forgot the
O.B. Appeal. It's only a token, of course, but Bouncer Acton was
always fond of the widow's mite parable."

The envelope contained a new pound note and he was far too
moved to protest. The poignancy of the gift nudged his memory,
so that he said, suddenly, "Look here, Chad, how would you like
to come back? To take my place as history master? We couldn't
pay a lot but we could improve on what you're getting, and at
least we'd put some Bamfylde beef on you. I can't guarantee, of
course, as to how they might feel about taking an Old Boy on the
staff, but I know Algy would approve. He was a kid here and came
back as head. I've been looking about for someone I really fancy
and if you'll give me a term to sort things out . . ."

He stopped there, as moved as he had been by any incident
over the last few years, for Boyer whipped out a handkerchief and
gave his nose a long fog-horn blast, of the kind he had often used
to infuriate Howarth in class. He said, "It's possible? Working
here under you, Pow-Wow?"

"The only thing I see against it is it might encourage other
O.B.s down on their luck to apply, and that might cause embarrassment in some quarters. However, leave that to me, and I'll
write you in time to give a term's notice. The time will come, I
hope, when the Ministry of Education will have to do something
drastic about some of these bloody little private schools dotted
about the country."

He was delighted to see the familiar grin split Boyer's face, who
said, "I may as well confess now. I wrote after a job at Carter's
school last term, and would have landed it, if another O.B. hadn't

jumped the queue. Needless to say, the chap who beat me to it was ex-Outram's."

"I don't blame Carter for that. We say we don't show favouritism but we do, all of us, and why not? Your epileptic fit was my first introduction to Bamfylde."

* * *

About a week later Nun Stratton-Forbes drove up in a black Austin Seven, a vehicle he managed to leave in the sidelong manner of a portly undertaker making an unobtrusive exit from a Rolls-Royce hearse. He looked like an undertaker, too, in black jacket, Homburg hat and owlish glasses, still fighting a losing battle with his squint. He made a businesslike entry, and after solemnly shaking hands told David he was in charge of the classics section of an old and reputable correspondence college. "It has a bearing on why I'm here, sir," he said. Alone among the Old Boys, Nun never addressed boy or master by nickname. "My work brings me into touch with a variety of educational establishments and I have a suggestion you might like to consider. It relates to that leaflet you sent through the post. I've given it some thought, sir, and I can't help feeling the appeal might be canalised by the introduction of a more specific scheme, promising a far better yield."

"Nun," David said, chuckling, "you always did make ten words do the work of two and you haven't changed a bit. What the devil are you driving at?"

"Geographical selection, sir."

He unzipped his brief-case and produced a sheaf of tabulated cards. "I did a trial scheme, sir. You see, Old Boys will be scattered all over the world and perhaps we have the addresses of several hundred of them."

"Just under a thousand, I believe."

"Well, then, of that total at least two dozen must be both centrally placed and attached to the school. My idea, worked out in detail here, is to enrol those O.B.s as agents, each giving an undertaking to make personal contact with all the Old Boys in his immediate area. Most of them will be known to them and within travelling distance. People ordinarily throw postal appeals in the wastepaper basket, but no one dismisses the direct solicitation of an old friend. You could even work out a quota for each area.

I'm based on North London and I'll be responsible for my district. I think I could undertake to raise three hundred, sir, either in covenants or direct subscriptions." He looked at David mildly. "Does the scheme recommend itself to you?"

"Nun," said David, respectfully, "you are Bamfylde's Carnot, organiser of victory. It's a brilliant idea. I could have sat here a month without producing anything half so good. Would you lend me those cards for a day or so?"

"Oh, you may keep them, sir. I prepared them with that in mind. And now, if you will excuse me, I must pay my respects to Mr. Barnaby. He would be hurt to learn I had been here and left without giving him a progress report."

"Barnaby will be delighted to see you, Nun. He regards you as his raison d'être for remaining in the profession," and Nun quietly withdrew.

"Extraordinary chap," David said aloud, as Grace wandered in, sketch-book tucked under her arm, and asked, "Who, Daddy?"

"Nun Stratton-Forbes, whose first notable feat here was to present himself at the long-jump pit and announce your arrival. He's just made me a gift of the product of the tidiest mind we've ever had at Bamfylde. What have you got there today?"

She opened her sketch-book and showed him a water-colour of a scene looking north-east from the corner of the planty, painted, it would seem, in the course of a cricket match, for in the distance were strategically-placed blobs, representing two elevens and the umpire. It was very good, he thought, impressionistic but sufficiently defined to catch a fleeting moment of the Bamfylde scene on a May evening. "Do you ever title your pictures, Gracie?" he asked, and she said she called this one 'Close of Play', one of a series she had done on the school year.

"I'd like to have them some day," he said. "They say more than a photograph. I'll tell you what, if this represents summer do one for the other three seasons and we'll get them framed and mounted and hang them in the study."

"Oh, I should have to talk to Spats about it," she said. "He's the only one who would know whether they were worth framing." Spats, of course, was Winterbourne, who now paid them monthly visits. It struck David, for the first time, that it was Grace, rather than Bamfylde, that prompted his twelve or more drives to and from London throughout the year. He said, teasing her, "Has Winterbourne always been hot favourite, Grace?"

"Not really," she replied, seriously, "but he's always in the first two. Sax is the other."

"Ah," he said, "you didn't have to tell me that. How about also-rans?"

"I should need pencil and paper for that," she said, and, giving him a shrewd glance, "Daddy . . . do I . . . I mean, is it absolutely a 'must' for me to start as a weekly boarder at Challacombe Convent School, in September?"

"I'm afraid it is," he said. "Frankly, I'd much sooner you stayed here, for you're a real help to me these days, with the name of every Old Boy back to 1925 in your head, but we can't have you as the only girl in a school of three hundred boys. At twelve it's bad enough, for you've already got more courtiers than Gloriana. At sixteen the competition would be frightful. After all, it isn't as if you were a plain, puddingy miss, is it?"

She drifted over to the convex mirror above the fireplace and studied her distorted reflection. "I look like one in this," she said, "and if it meant staying here, instead of spending Monday to Friday away, I wouldn't care if I *was* plain and puddingy."

"You wouldn't have any courtiers then. Go and give Rigby a hand with the lunch."

She went out and he stood thinking, one hand on the mantelshelf, the other still holding Nun's card-index. She was as much a part of the place, he thought, as Algy and himself, as integrated into the structure and texture of Bamfylde as Big School, the horse-roller and the planty, and the process had begun that autumn evening nearly six years ago, when he had lifted her from the taxi bringing her home from that convalescent home. He saw her now as his special bonus, something tossed him by the fate that had deprived him, in a moment of time, of Beth and her sister, Joan. She had come to represent all that part of his life between the plummeting descent of Beth's beret, from Colwyn Bay's pier, to the evening he stood on the plinth of the Founder's statue, taking his first roll-call as head. It would be a wrench to part with her, even for five days a week, eight months of the year, and if there had been a way of avoiding it he would have done it gladly, but there wasn't. She had to begin mixing with other girls, so that she began to think as a woman, and how was this possible so long as she remained here?

The bell clanged in the quad, the jangle reminding him of a parting shot of Algy's, when they had been discussing plans for the new buildings. "We'll have to crown that new wing with a bell tower," he had said. "We must be the only school of our size in the country that continues to regulate our comings and goings by that discordant clamour," and when David had reminded him of the special status of school bell-ringer, acknowledged by all as long ago as Nipper Shawe's day, he said, "We'll hold on to that. Imagine the status conferred on the chap who pulls the rope! We might even invest him with a ceremonial collarette, on the style of the Orange Order. Make a note of it, P.J., jot it down now, for these things count," and he had.

2

The old terminal pattern reasserted itself, the memorable incident surfacing among the flotsam of the school year, so that he could always look back on a specific period and say to himself, 'That was the time of poor old Lackaknacker Briggs' abduction . . .' or, 'That was about the time we had trouble with Crispin', and so on down the seasons, down the terms, down the years.

The two highlights of his first full year centred on misfits, similar in many ways. And yet, in retrospect, the one was quite ridiculous and the other something that could have ended in tragedy, but for luck, and the lessons he had learned since his first day here.

Briggs was the first celebrity, a boy whose unfortunate nickname, 'Lackaknacker', dated from the day it was broadcast that he had had a malformed testicle removed as a child. Anyone but Briggs would have filed this away as top secret, for what could be more certain than that it would earn him instant notoriety? It was nothing serious, it seemed, no more than a trifling piece of surgery, performed upon his undistinguished anatomy years before he ever set foot at Bamfylde, but the moment news leaked it found its way into school legend, so that Briggs was dubbed 'Lackaknacker', or alternatively, 'One Stroke', and the wags got busy on rhymes concerning his affliction, the most popular being a chant that ran:

> *Mr. Briggs is much improved*
> *Since he had a sphere removed.*
> *Shorn of passion, shorn of fire,*
> *He now sings alto in the choir.*

Most boys would have found the situation intolerable but somehow Briggs adjusted to it. Very easily, David would have said, for Briggs was an accomplished adjuster. You never found him out of humour and rarely out of mischief. Similarly, you never challenged him without hearing an excuse of marked originality. His excuses were, in fact, among the most original David had ever heard, and were offered with an air of innocence that exonerated him from any failing, save guilelessness. Briggs had the frank, slightly bemused expression of a cherub seen in a Renaissance painting, with blue, trusting eyes, heavy pendulous cheeks, a small, rosebud mouth, and no chin at all. A dullard at work, he was equally indifferent to games. Never once had he been known to catch a ball, or arrive anything but last in a heat over any distance, so that time would have hung heavily on his hands had he not possessed an inventiveness that led him into all manner of bizarre adventures during his rough passage through Lower School. The first, and possibly the most spectacular of these, was his alleged kidnapping that led to his acquisition of yet another reputation, that of Bamfylde's Baron von Munchausen, with a capacity for romantic lies that stunned the imagination. The story of Lackaknacker's abduction emerged at the time, of course, but the truth behind it had to be pieced together over the years, so that David, with an academic interest in such things, never got confirmation until Briggs himself admitted the facts as a returning Old Boy.

It all began with a raid upon Man Chilcott's orchard. Most of the farmers in the vicinity of the school had adjusted to the presence of some three hundred young savages, settled in their midst, but Chilcott, a particularly sour smallholder, never had, and for years maintained a running feud with boys who, for the sheer hell of it, would descend on his hen-roost and orchard.

It seemed that Lackaknacker was engaged in one of these forays when it happened—at least, that was his story when, tired and heel-blistered, he reappeared at school early one October morning, with a lurid tale to account for his overnight absence. He found Bamfylde alerted, despite the darkness of the hour before the dawn, for he had been missed at call-over, search-parties had been out and his parents had been notified by telephone that he would probably appear as a runaway on the milk train.

David saw that he was fed (he ate breakfast like a ravenous castaway), showered and sent to bed, after which he conferred with Barnaby, Briggs' housemaster, as to what should be done about him. Barnaby had already questioned him and rejected his bizarre explanation but confessed himself worried about the boy and inclined to lay the blame on that piece of surgery, carried out when Briggs was at kindergarten.

"Damn it all, P.J.," he said, "it can't be good for the chap's morale to have them chanting that obscene doggerel at him. You know how fiendishly cruel the juniors can be, and they've made hay over Briggs' missing equipment. I knew about it, of course. I've already warned Gosling, the house prefect, to report anyone ragging him on the subject, but it's turning the boy into a loner and we all know loners go one of two ways. Either they mope around, until they fall by the wayside, or they set about proving themselves by spectacular acts of brigandage. Briggs seems to have chosen the latter course."

Barnaby went on to relay Briggs' story of his truancy. He admitted frankly that he had gone to Chilcott's orchard to steal apples but had not, he said, had the chance to pocket any, not even windfalls. He was merely surveying the field of operations from inside Chilcott's hedge, when he heard the approach of a car and had dived for cover behind the gatepost. It had been touch and go after that. Somebody (he couldn't say who because he was crouched behind the gatepost) had opened the padlocked gate and entered the orchard and Briggs, seizing his sole chance of escape, had doubled through the gate but not, he claimed, to regain the road to Stone Cross. A blanket, 'smelling of linseed, sir', had been thrown over his head, he had been trussed with a coil of rope, 'smelling of creosote, sir', bundled into the back of a car and driven away at high speed.

He could give no details of the ride—'I think I must have blacked-out, sir . . .'—but when the car stopped he managed to wriggle free of bonds and escape into the market square. The town turned out to be Norton Dip, some twenty miles north-east of Bamfylde, and it was dark, so he at once set out to walk back to school. "I didn't catch a local train, sir, although I had the money for the fare. I thought I should get clear of those chaps, so I walked as far as Crosshayes, where I hid near the station until the slow goods came in. I got a lift there in the guard's van as far as Bamfylde Bridge Halt. Walrus Tapscott can back me up about that, sir, for he saw me. I told him I'd been lost on a run. Then . . . well . . . I just walked up, sir, and here I am."

"You don't believe a single word of this rigmarole, do you?" David enquired, but Barnaby said he was obliged to believe part of it, for he had checked with Tapscott at the station, and Briggs had indeed descended from the Crosshayes goods train at about five a.m. that morning. "He's also got marks on his wrists that could be caused by ropes," he added. "Otherwise he's in good shape."

"Then even if you believe some of it, it's a matter for the police, isn't it?"

"No," Barnaby said, "it isn't, but not for obvious reasons, the bad publicity we should get over a thing like this. I believe it's about half the truth, that is to say, I believe he did motor to Norton Dip, and return the way he claims, but don't ask me why, or how much he's hiding, or for what reason. All I can say is Algy's 'little man' tells me we should let well alone, P.J."

It was interesting, David reflected, how all of the old hands here borrowed from Algy's repertoire. Algy declared that he made his spot decisions according to the dictates of his 'little man', an inspired agent residing just below the navel and David recalled him consulting this infallible informant when they had been faced with Winterbourne's disappearance. He said, "Very well, Barnaby, I'll go along with Algy's little man. After all, you're his housemaster, and what you say about the ragging makes sense to me. But I'd better see the boy, hadn't I?"

"Rather you didn't," Barnaby said, "he might be encouraged to elaborate to a point where we should be obliged to investigate. Besides, between you and me I've a grudging respect for Briggs, dating from the day I caught him smoking, and he excused himself on the grounds that they were asthmatical cigarettes, recommended to him by his father. They were, too, for I checked on that. They smelled like incense when I burned the packet.

Wouldn't surprise me if Briggs didn't go into Fleet Street when he leaves here. First-class recruit for somebody like Rothermere or Beaverbrook, for whenever there's no hard news he invents some."

They left it at that, and it was years later when, propping up a bar at an Old Boys' annual dinner in London, an adult Lackaknacker told him the truth, amid shouts of laughter from former cronies. Finding no cover on the open road when he emerged from the orchard, he had dived into the back of Chilcott's Morris and crouched there, undiscovered, while Chilcott drove into Norton Dip and parked outside the Woolsack. He had then made his way back in approximately the way described. Briggs, as it happened, did not gravitate to Fleet Street but he did the next best thing, becoming a Public Relations officer for a big concern selling detergents. "A post calculated to give the utmost scope to his undoubted powers of imagination," commented Barnaby, when the story was relayed to him.

The Crispin story was equally sensational but had some alarming undertones. Crispin, a Sunsetter, and no relation to Howarth's Amy, was an exceptionally shy boy, who never seemed to make any friends but was tolerated as a hanger-on by other coteries all the way up to the Lower Fourth. Sensitive, withdrawn and intelligent, he arrived in Middle School before he was fourteen, but then, one bitterly cold day in early December, his frail roof fell on him in the form of a charge of shoplifting in the village shop.

Old Mark Trescott appeared with the felon in tow towards tea-bell, presenting evidence of the theft, one bar of Mackintosh's toffee, value twopence, and the shopkeeper was threatening to prosecute. "Tidden offen I ketch one red-'anded, as I did this jackdaw," he told David, while Crispin stood staring down at the carpet, and when David begged him not to go to these lengths over a bar of toffee, he growled, "Ah, tiz easy for you to talk, Headmaster, you don't have to make a livin' up there. Tuppence iz tuppence in my book."

David had been at Bamfylde long enough to know the real source of Trescott's resentment. Until the new tuckshop had opened in 1924, his confectionery counter had been one of his main sources of income, but latterly his takings had dwindled. Here was a splendid opportunity to drive what he would see as a straightforward peasant bargain. "I'll tell 'ee what," he went on, a shade too eagerly, "I won't press charges if you drop the hint to the bursar's missus to give over stockin' Mackintosh's. I don't want to zeem 'ardfaced, but toffee was my best line bevore she took it on."

"You really think I could persuade her to do that, Trescott?"

"Why not? Youm the Ade up yer, bain 'ee?"

"Well," David said, eyeing Crispin, "let me propose a slightly different bargain. I won't report you to the police at Challacombe for trying to blackmail me, providing you accept the price of the goods here and now. How's that?"

Crispin looked up quickly, perhaps not wanting to miss Trescott's outraged expression as he roared, "Tiz bluff an' you know it! I got a witness to 'im pinching that toffee but you abben got one to this bit of a tork we'm 'aving."

"Indeed I have. Crispin's a witness, aren't you, Crispin? And how do you know he didn't mean to pay, before you scared him half to death by pouncing on him? Good God, man—a twopenny bar of toffee—you'd be laughed out of court in three minutes. He's got a good character here and I'd say so."

There was a silence. Out in the quad the tea-bell rang. It always seemed to, David thought, at moments of crisis. Finally Trescott said, "You know and he knows, he 'ad no bliddy intention o' paying." Then, "You'll give 'im a damn good thrashing, I hope?"

"He'll get precisely what he deserves, Mr. Trescott, and thank you for bringing the matter to my attention."

With a long, resentful look at Crispin, Trescott withdrew, and David waited until he heard the door in Big School passage slam before saying, "Why, Crispin? You don't get much pocket-money but twopence—it's absolutely ridiculous! You see that now, I suppose?" but Crispin resumed his study of the carpet.

"You've stolen small things before? From Trescott's, from the tuckshop, the lockers?"

That found its mark. His head came up. "No, sir. *Never!*"

"Then there *must* be a reason, possibly a good one and I'd like to hear it. I've got to hear it, Crispin."

He said, carefully, "You wouldn't understand, sir."

"I might."

"Nobody would."

"You leave that to me, Crispin. Sit down and think it over.

We've got all evening if necessary, but you don't leave here until I know, understand?"

About a minute passed. "I suppose it was because of Towers, sir."

"Towers was with you? He suggested you took it?"

"Good Lord, no, sir!" He sounded even more outraged than Trescott. "Towers wouldn't do a thing like that!"

"Then how does Towers come into it?"

"He doesn't, sir, he doesn't know a thing about it. I meant to give it to him, that's all."

"Sit down, Crispin, and let's get this straight. You say Towers doesn't come into it, yet you admit stealing it for him? You hadn't the price of it on you?"

"Yes, I had, sir."

"You had? Do you often give Towers things?"

"Every Wednesday."

"Why every Wednesday?"

"Wednesday's pocket-money day, sir."

"Towers is a close friend of yours?"

"No, sir."

"But you'd like him to be?"

He didn't answer this. Neither did he accept the invitation to sit down. David said, "When you buy him things, how does he react?"

Crispin took his time. Finally he said, doggedly, "He doesn't want me. He's got chaps like Coxe and Nesbitt. I bought him a pot of Mrs. Redcliffe's baked beans last Wednesday but he sent it back."

It was one of the most complex cases he had ever handled and he thought longingly of Algy's vast store of experience. There was little to go on here save instinct, but instinct told him to tread with excessive caution.

"Listen, Crispin. I'm guessing and you aren't helping very much. Whatever's said here won't get around, it'll be between you and me, understand? I don't intend punishing you, either. What I said to Trescott was said to get rid of him. You're in bad trouble, sure enough, but it's not on account of that bar of toffee. Your people are a long way off. India, isn't it?"

"Yes, sir."

"When did you last see them?"

"I saw my mother last year, sir, just before she went out. I haven't seen my father in three years."

"Well, then, meantime I'm your father. That's how it has to be with most Sunsetters. Not perfect, but a lot better than nothing. Now tell me if I've got this right. You want Towers to accept you on the same terms as he accepts Coxe and Nesbitt, but he won't, so you buy him things. But that isn't working, so you go to the village and steal a bar of toffee from Trescott's counter. Can I assume you had already spent all your pocket money on that jar of beans?"

"No, sir, the beans were only fourpence. I had twopence left over."

"Then why the devil didn't you pay Trescott for the toffee?"

"Something Towers said, sir."

"What did he say?"

"He said you don't buy friends with beans or cream horns. Me and Towers—well—it just wouldn't work, sir."

"But after that you deliberately stole the toffee for him."

Crispin's lip quivered and his teeth clamped over his lip. "I'm sorry, Crispin, but if I'm to help I've got to know to understand. Maybe you find it difficult to explain, but try, boy, for God's sake, try!"

"It was *doing* something, sir."

"Doing something? You mean, *proving* something?"

"In a way, sir."

"To yourself or to Towers?"

"To both of us. If Trescott hadn't seen me I was going to tell Towers I'd pinched it."

"But you told me Towers wouldn't do a thing like that himself. Wouldn't he be even more inclined to turn you down when he knew you were a thief?"

"Yes, but it wouldn't have mattered, would it? I mean, he'd have thought about it, wouldn't he? You see . . . I can't *do* anything, sir. Towers knows it and everybody knows it. I'm no good at anything. I never have been."

The terrible poignancy of it assailed him. On one side Towers, a popular boy, strutting round with any number of friends to choose from, a boy with a father owning a big sports business in the Midlands, who drove up here in an Alvis and took his son and his son's cronies out for the day. And on the other side of the wire, looking in, Crispin; friendless, rejected and aware, every minute of the day, of his own inadequacy. There was no ready solution. It would need, he would say, a good deal of sober reflection, a careful weighing of every factor. He said, "Well, that's all for now, Crispin, and I'm glad you brought yourself to tell me. Go and have your tea and don't say anything about this to anyone, not even Towers. And don't worry about Trescott either. He won't do a thing, do you hear?"

"Yes, sir."

He went out, dragging his feet, and through the window giving on the quad David watched him, noting that he did not go through the arch towards Big Hall but across the quad towards the one-storey buildings that comprised the tuck-house, armoury, stables and coke-hole. He thought, "Let him mull it over tea-less if he wants to, he won't have an appetite to speak of," and rang for Rigby to order tea in his study, wishing that it was Friday, when Grace would be home. It was a problem he might, conceivably, have discussed with her. A twelve-year-old might be likely to approach it with more detachment than an adult.

He was crossing the quad an hour later when he saw Manners, a Sixth Former, emerge from the northern arch at a run. Seeing David, he changed direction rapidly, doubled round the Founder's statue and rushed up, gasping, "Better come, sir . . . that kid Crispin . . . down in the coke-hole, blue in the face . . . !", and spun round, rushing back through the arch with David at his heels.

They jumped the three steps into the coke-hole together. The low-powered naked bulb did not do much to light up the window-less interior but what light there was touched Crispin's right hand, flung out towards the squat boiler, as though to ward off the reek that filled the cellar. He was slumped on a coke-container and a glance showed him that Manners had cause for alarm. Crispin's face was purple, and his teeth were bared in a kind of snarl. David gathered him up and ran back up the steps where a long gust of the north-easterly wind caught them, strong enough to make him reel. He shouted, "After me, Manners . . . into the Third Form . . ." and ran past the entrance of Outram's, turning right at the foot of the slate steps that led up to what had once been Julia Darbyshire's quarters. The Third Form fire was dead and it was cold in here, with the sash cord of an open window rotating in the draught. He laid Crispin flat on the desk, tore away collar and tie, and began massaging his chest, throwing all his weight into the exercise as Manners said, distractedly, "Is he . . . is he *dead*, sir? He's my fag. I was looking for him, going to clout him . . . one of the kids said he'd seen him go into the coke-hole after tea . . ."

"He would have been dead in another ten minutes . . . get matron here . . . tell her one of the boys is sick but don't tell anyone else. Wait around until he's in sick bay and report back to me."

"I'm taking prep, sir."

"Find a stand-in."

"Yes, sir."

He ran off but before he had reached the far end of the room Crispin vomited, turning face downwards, gripping the edge of the desk and retching violently. David continued to work on his back. He knew little or nothing about artificial respiration, but applied his strength as common sense dictated and it appeared to work. Crispin, having emptied his stomach, drew several long, shuddering breaths and sat up as Ma Kruger sailed in demanding to know what had happened. He told her briefly that Crispin had gone into the coke-hole to warm himself and had been overcome by the fumes. "That place is out of bounds from now on," he said. "It's a marvel something like this didn't happen long ago. Put him straight into sick bay. Is there anyone else there?"

"No, Headmaster. The last 'flu case went out yesterday. Can he walk?"

"I can walk," Crispin said, thickly, and proved it by sliding off the desk and steadying himself on the nearest blackboard peg.

"You had a close shave, Crispin. He's had nothing to eat since lunch, Matron. Get him some soup, if he can keep it down, but get him to bed first."

"I know my job," said Mrs. Gorman, tartly, and he remembered, too late, that Ma Kruger could be very touchy if her methods were called into question.

*   *   *

He said nothing of his suspicions to Manners when the senior reported. In his own mind there was little doubt but that Crispin had gone there deliberately, seeking not warmth but oblivion, and the nearness of their escape made him catch his breath. He thought, "I didn't handle it right, I should have offered the kid tea and gone to work on him straightaway—anything but let him mooch off like that, with his packload of misery . . ." but Manners helped without knowing it, saying, "He's a frightful weed, sir, one of the worst we've ever had. He does everything you tell him but no more, if you follow me, sir. He's just the kind who would sit there like a kipper and wait to get cooked." He paused and it crossed David's mind that Manners might be wondering if his own approach to Crispin had not contributed to his fag's wretchedness. A moment later this was confirmed as he added, "I . . . er . . . I did try talking to him straight, sir. Early in the term I told him to pull his socks up and try harder at games. Would you like me to have another go at him, sir?"

"No," David said, definitely, "just try putting yourself in his place once in a while. He's cut off from his people, and hasn't the knack of making friends. Not everybody has, you know."

It was no use telling Manners to hold his tongue about the incident. It would be all over the school by now, and even if it wasn't it would leak as soon as he put the coke-hole out of bounds.

He went over to the library and browsed about looking for a book that might help to take Crispin out of himself. He found a copy of Williamson's *Tarka the Otter*, slipped it in his pocket and went up the slate staircase to matron's room. Crispin, she said, in her quaint hospital phrase, was 'comfortable'. The vomiting had probably prevented unpleasant after-effects, although he might have a bad headache for a day or so. He had taken soup, and kept it down, and later a cup of tea and a purgative. Ma Kruger was a great believer in purgatives and, crafty as some of her patients were, few found means to avoid swallowing them.

He said, "I'll pop in and have a word with him. He wanted a book," and left her to her darning, going through into the sick bay built the year after the fire.

Crispin was sitting up in bed looking at nothing. He said, as soon as David pulled a chair up, "I meant it to happen, sir. They say if you sit there long enough you pass out."

"Never mind all that, Crispin. It's time you and I put all our cards on the table. We've got to scrape a hole for you somewhere, and if you don't feel like co-operating try and see it from my point of view. What sort of headmaster would I be if I let boys get so depressed that they did what you did today? And don't kid yourself that your case is an isolated one. I've been at Bamfylde fourteen years, and there's always a few who can't settle in. You don't sing, I suppose?"

"No, sir." Mercifully he seemed to find the question amusing. "I sound like a stick on railings, so Mr. Renshaw-Smith says."

"And there's no one game you like more than another?"

"Not really, sir."

"You're not bad at English subjects. Maths aside, you've always had pretty good reports."

"That doesn't get you far at a place like this, sir."

"No, it doesn't." He thought hard. "There must be something you can do that nobody else can. There always is, Crispin. The key to getting by at a place like Bamfylde is to find that something, and build on it. It doesn't matter a jot what it is, so long as you're better at it than the next chap. Can you think of anything? Anything at all?"

"I play the handbells, sir."

"Handbells?"

"I've got a set, sir. My uncle left them to me when he died. He used to go around playing them at charity concerts, and . . . well . . . I got interested, so he taught me. They aren't as easy as they look, sir."

"I'll wager they aren't. Where are they now?"

"In my box in the Sunsetters' store, sir."

"You've never had them out since you came here?"

"No, sir. It seemed . . . well . . . a bit cissy, sir."

"Cissy my foot! It's a very old English craft, and very few people can play them as they should be played. You can ring out recognisable tunes?"

"Oh, yes, sir. I can do all the carols."

"The carols? Well, that's promising. We've got a carol service the night after the opera and that could be a star turn. Have you got the nerve to stand up on the stage in Big Hall and play, in front of the whole school?"

"I'd need to practise, sir. It's a long time since I had them out."

"Then I'll tell you what you do. You bring them over to my house after prep tomorrow night. Only my daughter and I will

be there and you can practise all you like. Then we'll make sure
you get star billing at the carol service, a surprise item on the programme that not even Mr. Renshaw-Smith knows about in advance. Will you do that?"

"Are you sure they won't laugh, sir?"

"At carols? Expertly played on old English handbells? You can
take it from me they wouldn't. Everyone will be pestering you for
a go at them, you see if I'm not right. How do you feel now?"

"Still muzzy, sir."

"Then get some sleep. Matron says you'll have nothing worse
than a headache in the morning. You needn't come in. Take it
easy over the weekend. Good night, then."

"Good night, sir."

He went out, feeling a good deal more hopeful than he went
in and thinking, "A purgative can't do him much harm but a big
hand up on that stage will do him untold good."

He went down and out into the quad, standing a moment with
the wind whipping his gown and sniffing the air for snow. It was
time it fell, having been threatening for two days now. From the
direction of Big Hall he could hear a solo—Frobisher, playing the
Grand Inquisitor in Algy's revival of *The Gondoliers*, and singing
'There Lived a King', one of Beth's favourites. A soft burst of
laughter came from the lighted windows of the Outram senior
dorm, then Vinnicombe's bellow at a skylarker making the most
of the few minutes before lights out. He thought, "God knows,
we get problems, but taken all round we seem to cope with 'em
better than the politicians."

He hunched his gown and turned in through Big Hall arch to
look in on rehearsals.

3

The thought returned to him often during the last fortnight of
term. An island in the torrent; a small bastion of refuge, where
some kind of order still prevailed, where most things worked fairly
well, where there was fellowship of a kind missing since Algy's
day, a time when the outside world had seemed to steady before
shooting off course again. Now, as Yeats might have said, 'all was
changed, changed utterly' out there beyond school bounds. The
old doctrine of Free Trade, bulwark of the Empire for so long,

discarded, alienating Philip Snowden, the one man of genius left in the Cabinet. Hunger-marchers proliferating. De Valera, arch-enemy of the old-style British, of which Bamfylde, like it or not, remained a symbol, triumphing at the Irish polls. World conferences that resolved nothing. Mosleyites confronting the militant Left on streets where, only a few years ago, a General Strike had been staged without a casualty. And it was worse still overseas. France, her President shot down, was in turmoil. The Japanese were making nonsense of The League of Nations covenant. And all about them was a confusion of tongues, a bankruptcy of policies. But at Bamfylde, in that final month of 1932, things were more hopeful. Algy's *Gondoliers* played to thunderous applause, and Crispin, darting up and down his trestle table in Big Hall, won the status symbol of Bamfylde with his handbell rendering of 'Silent Night' and 'The Holly and the Ivy', for thereafter he was known as 'Ringer' and with a nickname integration was achieved.

Watching his performance David felt he had earned the right to a little smugness, for Ringer Crispin was only one of many manifestations of the new reign. Aside from the Gilbert and Sullivan revival, Renshaw-Smith's Choral Society was thriving, spurred on by a Certificate of Merit gained in the Devon Music Festival, and his changes in discipline had produced no explosion. After the oppressive atmosphere of the Alcock era, there was a geniality in the common room that had not been evident in the 'twenties, when Carter kept tempers on edge most of the time. Hislop settled in effortlessly, a different Hislop to the bull-necked extrovert who had shouted the odds on the sports field. He had developed a flair for maths somewhere in exile and, even more surprisingly, a taste for authority, so that Gibbons, Havelock's new housemaster, appointed him house-prefect the day he reached the Sixth. David, watching him take parade one morning, wondered how he would act if he stumbled on a pontoon school in the old smokers' hideout behind the stacked trunks in the covered playground. Or what he would do if he caught one of his cronies studying the form-book. Howarth and Barnaby seemed to have entered into a tacit conspiracy to give him the kind of loyalty they had given Algy, and sometimes he saw the three of them as the new Magi, ageing harmoniously in the wilderness. Grace, her stillness seasoned by a developing sense of humour, was a great help to him during weekends and holidays, and even parents accepted her as his semi-official chatelaine, whereas Old Boys of recent vintage never thought of her as anyone but his deputy.

Thus, one way and another, the gap left in his life by Chris closed to some extent. He missed her, of course, but not as keenly as he would have thought. Mostly he was so busy, too busy indeed, to heed his publisher's plea that he begin work on another historical biography.

Financially he was better off than he had ever hoped to be, with a salary of six-fifty a year, free living expenses and about three hundred a year from royalties on *The Royal Tigress*. Chris told him his book was on display in Montreal bookshops, and that there were two copies in the University library. She wrote, on the average, once a week, chatty, mildly affectionate letters that seemed unrelated to the woman he had held in his arms in the seedy bedsitter at Bilhampton. She had detached herself, somehow, not only from him but from the British scene, so that sometimes he wondered if she would ever settle here again or, if she did, would see him as someone too pedestrian for her taste.

The centre of what he thought of as his political gravity was shifting and he was inclined, on the whole, to lower his sights and put his faith in tradition, in ripeness, habit and continuity. Even old Howarth commented on the change when David championed Britain at a gin-party discussion in Nicolson's on Howarth's fifty-sixth birthday.

"I can give you twenty years, P.J.," he said, jovially, "and Barnaby can give you fifteen, but at heart you're less of a radical than either one of us, notwithstanding that reputation you once had as a firebrand. You should watch it, lad, before the Bamfylde fungus gets a fatal hold on you."

But then, he told himself, he had excuses for feeling paternal these days. Chad Boyer appeared the first day of the Christmas holidays, seeking temporary quarters, and when David asked him what he meant by 'temporary' he looked, as Algy Herries would have said, 'felon-shy', and added, half-apologetically, "Well, the fact is I've just taken a three-year lease on your old cottage, over at Stone Cross, P.J. A bachelor room is out, I'm afraid. You see, there's Alison."

"Alison who?"

Boyer grinned. "My wife, Pow-Wow."

459

"Great God, you're not thinking of getting married?"

"I am married," Chad answered, grinning. "Alison and I are on our honeymoon, as from last Tuesday. We were married in a Manchester Register Office, and she's outside now, awaiting the abbot's permission to cross the monastic threshold. Shall I fetch her in?"

"Well, for God's sake," David said, quite taken aback, "you'll have to, won't you? You can't expect the girl to bivouac on Exmoor in December," and he ran to the window to peep out at a still, rather keyed up figure, hunched in the passenger seat of Boyer's ancient Austin Seven. She had flaming red hair, a small, pinched face, and a very definite air of uncertainty, so that he called, "Grace! Go out and fetch Mrs. Boyer in while I give this room a tidy."

It was very difficult to surprise Grace, even at twelve-and-a-half. She threw aside her apron and ran out into the forecourt, where they watched her trying to coax Alison Boyer out of sanctuary. Boyer said, "It's that Scots girl I mentioned at Easter, Pow-Wow, the one who was a domestic at the school, and came to me for coaching. I suppose you think I'm crazy on my salary."

"That depends," David said, remembering his own spot proposal on Colwyn Bay railway platform, in 1919. "How did it develop, exactly?"

"We were both lonely and very much down in the dumps, and . . . well, we kind of grew together. She's a real brick, and a tonic when she forgets to be shy. She's got the Celtic awe for all seats of learning. Oh, I daresay you'll think me an absolute idiot for saddling myself with a wife at this stage, but there it is and I don't regret it. I asked her to marry me the day I got your letter saying you'd wangled it."

He moved around the room, glancing at all the familiar pictures and pieces of furniture brought over from Havelock's. "It's like a dream, Pow-Wow. I mean, you being Gaffer here, and me on the staff. Sometimes I pinch myself and wonder if I'll wake up in that bloody awful attic I occupied in that prep school, or find myself back in the Havelock dorm, with Dobson and Ridgeway snoring away on either side of me." Then, seriously, "They say you're making a rare go of it, Pow-Wow. Would you say you were?"

"Feeling my way, Chad. It's trickier than it looked from the outside. I'm even beginning to appreciate some of Alcock's points of view, particularly as regards parents."

"But not us, I hope?"

"No, Chad, not you. The O.B.s have been marvellous, and so have Howarth and Barnaby. They're beginning to call us the New Magi now, the heirs of Judy, Bouncer and old Rapper Gibbs."

Grace came in with Alison, who looked even smaller and more uncertain in the open. She gravitated to Boyer at once and David noticed, with approbation, that she obviously adored him. Her red head finished level with his broad shoulders, and a gleam of sunshine, touching her hair, made it glow like a fire in a draught. She had cornflower-blue eyes, a small chin as resolute as Beth's and the kind of handknitted jumper that Beth had worn when she was dressing on a nurse's salary. He thought, "It's odd he should be bringing her to that old cottage of ours. Like watching yourself in a mirror of time . . . hard to believe Beth made her bow to Algy and Ellie in this room, thirteen years ago . . ." but then he remembered his manners and said, "I should be used to Chad surprising me, Mrs. Boyer. Congratulations, and I hope you'll be very happy here. Chad was, but it's going to take us a little time to get used to him at the distributing end of authority. He was a holy terror here in his salad days."

"Och, Chad'll do fine," she said, with almost staggering directness. "It was time he moved on. It was only a wee school. Nothing like this."

Her unexpected forthrightness made an immediate impression on him so that he thought, "She's just what he needed, come to think of it. Someone to rally on, someone who matters to him," and when Grace accepted Alison's offer to give a hand with the lunch, he said, in response to Boyer's interrogative glance, "You've got more sense than you think, Chad. I always had a morbid fear you'd turn up one day with one of those mincing little blondes, all promise and no performance. My mother would approve of Alison instantly, and so would Beth. They both had a preference for down-to-earthers."

Chapter Two

1

Chris wrote early in the new year, when he was beginning to wonder how soon it would be before he heard her pleasant Yorkshire brogue over the phone, asking when and where they could meet. But she wasn't coming home, after all, or not for some considerable time. She had been selected for what she described as a 'McKenzie-Solomon Travelling Scholarship, (financed by a couple of reformed robber barons, buying their way into heaven with an educational trust fund)' and would be working in Western Europe for six months, a trip that would take in shortened courses at Strasbourg, Rome and Munich Universities. And after that, on the strength of the travelling scholarship, she was committed to lecture her way across the States, all the way from the eastern seaboard to the Pacific.

She wrote, with a touch of her old breathlessness,

I was lucky to be selected but I was slow to accept. It meant not seeing you for almost another year, and even that isn't certain for, at this stage, I'm not sure how many cities the U.S.A. tour takes in. However, if I am to play fair with the people who sponsored me I owe it to them to be available for a candidature in early '34. I see the date of the next General Election as '35 but I may get pushed forward at a by-election much earlier. I've decided to resign the South Mendips candidature. Not even Keir Hardie could win that seat from the Tories, but that's enough about me. I treasure every scrap of Bamfylde news you send and am sure (despite your becoming modesty on paper) that you are proving a whale of a success as headmaster of that hallowed establishment! My love always, Davy dear . . . and I miss you so, and will go on missing you . . . your male gentleness and your sanity. Where did you get them both? Not in the trenches and not, I think, in the Valleys, where folk are exciting and amusing but intolerant. It follows that it must have been at Bamfylde, and that's funny when you think of it. I always saw those places as bastions of prejudice . . .

He accepted the letter, despite its breezy reassurances, as virtual disengagement, a gentle placing of their association on a platonic plane, and although this saddened him it was not unexpected. Like him, she was finding fulfilment and their inclinations no longer pursued parallel courses, but divergent ones, likely to carry them farther and farther apart as each of them spread their wings. He was sure now that she would never willingly exchange politics or even an academic life, for the role of a Martha, here in the wilderness. While he might have adapted, she never would. Always she would see herself as a walk-on player, meriting a leading role. Perhaps the only things they had ever had in common were physical hunger and a deep, personal loneliness.

He folded the letter, feeling that he needed time to reflect on an answer, and went into the Sixth to take his period on current affairs, beginning half-heartedly, his mind still on her implied renunciation but, as always, warming to his theme, and the rallying questions of Hislop and others, who enjoyed these occasions as much as he did.

The letter spurred him to make yet another decision, to enrol a commercial tutor and start courses in shorthand, bookkeeping and typing as soon as the new classrooms were ready. It had been put forward by several parents and at least one Governor a year ago, when he first took Alcock's place, but it had made no special appeal to him then. Bamfylde had produced several merchant princelings over the years, but few of them entered commerce at the clerical level, despite the usual poppycock talked by fathers about the importance of starting at the bottom. Businessmen's sons, he noted, invariably began their business life several rungs up, but now times were changing rapidly. More and more Old Boys came to him, or wrote to him, with tales of long spells of unemployment, and the inadequacy of a formal education in the scramble for jobs on an open market. It was time, he thought, to give seniors approaching school-leaving age a head-start, by introducing them to the kind of jobs they might have to use as footholds in the free-for-all of competitive business.

There was, however, another and strictly personal reason for introducing a commercial course, and it was Christine's letter that brought it into the open. Grace would be thirteen in May, and could expect about four more years at school. Nothing would please him more than to have her back here permanently. With the prospect of her acquiring secretarial skills at Bamfylde he could hope to reduce those four years to two. Bamfylde needed a woman's touch at the centre of affairs, and she was already half-qualified for the job. She knew hundreds of Bamfeldians by name and almost as many parents. Algy said she was tarred with the Bamfylde brush but in softer hues—"Shades of sweet pea, wouldn't you say, P.J.?"

The builders moved in during a dry spell in January and everyone had to adapt to the uproar and vast array of bricks, wheelbarrows and cement mixers about the place. When the foundations of the new wing were dug, and the first line of bricks had been laid, Stratton-Forbes wrote suggesting they should place a school muster-roll in a cavity, and this was done at an informal public ceremony. Even David, however, who thought himself attuned to Bamfylde's eccentricities, was surprised by the orgy of commemorative inscribing that followed. Half the boys in the school scratched their names in wet concrete, some of the bolder ones defacing the pier supporting the stone where the memorial plaque would be fixed. He took no counter action but mentioned the outcrop at assembly one morning, referring to that particular section of the foundations as the wailing wall, and advising vandals to beat their heads against it in moments of stress. It was a successful joke, of the kind he was beginning to fashion nowadays, and a matter for secret pride when he discovered that the facing side of the new block was permanently dubbed The Wailing Wall.

He gave Chad and Alison Boyer an unusual wedding present

that spring, undertaking to pay for the installation of an indoor
privy at the cottage. "Beth and I abominated that feature of the
place," he told them, when they were moving in. "It's no joke to
wade across that yard in dressing gown and slippers in a north-
easterly. I've given Grover instructions to take in a small section
of the landing and connect it with the kitchen wastepipe." When
Boyer said, chuckling, "It's lucky we aren't displaying our gifts
at a wedding breakfast, Pow-Wow," he said, "Ah, you may laugh
now but Alison will live to thank me for it."

The term slipped by and it was Easter before he knew it. The
sodden moor to the west came to life again and the Sunsetters
began their traditional task of preparing the cricket pitch. Then,
suddenly, it was full summer again, with extra half-day holidays
reintroduced for the important cricket matches, and the inter-
house drill competition, and Certificate 'A' examination, conducted by a spruce young captain sent from the War Office.

He was still disinclined to take an active interest in the Corps,
apart from keeping a fatherly eye on the band, now capable of
playing Sousa's marches, 'Soldiers of the Queen', and many another martial tune, but still saddled with the derisory title of
the Orpheans. The School Forum made progress, and another
innovation, a housemasters' fortnightly conference was successful,
although Howarth was cynical about it. "No more than a cast-
iron excuse to skip a period and sit around guzzling coffee, P.J.,"
he said, but Algy approved. He was over here a good deal nowadays, sometimes to the shameful neglect of his parish, and was
already recruiting for next term's *Pirates of Penzance*, but warned
that, when the nights drew in, David would have to take over
production. "My eyesight isn't what it was," he said, "and it would
be undignified to finish my time here upside down in a bog."

"No more than a case of the moor claiming its own," David
told him. "How many years have you been up here now?"

"Forty, counting my five-year stint under Wesker," Algy said.
"Half my lifetime, and I count the other half wasted. Look at me,
my boy, well beyond the allotted span and I could still head the
Second Form round the buildings, given a modest start!"

"I believe you could," David said. Then, diffidently, "How am
I making out, Algy? For my private ear alone?" and Algy replied,
cheerfully, "Fair to middling. What are your own conclusions?"

"Rather on the lines of a hospital report, 'as well as can be expected', but I still find authority over the senior staff a bit embarrassing. Can't help feeling, sometimes, that it's a bit of a liberty to give orders to chaps like Howarth, who were learning their trade when I was learning to read."

"The point is you don't, P.J. One of your rare qualifications—and I flatter myself I spotted it a week after you came here—is that you have the knack of gentle persuasion. Men like Howarth respond to it, even when they have reservations about your policies."

"They aren't my policies at all, they're extensions of yours, Algy."

"Perhaps, but where do you suppose I got mine? Invented 'em? Of course I didn't. Something rubs off from everything you read, observe and tinker with. The job's really no more than a lifelong process of subconscious distillation of other men's successes and failures. Point is, most chaps in our line of business let their arteries harden at thirty-five and become their own worst enemies on that account. Self-doubt never did anyone any harm, so long as it's offset by the gambling spirit. And by all accounts you've got your share of that. Your prefects don't beat any more, I hear."

"No, they don't and never will under me. That was something I always thought you'd sit on, Algy."

"Never had the nerve. I was lazier, too. But I approve, none the less. You seem to be bringing on a decent lot of seniors, but don't be surprised if you come across the odd rotten apple. You lay odds with yourself that you know how to spot them from afar but every now and again you come a mucker, particularly as regards the selection of prefects."

"What do you do then, Algy. Demote him on the spot?"

"Never. Bad for the system."

"Why?"

"Gives the old lags in Middle School the notion they can unseat any perk providing they go the right way about it. No, you tail him, everywhere he goes, until he gets nervous and keeps looking over his shoulder. That tames 'em. They either pull their socks up or leave a term or two ahead of schedule."

"You see, I still have to consult the oracle at least once a week."

"I should think so. I was the despot here nearly twenty-four years, and you're coming up to your second. Be reasonable, old

son. If you lived two lifetimes you'd still be carried away in a box
without knowing the half of it."

2

Sports Day, Whitsuntide Reunion and Opening Day.

Carter, suave and successful-looking, arrived for Sports Day,
telling David he now had over two hundred boys and was, in his
jubilant phrase, 'fairly coining it, old man'. David did not envy
him. His approach was too much like merchandising, as Howarth
was quick to comment on over a gin and tonic that night, when
dusk had fallen, and the last parental car had swept off down the
drive.

"Man might as well be churning out those bloody little gnomes
for suburban lily-ponds," he growled. "A place of that kind isn't
a school, it's an assembly belt, with the staff stationed at stipulated
intervals, screwing up nuts and applying the odd touch of solder."

Many others appeared that same day, some of them faces that
David had not seen in years, and a few he had never seen at all.
One comparatively new friend was Mrs. Hislop, whom he had
first met when she restored her son to them in his first term as
head. A Northerner, she found it difficult to express gratitude
but managed it somehow. "That man Alcock did the boy a good
turn," she said. "Pulled him up short and don't think I didn't
know he needed a jolt. But you did him an even better turn by
letting him come back again. My guess is you're going to be proud
of him before he's finished."

"In a way I already am," he told her, "but for Heaven's sake
don't tell him I said so."

At Whitsuntide there was a swarm of visitors, among them
Stoker Monk who, now that he was at liberty to smoke himself
to death, had taken up rowing and renounced the weed. Twitted
on this account, as he and David contributed their quota to the
sustained uproar in the Old Boys' bar, he justified his eccentric
behaviour. "After that first pipeful in the Third, when I wasn't
sick but everybody else was, I had a reputation to maintain," he
said, "but now, who gives a damn whether I smoke or not?"

Archer the Third elbowed his way forward, back for the first
time since leaving in 1924, and reminded David of the occasion
when he got lost during a run-in and the whole field had to be

467

turned out to search for him. Archer, now a captain in the Royal Engineers, had seen action on the North-West Frontier. "They recommended me for a decoration for completing a bridge under sniper fire," he said, "but I'd swop that experience any day for the two hours I sat under that hedge, waiting for you to show up. Never so pleased to see anyone in my natural, Pow-Wow."

It made him feel, as the day wore on, he was now a sizable thread in the Bamfylde pattern of legend. Skidmore drove up, confirming every phophecy made about him by appearing in a dog collar, just as they had feared when he spent so long at his prayers, but unlikely, David concluded, to qualify for martyrdom. He had charge of a big Methodist church in what he called 'the Yorkshire Bible belt', a place where 'the presentation of a good *Messiah* every year is the key to the kingdom of heaven'. It amazed David to hear Skidmore talk like that and he put it down to a general broadening of the mind among Methodists since the recent amalgamation of rival factions, a subject upon which Skidmore had some interesting comments. "If we can do it after all this time, then any denomination can," he declared. "Wouldn't that be something? An amalgamation of all the Christian churches in Britain?"

"I'm afraid it's a pipedream, Preacher," David said, but Skidmore said he wasn't so sure. "If things get rough enough it could happen," he said. "I think I'll live to see it."

"I hope you do," he said, and turned to greet the younger of the Kassava brothers, Jimmy, the eleven-year-old who had clung to the ledge until his brother had knocked him out so that he could be lowered into the quad like a sack of flour. Kassava was now a lieutenant in the Indian Army and his brother, he told David, was walking the wards in Manchester Infirmary and had plans to practise in Delhi. It made David glow a little to hear all these titbits but it also made him aware of his age, as though he had come to Bamfylde as a toddler instead of an old-young crock of twenty-one. Time, they said, speeded up after one's thirtieth birthday, and it seemed to be true in his case, for here he was, at thirty-seven, feeling as superannuated as Algy. Then something reminded him that others were growing older. Blades buttonholed him, in order to introduce his fiancée, a shy, extremely pretty brunette, with a pleasant smile and a low-pitched voice. Blades had gone into publishing and talked enthusiastically of David's best-selling account of the Wars of the Roses, tucking his publishing card into David's breastpocket—"In case you don't get the best terms with your people when you come up with something new," he said. "They say we don't poach authors, but that's a polite fiction." Talking to them David recalled a comment by Julia Darbyshire, after she had shown him Blades' parody of Herrick, written in her honour—"He'll make some lucky girl a wonderful husband one day . . ." and it looked as if Julia might be right, for the girl gazed at Blades all the time he was talking, glance steady and lips slightly parted, as though she could hardly wait to get him to bed. He wondered then whether Blades had told her about his brush with the Second Form mistress and decided he had not. She was the kind of girl who wouldn't want to know, and Blades was sharp enough to realise this.

He drifted off then, to take Alison Boyer in to tea, for Alison was quite overwhelmed by all this parading and gossiping, and all the smartly dressed women strolling about. She said, in an urgent aside, "They're awfu' fine, some of them. I hope my outfit didnae let Chad down."

"Don't ever worry about letting Chad down, Alison. One of the most sensible things he ever did, and in his youth he didn't do so many, was to marry you. How are your evening classes coming along?"

The evening classes were those devoted by Boyer to Alison and Chad had told him she tackled them with fanatical zeal. "She's even approached Barnaby about elementary Latin," he said. "I thought that was going over the top a bit. Damn it all, why does she need Latin?"

"To draw level with you and keep your end up with all the other masters' wives."

"But good God, Pow-Wow, no master's wife here knows a word of Latin."

"That's so, and acquiring some would give her the edge on them and you the edge on their husbands. The Scots are a very competitive lot, Chad. How do you suppose they managed to populate Canada single-handed, give or take a handful of English fur-trappers and remittance men?"

Opening Day was a more ceremonious occasion, with Lady Hopgood pulling the tapes on a sheet of tarpaulin screening the inscription plaque of the new wing, and any number of county dignitaries standing around to contribute a dutiful round of applause. The new block looked horribly raw against the grey stone and weathered red-brick of Big School but Algy, commenting on this in a breezy speech, said the sleet that came over the moor between October and March would soon take the gloss from it. By Christmas, he assured them, the block would have learned to lurch into the wind, like all the other buildings on the plateau.

The new hall was all but finished then and work began on the classrooms above. The O.B. Fund had topped the ten thousand mark, and the Governing Body were successful in getting an overdraft at the bank, so foundations were dug for the gymnasium and sports room that were to replace the covered playground, the fives court and library block. If the money ran to it there was provision in the plans for a dozen new studies but if subscriptions slowed down Fifth Form studies would have to wait on better times. David, contemplating the overdraft, extracted some comfort from the fact that the drop in numbers had levelled off and next term's figures promised an increase of about a dozen, with the waiting-list still fluctuating around a hundred mark. "We'll break even at about three-fifty," the bursar told him, but Barnaby came up with a very ambitious idea, although it was one that would have to wait upon a sizeable legacy or endowment. "The great thing nowadays," he said, "is to catch 'em young. What we ought to aim at, P.J., is our own prep department, catering for upwards of thirty nine-to-ten-year-olds, and a bright young graduate to run it. That way we should soon climb to four hundred again and be absolutely safe. Think about it. The country won't always be wallowing in this slough of despond. Even Wall Street is picking up a bit, I hear, in spite of that chap Roosevelt, who seems to have scared the bankers half out of their wits."

David did think about it but deferred it until they had a slice of luck, of the kind they had in 1912, when a wealthy and eccentric father, having lost his only son in an overseas drowning accident, died a widower, leaving twelve thousand pounds to Bamfylde solely because the school had been mentioned in his son's last letter home, written the day he died.

Then, with building progressing rapidly, the summer term slipped away, and everybody went home, and he and Grace toured the Western Isles as far as Skye, then came south again, where he left her to spend the last fortnight of the holidays with her grandparents at Elmer's End.

He had a big backlog of work before the new school year opened in mid-September, and was glad of Boyer's help, spending a good deal of his time in the cottage, where Beth's rowan tree and wild Devonshire garden were thriving.

It was after contemplating them, on his way back to school one warm September evening, that he turned aside at the lych-gate and went down the path to the Bamfylde preserve, on the excuse of satisfying himself that the sexton was mowing the grass.

He had no morbid feelings about being here, in the secluded spot under the yew where Beth and Joan had lain since that unforgettable summer of 1925. Over the years his memories of them had merged into the school, riding the western skyline. Their dust was as much a part of it as that of Judy Cordwainer and Bat Ferguson close by, and of his own flesh and blood too, he thought, as he stood with the evening sun warming his back and looking across the huddle of Ma Midden's farm and Chad's cottage to the higher slope of the moor. Blackbirds sang here and all but the Bamfylde headstones, or the few raised to newly dead villagers, leaned in one direction or another. Gray could have written another elegy here, he thought, and then doubted it as, beyond the low hedge, he saw a sports car rush past, hurrying towards the farm. A stray Old Boy, no doubt, anxious to assure himself that Ma Midden still made the tastiest pasties in Devon.

He went into the church and sat down to collect his thoughts. He often came here these days, ostensibly to work something out but actually to escape the clamour of school and yet remain within call. It was odd, he had told himself more than once, that a man born and raised a Welsh Baptist should seek and find peace here in what his mother would have dismissed as a Popish church, and he was recalling Preacher Skidmore's remark on the prospects of a sectless Britain, when he heard steps echo on the slate slabs outside the west door, then the door open, and a familiar voice said, "Had an idea I'd find you here. Boyer said you were on your way back but I didn't pass anyone." He stood up, dumb with amazement. "Yes, it's me! The perennial bad penny, home from the sea."

It took him ten seconds to convince himself that Chris was standing there, leaning against the oak door and smiling across at him. Chris Forster, sunburned, relaxed, and far more sure of herself than the girl he remembered even in their carefree Windermere days.

"Why the blazes didn't you ring or write? Why didn't you let me know you were home? I'd quite made up my mind you had gone for good. Damn it, you haven't sent so much as a postcard in weeks!"

She said, quietly, "Stop being a bear and come over here and kiss me. It wouldn't be the first time in this church, would it?"

He dived round the end of the pew and threw his arms round her and they stood there for several minutes saying nothing. Behind the swift rush of affection he was aware of a number of inconsequential things; the sunburned V on her neck; the fact that she wore her hair in the fashionable long bob; an unfamiliar perfume, that reminded him vaguely of sandalwood; a persistent blackbird, whistling a repetitive theme in the big yew clump beyond the belfry tower, things that somehow compounded Beth rather than her. She said, gently, "I'm not home for long, Davy. It's very much of a flying visit and I'll explain why. But first I've a surprise for you outside in the car. It's all right, don't scowl! It's male, but it isn't a husband."

They went out into the evening sunshine and up the path to the road where a little sports car was parked, the kind of silver grey toy some of the wilder spirits drove when returning to school a term or two after they had left. It was empty and he said, "You mean *that*? The car?" and she laughed, calling, "Ulrich? You don't have to hide! Where are you?"

A dark, rather sallow boy of about ten sidled into view, returning from the direction of the farm, hidden by the bend in the road. He was a continental. David could see that at a glance and this was established not so much by his clothes, grey knickerbockers and pork-pie hat, with a little feather tucked into the band, but by his bobbing little bow in David's direction. He was a spindly, undernourished little chap, with large, melancholy eyes that at once sought Christine's, apprehensively he would say.

She said, briskly, "This is Herr Powlett-Jones, Ulrich, headmaster of the school. Don't be shy. He's a very kind man. Come over and shake hands."

Ulrich approached gingerly, hand fully extended continental fashion, and when David shook and released it, he stepped smartly back, made another little bow and came smartly to attention.

"Ulrich," she said, "has just lost his father and his mother died a year ago. In a way I've adopted him, haven't I, Ulrich?"

The boy's defenceless eyes sought hers again, so that David thought, "He's in a rare pickle of one sort or another, and she's fishing him out of it," and Ulrich at once confirmed this, saying, "Always you have been most kind, Fraulein Forster."

"We'll go back to school now, Ulrich, for I have to make arrangements for you," and the child climbed obediently into the back seat, where he folded his arms and sat very erect, looking as expressionless as a page on ceremonial duty.

Chris said, as David squeezed in beside her, "His name is Meyer. I'll explain about him later. He's been fed. I introduced him to Rigby, who kindly took him down to the kitchen and while he was eating I looked for you but couldn't find you. Then a groundsman said you were down at Boyer's cottage so we both came looking."

She was like Grace in that way. She never forgot anything he told her about the school and was well aware Chad Boyer had been one of his favourites and had recently joined the staff. She was a fast and expert driver. In a flash they were shooting up the east drive and skidding to a halt on the forecourt gravel.

"Would it be asking too much to let Ulrich stay here with you until term begins, Davy?"

"That's no problem," he said. "I'll tell Rigby to bed him down in the sanatorium. The boys return on Thursday and when they do he can go in Nicolson's until you collect him." He turned to the child, now standing to attention. "You don't have to be correct here, Ulrich, and certainly not in the holidays. Go with this gentleman, and he'll show you where you can sleep," and as the door closed behind child and butler, "You're a great one for springing things on me. You haven't really adopted him, have you?"

"Not officially," she said, "but I intend to, providing it can be arranged."

"Well, it can't," he said. "I've had occasion to go into these things, and as our law stands someone in your situation wouldn't be allowed to adopt a boy. Maybe Canadian law is different. Has he any relatives in the States?"

"No, Davy. None."

"How long do you want to board him?"

She said, looking at him steadily, "Permanently, Davy. If it could be arranged. I'm getting him registered as an official refugee and in time, if all goes as I hope, he'll take up British nationality, but I don't want him regarded as a charity boy. I'll pay his fees."

"*You* will? Two-fifty a year?"

"Well, not me exactly, an organisation set up for cases like Ulrich by the Jewish Rescue Committee in the States. I'm not worried about that part of it, it's more or less fixed. The point is, I want him to have affection . . . help . . . someone to turn to. He's been through a dreadful time. His father was kicked to death in front of his eyes in July. I almost witnessed it myself. Those bloody Brown Shirts, out on the rampage."

"His father was anti-Nazi?"

"His father wasn't antianything. He was a harmless little jeweller and his shop was picketed in an anti-Jewish demonstration they staged. You must have read about what's going on in Germany since that foul little bastard took over but maybe it hasn't registered over here. Well, it's real enough there, a daily occurrence. There are scores of Ulrichs in Bavaria alone. I should like to have scooped them all up but I had enough trouble getting one out."

He looked at her with wonder. "Just how *did* you get him out?"

"Kept him hidden in my hotel for a fortnight, then passed him off as my nephew. The point is, it's all happened at a very awkward time for me. I'd have taken him back to the States and given him time to settle a bit, but I'm due to begin this lecture tour on Monday week, and I couldn't have got him a passage at such short notice. The only thing I could think of was to bring him here."

"Tell me about it. But first of all, have you eaten?"

"No, but any old thing will do. I've got to leave in an hour or so. I'm due in London by morning and I sail the day after, from Southampton."

He rang for Rigby and cold supper for two was brought in. She ate at speed, as though racing the clock, and he began to notice she did most things like this. Between gulps she told him how she came to be involved with Ulrich Meyer, towards the end of her three months' stay in Munich. "I'd heard about what was taking place over there but like you, like everyone else outside Germany, it didn't make an impact. I mean, one regarded it as a wave of street riots but it isn't like that at all. It's the end of the world for anyone opposed to Hitler, and for neutrals too. It's like living in Czarist Russia during a Cossack pogrom. Everyone's looking over their shoulder. They've set up camps for Communists, Socialists and Social Democrats, and for any Catholic or Lutheran who speaks out. Gangs of louts range the streets, knocking on people's doors and smashing windows. Before this happened to Herr Meyer, he had 'Juden' scrawled across his shop windows and men posted outside to turn customers away."

"You mean just in Munich and other Bavarian cities?"

"No, all over. Ever since the Reichstag fire in February. People outside have got to wake up, Davy. I'm going to start campaigning during my lecture tour but it needs far more than that."

"You mean it's likely to last? That there won't be a counter-revolution of some kind?"

"There might, but even that would mean civil war in the streets, and tyranny of one sort or another. Democracy is finished over there, so long as Hitler and his thugs are around. You can depend on that."

It made him acutely aware of his isolation, a political isolation that he would have found shaming a few years ago. He read the newspapers, and occasionally listened to radio bulletins on the library four-valve set, or one of the homemade radio sets built by radio enthusiasts, of which there were a dozen or so in Bamfylde. But strife and persecution on the scale she was describing, and of which Ulrich Meyer was living proof, had not emerged from news bulletins, only the political instability one had come to accept as the post-war norm in Germany, France and Italy.

He said, "You're right, of course. Down here we're cut off," but she countered, sharply. "No, Davy! Not just down here. Everywhere on this side of the Channel. I've heard Germans talk openly of 'Der Tag' again, the way they did before the 1914 war. It's no better in Italy. Fascists there kidnap political opponents, sometimes murder them, and dose others with pints of castor oil. Sooner or later everybody's got to face up to what's happening, and when I get a constituency I'm going to make sure they do."

"That won't win you many friends in the Labour party. They're all for disarmament, aren't they?"

"I can't help about that. I've seen what's happening and they haven't. Ulrich is going to be a *cause célèbre* before I'm done with him."

475

"And in the meantime I'm in *loco parentis?*"

"I can't think of anyone better suited for the job, can you?" She smiled, got up and came round the table to kiss him. "That's all about my obligations. How are you coping with yours, Davy? How is it working out?"

"Algy Herries tells me fair to middling," he said, "but I'll say one thing. Standing in for three-hundred-odd parents eight months of the year is an ageing process. Look at the hair above my ears."

"There would have been a lot more grey if you hadn't taken the bit between your teeth, Davy. You were a born worrier when I met you, muddling along under that man Alcock. Thank God somebody on that Board had the sense to push you forward. It'll be the saving of this place and the making of you. You already look fruitier than the old Davy."

"I wish I could say the same for you. When are you going to stop driving yourself, Chris?"

She gave him one of her half-humorous and speculative looks. "When I've dropped anchor, like you. When I can see where I'm heading. In that respect you're lucky, Davy. I'll keep in touch and you must write regularly, too, and tell me every last thing about that poor little beggar upstairs. Could I go up and say goodbye to him?"

"Surely. It's left at the top of the stairs, and the door facing at the end of the corridor."

She went out and he rang for Rigby to clear away, moving over to the windows where the last glimmer of light glowed in the far west. It was very quiet and still out there, as though the place was conserving its energies for the tumult of the approaching term.

3

Grace was due back the next day but in the meantime he took 'Stilts' Rhodes into his confidence, sensing that the Sunsetters, above all, would have to be briefed about the arrival of Ulrich Meyer in their midst. They had no continentals at the school and the fact that the boy spoke near-perfect English was a help. But those clothes, and that little bow, would mark him down from the first day of term, and he would have to rely on Stilts to weight circumstances in Meyer's favour.

Stilts was an immensely tall, long-legged Fifth Former, whose father was a railway superintendent in Lahore, an easy-going chap and a brilliant cricketer, who had captained the Bamfylde Eleven through the summer. He was head boy of the Sunsetters and although David did not credit him with much imagination, he relied upon Boyer to press the message home.

Stilts said, aghast, "A Jerry, sir? We've never had one of those, have we?"

"No, we haven't but if things continue to happen, like the circumstances that brought the poor kid here, we're likely to get a steady trickle in a year or so. The point is, I don't want him ragged, not even gently. You've got to behave to him 'correctly', as he understands that word. He's bright but he's had a pretty rough deal for a kid his age. His father was booted to death in front of him only a few weeks ago, and he's a refugee."

Stilts was visibly shocked. "*Booted*, sir? You mean mobbed—lynched?"

"That's exactly what I mean. He's a Jew, and they're attacking Jews on the streets all over Germany. He was smuggled out by a friend of mine."

"A kid his age? Good Lord, sir, they wouldn't have manhandled him, would they?"

"My information from an eye witness is that there's nothing they won't do. You probably read about how they set fire to the Reichstag and charged a half-wit with the crime."

"You mean I should . . . well . . . spread it around, sir? What happened, I mean?"

"Yes, but discreetly. It's the best way of getting him sympathy."

"Well, I'll do what I can, sir. He'll be going in with the Sunsetters, won't he?"

"As soon as term starts. Meantime I'll have to coach him a bit. I daresay he'll regard this place as another kind of bear-garden if I don't. Can I rely on your help, Stilts?"

"Well, yes, sir, under the circumstances . . . I mean, it's a bit much, isn't it? Kicking a chap's pater to death. But I suppose it's the kind of thing you can expect from them, isn't it?"

"I wouldn't have expected it. I fought the Germans for three years, and although I came across the odd brute, most of them seemed pretty decent fellows. I remember upsetting the Fifth when I first came here, telling them how two Jerry prisoners carried me across open ground under a barrage on the Somme, and how front-line infantrymen soon stopped calling them Huns. Some of the chaps thought it pretty odd of me to put in a good word for them. Now, I imagine, I shall have to do it again. The point to remember is it's only a section of Germans who go along with that kind of thing. I hope to God some of the better people sit on Hitler before he gets a real grip on the country."

"Oh, that chap won't last long, sir," Rhodes said, cheerfully, "I mean, he's nuts, isn't he, sir? He looks nuts and he acts nuts. Not like Mussolini."

"You admire Mussolini?"

"No, not exactly, sir, but I was reading in the Sunday paper during the hols that he's smartened the Eyeties up a bit—new roads and suchlike."

"Well, don't believe all you read. My information from the same witness is that he murders his opponents and doses others with pints of castor oil."

It did not seem to shock Stilts as much as the booting. "Is that so, sir? Well, you never can tell what they'll get up to over there," and David thought his attitude was probably reflected by almost every boy at Bamfylde, including the dozen or so coloured boys, and the odd Colonial on the muster roll. It made him reflect upon Chris's warning that, on this side of the Channel, everyone tended to lower a safety curtain.

He had a long talk with Ulrich that same day and took him to tea with the Boyers. Alison warmed towards him and he responded to her in the way he had to Chris. "Wouldn't it be a good idea to let him stay here for a term or so?" she asked, but David said no, it would only delay integration. The best way to drop him gently into the deep end.

"It won't be the deep end once the word gets around," Chad said. "If someone had shot his old man it mightn't have made much difference. But kicking, that's different. The chaps won't go for that."

The chaps didn't. Within two days of reassembly Meyer became an object of respectful curiosity. Nobody chivvied him, nobody jeered at his outlandish clothes, or his formal manners. He was an extraordinarily bright little boy. Barnaby and Howarth said he was up to Lower Fifth standard, and Renshaw-Smith discovered that he had a rare appreciation of classical music and was a promising pianist. "It only goes to show," Howarth grumbled, "that there's something bloody wrong with our system of education. Here's a child of eleven who is already at home with Goethe, and we have louts in the Sixth who make nothing at all of Goldsmith and Tennyson. I don't know, maybe we're all on a wrong tack, P.J."

"I wouldn't say that," David said, "there's nothing wrong with Continental academic standards but the boy's presence here proves they've got a hell of a lot to learn about the art of government. I know which slant Algy Herries would favour."

"Question of priority," said Barnaby, and came up with the inevitable tag from his favourite Tacitus—*'reipublicae forma laudari facilius quam evenire . . .'* translating it, in response to Howarth's bleak stare, as "It is easier for a form of government to be praised than brought about; if brought about it cannot be made lasting."

"I prefer Burke," grunted Howarth. "More down to earth. 'Among a people generally corrupt liberty cannot long exist.'"

David left them spouting at one another and went about his business, but Ulrich Meyer proved a springboard for some lively current affairs discussions with the Sixth that term, particularly as regards recent events in Germany. The trial of Van der Lubbe, for the Reichstag fire, followed by the threatened withdrawal of Germany from The League, were two sizeable straws in the wind and Meyer's presence among them gave both items an immediacy they would not otherwise have had. Hislop was particularly aggressive, declaring that Germany, left to herself, would soon prove the menace she was twenty years before, and 'ought to be sat on, pronto!' The mild-mannered Christopherson II took the pacifist line, declaring that a new armaments race was the most certain way of bringing about a second World War. Where did David stand, he asked, looking for support from such a well-known opponent of militarism but David, who always tried to be absolutely frank with the Sixth, had to admit that he did not know.

"The fact is," he said, "any sane man should prefer civilised discussion to war, as a means of settling international disputes, but what do you do against brute force? Meyer's father was a pacifist. It didn't stop the louts picketing his shop, kicking him to death and running off scot-free."

"There's provision in The League of Nations Charter for the

application of economic sanctions," protested Christopherson, but Hislop came back with, "Nobody seems all that anxious to stop trading with Japan since its invasion of Manchuria."

Christopherson, one of the few seniors with strong religious convictions, held to his point, aware that he was in a minority of one. "If a nation professes Christianity, oughtn't it to practise Christian virtues in politics, sir?" but before David could think of an answer Mainwaring growled, "Christian virtues, my eye! If anyone started shoving my Governor around he'd wake up in hospital if he woke up at all!" and everyone laughed as the bell rang, and the familiar hum of dismissal rose from surrounding classrooms. They hustled out, most of them, for a quick punta-bout until lunch bell, but Nixon, a boy who had travelled the Continent during his holidays, remained and seemed, David thought, troubled.

"Well, Nixon?"

"Excuse me, sir . . . something I didn't like to mention in front of the others—I mean—seeing we had a kid like Meyer here. Have you read *The Road Back*, sequel to *All Quiet on the Western Front*?"

"No, I haven't, Nixon. Does it have a bearing on what we've been discussing?"

"In a way it does, sir. It's concerned with what the Jerry front-line troops found when they went home after the war. The whole country had been sewn up by the war profiteers while they were away at the Front."

"That wasn't peculiar to Germany. Every country had its own crop of profiteers who made a pot of money while others slogged it out in the mud."

"Yes I know, sir. But I met a one-legged ex-service chap in St. Moritz when I was there in the Easter hols and he said the German Jews had sat up and begged for what they were getting. What I mean is, maybe it's a case of six of one and half a dozen of the other? Hitler recruits from ex-service chaps, doesn't he? I daresay a lot of them have got it in for the Jews. Mightn't that be a reason why a screw-ball like Hitler gets so much support?"

He was glad Nixon had asked that question. It gave him a chance to get the situation into a better focus. He said, "The fact is, Nixon, the two things don't match up. Jew-baiting has been a time-honoured sport on the part of despots for centuries, a means of diverting attention from failures on the part of the government. The Czars went in for it, so did the Spaniards. And Henry V—a chap I never could stand—kicked the Jews out of England at one time. It was Cromwell who had the sense to invite them back. I daresay there were Jewish war profiteers in Germany, but profiteering isn't a Jewish prerogative by any means, so don't fall for that one, however convincing that one-legged Jerry sounded. The Jews are singled out because they're easily recognisable."

"Yes, sir. Thank you. You didn't mind me mentioning it?"

"I'm very glad you did," David said, "but gladder still you had the sense to raise it in private. Baiting sects on account of race, religion or colour is wrong on any account, wouldn't you say?"

"Yes, I suppose it is, sir," and Nixon pottered off, still only half-convinced, so that David reflected both he and Bamfylde owed Christine Forster a debt for dumping Ulrich Meyer in their midst. The funny little chap was already serving as a catalyst.

He went through Big School door into his quarters and saw, on the hall table, a pile of letters that had arrived with the mid-day post. One from Chris was among them. She was keeping her promise to write once a week and this one was post-marked Cincinnati. She was well-launched on her tour, it seemed, and he was looking forward to the pleasure of reading her latest news when he heard an apologetic cough at his elbow. Little Meyer was standing there, as usual at attention. He was holding an unsealed letter, addressed to 'Fraulein Forster', but with nothing else on the envelope. He said, "Well, Meyer? What can I do for you today?" and Meyer said, "Sir, I have made my report to Miss Forster. I would be happy if you would address this letter for me. After approving it, of course."

"You mean you want me to look it over for grammar, Meyer?"

The child did not blink. "No, sir. The grammar is correct. I took great pains with the composition. But you will want to approve what I write."

"Censor your letter? I don't want to do that. We don't censor boys' letters home. Why should I have to read yours in particular?"

"Sir?"

He realised that Meyer was confused and said, "Come inside, I'll try and explain," and they went into the living-room where lunch was laid. "Sit down, Meyer, and listen. It was polite of you to invite me to read it and I will, of course, if you really wish it.

481

But don't get the idea it's standard practice here. Most of the boys would be angry if they thought masters read their private mail, and rightly so. Letters to parents and friends are personal, private things, and everyone is entitled to personal privacy as a right, do you follow me?"

"Yes, sir . . . but it is unusual, is it not? I mean, that would qualify as an English custom?"

"Well, you could put it that way. Now then, do you really want me to read it before I address it? Or would you honestly prefer that I didn't?"

Meyer seemed to give the matter considerable thought. Finally he said, extending his hand, "I wish to observe all your customs, sir. If I am to become an Englishman that is important, is it not?"

"I think it is, Meyer," and improbably he thought of Beth and how, in these circumstances, she might have reached out and hugged the child, as someone in desperate need of love. He experienced the same impulse, almost as though it was relayed to him, but all he said was, "Here's a letter from Miss Forster with her last address on the back. Copy it down, seal it and put your letter in the post-box."

"Yes, sir. Thank you, sir," and Meyer clicked his heels and gave his formal little bow.

He was relieved, a fortnight or so later, that Meyer had decided to observe English customs. Chris wrote saying

You might be interested to learn Ulrich sees you as a combination of Luther and Frederick the Great, with a dash of Moses thrown in. It's quite obvious he's settling there, as I knew he would with you to keep an eye on him, so I want to say thank you again, Davy, for making the effort, when you obviously have so much on your plate.

I'm two-thirds through this tour now and it looks as though I shall be home in the spring. There's talk of me being put forward for Ben Cathcart's constituency, in Openshawe South, when he retires and this is far better than I hoped. It has a Labour majority of over eight thousand, so, given ordinary luck, I couldn't fail to get elected. I won't catch you on the hop, again, Davy. We'll meet somewhere as soon as I get back, and if it's term-time you'll have to drop everything and come.

It was good to think of her impending return after all this time but he was resigned now to her marriage to politics. With a seat like Openshawe South in the offing she was already as good as elected, and once in Parliament she would be lost to him. He filed her letter with all the others and locked the file away. It seemed to him a symbolic gesture.

Chapter Three

1

The terminal-season rhythm caught him up again, so smoothly and compellingly that he often forgot he was now its arbiter here, with the power to vary the tempo and volume, to throw away the book if he felt like it, and replace it with a new one—but he did nothing so drastic. Most of the changes and adjustments he introduced were marginal, infiltrating themselves into the system within a matter of weeks or days, so that visiting Old Boys of Algy's vintage were rarely prompted to make disparaging comparisons, the privilege of all Old Boys everywhere. His life was a calendar within a calendar, so regulated that he could even predict the weather in advance. Mid-December, for instance, with Chad Boyer back in his former role as the pirate king in *The Pirates of Penzance*, a sequence of tingling, frosty days, when the ruts in west drive were coated with ice and Chivenor, head prefect, crossed the lighted quad at lock-up 'clothed in his breath' as Tennyson might have seen him, save that Chivenor carried a large bunch of keys instead of Excalibur. The Christmas lull, with light snow turning to slush, and the lowest boughs of the east drive beeches dripping down his neck as he walked, heavily muffered down to Chad's cottage for tea and muffins by a familiar hearth.

A new term, slowed by January mire, with a stream of cars arriving in slashing rain, disgorging cargoes of boys for the tight-rope term. Howarth's winter cough, booming a warning that his old enemy bronchitis would lay him low before March. The new buildings deserted by the builders' men, who could do nothing in this kind of weather, leaving the half-finished gymnasium raw and skeletal against a grey winter sky.

Then February, with everybody's tempers edgy, Molyneux and Howarth bickering over trivial issues and young Dennison, who had followed Irvine as geography master, resigning command of the Corps on account of cartilage trouble—few of these things actually impinged on him but the Corps vacuum did, and he made what seemed to those who remembered his earlier prejudices, a revolutionary decision, taking command himself and appearing in the quad for the first time in a brand new khaki outfit, with three pips on his shoulder.

"I feel a very bogus captain," he told Barnaby, when the latter ironically saluted him. "I would have wagered ten pounds to a penny you'd never see me in this rig again. But, hang it all, the Corps is there, and no one else seems to have a clue about how to run it. Besides, I'm only half a pacifist nowadays."

"I daresay the drill book is a bit above your head these days, P.J.," Barnaby said. "You won't have them kneeling to receive cavalry, I hope?" But the drill book hadn't changed all that much. They were still using Lewis guns, of the type David had lugged up the line in 1917, still forming fours, still singing the same old songs on route marches, choruses that had brought tears to his eyes on Armistice Day, in 1918, but now seemed as harmlessly nostalgic as carols.

One or two of the Old Boys pulled his leg about his conversion. One (it was Starchy Gosse, now a stockbroker) raising his hat and giving a cheer as he watched Captain Powlett-Jones dismissing his troops on the playing field after the drill competition.

"Permit me to recant too, Pow-Wow," he said, after following David to his quarters for the obligatory glass of Old Boys' sherry. "I once regarded you as the envoy of Lenin and Trotsky. You probably don't know how close you came to getting stuck with 'Bolshie' instead of the cosy 'Pow-Wow'!"

"I knew all right," David told him. "I overheard you or your brother discussing me while sitting on Algy's Mount Olympus, so let me tell you something in return. I'm still Bolshie as regards the fun and games chaps like you play in Threadneedle Street. If we'd guillotined the whole damned crowd of you in Trafalgar Square, maybe I wouldn't be doing this now."

Gosse took the gibe in good part, as they all did whenever they came back here, poking around and indulging in their orgies of reminiscence. His approach to them was that of an equal, with no obligation to counsel and patronise, now that they were out in the world.

March, with weeks of cold, drying winds, hardening the pitches, so that Nicolson's was able to confound the form book by winning the rugby shield, beating Havelock's, the hot favourites, by fourteen points. But March, for him, was a sad month, too, his sister Gwynneth wiring to say his mother had died in her sleep on Good Friday, a week before he was due to pay one of his bi-annual visits.

He and Grace travelled to Wales for the funeral, and Grace waited in the crowded little kitchen while he went into the front parlour to take a final look at her, surrounded by armfuls of daffodils and narcissi. She looked not merely peaceful but girlish, so that he caught his breath, wondering how so much sorrow, and so many years of unremitting toil, could leave so small a mark on her features. For her, for him too, at that moment, time stood still and he was looking at the same woman who had gone about her chores that summer evening he sat stunned in the kitchen, choking on the high tea she set before him only hours after they had told her that she had lost a husband and two sons in the pit explosion down the Valley. For sheer grit and stamina there had never been anybody like her, not even in the trenches. She had the kind of faith that made molehills of mountains of trouble, enabling her to absorb any shock, any disaster, any disappointment, with the dignity one associated with eighth-century saints.

He stood there aware of a sense of loss but no grief, for they told him she had given no sign of pain, or even discomfort, on retiring to bed the night she died. She had even spent the morning giving the parlour a spring-clean, as though she had a premonition it was likely to be seen by strangers within the week. All the wreaths and sprays surrounding the coffin trailed the usual black-edged cards, with assurances that struck him as a little smug, even though he was accustomed to the conventions of death in the

Valley. 'Safe in the arms of Jesus', 'Gathered to her eternal rest' and 'In the certain hope of a glorious resurrection'. He wondered if the neighbours who had penned them had possessed her kind of faith, a deep-rooted assurance in the natural order of things, an unassailable belief that a Blessed Redeemer would forgive her sins, if she had any, and reunite her with the stocky little man buried a few miles from here, far below the surface of the mountain. It was a faith that had sustained her through every trial and hazard, something intensely personal that had very little to do with the chants, prayers and affirmations proclaimed in the Elim Chapel down the hill. No one he had ever met had possessed such a faith, fused as it was with a sense of duty, and an obligation towards everyone her life had touched, a faith impervious to grief and penury, the faith of a child, buttressed by loving parents against every eventuality, even death itself. A faith like that was worth a million in the bank, and half a dozen Bamfyldes. Yet, in a sense, he had been able to borrow a little of it over the years. The spark it had lit in him as a child had never been entirely extinguished, as he had once believed, by the crashing bombardments of the Somme, and the long, dragging ordeal of Passchendaele. It had survived, to be blown upon by Algy and others on the moor, by the fortitude of kids like Briarley and Winterbourne, by Beth's love, by the patience of young Grace, by the friendship and encouragement of men like Howarth and Barnaby, but, above all, by a sense of contributing that had grown upon him like another skin, a little every year, a fraction every term.

He squeezed the small, cold hand and went back into the kitchen where Ewart, his brother-in-law, was sitting smoking half a Woodbine. Ewart said, "There's four years left on the lease yer, Davyboy. You wouldn't have no objections to me and Gwyn moving in, and taking it over, would you now? It's three shillings a week under the rent we pay for our rabbit-hutch, and me being on short-time . . ."

"Whatever bits and pieces she left are Gwyn's and Megan's, Ewart. That was always understood. Aren't things any better up here?" and Ewart said a little but not all that much. The Valley had never recovered from the strife and shutdowns of 1925 and 1926.

"Why don't you think about moving south? There's no future here and you're still in your prime."

"What else could I do, boyo? Been underground since I was fourteen, I have."

"How much do you earn in a good week?"

"Three-five," Ewart told him, "and I'm one of the lucky ones."

He thought, "We pay our groundsmen four pounds a week and they have accommodation thrown in. Old Westacott is due to retire in September, and that means everybody will move up one. I wonder if I could wangle Ewart the handyman's job? Or if he'd accept it, with me being head. I'll have a word with Gwyn after the funeral."

As he had half-expected, his sister had reservations. "Suppose I should talk him into it," she said, "would it be right? A headmaster, with a sister married to the odd-job man? What I mean is, wouldn't it make you look a little bit silly, Davy? Because if it did Mam wouldn't have heard of us going. You know that, boyo."

"Mam was old-fashioned that way. I tried to talk her into coming down when I first got the job but she wouldn't and I daresay that was the real reason. However, times have changed. I've got Old Boys with degrees taking jobs as counter-jumpers and clerks, and in one way it's a good thing. If things improved in the mines you could always move back. Why don't you think it over?"

"I'll do that," she said, "and thanks anyway, Davy," and she kissed him.

2

Chris rang as he had feared, in the first week of the new term, when it was impossible to snatch a weekend and meet her in London on her way up north, where she was due to be interviewed by the selection committee of the Openshawe South Division. Her candidature was regarded as a near-certainty, for she was on a short-list of two, opposed by another academic. "Male, of course," she said, "but wet. He's written a book on political economy. I tried to read it. It was like eating my way through four helpings of Bamfylde suet pudding."

"How old is he?" David wanted to know, and she said thirty-two or three. "He's a prominent pacifist, so at least our approaches offer alternatives. His father was a friend of Bertrand Russell, who served time during the war as a conscientious objector."

"Seems grass-rooted," David said, "you'd better watch him."

"Come, you don't really believe that, Davy. Not after what happened to Ulrich's father."

"I don't know what I believe any more. Sometimes I think the Sixth Formers have a clearer picture of what's happening than I have. Politically speaking I'm a museum-piece nowadays. Listen, hustler, it's hopeless for me to think of getting up there this weekend. Assuming you get chosen, when is your adoption meeting likely to be?"

"Second week in May, but how can you attend that? You know what happened last time."

He could chuckle at that. "It's not the same," he said, "these days I call the tune and they'd have the devil's own job to unseat me now. Algy and Howarth say I'd see 'em all off. How about the Saturday after next, in Manchester?"

"Please, *sir*," she said, and then, "I still love you very much, Davy."

"I'm delighted to hear it. But will it survive a wildly acclaimed maiden speech in the House?"

"It would survive me becoming the first Prime Minister in petticoats and you know it. You're just fishing for compliments."

He rang off, feeling braced. There was no positive future in their association but it was good to feel they still enjoyed the easy comradeship of the past, after such a long separation.

*　　*　　*

He had not expected her to meet him at the barrier, assuming she would be too busy, but she was there, peering anxiously at the stream of passengers from the West Country train, and he realised at once that something was amiss. She looked as bleak and tense as the night he had escorted her home to her lodgings, after that rowdy meeting, in the autumn of 1931, and bore no resemblance to his assessment of the eager girl he had talked to on the phone ten days before. He said, at once, "What's happened, Chris? That long-haired chap hasn't pipped you, has he?" and she said, "I could have faced up to it if he had, but you can't call a unanimous vote in his favour a pipping, can you?"

"The same old story? A woman can't win a Labour seat?"

"No, a very new story. They're incapable of facing facts and that's a tragedy, not just for me but for the party, and the country, too, in the long run. Where can we go? I need a drink."

"I booked the night at the Queen's and shall have to sign in. We can get a drink and a meal there. I'll get a taxi."

"It isn't worth it," she said, "it's just down the approach to Piccadilly," and she walked silently beside him down the setts to the hotel lobby, waiting while he signed in and sent the man up with his key and bag. He ordered two double whiskies and noticed she downed hers like a toper.

"Was it so very bad?"

"It's the end of everything for me. For some years, at least."

"But why, for God's sake? There'll be other vacancies, and there are rumours of an election next year."

"You don't get the message. I made a declaration. Some people would see it as tempting Providence, but I can't work any other way, and neither could you if you were in my shoes. The Labour Party is traditionally pacifist. I don't have to remind you of that, do I?"

"No, you don't, but hang it, Chris, even Baldwin is playing it in low keys these days. What the hell did you say to them to set them against you en masse?"

"I told the truth, as I saw it. They asked me my views on disarmament, and I told them it would be sheer madness in view of what's happening in Germany and Italy. Good God, they read the papers, don't they? They must know Jews are being forced to sweep the streets, that their property is being confiscated, that even the toddlers in Germany are being drilled, that anyone who questions Hitler and his Brown Shirts is dragged from his bed in the middle of the night and never seen again. I told them children in schools were being taught to inform on their parents, that the declared policy of Hitler is to build the biggest military machine in history. I told them Socialists were being murdered in Italy, and that newspapers were being sold on the streets of Berlin with cartoons showing Jews eating Christian children. I was there a mere three months but I saw some of these things, and what I didn't see was confirmed by people who had. I told them about Ulrich. Do you know what the Chairman said in reply? The only way to stop it was by Christian example—that disarmament on our part would be a gesture everyone else would follow! How's that for wishful thinking?"

"You don't have to convince me," he said, "I admitted I was confused but I've since had several talks with Meyer. As a matter of fact, I got him to come and talk to the Sixth. It set them thinking, I can tell you. The point is, where do you go from here? Newspaper articles, or a report to Transport House that the party should rethink its policy?"

She made a gesture of impatience. "What good would that do? I'm not the only one who understands what's happening, but how do you set about persuading a caucus to reverse its thinking? For that matter, how do you alert the right wing, never mind the left?"

"I suppose the same way you convince anybody of anything. By simply pegging away."

She said, thoughtfully, "There's more to it than that, Davy. The ability to use Ulrich to make your point for you, at a place as hidebound as Bamfylde, gives you the advantage on all of us. As a matter of fact, since they rejected me in favour of that self-opinionated little whippersnapper, I've been doing some rethinking myself. It's time I did. You can get punch-drunk on blue books and pamphlets and I'm beginning to suffer from a hangover."

"What does that add up to?"

She smiled. "Dear Davy . . . I can't tell you here. How well do you know the country about here?"

"Hardly at all. It's flat and built up, isn't it?"

"No, it isn't. It's only flat on the Cheshire side. We'll go to Dovedale, the best walking country in England. I was there last weekend, with a chum of mine from University days."

"I shall have to catch an early Sunday train back. It's slow and will take me eight hours. Howarth is standing in for me and he's not too well."

"I'll get you back in time."

He followed her out to catch a bus to Openshawe, where her bumble-bee car was garaged and an hour later, meeting little but cycling and hiking parties on the road, they were deep in the Dales, and he saw that he had underestimated Derbyshire, despite doing 'Peveril of the Peak' with the Middle Fourth, when Howarth was off sick last winter. The hills, shimmering in May sunshine, were crowned with masses of rock, and the slopes down to the Dove were clothed with older, more civilised woods than the straggling thickets on the banks of the Bray, Barle and Exe. They had tea in a pub and she led him down to the floor of the valley. Her spirits lifted when they saw the word 'Chatsworth' on a signpost and he reminded her that Mary, Queen of Scots, had spent part of her nineteen years' imprisonment up here. She said, "Another poor devil trapped in men's politics. Was she really guilty of all those plots, Davy?"

"As guilty as hell," he said. "She was party to a plot to assassinate Elizabeth by exploding gunpowder under the bed. But it never stopped her being a great favourite in the Junior School. She's got a romantic aura. I can always guarantee attention when I'm telling the Third about the last scene at Fotheringay. Especially that bit about the red wig coming off and exposing her as a grizzled old hag."

She laughed and he was glad to note a rise of her mercury. "You really do go for the gory details, Davy. But who are you to sneer at the romantics?"

"Oh, I don't. I make 'em work overtime for me. Until I get to the Fifth, that is," and suddenly she stopped in her stride, swung him round and kissed him on the mouth.

"You're wonderful medicine for me, Davy."

They were moving along a down-curving track, about some two hundred feet above the river. Oak, beech, thorn and chestnut grew in profusion, and although this was clearly a popular hikers' path they had met none over the last mile. She said, "In here, Davy . . ." and steered him off the track into a tiny glade, carpeted with the skeletons of last year's leaves and sown with bluebells and wood anemones. "We've waited long enough, Davy. Too long for our good. I'm sure of you, absolutely sure and, just for the record, there never was anyone else in Canada or the States."

"You don't have to justify yourself to me."

"I do. No one else means a damn to me."

Until then, until the moment she stopped, he had been aware on her part of something that had not been there in the serene days when they had been lovers on the shore of Windermere, or even that occasion he had been able to bring a measure of peace to her after that rowdy meeting at Bilhampton. But now, screened by the thickets, she seemed to reflect and as his arms went round her she said, mildly, "Here, Davy? Now?" and the way she said it gave him pause. He lowered his head and kissed the swell of her breast above the neck of her blouse.

"That's for you to say, Chris. At Bilhampton you needed me.

I'm not so sure now, in spite of what happened back there. You've grown a lot since then. You'll shake it off with or without me."

"I daresay. But I'll always need you. Not just when I've taken a tumble. I had a special reason for bringing you out here. If it had been simpler we could have stayed in town. I'll try and explain, but kiss me first. As though you meant it."

He kissed her mouth and felt her tremble. She said, "It's enough, you see. You've only got to touch me, Davy," but then, to his astonishment, she moved apart from him and taking lipstick and mirror from her handbag set about restoring her make-up.

He had a picture gallery then of the three women he had held in his arms, performing this same office, and in a way it emphasised their differences. Beth did it absentmindedly, as part of a daily routine. Julia Darbyshire did it painstakingly, as though the face she meant to show to the world was her sole capital, but Christine was different again. She applied lipstick, powder puff and comb with swift, impatient flourishes, the way she tackled most things, following through an impromptu plan but with half an eye on the clock. He said, "I wouldn't bother with the war paint. We're not going home yet, are we?"

"That could depend," she said, "on all manner of things."

"Such as?"

"Your tolerance, to start with."

"Take that for granted. Especially as you cheered me up by saying there was no one else in the picture."

"Not that kind of tolerance, Davy."

"Well?"

"I've always thought of you as my husband, my real husband, that is. If I hadn't I wouldn't have gone to bed with you, not even that night in Bilhampton when I was in the depths of misery. I'm not really promiscuous, although I suppose some people would say I was. I thought I loved Rowley. But I've known I loved you, from the second time we met and I went to confessional in that Newport pub. No, I mean something more important. I'm free, Davy. Or will be, in August."

She could not have said anything more calculated to astonish him. "Free? Rowley's agreed to let you divorce him?"

"Well, not exactly." Her smile was a little crooked, revealing a tinge of malice that was uncharacteristic of her. "I cornered him and forced him to let me go. On pain of being divorced the hard way. Now I suppose you'll want the entire sordid story."

"Don't you think I'm entitled to it?"

She considered. "Yes, you are. You've been very patient. A damned sight more than most men would have been!"

"You're saying we can get married? That you'd settle for Bamfylde?"

"I wouldn't marry you any other way, Davy. That would be treachery."

"Well, then," he said, catching up her hands, "to hell with how you got rid of him. I don't give a damn if you beat it out of him with a club," but she said, "Wait, Davy—you might as well hear it now. It isn't something I'm proud of. There was a lot to be desired in Rowley, but I never did doubt the sincerity of his religious convictions and I left more scars on him than he's left on me."

"Serve him damn well right."

"I can't look at it that way. I wish I could but I can't."

"What happened?"

"I got word of him through a mutual friend and dropped a hint that I'd be delighted to see him again. As an old friend. For a chat, say. He came over one day last summer all smiles and dear-old-girlish. After a pat and a pinch he implied he was all in favour of a form of reconcilation."

"How do you mean, a 'form of reconciliation'?"

"Rowley's kind. I was to remain his official wife, eager and available when he was randy, busy or between mistresses. He was to have a long leash. Say a couple of miles at full stretch. I saw my opening then and pretended to go along with the idea. I even let him get to the point where he was convinced the next time he'd make it all the way back. That wasn't difficult. Bright as he is, he's got a colossal male ego, and wrote off my reservations as a Nonconformist hangover on account of his other sleeping partners. It meant using my body as a bait but it worked like a charm."

"And after that?"

"I had him watched by the seediest little private detective you ever read about, if you read that kind of fiction. His work was a lot better than his appearance. He came up with cast-iron evidence in ten days and all I had to do then was threaten. Rowley holds an important position out there, and the Scots Presbyterian influence is strong in his university. He had no alternative but to cave in and

494

supply evidence for a divorce over here. The decree absolute comes through on August 1st. There's no prospect of complications, or not unless he's been watching us with a telescope this afternoon and that I doubt. He never was one for country delights."

It did not seem more than a defensive statement on her part but he knew she would not view it that way. She would be more likely to regard it as moral blackmail, and at the time it had probably disgusted her. He said, "You can't expect me to feel sorry for him. Plenty of women would have taken him for a lot more than a straight divorce, and you never spent a penny of his money on yourself. Put it out of mind. Look on it as a case of tit for tat." Then, with some difficulty, "In the preliminary skirmishes, didn't you feel anything of the very strong affection you once had for him?"

"Simply as a man? Yes, I did. You were a long way off, and I never did kid myself that celibacy is my strong suit. In that sense it was lucky it was Rowley, and not some other red-blooded male. But what came over to me again, this time in added measure, was his absolute bloody selfishness. Rowley is more than ordinarily selfish, anyway, but measured against someone like you he isn't much more than an animal. At least, that's how it seemed to me. I like to be wanted as a person, not as an instrument. That's important to me, Davy."

"It's important to most women, so don't be too generous with the haloes. If it wasn't I would have said to hell with it and gone off on the rampage now and again, and I daresay you'll discover I can run Rowley pretty close for selfishness sometimes. At least, as far as my job's concerned. Are you absolutely sure you want to take me on? A husband pushing forty is one thing. Motherhood to a horde of growing boys is another."

"I'll cope, somehow. Providing you've got more patience in reserve. In any case, it's you who are taking the risk, Davy. Maybe you should take time off to think about it."

"I've had all the time I need. Meantime I'm starving so why don't we celebrate? Do you think we could get a dinner at that place where we left the car?"

"If we can find our way back to it before dark."

He pulled her up and they went back up the long, winding path to the saddle of the two rock-strewn hills they had crossed an hour ago. In that brief interval or so it seemed to him, they had found a row of signposts pointing the way into a new era.

3

Not since the long, hot summer of 1919 had a term passed in such a succession of fleeting, sunlit days. His mood, in the span between early May and late July, was at one with the period just prior to his earlier marriage. There had been other smoothly running terms but always, at one or another stage of them, something sour or explosive had occurred, a flare-up with Carter, a confrontation with Alcock or even a let-down reminding him yet again that it was all too easy to grow too complacent about one's ability to judge character. But this term, with Bamfylde under his hand, it was all plain sailing and even the highlights were amusing.

There was Hislop's momentary reversion to his original form, when he hit a spectacular six that soared over the western boundary, ricocheted from the bonnet of a Governor's Daimler, and plopped through the open window of an adjoining car, where old Bouncer, back on a visit, was enjoying an afternoon nap. A dozen witnesses stepped forward to swear that Bouncer, leaping from his car, threatened the batsman with his statutory four penal marks for an act of lèse majesté.

There was the sudden appearance of Molyneux's outlandish Australian uncle, who looked exactly like a Colonial gent masquerading as Bernard Shaw, a man so unfamiliar with the taboos of English schools as to appear in the Upper Fifth one morning and address Molyneux by his carefully concealed Christian name, Aloysius, a gaffe that stunned the French master and bid fair to undermine his class discipline for all time. And soon after that there was the overnight visit of Sax Hoskins and his Rhythma-teers, touring the West Country resorts, who descended on Bam-fylde one Sunday afternoon and gave what Sax called a 'Bamfylde Benefit Session', an honour bestowed upon them in Grace's honour.

Sax had always been popular. Unquenchable high spirits, a rumbustious sense of humour and, above all, an uncanny mastery of many so-called musical instruments, dating from his Second Form variations of 'Alexander's Ragtime Band' on a mouth organ, had won him an enduring place in Bamfylde legend. His reappearance, at the head of a professional dance orchestra was a triumph and he played for two hours by Big Hall clock, the only man among his sweating Rhythmateers impervious to the heat, recorded as reaching the high eighties that night.

David had anticipated some difficulty with Grace concerning the prospect of a stepmother. Not much, perhaps, for she had always been an exceptionally biddable child, but their relationship was close and it would not have been surprising if she had viewed Christine with a certain amount of resentment. He told her of his plans the night he returned from Manchester, and was relieved when she took it calmly. Not as a matter of course, exactly, but more like an intelligent adult than an adolescent. She said, after he had outlined the history of his long, frustrating friendship with Christine, "Poor old Daddy! It sounds frightfully complicated. I knew you were keen on her, of course, and one time, two years ago it was, I made sure you'd marry her and was scared, even though she seemed nice that time she came here. But then, when you stopped talking about her, I made up my mind you'd stay single, especially now you're head."

"I'd come to the same conclusion myself," he said. "This came out of the blue. I didn't even know there was any hope for her getting a divorce, and even if there was there was always her determination to get into Parliament. She would, too, if she kept at it. She's that kind of person."

"Won't she ever try again?"

"I don't know. That'll be up to her."

"And what do you think about that?"

He was fortunate, he reflected, to be able to discuss the situation so frankly with a fourteen-year-old. Her objectivity had to do with her long isolation here among so many thrustful males, he supposed. Their resilience, their tendency to treat every new day as a fresh start, had rubbed off on her over the years. He said, "She might try for a local candidature, and I wouldn't stop her. This is Tory and Liberal country, and Labour are keen to get a foot in the door. I imagine it all depends on how she settles in here. She hasn't much confidence in herself as a headmaster's wife. It'll be up to you and me to try and give her some."

"You once had an idea of training me for the job, didn't you?"

"Yes, and in a way I still have. You could help a lot, Tuppence. The commercial courses start in September, when the builders' men move out, and after school-leaving certificate you can take

497

typing and shorthand. Then you can take Miss Rowlandson's place when she retires as secretary. Would that appeal to you?"

She told him it would and that she wanted, in addition, to improve her French and learn German. Her French was already good and she seemed to have a flair for languages. "Oughtn't I to meet her again soon?" she added, "I mean, *before* you get married? We shall have to have a good chin-wag about you," and he laughed, telling her that this was obligatory, if only to warn Chris of his likes and dislikes.

The meeting, when it came on Sports Day, was an unqualified success, adapting to the amiable pattern of the term. He had not realised how much he must have talked to Chris about Grace, or how observant Chris was when it came to assessing people. It was fun to watch Grace showing her round and familiarising her with every odd corner of the place, as though Chris had been a conscientious mother, hoping to send her son here in the autumn. And afterwards they gave him the slip and set out on a walk across Middlemoor, returning dusty and hungry, having achieved some kind of conspiratorial affinity while removed from the world of men and boys. It was only later, shortly before Chris set off north to pay a duty visit to her family in Yorkshire, that she indicated the level of intimacy they had achieved.

"She's an extraordinary little body, Davy. I don't think I've ever met anyone quite like her. Or not anyone under forty. Beth must have been a singular person. I mean, I'd expect any child of yours to be bright, and fairly easy to get along with, but she's more than that. She's . . . well . . . a born go-between. Now I'd say that's rare in a person her age. The really satisfying thing, however, is that she seems to have made up her mind that I'm the best of a bad job."

It was characteristic of her, he thought, to put it like that and he said, laughing, "Don't give me or Beth special credit for Grace. The boys have done that for her. I've always thought of Grace as a woman, even when she was six."

She had left her car up north for an overhaul, so he saw her off at yet another railway station, a familiar one this time, so that the parting was less urgent. When she had gone he walked home along a road cordoned by summer foliage, and rich with the scent of honeysuckle. At the playing field gate he paused, listening to the distant *snack* of the ball at the nets and the odd isolated shout that carried all this way in the evening lull, acknowledging both sounds as part of Bamfylde's summer pattern and welcome on that account.

Standing there, looking over his shoulder at the stark outline of the buildings silhouetted against a lemon, coral-streaked sky, he found it difficult to think of himself as a bridegroom-in-waiting, on a par with the callow young man who had passed this way on summer evenings in 1919. So difficult, indeed, that he could chuckle at the prospect, thinking, "It's impossible to think of oneself as young in this job . . . almost everyone around is so much younger . . . easier to see oneself as an up-and-coming Judy Cordwainer . . . I'm thirty-seven, sound of wind and limb, certainly in the right job, but there have been times over the past few years when I've felt as old as Jehovah in one of His Why-don't-I-give-it-all-up moods . . . ?" And then, unaccountably, he suddenly recalled that ridiculous incident in the train on their honeymoon trip to the Isle of Wight, when Beth had been so embarrassed by the onset of a period and he laughed, standing there by himself, for a thing like that wouldn't be likely to bother many couples nowadays.

As always, his reverie was terminated by the bell, ringing out over the plateau as Norman Minor, seventh in a long and distinguished line of bell-ringers he recalled, made his ritual circuit of the buildings, calling boys to prep like monks to prayer. He never had got round to replacing the handbell with a fixed one and now that he came to think about it he decided it could wait. The longer he stayed here the less he was inclined to disturb the old routine, even though, in a matter of thirty months, he had introduced a variety of new ones. It was a hangover of Algy's philosophy, he supposed—"Concentrate on essentials, expand all you like, but don't pull up anything by the roots before making absolutely certain it's dead."

He extinguished his cigarette carefully, for there were fire hazards in this kind of weather, then went along under a forest of six-foot cow-parsley stalks to the cloverleaf exit of the east drive. By the time he reached the forecourt the prep hush was on the school and he welcomed it. Four weeks wasn't long, for all the jobs he had in hand.

PART
EIGHT

Plenitude

Chapter One

Years later, when twenty-three new names had been added to the memorial outside, when he could look back on the period between his second marriage and the weeks preceding the summer of Dunkirk, he thought of the interval as his time of plenitude, strangely at odds with everything that was piling up outside. That, however, was an ultimate verdict, after he and Chris had met and survived a crisis that was new to him but morbidly familiar to her. So that, whereas he viewed it as no more than another sizeable hump in the rhythm of the years, she saw it as something infinitely more threatening and hazardous than he would have admitted at the time, shrugging it off as her playing-in period, the equivalent of a sensitive new boy's first school year.

It was at one with much that was happening in the world outside, where there seemed no prospect of harmony, where trouble flared in one capital or another, and her worst fears of the early 'thirties were justified, but her own inward struggle had no link with world turbulence, or the looming threat of war. It was a deeply personal challenge, fought without benefit of his armour, his sense of dedication, and there were times, many times, when she envied him his anchorage here in this small, close-knit community. His roots were well down and manifold. Hers, such as they were throughout that testing time, were pitifully shallow, save only the one, strong fibre of her love for him and what this place seemed to have made of him over the years.

* * *

It was a more sophisticated honeymoon than the sedate fortnight at Shanklin with Beth, in 1919. They took turns to drive her silver bumble bee all the way from Calais to Brittany, then down through the château country of the Loire, of which he had written in his single literary foray but had never visited. They enjoyed perfect weather, staying at old inns and eating alfresco meals beside the dusty high-roads. She found him an entertaining guide, for as they moved south to Gascony, then south-east to Carcassonne and Marseilles, and finally north to the battlefields of his youth, loose ends of his undisciplined reading would return to him, prompted by some place-name like Poitiers, or the signboard of an inn calling to mind some jack-booted, blustering character from the past, who had made his outcry and departed, forgotten by all but historical magpies.

In St. Emilion, for instance, he told her the story of Madame Bouquey, who had hidden the fugitive Girondins in her courtyard well, and paid for the impulse on the scaffold in Bordeaux. Near Chalons, his excitement describing the final rally of the Imperial Army in 1814 made her laugh aloud, but who could help sharing his enthusiasm? Farther north, when they drove through the miraculously restored pastures and red-brick villages of the 1915–18 battlefields, he again surprised her, for she had looked for a sombre approach to this tormented ground, where his generation had died, but found instead detachment, so that she said, "I made sure you'd sheer away from this part of France, Davy. I would have, in your place. What happened here, not so long ago, must have scarred every man who survived it."

"Yes, it did that," he replied, thoughtfully, "but I had to come back nevertheless. Perhaps just to satisfy myself how completely Bamfylde had exorcised the past. Maybe the equivalent happened with some of the others who came out of it with a whole skin. What I mean is, a man had to start fresh or cut his throat and, taken all round, I've been lucky."

"Tell me."

"I had a job I could lose myself in before the guns had stopped firing. I had Algy as counsellor and friend. I had Beth for more than six years, then Grace, and now I've got you. A fair deal all round, wouldn't you say?"

She wondered if it was, and whether it was the job, or a generous measure of domestic peace that had played the major part in his rehabilitation and thought, on balance, it was the former. For although she saw him as two men, the thruster with an *idée fixe*, for which he was prepared to sacrifice anything, and an amiable lover, respecting mental privacy and claiming his own as the price of that indulgence, it seemed to her that Bamfylde was never far from his thoughts. Or only in moments of rarefied intimacy, when he seemed to her very young and ardent for a man who, as he was fond of reminding her, was 'pushing forty'.

And here there was another aspect of him that surprised her. He had learned something very valuable from that girl Beth, whatever kind of person she had been, the trick of blending positive virility with an innate respect for a woman's body, so that she could never quite decide whether he approached her as conqueror or pilgrim.

He was surprisingly frank about his first marriage. He told her of Beth's eagerness to conceive a child as soon as they were married, and her recurrent disappointments at her failure to produce a son in the time left to them, and it made her wonder whether she, too, was likely to fail in this respect, for time was running on and she would be thirty next birthday. She said nothing of this to him, however. Although children were important to her, she had an idea they were not a vital factor to him. After all, he had so many substitute sons, with more coming all the time, and it was his passing reference to September's recruits that made her aware of this and vaguely uneasy regarding her ability to adjust to Bamfylde as effortlessly as he promised. It sparked off her very first doubt regarding the irrevocability of marriage to a school rather than a man.

They were on their homeward stretch, driving west from Newhaven across open stretches of the New Forest. He said, as they took the road to Ringwood, and pulled in to picnic at a spot overlooking a bramble-sown pasture, "It was just about here they ran that fool Monmouth to earth. He'd come a fair way from Sedgemoor, and what courage he had had run out of the toes of his boots."

"How was he caught?"

"He was collared by a couple of militiamen hiding in a ditch, with a few dried peas in his pocket. The real tragedy of that uprising was that Monmouth valued his head above his dignity."

"You can't hold that against him. Don't we all when it comes to the crunch?"

"His men didn't. They had everything to lose and damn all to gain, but at least they didn't crawl on their bellies, begging for mercy," and then he chuckled, saying, "There's a coincidence. John Churchill won that battle for James, and we've got a John Churchill coming next term. Youngest we've ever enrolled."

"How old is he?"

"Nine. We generally refuse 'em until they're eleven, but Churchill's people are abroad and he'll go in with the Sunsetters. Timid kid he seemed to me. Hope he doesn't find it too terrifying."

His casual tone irritated her a little. "Of *course* he'll find it terrifying! Who the devil wouldn't, at nine? I don't know what their mothers can be dreaming of to let them go at that age. Thirteen is the absolute minimum to my way of thinking."

He still seemed unconcerned. "Sometimes it's not a question of choice. All the Sunsetters' parents are abroad, some of them in places where there's no school. What do you do with kids in those circumstances?"

"Anything but isolate them from their families and plonk them down among a lot of young toughs."

"You'd be surprised how quickly they adapt. Better than some of those who come to us half-spoiled at around fourteen."

"They have to or go under, don't they?"

He gave her an amused, sidelong glance. "Well, that's part of your new job. To mother 'em a bit."

She said, experiencing her second identifiable qualm, "What gives you the idea I'm qualified for that? Herries's wife had years and years of experience."

He took her hand, alerted more by her expression than her tone. "You aren't getting cold feet already are you?"

"I don't know. Sometimes I'm scared for you more than myself."

"Don't be. I'll cope. A lot better with you around than on my own. You'll find it easier than nursing a constituency. A lot more rewarding too."

"Davy."

"Well?"

"I'll need time. And I'll need watching."

"You've got time. And I'll be watching." He seemed as though he was about to add something to this but checked himself, pretending to be busy spreading the rug and opening the sandwich lunch they had brought.

"You were going to say something else."

"Yes, I was. But it'll sound pompous. God forbid I should take that line with you, Chris."

"You say what you had in mind."

"Well, just this. I realise you've mortgaged your political prospects by marrying me. It was a spot decision on your part, brought about by hurt pride and the attitude of those idiots up in Manchester. I should be grateful to them, I suppose, but that's no reason why you shouldn't have second thoughts about it. You probably have already."

"About marrying you? No, Davy. Definitely not."

"I didn't mean that exactly. I meant about a candidacy somewhere fairly handy. Get this straight. I wouldn't stand in your way and I want you to remember that. And as for the school Governors, well, they couldn't either, for I'm beyond their reach now, so long as I'm up to my job." He faced her. "If you feel you have to try again and get back in the swim then for God's sake tell me, Chris. Don't bottle it up because you think it'll make things hellishly difficult for me. It won't, or not to any great extent, and even if it did I'd go along with you all the way."

His tolerance touched her deeply, the more so because she knew it cost him something to go as far as this and make so light of any complications that might result from her re-entry into the political arena. She caught his hand where it rested on the door of the car, pulled him down and kissed him.

"Thank you, Davy. That's you talking but this is my problem. I'll tackle it if I have to but I'm not going to anticipate it on my honeymoon. I love you very much and I'm sure you love me. So why don't we give me a term or two's trial?"

They left it there for the time being. The exchange had helped, if only in stiffening her resolution to do her damnedest to justify his faith in her.

2

There was more mothering to be done than either he or she had anticipated. Chance, plus a short waiting-list and an exceptionally high number of July leavers, had combined to lower the average age of the Second Formers by nearly two years and Churchill was not the only nine-year-old among the Sunsetters. There were two others, and several ten-year-olds not really up to the standard of the Second Form, so that David was obliged to improvise and split the lowest unit of the school into two unequal halves, the Second Form proper, comprising about a score of boys, and what amounted to a First Form approaching a dozen.

It was a great nuisance for it meant extensive revision of the timetable and a good deal of shuttling to and fro in the Lower School, but it was better than seeing their numbers drop, as they might well have done had he adhered to the earlier age limit.

He was so busy during those first hectic days that he had little opportunity to devote much of his time to Chris and was relieved when she admitted, without being asked, that Bamfylde was more terrifying at a distance than it was in close up. It seemed to him then that she was settling in very well, especially as she went on to say that the chief factor in her absorption was the unexpected warmth shown her by most of the staff, and all the senior boys, especially those who qualified as his secret favourites. It told him that she had been prepared for a certain amount of resentment on the part of the senior men, like Barnaby and Howarth, but it was soon evident to her that they both wished him well, and enjoyed the exceptional freedom he extended to housemasters. She got on very well with Alison, Boyer's Scots wife, and with many of the Old Boys, a proportion of whom seemed to share Boyer's almost mystical friendship with Davy. She took a great liking to Brigadier Cooper after he whispered, on being introduced to her, "Just what we were looking for, that husband of yours, m'dear. Been tellin' 'em so ever since we began casting round for someone to replace Herries. Difficult chap to follow, but P.J.'ll manage it, given time. Especially with a nice gel like you about the place."

"I think Briggy is an old duck," she told Davy later. "Has he always been a fan of yours?"

"I struck lucky with his boy my first term here. It works that way sometimes."

She derived a certain amount of amusement from learning her way around and discovering where to tread softly and where to take a chance. "It's a bit like the Habsburg Court," she said one day, "a frighteningly complex system of protocol, checks, counter-checks and balances, with all kinds of silent pressures and intrigues going on, and you hovering over the safety-valve watching for explosions. Really, you men are the most colossal frauds! For centuries you've been accusing women of gossip and backstairs politics, and we're absolute amateurs at the game compared with you!"

"It doesn't get you down, then? That aspect of it?"

"Not a bit. As a matter of fact, it makes me feel superior." And he had laughed and gone blithely about his business, unaware that there were other aspects of Bamfylde that were not so easily dismissed.

One was the obvious lack of flexibility about the system, despite the humanising effect David had obviously had on the school. Tradition, she supposed, was all very well at a remove, but the experience of the last few years, especially on the other side of the Atlantic, pulled against her ability to take the rigidity of the school calendar seriously, especially when it seemed to her to push education into second place. The high spots of each term were as fixed as the stars, beginning in October with the first of eight runs, and the play-offs of Senior and Junior house matches. Then there was the opera and ceremonial Middlemoor run, the Choral Society's concert, the drill competition, Sports Day, the War Office Certificate 'A' exam and interminable games of cricket. The new school year began with Speech Day and the Armistice Service and by then they were into the cross-country and rugby seasons again, and inside this framework of special occasions were countless minor rituals, so that she sometimes wondered what the parents were getting for their money in the way of down-to-earth education, for sport and red-letter days invariably took precedence over instruction. She raised this subject with David one night and found that he could be very touchy when the rituals of the school were questioned.

"I've been trying to explain for years that education isn't a matter of text-books and blackboards," he said. "At least, it isn't in schools of this kind. That was an article of faith with Algy."

She took a calculated risk then, saying, "But you're head now, Davy, and Algy, dear old chap that he is, stands for the past. The boys here are going out into a highly competitive world, aren't they?"

"Damn it," he said, irritably for him, "you're talking just like Carter before the Stoic outstepped his limits and he came over to our side. Of course they have to be taught something, and of course they have to be coached through the Cambridge Senior or some qualifying exam, but that isn't *why* they're here. Go and read *Tom Brown* and see what the old Squire had to say about it."

She was tempted to reply that Squire Brown had lived in the days of privileged classes and virtually no taxation, but she was not sure enough of her ground to risk a first quarrel. All the same, his extreme sensitivity bothered her, inasmuch as it threw her back upon herself and made her uneasily aware that she had no real place in his life in term-time. And term-time, she reflected, consumed two-thirds of the year. Clearly he was now a fervid convert to tradition and equally clearly she was not and never would be. From then on the open cheque he had handed her regarding her freedom to apply to Transport House for a candidature was prominent in her mind, so much so that twice she sat down and began a letter reminding the party of her existence and availability. She threw both letters in the wastepaper basket. Instinct warned her that, notwithstanding his pledge on the last day of their honeymoon, endless problems might result from taking up the challenge again. Instead, she looked around for some means of integrating more closely into the world of school and making some kind of attempt to justify her existence other than a kind of camp-follower.

She found it, oddly enough, through Howarth, whom she had come to like and respect as a man at war with humbug. Howarth gave her her first tenuous foothold by privately seeking her advice on Bradshawe, yet another of those unfortunates pulled apart by divided loyalties after his parents (surely, in this instance, the world's prize idiots!) sent him a stream of letters explaining their individual views on the rights and the wrongs of their divorce.

Bradshawe, an intelligent fifteen-year-old, was making heavy weather of the issue, or so Howarth told her. From a cheerful extrovert of a few months ago, he had become morose and solitary, and his work, according to a consensus of opinion in the common room had gone to pot. "Tell me, Mrs. P.J., as an expensively educated woman, how would you tackle it from my standpoint? Those fools are imposing unnecessary stress on the boy. As his housemaster I feel I'm falling down on the job and that really rattles me."

"What makes you think I'm qualified to advise someone who has been at the job as long as you," she protested, but he growled, "Oh, don't give me mock modesty! You're much nearer Bradshawe's age than I am and must have ideas, so let's have 'em! You can rely on me to throw 'em back at you if they're too academic."

"Well," she said, doubtfully, "you could try writing to each parent, pointing out the damage their letters are doing."

"I tried that at the beginning of term and all that happened was *I* got a blow-by-blow description of the fracas. Puerile nonsense it was, too—wretched woman can't even spell, and she finished her bleat with a split infinitive."

She laughed, deciding that, in this kind of situation, Howarth could be funny. "I'll tell you what might work," he went on. "I'll brief you on the case and you have a straight talk with the boy."

"Good heavens, how could I do that?"

"The same way as I'll have to if you don't," he said, "and passing the buck to P.J. won't work either. Too magisterial. Not him, of course, but his mantle of office. No, I'm serious. You'd be doing me a favour and, after all, it's a job that comes within the province of a head's wife. Ellie Herries got landed with it often."

She said, obstinately, "I won't do it without Davy's approval," and he said, with one of his rusty chuckles, "Leave P.J. to me. Told him a good many home truths in his time. Ask him if you don't believe me."

The upshot was that she made her debut as counsellor within forty-eight hours, trapping Bradshawe in her parlour when the treacherous Howarth sent him over with a note, with strict instructions to wait for an answer. The note read, 'Since you didn't see fit to invite me to the wedding I didn't buy you a wedding present. Here is a hot-plate for hot potatoes. Respectfully, Ian Howarth.' Below was a postscript, 'Fragile. Handle with care!'

She had the greatest difficulty in keeping a straight face as she said, "Er . . . do sit down, Bradshawe. I won't keep you a minute," and watched him out of the corner of her eye as she went across to the bureau and wrote, 'No hot-plate, thank you. I'm sitting on one, thanks to you', and sealed it.

She said, as he rose, "Hold on a minute, Bradshawe, we haven't met before, have we?" and he mumbled that they had not.

"I'm just making tea. Will you stay and have some?"

He looked at her suspiciously, she thought, but he could hardly refuse so he sat down again, stuffing the note in his pocket. She called through to Rigby, "Make it tea for two, please, Rigby," and then, deciding on the direct approach, "I had a chat with Mr. Howarth yesterday. He tells me you've had a wretched term so far. Would you care to talk about it, to someone right outside? It would be confidential. I wouldn't dream of passing it on to the headmaster or Mr. Howarth, if you preferred not." And when he said nothing, "You see, I've had personal experience of this divorce muddle myself. Nobody has to tell me how awful it can be."

He looked at her with a touch of wonder, a nice-looking boy, with serious grey eyes and a friendly mouth. Tall and well-made for his age and possessing, she would say, exceptionally good manners.

"Did Mr. Howarth tell you he had written to my people, ma'am?"

"Yes. But it didn't help, did it?"

Rigby padded in with the tray, set it down and went out again. She turned her back on him to pour and he said, "My mother keeps saying she put it off until I was old enough to understand. That if she had had her way they would have split up years ago. I . . . well, I don't really believe that. I mean, in a way it shifts the blame on me, doesn't it?"

"How does it?"

"Well, things must have been getting worse all the time. They quarrelled, of course, but everyone's people have a bust up now and again, don't they?"

"If they're human they do. What's your Christian name, Bradshawe?"

He looked surprised. "Nick . . . Nicholas, ma'am."

"Well, look here, Nick, it's time you faced up to something. As your mother implies, you're quite old enough. People drift apart for all kinds of reasons, but a divorce in the family isn't the end of the world. It used to be but it isn't now. I dare say more than a dozen boys here have parents who have got themselves divorced and married again, and nobody a penny the wiser. The thing is, everybody is an individual, and has his own life to lead. You can sometimes help but not all that much. Do your sympathies lie in one direction or the other?"

"Not really. I gather my father has been running around with his secretary but mother . . . well, in a way she asked for it. I mean, ever since I can remember she's filled the house with people, all kinds of people. Painters, writers and so on—drips most of them, and father was all for a quiet life."

"I see. Are you an only child?"

"I've got a brother older than me. He was here several years ago. He's married now."

"Have you discussed it with him?"

"He doesn't want to know. He says the governor is in his second childhood, and the mater isn't through her first yet, and all one can do is write 'em off. How can a chap do that? I mean, after all they are one's people."

"It's not bad advice for all that. Providing it's done kindly. Would it be so very difficult?"

He looked confused and she realised she would have to be more explicit. "Before this happened, did you get along with them? Both of them?"

"More or less. I didn't see much of the governor and, as I say, mother was always surrounded by long hairs. They left me pretty much to myself."

"Then what is it that's upset you so much?"

He said, with a baffled frown, "Well, it's being a sort of referee. I mean, a chap doesn't want to know all the grisly details, does he? They've split up and that's that. I'm sorry, but I can't do anything about it."

"Do you answer their letters point by point?"

"I try to."

"Well, here's my advice for what it's worth, Nick. Stop trying. Keep in touch, the way you used to, a letter every week to each of them but full of school gossip that they'll find frightfully boring. Don't comment on a thing they say, and if you see another appeal to the ref coming up throw that letter in the wastepaper basket without reading it. My guess is they'll soon leave you alone to get on with your own life. Does that make sense?"

Surprisingly, and rewardingly, he smiled. He had, she thought, a very wise smile for a lad of fifteen. "Yes, it does. It makes a hell . . . a real lot of sense." He stood up, carefully replacing his cup on the tray. "I'd better get back with this note. Mr. Howarth said he was waiting for it," but he didn't go and finally went on, "Er . . . was that note about me, ma'am?"

She said, with a smile, "Yes, it was, Nick. As a matter of fact, Mr. Howarth insisted I have a chat with you. He seemed to think I could do it better than he could, or the head could, but I'll tell you this. They're both very much on your side, and so am I after what you've told me. Will you give what I suggested a try for the rest of the term?"

"Yes, I will. And thank you, ma'am . . . I just had to spill it to someone. That's the trouble with a place like this . . . I mean . . . regarding things outside . . . a chap tends to go round in circles."

He held out his hand and she shook it, thinking as he left, "That's about right. That *is* the trouble with a place like this and not only for the Bradshawes." She was aware, however, of having made her first real contribution and it gave her a lift until she reflected that she had only been able to make it by chance. Very few boys would have been as frank and explicit as Bradshawe about a personal problem. To run a place like this had seemed a more or less straightforward job from a distance, a matter of training and educating boys within a system of do's and don't's, but it wasn't like that at all, not when you saw it from the inside. It was a task of fearful complexity, where it was so easy to lose one's way and flounder. All manner of unlooked for situations arose day by day and each demanded a personalised approach. In a way—and she grudged the admission—Davy was right. Education, of the kind outsiders associated with schools, was a relatively unimportant part of boarding-school life. The human side of it, the sheer effort needed to keep a place as unwieldy as this on a level keel, required infinite imagination, endless patience and heaven knows what else besides. The case of Nick Bradshawe, for instance, was no more than the tip of one iceberg, and here she was, preening herself for having smoothed it off, so to speak. Yet people like Davy and Howarth and all the other old stagers were expected to do what she had done off the cuff and still get boys through the examinations the outside world demanded of them.

*   *   *

The Bradshawe incident did have a side-effect, and that despite the fact that she did not discuss it with him. It made her aware of the true breadth of the demands made upon conscientious schoolmasters like Davy or Howarth, but it also increased the sense of her own inadequacy, so that it was fortunate that, within a month or so, her thoughts were switched by the near-certainty of a pregnancy, a circumstance that somehow surprised her, so much so that she kept her own counsel about it until the helter-skelter of the end of term was behind them and she had him more or less to herself.

The opportunity occurred on the last night of the old year, a few hours after she had received confirmation from Doc Willoughby. They had both attended a Sunsetters' party and after that a mild celebration with Howarth, Barnaby, Boyer and Alison, and he dropped off to sleep at once while she lay awake, listening to the storm getting up over the moor and marshalling its forces for an onrush on the school. Presently it struck and a dislodged slate from the roof went crashing down into the forecourt, landing with a noise loud enough to wake him.

"What was that?"

"A slate. You'd best get someone to look at that roof before term begins."

"Yes, I will," he mumbled sleepily but she said, "Don't go to sleep again, Davy. I saw Doc Willoughby this afternoon, while you were in town getting the party supplies."

He was wide awake now and sat up, switching on the bedside light. "You're okay? Nothing wrong?"

"Nothing to get worked up about. I'm pregnant," and his reaction to the bald statement was so dramatic that it reminded her of situations she had seen in so many bad films and plays, and had dismissed as improbable until now.

"Good God! This is a hell of a time to tell me. In the middle of the night, when we've accounted for half a bottle apiece!"

"I wasn't sure myself until teatime, and I could hardly tell you in front of the Sunsetters or a bachelor staff, could I?"

He laughed then and hugged her, holding her in a way that told her he was delighted but was attempting to play down his initial sense of shock.

"You're glad about it, aren't you?"

"Of course I am," he said. "Aren't you?"

"I'm not absolutely sure yet. Yes, I think so . . . but . . ."

"But what?"

"I would have liked a little more time to play myself in."

He rubbed his eyes. "Rubbish! You're doing fine . . ." but then, as an afterthought, "This will put paid to any prospect of a candidature. Does that bother you?"

"No. I've put that out of mind, Davy."

"You didn't have to. I told you . . ."

"I know you told me, but it wouldn't work. This will, maybe."

"What do you mean, Chris?"

She kissed his cheek. "Dear Davy. You're so bright in some ways and so dim in others. No, not dim exactly, but the tiniest bit prejudiced. That's Bamfylde's fault I suppose. You can't live and work in a place like this without taking it for granted that everyone else sees the place through your eyes."

"What are you getting at?"

"That a child of my own will give me real purpose in your life. I really haven't got one yet, you know."

He thought about this for a moment. She granted him that. He was always willing to take time to see someone else's view, a rare trait in schoolmasters in her experience. Finally he said, "I went through a longish period of uncertainty when I came here, Chris. Several times, during those long-drawn-out rows with Carter and Alcock I almost threw in the towel, but I'm damned glad I didn't. It's even more difficult for you, I imagine, without a defined role, and I'm only absolutely sure of one thing. You'll find one, with your brain and guts. I'd back all I have on that."

"You already have," she said, and then, "Go back to sleep now. We'll get around to making plans in the morning. We're not pushed for time. It isn't until the end of summer term."

The storm built up, prowling round the buildings like a sullen enemy looking for a chink in the defences, but it didn't bother her. She felt reassured somehow, and more hopeful of the immediate future than she had been since the Bradshawe incident.

3

The feeling grew on her isolating her from the place as a whole and even, to an extent, from him, so that she persuaded herself she was beginning to get things in proportion at last. It would be fun to have a child, especially his child, and the prospect released her into a more tranquil world, an intensively private one where she was content with her role as a bystander, a touchline supporter of Bamfylde's day-to-day being.

Her health remained good and the slight embarrassment she experienced moving among so many males with a swelling figure was a small price to pay for the mounting confidence she felt in herself. The winter tailed off, with its frosts and gales, and spring came, a dry, windy, sunny spell, lasting through April and May. But then, like a vicious kick from behind, her new-found peace was shattered in an hour and she was lost again, this time out of sight and sound of a guide.

It struck without even a token warning, a sudden spell of dizziness, and a single spasm of pain, as she was climbing the stairs to the first landing to see how the decorators were getting on with the little room overlooking the quad that had been selected as a nursery. She caught the iron rail of the banister and stood there, waiting for the spell to pass before moving up the last few stairs into the bedroom and finally she reached it with a sense of panic mounting in her as she hauled herself over the threshold and fell sideways across the bed.

The second spasm made her cry out and old Rigby heard her from the stairwell, calling up anxiously, "Is that you, ma'am . . . ?" and when she was unable to answer she had a terrible certainty that she would die here alone before anyone was aware of what was happening. Mercifully he called again, "Ma'am? Did you call?" and she knew then that Rigby was her sole chance of summoning help and shouted, "Rigby! Up here . . . !" and the old chap came at a trot, peering round the edge of the bedroom door and blinking at the sight of her sprawled sideways across the bed.

"The doctor . . . quickly . . . then the head, but phone first!"

He had his wits about him, senile as he appeared to most people, and was gone in a flash as the waves of pain crashed down on her submerging everything save a sense of maddening frustration that she was going to lose the baby within the hour. Then, unaccountably, the room seemed half-full of people, among them Davy and the matron, and her sense of time and place evaporated so that she was adrift on an ocean of pain and wretchedness, with only occasional glimpses of land in the form of Davy's anxious face and the fumbling hands of the matron as they wrestled with her clothes and tried to ease her into bed.

Willoughby must have arrived soon afterwards but there was little he could do but ease the pain to some extent and then, quite suddenly, she was aware that some hours must have passed for the sun patterns on the west-facing wall had lengthened telling her that it was evening. She heard Willoughby say, "Take it easy, now . . . it's all over," and she wanted to ask if there was any chance that a seven-month-old child could live but could not frame the question for her mind was still confused and her strength utterly spent.

It was nearly twelve hours later that she came to grips with it, opening her eyes to find the room empty save for the matron, who was standing by the tall window, her back to the bed, looking out on dawn creeping over the eastern edge of the moor. She looked cool and very clinical in her uniform, so cool that Chris found herself hating the woman's detachment. She said, "It was stillborn, wasn't it?" and the woman gave a slight start and turned back to the bed, saying, "I'm afraid so, Mrs. Powlett-Jones. A boy. I *am* sorry . . ." but stopped, looking troubled and embarrassed.

"Where's my husband?"

"He's asleep, I think. He was here until an hour or so ago. Doctor made him go and take a nap. Shall I fetch him?"

"No."

She didn't want him fetched and she didn't want his sympathy or anyone else's sympathy. Anything anyone said to her now would sound banal and would stoke the rage and bitterness that glowed in her like a furnace.

"Could you eat something? Some soup, perhaps?"

"Later. What time is it?"

"Getting on for six. At least let me get you some tea."

"Very well."

She did not want the tea but she did want to get rid of the woman, if only for a few minutes. The sense of doom and failure enfolded her like a huge, soggy blanket and she turned her face

518

from the wan light, lying still until matron came rustling in with the tea.

"Did Dr. Willoughby give any reason?"

"He said it might be one of many . . . maybe a fall, or some heavy exertion . . ."

She wanted to hurl the teapot at the woman's head. She had had no fall, had done nothing out of the ordinary beyond climbing a few extra stairs. But it was her second dead child and she remembered she had told Willoughby of the first.

Davy came in, saying little but sitting by the bed and holding her hand. What was there to say, anyway? Then Willoughby tried the medical guff 'Chance in a thousand . . . no reason at all why she couldn't bear a live child . . . happened sometimes quite inexplicably . . . touched off by an incident too insignificant to be recalled . . .' She wished them all to the devil, along with the scores of boys who erupted in the quad at stipulated intervals during the day, their assemblies and dispersals regulated by that damned bell.

A day or so later Davy tried a new tack. They would go away on a long Continental tour the day term ended. Down the Rhine, maybe, to Switzerland and then Italy if she fancied. Her responses were mechanical and he did not press her, sensing that the depression was too deep to be charmed away by reassurances and promised treats.

In another day or two she was allowed up but had no wish to go downstairs and still took her meals in the bedroom. They brought her books but she could never summon enough concentration to get beyond the first paragraph or two. All day the sun shone strongly through the southern window and in the evening, when Davy came up to take supper with her, the room was flooded with the pink reflection of sunset on the rim of the moor. On the third day she had been out of bed, he said suddenly, "You've got to snap out of it, Chris. Not for my sake but your own. God knows, I realise how keen you were to have that child and why, but this isn't *you*. You're a fighter and you've got to come to terms with it sooner or later. Willoughby swears there's absolutely no reason at all why you shouldn't have a child and I never once heard him use soft talk on a patient."

"How long did it take you to 'snap out of it'?"

"Me? Well, it's not the same for a man . . . I realise that."

"I'm not talking about losing the baby. I'm talking about the time you lost Beth."

She caught him off guard and he looked away. "A hell of a long time. But this place helped."

"It can't help me, Davy."

"It can if you'd let it."

She changed the subject. She could never make him understand her affections were centred wholly upon him, owing nothing to this great pile of brick and stone and timber that had succeeded, God alone knew how, in steering him through a succession of crises.

"Where's Grace? Why hasn't she been to see me?"

"She's still in France, brushing up for the exams."

She remembered then. Grace had gone off to spend a month with a pen-friend in Caen, with the object of improving her chances of getting a distinction in French, her best subject. She was glad the kid was out of it, glad too that she did not have to parry someone else's sympathy. The bell went again and he said, "That'll be the end of prep. There's a prefects' meeting in the Sixth and I promised I'd look in. I'll only be an hour. Will you go to bed now or would you like matron up for company?"

"No. Do what you have to, Davy. I'll be all right."

He went out with a troubled face and she heard him descending to the hall and the quad door opening and closing. The harsh clang of the heavy door decided her, symbolising what Bamfylde had become, a prison where every inmate, save only her, had become acclimatised to its routines and strictures. She knew then what she must do and went about her preparations with feverish haste, cramming a change of clothes into a night bag, checking the money in her handbag and detaching her car key from the ring on the mantelshelf. She opened the door and slipped on to the landing, listening for sounds from below. There were none. All the boys had gone into Big Hall for supper and the forecourt, overlooked by the landing window, was empty in the fading light of the sun's last rays. She hesitated a moment longer, wondering whether to leave a note but decided against it. A note would mean immediate pursuit and in any case what was there to explain that he hadn't already guessed. Prisoners didn't leave notes when they went over the wall to look for better luck on the outside.

She went down the stairs holding firmly to the iron rail, out of the front door and then round by the shrubbery path that led to the ramshackle car- and cycle-shelter. Nobody heard her go for the incline of the west drive was enough to coast down to the road without starting the engine. A minute later and she was turning right at Stone Cross and speeding between the huge clumps of rhododendrons in the direction of Bamfylde Halt.

4

It was by the merest chance Molyneux saw her. He was driving back from the village, after his customary two pints at the Fleur de Lys, when he saw the glint of the car as it coasted out of the drive and disappeared round the curve of the bank between the two exits. He recognised the beat of the engine and paid no particular attention to the incident until, an hour or so later, he happened to encounter David crossing the quad and say, "Glad to see the Missis is perking up, P.J.," a remark sufficiently puzzling for David to stop short and ask if he had been in to visit her while he was at the prefects' meeting. Molyneux said he hadn't but assumed, after seeing her drive off in the direction of Stone Cross, that she was up and about again.

"You *saw* her drive off? *Tonight?* Are you absolutely sure, Molyneux?"

"Well, it was her little roadster. About an hour ago. Caught a glimpse of it just as I was turning in the west drive."

"It couldn't have been her. She hasn't come downstairs yet. Somebody must be joy-riding."

"One of the boys?"

"Who else? No one on the staff would have borrowed the car without asking. I'd better check," and before Molyneux could reply he hurried off to the rear to the car-shelter behind the kitchen to confirm the fact that the car was gone.

Even then he had no inkling that it was Chris who had driven it off but it was just possible someone might have required transport in a hurry and, unable to locate him, had gone up to the bedroom to ask for the keys. He went into the head's house at a run and, hurrying upstairs, experienced an unpleasant qualm when he found the room empty and two of the drawers wide open. The nightdress and dressing gown she had been wearing were on the turned-back bed and he called, "Chris? Are you there, Chris?"

but then he noticed her handbag was missing from the dressing table and the near-certainty that she had gone hit him like a blow between the eyes.

He ran downstairs to the kitchen where old Rigby was having one of his stoveside naps.

"Did you see my wife go out, Rigby?"

The old fellow rubbed his eyes. "Out? No, sir. She's upstairs, isn't she?"

"No, she isn't. Has anyone been in while I've been with the prefects?"

"No, sir. No one."

Driven by instinct he ran back through the arch to the car-shelter and stood beside Molyneux's still-warm machine, trying to check the panic rising in him. Women who had recently given birth sometimes behaved very oddly and Chris had been frighten-ingly depressed since the loss of the baby. He felt the night breeze strike him cold under his arms and shivered. Where the hell could she have gone and why? He took several deep breaths and forced his mind to think logically. Stone Cross direction Molyneux had said, and about an hour since, for he had only been absent about ninety minutes. Stone Cross probably meant the road to the Halt but she couldn't take a train anywhere at this hour and, in any case, she had the car. A tiny gleam of hope pricked him. There was less than half a gallon in the tank. He knew that because he had used the car earlier in the day to get her tablets from Doc Willoughby's dispensary. The car averaged, on these gradients, no more than thirty-two miles to the gallon, usually less, and she couldn't get petrol until morning and even then no nearer than Cooper's ramshackle garage in Steepcote, ten miles or so on the road to Dulverton; providing she was heading for Dulverton and those open drawers indicated she had taken some luggage. Perhaps this in itself was reassuring. At least it indicated that she hadn't rushed off into the night in response to some half-crazed impulse.

He dashed back to Rigby, his profound agitation causing him to catch the old chap by the lapel of his old-fashioned tail-coat, a relic of pre-Herries butling. "Listen, Rigby. Find Mr. Howarth. Tell him I've got to dash over to Dulverton and I'll phone him inside two hours. Tell him to wait up in my study and that it's very urgent." And then, making a snap decision to half-confide in the old servant, "Mrs. Powlett-Jones seems to have overestimated her own strength. She took it into her head to go for a drive and I'm going after her. In the Dulverton direction. If I don't ring back after midnight ask Mr. Howarth to contact the doctor, do you understand?"

"Well . . . yes, sir. Certainly, sir."

The man looked more bemused than he had at the time of Alcock's fatal heart attack but there was no time to waste in further speculation. He ran back through the arch and wheeled out Molyneux's heavy machine. It started at the first kick and in less than a minute he was roaring down the drive and heading for Bamfylde Halt.

Rage as well as concern stirred in him. To go out like that without a word to anyone, at ten o'clock at night, was an utterly irresponsible action, providing she was in full possession of her faculties and he could not believe that depression had brought her that low. He took his profound irritation and anxiety out on the motorcycle, slowing it round the wide bends between the rhododendron clumps and screeching to a halt in the station approach. There was a gleam of yellow light on the platform. That would be Walrus Tapscott, stationmaster and signalman waiting for one of the two goods trains through here each week night. He called over the picket fence, "Tapscott! It's me, Powlett-Jones! How long have you been on duty?"

"Since around nine, sir."

"Did you see any cars pass either way?"

"Yes, sir. Just the one."

"What sort of car? Small or large?"

"I dunno, sir. I on'y got a glimpse as I was coming down the signal-box steps. Smallish, I'd say. It went by at a pretty good lick. Any trouble up at skuel, sir?"

"There might be. I'm finding out. Which way was it going?"

"Took the Dulverton road at the fork. Saw the tail light."

"Thank you."

"Anything I can do, sir?"

"No."

He was off again, roaring over the gritty surface to the fork and setting the machine at the one-in-six gradient that led over the shoulder of the moor. Ten miles of twisting by-road would bring him to the eastern edge of Middlemoor, looking down into the heavily wooded valley of the Barle and as he went his mind conjured with a variety of destinations beyond Dulverton or the nearest probable filling-station. It might be Taunton, or even London, if her strength held out that long. It might be the north. More likely it was anywhere chance took her, for he had nothing but instinct to help him follow a trail. In the heavy silence of the moorland night the motorcycle seemed to make a prodigious noise. A barn owl swooped out of a spinney and flew diagonally across his vision, causing him to swere so violently that he almost went into a speed wobble. After that he took a partial grip on himself, slowing down and peering about him in the darkness.

It was lighter when he emerged on to the open moor. A few stars were glimmering over Tarr Steps to his left and somewhere over on the right, in a fold of the plateau, they shone on a patch of water. He thought, savagely, "God damn my luck with women . . . first Beth, then Julia Darbyshire, now this . . . It's all so bloody disorganised . . . they all do the first thing that comes into their heads and jib at making a plan and sticking to it . . . they all get carried away by their emotions . . ." and in his misery he even found himself blaming Beth for not acting quickly enough to avoid that damned lorry on Quarry Hill. It was only when he caught himself thinking, "She could have slammed into reverse and shot off the road . . ." that he checked the onrush of hysteria and forced himself to review the wisdom of this blind pursuit into the night, thinking, "I'm just as bad . . . I should have seen Willoughby . . . consulted someone . . . anything but lose myself chasing a will-of-a-wisp."

* * *

He saw the reflection of his headlight beam with the tail of his eye as he shot past a wide open gateway on the very crest of the moor. Just a dullish flash but enough to bring him to a halt, abandon the machine in the hedge and run back twenty yards or so. The car was there, blocking the opening. The lights were switched off and it seemed to have been parked very carelessly on a hummock of dried mud.

He approached it with his heart in his mouth and saw, with a great surge of relief, that she was slumped in the nearside seat. She did not move when he went round the bonnet but when he reached through the open window and touched her shoulder she stirred and moaned before shaking herself and then sitting bolt upright, one hand raised as though to ward off a blow.

"Are you all right?"

She stared at him as though he had been a passing moorman. There was just enough starlight to see the bafflement in her eyes and the tight compression of the mouth. He went round the bonnet again and got into the driver's seat. Her hand, surprisingly, was warm. She said, slowly, "Where is this? What's happened?"

"You tell me."

Relief put an edge on his tongue. He had to make an effort to check an outburst of recrimination.

"I drove off by myself."

"Yes. You'd still be driving if the tank wasn't dry."

"It isn't dry." She sounded maddeningly rational. "I saw there wasn't enough to get me much farther so I pulled in."

"Why, Chris? For God's sake, why?"

She did not answer but half-relaxed again. "You must have known I'd be scared out of my wits. I only caught up with you by sheer luck. You don't even seem to know where you were heading."

"It didn't matter."

He had no answer to this, even though it went some way to explain her state of mind. Presently he said, "Do you feel all right? I mean, you got this far . . . we're only a mile or so short of Dulverton."

She said, "Odd how far you can get without trying. I had no idea where I was going . . . how far I'd come. First I wanted to break out and then all I wanted to do was sleep. Sleep and never wake up."

Compassion and concern returned to him with a rush. "That's no way to talk, Chris! People are concerned for you. Not just me but Willoughby . . . everybody. If only you'd tried to explain . . . Turn up that window. I'll back out and drive back. She might just make it."

"No, wait, Davy!" Then, "How did *you* get here?"

"Following my nose on Molyneux's motorbike. It's up there in the hedge. I can get someone to pick it up in the morning."

"Before we start back . . . we've got to talk. It might as well be now. I'm not ill, not physically ill, that is. It's quiet out here. Away from that bell."

It gave him a hint, broad enough to encourage him to humour her.

"It was pressing down on you?"

"Unbearably."

"There's a reason for it. After a pregnancy—even a normal one —women get all kinds of fancies, or so Willoughby told me a day or so ago."

"He told me, too. But there's more to it than that."

"You aren't happy—quite apart from the baby?"

"It's nothing to do with you, Davy. You must believe that."

"I'd like to, but how can I?"

"You must. I haven't stopped loving you."

"Then what? Try and tell me, no matter how crazy it sounds."

"I feel so bloody useless."

"Useless? You! But that *is* crazy! I thought you were settling in. Slowly, maybe, but a bit more every month. Then, when you were expecting the kid . . ."

"That led us both astray, gave a wrong impression."

"About what, exactly?"

"About me being someone, doing something useful, having a purpose back there."

"Isn't being my wife purpose enough?"

"No, Davy. Being anyone's wife wouldn't be. That's the way I'm made and I can't do anything about it."

"All right. The minute you're fit we'll go all out to get you a constituency. If it's so important . . ."

"I don't think that's the answer. I did once but I don't any longer."

"Then what? What kind of role would help?"

"If I knew that we'd be home in bed, Davy."

He thought, distractedly, "There's a way out of this mess somewhere, if I could find it. It's been half-suggesting itself for a year or more but it's so damned elusive neither of us can find it." He said, "At least you must know what isn't the answer. To cave in, to do the first damn silly thing that suggests itself, like coming out here on your own without letting any of us know how hard-driven you were. We've always been able to talk, or I thought so."

"Not really, Davy. Bamfylde's a big place. Most times I can't hear you and you don't seem to hear me."

He acted on impulse then as though he was faced with something more tangible than deep, personal despair. He reached over and swung her round roughly and shouted at her as though he was dealing with a case of hysterics. "That just isn't so! You know damned well it isn't so! You aren't making any allowances at all for your physical condition, for the fact that you've had your hopes dashed about the baby. You *were* settling in, and everything would have been plain sailing if the baby had lived."

She said, calmly, "Does it matter—the root cause of it? The fact is I made a hash of this, just as I did with Rowley, and the candidature, and two marriages, and everything else I've attempted."

"That's your view. It isn't mine and it isn't anyone else's and the sooner you get that into your head the better. I'll tell you something else. My Mam came home from the pithead after they told her she'd lost her man and two of her sons, and within five minutes of taking her coat off she was getting my tea and washing sheets in the copper. She wasn't all that singular. I daresay half the women in the terrace were doing the same—adjusting—facing up to what couldn't be altered. Hardly one of them could write or read English, or do more than scribble their names on a clothing club card, but you've had an expensive education. What's it worth if you crack up like this under a few bad deals? Will you think about that?"

She began to cry, quietly at first but then, both hands grasping one of his, unrestrainedly, so that her body shook and they sat there for what seemed a long time, with silence and emptiness all about them save for her dry, gasping sobs and the long sigh of the breeze. She was quiet at last and freed his hand, fumbling in the glove pocket for her handbag and dabbing her eyes with a crumpled handkerchief. She said, at length, "Take me home, Davy. Don't say anything more. Just drive on home."

He reversed out of the gate and switched on the lights. The beam seemed to probe a limitless expanse of the moor and away down by the tarn a nightjar screeched. He saw by the luminous dial that the petrol needle was not quite settled at empty. It was mostly downhill and there might be just enough to see them home. They did not exchange a single word until the car coughed at the summit of the west drive and ran over the flat to the forecourt, where the engine petered out. He saw it as a kind of sign, a pledge that his luck would turn and hers with it maybe. The study light was on. She said, "Is anyone else out looking for me?"

"No. I told Rigby to tell Howarth. That'll be Howarth in the study now."

"We can trust Howarth," she said, and scrambling out went swiftly in and up the stairs.

*   *   *

Howarth was sitting slumped in the swivel chair. The air in the room was thick with stale tobacco smoke and when David entered he hoisted himself up, then relaxed again.

"Well?"

"She's back. She had some damned silly idea about running away. I found her up on the moor, near Dulverton."

"She's all right?"

"As far as I can tell. Did you phone the Doc?"

"No. Had an idea you'd bring her in. Get Willoughby over here at this hour and everyone in the damned place would hear of it."

"Thanks, Howarth."

He went over to the decanter and poured two stiff whiskies. "Where do I go from here? Can you tell me? Can Willoughby . . . anyone?"

"We might. Between us that is. But if you'll take my advice you'll bring Barnaby in on it."

"Barnaby?"

"It was his idea, wasn't it?"

"What are you driving at?"

Howarth shot his legs out and savoured his drink. He looked particularly thoughtful and thought always made made him look disagreeable. "That prep class notion he had. The Second Form is hopelessly unwieldy. That woman we have can't cope with it. Too rule-of-thumb. Needs imagination. Christine might provide it. She seems to have a surfeit that needs siphoning off. Maybe you could solve two problems at a stroke."

He sat down, gaping at Howarth. The path out of the slough suddenly became clear, a tricky one, certainly, but at least some kind of promise to higher, safer ground. "You mean separate the under-elevens and put Chris in charge? Take her on the staff?"

"Why not. She's a graduate. She ought to be able to cope with a dozen youngsters that age. Give her something constructive to do. Keep her mind off her own fancied inadequacies."

He said, "That's a brilliant idea, Howarth. When did you think of it?"

"I've been sitting here twiddling my thumbs for three hours. Look at that ashtray."

The ashtray, a large one, was full of butts. The air in the study was like that of a taproom. David crossed and opened a window on the forecourt. When he turned Howarth was crushing out yet another Gold Flake and heaving himself up. "Give you another tip. Sleep on it before you put it to her and when you do have all the answers to her protests pat. Don't go off at half-cock again." He looked at David humorously. "You're inclined to do that, P.J. It's the Welshman in you, I imagine. Too damned impetuous, the Welsh! Good night to you." He went out, closing the door softly. In all the years they had worked together David had never known him bang a door or make any noise that could be avoided.

Chapter Two

So often it had happened that way, a sudden closing in of baleful factors that threatened to overwhelm him and then a single fissure that offered an escape route and, once exploited, presented a variety of alternative new courses. Within a day of his putting the proposal to her the means to achieve it without a great deal of fuss and improvisation came to hand in the form of a legacy, providing sufficient cash to expand Howarth's idea in a way that made it practical.

Until then he had not seen it as much more than a marginal involvement on the part of Chris, who could devote a couple of hours a day to the smaller, younger half of the swollen Second Form. But with the money, and the accommodation resulting from the new wing, he began to see the development as the founding of a bona fide preparatory department that could be expanded term by term, giving her all the scope she needed. He went about it with enthusiasm and when the builder's estimate for a junior dormitory was in hand he put the scheme to her in detail, expecting and getting some reservations on her part regarding her fitness for responsibility of the kind demanded.

"I don't know, Davy. You need special training for a job of that kind. I've had absolutely no experience with kids, or teaching of any kind, save that one term just after I left University. I don't think I could even keep order if it came to the point. Taking an odd class is one thing. Running a whole new department is quite another."

"I'd back you and so would Howarth, Barnaby and Briggy. They think you'd be ideal for the job. Give it a try, anyway. For all our sakes."

"Especially mine," and she smiled, wryly. "Well, that's the general idea, isn't it?"

"Up on the moor you wanted a role. Here's a real one and you'll get paid for it. Not all that much, for we can't afford it, but something."

"Won't you have to put it to the Governors?"

"Ultimately, but I don't expect any trouble there. I've got two trump cards. That legacy and your degree. Well?"

"I'll give it a go, Davy. I'll try. I'll try like hell."

"That's all I want to hear."

* * *

They soon had a nickname for it. The boys called it the Cradle and soon the term became general, even among the staff. The Cradle. Eight scruffy little first-termers and two more seasoned recruits, including John Churchill, the ten-year-old whose presence she had questioned at Ringwood on the last day of their honeymoon. From the first hour of the first day it was a resounding success so that within a week she came to accept the fact that she had a gift for teaching, an instinctive knowledge of how to estimate their potentialities, apply the spur to the embryo timewasters and nurture confidence in what Barnaby called 'the premature transplants'. Some of the enthusiasms of her own childhood and adolescence returned to her, so that she found herself rereading books and responding to them in a way she had all but forgotten. And at the same time she developed a fierce pride in obvious results, in seeing the timid take heart and the would-be jesters put firmly in their place. Young Churchill (whom she never ceased to regard as the rangefinder for the Cradle) took her fancy from the start, a sensitive, eager boy with a good memory, who had lost much of his initial shyness after a resounding success as Yum-Yum in last year's *Mikado*. The rest, for the most part, were a guileless, merryhearted lot and it was tremendous fun breaking them in, as Howarth put it, on *Poems of Action*, *The Water-Babies* and *Huckleberry Finn*. She liked her English classes best but they were quick to respond to elementary maths and the garishly illustrated *Le Livre Rouge* that she chose to give them their first lessons in French. Sometimes their high spirits were a little overwhelming.

"Please, miss, can we move on to the Sheperdson-Grangerford feud? I read it last night before lights out and it's spiffing . . ."

"Please, miss, what's the French for 'it doesn't matter'? Ford says it's 'Sanfairyann' but it isn't is it?"

"Miss, can I change places with Grisewood? He's a frowster and won't have the window open."

They all called her 'Miss' and when she asked Davy about this he said to let it pass. 'Mrs. Powlett-Jones' was too much of a mouthful and 'Ma'am' would make her feel like Queen Vic coming up to her Second Jubilee.

It was better therapy than any of them guessed and right through the tail-end of the summer term, the succeeding term and into the new year, she was aware of having got a grip on the situation, so that the memory of that humiliating surrender to what had seemed a conspiracy of events to wreck his life and hers receded into the subconscious. Both of them were happy to leave it there. It was a time of new experiences and a drastic reappraisal of her entire expectations up here on the plateau. But she realised he would be unlikely to see it as anything so dramatic. It was just one more tiresome problem solved, lost in the familiar pattern of humps, dips and level stretches of the school year although, every now and again, something occurred to make a period memorable in terms of Bamfylde history, Bamfylde lore, Bamfylde's ever-expanding gallery of oddities.

To her they were all oddities, but even by his standards there seemed to be a plague of them in 1935. Sometimes a new entry would yield a crop of faceless boys, who merged into the background like a stage chorus. At other times a clutch of singular personalities would emerge by the end of a full year. Nineteen-thirty-five was a vintage year.

Hookham, for instance. Thirteen when he arrived, and too old for the Cradle, he was sent instead to the Second Form, ruled by

Miss Nixon, spinster daughter of Prebendary Nixon, and known by the boys as 'Bo', herself quite a character.

Venn, in the long line of Bamfylde's official jesters, invented the name within days of Miss Nixon's arrival, the nickname emerging painlessly from a discussion in the Upper Fifth on her somewhat overbearing presence. Almost as tall as Frobisher, the lankiest boy on the roll, she was also broad-shouldered, bell-toothed and possessed of a furious energy that had her charges panting in her wake. Venn made a hobby of cataloguing staff idiosyncrasies and was currently regarded as Bamfylde's best mimic, so that idiosyncrasies were his stock in trade.

"The kind of woman one associates with the garrisons of beleaguered towns in the Indian Mutiny," he drawled. "True daughter of the regiment, don't you know? I see her as the unmarried elder sister of that nifty little brunette in the picture in Big School, 'The Relief of Arcot', where the nifty one is drawing attention to the approach of the pipes. However, seeing that even she could have landed a sex-starved subaltern in India, I think of Miss Nixon as someone more regal. How about a warrior queen, driving one of those chariots fitted with revolving meat slicers?"

"Boadicea," prompted Dodge, who was Venn's feed, and Venn said, "Right! Scattering arms, legs and helmets in all directions!" and Miss Nixon had been safely christened.

It was to Bo Nixon that David went, in puzzled mood, one November day, with a grubby note written on graph paper, seeking more precise information concerning little Hookham, but he was obliged to pretend to an absorbed interest in the skyline when Miss Nixon declared his evidence the clumsiest forgery she had seen in twenty years in the profession!

"Oh, I wouldn't say that," said David, gently pulling her leg, "I've seen worse, and you have to admit it's highly original. Let me read it again," and he took the note and read its contents aloud, savouring every laborious downstroke, "*Dere Headmaster, Please send Hookham home at wunce. I need him here. This is urjent. (Signed) Mrs. Hookham.*" And below, the inevitable postscript, "*Put the trane fare on the bill. L.H.*"

"You don't regard it as anything but an insolent joke, I hope, Headmaster? I know just how I should deal with it. Its perpetrator wouldn't sit comfortably for a week," but she added, as though not yet absolutely sure of her ground with an officer newly risen from the ranks, "Naturally, it's not my province to advise. It was addressed through the post to you."

"That's so," David said, "but to be frank I don't recall Hookham, save as a scared little beggar without a word to say for himself, and that's why I'm here, to get information. You've had him several weeks now, although I do seem to recall he arrived a week or so late."

Miss Nixon glanced at her register. "On October 1st. I'll tell him to report to you at once, Headmaster," and looked quite baffled when David said, hastily, "No, Miss Nixon! I don't want him reporting to me. That'll scare the living daylights out of him, and if he has any sense—and I'd say he had a good deal—he'll simply deny all knowledge of it."

"How could he do that? It's in his handwriting, if you call it handwriting."

"Well, that's one to us, but what's he like? To teach and handle?"

She said, knitting her brow, "You can judge his work standard from that ridiculous letter. As to handling him, there's no pertness or impudence as I recall. He's just a sack at the back of the class. As a matter of fact . . ." but she stopped, looking a little baffled.

"Well?"

"I was only going to add that, if it hadn't been Hookham's handwriting, I would have looked elsewhere for the authorship. A joke played on you and him by one of the others, possibly someone in the Third or Fourth."

"Thank you, Miss Nixon. You've been very helpful," and he sauntered away, with an uncomfortable impression that he had made an unwise choice as regards the Prebendary's daughter. Although undeniably a character, she was entirely without humour and therefore not the best Bamfylde material.

He was surprised when Chris affirmed that Miss Nixon was the right person in the right place at the right time.

"Is that based on what the women's magazines call feminine intuition?"

"I don't have intuitions here. I learned to discard them after a week. When I give you advice about anyone in this crazy place it's based on logic. I seem to be the only one capable of applying any up here."

"You're saying Bo Nixon is the right person to cope with thirteen-year-olds?"

"She fulfils a necessary function just now. Think back a bit. Before you set up the Cradle all the beginners looked for their mothering in the Second Form, right?"

"Right. Ma Fender, Mrs. Parminter that is, was said to press them to her bosom, and Mrs. Arscott was pretty soft with them."

"Well, now we've got some kind of prep department they arrive in the Second fully fledged, so they can do with a dose of Miss Nixon. But what's behind all this?"

He showed her the note, expecting her to laugh but she didn't. She said, seriously, "This poor little wretch is clearly an exception. He must have been desperate to go to these lengths. Has anything like this ever happened before?"

"Not to my recollection. I told Miss Nixon this took the Bamfylde biscuit for originality."

"Then do Hookham a favour. Let me deal with it."

"You really think that the kid is going to the wall? I mean, Miss Nixon's right in a way. We could regard it as an elaborate legpull."

"It isn't a legpull and could lead to a lot of unpleasantness." Without waiting for his assent she took the note and marched out, leaving him almost as baffled as Bo Nixon, but then, thinking it over, he remembered the rare tact she had shown in Bradshawe's case, and it occurred to him that she was already overhauling him at a breathtaking rate, overhauling them all, in fact. Hookham, he decided, was in safe hands.

* * *

She had observed the solitary paths taken by the loners. Always they followed the same spare time route between bells, when there were no compulsory games. Loners mooched off on a parallel line to the hedge dividing the main playing field from the Juniors' pitch, drifting towards the swimming bath, then turning off into the planty, where their heedless steps brought them to Towser's grave beyond the first of the trees.

Hookham took this route, book in hand, and she followed him, coming on him seated on a beech log, out of sight and sound of his private purgatory. She said, casually, "Hallo, old chap. What are you reading?" and he offered her the book, a battered library edition of *Treasure Island*.

"One of my standbys," she said. "The Cradle is halfway through it this term, reading it aloud. But you'll be done with all that, I suppose."

He was trying, she thought, to categorise her, to find her niche in his long, long catalogue of tormentors, and was finding it very difficult. It was therefore time to press her advantage and she said, turning the pages, "How far have you got?"

"I finished it," he said, guardedly, "and *Kidnapped* was out, so I didn't hand it in but started all over again." Then, very carefully, "Is that against the rules, miss?"

"Oh, no," she said, cheerfully, "quite the opposite. Mr. Howarth is a great believer in second readings. Who is your favourite character, Hookham?" and he replied, without a moment's hesitation, "Ben Gunn, miss."

"Oh? Why exactly?"

"Because he managed, I suppose."

"You mean he managed to survive on his own all that time?"

"He was the hero really. *They* wouldn't have managed without him."

Her opinion of Hookham shot up. She saw his line of reasoning at once, and it underlined not so much his originality but his remarkable powers of deduction. He would see himself as the maroon. Scoffed at, put upon, mocked and belittled, when justice, had justice been done to Ben Gunn and himself, proclaimed that their wits were so much sharper than those of Dr. Livesey and Captain Smollett.

She said, "You know, I think you're absolutely right, Hookham. They *couldn't* have managed without him. I'll tell my boys that this afternoon. Happy reading."

His startled gaze followed her all the way down the path to the planty's edge and it might have surprised him had he been in a position to notice that her eyes were bright with tears, but it all worked out satisfactorily and that within hours of the encounter. Hookham was demoted to the Cradle where his age and erudition gave him certain advantages and Chris was not slow to exploit them, going to work the second day Hookham had arrived among them, by announcing, during the reading hour, "Hookham has the advantage of us. He's read *Treasure Island* twice. He's an expert on it, aren't you, Hookham? That's why I'm going to ask him to judge the maps. Has every pair finished their map?"

Eager hands shot up and the maps were gathered in, blotched and grossly distorted variations of Stevenson's map, in the front of the standard edition. The Cradlers had been divided into pairs and told to assume the role of Jim Hawkins and make a treasure chart of their own devising.

Purposely she did not so much as glance at them but handed them all to Hookham, telling him to leave class and stay out until first bell in order to select the winner and runner-up. It was difficult to keep them quiet while he was absent and when the bell rang excitement erupted in squeals of glee and a great deal of bobbing up and down. Then, conscious of making an entrance, Hookham re-appeared. "This one, miss. It's easily the best," and he handed her a brownish roll of cartridge paper that had about it a definite stamp of authenticity. "Good. Help me unroll it, Hookham. You hold that end. Yes, this is very good indeed! It looks as though it might have come straight from Billy Bones's chest. Which pair did it?"

Gosse and Meadowes, both blushing, raised their hands.

"Well, come out and tell us about it. How did you make the paper and writing look so old, Gosse?"

Gosse expanded under her approbation. "We boiled it, miss."

"*Boiled it?* In what?"

"In tea, miss."

The Cradlers received this news with gasps of delight.

"That was really Meadowes' idea, miss."

"Good for you, Meadowes!" and Meadowes hung his head.

"And which of you did the drawing and invented the clues?"

"I did, miss. I borrowed Whatmore's fountain pen because of its green ink and crossed nib. It came out all spidery and faded-looking."

She pinned the map to the blackboard. "Twenty out of twenty for that, Gosse. And some of these others aren't bad at all. Dismiss now. I'm going to show the winning chart to the head. Wait a minute, Hookham. Off to tea, you others."

They scuttled out, with the usual desk-banging and competitive scuffling, while Hookham remained, looking at the floor. She said, "Thank you for helping, Hookham. It wouldn't have done for me to judge them."

His head came up. "Why not, miss? You're the teacher and give the marks."

"Yes, I know, but you see, I invented the exercise, and you noticed how they all accepted your decision. Would you like to be class monitor?"

"What does a monitor have to do, miss?"

"Oh, all kinds of things. Give out test papers, collect up books, clean the blackboard and even take charge if I have to pop out. You see, you're the biggest and the oldest now, and they'll take it from you. They'd skylark with any of the younger ones."

He said, doggedly, "I'll be monitor, miss." And then, warily, "How long will I stay in the Cradle, miss?"

"Just a term or two. Until you get the hang of things. You're beginning to settle, aren't you?"

"I'll get used to it, I reckon."

He said it as though addressing himself and she had a conviction that he had made the same affirmation many times over the last few weeks. He had surfaced, certainly, but she had an idea he would sink again if she let go too soon.

"Hookham?"

"Yes, miss?"

"What's your initial 'R' stand for?"

He looked surprised, "Roy, miss."

"I'll tell you something, Roy, something I wouldn't want the others to know. A secret between us. I'm fairly new here as well and getting used to it, a bit at a time."

"But how can you be? I mean, Dixon Major told us all you were the head's . . ."

"It doesn't matter who I am, I'm new. New at this job and new at the school, so don't think I don't understand how hard it is. Put it this way. To play me in they made *me* a monitor. Monitor of the Cradle."

Surprisingly, and to her great relief, he grinned. Davy was right about him. He really was an original, and the grin encouraged her to gamble again. She opened her handbag and extracted his grubby little note. "The head said I was to give you this. He's read it but he thinks you ought to stick it out a while longer, and so do I."

He took the note wordlessly and stuffed it in his pocket. Then, as a clamour rose from the quad, he said, "That's tea parade. May I go now, miss?"

"Yes, of course, but be here before first bell tomorrow. We're doing nature study and there's a lot to give out."

He nodded and hurried out and a moment later she heard the duty prefect's command, "Para*aade* . . . *shun! Dismiss!*" and the prolonged scrape of boots as the four contingents turned left and fell out. She took a closer look at Gosse's map, deciphering three blurred crosses, marking the treasure. The crosses were not scratched in green but in red, almost certainly in blood. Meadowes' blood, probably, for Gosse would see him as the obvious donor. She thought, "Davy's always said adults learn more than they teach in a place like this and, by God, he's so right!"

2

Despite his admitted experience, despite his sly Celtic trick of winning most people round to his point of view in the end, she did not wholly trust him with the Hookhams. It was very different, however, in the Middle and Upper Schools, where she would sometimes watch him at work.

He was, she decided, uniquely tailored for the job and once they were through the Upper Third, and beginning to notice such things, a majority of boys acknowledged this as freely as she did. This was particularly true in the Sixth, where he was able to step outside his tutorial role and move among them as a kind of group leader, appointed by popular ballot. She realised this one October afternoon when all the Cradlers were down on the lower pitch, practising for the Sevens Competition, and he invited her to attend a current affairs period on the dominant issue of the day, Mussolini's defiance of The League of Nations and invasion of Abyssinia.

Ordinarily, she said, she should have stood in the punishing wind on the touchline, pretending to take a professional interest in Lower School frolics in the mud, but she could never arouse more than a casual interest in their interminable games, and had, indeed, questioned the emphasis placed on them.

Up to a point he shared her view but added, on this occasion, "You'll find they grow on you. They did on me, after a year or so, but, strictly for your ear alone, I can still take 'em or leave 'em. Cross-country running excepted, that is, for that offers a change of scene. If you're at a loose end this afternoon, why don't you sit in on a Sixth Form current affairs? We often have the occasional visitor."

The Sixth subjected her to the half-amused appraisal that Beth and Phyl Irvine had received at their first Saturday dance, and he didn't fail to notice it, thinking, "It's good to have a pretty woman about the place again. Sweetens the atmosphere somehow," but took good care to ignore her during the discussion until Venn, with a brisk show of gallantry, turned to her and said, "What do you think?" and she looked apprehensively at Davy and then quickly away, for he was grinning. She said, "Coxe made a good point just now. Sanctions won't stop Mussolini. He'll be in Addis Ababa by the new year."

"But Coxe said we should have gone to war over it."

"It wouldn't have come to war. Bluff would have done the trick. We should have sent the fleet to Suez, and the whole thing would have fizzled out. As it is, who knows where it could lead?"

They were impressed, every last one of them, and Coxe, finding his minority views supported, was encouraged to prompt. "Could you say where, ma'am? To another World War?"

"It might. Mussolini isn't the only braggart on the rampage. There are plenty of others throwing their weight about in Berlin and Tokyo. How can they be anything but encouraged by the way he's getting away with it?"

After that she was embroiled and they went at it, cut and thrust, until the bell rang. It was not until after lock-up, when they were having their final cup of tea by the fire, that she glanced across at him and remembered how effortlessly he had chaired that lively discussion and how, in the end, every boy in the room turned to him, not to her, for the summing-up. She said, "It was very stimulating. But I won't come again if you don't mind."

"Why not? I thought you made out a pretty good case for military sanctions."

"So did I but they didn't think so. They were just being polite. Now if you told them the moon was made of blue cheese, they'd accept it as gospel, and that's victory, Davy. You're coming down the straight now, whether you realise it or not," but he said, seriously, "It's a damned long straight."

"Then, deep down, you're as scared as I am, especially since Mussolini got away with it. You're scared for boys like Venn and Coxe. And even for some of the younger ones. If it ever did come to the crunch, how would you regard them having to go through what you went through?"

He was a long time answering. It was something he had thought about very deeply. That much was obvious by his concentrated expression and the deliberation of his answer. He said, finally, "I'd feel like you, that I'd been right all along. Oh, not about politics, or the way things have drifted from bad to worse since Versailles. I'm not pretending to have foreseen that, or anything like it. All along the line you've been the only Socialist prophet of doom I've met, and every day's newspaper headline keeps reminding me of the fact. I'm talking about something different, more general, if you like."

"Could anything be more 'general' than another World War?"

"For me it could. Our approach to it, if and when it came. Looking back, that's what I've been working on ever since I settled in here, and saw things through adolescent eyes. But it's late for amateur metaphysics, love."

He was getting up but she stopped him. "Tell me, Davy. It's important."

He said, "I remember a story Algy told us to illustrate the same point years ago. The night of his farewell supper, it was, and it made a terrific impact on everyone at the time. They gave him a cheer for it. Loudest cheer I ever heard in Big Hall and won't hear a better, not if I'm here in my dotage."

He told her the story of Petherick, O.B.E. and 'Chuff' Rodgers, killed at First Ypres, of the train ride they shared with Algy over to Barcombe, the baby who was sick, and how Chuff had mopped up mother and baby with his handkerchief. It had always stayed in his mind so that gradually, over the years, it had become a kind of slide rule he applied to the potential of every boy he taught. There were the Pethericks, who went on to become presidents of insurance companies, who had their names in the Honours Lists, and there were the Chuffs, a majority he liked to think, although sometimes he wasn't sure.

"It's a good story," she said, "and very relevant. But shocking to my way of thinking."

"Why?"

"What you're really saying is that you accept the fact that the Chuffs will be sacrificed and the Pethericks, who stay put, will make a pile, grow fat and die in their beds."

"That's the way it usually goes."

"But it's too awful to contemplate, Davy. We ought to try and change it."

"You saw how difficult it is to change. The only consolation is that it seems to work and if I don't know who should? I came here absolutely convinced that every Chuff in the world had gone west, but they hadn't. They seed themselves somehow. I've got a good many of them here at this moment, nearly twenty years after they blew half-time out there."

"But that's what I mean, Davy, you're accepting it passively and that's as wrongheaded as that ostrich attitude that drove me out of politics."

"Not really. Neither is Howarth, Barnaby or any of the others who believe in what they're about. My job, yours too now, is to encourage the Chuffs and slap down the embryo insurance presidents, while grabbing their parents' money with both hands. The more we can swing our way the better our chance of survival, if it ever does come to another showdown."

3

There had been a time when his personal fortunes had seemed to run a parallel course with the roller-coaster ride of the world outside, a world where quarrelsome tribes continued to collide with one another all the way from Manchuria to Madrid. But things were different now. All about him, if the newspapers and radio bulletins were to be believed, was conflict and disarray, but here on the plateau it was sometimes difficult for a man, busy from rising-bell to lockup, to think of himself as involved in the ferment beyond bounds, and this despite the fact that he shared bed and board with a woman who was half-convinced they were all riding an express to perdition.

His own objectivity stemmed from several sources. His splendid health was one, and her presence was another, for sometimes, immersed like him in the come-day-go-day trivia of successive terms, she too could join him in looking at the outside world through the wrong end of a telescope. Her restored confidence and her new tendency to value the smaller bonuses of life, governed her moods so that for weeks together she could join him in forgetting what was going on outside.

She was made aware of this, and even acknowledged it with a private chuckle, when George V died a day or so after the Lent term began in 1936, and the boys put on their black ties and marched to Stone Cross Church for the memorial service. Everyone had liked harmless old George, whom they saw as a country squire, and everyone was sorry for Mary, but there was nothing personal about their regrets. Somewhere, two hundred miles to the east, a seventy-year-old stranger had died but that was less immediate than the Corps' attempt to play 'The Dead March from Saul' over the last two hundred yards of the journey to Stone Cross.

Now and again, of course, she was jolted out of her complacency and so, to a degree, were David and a few of the Seniors. As the months spent themselves in a succession of regularised assemblies and dispersals, in sports fixtures, Choral Society concerts, examinations, O.T.C. field days and the climactic event of the Christmas term, with Algy Herries as yet another Ko-Ko ("Seventy-five, by the Lord Harry, and still capable of warbling 'Tit-Willow' to Katisha!") the malaise of the world across the Channel would cross boundaries, and the Owl Society would debate the Popular Front in France, Mussolini's rape of Ethiopia, Hitler's re-occupation of the Rhineland and purges in Moscow. But as soon as the bell rang the inner rhythm of the place would reassert itself, and it would require something as immediate as the abdication of Edward VIII to turn Bamfylde eyes outward. But even then not for long. When a school had spent four months rehearsing *The Mikado*, even someone like Mrs. Simpson has to wait her turn.

Occasionally something would occur on the plateau that would make them aware that there were still abysses to be crossed on frail rope-bridges and usually they would cross in convoy, as in the case of young Driscoe's miry flirtation with death, in December.

Driscoe II was the youngest brother of the Driscoe who sang treble in the 1919 *Mikado*, when he was the third little maid from school, partnering Beth and Phyl Irvine. At the London dinner in January he reminded David that his kid brother would be arriving at Bamfylde in the summer term, and added, "Kid's a bit of a weed. As the youngest of five he's been spoiled to hell, particularly by the old lady, but he's okay upstairs. Might even pass an exam or two, and that's something I never did, did I, Pow-Wow?"

"You had compensating distinctions as far as I was concerned," David told him, and reminded him of his appearance on stage before an audience of four hundred beside an obviously pregnant Yum-Yum, but when Driscoe said, "Will you keep a special eye on the kid, Pow-Wow? Mater's orders, I'm afraid," he added, drily, "Hang it, I'm paid to keep an eye on all of them, but you can tell your mother I shall regard him as special if it's likely to stop her worrying."

But Driscoe II was seen to be something of a special case when he presented himself the following April, a morose little boy, light as a feather, with glasses, a slight stutter and exceptionally knobbly knees. It was those knees, singular enough to earn Driscoe II a lot of ragging, that encouraged David to put him straight into the Upper Third. Upper Third boys had discarded short pants and the boy's entrance exam paper justified a flying start. Moreover, it did not look as if Driscoe was likely to distinguish himself outside a classroom.

One could not always prejudge these things, however. Driscoe II, far too frail for rugby, showed unexpected promise as a cross-country runner, astonishing Outram's shield-holding team by averaging nine points in the first three runs of the season. Nine wasn't many, set against the impressive total of Outram's long-striding house-captain, Parker, but it was reckoned good for a shortsighted, knock-kneed first-termer, and Parker, a fanatic in this field, selected the boy as his fag, partly with the object of encouraging him when he was doing odd jobs about the study.

The result was predictable. Driscoe became fired with a desire to develop his unlikely talent to a pitch where the splendid Parker, an all-round sportsman, and in line for the house prefect-ship, regarded him as an asset to the house. When the run-in started from the crest of Middlemoor, the final run of the term, the new boy went off like a fugitive slave a few yards ahead of the bloodhounds.

He had no luck. At a gap in the hedge, dividing Man Dixon's sheep pasture from the marshy river bottom, he fell flat on his face and lost his glasses. Groping for them in inches of Exmoor mud he was trodden flat by a succession of runners determined to keep up with the leaders, and in a momentary lull between his involuntary prostration he decided to continue without them and return to recover them before first bell in the morning.

It was a reckless decision. Badly winded, and quite unfamiliar with the route, he ran far wide of the track, reaching the soggy floor of the valley at a point where the river bank was approached by a broad area of marsh, screened by a fringe of last year's sedge and partitioned off from firmer ground by a fence of two-by-four palings.

Any country-bred boy would have realised that a crossing here was impassable and that there was a very good reason for fencing out here on the open moor, but Driscoe had lived the whole of his life in Golders Green, and even his summer holidays had been spent with a doting aunt in Worthing. He made nothing of the flimsy barrier, scrambled over and plunged waist-deep into a slough as thick as black treacle.

He had time to yell and somebody heard him.

Gosse, maker of treasure maps, was passing the gap higher up the slope, moving at a deliberately leisurely pace, with the object of evading the whippers-in at the next belt of timber and making for Ma Midden's farm, where he could exchange a sixpence (carefully wrapped in his handkerchief) for two hot pasties, one for him, one for his crony, Meadowes.

Gosse, his curiosity aroused, changed direction, descended the steep field and stopped short at the barrier, appalled by what he saw on the far side. It was no more than half of Driscoe, who looked like the stump of a small tree hammered into soft ground.

Gosse was not only resourceful, he was also quick-thinking. Out of the corner of his eye he noted two things. One was his henchman Meadowes, who had followed his angled descent but stopped higher up the slope, puzzled; the other, a few yards to the right, was the remains of what had once been a wire fence, no more than a rotted post enmeshed in rusty wire. Above the frantic howls of Driscoe he put his hands to his mouth and shouted, "He's stuck! He'll never make it! Find the whippers-in—tell 'em a new kid is drowning in Man Dixon's bottom. Run like hell . . . !" and as Meadowes scudded off across the great, slab-sided field, Gosse made his own dispositions, slopping through mud on his side of the fence and dragging the isolated stake from its bed.

The wire was rusted and tangled, but it was a matter of seconds to unravel some ten feet of it and loop the free end round his shoulder. Then, wading as far as the fence, he threw the billet to Driscoe and was immensely relieved when he saw flailing hands grasp it either side of the staple, and a mud-spattered face stare up at him with an expression of baffled hostility—"Just as though I'd flipping well pushed him there," as he told an enthralled audience in the Outram dormitory that night.

The wire tautened and the strain paid out another three or four feet, so that Gosse, his shoulder wedged against the nearest upright of the fence, was able to get some kind of purchase and even attempt to twist the loose end round the lower horizontal. He did not ask himself how long he could hold on there but as long as the fence stood the strain, the billet held by Driscoe did not crumble, and the wire did not part, there was a prospect of supporting Driscoe until someone with more muscle and more practical apparatus arrived on the scene. In the meantime Gosse gritted his teeth and closed his eyes. He did not want to see Driscoe disappear under the mud, or watch his final struggles through the wide gap in the planks. It was enough to know he was still there, chest deep in the black, filthy stuff, and would sink no deeper so long as the wire remained taut.

*   *   *

Gosse did not see the combined approach of Coxe, Venn and Davidson, who arrived in a bunch, their whistling breath indicating that they had run a downhill mile in approximately the time it would take the best of them to complete the 880-yard circuit of Lower Side pitch. They crowded him even closer to the fence, Coxe taking the strain and Davidson, himself a moorman, straddling the fence and lowering himself on to the far side. Then, with what Gosse thought of as great cunning, making a bridge of his body by taking a grip of the lower horizontal and calling to Driscoe to grab his ankles. Venn, unable to find more wire, replaced Coxe as anchor, and Coxe, taking his cue from Davidson, scaled the fence farther along, noticing as he crossed it a section of loose planks. It took him only a moment to prise one loose and squirm along the inside of the fence to the spot where his friend Davidson was lying face downward in the mud. Driscoe was no farther down and had even contrived to flounder a few inches nearer the fence in order to improve his grip on Davidson's shins but it seemed that he had not entirely lost his head for he still held the wire between his teeth.

They huddled there, all five of them, in an ungainly group, a tableau that, viewed from a distance, looked like a clumsy exercise in gymnastics. Driscoe was hardly more than a black bubble on the surface. Davidson was only visible above the thighs. Venn was now flattened against the near side of the fence, with Gosse still trying to loop the fag-end of the wire to the cross-piece. There was progress of a sort, however, for Davidson, turning his head to spit out mud, saw Coxe's plank and shouted, "Under my knees, Frankie! Hard under my bloody knees! Quick, for Christ's sake . . ." so that Coxe, kneeling, plunged the board deep into the slime, aiming to burrow under Davidson's thighs. Despite ample lubrication, the passage of the rough timber made him wince but he found that it strengthened his purchase so long as Coxe remained kneeling on his end of the board. Beyond that, however, there was little they could do and glancing sideways Coxe saw that Driscoe could not hold on indefinitely. Then Venn called from the other side of the fence. "They're coming, Frankie. Pow-Wow and Man Dixon. They've got ropes!" and Davidson, ordinarily a very taciturn boy, made the only joke of the operation, grunting, "Shout up to them! Tell 'em not to hurry, will you?"

4

His instinctive front-line reactions were not as immediate as they had been, at the time of the Havelock fire. The war was a long time ago now, and although he thought of himself as very fit for a man turned forty, the habit of contemplation slowed him down when it came to making snap decisions.

He had been at the tail of the field, shepherding the few Second Formers running the course over the crest of the pasture and down into the valley, but once he saw the last of them wade the ford, and disappear into the spinney, he stopped to have a word with Man Dixon, remembering him not as he saw him now, a stolid, thickset moorman, but as the day-boy who, in 1925, had been credited with killing old Bat Ferguson with a buzzsaw rendering of the French adjective *vert*. He reminded him of the incident now and Dixon, as master of the family holding, could afford to grin. "Arr," he mused, never having lost his upland burr, "and there was a particle o' truth in it, Pow-Wow. I never could get my tongue round his ole French words, and I reckon he would ha' knocked me across the class if he hadn't seized up on the spot." He spoke philosophically and man to man, as though, at the ripe old age of twenty-three, he was David's contemporary. "Things are looking up downalong, I hear," he added.

All the local farmers, even those who had attended Bamfylde as day-boys, referred to school as 'downalong', just as they qualified for the majestic title of 'Man' when they became farmers in their own right. David confirmed that things were indeed looking up, that they now had more than three hundred and fifty on the roll, and a waiting-list of a hundred and seventeen. "Well," Dixon said, unsentimentally, "that'll be your doing, Pow-Wow. We never did take to that foreigner they brought in," and at that point three rearguard whippers-in came over the crest, Venn, Coxe and the local boy, Davidson, loping abreast and in no particular hurry, for they were all First Fifteen rugby colours and lukewarm concerning other sporting activities.

Then, plunging up the reverse slope, and sobbing for breath, Meadowes appeared, gasping out his news, and David's first impulse was to dash off down the steep slope but Dixon grabbed him, shouting, "Wait on! It's all but a mile. The youngsters'll make it in half the time. Wait, 'till I fetch tackle . . . had a heifer in that mire only last week . . . !" and he went off at a heavy run to his outbuildings farther along the crest, and David turned to speed the seniors on their way but they were already a hundred yards down the slope, heading for the sopt indicated by Meadowes' stabbing finger.

He said, making a tremendous effort to control himself, "How bad is it, Meadowes? How deep is he in?" and Meadowes, as blown as he had ever seen a boy, wheezed, "Deep, sir . . . Up to his waist" and was sick, bowing his head and sagging at the knees.

For a man weighing fourteen stone, Dixon was very quick on his feet. Almost at once he reappeared, pounding along the crest carrying a coil of rope and what looked like a leather harness. "Leave the kid here," he shouted, without checking his stride, "but look where you're going—bog patches right along that bottom," and went ponderously down the great, angled slope, and through a belt of brushwood that brought them to the river north of the ford.

He thought, as he ran, "Dear God, don't let it happen. Not *now*, not *this* way! A kid of thirteen, drowned in a bog . . . it'll be the end of everything . . ." and then he remembered that Coxe and Davidson would be there by now, and that both were tough and resolute, although he wasn't so sure about the jester, Venn.

They came on the group suddenly, at a spot where the cattle had churned the floor of the valley into a sticky, gluelike porridge, not unlike the crater-landscape of Passchendaele. They were still holding on, and his instinct for authority, trimmed and tested over the years, reasserted itself as he took in the situation at a glance. Coxe called, from the far side of the fence, "Throw us the rope over, sir! Davidson's got a good hold on the fence . . . !" and Man Dixon grunted, "Tiz harness, boy . . . Get it under his armpits somehow," but by then David was across the fence and crawling along to the point where Davidson was still lying prone, with the unrecognisable Driscoe clinging to his shins, both of them half-enmeshed in what looked like a coil of rusty wire.

They were only just in time. Despite Coxe's efforts, his success in reaching Driscoe's left arm, and his tremendous efforts to drag him closer to the palings, the boy was weakening and his fingers were slipping the length of Davidson's legs. He had also lost his end of the wire and with it the feeble anchorage it had provided. By wading in beyond his knees, however, David got a firm grip on Driscoe's right arm and his presence enabled Coxe to enlarge his hold on the left, so that between them they managed somehow to slip the leather harness over his shoulders. Floundering there, dragged forward into the mire, the task proved fiendishly difficult and even when it was accomplished they had no room to pay it out so that Driscoe could be dragged clear by sheer weight of muscle. But then, as though he had materialised out of the slime, another mud-spattered Junior appeared and David recognised Gosse, who piped, "*Leave it*, sir! Hold him, and I'll take it . . . !" and somehow he did, without rising upright, and the rope tightened almost at once as Venn began to haul.

They came clear in a flurry of mud, Coxe, Gosse, himself and Driscoe, whose legs, plucked from the slough, made a sound like a cork being drawn from a bottle. Even then, with Davidson lying prone between bog and palings, they would have got no farther forward had not Venn shown initiative by ripping away the bottom section of the barrier so that they could scramble through en masse, a jumble of arms, legs, wire, rope and splintered fencing.

Man Dixon took charge of them at that stage, lifting Driscoe in his arms and trudging back along the river to the point where a gravelled path climbed to his yard. The rest followed at a distance, with Davidson, the last to emerge, spluttering and coughing in the rear.

It was with a sense of wonder that he heard Driscoe speak, sitting with his head between his knees on Dixon's bagged-out sofa in the big farm kitchen . . . "Lost my glasses . . . went off the path . . ." but then he too was sick, obligingly on Dixon's hearthstones, clear of the sheepskin rug spread there. One of Dixon's Welsh collies drifted in, sniffing curiously at the vomit and Dixon, cuffing the dog, called over his shoulder, "Fetch a cloth an' bucket, Mother, and clean him up. We could all do with a wash, I reckon."

*   *   *

He remembered little of the shuffle home, with Driscoe carried pick-a-back by Coxe, and little Gosse, who had lost both shoes, picking his way fastidiously over the stretch of flint road beyond Stone Cross. Venn told him how they had managed until he and Dixon had arrived but it was not until later, when they had all had a shower, and Driscoe had been dosed and put to bed in the sanatorium, that he remembered to send for Coxe, senior of the trio, and get a detailed story.

Coxe said, "I did what I could, sir, but it wasn't much. Davidson took the brunt of it. I had to wedge one of those planks under his legs and it took the skin off his knees. There were old nails sticking in it. I think matron's bandaging him right now."

David said, "Go up and wait for him, Frankie. Then come down again, with Venn. You can skip prep, all three of you. And send someone else for those infants, Gosse was one . . . who was the other?"

"Meadowes, sir. Gosse was the one who saw him first. He's a plucky kid, and had his wits about him. He threw Driscoe the wire, but that was before we got there. He would have gone under but for that. I'll find Davidson, sir," and he left.

He sat at the desk stirring his tea, a desk occupied by a succession of Bamfylde headmasters, all of them, including Alcock, now gazing down at heedless newcomers in the Rogues' Gallery in Remove passage. He felt drained, used up and disconsolate, thinking, "My God, but it was a near thing. We should have been finished if it hadn't been for that bunch and that's a fact. I'd best write to Mrs. Driscoe tonight, for the kid will, as soon as he perks up," and then, following a perfunctory rap on the door, Miss Nixon appeared, holding an envelope that she laid on the desk. "Driscoe's glasses, Headmaster. He seemed anxious about them and Parker went out to look for them with a flashlight. They aren't broken, and I've cleaned them as best I can."

"Thank you, Miss Nixon," he said, absently, "and thank Parker for me, will you? Driscoe will be all right after a good sleep, or so matron says. He was sick and got the filthy stuff off his chest minutes after we pulled him out."

She withdrew quietly, disapprovingly he suspected, and he let his tea go cold. Presently there was a more subdued knock and all five of them sidled in, Davidson walking stiffly under his bandages, then Coxe, then Venn, miraculously transformed after his tussle with the mud, and finally the two Second Formers, Gosse and Meadowes. He said, "Find a seat somewhere. Nothing official," and they disposed themselves, only the dandy Venn at ease.

"That was a terrific show," he said, "and I wanted to thank you all in private before I do it in public. I imagine Mrs. Driscoe will write to you later. I'm not making any bones about what happened down there. But for you chaps Driscoe would be dead. And buried. You all appreciate that, I suppose?"

They said nothing and each of them studiously avoided his eye. "It's odd," he thought, "it's always so damned difficult to find the right words to compliment the English," but he went on, "I'll write an account of it exactly as it happened, and print it in this term's register. All I really wanted to say, beyond that, is don't play it down for fear of putting on side. I've a reason for saying that. I'd like to think we've all learned something about playing fast and loose with the moor in winter."

Gosse piped up then, so unexpectedly that Meadowes hiccoughed with embarrassment. "It wasn't Driscoe's fault, sir. He's as blind as a bat without his specs."

"I daresay. So the moral seems to be, no specs no movement.

And that goes for anyone overtaken by dusk on any of the runs.
Stay put and holler. Good night, and thanks again."

They got up and filed out but he sat on brooding. Presently
Chris came in, carrying the whisky decanter and soda siphon.

"You need a drink, Davy."

"I need a bottle," he said. "Neat. I've just had them all in and
thanked them. You've heard the full story I imagine?"

"Matron told me. You put up a pretty good show yourself,
Davy."

"I didn't," he said grimly, "and I've been sitting here coming
to terms with the fact that I'm slowing down. If it had been left
to me, or even to me and Dickie Dixon, that poor kid would be
as dead as Carver Doone. All we did was to speed it up a bit.
They'd have coped."

"You're forty plus," she said. "Most men your age wouldn't
have gone on the run at all, so don't sit there blaming yourself
for an unforeseeable accident."

"It wasn't unforeseeable. Or shouldn't have been. I've been
over that Middlemoor course every year since December, 1918,
and I knew there were patches of dangerous bog in that river bottom. I should have talked Dixon into fencing all the level ground
and putting up a damned great notice."

"Most boys will climb fences, and all boys will ignore notices.
Besides, you appear to have forgotten something."

"What?"

"Your indirect contribution."

"Come again?"

"Those five boys. Just tell me something, how long is their ag-
gregate stay here?"

He began to discern her line of reasoning. "I could work it out.
Venn is just entering his fifth year. Coxe and Davidson are old
stagers. They were here one term with the Stoic. The two Cradlers can only sport a year between them, they both arrived last
spring. That's a total of sixteen years, give or take a term or two."

"During which time they've all been taught and trained by you."

"Me among others."

"No, Davy. Not as regards what they did this afternoon. That's
your doing."

She got up, removed the tea tray and set the drink in its place
but then, noting his frown, took his face between her palms and

kissed his mouth in that asertive way of hers. "It's true," she said, "think about it. They all seem to me to qualify as handkerchief donors, and that's your doing. Not one of them was here when Algy Herries told that story."

His arm slipped round her. At times like this, when he was feeling vulnerable, he was immensely grateful for her and as always, when aware of a need of her, his senses stirred, demanding close physical contact. He said, "By God, I was lucky to talk you into coming here, and even more right to persevere when you wanted to pack it in. I couldn't cope alone any more."

"You've had to most of the time. Let's make an early night of it. Leave all that bumf on your desk. I'll get supper now and when it's lights out for them it'll be lights out for us."

"That's two hours or more. I'm not sure I can wait that long."

"You'll have to," she said, "for I'm hanged if I want last-minute interruptions by the duty prefect. It's happened more than once."

She switched off the desk lamp and they went through into the parlour where a bright log fire burned in the everlasting down-draught. Supper was laid. It looked very cosy in here. His overall grasp of the job returned to him a little soggily but definitely, like Driscoe emerging from the bog, and with it a buoyancy that stemmed, he supposed, from a sense of reprieve. He said, taking in the trim lines of her figure as she stooped to throw another log on the fire, "I wish it was holiday time. I wouldn't bother with supper or bed," but she was equal to him.

"There's always old Rigby, and even if he's asleep beside the kitchen stove, there are the Sunsetters. We haven't that much dignity to squander, sir."

Chapter Three

1

In his relaxed moods he could still think of himself as ruling an island in a stream, protected to some extent, from lethal flotsam that coasted by on either side, touching shore here and there, probing, fussing, worrying, but finally moving on round the bend in the river. But latterly lodgments were made, and unexpected pressures exerted, so that a certain amount of erosion was evident, fissures showing in his defences. Whenever this happened he was troubled, for they always appeared at places where he thought himself buttressed against adversity. Such a case was Christopherson's, in the spring of '37.

There had been a time when Bamfylde's remoteness made nonsense of faraway commotions but latterly, as the decade sped along, there had been dramatic improvements in communications. In the early 'twenties their newspapers had arrived almost a day late, while only the odd crackpot thought of wireless as anything more than an amusing toy. Today newspapers were delivered in bulk, and were distributed to classrooms before first period bell. There were also half a dozen wireless sets on the premises, some of them complicated-looking pieces of apparatus, and their stream of bulletins kept everyone informed of what was happening elsewhere. It made a difference, as his encounter with Christopherson II proved.

Christopherson, thought to be enjoying his first year up at Oxford, appeared on a motorbike in the middle of the Easter holidays and said, over a glass of Old Boys' sherry, "Glad I caught you, Pow-Wow. Had a feeling you might have taken Mrs. Powlett-Jones away for Easter. Should've rung, of course, but there wasn't time. I'm hellishly pressed as it is," and when David enquired where he was going, he replied, "You'll probably think I want my head examined. I know my people do, and so does my tutor, but there it is, a chap has to make his own decisions as regards fundamentals. I made mine in the new year. I'm off to Spain."

If it had been someone like Hislop, or a natural belligerent like, say, Paddy McNaughton, or Ruby Bickford, he might have been surprised, but not dumbfounded. He remembered Christopherson II as the most convinced pacifist they had ever had in the Sixth, a boy who supported Canon Dick Shepard's Peace Pledge Union, and God alone knew how many other pressure groups. Chris would remember him that way too, as the boy who took the unpopular pacifist line at that current affairs discussion a year or so back, when he insisted that confrontation with Mussolini would mean another World War and that this was unthinkable. Yet here he was, appearing out of the blue on an old Douglas motorcycle, announcing that he was about to embroil himself in the bloodiest civil war of the century.

"You're going as an ambulance driver, Chris?"

"No, Pow-Wow, to fight. To hell with turning the other cheek."

"Then I don't wonder your people think you're crazy, quite apart from the fact that Spain is Spain's business, whatever we may think of the rights and wrongs of what's going on there. You've only just started at Oxford and from all I hear likely to do well up there. What the devil do you imagine you can achieve singlehanded in Spain?" but before Christopherson could reply Christine came in, with an armful of daffodils and narcissi cut from the forecourt beds, and said, sharply, "Are you on your way to Spain?" and Christopherson, leaping up so quickly that he spilled his sherry, replied, smiling, "I always did think you were quick on the uptake, Mrs. P.J. I'm travelling overland to Bilbao, providing that old crank of mine outside stays the course. If it doesn't, I'll flog it and push on by train!" and she said, fervently, "Good for you. You won't get his blessing but you can count on

555

mine. Give him another sherry, Davy. He's spilled most of that being polite."

He took Christopherson's glass and moved over to the decanter, frowning at his reflection in the sideboard mirror and thinking, "She's already guessed his motives but I'm hanged if I can. That International Brigade everyone's yammering about will be full of starry-eyed amateurs like him, and the professional Communists will take full advantage of them if I know 'em!" He refilled the glass and came back to where the pair of them were talking in the window bay, saying, "You can't wonder I take a dim view of it. You were a pacifist when you left here, just over a year ago. Would it be too much to ask how pacifism fits in with what's going on over there?"

"He's asked for his card back and got it," Christine said, "and I think he's done the right thing. I wish to God more of Dick Shepard's converts had his moral courage," but Christopherson said, "Don't rub the salt in, Mrs. P.J. He had his basinful on the Western Front and I can understand his point of view." He turned back to David. "You don't think anything can be solved by war, do you, Pow-Wow? Or that was my impression after I got into Upper School."

"Then it was a wrongheaded one. I'm all for standing up to those bastards, and she'll tell you the same, but this is a local quarrel. Spain is still living in Philip II's time, and you won't be long finding that out. If you feel so strongly about it you would have done better to enlist in your college O.T.C. That way you'd be preparing yourself for the real show-down if and when it comes."

" 'If' is the operative word, Pow-Wow. Do you believe we'll ever have one?"

"Oddly enough, he does," Christine said, "he believes we'll wake up with the Fire Brigade on the doorstep and we've had any number of arguments about it. But I'm on your side. With Chamberlain and his set in Number Ten you'll be old to fight by the time our people realise what's happening. So good luck to you, and anyone else who takes a crack at Franco. Even P.J. will drink to that, won't you, Davy?"

He drank to it, but without enthusiasm. It was all very well for people like her and Christopherson, who saw everything in black and white, but you couldn't read history and teach history for thirty years without coming to a conclusion that almost every cause, from the Punic Wars onward, came in a shade of grey.

They gave him lunch and watched him chug away down the east drive on his elderly Douglas, trailing a cloud of blue exhaust, and signalling his departure with a series of sharp explosions, that reminded David unpleasantly of a machine gun sweeping a traverse. They never saw him again. Before Christmas news came that he had been killed at Teruel and that night, sitting alone in his study, he realised how Algy Herries must have felt when an early casualty list of the First World War had included Monson, killed at Château Thierry, in August, 1914. There was a difference, however. Christopherson, gallant idiot that he was, did not qualify for a place on the memorial outside. He died in what most people would think of as a foreign cause, and at a time when politicians were mouthing the newly fashionable phrase, Non-Intervention. But that did not make his death easier to bear. Not for him, who had always seen Christopherson as a warm, wise and lovable boy, and not for Christine, who wept when he showed her the letter from Christopherson's parents.

2

That was the very beginning as he saw it, the first major breach in his island defences, but thereafter, right through that year, the strength of the current increased to a point where it was impossible to stand off, in the manner of his early days as head, and leave the brawlers to get on with it. The war in Spain divided everybody, scoring a demarcation line not only through Westminster and Fleet Street, but through the Owl Society, solemnly debating the issue on an Exmoor plateau.

"Does Guernica mean battleships are out of date, sir?"

"The *News Chronicle* says Franco is relying on Moors, Eyeties and Germans!"

"*The Times* says the Reds are shooting nuns. Is it propaganda, sir?"

Questions fired at him not only by the Sixth and the Fifth, but the Fourth, so that he had to give them all a warning regarding the confusing references to the protagonists, variously styled Loyalists, Nationalists, Communists, Falangists, Reds, Fascists and even Liberators, according to the individual prejudices of correspondents and editors.

And, as if this was not enough, there was the occasional maverick like Hotchkiss, who subscribed, if you please, to the Left Book Club, and pressed Koestler's *Spanish Testament* upon him, declaring it made everything crystal clear. He obliged Hotchkiss on this occasion, and was shocked by Koestler's revelations, but the book did not rid him of a sour belief that Spain was a country full of gloomy bigots and that the Moorish streak in the Spaniard seemed to put a premium on acts of savagery.

Neither was Spain the only battleground. Some of the sharper ones had their eye on Paris, Berlin, Rome, Vienna, and even Manchuria.

"Sir, is there any chance of *us* forming a Popular Front, like the French?"

"What about the Anschluss, sir? Is it true all the Austrian Jews are jumping out of windows?"

"Does Japan's new invasion mean the Chinese Government and the Reds will join up, sir?"

He envied Chris, who seemed to have some kind of answers to these questions. For himself, it was getting a little above him, particularly as he had so much on his plate that summer.

He was still building, still encroaching bit by bit on their elbow room up here, and yet another Old Boy's legacy, enabling a sizeable reduction in the bank overdraft, encouraged him to push on after completion of the new wing that now comprised concert hall, classrooms, a new laboratory, seven studies, a gymnasium and a sports locker-room.

The familiar silhouette of the huddle of buildings, seen against the backdrop of a sunset, began to change, the looming bulk of the hall and classroom block rose only a few yards north of the last east drive beech, and what had been the old covered playground, once seen as a dip in the rooftop line, now straggled as far as the fives court on the northern boundary. The new buildings were, as Algy had predicted, mellowing rapidly, but there was still, in his mind at least, need for expansion since they were now aiming at a target figure of four hundred plus. The Cradlers were still without adequate quarters of their own but that, he decided, was less imperative than the provision of a real library, replacing what he regarded as a jumble of tattered books, mostly of the kind one might come across in an under-endowed convalescent home.

He put up a scheme to the Governors and they approved it at a single session. He had very little trouble with the Governors these days. Old Sir Rufus, still looking like a shrivelled walnut, continued to preside, and Briggy Cooper never missed a meeting. Between them they could always swing the waverers into line, so that he thought, "Next year will be my twentieth anniversary up here. I'll make myself a birthday present of that library," and the work was put in hand, the builder giving his completion date as August of next year.

Then, dramatically, other matters engaged his attention. Christine came to him with the news that she was pregnant again, and seemed cheerful and resolute about it, saying she intended to spoil herself throughout the spring, and would take no chances at all while on a course of tablets prescribed by the Bristol gynaecologist Willoughby had called in. She had no intention, however, of surrendering the Cradlers, now averaging twenty-five a term.

"They take very little out of me," she told him. "In fact, they'll keep me from worrying. This is the brightest bunch I've ever had, and I actually find myself looking forward to Monday, which is more than you can say of others. Yourself, included, on occasion."

But suddenly he found he had almost more than he could handle. Howarth went sick again, this time with pneumonia, necessitating a longish spell in hospital, and in his prolonged absence he was lumbered with Upper School English, and obliged to hand over his few Lower School periods to Boyer.

He did not mind the extra chore, despite the considerable pressures it exerted on his time. It was a pleasure, sometimes, to scamp the correspondence, letting Grace answer letters, guided by a pencil scrawl at the foot of the page, and spend an hour or two with his old favourites, Swift, George Eliot, Gray, Cowper, John Donne and even the war poets Owen and Sassoon, whom he had neglected lately.

He tried the Upper Fifth with Shaw's *Man of Destiny*, and found that they enjoyed it immensely, and this encouraged him to try *John Bull's Other Island*, when he heard himself recounting the story of Paddy McNaughton and his rusty revolver. He was still inclined to be a drifter in class and the boys knew it, and took shameless advantage of it, but that didn't bother him over-much. He had never seen any specific subject as watertight, so that his English had often spilled over into history, geography and even divinity, and sometimes, when the bell went, he would again remind himself he had learned more than he had imparted.

There was a price to be paid for this diversion, however, and it arrived on his desk one morning in the Lent term, in the form of an almost illegible letter from Howarth, asking him to drive over to the Challacombe Hospital, where he was convalescing. He went at once and was shocked, on being shown into a private ward, to note that Howarth was still a very sick man. He had lost a great deal of weight, and under his heavy woollen dressing gown he looked as shrivelled as Sir Rufus. He said, the moment they were alone, "You might as well have it straight, P.J. I'm finished. They can make as many cooing noises as they like, but it's a fact. I thought it only fair to tell you before the Easter break, so that you can start looking round for someone." Then, with some dif-ficulty, "That isn't the real reason I got you here. I'm asking a fa-vour, and I daresay you'll regard it as a big one when you hear it."

"You don't have to ask me to keep the job open, I'd do that in any case. I can cope. Grace does most of my correspondence, and Boyer has taken over my odd periods. As a matter of fact, I'm en-joying your work with the Fifth and Sixth," but Howarth made one of his irritable gestures. "I'm not talking about the job. I'm talking about dying, man."

"Dying?"

"That's what I said, so don't let any damned quack fob you off with anything different."

"But, good God, you're more or less over it, aren't you? A sum-mer in the south, the kind of sun-soak you always promised your-self and never took . . ."

"I left it too late." He looked at David very carefully, as though he had been an enterprising boy in Middle School, who had just presented him with an outrageous excuse for a scamped essay. "I finally got the truth out of them. I have about six months. Can-cer, here," and he tapped his chest.

It was particularly surprising. For a year or so Howarth's boom-ing cough had been as much a part of Bamfylde's background as the iron notes of the bell. Howarth had even made jokes about it calling it his forerunner. "Not the John the Baptist variety. Hairy

John promised eternal life, didn't he? Mine tells me they'll soon be burning a pile of rubbish somewhere."

It might be rooted, David supposed, in Howarth's lifelong addiction to tobacco, and he said feebly, "If you cut out cigarettes . . ." but at this Howarth snarled, "Don't give me that, P.J.! I've already given 'em up, or they think I have. But if I had done it when it meant anything I should have been carted away from that barn frothing at the mouth years ago. Tobacco is an absentminded habit with most people. It never was so with me. It was a source of enormous comfort to know that, the minute that bloody bell went, I could light up, and there it is. Some take to drink, and some can't get by without women. I liked my gin, yes, but it was never important to me. Neither was I ever in your category, with my eyes on the stars. You're fortunate to be committed to a job and I hope you've sense enough to realise it."

"What was the favour, Howarth?"

"An eccentric one and you'll have to bend rules to grant it. I'm not scared of dying but I'm scared to hell of dying here, among the sick, sorry and senile. I want to die where I belong, within scent and earshot of familiar smells and sounds. If I discharge myself, can I come back to my own quarters? I've plenty of money to pay for a day and night nurse later on and I wouldn't be a bother. You and Barnaby would be handy for a chat, and all the latest scandal. Is that asking too much? Because if it is, say so and be damned to you."

"I daresay it can be arranged, so long as you don't tell anyone else what you've just told me. If that got out we should all be in trouble."

Howarth relaxed and said, "I'm much obliged to you, P.J.," and then, with a twitch of a smile, "Wouldn't be the first rule we've bent, eh?"

He left him feeling absolutely desolate. Ever since that first exchange of conversation in the common room twenty years ago, he had leaned heavily on Howarth, more so since he had taken Alcock's place. The man's enormous experience, and his deep love of Bamfylde that he was always at such pains to conceal, had proved rallying points time and again over the years. If it had been difficult to picture Bamfylde without Algy it was impossible to imagine it without Howarth. He never had believed that story of his about scuttling off to the Riviera the moment he was pensioned. "You can't love bricks and mortar," had been one of Howarth's favourite maxims but he had belied it every time a fresh crisis blew up, and here he was begging to be allowed to die on the premises. He drove back to Bamfylde very slowly, coming to terms not only with the fact but with his decision to confide in nobody, not even Chris.

3

Howarth installed himself in his old quarters, just before the summer term opened and seemed to rally, shuffling out and about on sunny days, and sometimes making his way as far as the nets, where he would sit on the roller, his rimless glasses flashing in the sun, as he drew carefully on a forbidden cigarette, holding it under his hand, like a Fourth Former in one or other of the smokers' hideouts about the place. David and Chris spent a good deal of time with him, and so did Barnaby, who probably guessed the truth, but he must have fooled most of the others, for every now and again the bursar, or one of the junior staff, would refer to his impending return to work with phrases like, "When Howarth is fit . . ." or "Just until Howarth is back on the job."

But then, in the latest flare-up over the Sudetenland dispute, and the sordid scuttling to and from Bad Godesberg, Berchtesgaden and finally Munich, even Howarth was all but forgotten; and the writing on the wall became so stark and clear that sometimes, reading the latest headlines, he felt physically sick, as though he had eaten an indigestible meal. Possibly he had. It was not pleasant to see the sons and daughters of the men who had stormed Vimy Ridge squealing with glee over the human sacrifice of Czechoslovakia.

He was very glad then that Chris was so obsessed with her child that her approach to politics was muted, although, every now and again, she would curse Chamberlain as a fool and a coward. Like him, she winced at Chamberlain's brief triumph, when he arrived back from Munich, to be received with hysterical cheers as he waved his absurd bit of paper.

"It's the most terrifying spectacle I've ever seen," she told David, when they watched a news-reel on a rare visit to the cinema. "Nobody sane could believe in it and I don't think any informed person does. They'll be evacuating children and digging air-raid shelters in a week or so, and I hope to God somebody somewhere profits by the time that idiot is supposed to have bought us. But I wouldn't bet on it, would you?"

No, he told her, he would not, and with the onset of the new school year a sombre mood settled on him, not improved by a surprise visit from Carter, with an even more surprising proposition in his brief case.

Carter, it seemed, was someone else who wasn't taken in, and was making his dispositions well in advance. "If it does come to a show-down they'll evacuate my beat on the coast," he said. "We'll qualify as bona fide evacuees, and I want to get in on the ground floor. I don't want them sending me and the left-overs to some Godforsaken place up north, where I've no local contacts. You have plenty of room here now. Could you accommodate, say, an extra fifty under fourteen, if you had to? It would let you out too. They're bound to regard you as a host school. The Luftwaffe isn't likely to bomb Middlemoor, is it?"

The scheme had a good deal to recommend it. Carter's venture had prospered, and he could pay a good rent. It would also mean that at least some of his youngsters would automatically qualify as Bamfeldians as soon as they passed their fourteenth birthday, so he gave Carter a promise that he would put the proposition before the Governors and ring back within a fortnight.

He carried out the first half of his promise and, as he had fully expected, the Governors approved. But then, like balanced buffets to the left and right of his head, two other events put everything else out of mind. In the second week of a new term Chris was rushed off to the nursing home, and he had barely settled her in, horribly anxious but outwardly bearing up, when Howarth died, a week or so short of the six months given him by the specialist in the spring.

*   *   *

They sent for him early in the morning and he found Howarth conscious and very restless. His blanched face was a parody of the man he remembered. It looked like the face of someone in the final stage of starvation, but the breakfast bell seemed to alert him, as though that same sound, repeated down three decades, at precisely the same hour of the day, was still able to recall him to duty.

He opened his eyes, gestured feebly to the nurse, then fixed his gaze on David. The male nurse got up and left, obviously in response to some previous instruction and Howarth whispered, as the door closed, "This is it, P.J. Wanted to see you . . . know you were still around . . ." and he moved his left hand in a way that impelled David to take it. They sat there for a minute or so, listening to the clamour of boys hurrying down the long stone passage to Big Hall and breakfast. Then, after the hall door had banged on a prolonged bumping of forms and rattle of crockery, he said, "Curtain . . . what kind of day?"

David got up and pulled the curtain of the window facing southeast across ploughland and the blur of copses screening Bamfylde Bridge Halt.

"Very clear," he said. "No rain about. Can you see it from where you are?"

Howarth nodded briefly and said, "Wife all right?"

"Any minute now," but Howarth seemed not to be listening. With his free hand he made an attempt to reach under the pillow, finally succeeding in exposing a stiff folded document that David recognised as his will. In response to Howarth's nod he opened it out. It was a very simple will. Everything Howarth possessed had been left to the school. There was a brief codicil, dated two days before, naming Chris as the beneficiary of two hundred pounds, and meeting David's questioning glance, Howarth said, with a grimace that might have been one of his wry smiles, "Not for her really. For that boy . . . if you get one."

"I'm going out there this afternoon. This is very good of you, Howarth. Chris will be touched," and Howarth, husbanding each syllable, said, "Never . . . touched . . . anyone . . . Never . . . wanted . . . to . . ." Then, framing the words clearly, "Bureau. Top drawer," and David knew what he sought. He crossed to the bureau and opened the drawer. The portrait of Amy Crispin still lay on top of a pile of neatly laundered shirts and he took it out, holding it so that Howarth could see it. Perhaps a minute passed before he said, just audibly, "Wish I'd been able to believe. Leave it when you go."

He put the photograph on the cluttered night table and tried to think of something comforting to say, something that Howarth would not find embarrassing. It was not easy. All his life Howarth had been trying to increase the thickness of the shell that encased his emotions. He took his hand again and said, carefully, "Can you hear me? Don't talk, just nod," and Howarth nodded, so obediently that the gesture seemed grossly out of character. "You've done a thundering good job here. That's something to believe in. I won't ever forget you. Neither will any of the old stagers, or any of the boys you taught. As for me, I'd like to say thank you, from the bottom of my heart. But for you I wouldn't be here. Since I am, I'd like you to know nothing is going to shake me loose now, Howarth. Did you get that?"

Howarth nodded twice and closed his eyes, lying so still that David thought he had slipped away, but he hadn't. Presently he began to cough, and half sat up, his eyes blazing with fury, so that for a moment he looked his old self as he spluttered, "*Bloody* cough —fetch him . . ." and David called the nurse, who sidled in and picked up a beaker half-full of barley water.

He left then, his thoughts in a whirl, and it was not until he reached the sanctuary of his study that he realised he was still holding Howarth's will. He glanced at it again, realising that Bamfylde was richer by something like eleven thousand pounds.

*   *   *

The nursing home matron rang soon after lunch and he almost choked on the words identifying himself. She said, coolly, "No panic, Mr. Powlett-Jones. Dr. Willoughby thought you'd like to know it's started. He seems very pleased with her. Will you be coming over?"

"Now?"

"Whenever it's convenient."

He wanted to shout, "Of course I'll come! Get back to her, you idiot!" but then he remembered Willoughby and the specialist would be with her, for the Bristol man had promised to make a special trip down that day and had phoned mid-morning to say she was in excellent shape. He said, hoarsely, "I'll come within the hour," and she said, impersonally, "Good . . . good . . ." and rang off.

He stood there holding the receiver, his mouth parched and dry, his knees trembling so violently that he had to brace them against the door of the cupboard supports of the desk. The bell rang for the first period. "It would," he thought, savagely, "it always does somehow . . ." but then he got hold of himself and went in search of Barnaby, catching him crossing the quad on his way to the Sixth.

"Chris is having her baby," he said, breathlessly. "Can you take the Sixth for Howarth?" and as he said it he realised that, like everybody else, he was assuming Howarth would be back on the job in a day or so. Barnaby said, gently, "Don't worry about a thing, P.J. I've got a free period myself mid-afternoon. You're driving over now?"

"Right away. Thanks, Barnaby. Have you looked in on Howarth today?"

"No, the night nurse told me he was having a bad spell . . ."

"He won't last the day but keep it to yourself. Sorry to put so much on you. I'll ring if I'm delayed." He left Barnaby looking very startled and went round to the cycle sheds where Bamfylde's few cars were parked. Chris's silvery bumble bee stood there under a tarpaulin and his mind, conjuring with possibilities as it always did when he was seeking escape from unpleasant thoughts, toyed with the idea of pulling down the ratty old sheds and building a garage block here. In the years ahead, he supposed, almost every adult at Bamfylde would own a car or motorcycle, and they wouldn't want them kept under tarpaulins.

He headed west into a golden afternoon, thinking of Chris, of all the high hopes she had pinned on this moment, and of poor old Howarth, gasping his life away in those bachelor quarters, off Nicolson's landing. It would take him a long time to get accustomed to life up here without Howarth. Algy had gone, but Algy was still available when he was needed. With Howarth gone he and Barnaby would be the only survivors of the First World War rump, and it would seem lonely, just the two of them. Staff were not much different from boys in that way. They came, stayed a little longer than the average boy, and then left, either by way of Bat Ferguson and Judy Cordwainer, or by way of Carter and Irvine. The same thing had happened with two of the three women in his life, Beth and Julia Darbyshire. One day they were there, the next they were gone, and it was of Beth he thought as he dropped into second gear to tackle Quarry Hill, remembering passing this way in a more carefree mood one sunny May afternoon in 1920, when he had driven over to take his first peep at the twins. Howarth's enigmatic remark returned to him—'Wish I could have believed . . .' Believed in what exactly? In God? In marriages made in heaven? In Amy Crispin's lasting affection for him? Probably the first, for Howarth, although a born cynic, had never professed himself an atheist. Just one of the bewildered majority facing the fact that they had no way of knowing whether life was a planned process or a cosmic accident. It was strange, he thought, that in all their discussions, talk that had ranged over almost every conceivable topic, they had so rarely touched on faith.

*   *   *

He read the good news in Willoughby's face the moment he ran up the steps and met him in the act of lighting his cherry-wood pipe beside the receptionist's desk.

"Went like clockwork," he said, eagerly. "A boy. Seven pounds, three ounces, and yelling his head off! About an hour ago, soon after matron's phone call actually."

"Chris?"

"She's bonnie. And drunk with triumph. Never knew such a stayer. She'd absolutely made up her mind to it. She'll take me more seriously in future, I hope. I was always telling her there was absolutely nothing to stop her producing a live child."

"An hour ago, you said? Should I go in?"

Willoughby considered, drawing noisily on his pipe. "I'd leave it a bit if I were you. She's asleep. It's only three-thirty yet. Suppose you accompany me on a couple of local calls, we take a dish of tea in Glossops then pop back here about five-thirty? They can manage headless for that long, can't they?"

"Yes, but poor old Howarth is dying, Doc."

The news didn't surprise him. He said, "Amazed he lasted this long. Tough old bird." Then, shrewdly, "He talked you into letting him go back there, I imagine?"

"I don't regret it. Should I?"

"No, no. Kindest thing to do. Made it much easier on him, but you'd better go on pretending to be shocked. Some of the parents might think it wasn't quite the thing in the circumstances," but David said, "To hell with that. If Alcock could die on the premises why couldn't Howarth? He was as much a part of the place as Algy and I'm going to miss him like hell."

"Queer chap," Willoughby said. "Frankly I have always respected him without being able to like him. But you did both, didn't you?"

"I knew him better than most people."

* * *

He found her much as he had found Beth when he had called in this same place for the same reason eighteen years before. Radiant, and extraordinarily pleased with herself, so much so that he thought, smiling, "Why the devil did she ever bother with politics? This is what she really wanted. Maybe it'll take some of the steam out of her and that can't be a bad thing. We've all got too much head of steam these days."

She said, "Have you seen him yet? He's an absolute cherub, Davy, and very much the Celt. Or will be, as soon as he loses that outraged look they all seem to start off with. Long bones and lots of dark hair. No doubt at all about him being yours," and he said, letting his hand run over her own smooth brown head, "Fine time to be telling me that. Was it as bad as you thought?" and she said, no, not as bad as the last miss, and a lot more rewarding.

He didn't stay long. He had a suspicion amounting to a certainty that Howarth would have gone by the time he got back, and it seemed a shabby thing to cloud her happiness with such dismal news. He drove back through the gathering dusk and stopped a mile or so beyond Quarry Hill, where he could just see the lights of Bamfylde winking under long, blue trailers of mist. The day had brought good news and bad, like most other days up there, and it crossed his mind that it might be an idea to marry the events by naming his son Ian, after Howarth. In a way, the crusty old chap had seemed to move on to make room for the child. Chris had wanted to call him David but he had had too much experience with duplicated initials to agree to that. In a place like Bamfylde identity mattered, and two David Powlett-Joneses about the place simply wouldn't do. He wondered how Grace would take it, a baby brother eighteen years her junior, and decided it didn't really matter much, for Grace wouldn't stay indefinitely. One or another of her swains would come asking for her in a year or so and he wondered, briefly, which of them it was likely to be. His money was on Winterbourne, who made no secret of his affection for her. He remembered seeing them only last summer, strolling up towards the planty hand in hand, not the least bit interested in the match against Somerset Stragglers being fought out on the pitch.

It was curious how life seemed to weave a pattern that was not in the least haphazard, as it so often seemed to be. His own, for instance, and Keith Winterbourne's and Grace's, all linked by the fatal circumstances of that sultry day in 1925, when Winterbourne had appeared out of a blinding rain-storm and drawn him into that hideout he had beside the rushing stream.

He restarted the engine and went along the level stretch to the foot of the plateau, where a rather fussed Renshaw-Smith signalled him as he turned in at the corner of Nicolson's to head round the main buildings.

"You won't have heard about poor Howarth," he said. "He died, quite suddenly, about two hours after you left. I was going to ring the nursing home but Barnaby said you had other things to worry about. How is Mrs. Powlett-Jones, Headmaster?"

Renshaw-Smith had never been able to bring himself to use an informal mode of address and David had been obliged to accept his rectitude.

"She's fine. Just presented me with a seven-pound boy. You're the very first to know."

"I *am*? She *has*? But that's splendid! . . . Absolutely splendid! . . . Congratulations, Headmaster!"

He was so delighted that chance had chosen him for the honour of being the first Bamfeldian to hear the great news that he forgot for a moment he had been the bearer of such gloomy tidings. David said, to correct any impression Renshaw-Smith might have that he was taking Howarth's death calmly, "I saw Howarth this morning and realised then that he was critically ill. I've just been talking to Dr. Willoughby about him. I'll have to get him over right away."

He parked the car and stared up at the windows of Nicolson's, relieved in a way that old Howarth was released, but sorry he died without learning that Chris's guts and determination had been rewarded. They had always got along very well, Howarth having seen her as a fighter the day she arrived and he recalled again that it had been Howarth who urged him to put Chris to work in the Cradle.

He cut through the kitchen passage, out into the quad, then into his own house, where Rigby told him Grace was with matron, tracing laundry that had gone astray and been the subject of tiresome correspondence.

"Shall I tell her you're back, sir?"

"No, Rigby. I'll see her at dinner."

"Very well, sir. I'll be serving in twenty minutes."

He went into the study, where the day's correspondence was spread out on the right-hand side of his desk, with a note from Grace telling him which letters had been answered, which were pending. One unopened letter marked 'Personal' lay there. It had an American stamp and a Boston postmark. He opened it absent-mindedly and was amazed to find it was a letter from Julia Darbyshire, the first he had received since that day in 1927, when she had written telling him of her marriage to Sprockman, the restaurateur. He let his eye run down the pages with a sense of wonder that the letter should reach him today of all days.

It had a breezy, impersonal note, almost as though they had been corresponding regularly all these years, and concerned her eldest son, Charles, now almost eleven. She was asking if he would have room for him next term, when he would be coming up to twelve. She had two other children, both daughters, but Hiram Sprockman had died the year before, leaving her comfortably off. She had a poor opinion, it seemed, of the American educational system,

You recall what an Anglophile Hiram was and he was determined to send the boy to an English school as soon as he reached his teens. He liked you, and I told him everything I remembered about Bamfylde, even the reason I left. That made him laugh for nearly a week. Shortly before he died he asked me to try and get Charles fixed up there as soon as he was old enough, so here goes. If there's no vacancy, or if you have any prejudice against Americans, I'll understand, but I'm sure Charles could manage the entrance exam. Drop me a line saying yes or no, because if it's no I shall send him to Canada. And if you're wondering how I knew you were still there (and headmaster to boot!) put it down to our business efficiency over here. All I did was to call our advertising agency, giving the name and location. They called me back in twenty minutes with all the details, including the fees. I hope you're well and happy, P.J. I've never ceased to think kindly of you. Affectionately, Julia Sprockman (née Darbyshire in case you've forgotten all about me!)

He poured himself a whisky and sat at his desk, trying to imagine what she looked like now, what her son and daughters were like. He had no snapshot of her and could only recall, at this distance, that she was pretty, broad-featured, and had once had luxuriant hair, tresses she used to torment poor Blades, down in the goyle that summer day so long ago. Yet, although his memory of her was vague, erased perhaps by Beth and Chris, he found the prospect of Charles Sprockman coming here a pleasing one, partly because Sprockman had seemed so English somehow, and recalling this there came to him the American's quote from one of Rupert Brooke's letters: 'There walk, as yet, no ghosts in Canadian lanes . . . at a pinch one can do without gods, but one misses the dead . . .' One did miss the dead and he wondered if he should go and look at Howarth, but he did not feel equal to it. The boys would have to be notified officially, and he supposed he would have to make an announcement in the morning, but there would be no service at Stone Cross. Howarth had left explicit instructions concerning that, and had asked to be cremated. He heard the quad door bang and Grace's footsteps on the flags and rose quickly, suddenly glad of her company.

4

He told them at breakfast, letting the house prefects know in advance that he would ask for a moment's silence in Big Hall, so that the moment he mounted the dais every face turned to him expectantly. He said, once they had resumed their seats, "You will have heard that Mr. Howarth died yesterday. At his own request we won't be having a special service. Everyone who remembers him, before he was taken ill, will recall how much he disliked fuss and ceremony. But I should like to say a word or two about him, and how much he meant to the school. He was a very good friend to me, ever since I came here as a young man, before any of you were born. Hardly a day passed when he didn't give me the benefit of his experience, and when I became head I couldn't have managed without him. Bamfylde owes him a very great deal. He was a first-class teacher, and I suppose those of you who didn't have time to know him well were sometimes a little scared of him. I know all the new boys were, but the Upper School, and even some of the Middle School, soon realised how wonderfully kind he was. I could give you many instances of his kindness but he would have hated that. I see no reason why I shouldn't tell you, however, that he left everything he had to Bamfylde. Perhaps we should acknowledge his great love of the school by standing in silence for a moment."

The house prefects took their cue from him and stood, more or less in unison, so that upwards of four hundred heads bobbed up, and upwards of four hundred pairs of eyes studied porridge plates for what seemed to him a long sixty seconds. Then he stepped back and they sat again, subdued and a little embarrassed, so that it occurred to him that he might have chosen the wrong moment. Barnaby disposed of the doubt at once. Leaning forward he said, quietly, "Thank you, P.J. That was just right, I think. He wouldn't have approved, of course, but we owed it to him, anyway."

Immediately below, the continuous murmur rose steadily, falling short of its usual breakfast crescendo, a low buzz of conversation against a sustained rattle of china and cutlery. A very Bamfylde sound at this time of day. Some of them, he supposed, might be exchanging comments not on Howarth but on the arrival of Chris's boy at Challacombe, for that, too, would be common knowledge by now. Howarth had often voiced his respect for the speed and deadly efficiency of the Bamfylde bush-telegram. "Bulletins, I am persuaded, are issued regularly on the hot-water pipes. The way they circulate in gaol," he had said, and David, remembering this old joke, discovered to his surprise that he could already think of Howarth, not as he had seen him twenty-four hours ago, sick and ravaged, but as Bamfylde would always see him in the future, irascible, frigid and occasionally frightening, but underneath all that as soft as thistledown.

That wasn't quite the end of it, however.

At the Old Boys' Annual Dinner in London not long afterwards, Masterson, that year's president, paid a warm if jocular tribute to Howarth in his speech, making gentle fun of his acidity, and even giving an excellent imitation of one of Howarth's quiet eruptions in class. It was well received, for the three hundred assembled here recalled Howarth in his prime and not, as David's audience would remember him, as a tired, ageing man, racked by 'that bloody cough'. But Gilmour, a plump, rosy man in his mid thirties, sitting at the far end of table 'D', had a sobering surprise for everyone when he rose to reply to the last speech of the evening. He said, half-apologetically, "The president referred to Mr. Howarth and I should like to add something to that, something I never felt free to tell anyone until now, for had I done so Howarth would never have forgiven me. Back in 1923, when I was sixteen, and in the Lower Fifth, my father died suddenly, and in tragic circumstances. I won't bore you with details but I have to tell you this. There wasn't much money to go round at the time, and my mother at once gave notice that I would be withdrawn at the end of term. Howarth wrote my mother a letter and, having heard of his death in October, I looked it out and brought it with me. It's short, and like all Howarth's letters, very much to the point. Have I your permission to read it, sir?"

He had everybody's attention now and waited for the murmur of assent to die down.

Dear Mrs. Gilmour,
I heard of your loss from the headmaster, and write at once to express my sympathy. In the meantime I take the liberty of expressing an opinion that you would be ill-advised to remove your son before he qualifies to sit the Cambridge Senior examination. In my view he has every chance of achieving a creditable result, particularly in English subjects, and I am given to understand, again by Mr. Herries, that the reason you are removing him is financial. If I am wrong, please ignore this letter. If I am right, may I make a suggestion? I would take it very kindly if you permitted me to contribute one half of Gilmour's fees until he arrives in the Sixth, and I do not advance this somewhat impertinent offer in what some people would regard as a spirit of charity. Gilmour has ability, of the kind that I regard as rare, at least in one respect. He can express himself simply and clearly and if, as I understand was your intention, he enters the Civil Service on leaving here, that facility alone should stand him

in good stead, and benefit us all. Please let me know if this is acceptable,

Sincerely, Ian Howarth.

The effect of this letter upon the audience reminded David of the reception accorded Algy Herries's speech at his farewell supper. No after-dinner speech that he had heard on these convivial occasions had been received so spontaneously and Gilmour, flushing, was obliged to wait for the clamour to subside. He concluded, "My mother accepted that offer. I stayed on another two years, and it cost Howarth three hundred pounds, or one year's assistant master's salary at that time. Like everyone here there are times when I feel I owe Bamfylde a good deal. But looking back on what happened at that time I think I owe Howarth more."

Gilmour sat down amid tremendous applause and was further embarrassed by a standing ovation, something no one had ever previously witnessed at an O.B.A. dinner, usually no more than a beery get-together. But the ovation, David realised, wasn't for Gilmour at all. It was for Howarth and, to his way of thinking, not only deserved but years overdue. As they crowded round Gilmour at the bar afterwards he remembered Barnaby's almost obligatory quotation the day after he told him he had scattered Howarth's ashes on the Bamfylde preserve at Stone Cross. Something from Horace, Livy or Plautus, he had forgotten which: 'Love is very fruitful, both of honey and gall.' Like most of Barnaby's quotations it was extraordinarily apt.

Re - Run

Chapter One

1

Prague occupied, Albania overrun. A sense everywhere of living on borrowed time and yet, for him more than anyone on the plateau that spring, there was still an inner fortress into which he could retreat, slamming the door on the babel outside with a finality never quite achieved in the tranquil days, before he was head and before Alcock walked among them. And this, he supposed, stemmed more from her and the child and Grace, than from his own convictions, or from a persistent hope that somewhere something would happen to arrest the movement of the long creeping shadow over the Western World.

There were moments when he could even see himself, half-humorously, as a Victorian paterfamilias, presiding over a complaisant household comprised of dutiful wife, young girl in the first bloom of womanhood, baby with powerful lungs and a phenomenal appetite, and creaking manservant, as though, in unspoken agreement one with the other, all five of them had agreed to enact a charade that had, as its keywords, felicity and domesticity.

The child had this effect on her, a very surprising one to any who had known her in her electioneering days, so that sometimes he wondered if she wasn't overdoing it a little, or perhaps con-

577

serving her nervous energy for some tremendous challenge that lay in the future. The question teased him so persistently that one evening, shortly after the opening of the summer term, he said, watching her powder the baby after his bath, "Am I right about you? Has that child taken over the Chris Forster of the barnstorming days?" and she threw him a saucy look over her shoulder and replied, "If he has are you complaining, Davyboy?" and he admitted cheerfully that he wasn't but that it surprised him none the less. With everybody finally convinced that Armageddon was just over the hill he would have looked for a little crowing on her part, or at least an occasional comment on the day's headlines.

She said, dumping a drowsy Ian into his cot, "Maybe I am crowing inside. I've been wrong so often it's a rare pleasure to be right for once. But don't misunderstand me. I'm not blind to what's going on. It's just that none of us can do a damned thing about it at this stage but sit and wait. And hope, maybe."

"Hope?"

"That's what I said. I did my best to stir 'em up, and they are beginning to stir a little. A possible Polish guarantee, evacuation plans and air-raid trenches in Hyde Park establish that, if nothing else. You've done your bit, too, in a different way right here, on your home ground. I imagine you'll go right ahead doing it while there's breath in your body."

"I still don't see that as grounds for hope," he said, remembering Christopherson II on his way to Spain.

"You will, Davy, when it happens. Read your Froude again, that chapter on the early summer of 1588. Or read Churchill and L.G. come to that, writing of what they call the last summer of the old world, in June–July, 1914," but he was not to be fobbed off so easily.

"We left it until five minutes to twelve on both those occasions, and we had a hell of a lot of luck into the bargain. This time it only wants about thirty seconds to midnight and that little bastard will pick his own time, won't he?"

"Well," she said, philosophically, "it's not for me to remind you of that old jingo nostrum about England losing every battle but the last. You have a chat to the Sixth and Fifth, and then come back and convince me that Hitler and Musso are going to push us around indefinitely."

After that she wouldn't be drawn. Indeed, once a reliable nanny had been found in the village, and she could return to her beloved Cradle, and their halting readings of *Huckleberry Finn, Treasure Island* and *Robinson Crusoe*, he did not see very much of her, for he still had his hands very full, with a muster of four hundred and two boys, and a record number of thirty-eight new arrivals down for September.

He did take her advice, however, and raised the subject with the two Sixth forms and three Fifth forms. Nobody seemed to share his lack of confidence. All appeared to regard an ultimate confrontation with Hitler as a certainty, but the prospect of squaring up to his enormous army and air force, with dubious allies, and a totally inadequate armament, did not seem to daunt them. Perhaps their forefathers had won too many battles. Or perhaps, like Fleet Street, they fell for all those tales about Hitler's cardboard tanks and dummy submarines.

He was taking no chances, however, and that summer the Corps had a lively time of it, with new exercises on open warfare, Lewis gun and grenade training, and a concentrated programme of long-range shooting down at the Bamfylde Halt butts. Anything he could teach them he taught them well, and they seemed to respond to his zeal, sometimes calling him a slave-driver with the wind up, but doing their best, none the less. A young and rather foppish War Office captain, down for the Certificate 'A' pass out that year, complimented him on their keenness and turnout, saying, over a farewell gin, "Heard you were in France for four years, Headmaster. Maybe that accounts for the high morale of the chaps," and David, suddenly seeing himself as a kind of Blimp, mumbled that he had served three years in the line but left it vowing he would never be caught in khaki again.

The young officer looked a little outraged. "But you're the official C.O. of the outfit, aren't you?"

"Yes, I am," he growled, "for I've since come to the conclusion that if some of us don't make a stand soon it'll be all over bar the Sieg Heils." The War Office man, who would have been about five years old when Passchendaele was fought, raised an eyebrow. "You mean you don't think that chap's ravin' is four-fifths bluff?"

"Do you? After Munich?"

The officer shrugged. "Never meddle in politics. Just get on with the job. It's done one thing for us, I will say. The Territorials are up to strength for the first time since I left Sandhurst," and he excused himself with a nod, leaving David with the impression that Whitehall could still count on its Haigs and Robertsons.

A week later, however, he had unexpected proof of the man's claim concerning the sudden popularity of the Terriers. Spats Winterbourne turned up in uniform, on his way to summer camp on Bodmin Moor, a trim, uncharacteristically subdued young man, who looked very smart in his uniform, but reminded David poignantly of youngsters like Nick Austen and Robin Barnes, killed on the Somme. He said, apologising for what he called his fancy dress, "Had to do something, Pow-Wow. If it does come there'll be conscription, and a chap might as well get in on the ground floor. I'm ack-ack, actually. Is Grace around?"

Grace was around and they went off together in Winterbourne's rakish car. Late that night he heard the car roar into the forecourt and then Grace's hurried footsteps on the stairs, but she didn't look in to say good night. Neither did Spats, for the usual nightcap, a circumstance he thought little of at the time but was to remember a few months later, when he had occasion to put two and two together.

The term seemed to pass very quickly, with no improvement in the situation, so that he abandoned a half-formed plan to park Ian with the Boyers for a fortnight, and take Chris across to the Continent to make his own soundings, and went instead on day-trips into Cornwall and South Devon. It was as well he stayed home. News came of the Russo-German pact, and on its heels renewed outcry about the Polish Corridor, so that he wasn't much surprised to hear Carter's voice on the phone one morning in late August, suggesting they meet before the new school year began and finalised the evacuation plan, agreeing to meet in London on Saturday, September 2nd.

In the last week of August he interviewed Howarth's replacement, a cheerful, thirty-two-year-old Cornishman, called Heathcott, who seemed by far the best of the bunch, even though he had been slightly crippled in a road accident, leaving him with a limp that reminded David of Grace's handicap before her determination (plus Sax Hoskins' unconventional exercises) had strengthened the damaged muscles of her leg. Heathcott had been teaching at a grammar school in South London and wanted to get away to the country, chiefly on account of his wife's health, for she had spent some months in a tubercular clinic. "The doctors say it will do her all the good in the world to live up here," he said, enthusiastically, as soon as he knew he had been accepted.

"They told me the same thing when I was discharged from the army in 1918," David said, "and they were right. But she might find it deadly dull after a place like Croydon."

They had dinner together and David decided he was going to like the talkative, freckled young man—he had begun to think of everyone under forty as young—and they chatted far into the night, discovering that they shared many old favourites, among them Gray, Goldsmith, the Restoration poets and even Tennyson, whom David would have thought a chap like Heathcott would regard as old hat. Heathcott was interested in history, too, and had made an amateur study of the early Plantagenets. His clear favourites were the obscure Henry III and his more popular son, Edward I. "They each gave the country something lasting," he said. "Henry built most of the best cathedrals, and I always see Edward as the real originator of our legal system."

"What did you make of Heathcott?" he asked Chris when they were going to bed, and she replied, predictably, "Liked him. If his wife is half as intelligent they're going to be assets. I had a word with him on politics when you were talking to the bursar, and discovered that he's an old-fashioned Liberal. Thinks the balloon will go up in a year or so, unless we decide to get in first, and I can't see that happening."

Heathcott was over-optimistic. He drove off to collect his wife and arrange his move, but four days later the school radios crackled with news of Hitler's onslaught on Poland. It was here again, two months short of the twenty-first anniversary of the night he and Howarth had escaped from the Armistice celebration concert in Big Hall and sat under the fives court, discussing the poet Heine.

2

It fell upon them like a cataract, days before the twin drives were jammed with cars bringing boys back for the opening term, such a coming and going as nobody at Bamfylde could recall, even at Whitsuntide reunions in the halcyon days. Carter's contingent of fifty arrived, sleeping rough in classrooms until they could be sorted out and organised as a separate unit, with headquarters in a couple of Nissen huts erected just short of the Junior rugby pitch. Official forms arrived in a steady stream, 'a flood-tide of bumf', the overworked bursar called it, and David sympathised with him, cowering under the Whitehall bombardment concerning rationing, blackouts and emergency regulations. And then, while they were still in a hopeless muddle, the term began, and what had seemed confusion slipped into chaos, with a new timetable to be drawn up, extra domestic staff signed on, the workshop set busy making trestle tables and forms and a miniature farmyard established down by the piggeries, with a nucleus of a hundred White Leghorns, and a dozen ravenous Saddlebacks.

"Damn it," he complained to Chris, soon after the start of term, "it's like preparing for a siege, with the place full of peasants fleeing from the surrounding countryside," and she said that that was what it amounted to, although the anticlimax of those early autumn days did not confirm her view. Nothing seemed to be happening in the Maginot Line, so that he wondered whether there might not have been some substance in that War Office man's comment about Hitler's diatribes being bluff, and even relayed the possibility to Chris, whom he had come to regard as an oracle since the day she had appeared with little Ulrich Meyer in tow. And thinking of Meyer, he remembered to tell her that he had promoted the German boy to the rank of sergeant-major of the Corps. Ulrich was eighteen now, and in line for a prefecture if he stayed on.

"Can't help laughing when I think of his transformation," he told her, describing Meyer's first parade, north of the cricket pitch. "He was a weedy little beggar when you dropped him off but the traditional Prussian in him has begun to emerge. Adolf missed a good thing when he forced that boy into exile. There's Potsdam in his ancestry somewhere. He regards drill as poetry, and his voice, hectoring the awkward squad, carries farther than the bell. Scares the living daylights out of some of the recruits."

There were unexpected departures, as well as a flood of new arrivals. Five of the Upper Sixth, scheduled to stay on until March, did not return, among them, Crispin, handbell-ringer and stealer of toffee bars. And after Crispin, Keithley, the tiny Mancunian who had the honour of being the first new boy David had welcomed as headmaster in January, 1932. And after that Lackaknacker Briggs, still secretive and evasive about his alleged kidnapping.

Crispin and Keithley, both members of a gliding club, went straight into the R.A.F. Lackaknacker took up a commission, wangled for him by an obliging uncle at the War Office, sailing the day after he had passed out to join Wavell's army in the Near East.

Among the newcomers that term was somebody he had forgotten in the rush of events. Julia Darbyshire's boy, Charles Sprockman, of whom both he and Chris instantly approved, a tall, confident youngster, likely to be popular, despite his transatlantic drawl, that won him the overnight nickname of 'Clark', Clark Gable being the current favourite among Bamfylde's many cinema addicts. Julia had sent a letter with him, that went some way towards explaining why she had taken the momentous step of sending her son east, when everybody who could afford it was shipping his children out of harm's way. "He's half-English," she wrote, "and I'm sure his father would have approved. I think he ought to be in on anything that happens, and not dodging the column, likes scores of Britishers I'm meeting over here, all busy explaining they're over here on official business." He thought it worth while to mention this eccentric approach to young Sprockman and discovered that he had already discussed it with his mother and endorsed her view. "I was looking forward to coming, sir," he said, "and I can't see what the fuss is all about. It won't last all that long, will it?"

"I don't know about that," David said, with a glance over Sprockman's shoulder at the rehung photograph of Algy's 1913 Rugby Fifteen. "The last war was supposed to be over by Christmas and it lasted more than four years. My guess is we'll be lucky to settle Hilter's hash, in less." Then, as the boy looked puzzled, "I've fought Jerry, lad, and he's tough. Don't let anyone fool you into thinking he'll cave in quickly, the way the Italians will, if they're crazy enough to get mixed up in it," and the boy said, "No, sir. Guess I won't," and politely excused himself.

But then somebody appeared who succeeded in putting his manifold problems out of mind for a day or so. One wet and windy November afternoon Sax Hoskins knocked on his study door and said, with rather less than his usual assurance, "Er . . . have you time for a word, Pow-Wow? Kinder personal?"

Since taking up a professional career among musicians, and playing so much blues music, Sax had dropped into the habit of using American idioms and sounded, David thought, more Ameri-

can than Sprockman. He said, "You know I've always time for
you, Sax. What's your problem?"

"Well, I guess it could be yours as well," Sax said, smiling uncertainly. "Grace and me . . . well, we figured on getting married
before Christmas. Providing you'll wear it, that is."

David opened his mouth, closed it again, and ran his hand
through his greying hair.

"Married? You and Grace? Christmas, you say?"

"You mean you didn't figure on it? Not ever?"

"Well, no . . . that is . . . I had some sort of idea that when
she did marry . . . if she married, it would be you or Spats Winterbourne—I never could decide which. But good God, Sax, she's
only nineteen . . ."

"She tells me her mother was nineteen when she married you,
Pow-Wow."

He hardly knew what to say. He had always liked Sax, and he
knew that Grace had been very devoted to him since that far-off
day in 1926 when, as a lad of fifteen or so, he had marched into
Havelock's and asked if he could teach Grace some of the latest
dance steps, partly to boost her morale, partly to supplement
the exercises she had been doing at that time. Now that he came
to think about it he would have said Sax didn't stand much chance
while Winterbourne was in the offing, and Spats had never ceased
to be in the offing, since leaving Bamfylde almost nine years ago.
Winterbourne had a lot to offer, not because he was the only son
of a rich man but because he was more serious-minded than Sax,
who was reckoned a bit of a gadabout, not the kind of chap likely
to clutter himself with a wife, unless there were bonuses of one
sort or another. He was a rover, too, here today, up north tomorrow, and playing a date in a Continental resort the day after. He
just couldn't imagine Grace opting for that kind of life. She had
always seemed so wedded to Exmoor.

Sax said, amiably, "If you've got any objections you'd better
spill 'em, Pow-Wow. I've always had a hell of a lot of time for you,
and nobody could kid me you don't top the bill with Grace. So
if you put your foot down we'd wait until we could see further
ahead. The point is," he continued, "it's not really as simple as
that. I'm starting my A.G. course at Jurby, Isle of Man, on Monday, but there, I haven't told you I'm in the R.A.F. have I?"

584

"No, you haven't, and while you're at it, what the devil is an A.G. when he's at home?"

"Air Gunner. I was lucky to get signed on aircrew at my age. I'm twenty-six, Pow-Wow."

"You don't have to tell me how old you are," David said, still trying to absorb the situation, "but if you're already in the services why are you wearing civvies?"

"Oh, that? Well, my rig doesn't fit. The tunic makes me look like Joan of Arc and I'm having it tailored."

"But why is twenty-six reckoned old for flying? There must be pilots and observers older than that in the regular service?"

"Oh, there are," Sax said, "but they qualified on long, peace-time courses. Our A.G. course is only six weeks, and there are scores of kids queueing for it, some of 'em with the cradle marks still on their backside. I had to use a drop of the old palm oil with a recruiting sergeant and he put me down as twenty-three. Cost me a fiver as a matter of fact."

He gestured, hopelessly, "Look, sit down, Sax . . . give me a minute or two. Where is Grace right now? Listening outside the door, as they do in Victorian novels?" and she said, laughing, "Yes, I am," and then to Sax, "You might have closed it properly. Prefects are always using this passage as a short cut to the linen room. I had to head one off or your proposition would be all over the school by now."

She slipped inside, looking, he thought, as pretty as he had ever seen her, in her new blue two-piece, bought, he guessed, with a honeymoon in mind on her last trip to town just before term began. She said, casually, "I didn't hear everything. Daddy isn't making a song and dance about it, is he?" and Sax said, "Not really, though he has mentioned your age, just as you said he would," and David thought, "My God, there must have been some odd conversations in this room over the last seventy years but never one quite like this . . ." But then, right on cue, the bell began to clang in the quad and he said, shutting the door, "I've no objections at all in principle. You must know I haven't, the pair of you. But why all the rush? I mean, you'll be home-based for some time, won't you, even if you pass out. And talking of passing it would be the first time you ever did pass an examination."

"Oh, I'll walk this," Sax said. "Piece of cake. I'm genned up on it," and years later David realised that this was the first time he ever heard the new R.A.F. slang, that was to pass into the language in a matter of months. Grace said, "It's like this, Daddy. Once he's passed he gets a week's leave, but after that he could be sent absolutely anywhere, couldn't you, Sax? I mean, it might be years, and we couldn't wait that long, not when we don't have to. We're in love, Daddy, and he's too bashful to tell you. I daresay we would have been married in the spring, anyway, if there hadn't been a war. Isn't that so, Sax?"

The way she kept referring everything back to him robbed her of maturity somehow, so that he saw her, not as a woman of nineteen, but as a seven-year-old, skipping round the Havelock parlour with the gangling Sax, to the strains of ''Bye, 'Bye, Blackbird', played on his portable gramophone. Sax had gone red in the face, shamed by her forthrightness, but he stood his ground, just the way he had that night in Big School, when he owned up to finding Alcock's pipe-smashing ceremony very funny. "It's true," he said, doggedly. "There's never been any other Judy for me, Pow-Wow. How about it, then?"

"Well, you'll suit yourselves, I suppose, for it's clear you've made up your minds anyway. Coming here was a formality. Will you be getting married in church?"

"Good Lord, yes," Sax said, as though someone had questioned his integrity. "We'd like to be married at Stone Cross. Grace would like that, and I think it's a bit of a lark, I mean, getting married where I've sat through so much jaw. How about the seventeenth? That's the day after I complete the course."

"And the last full day of term," Grace added, "so everyone can come who cares to."

He got out his day-book and marked the date, and as he did it struck him that Grace and Sax had almost certainly taken instruction from someone on how to play this rather old-fashioned scene. "That could only be Chris," he thought, "and they aren't going to get off scot-free and write me off as a dimwit," and he said, artfully, "Why don't we go in and get Chris up to date? She'll be so surprised she'll probably drop the baby."

He had his small revenge. They both looked a little outfaced and then Grace said, "Er . . . she won't, Daddy . . . be surprised, I mean. She might pretend to, but the fact is we talked it over with her an hour ago. She took it very calmly."

"She was flat out for it, as a matter of fact," admitted Sax, "so let's go back into the parlour and drink on it. You've got Scotch in there. You can't oil a prospective son-in-law with Old Boys' sherry."

*　*　*

They were going to bed about midnight before he made his first direct reference to the query uppermost in his mind. "I always thought it would be Spats Winterbourne if it was anyone. I would have bet on it, wouldn't you?"

She didn't answer for a moment, tugging at a knot in her hair, with her head on one side, so that he could see three aspects of her face in the three-sided mirror and reflect, idly, how young she had looked since coming home with that baby, as though she had just won first prize in the Irish sweepstake. Then she laid aside the comb, pivoted slowly on the stool and looked him over carefully and judiciously. "Your trouble is you have a surfeit of males and male psychology, Davy. No, I wasn't in the least surprised to discover it was Sax. In fact, I would have been very surprised to learn it was Winterbourne, poor devil."

"Oh, he'll get over it at his age. They all do."

"It'll take him longer than most."

"If he was so keen why didn't he put up a fight for her?"

"How do you know he didn't?"

"I don't know. He was here on a flying visit in the summer. Come to think of it he went off without saying goodbye, and hasn't been near us since."

"Well, that isn't hard to explain. That would be the day Grace told him the score."

"You mean that she was always in love with Sax?"

"Rather more, I suspect. That Sax needed her more than he did, and Grace is a woman who has to be needed. Keith Winterbourne is a sensitive, civilised human being, and he would have made her a good husband. But Grace wanted more than that. She wanted someone to spoil and that disqualifies anyone as self-sufficient as Winterbourne."

He thought about this and then about her, how wise she was in so many ways, how well endowed to operate at a far wider range than he, whose talents were confined to handling males between the age of about thirteen and eighteen. He said, "I think Grace

587

is damned lucky. She not only had a stable to pick from when it comes to a husband, she got a Grade A stepmother for good measure."

"I don't take much credit for that. Anyone could get along with Grace."

"Anyone couldn't."

"Well, anyone you picked for her stepmother could."

She got up and moved between him and the dressing-table light, so that the lines of her figure—the figure of a girl athlete he sometimes thought it—were displayed through the flimsy material of her nightdress. It struck him then what a tremendous part she had played in keeping him young in heart, warding off the fossilisation that threatened all men in his profession after more than ten years on the job. "You don't look much older than Grace in that get-up," he said, and she replied, switching off the light, "I know a lot more about men. Notwithstanding the head-start she's had over most of her sex."

"I'm glad to hear it. It follows you probably know what I'm thinking."

"I knew before you did. Wedding talk always makes men randy. Women too, sometimes. Me, for instance."

She stood still in the darkness for a moment, out of immediate reach but close enough for him to hear the soft rustle of her nightdress as she shrugged herself out of it.

3

Twice during that winter of war that was not war the battle flared, two live coals in an otherwise dead fire. H.M.S. *Royal Oak*, at anchor in Scapa Flow, was torpedoed by a U-Boat and sank at dead of night, taking with her Lieutenant Graves-Jones, who had served in the Navy since leaving the plateau in the mid-twenties. Beth would have remembered him well, for he had been the least shy guest at her first new boys' party in 1919, acknowledging her hospitality with a Prussian heel-click when saying good-bye in the garden of the cottage. Always a bit of a ladies' man, Graves-Jones, but a credit to Bamfylde, for he was naval cadet of the year when he passed out at Dartmouth. But David recalled him for another reason, seeing him as a self-assured senior standing on the threshold of Havelock's parlour the night they buried

Beth and Joan up at Stone Cross, holding a bunch of flowers he had intended laying on the grave and suggesting they went instead to Grace, lying trussed in hospital at Challacombe. "She won't see them, sir, but maybe she could smell them. The freesia has a lovely scent . . ."

He wrote his name, achievements and dates in the rearward section of his day-book, on a page that was blank save for the name of Christopherson, killed in Spain two years earlier, and as he made the entry he shuddered at the prospect of seeing the page studded with names. But records would have to be kept. Already letters were beginning to trickle in from all over the world, so that he found himself stuck with his old job of O.B.A. Secretary, a task he had cheerfully surrendered to Howarth but did not care to entrust to anyone else these days. Not even Barnaby who, with the best will in the world, would be likely to revere the dead of Thermopylae and Salamis above those doing battle in aircraft and tanks. Bamfylde's naval minority had it very much their own way that season. Letherett was aboard one of the destroyers that pursued the *Graf Spee,* and Ruby Bickford, surely tailored for the role, was aboard *Cossack* when she intercepted the prison ship *Altmark* in such dashing style, the boarding party leaping on deck like Elizabethans capturing a Spanish treasure galleon off Panama.

Then, for the first time since any of them could recall, there was a school wedding at Stone Cross, almost a fairy-tale wedding it seemed to him, when he came in by the west door with Grace on his arm, and moved up the aisle to join Sax Hoskins, in R.A.F. uniform, with sergeant's stripes up, evidence of promotion that had astonished him until Sax explained "Aircrew get their third automatically . . . Can't have A.C. plonks flying kites, can you, Pow-Wow?" Sax was good enough to offer a free translation of this jargon for the benefit of those who did not yet speak the strange new language, a language that was already invading civilian sectors.

Algy Herries married them, and besides a full congregation of staff and boys there were one or two former cronies present, down to give Sax moral support. Massa Heilbron was one of them, the West Indian Sunsetter, over here on a gunnery course. Rowlandson was another, who might have remembered upsetting the teapot at the new boys' party, in 1924. David kept hoping to spot

Winterbourne but he did not, and when he asked around nobody seemed to have news of him.

There was a lively reception back at the school, and the rowdy send-off he would expect in the forecourt as the short afternoon died, and the couple drove off to catch their train to Taunton and Paddington. The finality of the event did not strike him at the time, for so many old friends hung about the place until late that night, and there was the usual end-of-term tumult at first light the following morning.

"Have a good hols, sir . . . !" "Don't join up while we're gone, sir . . . !" and the inevitable sober note, this time from Vicary, head boy and due to join the Royal Marines in the new year— "I'll keep in touch, sir . . . Might even be handy for a spell. They tell me there's an R.M. training camp at Lympstone, just south of Exeter."

He stood on the steps and watched the last of them go, and it was then that he missed Grace most keenly, and was glad that she was likely to be back for a spell, at least until Sax found out where he was posted, and could wangle a living-out pass near the camp. He would miss her secretarial work too, for the post did not get any lighter, and Chris couldn't help him much, with her Cradle at full muster, and Ian at the toddling stage. Chad Boyer nudged him, collar turned up against the biting north-easterly and said, "How about a coffee, Pow-Wow?" in a way that suggested a confidence of some kind, so he went back into the house and told Rigby to bring coffee into the study, where a mountain of work awaited him. Chad said, when the door had shut on the old man, "Are all those letters from Old Boys overseas, Pow-Wow?"

"Most of them. Care to read some? There are several from chaps here in your time."

"Not in my present mood," Chad said, and when David asked what was amiss he said, gloomily, "I don't know. I feel out of it somehow. All the old crowd are doing something—Letherett, Dobson and even the Gosse brothers."

"A lot of the older bunch made a career of the services, Chad. It's no more than their job. Yours is right here, especially with Alison, one boy, and a second child on the way."

"Sure, sure but . . . I don't know . . . I still feel out of it. Is that so crazy?"

"I think it is. You're not much younger than I am, and from all

I hear they can't cope with more men at the moment. Nothing seems to be happening, does it? Sometimes I see it as a kind of mime, a ritual squaring up to one another that will end in a compromise."

"Does Chris see it that way?"

"No. She says it'll get going in the spring, but she could be wrong. Frankly, I never imagined anything like this. The last war started off at a rare gallop. Mons was twenty days after declaration and I was in action three months later. Do you really want my advice?"

"I don't. Alison does."

"Well, for God's sake go back and tell her I said don't do any enlisting until it's absolutely necessary. For one thing I'd find it damned hard to replace you. For another you've got her and the kids to consider. But quite apart from all that, I think you'd find it difficult to land anything but a stooge job, in one or another of these new ministries. You'd be making a far better contribution here than getting bogged down at a desk."

Chad said moodily, "You were under eighteen when you signed up," and he snapped, "I was a bloody fool and lived to regret it. Besides, nobody knew a damned thing about war in those days."

He foraged among the incoming mail and found a single-sheet letter. It was from Gilbert, the Tory M.P.'s son, a contemporary of Boyer's and postmarked Tiree, in the Hebrides. "Listen to this. It illustrates my point.

Dear Pow-Wow,

You'll note from the above address the Governor managed to get me into the R.A.F. after all. You need a lot of influence to get in, I can tell you. I tried half a dozen things off my own bat up to the end of October, but they didn't want to know. I couldn't even get into a line regiment as a ranker, and as for Cert 'A', nobody seemed to have heard of it. They probably regard it as a passout at the archery butts, or the Bamfylde certificate of proficiency for pike-drill. I was chuffed when I made it to O.C.T.U., but I might just as well have stayed put. I was failed aircrew on account of age (!) and given an admin. job up here, and I've never been so brassed off in my natural. All I do is look at the sea, sign chits for crafty weekends, and churn out daily returns that nobody reads. Believe me, it's all a big-scale hoax.

Drop me a line if you've time, and tell me how my lot are making out. And tell old Barnaby, preferably in Latin, that the pen is not only mightier than the sword, it's a hell of a sight more universal in this man's army.

Warmest regards, R. S. Gilbert."

He was relieved to look up from the letter and see Chad grinning. "You're wasted as a schoolmaster, Pow-Wow," he said. "You ought to have been one of those barristers who sit waiting for hopeless briefs handed down from the Bench. If ever I fall foul of the law I'll engage you. You'd come up with something proving I had a damned good reason for having the spoons in my pocket."

Chapter Two

Chris was right, as usual.

In April, Chamberlain was talking about Hitler missing the bus. A fortnight later Denmark and Norway had fallen, and the summer term was less than a month old when Rotterdam was reduced to rubble and the distracted French Government had scuttled off to Bordeaux. The river of steel poured unchecked through the Low Countries, leaving in its wake a Maginot Line as obsolete as Martello towers, built to resist invasion in 1805. It was too late to do anything but run for cover, if cover was to be found.

The speed, and horrid finality of the onrush, stunned a man conditioned to think of an offensive's territorial gains in terms of yards, and those yards won at a cost of a hundred thousand casualties. It was an entirely new concept of war. He could think of no historical equivalent. The Napoleonic swoop on Ulm, culminating in Austerlitz, and the encirclement of Sedan, in 1870, were measured manoeuvres compared to this. At a stroke, huge French armies were dispersed and isolated, and the B.E.F., pushed back on three Channel ports, was reckoned lost.

*　　*　　*

He could not remember feeling so desolate since they brought him news of the accident on Quarry Hill. Catastrophes fell one upon the other like the subsiding storeys of a row of tall houses, overwhelmed by a hurricane. Belgium surrendered, then France, whereas over here all was confusion and dismay, even after Churchill had ousted Chamberlain, and thundered defiance in cadences that struck the ear like parodies of Henry V's oration before Harfleur. Soon long-range shells were falling on Folkestone, road blocks were set up, even down here in the wilderness, and a local L.D.V. force, armed with rook rifles, old army Webleys and farmers' shotguns, patrolled the moors and coastal sectors. There was a sense of unreality and lack of purpose about everything one did, as if the ordinary processes of life, governed for so long by bells, by the school calendar, by arrivals and departures at the beginning and end of each new term, had lost their significance, were mere gestures in a compulsive ritual initiated long, long ago and persisted in from habit. A terrible sense of urgency, seen on the faces of adults, spread downwards to the Middle and Lower Schools, where he found himself the target of repeated questions for which he had no kind of answers.

"Will they invade, sir?"

"How about the navy, sir?"

"Is it true they're dropping paratroopers disguised as nuns, sir?"

"Will France fight in North Africa, sir?"

"Can't we join the L.D.V.s? There are rifles in the armoury, aren't there, sir?"

At least he could answer that one truthfully. There were no rifles in the armoury, not even the much-derided dummies, issued to the very youngest recruits in the Corps in their first month of training. Only a week ago a detachment of Terriers had arrived in a lorry, and carted them all away, together with what small arms ammunition was available. By now, he assumed, those same rifles, that had been humped up and down the playing fields since the days when Carter had been Corps Commander, were in the hands of half-trained men drawing army pay, awaiting the first shock waves of German invaders behind the beaches of Sussex and Hampshire, and in the hopfields of the Kentish Weald.

But then, like a blessed spate of silence after an earsplitting cacophony, came whispers of a fleet of small ships, and the lifting of 360,000 castaways from the littered beaches of Dunkirk. No more than a rumour at first, but a persistent one, that presently emerged as a fact, a kind of massive lifeboat snatch from a foundering vessel, surrounded by bobbing heads and upraised arms, and after it a vast wave of thankfulness, followed by a mood of buoyancy not unlike the first stage of intoxication. Apparently it was not the end of everything, or not quite, so that, like everybody about him, he plucked up heart and took up the threads of authority again, snatching a moment here and there to collate the snippets of news that found their way to his desk via post and telephone, and the occasional appearance in his parlour of a harassed parent, past or present. It seemed a miracle that, of the score of Bamfeldians serving with the B.E.F., fourteen were already reported safe and well, and one or two had actually rung through while on survivors' leave. He conceived the idea then of posting a list of them on the quad notice board, announcing details within minutes of receiving his stream of messages, then squinting through the window of Algy's Mount Olympus, where he could see them crowding round the slip of paper hanging there, relaying the news to the outer fringes of the crowd.

More and more news filtered in, almost all of it good. Gilbert, last heard of looking out at sea, and signing chits on a lonely Hebridean Isle, was spirited from a French beach by an amateur yachtsman, and confirmed as much in person, writing cheerfully from Newhaven where he was set ashore. Kassava II, he who had clung to the guttering of the blazing Havelock dorm until his brother knocked him senseless, showed far more initiative at Calais, hiding in a partially collapsed slit trench until it was dark, then making his way along the tideline to the nearest evacuation point, where he was taken off by the boat's crew of a destroyer.

Through the blazing summer days the list lengthened until it ran off the page and was replaced by a larger, more comprehensive one, with notes beside every name, Daffy Jones, Nipper Shawe, Gage and Stilts Rhodes rescued by destroyers, and set ashore at Dover; Bummy Bristow, whose elder brother had been Bamfylde's last casualty in the First World War, having more luck than his brother, this time off Bordeaux, where he got off in the *Lancastria*, went down with it, but bobbed up and was hauled aboard a trawler and carried into Falmouth; Johnston, the indirect cause of Winterbourne's flight in 1925 (he had told him his mother's divorce was all over the Sunday papers) taken prisoner at St. Malo but dodging the column (Johnston was always a bit of a column dodger, David reflected), and making his way to Brest, where he caught the last refugee boat out of the harbour; Maxton, third official bell-ringer in David's recollection, together with Heffling and Keith Blades, rescued by the navy at Dunkirk; Parker and Morgan-Smith carried home on a paddle steamer that had once plied for hire from the Isle of Wight; Cookson, whose father had once shamed him by appearing on Sports Day in a chauffeur-driven Rolls-Royce, using more plebian transport and landing, black as the Ace of Spades, from a collier at Newport, Monmouthshire. Some fifteen in all, the last being Driscoe who had partnered Beth and Phyl Irvine as the third of the three little maids in the 1920 *Mikado*, reported safe a week after having been listed a P.O.W. Driscoe, it seemed, had made it all the way to Marseilles in an elderly Citroën, found by the roadside near Abbeville, paying his way with cigarettes, looted from an abandoned N.A.A.F.I.

And after that a lull, while David was seeking, and getting, confirmation of their two known casualties, a sad pair to anyone's way of thinking. For Briarley, serving as a captain in the Calais garrison, was killed some thirty miles from the river Lys, where his father had died in the Big Push of 1918. Details concerning Skidmore's death were more confused but it looked as if he had achieved a kind of martyrdom after all. Serving in the B.E.F. as a Methodist padre, he had remained behind to tend to the wounded and was now reported missing, believed killed.

* * *

The day he got confirmation of Briarley's death he went out across the forecourt to the big cedar beside the tennis court, sitting near the spot where he had talked to the boy twenty-two years before, after Ellie Herries had sent him out to offer what comfort he could. He wondered if Briarley's mother was still alive, and if she was, how would she take this second blow? Bitterly, he would say, for Briarley Senior had died in what was reckoned a war to end war, and Briarley Junior, he recalled, was an only son.

The boy's voice seemed to speak to him over the years—"Didn't see a great deal of him, sir . . . when I was small he was mostly in

India or Ireland . . ." and a later question, "Would it have been quick, sir? I mean, you'd know . . ."

He sat there in the blinding heat, biting his lip and silently cursing the fools who had let things drift and drift until they had reached an impasse where the only hope of a future rested on the wanton sacrifice of boys like Briarley, boys with guts and imagination, now called upon to go out and do their fathers' work all over again. The bell rang for lunch but he did not hear it and later Chris found him there, staring into the heat haze shimmering on the western slopes of Middlemoor.

She said, quietly, "What is it, Davy?" and he told her of all three Briarleys, father, thirteen-year-old son who had sat here beside him, and thirty-five-year-old regular, left behind in Calais to stop Panzers with hand grenades and a standard issue revolver.

She said, taking his hand, "All in all, we've been lucky, Davy. In two ways if you can bring yourself to see it in that light. Fifteen out of seventeen saved by a miracle, or a string of miracles. But that isn't what I mean."

"Well?"

"God knows, I've never seen you or myself as people subscribing to those platitudes about the nobility of sacrifice—*pro patria mori*, and so on. I never was entranced by Kipling, or that chap Newbolt, who wrote that slosh about the voice of the schoolboy rallying ranks. But this is different, utterly different. I think it's important you should face up to it now, for it looks to me as if there's worse to come."

"How is it different? Briarley, father and son, died in the same war, on the same ground, fighting the same enemy. What's different about it?"

"I don't think I have to go over that again. I made it clear five years ago, when I backed down on every principle I ever held. This time it isn't a question of dying for king and country, for the flag, for honour and glory and all that rubbish."

"It never was," he said, "for the chaps called upon to do it."

"But it was for the people who weren't, people like me standing on the touchline. Only now there isn't any touchline. We're all in it, right up to our necks, and that's a point in our favour, I'd say. At least, there's no more bloody hypocrisy, no more do-your-bit-son, no more white feathers and promises of homes fit for heroes to live in. This is total war, with nothing but survival as the prize-money. More muddle if we win, a living death if we don't. It's worth dying for if that much is clear. Briarley was killed at Calais, you say?"

"Left to his fate, back to the sea. Bombed from above, fired on by God knows how many tanks."

"But if it hadn't been for Calais, what would have happened up the coast at Dunkirk?"

"I'm damned if I know and I don't see how you could know."

"It so happens I do," she said, "for Bradshawe told me. He plied one of those small boats, and that's something else you should put on your little list before you draw a line under it. Don't look so outraged—Bradshawe was here and I tried to find you but you were over at Challacombe at that L.D.V. conference. He couldn't wait. He was on his way to Plymouth to join the navy."

"What exactly did Bradshawe tell you?"

"A lot they didn't print about Dunkirk. More than he's told anybody, I'd say. I have a very special relationship with Bradshawe."

She had too, beginning that day during her first term here, a month or so after they were married, when Howarth, the old fox, had persuaded her to mediate between Bradshawe, then fifteen, and his parents, plaguing him with their respective versions of the family divorce. "He picked nine out of the water, close inshore. I didn't know he was a yachtsman, did you?"

"No," he said, the weight beginning to lift from his shoulders, "but I settled years ago for learning something new about every damned one of them every day I make contact. Both during and after their time here."

He stood up. "That's not such a bad idea, either—adding Bradshawe to the list, I mean. He only left in 'thirty-eight, and there'll be quite a number here who remember him. They'll be excited to hear we had someone who took part in that crazy armada."

He made no excuse for his sudden change of mood and she watched him move with long strides across the sunlit tennis court, over the forecourt and through Big School arch to the quad. He already had his fountain pen unscrewed and she thought, "He's no more than a Briarley or a Bradshawe himself some days. But, just occasionally, he's as old as God. That's the way of it in his job, I imagine . . . my job, too, now, if I'm honest with myself . . ."

She got up, smoothed her skirt and walked thoughtfully across the sunbaked lawn to the steps, meaning to pass straight through into the kitchen and warm his untouched lunch, but tempted, en route, to use his Judas window in the lavatory. She was in time to see him repin the notice and stand back to let the first quad loungers read the addendum.

2

She had promised him worse and he had learned to trust her judgment in these things, yet the summer blazed on tranquilly enough, with plenty of bustle, and a steady bombardment of officialdom certainly, but as yet no cataclysmic sequel to the epic of Dunkirk.

World War was lapping into the quadrangle, into the nooks and crannies of the old place in a less dramatic way, creeping paralysis rather than a seizure, for the very influx of boys that summer slowed them down, sometimes to a virtual standstill. Seemingly the reverse of the 1931 slump was at work in the minds of parents, particularly those living in Greater London, and the threatened south-eastern areas. Younger brothers arrived out of nowhere, often at short notice, so that the waiting-list, that had always had to be nursed, shook itself out well ahead of time as people remembered the relative immunity of the plateau.

In addition to their own swollen complement of four hundred and seventeen, there was an increase in Carter's contingent. 'Minimals' Barnaby called them, a play of their school's official name, St. Magnus, and Carter was very jealous of their identity, keeping them within their perimeter, which was just as well in view of the chronic shortage of dormitory, classroom and playing field space. There were now over sixty Minimals, living like a dependant and slightly disreputable tribe under the lee of the planty, where two more Nissen huts were erected to serve as dining-room, kitchen and communal classroom. Carter managed them with one assistant master, an elderly man called Badger, said to be an amateur archaeologist, with extravagant theories about Middlemoor being the real site of Arthur's Camelot.

They lost Molyneux towards the end of term. It seemed that he, too, heard the call of duty, in the form of a muted 'Marseillaise', played by the exiled de Gaulle. He was not a Frenchman but had many Gallic friends and one of them, a certain Capitaine d'Orley, appeared in uniform one morning and talked him into joining the nucleus of the French Resistance Group as an official interpreter.

He went off gaily, despite David's indignant protests. He had never really integrated into the school but his work was first-class, and David was reluctant to lose him. He said, by way of valediction, "I've been stuck here fifteen years, P.J. and I've never had any *fun*. I'm nearly forty now, and if I turn this down I'll marry a local peasant and grow a turnip for a head. Time I moved on, but it took a thing like this to shake me loose. Never had enough initiative, but d'Orley tells me there's a prospect of seeing the world once we get properly organised. It was that that decided me."

He was replaced, almost at once, by an elderly Belgian refugee, a Monsieur Oujardier, a name that the boys instantly converted into 'Oojah', without waiting for Barnaby's cue. In some ways the Belgian reminded David of the long-dead Bat Ferguson, in that he was excitable and very voluble, but he showed promise of being adequate, and at least qualified as an eccentric, an honour that Molyneux had never achieved, notwithstanding his middle name, Aloysius, and that awful Australian uncle who looked like a Colonial pretending to be Bernard Shaw.

Then, in the final week of term, when he was in the throes of making arrangements to house an additional fifty boys for the holidays, on the lines of the Sunsetters, a much heavier blow fell on him. A grim-faced Boyer invited him and Chris down to the cottage for tea one baking Sunday afternoon, and announced in the momentary absence of Alison, that he was enlisting in the merchant navy as soon as their second child was born, and that it was no good trying to talk him out of it because he had been to Plymouth and signed on the previous Saturday.

In the last twenty-odd years there had been many occasions when Boyer had exasperated him but never more so than now. He said, explosively, "But that's absolutely crazy, Chad! The merchant navy! Good God, what the hell do you know about the sea? It's no more than a Quixotic gesture. Why don't you borrow a suit of armour while you're at it, and charge Man Bullivant's bloody windmill at Bamfylde Halt?"

Chris said, "Keep your voice down, Davy. Maybe he hasn't told Alison," and Boyer said, calmly, "Yes, I have, and she's behind me, odd as it may seem. Or not so odd, perhaps. Her kid brother,

Hamish, went down on the *Jervis Bay* last winter. She was very fond of Hamish. He was only seventeen."

"I never heard that," said David, checked somewhat. "She kept it very much to herself, didn't she?"

"She isn't a song and dance artist, Pow-Wow, but it left a scar. I was scared of admitting how I felt about things, but when I did she saw my point of view, particularly as I've every hope of training as a gunner, although my real duties will be steward."

"Steward!" David growled, warming up again, "Steward, with a good degree and a reserved occupation!" but Chris intervened again, saying, "Do stop erupting, Davy. Let Chad explain if he wants to."

"He already has. He came to me when the phoney war was still on, mumbling about missing out, but I thought I'd talked him out of it. Damn it, I could understand it if you were in the Sixth, or still up at university. But thirty-five, with one toddler and another expected in October!"

Chad said, addressing Chris, "The trouble with Pow-Wow is that he won't accept the end product of his own gospel. He's like an apostle of the early Christian Church who gets cold feet and urges his converts to pay homage to Nero the minute he hears the lion roar," and Chris said, laughing, "That's a pretty good analogy, Chad. Go on."

"I don't know whether or not you realise it, Pow-Wow, but all these years, ever since you walked into Big School with the shakes on you before that last show ended, you've been preaching tolerance, equality of opportunity, the true essence of democracy, small 'l' liberalism, and British standards of equity and fair play. Everything, in fact, that places like Bamfylde are supposed to stand for. All that red flag flapping never fooled me, and it never fooled anyone else except that idiot Alcock. Even Sir Rufus Creighton saw through it the moment he put his glasses on and that's what got you the job. We almost nicknamed you 'Bolshie' your first term but if we had it would have been ironic. You're no more than a Tory, slightly left of centre, and as a rebel Welshman you're a damned fraud. Bamfylde took you over body and soul and did it in a matter of weeks. It beats me why you haven't admitted as much to yourself."

"I don't see what my political outlook has to do with you throwing up a responsible job and risking your life in order to bring the skipper a mug of cocoa at six bells."

"Tell him, Chad," Chris said, "you're doing fine so far."

"Well, the fact is, all your own chickens, and those you inherited from Algy, are coming home to roost. God knows we've had proof of that lately. For years and years you've been jawing about the struggle of the British tribes to hammer themselves into a unit qualified to make a contribution to real civilisation and you seem to have done a pretty good job one way and another. On my reckoning we've already got around sixty Old Boys in the scrap, all squaring up to that bastard and his thugs, and pretty sure to make mincemeat of 'em given time and equipment. Fifteen slipped the collar at Dunkirk and lived to fight another day, and three, four if you count Christopherson, who was too quick off the mark, have already died for what you and they believe in. Well, you have to take some of the responsibility for that, and for any more chaps who go west before it's over. But would you be any more pleased with your work if nobody stepped forward? What would you have done then? Taken to recruiting, I wonder, or gone back yourself to take a second crack at Jerry? Pour him some more tea, Chris, and call up to Alison to bring Robbie down. If he sleeps any longer he'll keep us awake all night."

So there it was, his philosophy, his ultimate responsibilities, fed back to him, spoonful by spoonful, by one of his own converts, and there was no alternative but to open his mouth and swallow it. The flavour was sharp at the time. Within a month its bitterness set his teeth on edge.

*   *   *

The tempest rushed down on them again about the time a majority were leaving for the summer holiday. Radio bulletins told of massed air attacks on Channel shipping, on port installations, on fighter airfields, and finally on the Port of London itself, so that the Armageddon everyone had looked for on that clear September day almost a year ago was here now, and the more thoughtful among them began to understand why the R.A.F. had made such a modest showing over the beaches at Dunkirk. Defence squadrons had clearly been held in reserve, against just such a contingency as this.

They saw nothing of the air battles, of the twisting vapour trails in the clear blue sky to the south-east (the summer seemed endless that year) but the B.B.C. soon evolved a cricket score technique concerning the state of play, and it caught on at once, after he had installed their most powerful radio in Big School, so that no one missed any bulletins, and they could use the blackboard for a score board. Even the rump of the Cradlers, and the junior Sunsetters, were given permission to stay until the last bulletin of the day.

The damage inflicted on the attackers was astounding if true. Squadron after squadron decimated between the Normandy airfields and the Home Counties, where a junkyard of Luftwaffe hardware was said to be building up in fields and coppices of Sussex, Kent and Essex.

There was a price to pay, of course, but it seemed, to most onlookers, a modest one, again if the bulletins were true. For every Spitfire or Hurricane lost Goering had to sacrifice three aircraft, and the R.A.F., fighting over its home ground, had the advantage as regards pilots parachuting to safety.

But again, as snippets of news filtered on to his desk, he began to feel more and more like Algy Herries during the Somme and Passchendaele offensives of 1916 and 1917. The price might be modest in terms of men and machines, but it was terribly high to him, and mounting week by week, for the Junior Service seemed to have attracted a swarm of Bamfeldians, mostly the younger ones who had been here as recently as 1938 and 1939, and were now, unbelievably, among those spearheading the battle.

News had reached him via telephone in late July that Hislop had been shot down off Folkestone. Hislop, who had once stood in this very room, and told the Stoic the truth concerning his exploits as school bookmaker, and had then disappeared from their midst, to reappear more than a year later, with his sights set on a commission in the R.A.F.

Mrs. Hislop rang late one night, when he was wrestling with the September timetable. She was extraordinarily resigned, he thought, but he pitied her from the bottom of his heart when she said, "He was something of an ace, P.J. I had that from one of his squadron, who brought me the news. He shot down three M.E.s in France, and was credited with five certainties over here, one Heinkel, one Dornier and three Junkers, I think they said. I haven't told his father yet. He's away up North, attending a relative's funeral, but I had to talk to someone tonight."

David said, "He was everything I hoped in the end, Mrs. Hislop, and I'll never cease to be grateful to you for letting him return here. It turned out splendidly. He was one of the best seniors we ever had. But what comfort is that to you now?"

She said, quietly, "Some comfort. More than you'd think, maybe. I'm proud of him, and his father should be. I hope so, anyway, for it's all he'll have to hang on to. I keep telling myself that if it hadn't been for trained pilots like him we'd be finished by now. You think that too, don't you?"

"I've thought it ever since Dunkirk," he said, fervently. "The Services didn't get much of a show before the war. People thought of them as old hat I suppose, but it's a damned good job some youngsters opted for them."

"Will you pass it around among his old friends?" she concluded and he said he would, and thanked her for ringing. "Don't thank me," she said. "He 'went a bundle' as they say, on you, and on that place of yours. In spite of that silly business with Alcock. Good night, P.J."

"Good night, Mrs. Hislop."

He replaced the receiver, with no stomach to return to the madly complicated timetable. Hislop's death made four certainties in less than a year. The list was lengthening. All one could do was pray it wouldn't be as long as the one on the cross outside before they blew the Cease-Fire.

He thought about prayer for a moment. Almost nothing remained of the conventional faith of his Valley upbringing, the chapel-based certainty of a glorious resurrection, that had proved such a rock of comfort to his mother. He supposed himself an agnostic, like old Howarth, but he wasn't even sure of this. The outlines of his earthly beliefs were well-defined, but he had never exercised his mind to fill the spiritual vacuum, created by his first few weeks in the trenches. There might be something, he supposed, some vague creative force, impossible to define in words, or even contemplate in solitude. Prayer would be a help now, he imagined, but the best he could do was rally on what he thought of as the Abu Ben Adam philosophy, the substitution of faith in one's fellow man as a workaday equivalent for faith in God. Given there was a God.

He turned off the desk light and went out into the passage, passing through the door leading to Big School passage, then out on to the playing field.

A harvest moon hung over the moor. He could see the dark line of the planty all the way from the spot where it turned a right angle to run the full length of the crest as far as the cricket pitches. Below it, fifty yards or so nearer the school, was the stark silhouette of Algy's thinking post, and he bent his steps there, lighting a cigarette, leaning against its brittle bark, and remembering not only Hislop, who had once hit a stupendous six about here, but other moments he associated with this spot. It soothed him somehow, so that he could find some kind of anchorage for his confused thoughts. He was by no means sure about a God but he acknowledged the clear difference between good and evil, and according to Chris there had never been a war in which the options were so clear. That ought to help, and might, perhaps, as time went on, and you could see a pinpoint of light at the end of the tunnel. But so far evil seemed to be winning hands down, with a Continent enslaved, and Britain hanging on to the coat-tails of a few thousand boys like Hislop. There was only so much they could do and they had already achieved far more than he, and all the other anti-militarists of the 'twenties, had the right to expect. He thought, bitterly, "By God, we've got a lot to answer for—not just the politicians but all of us, Left, Right and Centre, from Versailles onwards. I saw the red light before the majority, but I wouldn't have if Chris hadn't had the moral courage to point it out, and bring me evidence in the person of that kid Meyer. It's our fault the odds are so long up there. Who the hell am I to put the responsibility for Hislop's death on politicians?"

Prayer was denied him but there was its equivalent, a mute appeal to the ageing ghosts of all those names on the memorial, and the newcomers to Valhalla, like Briarley, Christopherson, Graves-Jones, Hislop and old Preacher Skidmore, and he made that plea, now, standing in a flood of moonlight, his back against Algy's thinking post. "Get us out of this somehow. Show us the way. Give us the guts and stamina, but don't be too greedy for company . . ."

One of the planty owls hooted, perhaps with derision at his naivety, but he felt a sense of release, as though the soft night breeze, gusting down from the moor, carried the hopes of all Bamfeldians who had stood at this spot across four generations and seen below a sprawl of buildings that was something more than a seat of elementary learning, a place where, in their brief span hereabouts, they had imbibed a little of the ethos of the island, and its struggle over twenty centuries to fashion apparatus capable of accommodating free will with justice and human dignity.

He extinguished his cigarette and went down the slope to the fives court, round the promontory of the Bog and through the flagged court that led, via Outram's and the Third Forms, to the quad. Everyone was asleep but him, moonlight reflecting on the windows of the Sunsetters' dormitory, and the steep, tiled roof of the new labs. The place looked washed clean in this strong, bluish light, looked as if nobody had ever trodden the asphalt circuit about the Founder's statue, and as he passed it, on his way to his own back door, he gave it a new boy's bob. For tonight he felt more defenceless than Endsleigh Minor, youngest of last term's Cradlers.

Chapter Three

And that was really no more than the beginning. The end of the beginning, as Churchill would later describe it.

On through an endless succession of blazing summer days the battle continued, rising to three screaming crescendos on August 13th, August 18th and September 15th, the day school reassembled for the start of another year. On that day alone, Buck Suttram, the West Indian Sunsetter, who had been keeping score, chalked up a total of fifty-six German aircraft destroyed.

On through the full month of October it continued to rage, when Suttram, reduced to keeping a private record after Big School blackboard had been restored to normal use, told David that the R.A.F. and anti-aircraft defences had accounted for just over two thousand enemy aircraft between July 10th and the last day of October. The figure was duly entered up in the records and Suttram wasn't so far out at that. Years later, when official figures were reissued after the capture of Luftwaffe documents, it was seen that, between the dates quoted, an admitted total of German planes destroyed was one thousand, seven hundred and thirty-three, with a further six hundred and forty-three damaged.

Suttram had not kept tally of R.A.F. losses but David had, in terms of lives if not machines. Of the one thousand, four hun-

dred and ninety-five R.A.F. personnel killed, four, including Hislop, were Bamfeldians. A fifth, Crispin, was so badly burned over
the Thames estuary, that he was in Halton Hospital for months
and left it on crutches.

*   *   *

Alone among those who stayed on at school throughout that
unforgettable seven weeks, David was unable to share the Test
Match excitement prevailing in Big School around the Sunsetters'
radio. How could he? The impersonal announcements, relevant to
the cost of victory, were translated, figure by figure, into a sombre
parade of faces recalled over recent years, all linked in his mind to
some quirk, nickname or exploit, attaching itself to every boy who
had mooched about the quad, or added his quota to the changing-
room cacophony attending the end of every rugby game.

News of Towers's death, for instance, received the same week
as that informing him of Crispin's terrible injuries, touched him
almost as deeply as the loss of Hislop and Briarley. For he saw it
as an ironic adjustment in the balance sheet of life, recalling how
once—long ago it seemed now—Crispin, alone and friendless, had
worshipped Towers from afar, and had stolen a bar of Mackintosh's toffee from the village shop simply in order to register with
his hero. Now they were level pegs, or almost so. Towers, shot
down over Maidstone, was dead. Crispin, trapped in blazing debris at a satellite field in Sussex, was half-dead, 'cooked' they
would say, in their pitiless new slang, and in the hands of the
skin-grafters for months to come.

He wrote to both boys' parents and Crispin's mother replied at
once, promising to keep him informed on her son's progress. But
then, for a brief spell, his attention was switched to more personal
concerns. Grace, who had been living with them since she returned from her honeymoon, was whisked away at a day's notice
by Sax Hoskins, now commissioned and stationed in Yorkshire,
on a basis that enabled him to live out of camp.

He had a few minutes' garbled conversation with his son-in-law,
due to begin yet another course the following day, and nervous of
missing his connection if the London termini were blitzed. Sax
was developing a variety of new skills in his wartime profession,
even showing marked proficiency in maths, something that would

have astounded his Bamfylde mentors. Gunnery was behind him now and he was moving on to qualify as a navigator.

"Will it keep you out of harm's way for a few months?" David asked anxiously, and Sax replied gaily that it would, for the R.A.F. did not yet possess the means to mount a sizeable bombing offensive on Germany.

"We won't start dishing it out on their scale for a year or so," he said, "but when we do, oh boy! Hamburg, here I come!" David gathered there was a certain amount of rivalry between the men who flew bombers and those who flew fighter aircraft. Sax said, "So far the Spits and Hurrys have had all the glam but the war won't be won by the Brylcreem boys. We've got to go over and sort 'em out on their own ground, and we've got some real beauts on the assembly lines." Then, less breezily, "You don't mind me taking Grace off your hands, do you? The way I see it we might as well spend what time we can together. It won't be all that much, with me genning up like a bloody boffin."

He said his next farewell, in early November, to Boyer, off on the first stage of his Quixotic odyssey, an odyssey that was to take him, in the next few years, all over the world. Chad's second child, a daughter, had been born in early October, and his place at the little cottage had been filled, to some extent, by a landgirl who lodged there. "I was chuffed to get her," Chad said, "for she's another Scots girl, and will be great company for Alison. But you'll keep an eye on her, won't you, Pow-Wow? And I'll keep in touch wherever I am, whatever I'm doing."

Everybody but himself, it seemed, was either dying or tearing about the country in a prodigious hurry, and his very rootedness made him feel his age. Boyer, had he stayed on, would have become housemaster of Nicolson's in place of Howarth. As it was, he made do with the new man, Heathcott, and judged himself lucky to have him, for Heathcott, like his wife, was not strong and unlikely to disappear into the blue like so many others. He came to like Mrs. Heathcott, whose health improved as soon as she settled on the plateau, so that Heathcott said, "Gladys and I are a couple of creaking doors, I'm afraid, P.J., but these days that's insurance."

It was at that, as he found himself thinking when he had final confirmation to two more casualties, Churchill and Keithley, both reported missing earlier in the term. He thought of them as hardly the scatter of friendly lights lower down the slope had warmed his heart, a fire to go home to whenever he needed one. He had need of it now for suddenly, out here in the frosted silence, he felt not cold but frightened. The moonlight held on long enough for him to stride down to within ten yards of the fives court and then, just as it clouded over again, he saw Chris, muffled to the ears, move into the fleeting patch of light. She called, "Davy? Is that you, Davy?" and, when he answered, "Anything wrong?"

"No," he said, "just popped out to blow the cobwebs away," and sought her hand.

"I told them you wouldn't mind them staying up to see the New Year in. Is that all right?"

"Yes, it's fine. They'll do it anyway, and we might as well join them. But how about some tea first?"

"I'll make some." Then, as they moved round the bulk of the new wing to the forecourt, "You'll be glad to wave goodbye to this one, Davy. The next can only be for the better, can't it?"

"Yes," he said, with certainty, "it'll be that all right."

He spun her round as she went up the two steps and kissed her mouth, finding her lips as warm and reassuring as her hand. "This won't do at all, sir," she said, laughing. "Not in front of the children," and steered him into the hall, slamming the door before she reached for the light switch. "It's okay," she said, off-handedly, "I saw to the blackout on the way through," but somewhere, probably in old Rigby's kitchen, there was a window open for faintly, carried on the downdraught in that funnel of a passage, came the sound of the Sunsetters, singing to Buck's accordion. He was leading them in an old community favourite, 'Shenandoah', and the sound had within it comfort and continuity.

3

It was inconceivable as well as unforgivable that he had completely forgotten his appointment with Earnshaw at eleven on New Year's Day.

He had just popped down to the cottage to wish Alison a happy new year and was walking back when he spied Buck Suttram scudding across the rimed football pitch towards the field gate. Buck gestured urgently, and changed direction, arriving out of breath, and saying, "Someone waiting, sir—been waiting half an hour. Said